What the
YANKEES
Did to Us

MERCER
UNIVERSITY PRESS

Endowed by
TOM WATSON BROWN
and
THE WATSON-BROWN FOUNDATION, INC.

What the

YANKEES

Did to Us

SHERMAN'S BOMBARDMENT AND WRECKING OF ATLANTA

STEPHEN DAVIS

For Cmdr Tom Stevens
Gen Edward Dorr Tracy
Camp

MERCER UNIVERSITY PRESS | MACON, GEORGIA

Stephen Davis

Aug 22, 2013

MUP/ H859

© 2012 Mercer University Press
1400 Coleman Avenue
Macon, Georgia 31207

First Edition

Books published by Mercer University Press are printed on acid-free paper
that meets the requirements of the American National Standard for
Information Sciences—Permanence of Paper for Printed Library Materials.

Mercer University Press is a member of Green Press Initiative
(greenpressinitiative.org), a nonprofit organization working to help publishers
and printers increase their use of recycled paper and decrease their use of fiber
derived from endangered forests. This book is printed on recycled paper.

ISBN   978-0-88146-398-9
Cataloging-in-Publication Data is available from the Library of Congress

CONTENTS

Origins in the 1830s—"Terminus," the Southern end of a
proposed railroad, becomes Marthasville in 1842—connected by
rail to Augusta, fall 1845, the place takes a new name—
continued growth, and rail linkage to Chattanooga in 1850—
growth of the city's central business area, and a fourth rail line to
Montgomery in 1854—US Censuses of 1850 and 1860—The
Passenger Depot ("Car Shed"), roundhouses and freight depots
for the four rail lines—factories and manufacturing shops—
churches, schools and public buildings—citizens' residences—
secession of the Southern states and Lincoln's election portend
war.

Atlantans prepare for war—the city becomes a military hospital
center—growth in Atlanta's population—newspapers—various
Confederate bureaus in town—manufacturers of arms and
military equipment—the Atlanta Arsenal—suppliers of
quartermaster and commissary stores—Atlanta as railroad
center—the Andrews railroad raid—worries over Northern spies
and sympathizers lead to calls for martial law—Streight's
Yankee cavalry get to within 80 miles of Atlanta, May 1863—city
fathers plan for defense—the CS Bureau of Engineers takes over
the construction of defenses—Capt. L. P. Grant supervises the
work—Gen. Johnston takes interest in the defenses—Atlanta
braces for the Yankees' advance in north Georgia, spring 1864.

shelling—damage to suburban buildings—deaths of Joseph Warner and his daughter Elizabeth, 3 August—the problem of burials—Carrie Berry chronicles the shelling—Isaac Pilgrim reports for the *Intelligencer*—Sherman intensifies his cannonade—arrival of the 4.5-inch siege guns—heavy bombardment of 9 August—Gen. Hood comes under shellfire—the Yankees admire their cannon-work—hot shot upon the city—fires downtown—casualties among the people—bombproofs and cellars save lives—nighttime pyrotechnics—death of Sol Luckie, free black barber—surgeons care for shell casualties—Sherman plans to break the semi-siege—Confederates' 64-pounder Dahlgren—the Willis bombproof—food supplies inside the city—church services—cautious ambulation—years later, memories of the shelling—Frances Hale, shell-casualty—more talk of civilian deaths—fires of 23–24 August—the Yankees try to evade responsibility—shells stop, 26 August—Sherman marches most of his forces toward Jonesboro—the Southern press vilifies Sherman—Federals cut the Macon & Western near Morrow—Confederates evacuate Atlanta—did the bombardment help Sherman take Atlanta?—how many Atlantans died?—final assessments.

Confederate evacuation—explosion of the reserve ordnance train—Union forces advance closer, morning of 2 September—Mayor Calhoun surrenders the city—Federal troops occupy Atlanta—looting by the Yankees—Col. Cogswell imposes order—Union forces continue to march in—what they saw—Northern officers and men find quarters—identifying loyalists among remaining Atlantans—Sherman orders the civilian population to leave—generals Hood and Sherman exchange barbed letters—the expulsion of Atlantans to Rough and Ready—Sherman's men react—response in the North—Cump meets with Bishop Lay—Atlantans also travel northward—some civilians are allowed to stay—Federals commandeer all property in the city—dismantling buildings to construct their shanties—the Northerners settle into their occupation—amusements for the officers and men—Sherman follows Hood's army into north

Georgia— Capt. Poe oversees construction of inner
fortifications—Rebels cut the railroad between Big Shanty and
Tunnel Hill—pinched subsistence among the XX Corps
occupiers—the four foraging expeditions.

Reviewing the causes of damage to Atlanta—the Federals'
destruction of railroads around the city—Sherman plans his next
campaign—Col. Cogswell begins planning the destruction of
downtown—rumors circulate in the ranks—press leaks of
Sherman's purported plans—the three provost regiments'
proposals for destruction—Sherman shifts the demolition work
to Capt. Poe's engineers—remaining civilians in the city, already
apprehensive, are ordered to leave, 8 November—Northern
soldiers vote in the presidential election—Sherman, with the
XIV, XV and XVII Corps in northwest Georgia, begins marching
back to Atlanta—"last train from Atlanta," morning of 12
November —Poe's engineers begin their track demolition in the
city—Federals tear up the rails from the Etowah to the
Chattahoochee—burning towns and blaming "Jeff Davis"—
Sherman's orders for only military structures to be burned, and
their violation—Poe's cant hook—US engineers begin tearing
down the city's railroad structures—unauthorized fires break
out downtown, night of 11 November—soldiers marching in
from northwest Georgia are blinded by the smoke—final
destruction of Atlanta's railroad complex—15 November, day of
the most extensive burning—Northern soldiers' opinions—
Sherman and the last Federal soldiers leave Atlanta, morning of
the 16th—how much of the city was burned?— Z. A. Rice's
newspaper letter, 20 November, first of seven eyewitness
reports—James R. Crew's letter of 1 December—Militia general
W. P. Howard's letter to Governor Brown, most extensive
evaluation of the burning damage—the myth of Father O'Reilly
saving downtown churches—the *Intelligencer's* account, 10
December—report in the *Augusta Chronicle & Sentinel*, 14
December—"Civis" reports the damage for the *Augusta Chronicle
& Sentinel*—the *Intelligencer* offers a final report, 20 December—

evaluating the extent of the fires, 11–15 November—the burning in final context.

PICTORIAL COMPLEMENT.
Captions and Sketched Maps by the Author.

1. The downtown passenger depot or "Car Shed." George N. Barnard photograph. (Atlanta History Center)
2. Edward Vincent's map of Atlanta, 1853. (Atlanta History Center)
3. Sketched map: Atlanta's downtown railroad complex and leading manufactories on war's eve.
4. Sketched map: Atlanta's six hotel sites downtown, 1859; churches, major schools, and selected public buildings.
5. The "Calico House" of Marcus Aurelius (Mark) Bell. Walton Taber illustration, Battles and Leaders of the Civil War. (Atlanta History Center)
6. Sketched map: Atlanta's Six Hotels in 1859..
7. Captain Lemuel P. Grant's map, "City of Atlanta and Line of Defenses," dated 12 April 1864 by Colonel Moses H. Wright. Official Records Atlas. (Atlanta History Center)
8. Sketched map: area of the Atlanta Campaign, May–September 1864.
9. Confederate fortifications northwest of the city. George N. Barnard photograph. (Atlanta History Center)
10. Sketched map: situation at nightfall 17 July, when General Johnston was relieved of command.
11. Wilbur G. Kurtz, "Map of Atlanta as of 1938, Showing the Field and Fortified Lines of the Confederate Forces, Together with Those of the Federal Armies." Atlanta Chamber of Commerce, 1938. (Atlanta History Center)
12. The white stucco home of Ephraim and Ellen Ponder. Photograph by George Barnard, showing effects of Federal artillery fire. (Atlanta History Center)
13. Detail of Kurtz 1938 chamber of commerce map, showing positions of three 4.5-inch rifled siege cannon. (Atlanta History Center)
14. L. Windsor Smith house on Whitehall Street, headquarters of General Hood, ca. 10 August–1 September. *Frank Leslie's Illustrated Newspaper, 29 October 1864.* (Atlanta History Center)
15. A bomb-proof, photographed by George Barnard after the fall of the city. (Atlanta History Center)
16. Solomon Luckie, African American resident killed by one of Sherman's shells, August 1864. (Atlanta History Center)
17. The shell-damaged lamppost, last relic of Sherman's shelling in downtown Atlanta. (Atlanta History Center)
18. Wilbur G. Kurtz drawing accompanying his article, "Dugout Home in Atlanta," *Atlanta Journal Sunday Magazine,* 10 July 1932. (Atlanta History Center)

19. Ruins of the Atlanta Lard Oil Factory and adjacent wholesale grocery, destroyed by a shell-caused fire, 24 August. George Barnard photograph. (Atlanta History Center)

20. Imaginative Northern map, placing Rebel fortified lines well within the Atlanta city limits. *New York Herald*, 5 August 1864.

21. John Neal house, Sherman's headquarters, 7 September–16 November. (*Frank Leslie's Illustrated Newspaper*, 29 October 1864. (Atlanta History Center)

22. Col. Henry A. Barnum and staff on the front porch of the Windsor Smith house. George Barnard photograph. (Atlanta History Center)

23. "Provost Marshal's office, Atlanta—Citizens getting passes to go north and south." *Frank Leslie's Illustrated Newspaper*, 29 October 1864. (Atlanta History Center)

24. "Rebel Citizens Leaving Atlanta, Ga., for the South, in U.S. Army Wagons, in Compliance with the Late Order of General Sherman. From a Sketch by Our Special Artist." Frank Leslie's Illustrated Newspaper, 12 November 1864. (Atlanta History Center)

25. "Rebels Moving South from Atlanta. Sketched by D.R. Brown." *Harper's Weekly*, 15 October 1864. (Atlanta History Center)

26. "U.S. Soldiers, at Atlanta, Ga., Tearing down Buildings Shattered during the Late Bombardment." *Frank Leslie's Illustrated Newspaper*, 12 November 1864. (Atlanta History Center)

27. Camp of the 2nd Massachusetts in City Hall Park. George Barnard photograph. (Atlanta History Center)

28. General Sherman at Federal fort 7. George Barnard photograph. (Atlanta History Center)

29. Federal map showing Confederate fortifications surrounding Atlanta, and Captain Orlando Poe's interior defensive line. *OR Atlas*. (Atlanta History Center)

30. "Atlanta. before Being Burnt by Order of Genl. Sherman. From the Cupola of the Female Seminary." George Barnard "stereoscopic" photograph. (Atlanta History Center)

31. William Solomon House, Mitchell Street, with Federal fortifications in front yard. George Barnard photograph. (Atlanta History Center)

32. "Whitehall Street, Atlanta, Georgia.—Sketched by D.R. Brown." *Harper's Weekly*, 8 October 1864. (Atlanta History Center)

33. "View of Decatur and Peach Tree Streets from Marietta Street." D. R. Brown lithograph 2. (Atlanta History Center)

34. The wrecked Georgia Railroad east of Atlanta. George Barnard photograph. (Atlanta History Center)

35. Sketched map: downtown Atlanta, with structures designated for destruction by men of the 2nd Massachusetts, 33rd Massachusetts and 111th Pennsylvania regiments.

For my loving wife Billie, without whose sweet patience and kind support this

work would never have come to be.

Amor omnia vincit.

* * * * * *

And in memory of Joseph Warner and his daughter Elizabeth, both killed by a Northern artillery shell while sleeping on the night of 3 August 1864, in Atlanta, innocent victims of "Sherman's murders."

ACKNOWLEDGMENT

THE ATLANTA HISTORY CENTER

Whatever strengths this work may possess are due to the rich resources and superb staff members of the Atlanta History Center. I wish to acknowledge my thanks to the institution, and especially to the wonderful people who have helped me to build this book.

The History Center was chartered back in 1926 as the Atlanta Historical Society, a group of community-conscious citizens seeking to provide a needed cultural resource for our city. With growing memberships and donations, the society bought land and in 1946 had a headquarters and exhibit room at Peachtree Street and Huntington Road (I have a dim memory of coursing through it as a youngster). The society acquired more property in northwest Atlanta in the 1960s; staff officers were in the basement of the Swan House. Construction of McElreath Hall in 1975 gave the society's library and archives an attractive and substantial home. Diaries, letters, artifacts, books and all sorts of important memorabilia formed such an important collection that, say, after the late 1950s (when A. A. Hoehling published *Last Train from Atlanta*) no scholar could write about our city without visiting the society's collections.

Meanwhile, the Historical Society became the History Center; Tom Watson Brown, a generous benefactor, once explained to me the reasons for the change. The Center's collection has increased in size to 2.5 million items, spanning the entire history of Atlanta, including the Olympics of 1996. More important to me, the History Center has become one of the nation's best storehouses of Civil War artifacts. The Beverly M. DuBose Collection and Thomas Swift Dickey Civil War Ordnance Collection are legendary, featuring objects not to be seen elsewhere. (Just try finding a Union army ordnance wagon near you!) The permanent "Turning Point" exhibition explains the Atlanta Campaign with a comprehension and color to reward Civil Warriors from around the world.

So, I express my sincerest gratitude to all of the gracious staff members of the History Center, and specifically its James Kenan Library, Archives and Research Center. I think I started my regular visits to the library back in the 1980s. Delving into the Wilbur G. Kurtz Collection, my research notes show that Sara Saunders, Helen Mathews, Frances Westbrook, and Tammy Galloway all helped me during those years. Sara is today at the Carter Center and Presidential Library in Atlanta. Behind the front desk staff was Library Director Anne Salter, now at Oglethorpe University's Philip Weltner Library, still helping me with source searches.

Preparing this manuscript has given me the opportunity to add new friends. Sue Verhoef, archivist, cheerfully procures manuscript files during my visits. Melanie Stephan, senior archivist, knows more about the famed Kurtz Collection than anyone, and has given me wonderful assistance. Helen Mathews, librarian, continues to assist in my research, as does Laura Starratt, archivist. Michael Rose, executive vice president, and Paul Crater, vice president of research services, have allowed me to draw on the History Center's vast visual arts collection for the illustrative material complementing my text. Melanie and Paige Adair, reprographics manager, have identified the images I have sought and—to the astonishment of one for whom "digitization" is a new word— prepared them for publication. Finally, to Dr. Gordon Jones, senior military historian, I want to say thanks for his years of encouragement on this book project. Back at Northside High School, we learned in Latin from Aeneas's companion, *fidus* Achates, that faithfulness is the staple of friendship, and I thank Gordon for it.

—S.D., July 2012

A NOTE ON THE TITLE

On 31 December 1861, Samuel P. Richards—who had moved to Atlanta a few months before, settled his family into his brother's house, and who co-owned a prospering book and stationery store on Whitehall Street—recorded in his diary that "the great things that the Yankees were going to do to us…have not yet been done."[1] At the time, Richards wrote more as a Southerner than as an Atlantan. But in 1864, when the Confederacy's military frontier had shrunk with the advance of Union armies, the grim prospect of Yankees reaching Atlanta seemed more and more likely. Richards's forecasting of what the Yankees were going to do to us became reality in summer and fall 1864, when Major General William T. Sherman's Federal armies approached Atlanta, battled the defending Confederate army, besieged and bombarded the city, and finally took it. Then they stayed in Atlanta for two and a half months. Before they left, Sherman's engineers destroyed the city's railroad infrastructure and what remained of its industrial complex. Although Sherman never called for the burning of private homes, in the final days of the occupation, soldiers torched countless dwellings throughout the city where either provost guards could not prevent unauthorized arson or officers looked the other way. When he rode out of Atlanta on the morning of 16 November, Sherman looked back on a city that his troops had thoroughly destroyed.

This is what the Yankees did to us, and it is the story that I aspire to tell. It has a number of different elements, most important among them Sherman's artillery bombardment of Atlanta from 20 July 1864 to 25 August. The story of Sherman's shelling has for more than a century not been extensively related—as Russell S. Bonds has recently written, "most historians and biographers minimize, excuse or entirely ignore the five-week bombardment of Atlanta."[2] In relating the shelling of Atlanta in what I believe to be its most thorough account yet, I am following my friend and mentor Albert Castel's advice that with so many books and articles printed on the Civil War, an author's challenge should be to describe events "in far greater detail than they have ever been described before."[3] In my analysis I note that the Federals' cannonade of Atlanta was not the longest bombardment of the war—Charleston and Petersburg earned that dubious distinction. Yet the Union shelling of Atlanta was arguably the bloodiest

---

[1] Wendy Hamand Venet, ed., *Sam Richards's Civil War Diary: A Chronicle of the Atlanta Home Front* (Athens: University of Georgia Press, 2009) 87.

[2] Russell S. Bonds, *War Like the Thunderbolt: The Battle and Burning of Atlanta* (Yardley PA: Westholme Publishing, 2009) 454n16.

[3] Albert Castel, *Winning and Losing in the Civil War: Essays and Stories* (Columbia: University of South Carolina Press, 1996) 201.

urban barrage in the Civil War, inflicting more civilian casualties than any other. We will say more about this later.[4]

Although "Sherman's burning of Atlanta" is a well-known phrase, the Federals' destruction of the city's buildings had begun well before their fires of 11–15 November. The artillery shelling damaged numerous structures in the city and destroyed others by fire. During their occupation, Union soldiers stripped houses and other buildings of their planking so they could build huts and shanties. More structures came down during October when Union engineers built defensive fortifications well within the city. The Northerners bashed and battered many buildings before they set their fires of mid-November. For all of these reasons, "wrecking" seems to me to be a better term than "burning" to explain what the Yankees did to us. Even the phrase "what they did to us," plays upon legends that Southerners after the war spoke and wrote about, trying to explain their defeat and devastation, how their world had come to end. One of my favorite stories comes from Father Abram Ryan, the poet-priest who after the war glorified the Lost Cause. Then he saw his young niece gazing upon a painting of Jesus' crucifixion. He asked her if she knew of the infidels who had crucified her savior. "O yes I know," she said, "the Yankees."[5]

I should comment on the term Yankees itself. As Mencken points out, the word (originally for Dutchmen in New York, Jankees) had before the American Revolutionary War been applied to New Englanders "as a term of derision." Yankees turned it into something prideful (as in "Yankee ingenuity"). But, Mencken continues, "during the Civil War, as everyone knows, Yankee became a term of disparagement again, applied by the people of the South to all Northerners."[6] The latter point is important, as most soldiers in Sherman's army were not New Englanders (Yankees in the strictest sense), but men of the Old Northwest and beyond. I use the term here as Southerners did in the war; it's just what we called them. (Try finding Scarlett or Rhett referring to "Federals" or "Northerners" in *Gone With the Wind*.) At the same time, if there is a wartime term of derogation, it is not Yankees (which had a geographic origin dating from a century before the Civil War). Rather, it would be Rebels, which is what Federal soldiers called Confederate soldiers, based not upon an unarguable fact of geographic origin, but upon a very arguable political and constitutional point

---

[4] As example, Chris Phelps, chronicling the Union bombardment of Charleston, August 1863–February 1865, concludes that five civilians had been killed and six wounded as of January 1864. He does not, however, offer a final casualty count (W. Chris Phelps, *The Bombardment of Charleston 1863–1865* [Gretna LA: Pelican Publishing Co., 2002] 150).

[5] Charles Reagan Wilson, *Baptized in Blood: The Religion of the Lost Cause, 1865–1920* (Athens: University of Georgia Press, 1980) 25.

[6] H. L. Mencken, *The American Language: An Inquiry into the Development of English in the United States* (New York: Alfred A. Knopf, 1936) 110–11.

of view.[7] That being said, in these pages I will use Federals, Northerners, and Yankees interchangeably. And when I assume the Federals' point of view, sometimes I will refer to Confederates as Rebels.

And there is that word, us. In adopting it in both my title and text, I mean us as a deliberately vague combination of the people of Atlanta as well as the physical structures that defined our city, and that together—people and buildings—made us "Atlanta." In summer 1864, civilian residents still in the city—white, black, free and slave, male and female, young and old, native-born or immigrant—all endured the same frightening ordeal of Yankee bombardment, occupation, and eventual expulsion. To that extent, we who are Atlantans, though we do not share a common ancestry, do nonetheless share a common history of the war, and a collective memory from it. So us does not mean solely white Southerners fighting the Yankees. Even if it did, we have accepted the verdict of the war, and have transcended defeat, just as Henry Grady declared in his famous "New South" speech of 1886: "There was a South of slavery and secession—that South is dead. There is a South of union and freedom—that South, thank God, is living, breathing, growing every hour." In the century-plus since then, Americans have continually redefined the meaning of the Civil War. Particularly important has been the African-American narrative of the war, which has enriched our understanding of the nation's greatest conflict.[8]

And just as Henry Grady's New South meant a rebuilding from war's ashes, so do I add a further note on us. In this volume, I will be emphasizing the wartime harm done to Atlanta's buildings at least as much if not more than that done to the city's civilians. A. A. Hoehling, Samuel Carter, and others have told the story of Atlanta's people in summer 1864, so the tale need not be recounted.[9] Along its way my narrative will also veer to subjects I think merit a bit more attention, such as Atlanta's wartime newspapers, my richest source of information on Sherman's shelling. Similarly, I will look at how the Yankees

---

[7] Few Northern soldiers referred to their enemies as "Confederates": usually they were "Rebels," or better yet, "rebels." Later ex-Federals objected to the term *Confederate,* as shown by a complaint to the editor of the *Ohio Soldier,* a Union veteran's magazine, concerning postwar Gettysburg tour guides' references to "the Confederacy," which one veteran contemptuously dismissed as a "thing that never had an existence except in the diseased imagination of rebels." The proper term, the Ohioan suggested, should be *rebellion* or *conspiracy* (James Marten, *Sing Not War: The Lives of Union & Confederate Veterans in Gilded Age America* [Chapel Hill: University of North Carolina Press, 2011] 136).

[8] Harold E. Davis, *Henry Grady's New South: Atlanta, a Brave and Beautiful City* (Tuscaloosa: University of Alabama Press, 1990) 176. David W. Blight offers a wonderful account of the African-American narrative of the war, and how for so long it was forgotten in the national discussion, in *Race and Reunion: The Civil War in American Memory* (Cambridge: Harvard University Press, 2001).

[9] A. A. Hoehling, *Last Train from Atlanta* (New York: Thomas Yoseloff, 1958); Samuel Carter III, *The Siege of Atlanta, 1864* (New York: St. Martin's Press, 1973).

whiled their time as occupiers of Atlanta, September–November 1864. With a few exceptions (such as Lee Kennett's and Russell Bonds's narratives[10]), the occupation is untreated in most war histories, which move from the Northerners' entering the city on 2 September to their marching out 15–16 November, generally in the flip of a page. For this reason I give the Union occupation a little more attention in the desire to contribute to the literature.

Finally, I attempt to give the real "burning," the fires of 11–15 November, its most thorough examination, calling on several accounts that have surprisingly been unheeded by earlier students. Thus in the end, I will attempt to focus on the physical city, the structures that were victims of Sherman's hard war, as much as the resident noncombatants who inhabited them.

All in all, mine is a story that I regard as not yet having fully been told before—others after me will generously add to it. But it is a story that I have wanted to tell for a long time.

---

[10] Lee Kennett, *Marching through Georgia: The Story of Soldiers and Civilians during Sherman's Campaign* (New York: HarperCollins, 1995).

FOREWORD

GROWING UP IN ATLANTA

I cannot put my finger on what triggered it, but sometime around 1957 (my fourth grade year) cemented my lifelong avocation, that of a Civil War enthusiast, a "buff," a "Civil Warrior," a devotee of what must be admitted as a slender fragment of United States history. Was it then that I first viewed the Cyclorama? When did my parents first take me to Kennesaw Mountain Battlefield? Was it another showing of *Gone With the Wind* (and at the Loews Grand)? Or maybe even that television series, *The Grey Ghost* that aired on CBS in 1957–1958 (Tod Andrews as Major Mosby!). Maybe it had to do with my attending Margaret Mitchell Elementary School and seeing Mrs. Marsh's novel in the display cases translated into so many languages (German! Japanese!). Maybe it was sitting in the school auditorium beneath the imposing, full-length portrait of Scarlett O'Hara (the same as in the movie) with her determined, imperious gaze cast down upon us (it now hangs in the Margaret Mitchell House in Midtown). Another factor may have been all the roadside historical markers one saw throughout the city beginning in the late 1950s—e.g., "O'Neal's Brigade at the Ravine," by Bobby Jones Golf Course—which collectively reminded all of us that the war had come to our very backyards.

Whatever the cause, I was certainly ready for the Civil War Centennial of 1961–1965. For us Atlantans, the vicarious "war years" were a particularly meaningful time. To be sure, it was a troubled one. Segregation was at last crumbling in the early 1960s, and we were right in the middle of it. Northside High received its first black students as I entered the eighth grade there, and I still recall the pride with which we saw President Kennedy that evening commend the people of Atlanta for peaceful acceptance of progress. But even while we were making history, we were remembering it. Atlanta public television's *Sunrise Semester* featured Colonel Allen P. ("Ned") Julian, then director of the Atlanta Historical Society, in a half-hour broadcast on the war in Georgia (my friends wondered why I set my alarm so early). And there was Norman Shavin's weekly page in the Sunday *Journal-Constitution*, "The Atlanta Century," which ran during the centennial years, recasting war news as if it had just happened that week.

In other words, the war seemed to be everywhere for me, and like a lot of Atlantans I pondered how our city fared during it—no more so, I suspect, than history-conscious residents of other places, but when we did, it was in the knowledge that Atlanta had suffered specially from the hard hand of war. Indeed, this study may be said to stem from my desire to know just what happened to the city in which I grew up. (What?! A Yankee shell fou[?] the downtown Rich's department store, in which as a kid I rode the fabl[?] Pig"!?) This physical and emotional closeness to our city's war hist..., ..c..ps explain my yearning to learn more about it. Gradually my adolescent avocation became more than a hobby, merging into a lifelong pursuit of knowledge about the American Civil War. At Emory, my history professor, the great Bell Irvin Wiley, guided and confirmed my interest into something that at the time might have been called youthful scholarship. Master's degree study at Chapel Hill steeped me further in my war-interest. For my doctoral dissertation at Emory, of course I focused on the war, although not on the Atlanta Campaign (Richard McMurry had already done that, under Dr. Wiley). Research and publication— my first article in *Civil War Times Illustrated* (1976) was on the big snowball fight among Confederate soldiers in winter quarters at Dalton in March 1864— whetted my desire for still more. Teaching and writing followed, even editing. Here my thanks go to David E. Roth for giving me the opportunity to serve as book review editor for *Blue & Gray Magazine* for two full decades. In Dave's issue of August 1989, I finally got a chance to write a short narrative of the Atlanta Campaign. Since that time I've written more, especially my *Atlanta Will Fall: Sherman, Joe Johnston and the Yankee Heavy Battalions* (2001).

Talking to Civil War groups around the country has further sharpened my interest in what we Atlantans endured in the war. And—full disclosure—as a white Southerner, my perspective on the war has become a tangle of academic dispassion and unabashed partisanship, occasionally drawing criticism from my audiences (and rightly so). I recall my coaching from the president of the Atlanta Civil War Round Table before I addressed it on Sherman's bombardment of our city. To his cautionary words—that certain of the membership were descended from Union veterans—I commented, "That's all right, Mac; in the eyes of God we're all sinners." Yet it goes without saying that regional partisanship must not be construed as racial prejudice. In my class at Oglethorpe University, I once marveled that we—Caucasians, African Americans, males, females—could approach a subject as volatile as "The Civil War in Myth and Memory" with such frank and open opinions. In the end we settled upon the wisdom of Donald Davidson's observation that when it comes to the Civil War, we are still Rebels, still Yankees.

With this perspective, I wish to commend Dr. Marc Jolley at Mercer for his faithful patience with my manuscript through these years, and for his commendable adherence to the standards of a university press. For instance, MUP's style sheet calls for the historical profession's traditional method regarding dates; in returning to it, I recall my first research paper for Professor Wiley, 9 December 1968. More importantly, the Press continues to print footnotes, eschewing the (to my mind) lamentable current fashion of endnotes. I thank Marc too for allowing me to prepare my own sketched maps. The best example to me of the author-as-cartographer is Allen Tate, who drew his own battle maps for his great biography of Stonewall Jackson in 1928. Mine here are not as messy, but they follow the idea that an author's closeness to subject is reflected in cartography.

For his years of support and encouragement, I thank Dr. Gordon Jones of the Atlanta History Center, who more than anyone I know understands the role of Atlanta in the war. I also wish to thank Drs. Richard McMurry and Albert Castel for reading early drafts of this manuscript. Of their many helpful suggestions, I have heeded a good number; I trust they will pardon me for those I did not. As always, I stand alone in blame for every error of fact. Imperfections in my scholarship will summon future students to improve our narrative, which, in the end, is the object we all seek.

And so I prepare to tell an Atlantan's story, returning to the time of war, when our city was Sherman's target. Few of us would then have predicted that he would capture Atlanta, let alone wreck it. When it was all done, recalling the words of Professor Vann Woodward in one of his seminal essays, we truly knew that history had happened to us.

Stephen Davis

The downtown "Car Shed," the 100-feet-wide-by-300-feet-long brick passenger depot completed in 1854. The structure was in use through the war until its demolition by Northern troops on 14 November 1864. George N. Barnard photograph. (Atlanta History Center)

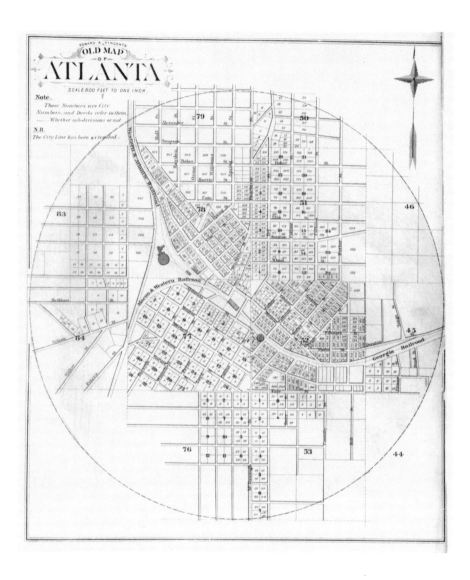

Edward A. Vincent's map of Atlanta, 1853. The circle of Atlanta's city limits extended by radius of a mile from the zero mile post. (Atlanta History Center)

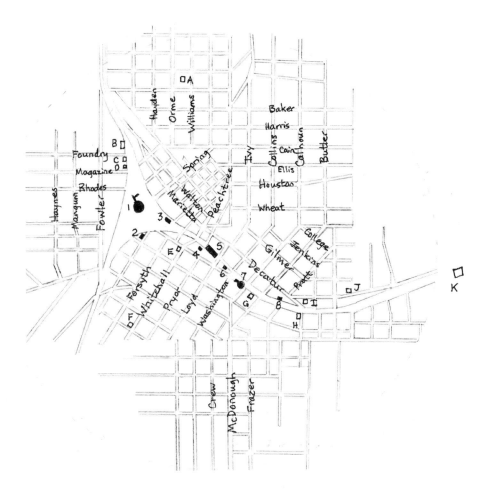

Map of Atlanta's downtown railroad complex and leading manufactories on war's eve.

1. Western & Atlantic locomotive house   2. Macon & Western locomotive house
3. Western & Atlantic freight depot   4. Macon & Western freight depot
5. Passenger depot/car Shed   6. Georgia RR freight depot
7. Georgia RR locomotive house   8. Atlanta & West Point freight depot

A. Atlanta Steam Tannery   B. Atlanta Gas Company
C. Winship's Iron Works   D. Pitts' & Cook's Planing Mill
E. Tomlinson & Barnes   F. Reed's Tannery
G. Peters' Steam Flour Mill (closed 1858)   H. Atlanta Machine Works
I. Peck's Planing Mill   J. McMillan's Tannery
K. Atlanta Rolling Mill

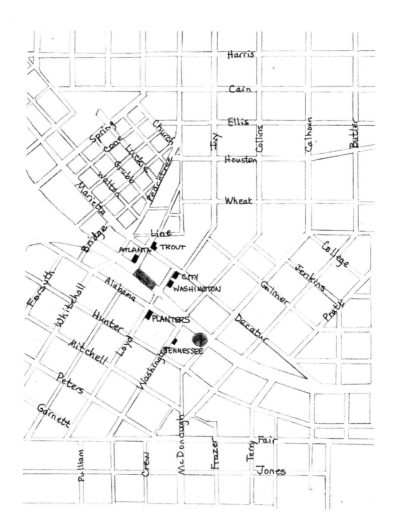

Sketched map. Atlanta's six hotels in1859.

The "Calico House" of Marcus Aurelius (Mark) Bell, a few blocks northeast of the Car Shed at Wheat and Collins streets. During the Federal occupation, Union engineer Captain Orlando Poe stayed in the house 3 September–10 November. Walton Taber illustration from George Barnard photograph lent by Ms. Orelia Key Bell; *Battles and Leaders of the Civil War*. (Atlanta History Center

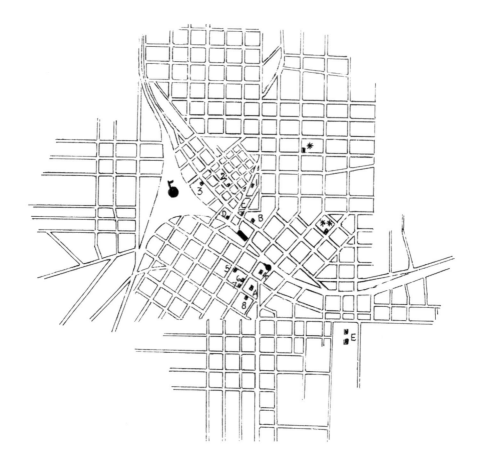

Sketched map, Confederate Ordnance Department facilities, naval works and major privately owned manufacturers. Based primarily on Capt. L. P. Grant's map "City of Atlanta and Line of Defenses."

1. Wesly Chapel	A. City Hall
2. First Baptist	B. Masonic Hall
3. First Presbyterian	C. Atheneum
4. St. Philip's Episcopal	D. Concert hall
5. Immaculate Conception	E. Fair Grounds
6. Central Presbyterian	
7. Second Baptist	* Female Institute
8. Trinity Methodist	** Medical College

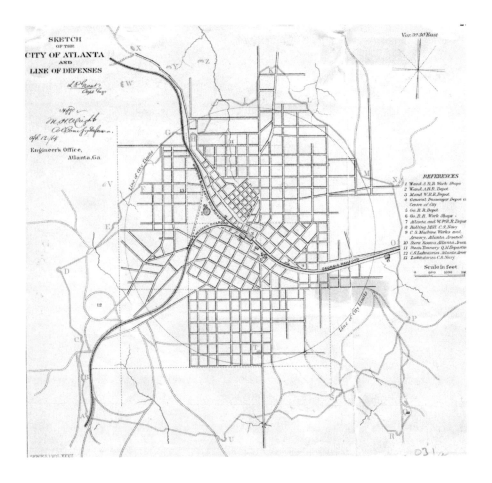

Captain Lemuel P. Grant's map "City of Atlanta and Line of Defenses," dated 12 April 1864 by Colonel Moses H. Wright, commanding defenses of the city. *OR Atlas*, plate 51, 2. Note keyed references to railroad structures, rolling mill, and arsenal facilities. (Atlanta History Center)

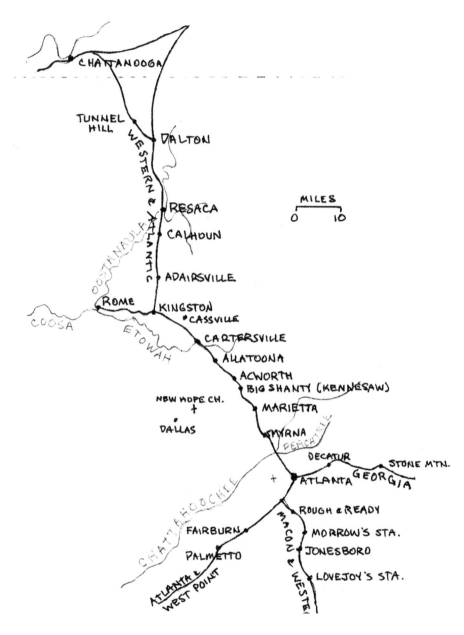

Sketched map of North Georgia involved in the Atlanta Campaign, May–September 1864.

Confederate fortifications northwest of the city. George N. Barnard photograph taken from Fort Hood, fall 1864. Shown are chevaux-de-frise, palisades and abatis in front of a sandbagged artillery emplacement. Nearby structures have been stripped of their planking. The Ponder house stands in the background. (Atlanta History Center)

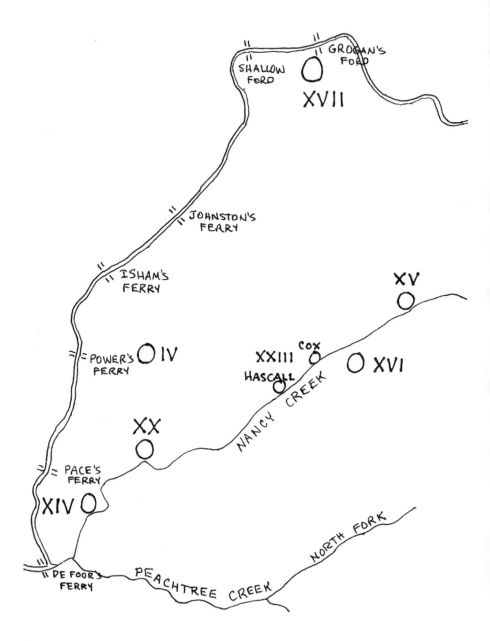

Sketched map, situation at nightfall, 17 July, when General Johnston was relieved of command. All seven Federal infantry corps were across the Chattahoochee and had advanced to Nancy Creek (approximately 8 miles north of the Car Shed).

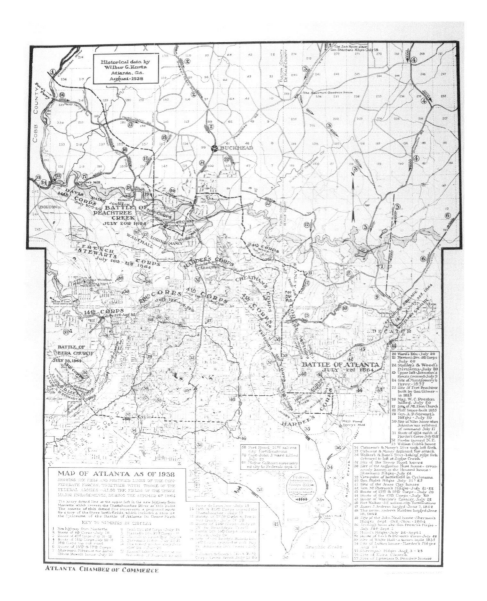

Wilbur G. Kurtz, "Map of Atlanta as of 1938, Showing the Field and Fortified Lines of the Confederate Forces, Together with Those of the Federal Armies." Atlanta Chamber of Commerce, 1938. (Atlanta History Center)

The white stucco home of Ephraim and Ellen Ponder, 3/4 of a mile outside of Atlanta's
northwest city limits, an example of a prominent house in the suburbs. showing effects of
Federal artillery fire; the Ponder home was located near Confederate Fort Hood. Photograph by
George N. Barnard, fall 1864. (Atlanta History Center)

The Ponder house was likely that referred to in the report of signal officer Lieutenant W.
W. Hopkins, 9 August, who sat perched in a tree near Geary's headquarters. Observing the
effects of the bombardment, Hopkins wrote, "the most noticeable effect of the shelling was in
front of General Geary's division at a fort and house. This fort was struck; also the works near
it, and the house had a large hole knocked in it besides being riddled." The Ponder place was
also that most likely referred to by a correspondent of the *New York Times*, writing from the
Federal lines on 18 August: "Bundy's battery (Thirteenth New York) has been making a target
of one very fine house, until now it presents a very highly ventilated appearance." Bundy's 13th
New York was attached to Geary's division.

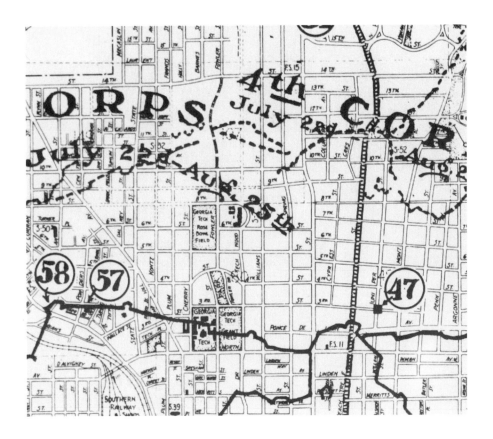

Detail of Wilbur G. Kurtz, "Map of Atlanta as of 1938," siting positions of three 4 1/2-inch rifled siege cannon. Shown near today's Cherry and 11th streets are three Union artillery emplacements that Kurtz discovered in the late 1920s (in top left, below the "S" in "CORPS"). Kurtz concluded that they were the probable positions of the three 4 1/2-inch siege rifles emplaced on Geary's division's front in August 1864. (Atlanta History Center)

L. Windsor Smith house on Whitehall Street, headquarters of General Hood, ca. 10 August–1 September. Hood moved to this house after he had come under enemy shellfire on 9 August at newspaperman John S. Thrasher's, also on Whitehall but closer in downtown. *Frank Leslie's Illustrated Newspaper*, 29 October 1864. (Atlanta History Center)

A bomb-proof, photographed by George Barnard after the fall of the city. The building behind has been identified as the Charles E. Grenville Flour Mill, east of Forsyth Street in the southwest suburbs. (Atlanta History Center)

Solomon Luckie, African American resident of Atlanta killed by one of Sherman's shells, August 1864. (Atlanta History Center)

IMAGE 17 CAPTION: The shell-damaged lamppost, last relic of Sherman's shelling in downtown Atlanta. Originally at Alabama and Whitehall streets, the post today stands in Underground Atlanta.

The upper of the two plaques, placed in 1919, honors Andrew West, a general in the United Confederate Veterans. The second notes that the "damage at the base of this post was caused by a shell during the War Between the States, Battle of Atlanta, July 22, 1864." Besides erring on the date, there is no mention of Solomon Luckie, the free African American barber, who was mortally wounded by the deflected shell. (Atlanta History Center)

The dugout was back of the house and kitchen

Wilbur G. Kurtz drawing of the Willis family bombproof. Accompanies his article, "Dugout Home in Atlanta," *Atlanta Journal Sunday Magazine*, 10 July 1932. (Atlanta History Center)

Ruins of the Atlanta Lard Oil Factory and adjacent wholesale grocery, destroyed by a shell-caused fire, 24 August. Barnard photograph, looking west from the bridge over railway. The Macon & Western arcs toward the southwest at right. The view was clearly taken during the occupation: note "U.S.M.R.R." (United States Military Railroad) on the car in the foreground. (Atlanta History Center)

THE CITY OF ATLANTA.

The Defensive Works of the Rebel Army at Atlanta and the Position of Sherman's Lines on July 27.

Imaginative Northern map, placing Rebel fortifications improbably within the city limits. *New York Herald*, 5 August 1864. Also see A. A. Hoehling, *Last Train from Atlanta*, with a caption that accepts it as fact. (Atlanta History Center)

The John Neal house, Sherman's headquarters, 7 September–16 November. Also known as "Judge Lyon's." *Frank Leslie's Illustrated Newspaper*, 29 October 1864. (Atlanta History Center)

Col. Henry A. Barnum and staff on the front porch of the Windsor Smith house, photographed by George Barnard. Note the US flag over the porch. Because the Smith house had become so well known as Gen. Hood's headquarters, Northerners made a special point of advertising who now occupied the place. (Atlanta History Center)

In September 1946, Wilbur G. Kurtz received a copy of this photo from one Charles E. Seng of Atlanta, who had found its original at the Onondagua Historical Society in Syracuse NY, having been donated by one of the Union officers pictured. On the back were listed the names of the eight officers on the porch. Kurtz copied them (left to right): Capt. O. E. E. Brown, 149th NY, brigade topographical engineer; Capt. Lester D. Wilson, 60th NY, brigade inspector general; Dr. James V. Kendall, 149th NY, brigade surgeon; Col. Henry A. Barnum, commander, 3rd Brigade, 2nd Div., XX Corps; Capt. O. T. May, 149th NY, brigade assistant adjutant general; Capt. Moses Summers, 149th NY, brigade quartermaster; Capt. Winchester; Lt. Loren Fuller, 60th NY, brigade aide-de-camp.

Barnard took another picture of these officers standing in front of the Smith house, which is often seen in print. Neither this view nor the list of officers' names has ever been published.

"Provost Marshal's office, Atlanta—Citizens getting passes to go north and south in consequence of General Sherman's order for the departure of all citizens." *Frank Leslie's Illustrated Newspaper*, 29 October 1864. (Atlanta History Center)

In Civil War America, the two leading newspapers specializing in illustrations were both based in New York, *Harper's Weekly* and *Frank Leslie's Illustrated Newspaper*. Each had a professional illustrator with Sherman's army who produced a handful of contemporary drawings during the occupation of Atlanta. Their pen-and-ink drawings were sent back to New York by train and there rendered into woodcut for printing. This woodcut engraving is based on a drawing by C. E. F. Hillen, the paper's "special artist" traveling with Sherman's forces.

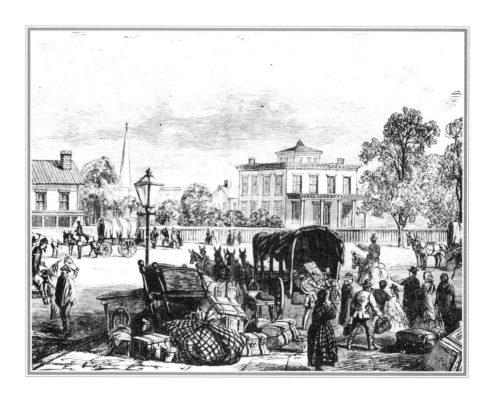

"Rebel citizens leaving Atlanta, Ga., for the south, in U.S. Army wagons, in compliance with the late order of General Sherman. From a sketch by our special artist, C.E.F. Hillen." *Frank Leslie's Illustrated Newspaper*, 12 November 1864. (Atlanta History Center)

"Rebels Moving South from Atlanta. Sketched by D.R. Brown." *Harper's Weekly*, 15 October 1864. (Atlanta History Center)

Harper's Weekly accepted several illustrations from David R. Brown, captain of Company F, 20th Connecticut, and printed them as woodcuts. In "Rebels Moving South from Atlanta," crowds of civilians are shown piling their possessions on wagons, some marked "U.S.A." Brown clearly wanted to show the helpfulness of Sherman's soldiers; men in kepis help lift furniture while women and children watch. In the foreground, a Federal officer politely tips his hat to a bonneted lady, who frowns and crosses her arms.

"U.S. Soldiers, at Atlanta, Ga., Tearing down Buildings Shattered during the Late Bombardment. From a Sketch by Our Special Artist." *Frank Leslie's Illustrated Newspaper*, 12 November 1864 (Atlanta History Center). The Northern caption puts the best possible light on Federal soldiers tearing down wooden structures in the city: the editors imply that the men are seeking to eliminate damaged buildings that could be public health hazards, instead of getting boards and planks to build their quarters.

Here the artist (presumably C. E. F. Hillen) depicts damage to buildings in the city, both from Union shells and Union soldiers. The drawing shows a large stack of lumber in the foreground; evidently a private house has been torn down. Soldiers are loading some wood, including a door, onto a wagon.

George Barnard's photograph of the camp erected by the soldiers of the 2nd Massachusetts in City Hall Park during the Federal occupation. Barnard took at least three views of the encampment. The huts were built on the south side of the park; this view looks northeast from Mitchell near Collins Street. (Atlanta History Center)

According to Georgia militia general W. P. Howard, the bricks for the soldiers' chimneys came from the three-story Atlanta Female Institute, torn down on 23 October to make room for Federal fortifications.

General Sherman in Federal Fort 7, photographed by George N. Barnard, late September 1864 (Atlanta History Center). The general sits his horse, Duke. On 1 October, Sherman wrote his wife Ellen: "I sent you a few days ago some photographs, one of which Duke was very fine. He stood like a gentleman for his portrait and I like it better than any I have had taken."

Barnard marked the site as "Federal fort No. 7, new line of defenses, (old rebel fort remodelled)," and "large rebel fort west of Atlanta (No. 7, new line of defense)." This would have been Confederate Battery E on Captain Grant's map of April 1864. (The site is on today's campus of Atlanta University.)

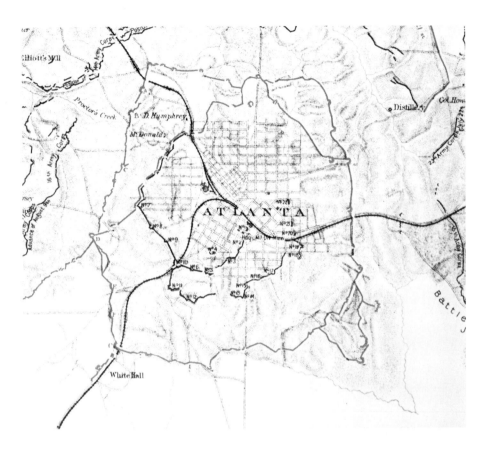

Federal map showing Confederate fortifications surrounding Atlanta, and Captain Orlando
Poe's inner defensive line, constructed in October 1864. Letters refer to Confederate artillery
forts, numbers to Federal. Note that Federal fort 7 coincides with a Confederate fort in Captain
Grant's original line. *OR Atlas*, plate 88. (Atlanta History Center)

"Atlanta. Before Being Burnt by Order of Genl. Sherman. From the Cupola of the Female Seminary." Barnard "stereoscopic" photograph (Atlanta History Center). Barnard used the cupola of the Female Seminary at Collins and Ellis streets to capture this memorable image of the city on a clear autumn day—probably in the first half of October, before the engines tore the building down on 23 October.

Barnard titled his image "Panoramic view at Atlanta, from the top of the female seminary, extending from the Medical College on the South East around by the South, to a point, on Peach Tree Street a little North of West. Three prints joined, 10" x 12"." The panorama takes in everything from the Medical College at Jenkins and Butler (now Grady Hospital) to Austin Leyden's residence on Peachtree, north of Ellis—an area of at least seven blocks, and a line a half-mile long.

William Solomon house on Mitchell Street, quarters of Col. William Cogswell and Lt. Col. Charles Morse. Photographed by George Barnard, ca. 18–19 October, when he was photographing the camp, officers, color bearer and men of the 2nd Massachusetts, according to Capt. Henry Comey of Company F. By that time, Federals had constructed their interior line of defense in Atlanta; earthworks in the right foreground come up to the Solomons' front yard. (Atlanta History Center)

"Whitehall Street, Atlanta, Georgia.—Sketched by D.R. Brown." *Harper's Weekly*, 8 October 1864 (Atlanta History Center). The view is to the southwest, at the intersection of Alabama Street. Brown shows a broad series of five imposing, ornate, three-story buildings, all brick and at the heart of the city's commercial area. None shows any damage from the bombardment. After the war this and five other of Brown's Atlanta drawings were printed as lithographs. In the lithographed version of this picture, the flag aloft the the tall building in the center is clearly shown to be the "white star" banner of the Union XX Corps.

"View of Decatur and Peach Tree Streets from Marietta Street." From a drawing by David R. Brown; lithograph by E. B. & E. C. Kellogg, Hartford CT (Atlanta History Center). Second in a series of six postwar lithographs made from wartime sketches by Capt. Brown while he was in Atlanta. The center of the drawing is Hunnicutt and Taylor's three-story drugstore on the northeast corner of Peachtree and Decatur. Next to the drugstore, looking down Decatur, is the Atheneum, where Welch and the 33rd Massachusetts band performed. Beyond that, looking southeast, is the Trout House, where early Federal arrivals into the city, such as Generals Slocum and Geary, took their first quarters. Brown's vista also looks north, to the block beyond Hunnicutt & Taylor's; there he noted "WM Clark" had his hardware store; it was Thomas M. Clarke & J. Thomas Lewis' "Hardware, Cutlery, Iron, Nails, &c." establishment (according to the city directory of 1859). To round out his picture, Captain Brown showed in the middle of the main intersection a US army wagon whose canvas top is conspicuously painted "3 Brig 3 Div 20 Corps"—the brigade to which the 20th Connecticut, Captain Brown's regiment, belonged in fall 1864. Around it, on what was once one of Atlanta's busiest intersections, are to be seen not even a dozen civilians.

George Barnard's photograph "Rebel lines east of Atlanta, Ga. Looking towards Decatur," shows three physical traces of war in the city suburbs. Cut foliage forms an abatis in front of Confederate entrenchments. A locomotive and tender sit stranded on the Georgia Railroad; Federal soldiers have taken up all rails, and piles of embers mark the burning of crossties. A house, caught in no-man's land, has been burned. (Atlanta History Center)

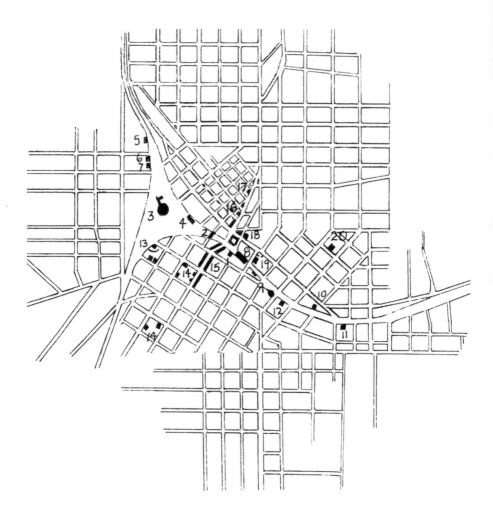

Sketched map of downtown Atlanta with general areas designated for destruction by men of the 2nd Massachusetts, 33rd Massachusetts, and 111th Pennsylvania regiments, based on reports submitted by Lt. Col. Morse, Lt. Col. Doane, and Lt. Col. Walker.

1. Macon & Western freight depot   2. Bridge
3. Western & Atlantic roundhouse   4. Western & Atlantic freight depot
5. Gas works   6. Winship's foundry
7. Pitts' & Cook's planing mill   8. Car Shed
9. Georgia R.R. roundhouse   10. Atlanta & West Point freight depot
11. Atlanta Machine Works   12. Peters' flour mill
13. Stable and corral   14. Shops
15. Whitehall Street   16. Georgia Railroad Bank and Peachtree Street
17. Barracks   18. Trout House
19. Washington Hotel   20. Medical College

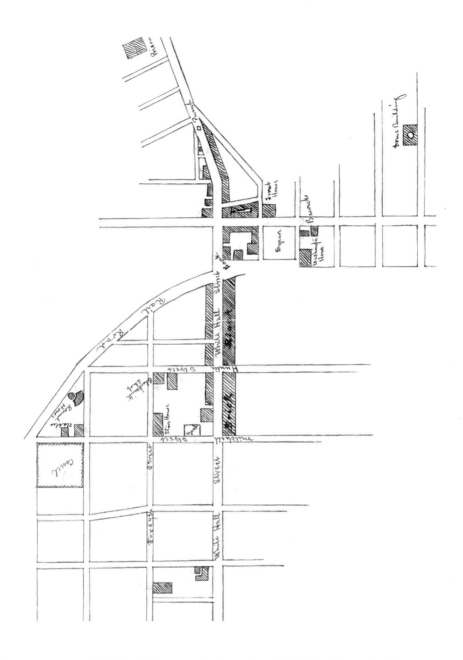

Map accompanying the "Plan of Destruction" submitted to Col. William Cogswell, with structures designated for demolition by the 33rd Massachusetts. (William Cogswell Collection, Phillips Library, Peabody Essex Museum, Salem MA)

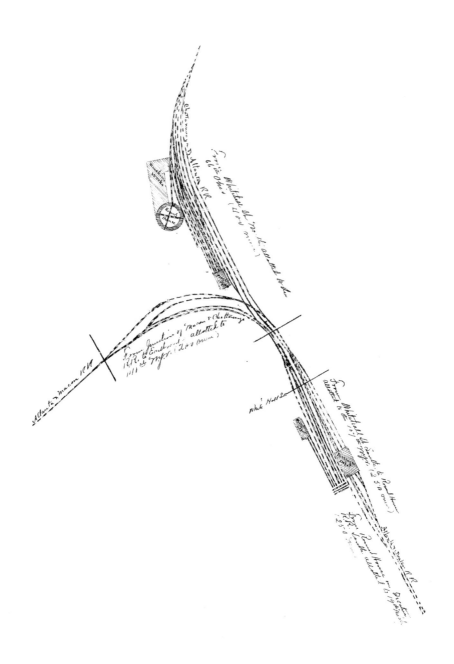

Map showing downtown sections of the three railroads converging on the Car Shed, with regiments of Powell's provisional brigade assigned to destroy them. E.g., "From Junction of Macon & Chattanooga R.R. to Earthworks Allotted to 141st N.Y.V. (200 men)." (Accompanies Lt. Col. Eugene Powell to Col. Cogswell, 4 November, William Cogswell Collection, Peabody Essex Museum)

Train being loaded at the Car Shed with possessions of northbound civilians, ca. 8 November. Barnard photograph (Atlanta History Center). In the background, the Atlanta Hotel, Trout House, and Masonic Hall are pictured, as well as quarters of the 111th Pennsylvania.

Ken Denney of Carrollton GA has focused on the posters attached to the *Intelligencer* building in right foreground; they publicize two concerts, "The Cobblers Frolic Atheneum Sat Nov 5" and "Wentworth's The New American Hercules Tonight Nov. 8." I thank Ken for this and also for his keen observation that the equipment on the loading dock appears to be a fire engine, intended for transport north. Capt. David Conyngham, correspondent for the *New York Herald*, recorded, "The fire engines were about being shipped for Chattanooga" when the first blazes broke out in the city on 11 November; the engines were returned to fire-fighting service in the city.

Northbound train, being loaded with possessions of civilians seeking to leave the city, ca. 8 November 1864. Barnard photograph (Atlanta History Center). Ken Denney noticed that the wagon in midground carries a poster advertising a concert at the Atheneum on 8 November.

Barnard took at least four shots of this train at various stages of its being loaded. While the open doors suggest that the cars themselves will be filled with army property, bags and bundles belonging to civilians are piled on the tops of the cars. The people themselves— probably African Americans, among the last civilians to leave Atlanta before the destruction—are seen in front of the arched doors of the Car Shed, awaiting their transit northward.

Sherman's troops destroying railroads at Atlanta. George Barnard photograph (Atlanta History Center). Barnard's photograph of Northern troops wrecking the railroad in downtown Atlanta was rendered into a drawing by Walton Taber for the famed *Battles and Leaders* series of the 1880s. When the men of the 1st Missouri Engineers (one of Poe's two engineer regiments at Atlanta) saw the Taber illustration, they apparently recognized themselves, to the point of reprinting the drawing in their regimental history of 1889 with the caption, "The First Missouri Engineers destroying a railroad showing the use of hooks made by them for the purpose." Note that the Car Shed has been taken down, meaning that Barnard probably took this photograph on the afternoon of 14 November. The Concert Hall and Georgia Railroad Bank Agency are still standing. They were destroyed in the fires of 15 November.

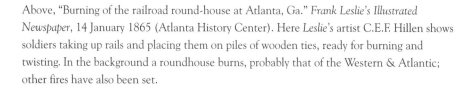

Above, "Burning of the railroad round-house at Atlanta, Ga." *Frank Leslie's Illustrated Newspaper*, 14 January 1865 (Atlanta History Center). Here *Leslie's* artist C.E.F. Hillen shows soldiers taking up rails and placing them on piles of wooden ties, ready for burning and twisting. In the background a roundhouse burns, probably that of the Western & Atlantic; other fires have also been set.

Below, "Destruction of the Depots, Public Buildings, and Manufactories at Atlanta, Georgia, November 15, 1864." *Harper's Weekly*, 7 January 1865 (Atlanta History Center). *Harper's* artist Theodore Davis witnessed the destruction in the last days of the Federal occupation. Maj. Henry Hitchcock, of Sherman's staff, recorded in his diary, 13 November, "glad to see Davis in rear sketching." In this woodcut made from Davis' drawing, the city blazes in the background as the Georgia Railroad roundhouse lies in ruins.

"Near the foot of Whitehall Street, Atlanta." Barnard photograph (Atlanta History Center). The Crawford, Frazer & Co. slave market on Whitehall Street had been an eyesore to Union soldiers occupying the city. "Nickajack," correspondent for the *New York Times*, noticed that the slave market had been struck by a Federal shell. To him, the Northern artillery "was but uttering the condemnation of God and the civilized world, against the diabolical traffic." Col. Adin Underwood of the 33rd Massachusetts later recalled his satisfaction at knowing the building had been destroyed in the fires of 15 November.

There has been speculation about the African American soldier shown seated and reading in front of the market. Sherman's forces engaged in the Atlanta Campaign included no unit of the US Colored Troops, so the photograph appears to have been "staged" as an ironic affirmation of the demise of slavery.

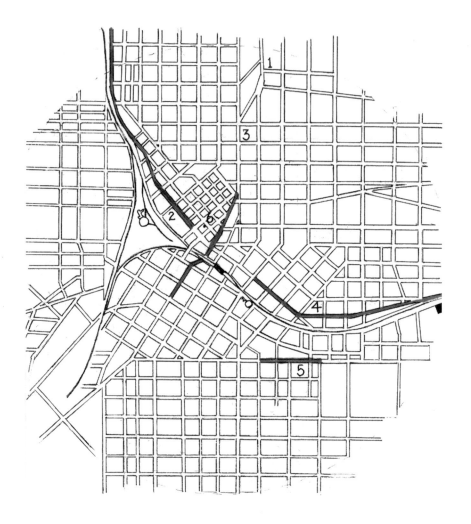

Sketched map. Streets are shaded to show general areas of destruction, as described by letter of Zachariah A. Rice, 20 November.

1. Downtown Whitehall-Peachtree axis.   2. Extensive damage along Marietta Street.
3. No houses burned on Peachtree Street beyond Wesley Chapel.
4. Extensive burning along Decatur Street.   5. Several blocks along Fair Street.
6. Saint Luke's Episcopal Church burned

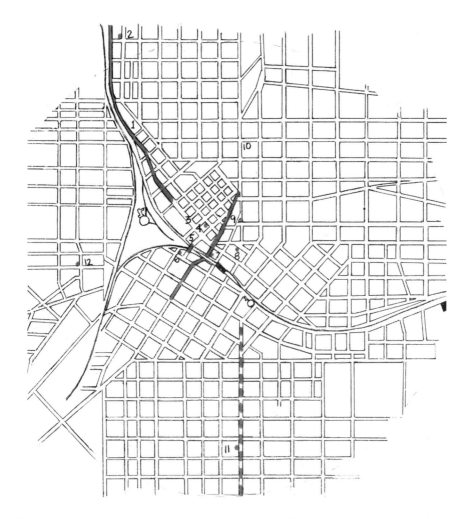

Sketched map showing city streets shaded with substantial fire-damage and other burned structures, as described by James R. Crew in letter to wife, 1 December.

1. "Between Judge Clayton's and Mrs. Ponders, I think that not more than half Doz houses are Standing."

2. "Pains Chapple is also distroyed."

3. "On Marietta St from Bridge St to Judge Clayton's, all the buildings are standing."

4. "Dr. Quintard's church"—St. Luke's Episcopal—burned

5. Bridge over railroad destroyed

6. Mrs. U. L. Wright's burned

7. "The RR bank"—Georgia Railroad Banking Agency—destroyed

8. Home of Dr. Taylor burned

9. "From Roarks Corner to Wesley Chapel not one Single house is standing."

10. "From Wesley Chapell to Billy Mim's new house on Peachtree Street all the houses are Standing in good order; not one distroyed."

11. "Mr. Cooks fine house on McDonough St distroyed. About one half the houses on this street distroyed."

12. Home of Thomas G. Healey burned

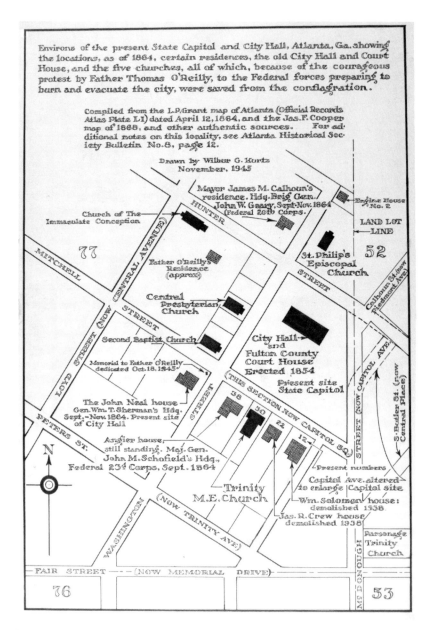

Wilbur G. Kurtz map, "Section of Atlanta Saved by Father Thos. O'Reilly, 1864, Showing Army Headquarters, Churches and Portion of Many Homes Saved." *Atlanta Historical Bulletin*, October 1945 (Atlanta History Center). Cartographic depiction by the respected Kurtz helped strengthen the very disputable legend that Father O'Reilly "saved" the downtown churches from being burned by Sherman's Yankees.

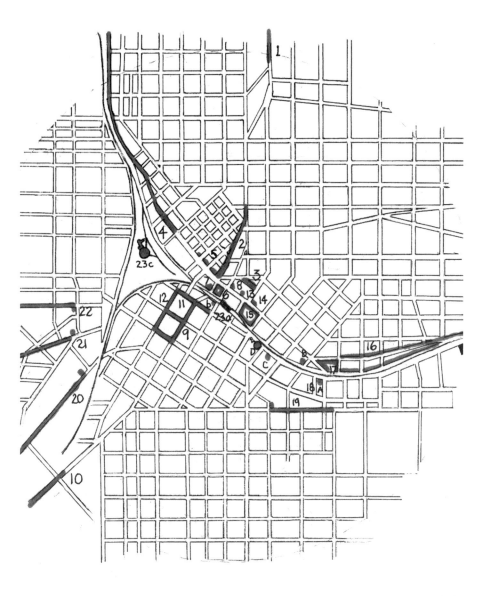

Sketched map of burned areas, as reported by "Civis," in the *Augusta* Chronicle & Sentinel of
15 December 1864.

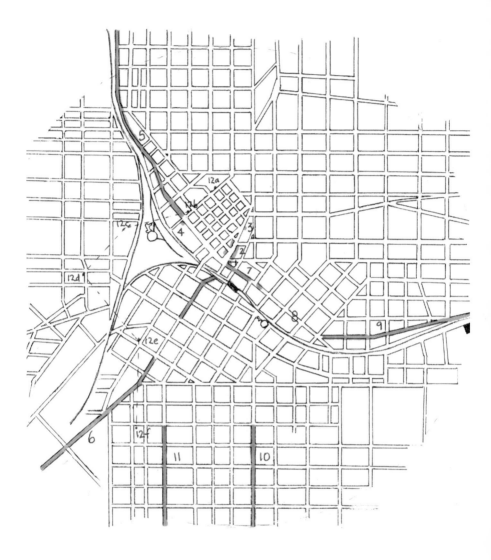

Sketched map of areas burned, described by *Atlanta Intelligencer*, 20 December 1864.

"City of Atlanta, Ga. No. 2." Barnard photograph, May 1866 (Atlanta History Center). The Georgia Railroad Bank, gutted on 15 November, is still in ruins. The buildings beside and behind are reconstructions, closely resembling their torched predecessors. The site of the Atlanta Hotel at right is marked only by brick foundations. In place of the Trout House, also destroyed by the Federals, a new building has risen, topped by a sign reading, "PHOENIX."

What the

YANKEES

Did to Us

CITY ON THE MAKE, 1837–1861

The proud, confident city that Sherman wrecked had humble beginnings. A mere generation before the Civil War, the area destined to become Atlanta was only a thick, wooded wilderness. The Creek had gone, forced to cede their lands south of the Chattahoochee and forcibly removed far to the west. A few white settlers had moved in, built log cabins for their families and cleared the woods for farming; one Hardy Ivy is credited as being the first resident of the city-to-be. Some roads wended through the land, chiefly the east-west stage route connecting Decatur and Newnan. Serving its travelers were such isolated taverns as Charner Humphries's "White Hall," built about 1835. By that time, the Cherokees had lost their claim to North Georgia and been forced to sign a treaty promising to leave within two years.

Even before the last Native Americans had left Northwest Georgia, state legislators called for a railroad through the territory. In late 1836, the Georgia General Assembly passed the railroad law that made Atlanta possible. Incorporated as the Western & Atlantic Railroad, the line would connect the town of Ross's Landing (soon to be Chattanooga) with some point on the southeastern bank of the Chattahoochee River, more than 100 miles to the south. From there, as-yet-to-be built other rail lines would link Augusta and Macon, bringing the state's major cities into commerce with the Tennessee River and the vast Midwest beyond. It was an ambitious plan. In fall 1837, Stephen H. Long and other engineers, surveying the proposed W & A, fixed the southern terminus of the lines at a point 7 miles south and east of the Chattahoochee. The site today is in the heart of downtown Atlanta; back then it was an uninhabited pine and scrubby oak forest amid thickets of sourwood and gooseberry.[1]

Around this terminus grew the village that would be Atlanta. The place was in fact called Terminus even when there was as yet no town. A young,

---

[1] James Michael Russell, *Atlanta, 1847–1890: City Building in the Old South and the New* (Baton Rouge: Louisiana State University Press, 1988) 20; Franklin M. Garrett, *Atlanta and Environs: A Chronicle of Its People and Events*, 2 vols. (New York: Lewis Historical Publishing Co., 1954) 1:48 (Treaty of Indian Springs), 115–16, 129–31, 145 (state railroad act), 149–50; Theda Perdue and Michael D. Green, *The Cherokee Nation and the Trail of Tears* (New York: Penguin Books, 2008) 110–11, 127–32 (forced removal in 1838); [Louis L. Parham, ed.], *Pioneer Citizens' History of Atlanta, 1833–1902* (Atlanta: Byrd Printing Company, 1902) 11–13; Wallace P. Reed, *History of Atlanta, Georgia, with Illustrations and Biographical Sketches of Some of Its Prominent Men and Pioneers* (Syracuse NY: D. Mason & Co., 1889) 26–27.

twenty-one-year-old John Thrasher arrived and opened a store to serve the increasing number of families, all forming "a right smart little town," and hopefully awaiting the arrival of the railroad. For several years, though, there was not even a railroad. By late 1841 not a single iron rail had been laid on the proposed Western & Atlantic, although engineers had been busy surveying and grading.

An important step was taken in July 1842 when W & A officials, after relocating their southern terminus site some 400 yards eastward, acquired land for a depot. The 5-acre tract eventually became known as State Square and around it was laid out lots for a township. Within a few months, the depot, a two-story engineer's office and several other buildings were constructed; tracks also began to be laid northward. As the village began to take shape, the United States Post Office graced it on 22 December 1842 with a name: Marthasville for the daughter of then-Georgia Governor Wilson Lumpkin. Two days later, Marthasville became a true railroad town when a locomotive and two cars, hauled overland for the occasion, stoked up and carried a throng of excited passengers (from Decatur and thereabouts) from the Terminus depot northward on the 20 miles of track that had been laid to date across a rickety Chattahoochee bridge and on to the trackside township of Marietta.[2]

Before completion of the railroads, Marthasville held little lure to would-be residents. In early 1842, perhaps seven families had built homes in the village. Most folk felt the little burg would be no more than a waystation on the rail lines. For several years, most of the original seventeen house lots laid out in 1842 around State Square remained unsold. A few streets were drawn, merging with the old Indian trail northward (Peachtree), leading to nearby boroughs (Marietta and Decatur) and carrying their names, or named for early residents (such as James Loyd, who opened a general store in spring 1844). These ragged thoroughfares ran from the town's center-of-sorts outward, eventually fading away in the surrounding forest. A few other businesses took hold, such as Jonathan Norcross's sawmill, which provided for villagers' building needs. George W. Collier's grocery store, at Peachtree and Decatur streets, doubled as the town's first post office—meaning that storekeeper Collier also doubled as town postmaster.

Still, Marthasville's population numbered only 100 to 200 in 1845, the year the town's first physician (Dr. Joshua Gilbert) and attorney (Leonard Simpson) arrived. Much more significant, in 1845 the Georgia Railroad being built from Augusta finally connected with the W & A terminus to provide a 169-mile rail line running roughly east to west. Arrival of the first train from Augusta, September 1845, was the occasion of wild excitement, as folk came in from all

---

[2] Garrett, *Atlanta and Environs*, 1:150, 165, 179, 185, 189–90; James G. Bogle, "Civil War Railroads—Georgia and Tennessee," *Atlanta Historical Bulletin* 12/3 (September 1967): 33 (on train trip of 24 December 1842).

around to see the locomotive, examine the cars, interview the engineer and foreman, all in the mood of a public celebration. Linked now to one of the state's principal cities, forward-looking businessmen resolved to discard the somnolent village name of Marthasville. Atlanta came to fore as the new name, derived from the name of the railroad, Western & Atlantic. From fall 1845, Georgia railroad circulars began to be printed with "Atlanta." Senator John C. Calhoun used that name, too, in a speech to railroad businessmen in Memphis, 13 November 1845, when he predicted a great future for the place as a rail junction. The state legislature formally ratified the town's new name a month later.[3]

Atlanta's rail connections strengthened in October 1846 with the completion of yet another railway, the Macon & Western, into the city. The three lines—the Georgia, M & W, and still as-yet-uncompleted W & A—converged in State Square, upon and around which freight depots, engine houses, and rail company machine shops arose. Serving the now-thriving town were, by late 1847, two schools, a post office, a non-denominational church building, and several newspapers (the *Luminary, Enterprise,* and *Southern Miscellany*). There were also two hotels, the Atlanta and Washington Hall, each capable of accommodating 150 guests; the hostelries were the town's first brick buildings (the Atlanta Hotel rising to an impressive two stories). At that time, in December 1847, Atlantans took the further step of incorporating the city with a mayor, city council, and formal limits, the latter a 1-mile-radius circle drawn out from the railroad depot in State Square.[4]

The arrival of the Georgia and M & W Railroads brought more folk, so that 2,500 people called themselves Atlantans by the end of 1847. "The streets are alive with people," wrote an early Atlantan, Dr. William White in 1847, and the stores, perhaps thirty in number, were "full of trade, and bustle." So many strangers were arriving, Dr. White recorded, that "the people here bow and

---

[3] David F. Weiman, "Urban Growth on the Periphery of the Antebellum Cotton Belt: Atlanta, 1847–1860," *Journal of Economic History* 48/2 (June 1988): 263; Garrett, *Atlanta and Environs*, 1:199, 205, 207, 216–17 (on Gilbert and Simpson), 224–25; Frank K. Boland, "Atlanta's First Physician," *Atlanta Historical Bulletin* 7 (June 1933): 16; James Walter Mason, "Atlanta's Matronymic," in Walter G. Cooper, *Official History of Fulton County* (Atlanta: History Commission, 1934) 68–71; [Greene B. Haygood], "Sketch of Atlanta," in *Williams' Atlanta Directory, City Guide and Business Mirror* (Atlanta: M. Lynch, 1859) 10 (Haygood notes that for awhile the town's name was written Atalanta); Reed, *History of Atlanta*, 41–42, 48–49; Richard K. Cralle, ed., *The Works of John C. Calhoun*, 6 vols. (New York: D. Appleton and Company, 1856) 6:276. A commemorative plaque excerpting Calhoun's address can be seen today in downtown Atlanta at Park Place and Edgewood Avenue.

[4] Garrett, *Atlanta and Environs*, 1:234–37; 247–48, 251 (on Atlanta's early newspapers), 260; Reed, *History of Atlanta*, 38.

shake hands with everybody they meet, as there are so many coming in all the time that they cannot remember with whom they are acquainted."[5]

Yet all was not gentility, as young Atlanta gave every appearance of a frontier town. The "streets" were of course unpaved, full of stumps and roots. Livestock roamed about freely; sometimes their carcasses littered the thoroughfares and had to be removed by the town marshal. Just north of State Square, a block of wooden shanties running along Decatur Street east from Peachtree to Pryor, known locally as Murrell's Row, housed saloons, cockpits, faro banks, and brothels. Against the rowdies, gamblers, and prostitutes frequenting this area stood only one town marshal and a deputy, who had at their disposal a tiny, single-cell jail. This log calaboose was so small (12 feet square) and so unfounded that at least once the buddies of the prisoners inside stormed the jail, heaved-to, and lifted the structure off the ground so the inmates could crawl out. Less violent than the toughs of Murrell's Row were the gangs of wild boys, "dirty, mischievous urchins running at large...in our streets," one newspaper complained. One of their favorite pranks was to round up four or five pigs, put them in a barrel, and roll it down the Alabama Street hill, from Whitehall to State Square. The grunters' wild squealing would invariably raise a huge ruckus, as everyone rushed outside to see the commotion.

Gradually the town's rough appearance smoothed. The erection of worship places helped: the Methodists' Wesley Chapel, the Episcopalian St. Philip's Church, and First Baptist all opened in 1848. The city's first telegraph office followed the next year. The city council provided for a new cemetery as well as a volunteer fire company in 1850—the year that the Western & Atlantic cleared the final mountain in North Georgia and linked Atlanta to Chattanooga. A stone zero-mile post, formally marking the southern end of the W & A's 138 miles of track and its junction with the Georgia Railroad, was at the eastern edge of State Square. As Atlanta's oldest landmark, the post may be seen today beneath the Central Avenue viaduct, near Underground Atlanta.[6]

---

[5] William Stafford Irvine, ed., "Diary and Letters of Dr. William N. White, a Citizen of Atlanta Written 1847, 90 Years Ago," *Atlanta Historical Bulletin* 2/10 (July 1937): 39, 41.

[6] Irvine, ed., "Diary and Letters of Dr. William N. White," 39 ("streets are still full of stumps and roots"); Garrett, *Atlanta and Environs*, 1:190 (zero mile post), 205 (seven streets in 1844), 265–66, 268–70, 278, 282, 298 (one marshal and deputy), 310, 315 (the Atlanta or City Cemetery, named Oakland in 1876), 317–18, 359, 373; Annie Laurie Fuller Kurtz, "Atlanta's First Jail Break," *Atlanta Journal Magazine*, 11 February 1934, 10; Russell, *Atlanta, 1847–1890*, 64 ("dirty, mischievous urchins"); Russell S. Bonds, "Sherman's First March Through Georgia," *Civil War Times* 46/6 (August 2007): 35 (on Tunnel Hill).

Completion of the W. & A. gave tough guys another means of upending the cabin-jail. It is recorded that once boys roped the caboose to a departing engine; the unsturdy structure was ripped off, and its inmates made their getaway ("Atlanta Police. From the Days of Marthasville, in '44, to Atlanta, in '88," *Atlanta Constitution*, 12 August 1898, 2).

The Federal Census of 1850 confirmed Atlanta as a town a-building. Among its 2,500 residents (2,058 whites, 493 enslaved blacks, and 18 free blacks), the leading occupation was that of carpentry. A good many Atlantans, too, were merchants, reflecting the tilt of the town's economy toward commerce over manufacturing. An array of wholesale and retail stores grew up—the number increased from twenty to fifty-seven between 1849 and 1854 alone—selling Northern-made hardware, farm tools and other goods to farmers and country store owners in the surrounding area. A number of vendors advertised Yankee-made sewing machines for the city's clothing-makers and seamstresses. Moreover, carried by wagon and train from Georgia's upper piedmont and east Tennessee, food crops were brought and sold, along with cotton from middle and South Georgia. Cotton warehouses were accordingly scattered throughout the city.[7]

Not surprisingly, Atlanta's business district emanated from the railway facilities in the heart of town, developing along Whitehall, Alabama, Peachtree, and Decatur streets. A resident later described the cluster of shops and vending places that extended up Whitehall from the railroad.

> ...the first house was the new grocery of John and James Lynch.... They did a large grocery trade and bought cotton. Across Alabama Street, Smith, Smith, Jones & Johnson had a general supply store.... Cooper Holiday had a barroom a little up the street. [Robert M.] Clarke & [Thomas F.] Grubb had a general supply store at or near that time, and they packed a very large amount of bacon. Dr. [Benjamin] Bomar had a general grocery store. The dry goods store of Dr. Angier was on the corner of Hunter and Whitehall. On the side beyond Hunter and on the right was an almost unbroken row of small store houses to Mitchell, where the store houses ended. On the other side Scott, Carhart & Co. had a very large grocery on the corner of Alabama. Their managing partner, U.L. Wright, was a great cotton buyer. The Sternberger Brothers...was next; then [John J.] Thrasher & Schife, who had a large variety store; then Old Billy Mann, and then Terrence Doonan, a great cotton buyer, who had a large grocery store. On the corner of Hunter and Whitehall was the only brick store in town, occupied by [Ira O.] McDaniel, [Alexander W.] Mitchell & [Eli J.] Halsey. Before coming to them was the large dry goods and clothing store of Jacob Haas & Bros.... On the south sides of Hunter,

---

[7] Garrett, *Atlanta and Environs*, 1:305–306; Russell, *Atlanta, 1847–1890*, 40–41; Weiman, "Urban Growth," 264, 268.

on Whitehall, was J.T. Doane and Co.... They sold everything the country trade wanted....[8]

Sprinkled amid these mercantile establishments (seventy-seven in 1859), were a few manufactories, such as Austin Leyden's foundry and machine shop, Joseph Winship's freight car factory, or Richard Peters's steam-powered flour mill, built in 1849. The Atlanta Rolling Mill was established in 1857 at the city's eastern limits alongside the Georgia Railroad. Under the management of Lewis Scofield and William Markham, the facility specialized in rolling iron rails for the South's growing railroad lines.

Throughout the city were the many other enterprises serving Atlanta's growing population. The city's first successful bank, the Bank of Fulton, opened in 1856. New newspapers had arisen to replace those that had dried up; but others showed staying power, such as the *Southern Miscellany*, which changed to the *Atlanta Weekly Intelligencer* in mid-1849, and transformed into a daily five years later. There were more hotels, such as the four-story Trout House, completed in 1854 at the corner of Decatur and Pryor Streets. There were more schools, too; seven opened in 1851 alone. All were private enterprises vying for profitability, as public education for Atlanta's children was still a long ways off. There were more churches, too: the Catholic Church of the Immaculate Conception (1851), First Presbyterian (1852), Trinity (or Second) Methodist (1854), and Second Baptist (1854). Among the town's other amenities were a theater, the Atheneum (built in 1857); whose bills boasted minstrel shows and such comedies as *Toodles, the Gambler's Wife*. Just north of the passenger depot in State Square was laid out a public park; farther off to the south, below Fair Street, a multi-acre fairground was dedicated to luring regional farm shows to Atlanta (the city council also dubbed the land as the "hospital lot"; it was here that a smallpox hospital opened in July 1853). Eventually, a new jail was built at Bridge Street near the railroad. Then in 1854 came a new city hall on Collins Street two blocks south of the railroads. As the state legislature had just created a new county for the Atlanta area (named for a local civil engineer, Hamilton Fulton), the city hall doubled as county courthouse.

Signs of a town struggling to become a city were plentiful in the 1850s. Atlanta's development as rail-fed commercial center was furthered in 1854 by the arrival of the city's fourth railroad, the Atlanta & West Point. Actually the road terminated at an "East Point" on the Macon & Western, 6 miles southwest of State Square. From there the A & WP led 87 miles farther southwest to West Point, Georgia, where other lines connected to Montgomery, Alabama, and eventually Mobile and New Orleans. Completion of the Memphis & Charleston,

---

[8] Franklin M. Garrett, *Yesterday's Atlanta* (Miami: E. A. Seemann Publishing, 1974) 8 (the city's official seal); George Gilman Smith, "Recollections of an Atlanta Boy, 1847–1855," *Atlanta Journal*, 2 October 1909, quoted in Garrett, *Atlanta and Environs*, 1:287.

heading west of Chattanooga in 1857, also strengthened the city's railway ties to the Mississippi Valley, a link that Charlestonians recognized by dubbing Atlanta the "Gate City." Atlantans liked the nickname, as shown when a new militia company in early 1858 took the title of "Gate City Guard." Status as a "gate city" was certainly supported by the volume of Atlanta's commercial traffic. Forty-four freight and passenger trains were said to arrive and leave every day, while wagon traffic seemed equally heavy. One resident recalled that at times "wagons would line Peachtree road thickly for miles…. Some were one-horse or ox, some six horses or mules," and all bringing goods for sale or transport from as far away as North Carolina. Rail passengers to and from the Gate City were accommodated by the big (100 feet by 300 feet) "Car Shed," the brick passenger depot in State Square completed in 1854 as replacement of the original wooden depot building. The clanking of trains back and forth between the Car Shed, freight depots, and locomotive houses downtown inconvenienced many pedestrians, who at times stood angrily on street corners for up to half an hour trying to cross the tracks. Only one downtown bridge built in 1852 (and replaced in 1858) at Bridge Street (eventually Broad) near the W & A freight depot gave wagons and other traffic a means of passing over the busy rails.

Though called for by the city council as early as 1850, plank sidewalks along the city's downtown business streets did not abound before 1856, largely because they were to be funded by levies against the property owners. Streets themselves remained unpaved, although oak planking had been laid down on Whitehall as early as 1849 to help with wagon traffic. Grading and smoothing improved the thoroughfares, as did the city council's occasional provision of dumped gravel during winter rainy seasons. Finally, in 1857 the city called for brick or flagstone paving of the "business portions" of Peachtree, Alabama, Marietta, and Decatur streets. Such ordinances as that passed by the council on 27 August 1858, ordering that garbage from the Trout House hotel could henceforth not be dumped in the streets, also helped. Gas-lit streetlights also appeared in the business district in late 1855 when, following the creation of the Atlanta Gas Light Company, pipes were laid down and the city's first fifty street lamps went up. Other early if faltering efforts at providing public services came in the area of fire protection. By 1860 four fire companies had been formed in Atlanta. All were staffed by volunteers, but the city helped fund their water-wagons, hoses, and station houses. Several water cisterns in the business district, called for by the city council as early as 1851 with their adjacent wells, were kept full against the periodic blazes that broke out among the wooden storefronts. With such destruction by fire, however, occasionally came better reconstruction with brick. Indeed, in December 1857 the city council set as "fire limits" the roughly ten-block area around State Square, inside which no wooden residence could henceforth be built. Nineteen brick stores were built in 1858 alone.[9]

Periodic censuses recorded the growth of Atlanta's population from the 2,500 individuals enumerated in 1850. A local census four years later counted 6,025 people, and the number seemed to grow by a thousand each year, to 8,000 in 1856. The first city directory of 1859 boasted 11,000 residents. The Federal count of 1860 established Atlanta as Georgia's third largest city, behind Savannah and Augusta (it had been fifth in 1850). The census takers' detailing of Atlantans' occupations suggested a fast-growing, commerce-fed city; "laborer" and "carpenter" were still the two largest categories, as from the decade before; then came clerk and merchant. Next in frequency were other workingmen's trades that not only showed Atlanta's reliance on the railroads (machinist, locomotive fireman, locomotive engineer) but also allowed local observers to claim that a "mechanical element prevailed in the city." The number of brick masons and painters, over 100, further confirmed all the construction underway. And where there were so many workingmen, there were workingwomen, too; prostitution ranked as Atlanta's tenth-largest occupation. There were almost as many railroad conductors as attorneys, and almost as many "train hands" as physicians. The number of men in other categories—bookkeeper, stonemason, printer, shoe and boot maker—altogether demonstrated why skilled laborers comprised 44 percent of the city's working population in 1860. Not surprisingly for an upcountry city, there lived in Atlanta only a few farmers and planters (twenty-eight all told, or 1.7 percent of the population). As a consequence, comparatively fewer slaves lived in Atlanta than in low-country cities sustained by cotton and black-belt agriculture. Indeed, Atlanta's largest slave owners were men like the hoteliers James Loyd and Joseph Thompson, or Joseph Winship and Julius Hayden, whose foundry and brickyards used slave labor.

Given other contemporary accounts, the 1860 Census figure of 9,691 Atlantans—7,751 whites, 1,917 enslaved blacks, and 23 free blacks—seems low. Doubtless, it excluded residents living outside the city limits. In fact, so many folk lived in the "suburbs" that the council in October 1860 considered extending the city limits to a 2-mile radius from the Car Shed. The motion failed, but the

---

[9] Garrett, *Atlanta and Environs*, 1:273, 279 (*Atlanta Weekly Intelligencer*), 282, 309 (city council and sidewalks), 324, 333–34, 350, 354–56, 362–65 (on Robert or Hamilton Fulton as source for county name), 373–75, 379 (new city hall, October 1854), 382, 391 (jail), 397, 406 (Bank of Fulton), 427, 432 (Atlanta as "Gate City"), 437–39, 440, 457, 466, 483, 488; Russell, *Atlanta, 1847–1890*, 32–33 (on bridge), 42–43, 46–47 (Atlanta Rolling Mill), 50–52, 59–60; [Haygood], "Sketch of Atlanta," 14; [Parham, ed.], *Pioneer Citizens' History*, 233; Reed, *History of Atlanta*, 65–68, 78, 82–83.

Local historian Wilbur G. Kurtz concluded that Hamilton Fulton, surveyor of railroads, was the source of Fulton County's name (notebook 9, 69–70, Wilbur G. Kurtz Collection, Atlanta History Center). Though Garrett, above, concludes that the honor belonged to the steam boater Robert Fulton, I side with Kurtz's logic.

official limits had already been extended by the addition of a "handle," 600 yards wide, extending to the southwest along the Macon & Western Railroad. With this exception, Atlanta's demarking circle, as set originally in 1847, remained in place.[10]

City limits, major streets, and railroads are all depicted on Atlanta's first map, commissioned by the mayor and executed in 1853 by Edward A. Vincent, an English-born architect who had settled in Atlanta. With the aid of Vincent's map and Williams' directory for 1859, one can see the layout of the city just before the Civil War. The business district, of course, was concentrated along the Whitehall-Peachtree axis between Alabama and Decatur. Here were almost all of the city's more than 200 stores and wholesale outlets, as well as various enterprises that supported them. The city's several banks, for example, were all located within three blocks of the railroad, along Whitehall.

More than any store or bank, however, the passenger depot or "Car Shed" in State Square represented the center-point of the city. Built according to plans by Vincent, the shed's huge arched roof covered four rail lines, ticket and baggage offices, and waiting rooms—everything a busy railroad station needed for its passengers. Not surprisingly, all of Atlanta's six hotels in 1859 clung to the periphery of the square: the Atlanta, City, and Planters' hotels, Trout and Tennessee Houses, and Washington Hall.

Strung out along the tracks east and west of the Car Shed were the various depots and engine houses serving the four railroads. West of the Bridge Street span over the tracks lay Western & Atlantic's locomotive roundhouse and freight depot. The Macon & Western locomotive house was to the south, at Hunter Street's junction with the tracks, but the M & W freight depot was three blocks away, near the Car Shed. To the east of the shed, the Georgia Railroad had its freight depot and locomotive house. Farther east, at the railroad and Pratt Street, was the Atlanta & West Point freight depot.[11]

More a commercial and railway distribution center than an industrial city, antebellum Atlanta nevertheless had several factories and a number of smaller shops. The Federal Census of 1860 counted fifteen manufacturing concerns worth the name. Seven of them, and the largest enterprises, involved metals. The Atlanta Machine Works, the foundry established in 1848 by Austin Leyden, was

[10] Garrett, *Atlanta and Environs*, 1: 305, 373, 406 (8,000 in 1856), 479, 489–91 (census of 1860); Ralph Benjamin Singer, "Confederate Atlanta" (Ph.D. diss., University of Georgia, 1973) 12–13 (on Atlanta's population ranking); Russell, *Atlanta, 1847–1890*, 70–71; [Haygood], "Sketch of Atlanta," in *Williams' Atlanta Directory*, 11 (6,025 in 1854), 13–14.

[11] Garrett, *Atlanta and Environs*, 1:353–54, 382 (Car Shed completion date); Annie Laurie Fuller Kurtz, "Departed Glory of State Square," *Atlanta Journal Magazine*, 1 December 1935, 16; Elizabeth Catherine Bowlby, "The Role of Atlanta during the Civil War" (Master's thesis, Emory University, 1938) 4–5. A summary of Bowlby's thesis is printed as Elizabeth Bowlby, "The Role of Atlanta During the War Between the States," *Atlanta Historical Bulletin* 5/22 (July 1940): 177–96.

eventually bought by James L. Dunning. Advertising itself in Williams's 1859 city directory as "builders of steam engines," the company turned out sawmills, boilers, waterwheels, and other machinery. Its plant was located south of the Georgia Railroad at King Street. Another early manufactory, Joseph Winship's car works, had been destroyed by fire in 1856. Undaunted, Winship founded another company, specializing not only in rail cars but boilers, engines, mining machinery, circular saw mills, as well as iron and brass castings. Eventually managed by Winship's brother and two sons, Winship's Iron Works was located at the W & A RR and Foundry Street (so named because of Winship's business). Nearby, the Western & Atlantic's machine shops not only met the W & A's maintenance needs, but even built a few passenger cars. One of them, on display at a regional trade fair in 1857, won a prize for equaling "any brought from the North." The Georgia Railroad also had shops in the city for its machinery and engines. Two other concerns dealt in tin, copper and sheet ware. One of them, John T. Tomlinson and William B. Barnes's at Whitehall and the railroad, manufactured and dealt in stoves, copper stills, gas fixtures and tin ware. But by far the largest metal fabrication plant in the city was the Atlanta Rolling Mill, well east of downtown at the Georgia Railroad. With six big furnaces and two strong engines to drive the rollers, the plant could produce 18,000 tons of iron rails a year and at capacity employ 150 workers (although actual operations fell far short). Nevertheless, Scofield and Markham's rolling mill was the largest of its kind south of Richmond, Virginia, where the Tredegar Iron Works ranked as the South's largest.[12]

Other enterprises processed grain, leather, and lumber. Near the Georgia Railroad yards between Calhoun and Butler streets in 1849, Richard Peters had set up his Steam Flour Mill. At peak capacity, the concern turned out 280 barrels of flour a day with its two powerful engines, but freight rates and distance from wheat farmers forced Peters to shut down his mill in 1856. The machinery remained, however, ready for application to other purposes. Another flour mill, James A. Stewart and William C. Moore's Greenwood Mill, was located in the city's northwestern fringes, Marietta Street near the city limits line.

Tanneries and boot and saddle makers represented another thriving line of business: leather goods. Two tanneries, as shown in Williams's 1859 directory, operated in the south part of town: William H. McMillan's, on Decatur Street between Bell and Gartrell, and Harvey Reed's, south of Garnett at Whitehall. On the other side of town, near the northern circle of the city limits, stood the Atlanta Steam Tannery of J. Christian Orme. Established in 1852 at Orme and Simpson Streets, Orme's was the city's first tannery and shoe factory. Closer into

---

[12] *Manufactures of the United States in 1860; Compiled from the Original Returns of the Eighth Census...* (Washington, DC: Government Printing Office, 1865) 68; Russell, *Atlanta 1847–1890*, 45–47; *Williams' Atlanta Directory*, 36, 39, 86, 141, 145, 147; [Parham, ed.], *Pioneer Citizens' History of Atlanta*, 117–18; Garrett, *Atlanta and Environs*, 1:350.

town were several more enterprises specializing in boots, shoes, brogans, saddles, and harnesses, but located along Whitehall and Peachtree streets, these firms (Loderick Dimick, William Wilson & Co., Francis Eddleman & Isaac Banks, and Daniel Miller and Ezra Andrews) were more wholesale and retail outlets than industries.

Of the two main lumber-processing companies, Columbus A. Pitts and George W. D. Cook's was the larger and more varied in product. Their "Atlanta Steam Planing Mill, Cotton Gin, and Thrashing Machine Manufactory" turned out not only agricultural machinery but also planed wood for the city's busy construction trade: tongues and grooved boards for floors and ceilings, sashes, doors, and blinds. Pitts and Cook's lumberyard was in the northwest part of town, at the railroad opposite Foundry Alley. On the other side of the Car Shed, Aaron H. Brown, Edwin P. Priest, and John C. Peck's "Lumber Yard and Planing and Flooring Mill, Sash, Door and Blind Manufactory" was sited at Decatur and Pratt.

In addition to these manufacturing concerns, there were of course smaller enterprises, such as Muhlenbrink's Atlanta Cigar Manufactory on Whitehall, H. G. Gardner's carriage shop at Hunter and Forsyth, or P. J. Immel's candy-makers on Alabama Street. Altogether they were clustered more toward the center of town than were the bigger industrial plants and mills. Clothes-making in 1859 was said to employ more than seventy-five workers, mostly women; by and large these shops fronted on Whitehall and Peachtree streets, as did the city's several furniture-making businesses. On the other hand, Thomas C. Howard's Empire distillery made whiskey out on Houston Street, slightly beyond the city limits.[13]

Centered downtown were most of the city's churches, schools, and other public buildings. Atlanta's earliest houses of worship—Wesley Chapel (or First Methodist), First Baptist, and First Presbyterian—were built several blocks north of State Square. Others eventually ringed city hall: St. Philip's Episcopal, Immaculate Conception, Trinity Methodist, Second Baptist, and Central Presbyterian (1860). Five other Christian congregations, mostly Methodist, had arisen in various locations throughout town by 1859. One was located at Garnett and Forsyth in the city's southwest quadrant. Another was an African Methodist church for the city's free blacks.[14]

---

[13] Russell, *Atlanta 1847–1890*, 47–48; Sarah Huff, *My Eighty Years in Atlanta* (Atlanta: n.p., 1937) 65; *Williams' Atlanta Directory*, 53, 70, 74, 80, 96, 117, 124, 126, 129, 138; Singer, "Confederate Atlanta," 22–25; [Haygood], "Sketch of Atlanta," 12; [Parham, ed.], *Pioneer Citizens' History*, 119; Weiman, "Urban Growth," 268–69; [Franklin Garrett and Wilbur J. Kurtz], "Key to Map," *Atlanta Historical Bulletin* 2/8 (September 1934): 5.

[14] Garrett, *Atlanta and Environs*, 1:268–71, 333, 347, 439; [Parham, ed.], *Pioneer Citizens' History*, 140–56; *Williams' Atlanta Directory*, 14, 22–23. Atlanta's Jews had no formally dedicated temple until after the Civil War, in 1877 (*Pioneer Citizens' History*, 390–91).

Antebellum education in Atlanta, without municipal funding or administration, relied largely on the efforts of entrepreneurs or charitable volunteers. Most "teachers" of young people were women who conducted classes out of their homes, such as Mrs. T. S. Ogilby, who charged female pupils $4.00 per term for "orthography, reading, writing, and arithmetic"; $6.00 for instruction in "geography, botany, grammar, philosophy, rhetoric, astronomy, geography of the heavens, ancient and modern history, moral and intellectual philosophy"; plus other enrichment courses such as "waxwork, fruit and flowers" ($10.00). Similarly, the wife of attorney Greene B. Haygood operated a school for girls, Haygood's Academy; but the academy itself was merely the Haygood house at Mitchell and McDonough.

Of actual school buildings there were thus but a few in town. Atlanta's first non-denominational church, the Atlanta Union Sabbath School, not only housed Sunday school classes, but became a kind of community schoolhouse used by schoolmasters-for-hire. Known variously as the Union School or "triangle schoolhouse," the small weatherboarded structure was located in the triangular lot bounded by Peachtree, Pryor, and Houston streets. In the late 1850s, the triangle schoolhouse was used by Alexander N. Wilson, a schoolmaster from east Tennessee, for his "Atlanta Classical School" for boys. Another educational edifice was established by the physician Needom L. Angier, a schoolhouse at the corner of Forsyth and Garnett in the southwestern quadrant of the city. The Angier Academy proved to be impermanent (as did so many of early Atlanta's "schools"); Dr. Angier eventually turned to banking and insurance. A public-spirited citizen, Edward W. Holland, in 1853 bought Angier's little building and lot and offered it to the city fathers as a free school. The Holland Free School thus became Atlanta's first try at public education. Funded in part by the city council, the enterprise lasted a rather respectable five years.

The collapse of the free school spurred several leading residents to pool their resources and raise money for a women's school. Built on the northeast corner of Collins and Ellis, the Atlanta Female Institute (or Seminary) opened in 1860, offering preparatory and collegiate curricula under "Professor" J. R. Mayson, a Methodist minister. More significant still as an educational institution was the Atlanta Medical College. Conceived by Dr. John G. Westmoreland and other physicians in the city, the Atlanta Medical College began classes in 1855 at city hall with an eight-physician faculty. That year the cornerstone of a college building was laid at the corner of Butler and Jenkins. Within a year, a two-story building, topped with an imposing dome, had been completed, the present-day site of the Grady Memorial Hospital. Under the deanship of Westmoreland, the medical college faculty in 1859 included Drs. Thomas S. Powell, professor of obstetrics, Joseph P. Logan, physiology and pediatrics, and Willis F. Westmoreland, surgery.[15]

Along with churches and schools, Atlanta's urban landscape included other public facilities. At opposite ends of the W & A Railroad axis were the gas works and fairgrounds. Incorporated in 1855 by the state legislature, the Atlanta Gas Light Company was, after the railroads, the city's oldest corporation. Its plant was sited in the northwest quadrant, near Winship's Iron Works. Across town were the city's fairgrounds, 10 acres acquired in 1850 by the city council in hopes of hosting the annual fair of the Southern Central Agricultural Society. A few blocks to the west of the grounds, at Fair and Fraser streets, was the county jail. The two-story brick structure completed in 1856, replaced Atlanta's early, ineffective log calaboose. The center of municipal authority was the Atlanta City Hall/Fulton County Courthouse, located in the block southeast of Hunter and Collins. The open space around the courthouse, with trees and shrubbery, served as an informal park. Indeed, the only public park so designated in the city was the north end of State Square, which the city fathers in 1858 arranged as the site for benches and lawn, bounded by Decatur, Pryor and Loyd streets.

Other public services included the fire companies. The four organizations had their engine houses sited close to the business district: the Atlanta Fire Company (no. 1), Bridge Street at the railroad; Mechanic Fire Company (2), Washington Street north of St. Philip's; Tallulah Fire Company (3), on west Bridge, between Marietta and Walton; and the Atlanta Hook and Ladder Company, east Pryor between Alabama and Hunter. Sited as they were, the firehouses were intended to protect the businesses and buildings along the Peachtree-Whitehall axis as well as the area around city hall.

Public buildings downtown were numerous. The imposing, three-story brick Masonic Hall was completed in June 1860 just east of the Trout House on Decatur Street. On the other side of the Trout hotel, the Atheneum theater, with its row of white fluted columns above the ground floor, fronted on Decatur Street between Pryor and Peachtree. To Atlantans of the time, it was the only place for public performances. The theater's site, a triangular demi-block bounded by Decatur, Cherokee, and Pryor, was known as "Silvey and Glazner's Block," for George Glazner and John Silvey's saloon and billiard hall. (The next block northward also had a name, "Cherokee Block," distinguished on its Peachtree side by the sign of a big boot, the logo for Dimick and Wilson's boot and shoe shop.)

South of Silvey and Glazner's, the corner of Peachtree at the railroad was marked prominently by the Georgia Railroad and Banking Company's

[15] Meta Barker, "Schools and Teachers of Ante–Bellum Atlanta," *Atlanta Historical Bulletin* 4/16 (January 1939): 31–33; "Atlanta's Early Schools," in [Parham, ed.], *Pioneer Citizens' History*, 133–36; Garrett, *Atlanta and Environs*, 1:247–49, 356–57 (Holland Free School), 375–76, 456–57; *Williams' Atlanta Directory*, 39, 146.

building—two stories, stone and as substantial-looking as one might expect for one of Atlanta's premier structures. Across the street, on the west side of Peachtree, stood Atlanta's three-story concert hall, as painted prominently at its corner, although there was no auditorium inside (the real concert hall was the Athenaeum). The building's levels held offices for such firms as Marcus Bell and Daniel Pittman's law practice, and Bartley M. Smith and William L. Ezzard's drugstore. The concert hall was in "Norcross' Block," named for the Norcross Building at the corner of Peachtree and Marietta. On this site one of Atlanta's pioneer settlers, Jonathan Norcross, had built his general store; Norcross's purchase of the corner dated from 1846. The city's telegraph office was located in the Dougherty Building next door, whose ground floor offered office space, and whose upper-story rooms were let out as a hotel. The first telegraph office had but a single machine, with the wire leading only to Macon, thence to Savannah. The novelty of the contraption was such, in the early days, as to draw curious onlookers. It was said that General Sam Houston of Texas, passing through town on his way to the national Congress, caught his first glimpse of the telegraph in Atlanta. Also operating out of the Dougherty Building was one of the city's specialty publications, the *Georgia Temperance Crusader*, edited by John H. Seals as "the family paper of the South, devoted to temperance and literature."

South of the railway Peachtree became Whitehall Street, running southwestward with its many stores and offices. The whole block on the western side of Whitehall from the railroad to Alabama was known as Muhlenbrink's Block, for the cigar factory in its center. On the east side of the street, at the railroad, offices for the *Daily Intelligencer* were located in the second floor over M. Wittgenstein's wine, liquor and cigar shop. At the other end of the block, the northeast corner of Whitehall and Alabama, stood the Holland House Building, or Holland Reserve. Three stories tall and brick, the structure served as a hotel, headquarters of the *Examiner* (before its merger with the *Intelligencer* in 1857), and one-time post office, until this latter institution moved down the block to a two-story frame building of its own.

Across Whitehall, on its northwest corner with Alabama, Lynch's Building held the grocery store of John and James Lynch, Irish brothers who had come to Atlanta in 1847. To its west on Alabama could be seen the city market, where stalls were rented out to farmers retailing their produce. Across Alabama, the entire block was named for William Markham, early co-proprietor of the rolling mill and real-estate investor. On the northeast corner of Markham's block was the building of Lewis J. Parr, hardware merchant. Parr's Hall was site of some of Atlanta's first theatrical efforts (before the Atheneum was completed in 1857). Down from Parr's Hall along Whitehall were the storefronts of R. S. Dunning's boot and shoe shop and John Beach and Sidney Root's dry-goods establishment. Beach and Root's building distinguished itself as the "Iron Front Store," noticeably different from the much more common brick and wooden edifices gracing the city's business district. Another downtown landmark, the Johnson

House, was built by Allen E. Johnson in the early 1850s as a hotel, and the surrounding block (west side of Whitehall between Hunter and Mitchell) came to be called Johnson's Block. But the Johnson House itself, like the Dougherty Building, had by 1859 become partially an office site, such that it was not listed among Atlanta's six hostelries in Williams's 1859 directory.[16]

Much more so than in modern Atlanta, or in any modern city for that matter, residents lived much closer to the central business district. Indeed one urban demographer has concluded that white-collar males were more likely to live closer to antebellum Atlanta's center—say, within a half-mile of the zero-mile post—than were working-class whites. The latter tended to live nearer the periphery of the city (close to the rolling mill, for example, Winship's foundry, or the railroad machine shops). Hence one could see some of Atlanta's most stylish and eye-catching residences within a few blocks of State Square. Across the street

---

[16] Garrett, *Atlanta and Environs,* 1:207, 255–56, 318, 355–56 (new city hall), 375, 391, 397, 410 (Mechanics No. 2), 438, 454–56; *Williams' Atlanta Directory,* 23–24, 26, 40, 45, 56, 90–91, 98, 118, 127, 148; [Parham, ed.], *Pioneer Citizens' History,* 120–25, 127; Reed, *History of Atlanta,* 44 (on Houston in Atlanta, "at the time a congressman"); Robert Scott Davis, *Civil War Atlanta* (Charleston SC: History Press, 2011) 18–19 ("Concert Hall" was not the concert hall; the Athenaeum was); Piromis H. Bell, "Drama Behind Oil Footlights," *Atlanta Journal Magazine,* 31 July 1932, 9; Wilbur Kurtz, notebook 6, 153 (on site of downtown post office, "Whitehall St.—east side–between Alabama St. + R.R....Frame building—standing on ground lower than the street–grade—so that public entered on 2d. Floor of bldg." [Kurtz interview, July 1933, with William Fort Williams]), Wilbur G. Kurtz Collection, Atlanta History Center.

Wilbur Kurtz notes that the northwest corner of Marietta and Peachtree was known as Kile's Corner (for Thomas Kile, 1818–1894). The southwest corner is present-day Five Points. Although Albert Castel, Lee Kennett, and Marc Wortman, chroniclers of the Atlanta Campaign, refer to "Five Points" as the name of the intersection at the time of the Civil War, Kurtz sagely observes that Sarah Huff, nineteenth-century city resident, said that she never heard of the intersection referred to as Five Points until after the war (Albert Castel, *Decision in the West: The Atlanta Campaign of 1864* [Lawrence: University Press of Kansas, 1992] 69–71; Lee Kennett, *Marching through Georgia: The Story of Soldiers and Civilians during Sherman's Campaign* [New York: HarperCollins, 1995] 199 [Confederate picket at "an important downtown intersection called Five Points"]; Marc Wortman, *The Bonfire: The Siege and Burning of Atlanta* [New York: Public Affairs, 2009] 263 ["the riot in Five Points" of 21 July 1864]; Wilbur Kurtz, notebook 10, 26, Wilbur G. Kurtz Collection, Atlanta History Center). Moreover, after Atlantans in 1936, upon publication of *Gone With the Wind,* noticed that Margaret Mitchell referred to "Five Points" during the war, *Atlanta Journal* columnist Ralph Smith began asking longtime Atlantans and concluded that the name for the busy intersection came about in the early 1900s. Mrs. Walter Taylor, whose husband had been editor of the *Journal,* believed it was around 1904 or 1905. "Walter used to write a column of city chatter, called Curbside Gossip, and it was during this time that he gave ...to the heart of Atlanta the name of Five Points" (Ralph Smith, "Crackerland," *Atlanta Journal,* 17 December 1936, 11).

from city hall, on the southwest corner of Washington and Mitchell, stood the stately home of John Neal, the planter and merchant of Pike County who had moved his family to Atlanta in 1858. After buying his lot (for $2,000), Neal saw to the construction of a big house—deliberately so, as he prepared it for his children to inhabit even after they were married. When finished, the place rose two and a half stories, graced by Corinthian columns at its front and a cupola of stained glass at its top.[17]

Three blocks west, on 2 acres of well-landscaped grounds at Forsyth and Mitchell, rose the two-story, L-shaped home of Richard Peters, one of Atlanta's five wealthiest citizens, to judge from their taxable real estate holdings. Peters, owner of a prosperous plantation in Middle Georgia, was better known locally as an active real-estate investor and railroad promoter, as well as owner of the Steam Flour Mill. Departing from the heavy Greek columns of the Neal home and others, the Peters house was marked by the lighter, Victorian architectural touch of latticed porches on both lower and upper levels.[18]

Atlanta's attractive homes boasted both wood, as in the fine weatherboarding of the Peters place, and mortar and brick. Judge Julius A. Hayden's two-story brick home, on the south side of Marietta between Wadley and Spring, suggested its owner's side-vocation as co-proprietor (with Thomas G. Healey) of a brick works across the tracks near the W & A roundhouse. It also justified one observer's opinion that Atlanta's finest residences "were located on Marietta Street, on both sides, and extending westward for the distance of about a mile." Actually, attractive homes were scattered throughout the city, south of State Square as well as north of it. John Collier's huge stone dwelling on Nelson Street west of the Macon & Western Railroad, with two massive pillars peculiarly placed on only half of its face, eclectically mixed Greek Revival facade, Victorian bracketed cornice, and a mansard roof.[19]

A ways south of Collier's, on Whitehall very near the city limits, stood the two-story weatherboarded dwelling of L. Windsor Smith, with a columned, sheltered porch on each of its four sides. Smith, an attorney, ranked with Julius Hayden and Richard Peters among Atlanta's dozen wealthiest property owners. A few blocks east was the estate of prosperous hardware merchant Edward Everett Rawson, bordered by Pryor, Formwalt, and what came to be called

[17] Russell, *Atlanta, 1847–1890*, 60–62; Elinor Hillyer, "New City Hall Where Sherman Made Headquarters," *Atlanta Journal Magazine*, 4 September 1927, 11; Garrett, *Atlanta and Environs*, 1:638.

[18] City of Atlanta Tax Digest, 1858–1860, Atlanta History Center; Royce Shingleton, *Richard Peters: Champion of the New South* (Macon GA: Mercer University Press, 1985) 34–35.

[19] Reed, *History of Atlanta*, 56; *Williams' Atlanta Directory*, 99; Garrett, *Atlanta and Environs*, 1:351, 466; Thomas H. Martin, *Atlanta and Its Builders: A Comprehensive History of the Gate City of the South* 2 vols. (Atlanta: Century Memorial Publishing Company, 1902) 1:500 (photograph of Collier house); Harold Bush-Brown, "Architecture in Atlanta," *Atlanta Historical Bulletin* 5/23 (October 1940): 282.

Rawson and Clarke streets. The terraced grounds were logically labeled "The Terraces," and showcased ornamental topiary, box garden, and striking conifers.[20]

Residential fashion was evident well north of the Car Shed, too. Gracing Peachtree between Ellis and Cain was the handsome Greek revival residence of Austin Leyden. Its broad colonnade and second-story balcony presented an imposing white-paned facade on Peachtree; the columns themselves extended around both sides of the house. The structure was built during 1858–1859 by Atlanta architect John Boutelle, whose own home stood two blocks away at Collins and Ellis.[21]

Attorney and realtor Marcus Aurelius Bell's home, the Calico House, on the southeast corner of Wheat and Collins, was one of the city's talked-about residences. Built in 1860 of stone from the local quarry of Patrick Lynch (as was John Collier's home), the structure took its name from its bright, pastel-painted colors. After the rock exterior had been covered with plaster, subcontractor Frank Rice took paints of light blue, yellow and red, and applied them in swirls similar to the marbling seen inside books (young Rice had learned the technique from William Kay, Atlanta's first publisher). "About this time," later recalled Bell's son Piromis, "a popular pattern of calico appeared on the market with the same sort of coloring, and some one remarked that the house 'looked like this calico,' and the name of the house was thus made common."[22]

Bell's Calico House as well as the Neal, Hayden, Peters, and Leyden residences all stood well within half a mile of the zero mile post; but some prominent homeowners availed themselves of larger acreages outside the city limits. Such a leading suburbanite was Lemuel P. Grant. Grant, who had begun buying real estate in Atlanta as early as 1844, owned hundreds of acres in the city's southeastern quadrant. About 1858 he built a very solid stone and brick, two-story home on his property. With columned porches on three sides and buff-colored stucco exterior, L. P. Grant's home boasted twelve big rooms separated by solid brick walls 18 inches thick—surely a statement of permanence. (The Grant house survived the war, according to legend, because the Yankees discovered Masonic paraphernalia there.)[23]

[20] *Williams' Atlanta Directory,* 136; City of Atlanta Tax Digest, 1858–1860, Atlanta History Center; illustration of Smith house, *Frank Leslie's Illustrated Newspaper,* 29 October 1864, 93; Garrett, *Atlanta and Environs,* 1:431.

[21] "Here Are Some Last Farewell Views of the Old Leyden House," *Atlanta Journal,* 23 February 1913, 8; Garrett, *Atlanta and Environs,* 1:639; Garrett, *Yesterday's Atlanta,* 19.

[22] Reed, *History of Atlanta,* 44, 56; Shingleton, *Richard Peters,* 34; Piromis H. Bell, "The Calico House," *Atlanta Historical Bulletin* 1/3 (May 1930); 28–29; Garrett, *Atlanta and Environs,* 2:103.

[23] Russell, *Atlanta 1847–1890,* 55; "Colonel Grant's Historic Home, Atlanta Battle Survivor, Sold," news clipping in notebook 12, 245, Wilbur G. Kurtz Collection, Atlanta History Center; "Grant Home, Built in '50s, Historical Site," *Atlanta Constitution,* 1

Equally imposing was a stately residence clear on the other side of the city, that of Ephraim G. Ponder. A planter from southwest Georgia, Ponder moved to Atlanta with his wife Ellen in 1857. After buying more than 25 acres along Marietta Street three-fourths of a mile outside the city limits, Ponder saw to the building of a two-story stone mansion covered in white plaster and sporting a banistered observation deck. Boxwood and fruit trees adorned the grounds in a landscape every bit as fine as that of Rawson's Terraces; a double-row of hedge-apple trees lined the driveway leading uphill to the Ponder mansion. The decorum and grace of the Ponders' estate, however, belied the couple's relationship inside the house. Ephraim had long suspected his wife of infidelity; in March 1861 he became convinced of it. Ponder moved out of the house, back to Thomasville, leaving Ellen behind—but not before filing for divorce, labeling his estranged wife a drunkard who had become verbally abusive (even threatening him once with a pistol), and charging her with adultery. Ephraim eventually named the other party, one Ben May, a prominent state railroad official. (It was said that May habitually boarded a northbound train at the depot and rode out to near the Ponder house, where the train slowed for May to hop off.)[24]

The end of the Ponders' union in spring 1861 coincided with the more titanic and far more tragic breakup of the national union. After Lincoln's election in November 1860, the Southern states seceded to form their own confederation, resolving to protect their institution of slavery. At that time, no Atlantan—not Ellen Ponder, Ben May, or Mark Bell—could have foreseen what the Yankees would do to them. Indeed, while many Southerners realized that the election of Abraham Lincoln forebode conflict between North and South, most viewed the prospect of war optimistically, even boastfully. Such was the spirit of the *Atlanta Intelligencer*, as it editorialized just after Lincoln's inauguration in March 1861. "On last Monday, the 4th inst., Abraham Lincoln was inaugurated President of what is left of the United States of America," the editors affirmed, pointing to his inaugural address.

> Upon one point he is perfectly plain. He decides for war. We are prepared to meet it. We are a united and a homogeneous people.... Our Government is now firmly established, and will soon be acknowledged by the great European powers. Our Executive and the heads of the various departments possess the unlimited confidence and affection of

September 1942, 4E; Margaret Shannon, "Court Asked to Save Historic Home Here," *Atlanta Journal*, 10 December 1947, 20; Frank Daniel, "Only 2 Ante Bellum Homes Now Standing in Atlanta," *Atlanta Constitution* or *Journal* (*ca.* 1953, with picture of Grant house), Wilbur G. Kurtz Collection, box 29, folder 1, Atlanta History Center.

[24] Garrett, *Atlanta and Environs*, 1:511–12; Wilbur Kurtz, notebook 10, 222 (Kurtz conversation with James Bell, 31 May 1935, *re* the Ponders), Wilbur G. Kurtz Collection, Atlanta History Center.

the people. Every man in the South is a soldier, and even the women and children, if needs be, will stand by the side of their fathers, husbands and brothers, in defense of their altars, their hearthstones and their firesides. We have the munitions of war in the accumulated wealth of the richest agricultural region on the habitable globe.

With these presumed advantages on the side of the Confederacy, the *Intelligencer* voiced its defiance: "we say then, to Lincoln and his myrmidons, come on!"[25]

---

[25] "Inaugural of President Lincoln," *Atlanta Intelligencer*, 6 March 1861, 2.

2

CONFEDERATE WAR CENTER

In the heady, exciting days after Georgia's secession in mid-January 1861, Atlantans saw opportunity ahead. Talk of the seven seceded Southern states coming together in a national confederation allowed some to pitch the Gate City as the ideal site for the forthcoming Confederate Provisional Congress. Atlanta was centrally situated in the region, well connected by railroads, and now boasted seven hotels. It possessed a salubrious climate, one that was free of yellow fever, as the *Gate City Guardian* crowed; plus it had plenty of peanuts, "goobers," politicians' perennial snack. For these reasons and others, some began to promote Atlanta as capital for the new Confederate nation. One city newspaper even hailed nearby Stone Mountain as abundant source of granite, ready for the many public buildings sure to be constructed if the city won the award as capital.

When Montgomery was nonetheless selected as the seat of the new national government, Atlantans consoled themselves with a brief visit on 16 February by the Confederacy's president-elect Jefferson Davis, who was travelling from Washington to Montgomery en route for his inauguration. A large crowd greeted him at the Car Shed; Mayor Jared Whitaker pronounced a cordial welcome and militiamen fired a rifle salute. Before he left, Davis delivered a speech in which he castigated the North for its subversion of the Constitution and praised the South for its patriotic people. Later, Vice President Alexander H. Stephens also visited the city, receiving the same enthusiastic welcome, including a downtown military parade. Stephens addressed the assembled crowd in a speech of "surpassing eloquence and breadth of statesmanship," according to one source, in which he predicted that the South would achieve its independence without resort to war. Notwithstanding, the vice president warned that the new Confederacy should embark upon military preparation against the North's miscreants.

At the time of Davis's and Stephens's stop-overs, military organizations had already begun forming in Atlanta. The city already had two militia companies, the Gate City Guard and Atlanta Grays, but more came forth in the next few weeks. The Georgia Volunteers and Davis Infantry emerged by 1 March. A month later the Gate City Guard entrained for Pensacola, Florida, as part of the Confederate forces keeping watch on the Federal garrison at Fort Pickens. When war broke out in April 1861, Atlantans felt the war-fever like everybody else. More infantry companies were organized in late April and May: the Confederate Volunteers, Stephens Rifles, Atlanta Volunteers, Confederate Continentals, and Atlanta Rifles, as well the Silver Grays (of men over forty-five).

The city's ethnic blend showed with the formation of the Steuben Yagers (exclusively Germans) and the Atlanta Irish Volunteers. Atlantans volunteered in such numbers that they comprised the bulk of the eleven companies of infantry (and one of cavalry) raised in Fulton County by early August. When it was all over, Atlanta and Fulton had given 2,660 men to the national service. As these units were armed and equipped they were transferred to Confederate authority and merged into Georgia regiments. One such was the 7th Georgia Volunteer Infantry, organized in early May from the Confederate Volunteers, Davis Infantry, and eight other companies from Cobb, DeKalb, Paulding, and Coweta counties. As these units left for the front in Virginia, citizens saw them off with vast demonstrations of support, including fundraising events. An embarkation event for the Atlanta Volunteers and Confederate Continentals was held 24 June at the downtown Atheneum, where the "Atlanta Amateurs" performed familiar songs and patriotic airs such as "Dixie Variation" and "Our Southern Land."[1]

Atlantans kept up with the war-news from the major fronts in Virginia and Kentucky-Tennessee through the city's two daily newspapers, the *Intelligencer* and the *Southern Confederacy*. The latter had been founded in 1859 as a weekly, turning then into a daily when its management bought out the rival *Gate City Guardian* in early 1861. With offices on Alabama Street between Pryor and Loyd, across from State Square, the new Atlanta *Southern Confederacy* put out its first issue 4 March 1861—the day Abraham Lincoln was inaugurated.[2]

---

[1] Ralph Benjamin Singer, "Confederate Atlanta" (Ph.D. diss., University of Georgia, 1973) 65–66; Thomas H. Martin, *Atlanta and Its Builders: A Comprehensive History of the Gate City of the South,* 2 vols. (Atlanta: Century Memorial Publishing Company, 1902) 1:165–72; Clement A. Evans, ed., *Confederate Military History,* 12 vols. (Atlanta: Confederate Publishing Co., 1899) 6:31; Richard Barksdale Harwell, "Civilian Life in Atlanta in 1862," *Atlanta Historical Bulletin* 7/29 (October 1944): 217 (on Atlanta Volunteers and Confederate Continentals); Wallace P. Reed, *History of Atlanta, Georgia, with Illustrations and Biographical Sketches of Some of Its Prominent Men and Pioneers* (Syracuse NY: D. Mason & Co., 1889) 110–18; Robert Scott Davis, *Civil War Atlanta* (Charleston SC: History Press, 2011) 31 ("Fulton County gave at least 2,660 men"); Mary A. H. Gay, *Life in Dixie During the War* (Atlanta: Charles P. Byrd, 1897) 39–41 (playbill for the Atlanta Amateurs' concert).

As for Atlanta's seven hotels in spring 1861, city boosters were counting not only the six listed in *Williams' 1859 City Directory* (Atlanta Hotel, City Hotel, Planters' Hotel, Tennessee House, Trout House and Washington Hall) but also at least one more, either the Johnson House on Whitehall or the Dougherty Building at Peachtree St. and the railroad (*Williams' Atlanta Directory,* 155; [Louis L. Parham, ed.], *Pioneer Citizens' History of Atlanta, 1833–1902* [Atlanta: Byrd Printing Company, 1902] 126–27).

[2] Henry T. Malone, "Atlanta Journalism during the Confederacy," *Georgia Historical Quarterly* 37/3 (September 1953): 211–12; Rahun Lee Brantley, *Georgia Journalism of the Civil War Period* (Nashville: George Peabody College for Teachers, 1929) 58. About the same time, March 1861, in addition to the two morning papers, an evening issue was founded, the *Commonwealth.* It, however, was destined to fail the very next year (Malone, "Atlanta Journalism," 212–13). For more on the *Intelligencer,* see Henry T. Malone, "The Weekly

War news in the papers highlighted the opening battles, which in turn brought word of casualties. The city's papers honored the nearly dozen Atlantans killed or mortally wounded at Manassas, 21 July. Months later a memorial service was held in the city for attorney Thomas L. Cooper, captain of the Atlanta Grays, who died the day before Christmas 1861, unheroically enough, from a fall off his horse in Virginia. Such fatalities left families grieving and in some cases financially straitened. To assist them, several fund-raising societies were formed in the city. Atlanta's physicians, including Drs. T. S. Powell, J. G. Westmoreland and J. P. Logan, resolved just after Fort Sumter to treat soldiers' destitute families for free. These and other physicians on the faculty of the Atlanta Medical College suspended all classes in August 1861; the college building henceforth served as a hospital. In a letter to the *Southern Confederacy*, respected Atlanta physician Noel D'Alvigny urged medical students to seek work as nurses in soldiers' hospitals since such clinical experience there would be more beneficial than mere "theoretical lectures." Meanwhile, the wife of Dr. Willis Westmoreland had helped organize a women's aid society to make bandages and lint for the wounded away at the battlefront.[3]

The front itself moved menacingly closer to Atlanta in early 1862 after the surrender of Forts Henry and Donelson in Tennessee forced the Confederate evacuation of Nashville on 23 February. On that very day the *Southern Confederacy* reported the arrival of some 500 sick or wounded soldiers by train from Chattanooga. The *Intelligencer* on 25 February thanked the "Medical Fraternity of the city" for springing to action. The mayor and authorities were credited, and so were "the LADIES, too, God bless them." Martha Winship had assumed leadership of the Atlanta Hospital Association, formed in winter 1862 to solicit and disburse contributions to Atlanta's hospitals. The ailing soldiers were accommodated by the medical college and other facilities hastily converted into hospitals. The Atlanta Medical College Hospital specialized in surgical cases—the laboratories were operating rooms and classrooms were the wards. Confederate medical officers from the Army of Tennessee worked with the city government and private citizens to organize hotels and municipal buildings for use as other hospitals. The army's assistant medical director, Dr. Lewis T. Pim, was in Atlanta in late February looking for sites. Dr. Pim applied for use of city hall as a hospital, but the city council made it clear that such occupancy would be granted only under the direst of circumstances. Apparently those circumstances

Atlanta Intelligencer as a Secessionist Journal," *Georgia Historical Quarterly* 37/4 (December 1953): 278–86; and Alan Bussel, "The Atlanta *Daily Intelligencer* Covers Sherman's March," *Journalism Quarterly* 51/3 (Autumn 1974): 405–10.
[3] Franklin M. Garrett, *Atlanta and Environs: A Chronicle of Its People and Events,* 2 vols. (New York: Lewis Historical Publishing Co., 1954) 1:509, 516–17; Reed, *History of Atlanta,* 113–18; L. R. Hilde, *Worth a Dozen men: Women and Nursing in the Civil War South,* 138; L. B. Wylie, "Interesting Sketches of Pioneer Women: Mrs. Isaac Winship," S1.

soon prevailed, as city hall took in ailing soldiers by the end of the month, according to the letter of Susan Lin to her brother "Bud" of 28 February: "If you could be at home now to witness the suffering of our sick soldiers, you would not be so anxious to go to war," Susan explained; "Atlanta is completely run over with them." The fall of Nashville had sent a wave of sick southward. "There is six or eight hundred here now and more are coming every day," Lin described. "Nearly every house is town is filled with them." Susan predicted her mother would do the same. She listed the public buildings converted into medical wards: "The City Authorities have turned the medical college Fulton House, negro church, City Hall, Hayden Hall the halls over the stores of Clark & Gilbert, Hunnicutt and Taylor and Kile into hospitals." Particularly important were those structures near the passenger depot, where patients were first unloaded from the cars (indeed, the Car Shed itself became an open-air ward for some cases too grievously hurt to be moved farther). Accordingly, the Gate City Hotel (formerly Planters', at Alabama and Pryor) became the Gate City Hospital. Likewise, the City Hotel Hospital, at Decatur and Loyd, was within 150 yards of the depot. By mid-March, according to rather gruesome hospital mortality lists published daily in the *Intelligencer,* other makeshift hospitals had been set up in boarding houses or office buildings along Peachtree: Hayden's Hall, Hindman's Hall, Holland's Hall, and Howell's Hall, all dignified by the term "hospital," as was Bank Hospital, also on Peachtree. On Whitehall Street, between Hunter and Mitchell, the Empire House, previously for boarders in Atlanta, now tended to hospitalized Confederate soldiers. Farther north, as mentioned by Lin, the African Methodist Church was given over to military medical use, at least for a while. Hospital casualty reports show that the black church and several of the "hall" hospitals had very brief existences, perhaps only a month or two, while Gate City, City Hotel, Medical College, and Empire House hospitals proved to be more lasting facilities. (The medical college was especially important because of its large classrooms. After a visit on 27 February, Susan Lin wrote, "in each room there is 10 or 15 men.") Sick and wounded were also tended in the Franklin Printing House, Kile's Building (southeast corner of Decatur and Loyd), and even private homes, such as the Bells' "Calico House." Marcus Bell's son later remembered Dr. James Alexander, the Westmoreland brothers, Drs. Daniel O'Keefe, Noel D'Alvigny, and others walking about the rooms of his home treating ailing soldiers. After Shiloh, Martha Winship sent her husband Isaac and children downstairs, and turned the upper floor of her house into a hospital ward. All six rooms and a wide hall were soon crowded with cots.

Felix Gregory De Fontaine, war correspondent for the *Charleston Courier,* was in Atlanta in mid-March 1862, quite struck by the widespread, makeshift hospital facilities and their large numbers of patients. "Fully thirty five hundred soldiers are now lying here restive and impatient under the restraints of disease," De Fontaine reported. "All the principal halls and upper stories of buildings in the City have been given up to hospital uses, and the invalids lie in rows two deep with only room enough between the cots to allow the passage of a physician." Unfortunately, this crowding seemed not merely "inconvenient and unhealthy," but an evil that seemed "not directly remediable," at least until more hospitals opened up.

More hospitals in fact opened up in the ensuing months. Ironically, the City Cemetery's list of soldier interments, attributed to the various hospitals, serves as a guide to when these facilities began their services. The concert hall had been converted to a hospital by 9 May 1862, as that was when its first failed case was buried (Andy Sprinkel, of Company C, 29th Tennessee Infantry). By mid-June Jones' Hospital had been set up on Whitehall, opposite the Empire House; at that time also Atlanta physician Daniel Heery oversaw a facility, "Heery's Hospital," in the same area. Dr. Thomas S. Denny's hospital was sited at Whitehall and the W & A Railroad. Similarly Dr. James Alexander operated "Alexander's Hospital" on Peachtree, not more than 150 yards from the Car Shed.

Ailing, convalescing or dying Confederate soldiers could be seen throughout the city's downtown sections in spring 1862. By that time, military authorities already planned a big general hospital complex at the Fair Grounds. Contracts went out for construction of dozens of wards; in June medical officers authorized forty buildings. Soon thereafter "Fair Ground Hospital" began treating patients. By next spring, "Fair Ground Hospital No. 2" was also in operation. Expansion of these facilities allowed most of the downtown hospitals started in 1862 to close, although a few stayed open, such as the Gate City, which began serving as a receiving and distributing hospital because of its proximity to the Car Shed (at the "R & D," patients were entered into hospital records and assigned transfer to other hospitals either in the city, or facilities linked by railroad beyond Atlanta). By spring 1863, the Fair Grounds and other hospitals in Atlanta possessed 1,800 beds—an impressive number, yet woefully inadequate for the thousands of wounded flooding in after a major battle. The big fight at Murfreesboro, Tennessee, 31 December 1862–2 January 1863, brought an avalanche of wounded Confederates that overwhelmed the medical staff at the Fair Grounds. Dr. Ira Gunter was working there, and could not refrain from detailing the clinical horrors he encountered in a letter to his wife, written on 6 January.

> Since the battle all the Hospitals in this place has been filled to overflowing with the wounded and the cry is still they come on every train. We have received in the Fairground Hospital between five and six hundred, and making preparations with all our might for the reception of more. The poor fellows are wounded in every way and almost in every portion of the body and limbs. And taken collectively exhibit an amount of physicial suffering which is heart rending to contemplate. Some have their lower jaw shot all to smash while [others] have the upper jaw mangled. Others have extensive and ugly wounds in the fleshy parts of

the systems produced by the explosion of shells. Others again have the flesh and bones of their limbs torn all to pieces presenting wounds of a very ghastly character. I have to assist and see to the dressing of between fifty and one hundred wounds every day, and [this] keeps me busy the greater portion of my time. I have assisted in amputating two or three arms and today I assisted in splitting open two poor fellows arms making a gash six inches long clear down to the bone above and below and through the elbow joint.

Gunter's work was shared by many other army physicians, all serving the numerous hospital wards in the city. Four facilities alone housed more than a thousand beds: Fair Grounds, 800; Medical College, 200; Empire, 250; and Gate City, 300. For patients on the mend, a convalescent camp was established out near the Ponder estate by the W & A Railroad. When smallpox broke out in Atlanta in early 1863, military authorities had a hospital for contagious disease erected in a remote area beyond the city's southeast limits. In September 1863, the three-story Female Institute building was commandeered as a hospital just in time for the avalanche of wounded from the battle of Chickamauga.[4]

---

[4] Stephen Davis, "Another Look at Civil War Medical Care: Atlanta's Confederate Hospitals," *Journal of the Medical Association of Georgia* 88/2 (April 1999): 9–17; Stephen Davis, "An Avalanche of Wounded: Atlanta's Confederate Hospitals and the Challenge of Chickamauga, Fall 1863," *Atlanta Medicine* 78/3 (2005): 7–9; "The Sick and Wounded," *Atlanta Intelligencer*, 25 February 1862, 2; Wylie, "Interesting Sketches of Pioneer Women: Mrs. Isaac Winship"; Robert Scott Davis, Jr., ed., *Requiem for a Lost City: A Memoir of Civil War Atlanta and the Old South* (Macon GA: Mercer University Press, 1999) 82 (on Atlanta Hospital Association); Susan B. Lin to Charles B. "Bud" Lin, 28 February 1862, Lin Family Papers, MSS 849, box 1, folder 6, Atlanta History Center; Mildred Jordan, "Georgia's Confederate Hospitals" (Master's thesis, Emory University, 1962) 44–48, 73–76; Singer, "Confederate Atlanta," 150–54; Garrett, *Atlanta and Environs*, 1:530; "The Dead," *Atlanta Intelligencer*, 1 June 1862, 1; Bell, "The Calico House," 30–31; "Mrs. Peel's Essay Is Tribute to Mrs. Winship, War Heroine," *Atlanta American*, 16 April 1922, typescript, box 1, folder 13, Atlanta Women's Pioneer Society, MSS 391, Atlanta History Center; James M. Merrill, ed., "Personne Goes to Georgia: Five Civil War Letters," *Georgia Historical Quarterly* 43/2 (June 1959): 209; "List of Confederate Soldiers Buried at Oakland arranged by Hospital," Oakland Cemetery Collection, Atlanta History Center; *Williams' Atlanta Directory*, 37, 75, 101; Atlanta City Council Minutes, 4 March 1862, Atlanta History Center; Glenna R. Schroeder-Lein, *Confederate Hospitals on the Move: Samuel H. Stout and the Army of Tennessee* (Columbia: University of South Carolina Press, 1994) 92, 129; Ira L. Gunter to wife, 6 January 1863, in possession of Jim W. Latimer, Jonesboro GA. I thank Dr. Latimer for making his ancestor's letters available to me.

Jack D. Welsh, *Two Confederate Hospitals and Their Patients: Atlanta to Opelika* (Macon GA: Mercer University Press, 2005), is the definitive source on Atlanta's Fairgrounds Hospital complex.

Arrangements had also to be made for the hospitalized soldiers who had died. The city council had, as early as June 1861, begun to discuss expanding the City Cemetery's 25 acres for military burials. The need increased markedly in 1862, as the council realized from quarterly reports submitted by the cemetery sexton of soldiers' burials: 157 interred January–March, 181 the second quarter, 159 the third, and 135 the fourth—632 in all. Negotiations with the Confederate government for money to buy more cemetery land began in mid-1862. While the deal was being struck Confederate authorities had the land to the east of the cemetery cleared of trees, and it was there that the war dead were eventually interred. The situation was helped a bit the next year when army medical directors began establishing hospitals farther south of Atlanta (by October 1863 surgeon Samuel H. Stout, medical director for the Army of Tennessee, had facilities in Newnan, LaGrange, Griffin, and Forsyth, and soon got permission to set up even more). At the same time, however, from the army hospitals remaining in the city, the number of deaths increased: 625 unlucky men in the first three quarters of 1863 (including, according to interment records, a box of amputated arms and legs from Gate City Hospital, buried 13 February in block F, row 10). The battle of Chickamauga in north Georgia, late September, led to 743 soldier burials in the city during the last three months of 1863. There were Yankees to be buried, too, wounded prisoners treated awhile in the hospitals before their demise (the cemetery today holds the graves of twenty Northern soldiers). All in all, the exigencies of war kept Atlanta's "city of the dead" a very active place.[5]

Advances of the Union armies in Tennessee and Mississippi during 1862–1863 also made Atlanta a city of refugees. From an estimated 13,000 residents of both city limits and suburbs at the start of the war, Atlanta's population rose quickly as displaced persons overwhelmed hotels and boarding houses. After visiting Atlanta in mid-1862, a Confederate artilleryman believed its population had risen to 17,000. A year later a visitor to the city who had seen it in 1845 was

---

[5] Singer, "Confederate Atlanta," 80; Garrett, *Atlanta and Environs*, 1:530, 548; "List of Confederate Soldiers Buried at Oakland," Atlanta History Center; Schroeder-Lein, *Confederate Hospitals on the Move*, 129–30; Kent Moore, "Atlanta's Pride and Problem," *Atlanta Historical Bulletin* 20/2 (Summer 1976): 23 (on the City Cemetery, which officially became Oakland Cemetery in 1876); S. H. Stout to S. P. Moore, 11 October 1863, in US War Department, *The War of the Rebellion: A Compilation of the Official Records of the Union and Confederate Armies*, 128 vols. (Washington, DC: Government Printing Office, 1880–1901) ser. 1., vol. 30, pt. 4, p. 736 (hereafter *OR* and all references will be to series 1 unless otherwise indicated); "Oakland Cemetery: Alphabetical List of Confederate Soldiers," Oakland Cemetery Collection, Atlanta History Center; Atlanta City Council Minutes, 1 April, 20 June, 4 July, 3 October 1862; 2 January, 3 April, and 16 October 1863; 1 January 1864, Atlanta History Center; Robert E. Zaworski, *Headstones of Heroes: The Restoration and History of Confederate Graves in Atlanta's Oakland Cemetery* (Paducah KY: Turner Publishing Co., 1998) 6.

now amazed to behold "more than a thousand houses and twenty thousand inhabitants." By then even more refugees had arrived, spilling into the streets or vacant lots, struggling to find shelter. An army nurse, Kate Cumming, recorded in her diary on 9 September 1863—the day after Confederate forces evacuated Chattanooga—that she saw families all around the passenger depot, sheltered only by tents or inhabiting old railroad cars. So many strangers were about that the city council voted in May 1863 on something that had heretofore never been needed: street signs at the corners of major thoroughfares to help newcomers find their way around. By late spring 1864 before Sherman's armies approached, Atlantans believed their city had become home, permanent or transient, to as many as 22,000 souls.[6]

Atlanta had also become home, permanent or transient, to two more newspapers besides the *Intelligencer* and the *Southern Confederacy*. When Knoxville fell in late August 1863, its *Register* took flight, nesting in Atlanta to resume as a daily publication. Taking up residence in the printing offices of the *Georgia Temperance Crusader* near Alabama and Whitehall, the paper's headquarters became the informal meeting place of East Tennessee refugees. Into Atlanta as well, alighting on Whitehall Street between Decatur and the railroad, flew the *Memphis Appeal*, which actually had become the Memphis-Grenada (Mississippi)-Jackson-Meridian-Atlanta *Appeal* by the time of its first issue in the Gate City, 6 June 1863. Thus by the spring of 1864, four daily papers in town scavenged for news and subscribers. A printer's strike in mid-April 1864 shut down the city's major papers, but only for a while. The editors of the *Intelligencer*, *Southern Confederacy*, *Register*, and *Appeal* collaborated to crank out a little paper, the Atlanta *Daily Press*, but it was only one side of a small sheet. The strike was notably short lived. It lasted all of four days, 12–15 April, whereupon the printers came back to their presses, lest they lose their military exemption. To force their

---

[6] C. Mildred Thompson, *Reconstruction in Georgia: Economic, Social, Political, 1865–1872* (New York: Columbia University Press, 1913) 98; Lt. Charles C. Jones, Jr., to the Rev. C. C. Jones, 25 July 1862, in Robert Manson Myers, ed., *The Children of Pride: A True Story of Georgia and the Civil War* (New Haven: Yale University Press, 1972) 938; "A Trip to Atlanta," *Atlanta Southern Confederacy*, 23 May 1863, 2; Richard Barksdale Harwell, ed., *Kate: The Journal of a Confederate Nurse* (Baton Rouge: Louisiana State University Press, 1964) 83–84; Atlanta City Council Minutes, 8 May 1863, Atlanta History Center; Valentine T. Barnwell, "Condensed History of Atlanta," in *Barnwell's Atlanta City Directory and Stranger's Guide...for the Year 1867* (Atlanta: Intelligencer & Job Office, 1867) 24.

In accepting 22,000 as Atlanta's population in 1864, David Coffey nonetheless errs in calling it "the second largest city still held by the Confederates (only Richmond was larger)" (Coffey, *John Bell Hood and the Struggle for Atlanta* [Abilene TX: McWhiney Foundation Press, 1998] 62). After the fall of New Orleans, Charleston would have rivaled Richmond as largest city in the Confederacy; in 1860 it held a population of 40,522, while Richmond held 37,910 (E. Merton Coulter, *The Confederate States of America, 1861–1865* [Baton Rouge: Louisiana State University Press, 1950] 409).

employees back to work, the editors had approached the local conscription officer and suggested that he draft the idle printers. The officer liked the idea, and turned it against the editors themselves: without printers, the editors too were out of a job, hence draftable. Needless to say, the two sides in the labor dispute readily resolved their disagreements and went back to work. Another product of the printers' strike seems to have been another small paper (front-and-back only), the *Atlanta Reveille*, whose first issue appeared on 16 April. According to some sources, it lasted until the fall of the city.[7]

An influx of military personnel and government employees, both Confederate and state, also helped swell the city's population. Enough of these had found office space throughout the city by May 1864 that a directory of their

---

[7] J. Cutler Andrews, *The South Reports the Civil War* (Princeton: Princeton University Press, 1970) 38–39; "Destructive Fire in Atlanta," *Augusta Chronicle & Sentinel*, 24 July 1864 (on fire of Connally Building at Alabama and Whitehall of 19 July, report of which mentions the *Atlanta Register* headquarters); Mary Elizabeth Massey, *Refugee Life in the Confederacy* (Baton Rouge: Louisiana State University, 1964) 167; B. G. Ellis, *The Moving Appeal: Mr. McClanahan, Mrs. Dill, and the Civil War's Great Newspaper Run* (Macon GA: Mercer University Press, 2003) 225–26; Thomas Harrison Baker, *The* Memphis Commercial Appeal*: The History of a Southern Newspaper* (Baton Rouge: Louisiana State University Press, 1971) 91–111 (See also Thomas H. Baker, "Refugee Newspaper: The Memphis Daily Appeal, 1862–1865," *Journal of Southern History* 29/3 [August 1963]: 326–44, and B. Kimball Baker, "The Memphis Appeal," *Civil War Times Illustrated* 18/4 [July 1979]: 32–39.); R. A. Halley, "A Rebel Newspaper's War Story: Being a Narrative of the War History of the Memphis Appeal," *American Historical Magazine* (April 1903), reprinted in Tennessee Historical Commission, *Tennessee Old and New*, 2 vols. (Nashville: Tennessee Historical Commission, 1947) 2:247–72. On the printers' strike, the *Press* and *Reveille*, see Malone, "Atlanta Journalism," 212–13, 217–18; Richard Barksdale Harwell, "Atlanta Publications of the Civil War," *Atlanta Historical Bulletin* 6/25 (July 1941): 193–94; Reed, *History of Atlanta*, 185–86; Ruth Elaine Feldman, "A Checklist of Atlanta Newspapers, 1846–1948" (Master's thesis, Emory University, 1948) 29–34. Issue 5 (21 April 1864) of the *Reveille* is described in "Old Newspapers; Relics of the War," *Atlanta Constitution*, 20 July 1898 ("The paper is five columns wide and is one sheet printed on both sides").

The *Chattanooga Rebel* is mistakenly sometimes listed among Atlanta's wartime refugee newspapers (Andrews, *The South Reports the Civil War*, 39; Reed, *History of Atlanta*, 184; and Elizabeth Catherine Bowlby, "The Role of Atlanta during the Civil War" [Master's thesis, Emory University, 1938] 61). The *Rebel*, shelled out of its hometown in August 1863, moved to Marietta, and there resumed publication for nine months. It then retired to Griffin, south of Atlanta, in spring 1864 when Sherman's armies approached. Franc M. Paul, publisher of the *Rebel*, writing in the Nashville *American* of 4 May 1890, pointedly asserted, "The *Rebel* was never published in Atlanta.... It remained in Marietta until the advance of Johnston's retreating army got in sight of the town, when it was transferred to Griffin" [reprinted in *Tennessee Old and New*, 2:277]). See also James W. Livingood, "The Chattanooga Rebel," *East Tennessee Historical Society Publications* 39 (1967): 50–51; and Roy Morris, "The Chattanooga Daily Rebel," *Civil War Times Illustrated* 23/7 (November 1984): 22–23.

whereabouts, as published in the *Intelligencer*, made for a column a whole page long. For example, where there were hospitals, there were hospital administrators. The Army of Tennessee's director of hospitals, Samuel H. Stout, who moved to Atlanta in December 1863, had his office on Whitehall Street, below Mitchell. Atlanta physician J. P. Logan, serving as senior post surgeon, conducted his affairs over (Calvin W.) Hunnicutt & (James A.) Taylor's Drug Store; the sturdy, three-story brick structure overshadowed the northeast corner of Peachtree and Decatur. Across the street, over Thomas M. Clarke's hardware store, surgeon George S. Blackie, medical purveyor, oversaw the distribution of military medical supplies; assistant surgeon J. F. Young also had his office on Peachtree.

Other government bureaus had offices about town. In the *Southern Confederacy* building on Alabama Street, Major George W. Lee headed up the local conscript department, enforcing the Confederate draft law passed in spring 1862 (a camp for recruits was established outside the city's northeast suburbs, on land of the Richard Todd plantation). At the north end of the square, in the Masonic Hall on Decatur Street, Lt. J. M. Harwell served as enrolling officer. Army of Tennessee paymasters had offices on Marietta Street near the First Presbyterian Church and on Whitehall south of Mitchell. In the same area, at the southwest corner of Whitehall and Mitchell with William W. Roark's grocery store, was an office for the Transportation Department; another was two blocks north at Alabama and Whitehall. At the southwest corner of the same intersection, in the old Parr's Hall building and over the Atlanta Insurance & Banking Company offices, were the headquarters of Colonel Moses H. Wright, Confederate officer in charge of troops and defenses of the city. Across the street in James J. Lynch's three-story building, Confederate chief engineer Captain Lemuel P. Grant—one and the same as the prosperous eastside Atlanta homeowner and property holder—had his departmental office. Also on Whitehall, a door or two closer to the railroad, were the offices of the Confederate provost marshal and Georgia Governor Joseph E. Brown's aide de camp, Sam Hoyt, who kept the governor informed of military goings-on in the bustling Gate City.

As a major railway hub, Atlanta became a busy scene of logistics—the accumulation, warehousing, and transportation of military supplies. Administrative offices for these activities dotted the city. Confederate Commissary Department officers, overseeing food supplies for the Army of Tennessee, had headquarters along Whitehall: Major James F. Cummings, department chief, and Major R. T. Wilson, commissary officer for Confederate forces in East Tennessee, were at Whitehall near Alabama; so was Captain W. R. Cox, on the west side of Whitehall between Alabama and the railroad (across the street from the post office). State commissary department officers, charged with supplying the Georgia militia and other state troops that Governor Brown zealously maintained, also were on Whitehall, including Colonel Jared I.

Whitaker, former Atlanta mayor and now commissary-general of Georgia troops. (One of Whitaker's duties was the procurement and distribution of salt; in October 1863, Governor Brown asked Alvin K. Seago to take the locomotive *Texas* and cars to Saltville, in southwest Virginia, and bring back a cargo for the state commissary.) Other military supply offices ranged down Whitehall as well: state purchasing commissary, between Alabama and Hunter; CS Post Commissary over William McNaught and James Ormond's wholesale grocery between Hunter and Mitchell; and the state salt agent on the corner of Whitehall and Mitchell.

Quartermaster's department offices, both state and national, also clustered on Whitehall. Major G. R. Fairbanks, hospital quartermaster, worked in the same building as the post commissary. State quartermaster for leather and shoes shared first floor offices near Whitehall and Hunter with the state QM for clothing. On Whitehall, too, were the offices of Confederate Post Quartermaster (over W. Herring and Son's Clothing Store between Alabama and Hunter); and Confederate Inspector of Field Transportation Captain J. A. Anderson. Near the corner of Whitehall and Alabama the quartermaster general for the state of Georgia, Colonel Ira R. Foster, had his upstairs offices over McPherson's Book Store. Likewise, on Alabama one door east of Whitehall, Major George W. Cunningham supervised clothing supply for the Army of Tennessee. Major William Bacon's office on Alabama coordinated goods obtained through the Confederate tax-in-kind (a measure passed by congress in April 1863, entitling the government to 10 percent of all crops grown or livestock slaughtered in the year). Military storekeeper for Georgia's commissary department, A. B. Forsyth, likewise worked on Alabama Street.

There were also military offices north of the railroad and Car Shed; Forsyth's counterpart for the state quartermaster's department, C. M. Wellborn, administered from Peachtree Street, as did the Confederate military storekeeper for ordnance, Lieutenant John U. Ansley (Augustine C. Wyly's building at Peachtree and Walton). A block or two to the north, at Peachtree, Houston and Pryor, the Confederate Commissary Department acquired land and had a building constructed for its operations. A little to the west, in the area bounded by Walton, Cone, and the First Baptist Church on Wadley, the Atlanta post garrison headquarters were located. On Marietta, the Confederate naval department maintained a presence in the city, through Chief Engineer T. Alphonse Jackson. In the same direction, on the W & A Railroad a mile northwest of the depot, were offices for the CS Nitre and Mining Bureau, which directed the procurement of the raw materials for making gunpowder, especially saltpeter and nitre.[8]

---

[8] "City Military Directory," *Atlanta Intelligencer,* 11 May 1864; Allen D. Candler, ed., *The Confederate Records of the State of Georgia,* 6 vols. (Atlanta: Charles P. Byrd, 1909–1912) 2:477–78 (on Seago procuring salt in Virginia; as also noted in Wilbur G. Kurtz, notebook

All of this administrative apparatus suggested Atlanta's importance as one of the Confederacy's most important supply centers. To be sure, from the start of the war, numerous factories and shops throughout the city turned out much military material, but without doubt the most essential plant in the city for the Confederate war effort was the Atlanta Rolling Mill. At the outbreak of the war, Scofield and Markham's enterprise was one of only two in the entire South that had turned out rails for the region's train lines; the other was the Tredegar Iron Works of Richmond. In 1860, the Atlanta mill had turned out 2,000 tons of rails. Logistical demands for railway transport made such capacity critical. The rolling mill was soon called upon for another wartime need: armor plate for the South's new ironclad warships. Builders of one such gunboat in New Orleans, the Tift brothers (Nelson and Asa), negotiated with the Atlanta factory in November 1861 to convert some of its machinery to turn out 2-inch-thick plates. At first Scofield and Markham refused, stating that their rollers could not be made to produce plating of the desired thickness. Nelson Tift persisted, though, with the offer of a better price, personally coming to Atlanta to close the deal. He did so on 14 November, offering contract for a thousand tons of plate at 6 1/4 cents per pound drilled for fastening, or 6 cents undrilled, as well as for 160,000 pounds of bolts. Within a month or so, the Atlanta mill was rolling 150 plates daily; as of 10 January 1862, Scofield and Markham had shipped almost 200 tons of them. The plating failed to reach New Orleans, however, largely for want of rail transport. After delays in shipment via Memphis, the Tifts tried other rail routes through Montgomery and Mobile, which still proved exasperatingly slow. In March '62 the Tifts and their vessel, to be named the *Mississippi*, were still awaiting armor plate. A particularly valuable load of the material arrived just about the time that New Orleans fell to Union forces in late April. The evacuating Confederates were compelled to blow up what had been built of the *Mississippi* and her sister ship *Louisiana*. Despite this loss, the Confederate navy continued to call for ironclad warships, and the Atlanta Rolling Mill continued to serve as naval armorer. By mid-1863, another huge ironclad, the *Tennessee*, was under construction at Selma, Alabama; its 7-inch-long, 2-inch-thick plating was being rolled at Atlanta.

In 1863, the mill was bought by Trenholm, Fraser & Company, the Charleston-based import-export firm that under George A. Trenholm purchased munitions supplies for the Confederate government. As the Confederate Rolling Mill, it continued its vital roles, producing naval gunboat iron plate and iron rails, which were in constant demand. A railroad official in spring 1863 estimated

12, 27, Wilbur G. Kurtz Collection, Atlanta History Center); Garrett, *Atlanta and Environs,* 1:496, 551–52; Stephens Mitchell, "Atlanta the Industrial Heart of the Confederacy," *Atlanta Historical Bulletin* 1/3 (May 1930): 25–27; Schroeder-Lein, *Confederate Hospitals on the Move,* 131n19; Emory M. Thomas, *The Confederate Nation, 1861–1865* (New York: Harper & Row, 1979) 198 (on the Confederate tax-in-kind). The *Atlanta Intelligencer* "Military Directory" is reprinted in Garrett, *Atlanta and Environs,* 1:590–93.

that to replace tracking either worn out from use or destroyed by the enemy would require nearly 50,000 tons of rails annually. The Atlanta mill, if dedicated to that purpose alone, was thought capable of only 10,000 to 12,000 tons a year. This disparity demonstrates both the Atlanta Rolling Mill's vital importance to the Confederate transportation system, and the ultimate failure of that system to operate as Confederate war fortunes waned.[9]

---

[9] Mary A. DeCredico, *Patriotism for Profit: Georgia's Urban Entrepreneurs and the Confederate War Effort* (Chapel Hill: University of North Carolina Press, 1990) 36–37; Thomas G. Dyer, *Secret Yankees: The Union Circle in Confederate Atlanta* (Baltimore: Johns Hopkins University Press, 1999) 77–78; Charles B. Dew, *Ironmaker to the Confederacy: Joseph R. Anderson and the Tredegar Iron Works* (New Haven: Yale University Press, 1966) 87 ("only one of the Tredegar mills and the Atlanta mill had ever rolled rails"); William N. Still, Jr., *Confederate Shipbuilding* (Columbia: University of South Carolina Press, 1987) 30, 35, 77; Maurice Melton, *The Confederate Ironclads* (New York: Thomas Yoseloff, 1968) 72–74, 82–83, 205; Mitchell, "Atlanta the Industrial Heart," 22; Stephen R. Wise, *Lifeline of the Confederacy: Blockade Running During the Civil War* (Columbia: University of South Carolina Press, 1988) 46, 151–52; P. V. Daniel, Jr., to Secretary of War James A. Seddon, 23 April 1864, *OR*, ser. 4, vol. 2, p. 512; statement of Nelson Tift, 12 June 1863, *OR*, ser. 4, vol. 6, p. 626; N. & A. F. Tift to naval secretary Stephen R. Mallory, 27 November, 6 December 1861; 10 January, 26 August 1862, in US Navy Department, *Official Records of the Union and Confederate Navies in the War of the Rebellion*, 31 vols. (Washington, DC: Government Printing Office, 1894–1922) ser. 2, vol. 1, pp. 581, 583, 586, 599 (hereafter *ORN*).

Unfortunately, a mistaken legend has developed that the Atlanta Rolling Mill produced plating for the Confederate ironclad *Virginia*. The error is traceable to an early city history ([Parham, ed.], *Pioneer Citizens' History of Atlanta*, 116), and has been sustained by other local writers, working its way without challenge into even scholarly studies. Examples are "Atlanta Made Armor for the Famous Merrimac," *Atlanta Journal*, 21 September 1930; Garrett, *Atlanta and Environs*, 1:532; Singer, "Confederate Atlanta," 138; and James Lee McDonough and James Pickett Jones, *War So Terrible: Sherman and Atlanta* (New York: W. W. Norton & Company, 1987) 82.

In his study of the Tredegar Iron Works, on the other hand, Charles B. Dew makes it clear that the Richmond factory's work in producing armor plate, September 1861–February 1862, was exclusively for the *CSS Virginia*, then under construction at Norfolk. Besides Tredegar Company records as his basis, Dew shrewdly observes that "Southern railroads could not have delivered the iron to Norfolk from any plant much farther away than Richmond. Getting the armor from the Tredegar works to the Gosport Yard was difficult enough" (Dew, *Ironmaker to the Confederacy*, 117). Raimondo Luraghi also used Tredegar Company papers to prove the Richmond firm's armoring of the *Virginia* (Raimondo Luraghi, *The Rise and Fall of the Plantation South* [New York: Franklin Watts, 1978] 124–25). Regrettably, Dew's and Luraghi's findings have not countered the longstanding legend of Atlanta's link to the *CSS Virginia*. Most recent example is Marc Wortman, *The Bonfire: The Siege and Burning of Atlanta* (New York: Public Affairs, 2009) 126: "second only to the Tredegar Works in Richmond, the Atlanta, later the Confederate, Rolling Mill produced cannon, rails, and armor plate, including iron sheathing used on the *Merrimac* [sic] and other ironclads."

Atlanta's manufacturing importance rested not only on rails and plating, but also armaments and accoutrements. The former were the domain of the CS Ordnance Department, whose chief officer in Atlanta as of May 1864, was Colonel Moses H. Wright. Wright also served as commander of Atlanta's Confederate arsenal. He worked closely with Major G. W. Cunningham of the quartermaster department, who supervised the supply of uniforms, clothing, shoes, and equipment. Together the two departments, ordnance and commissary, had much activity to oversee.

Early in the war the city's privately owned manufacturing firms were converted to war purposes when the Confederate government offered lucrative production agreements. Colonel Wright contracted with numerous firms in the city to manufacture various goods. James L. Dunning's Atlanta Machine Works were given over to the production of artillery ammunition, but not before Superintendent Dunning expressed some Unionist feelings. When Dunning refused to accept a government contract for shell castings in mid-1861, military authorities arrested him for a few weeks, releasing him only after Dunning promised he would not impede the war effort. The plant then very efficiently turned out war goods, especially after the government took it over in March 1863 in its well-nigh revolutionary nationalization of essential war industries. Managed by Gullatt & Company, the machine works produced artillery shells, small arms, and swords. Between August and December 1863 alone, some 2,300 rounds of shot and shell were manufactured under contract with the Atlanta arsenal.[10]

Joseph R. Winship's Iron Works, at the southeast corner of Foundry Street, was ready and eager for the profitable contracts generated by the nation's war effort. Winship's barn-like main building housed three planing machines, four circular saws, a drill press, woodturning lathe, and other implements, including a bolt-cutter useful in naval armorclads' bolting. (For the ill-fated *Mississippi*, Nelson Tift contracted with Winship & Company for bolts to secure plating and gunport doors.) The plant put together machinery of its own, such as a screw-cutting lathe ordered by the Confederate Naval Ordnance Works in Selma (though the works superintendent had to write a letter of complaint about its quality in January 1863). In the main, though, the Winship ironworks served the Confederacy by pursuing its specialty, the manufacture of railway freight cars and other railroad supplies.

The machine shops of both the Georgia and the Western & Atlantic also adapted themselves for government work. William Rushton, master mechanic at

---

[10] Dyer, *Secret Yankees*, 102, 113; Ginger, "Confederate Atlanta," 103–104; Reed, *History of Atlanta*, 188; Mitchell, "Atlanta the Industrial Heart," 22–23; Garrett, *Atlanta and Environs*, 1:532; Emory M. Thomas, *The Confederacy as Revolutionary Experience* (Englewood Cliffs NJ: Prentice-Hall, 1971) 67 (on the Confederate government's nationalization of war industries).

the Georgia Railroad machine shops, experimented with making cannon from the crank axle of a train engine; his weapon, called a "Sumner Oscillating Breechloading Rifled Gun," received favorable comment in the press in August 1861. The State of Georgia awarded to the railway company a contract for six rifled cannon. At least two of these 3-inch bronze breechloaders were produced, for they passed through Colonel Wright's Atlanta arsenal later in the war. One of them, stamped "Rushton," attested to its origin at the Georgia railroad shops, just east of Atlanta's Car Shed.[11]

Smaller shops, too, did their part. Atlanta's large working force of railroad machinists and artisans, such as Charles Heinz (the gun- and blacksmith whose store stood on Alabama between Whitehall and Pryor), enabled Governor Brown to call a gunsmiths' convention in the city after the war broke out. Determined to begin a state program of weapons production, Brown expropriated some of the forges in the state-owned W & A machine shops for the making of gun barrels. John C. Peck and his partner, Francis Day, owners of the planing mill at Decatur and Pratt, accepted the governor's contract for gunstocks as well as the responsibility for delivery of finished weapons. Others also got involved. Heinz showed Peck how to rifle the bores; Atlanta's Gullatt brothers, James and Henry, cast the metal mountings, while Peck found still others to operate the boring bits and other machinery. After much time-consuming labor, all of twenty-three firearms, complete with special bullet molds and tripod rests, were handed over to the governor's office in December 1861. Peck made further but equally insubstantial contributions to the Confederate war effort through his pursuit of another of Governor Brown's enthusiastic projects, the design and manufacture of 6-foot wooden pikes, each topped with a 16-inch blade. Despite their obvious absurdity—men armed with sharp sticks could not stand long against rifled musketry—the governor called for patriots throughout the state to make pikes, and in 1862 over a hundred smiths and manufacturers turned over to the state arsenal (for $5 each) at least 7,000, perhaps as many as 12,000 pikes. As they did with the Peck rifles, blacksmiths at the W & A shops helped out in the governor's misguided initiative, and eventually 800 of these "Joe Brown Pikes" were sent off to the Army of Tennessee (where they were probably used as firewood). For good reason then, one authority has surmised that the patriotic Peck's most

---

[11] DeCredico, *Patriotism for Profit*, 37; Bowlby, "The Role of Atlanta," 31; Maurice Melton, "Major Military Industries of the Confederate Government" (Ph.D. diss., Emory University, 1978) 77; Mitchell, "Atlanta the Industrial Heart," 22; Statement of Nelson Tift, 11 June 1863, *OR*, vol. 6, p. 625; Larry J. Daniel and Riley W. Gunter, *Confederate Cannon Foundries* (Union City TN: Pioneer Press, 1977) 87, 106 (on the Rushton cannon, made at the Georgia Railroad machine shop); Robert C. Black III, *The Railroads of the Confederacy* (Chapel Hill: University of North Carolina Press, 1952) 60.

significant wartime contribution was the construction of a magazine, laboratory, and other buildings for the Confederate arsenal in Atlanta.[12]

Other businessmen either adapted their shops to war goods or started enterprises from scratch. Adolph Brady and Solomon Solomon, who before the war owned a hardware store on Whitehall between Hunter and Mitchell, organized a "Fulton Novelty Works," which by April of 1862 was advertising in the *Intelligencer* as manufacturer of buckles and harness mountings. At the time Brady and Solomon were also under contract with the Atlanta Arsenal for musket nipples and percussion caps, the essential items for soldier's firearms. The Novelty Iron Works was located on Marietta Street near the W & A Railroad, according to Fulton County deeds from Brady and Solomon later located by Atlantan Stephens Mitchell. Within several months, Brady and Solomon apparently sold the firm to the prominent Atlanta businessmen William McNaught and James Ormond. McNaught is named as president of Novelty Iron Works in an October 1862 agreement that linked the Atlanta firm to iron furnaces located in Bartow County.[13]

With W. S. Withers, Solomon evidently then formed another manufacturing company, the Atlanta Iron and Brass Works, on Marietta Street near Hunnicutt. In a January 1863 *Intelligencer*, Solomon advertised for "mechanics, moulders, negro blacksmiths" and other craftsmen, all entitled to "good wages on Government Work." The Iron and Brass Works made buttons and buckles for soldiers' uniforms, as well as spurs, bridles and bits for cavalrymen's use. (Another "button factory" was started in August 1863; its material was not brass, but bones. According to the *Intelligencer*, a small steam engine and wooden shop

---

[12] *Williams' Atlanta Directory*, 101 (on Heinz); Singer, "Confederate Atlanta," 95–96; Bowlby, "The Role of Atlanta," 27–29; Garrett, *Atlanta and Environs*, 1:509; William A. Albaugh and Edward N. Simmons, *Confederate Arms* (Wilmington NC: Broadfoot Publishing Company, 1993) 126–28; T. Conn Bryan, *Confederate Georgia* (Athens: University of Georgia Press, 1953) 26; DeCredico, *Patriotism for Profit*, 36. A detailed and entertaining account of Peck's travails with the twenty-three rifles is to be found in Mary A. H. Gay, *Life in Dixie During the War* (Atlanta: Charles P. Byrd, 1897) 320–24.

[13] *Williams' Atlanta Directory*, 51 (on Brady and Solomon); Fulton Novelty Works advertisement, *Atlanta Intelligencer*, 28 February, 3 April 1862 (Brady, Solomon & Co. as Fulton Novelty Works); "Cash-Book, Nashville and Atlanta Arsenals, 1862," in "Records of Ordnance Establishments at Dalton, Savannah, Augusta, and Atlanta, Ga., and Nashville, Tenn.," National Archives, RG 109, microfilm reel 7, University of Georgia (payments to Brady & Solomon, 29 March 1862, for percussion caps and "gun nipples"); Mitchell, "Atlanta the Industrial Heart," 21; Dyer, *Secret Yankees*, 16 ("the mercantile firm of McNaught and Ormond, one of Atlanta's largest and most successful businesses"); agreement between J. A. Howard of Cartersville and William McNaught, 7 October 1862, McNaught Papers, box 3, folder 7, MSS 156, Atlanta History Center. The Atlanta History Center also has on microfilm the Confederate Ordnance Bureau records from the Nashville and Atlanta arsenals.

had been set up in a suburban area where dead horses and cows had been buried. Animal bones were boiled till soft, then cut and shaped for pants buttons.)

Besides Solomon and Withers's venture, other metal works in the city also turned out military wares. The enterprising James Gullatt and William Barnes opened the Confederate Iron and Brass Foundry on Hunter Street, turning out such sundries as metal mountings for John Peck's ill-fated firearms. In May 1863, Kentuckian Hammond Marshall opened the Atlanta Sword Factory on the southwest side of Marietta between Simpson and Latimer Streets. In May 1862, the firm had secured contract with Moses Wright of the Atlanta Arsenal for 1,000 artillerymen's swords and 3,000 cavalry sabers with scabbards; another 3,000 were ordered six months later. The sword factory soon produced 170 edged weapons per week. Not all of its work proved satisfactory. Wright complained in a letter that he had destroyed a lot of scabbards produced by Marshall: "I must confess my astonishment at the inferiority of your work." By mid-1864, H. Marshall & Company was also under contract with the government for horse bits and shoes, and doubtless other metal gear as well. In May 1862, Wright also signed orders with J. B. Langford & Son for 200 cavalry saddles with bridles and bags and with S. A. Durand for 2,000 haversacks (the shoulder-slung canvas bag for rations). With other enterprises, Wright signed for infantrymen's accoutrements, each set consisting of cartridge box and belt, bayonet scabbard, shoulder strap, and percussion cap box. Daniel Miller and Ezra Andrews's saddle and harness shop, southwest corner of Whitehall and Hunter, worked under government contract as well.

As commander of the Atlanta arsenal, Colonel Wright did not deal with in-town businesses alone. Barber Greenwood & Company, a Cartersville firm, was to deliver 5,000 knapsacks and 200 saddles; from Coweta County were to come 1,000 wooden canteens; the A. H. DeWitt Company in Columbus signed with Wright for sabers and belts at $20 each. Colonel Wright even let out work to the spouses of his arsenal employees; in 1862–1863 these women produced 8,188 haversacks. This entire equipage was delivered to the government under stringent demands from the Confederate Ordnance Department in Richmond. For example, in late February 1864, Colonel Josiah Gorgas, Confederate ordnance chief, informed Wright that he was expected to produce in the next four months 2,500 sets of infantry accoutrements, 500 sets of cavalry equipment, and as many artillery harnesses.[14]

---

[14] Mitchell, "Atlanta the Industrial Heart," 23–24 (on deed site of "the Foundry of Solomon & Company"; citation of deed book reference, May 1863, to "Marshall's sword factory...containing 1/4 acre, more or less, together with all of the machinery, engines, fixtures and tools"; and contracts for Miller and Andrews's saddlery); Iron and Brass Works advertisement, *Atlanta Intelligencer*, 13 January 1863; "Button Factory," *Atlanta Intelligencer*, 21 August 1863; Sarah Huff, *My Eighty Years in Atlanta* (Atlanta: n.p., 1937) 21

With war demands so high, all resources were put to use, including the building and machinery of Richard Peters's steam-powered flour mill, which had been idle since 1858. The 130-horsepower engine was spotted as early as July 1861 by organizers of a big gunpowder plant to be erected in Augusta. After Peters sold this (for $120,000 in Confederate bonds), the engine, its two cylinders, five boilers and 14-ton flywheel were sent to Augusta and became part of the Confederacy's largest gunpowder factory. The flour factory building itself was also converted to military purposes. Two out-of-towners, Edward N. Spiller of Baltimore and David J. Burr of Richmond, had entered into agreement with the Confederacy in November 1861 to establish a pistol factory and produce 15,000 .36-caliber handguns, similar to the popular Navy model. The two entrepreneurs' initial intention was to set up their works in Richmond, where Burr had headed a company specializing in steam engines, and where they got assistance from James H. Burton, superintendent of the Richmond armory. But when Burton was reassigned in late May 1862 from the Richmond armory to Atlanta to establish a Confederate armory there, too, Spiller and Burr moved with him. The city council learned of Burton's plans and resolved to help secure land or buildings for the proposed armory. The city fathers failed, however, to suppress landowners' greed and high prices for use of their property. Burton became exasperated and moved on to Macon, where he eventually built his armory. But the Spiller and Burr pistol factory made its start in Atlanta. Meeting Burton there, Spiller in early June settled on the abandoned Peters flour mill as a suitable site for the enterprise—a solidly built, three-story frame building just south of the Georgia Railroad, between Butler and Calhoun Streets. During the latter half of 1862, the cylinder drills and other machines were installed and workers hired, so that by the end of December Spiller and Burr were ready to present a few sample models of their pistol to government officials in Richmond. Woefully behind schedule—their contract called for the delivery of 4,000 weapons by 1 December 1862, and 7,000 more the next year—Spiller and Burr's pistol factory succeeded in turning out no more than 800 handguns in 1863. Then, in January 1864, to

---

(reference to the "button factory" and its proprietor, George Edwards); Bowlby, "The Role of Atlanta," 28, 32; Marshall & Co., Atlanta Sabre Manufactory advertisement, *Atlanta Intelligencer*, 10 October 1862; Singer, "Confederate Atlanta," 141; "Contracts, Nashville and Atlanta Arsenals, 1862–1864," in Records of Ordnance Establishments, National Archives, RG 109, microfilm reel 6, University of Georgia (contracts to Marshall, Langford, Durand and Barber Greenwood); William A. Albaugh III, *Confederate Edged Weapons* (New York: Harper, 1960) 192 (Major Wright's complaint); Bryan, *Confederate Georgia*, 24 (Coweta County canteens); Albaugh and Simmons, *Confederate Arms*, 215 (DeWitt Company); "Annual Report of operations at the Nashville and Atlanta Arsenals, Confederate States of America, commanded by M.H. Wright, Ord. Offr., during the current year ending June 30th, 1863" (women as haversack makers) and Gorgas to Wright, 27 February 1864, Moses H. Wright Compiled Service Record, RG 109, National Archives (microfilm copy, Georgia Department of Archives and History).

secure firmer control of production, the Confederate government bought the pistol factory, soon moving all machinery and tools to its armory in Macon.[15]

During the course of the war Atlanta had other private enterprises engaged in the manufacture of ordnance. Charles Heinz's gun and lock shop at Alabama and Whitehall converted old flintlock muskets into percussion pieces. There is some shadowy evidence of an Empire Manufacturing Company just outside the city limits near the Western & Atlantic line, in the business (like Winship's works just down the tracks) of making railroad cars. Some shop in Atlanta carrying the name of Bell & Davis made Bowie knives in July 1861, for at least one such weapon has turned up for modern-day Civil War arms collectors. From his advertisements in the *Atlanta Intelligencer* and *Southern Confederacy*, we also know of one C. J. Christopher, who made and repaired swords from his shop on Bridge Street, near the railroad. Such weapons works sprang up particularly as Confederate territorial losses forced the relocation of munitions machinery from New Orleans, Nashville, and other places. A machinist from New Orleans received a cordial greeting from Atlantans for having, in the words of one Southern newspaper, "removed the valuable tools from an occupied area and put them to work for the Confederacy"; he reestablished himself in Atlanta as fabricator of artillery shells, solid shot, and gun carriages.[16]

While Atlanta's privately owned arms facilities operated under government contracts administered by Colonel Wright and the arsenal, the arsenal itself was not an arms manufactory. By definition an *armory* (such as Colonel Burton's plant

---

[15] George W. Rains, *History of the Confederate Powder Works* (Augusta GA: Chronicle & Constitutionalist Printing, 1882) 9; Matthew W. Norman, *Colonel Burton's Spiller & Burr Revolver: An Untimely Venture in Confederate Small-Arms Manufacturing* (Macon: Mercer University Press, 1996) 22–27; Royce Shingleton, *Richard Peters: Champion of the New South* (Macon GA: Mercer University Press, 1985) 43, 81–82; George W. Rains to Josiah Gorgas, July 25, 1861, in *OR*, ser. 4, vol. 1, p. 557; William A. Albaugh III, Hugh Benet, Jr., and Edward N. Simmons, *Confederate Handguns* (Philadelphia: Riling and Lentz, 1963) 61–77; "Mitchell, "Atlanta the Industrial Heart," 21; Atlanta City Council Minutes, 27 June, 4 July 1862, Atlanta History Center; Frank E. Vandiver, *Ploughshares into Swords: Josiah Gorgas and Confederate Ordnance* (Austin: University of Texas Press, 1952) 114; Spiller & Burr contract with government, 30 November 1861 (typescript copy), Spiller and Burr Pistol Factory Records, 1861–1863, MSS 334F, Atlanta History Center.

On the pistol factory, see also Matthew W. Norman, "Spiller & Burr: One Confederate Manufacturing Firm's Struggle for Survival During the War Between the States," *Man at Arms* 17/1 (January-February 1995): 30–38. Colonel Burton's further activities are described in Frank E. Vandiver, "A Sketch of Efforts to Equip the Confederate Armory at Macon," *Georgia Historical Quarterly* 28/1 (March 1944): 34–40.

[16] Albaugh and Simmons, *Confederate Arms*, 202, 209, 228; Mitchell, "Atlanta the Industrial Heart," 22; Atlanta *Intelligencer*, 4 August 1864 (announcement of Christopher's sword manufactory relocated in Macon); Albaugh, *Confederate Edged Weapons*, 183 (Christopher advertisements); Massey, *Refugee Life in the Confederacy*, 169.

in Macon) produces new weapons; an *arsenal* repairs and stores them. But an arsenal often has attendant laboratories and shops, manufacturing ammunition. Such was the case in Atlanta, where the government arsenal included laboratories for making cartridges and shells. As supervisor of all this work, Moses H. Wright performed his duties admirably. He had begun work for the Confederate Ordnance Department at Nashville, where with the rank of artillery lieutenant he commanded the Nashville arsenal beginning in September 1861. Five months later, in February 1862 with the fall of Fort Donelson (downriver from the state capital), Lieutenant Wright was ordered to dismantle and pack up his cap-making machinery and laboratory supplies. The order from army headquarters, dated 16 February, warned of the enemy's imminent advance: "Your services are more valuable than your stores. Save both if you can; if not both, then the former." Actually, Wright was able to get himself and all his machinery plus other material out of Nashville by train on 19 February, six days before the Yankees entered the city. He even brought out some of the mechanics trained in working his percussion cap machines, together with their families.[17]

Charged with establishing a new Confederate arsenal in Atlanta, Wright had first to find or erect buildings suitable for his varied enterprises. Arriving in the city on 5 March 1862, the lieutenant soon rented rooms and buildings around town for his ordnance department office, his laboratories and cap factory, plus a storehouse, 1-acre gun yard and stables for government horses. (For instance, Wright paid Lemuel P. Grant $125 a month to rent "Stables & Lots for use of Atlanta Arsenal.") Some of these facilities were meant only as a stopgap,

---

[17] Albaugh and Simmons, *Confederate Arms,* 76 (definitions of armory, arsenal, and laboratory); "Annual Report of operations…1862," Wright service record, Georgia Department of Archives and History, Atlanta; W. W. Mackall to Wright, 16 February 1862, Moses H. Wright Papers, MSS 386f, Atlanta History Center.

M. H. Wright, as he signed himself, has sometimes been confused by students of Atlanta history with another Confederate officer, Brig. Gen. Marcus Joseph Wright, commander of the army's Post of Atlanta (see Singer, "Confederate Atlanta," 159, 240; Beverly M. DuBose III, "The Manufacture of Confederate Ordnance in Georgia," *Atlanta Historical Bulletin* 12/4 [December 1967]:18; DeCredico, *Patriotism for Profit,* 37; and Davis, *Civil War Atlanta,* 38 ["Colonel Marcus H. Wright's Atlanta Arsenal"]). *Moses Hannibal Wright,* Tennessee-born graduate of West Point in 1859, received a US officer's commission and at the outbreak of war was serving as ordnance officer at St. Louis Arsenal. He resigned to fight for the South, taking with him US Army guides for the conversion of flintlock muskets to percussion. Appointed captain of ordnance in Tennessee's provisional army by Gov. Isham Harris, Wright applied for Confederate commission in July 1861 and was soon made lieutenant of CS artillery. In this capacity he assumed command of the Confederate arsenal works at Nashville, which began operation that September (Wright to Samuel Cooper, 1 July 1861, in Wright service record, Georgia Department of Archives and History, Atlanta; S. Williams to P. V. Hagner, 10 April 1861, *OR,* vol. 1, p. 664; Albaugh and Simmons, *Confederate Arms,* 198).

especially as the "Pyrotechnical branch of the Laboratory" had to be located well outside of the city, in case of ammunition explosion. Accordingly, Wright secured use of the "Old Race Track," an antebellum amusement site outside (to the southwest) of the city limits, and leased adjoining land from private owners. On this site, altogether 50 acres, Wright arranged for John C. Peck, the wood planer and would-be rifle-maker, to construct nine separate buildings, each designed for a specific function: magazine, laboratories, cap and cartridge factories, etc. All these were completed so that Lieutenant Wright was gradually able to move his labs and ammunition facilities outside the city. But it took some time. For a while, part of the laboratory was housed on Washington Street on the city's southside; the Confederate Cap Forming Department operated on Mitchell Street, two doors down from Whitehall. This offered some distressingly explosive potential, of course, as was noted by Captain John W. Mallet, head of Confederate ordnance laboratories. After an inspection of the arsenal works, Mallet wrote Colonel Gorgas in late May 1863 that Wright's artillery ammunition, friction primers, and fuses were "all still prepared within a two-story building in town, which looks to me very dangerous. If an explosion should occur it would be a very serious one." Mallet noted, though, that the arsenal commander intended to remove these operations, and so he did. Writing Gorgas in Richmond on 30 June, Wright affirmed that "the laboratories were, during the current year, all removed to the new location at the 'Race Track,' one mile from the center of the city." By March 1863, the Race Trace works encompassed thirteen buildings, each housing operations potentially too dangerous to be sited downtown.

In early August 1862, Wright (by then promoted to captain) reported his cartridge works alone could turn out 75,000 rounds per day, if lead supplies permitted. Actual output, however, was far lower, if only because the chief of ordnance in Richmond, Lieutenant Colonel Josiah Gorgas, that November set less ambitious rates for daily ammo production for Atlanta and his seven other arsenals then in operation: the Atlanta arsenal was charged with 25,000 rounds per day. Altogether, in the year 1 July 1862–30 June 1863, Wright reported to Colonel Gorgas with evident satisfaction that his laboratories and factories manufactured 4,164,050 small arms rounds, almost 19.5 million percussion caps for muskets and 3.75 million pistol caps, over 300,000 artillery friction primers and priming tubes, and just over 20,000 rounds of field artillery ammunition, with another 9,000 repaired or refixed. Wright's "pre-eminent service" (Gorgas's words) did not go unnoticed; he was promoted to major in fall 1862 and again to colonel the following July.[18]

---

[18] "Annual report of operations…1862," and "Annual Report of Operations…1863," Wright service record, Georgia Department of Archives and History, Atlanta; J. W. Mallet, "Work of the Ordnance Bureau," *Southern Historical Society Papers* 37 (1909): 14; receipt for rental of land by Arsenal, 1 May-31 July 1862, Lemuel P. Grant Papers, box 7, folder 5, MSS

Wright's other operations were kept inside the city. The arsenal commander worked a deal with John Peck for use of his carpentry and blacksmith shops, wood-drying kiln and other facilities, along with the right to construct other such buildings as might be needed. (Peck's enterprise was bought outright by the CS Ordnance Department in 1863.) As a result, the Atlanta arsenal's machine, blacksmith, carpentry, and gun carriage shops were all located on or about the grounds of Peck's lumberyard and planing mill, Decatur and Pratt streets just north of the Georgia Railroad (and across the tracks from Dunning's Machine Works). These facilities repaired artillery carriages, caissons, and wagons, primarily for use by the Army of Tennessee. For example, when a train which carried six new 12-pounder cannon to General Bragg's army at Chattanooga derailed in July 1863, it was the Atlanta arsenal that repaired the smashed carriages and caissons. The machine shop also turned out spare parts for weapons and tools, such as bullet molds and gauges for the other government arsenals. The facility also repaired weapons gathered from battlefields. In March 1863, ordnance officers for the Army of Tennessee relied on the arsenal to restore at least 500 small arms per week. Actually, in the 1862–1863 reporting year, Wright counted 9,344 muskets and pistols repaired and returned to service by his arsenal. All of this production required storage space; storerooms were leased in A. C. Wyly's building on the northwest corner of Peachtree and Walton. But Wright's operations were not confined to armaments. A tin shop over the Wyly storehouse specialized in canteen work; during 1862–1863, over 9,000 canteens were made. Other rooms were obtained on Whitehall Street for Wright's harness and saddle shop, which turned out artillery harness, cavalry saddles, bridles, cartridge bags and box belts, cap boxes and waist belts. Between mid-1863 and mid-1864, the shop produced 2,000 saber belts, 16,000 spur straps, 2,200 pistol holsters, and 1,200 rifle slings. Another two rooms and

---

100, Atlanta History Center; Contracts #1–5, 15 March 1862 (between Peck and Wright) and #6, 1 May 1862, in "Contracts, Nashville and Atlanta Arsenals, 1862–1864," Wright service record, Georgia Department of Archives and History, Atlanta; Albaugh and Simmons, *Confederate Arms,* 198 (listing of downtown buildings used by the arsenal, March 1863); Mallet to Gorgas, 29 May 1863, Melton, "Major Military Industries," 409; Wright to R. M. Cuyler, 10 August 1862, *OR,* vol. 16, pt. 2, p. 749; Vandiver, *Ploughshares into Swords,* 148n1; Gorgas to George W. Randolph, 3 September 1862, Wright service record, Georgia Department of Archives and History, Atlanta; statement of commission (captain of artillery), Confederate War Department, 9 June 1862 and commission (major), 10 October 1862, Wright Papers, Atlanta History Center.

A good review of the work of the Atlanta Arsenal is to be found in John M. Murphy and Howard Michael Madaus, *Confederate Rifles & Muskets: Infantry Small Arms Manufactured in the Southern Confederacy, 1861–1865* (Newport Beach CA: Graphic Publisher, 1996) 63–70.

buildings were obtained (without charge from their owners) for tanning and finishing leather.[19]

In Richmond, ordnance chief Josiah Gorgas placed particular demand upon the Atlanta arsenal for percussion caps. By early 1864, he had devised a program of specialization for the eight arsenals then in operation throughout Confederate-held territory. Gorgas called on Richmond and Atlanta to turn out caps for rifles and pistols; the former worked primarily for General Lee's army, the latter for the Army of Tennessee. Over 41 million percussion caps for muskets and another 5 million pistol caps were thus produced in Atlanta between 1 July 1862 and 30 June 1864.[20]

Atlanta's government-owned war plants were not devoted exclusively to the army, for the Confederate navy had an ordnance depot and laboratory facility in the northwest part of the city (west of Fowler Street, not far from Winship's Iron Works). These naval ordnance works were set up in early summer 1862 by Lieutenant David P. McCorkle, based on stores and machinery McCorkle was able to bring away from New Orleans before that city's fall. For his operations, the lieutenant had buildings erected that one inspector in mid-August 1862 judged "as suitable as such temporary wooden structures can be for ordnance purposes." There McCorkle's blacksmiths, machinists and other workers operated lathes, planes, and steam hammers to manufacture gun carriages and shape 7-inch rifle shells and other ammunition for the navy's big guns. With manpower always in shortage, women helped strap, fuse, and fit the shells, packing them in wooden boxes for transport.[21]

---

[19] "Annual Report of operations...1862," "Annual Report...1863," and "Annual Report...1864," Wright service record, Georgia Department of Archives and History, Atlanta; Lt. Col. H. Oladowski to Col. W. P. Johnston, March [—], 1863, *OR*, vol. 23, pt. 2, p. 762; L. P. Grant, map, "Sketch of the City of Atlanta and Line of Defenses" (dated 12 April 1864 by Colonel Wright), plate 51, 2 (location of "C.S. Machine Works and Armory, Atlanta Arsenal"), in Calvin Cowles, comp., *Atlas to Accompany the Official Records of the Union and Confederate Armies*, 3 vols. (Washington, DC: Government Printing Office, 1891–1895) (hereafter cited as *OR Atlas*); Albaugh, *Confederate Edged Weapons*, 194; Larry J. Daniel, *Cannoneers in Gray: The Field Artillery of the Army of Tennessee, 1861–1865* (Tuscaloosa: University of Alabama Press, 1984) 76–77.

[20] Melton, "Major Military Industries," 126–27, 353–54, 451; "Annual Report of Operations...1863," Wright service record, Georgia Department of Archives and History, Atlanta.

[21] Grant map, "Sketch of Atlanta Defenses," *OR Atlas* ("Laboratories, C.S. Navy"); George Minor to Confederate naval secretary Stephen R. Mallory, 15 August 1862, *ORN*, ser. 2, vol. 2, pp. 250–51; Lt. D. P. McCorkle to Cmdr. C. Ap R. Jones, 8 June [July] 1864, *ORN*, vol. 21, p. 901; Tom Henderson Wells, *The Confederate Navy: A Study in Organization* (University: University of Alabama Press, 1971) 53, 55–56; William N. Still, Jr., "Facilities for the Construction of War Vessels in the Confederacy," *Journal of Southern History* 31/3 (August 1965): 302.

Because of its multiple operations, the Atlanta arsenal was the city's largest employer, with some 5,500 men and women working in 1863–1864. Even children were hired. In late October 1863, Colonel Wright advertised in the *Appeal* for "one hundred boys and girls" to help out at the racetrack laboratories. To an extent, Wright was trying to aid the city's destitute families: "the labor is light and the buildings comfortable, and industrious hands can make from one and a half to three dollars per day."

After the arsenal, probably the city's second-largest employer was the Confederate Quartermaster Department, which was responsible to the army for uniform clothing, shoes, blankets, medicines, and other camp equipage. In April 1863, Major George W. Cunningham reported he had some 3,000 women working for him as seamstresses. Their collective output was prodigious, as demonstrated in the last three months of 1862 alone: 37,000 wool jackets, 13,400 pairs of pants, 10,000 cotton shirts, 13,700 pairs of drawers, 1,500 flannel shirts. In the first quarter of 1863, Cunningham reported that production of pants had more than doubled; that of cotton shirts zoomed more than eightfold. "No part of this clothing," Cunningham proudly noted, "is made under contract"; it had all been sewn by employees under direct government hire (and therefore, presumably, more efficiently and inexpensively). Contractors, of course, did more, such as Lewis Lawshe and James Purtell's tailoring establishment, as well as Herring and Son clothiers, both on Whitehall Street. A hatmaker in the city advertised in the *Southern Confederacy* as early as March 1861 for workers to help meet the army's impending need for wool hats. Even volunteers contributed. One Atlanta woman recalled long after the war how she and other ladies took their sewing machines to city hall to help make soldiers' uniforms. Many did their part for the cause (and to make some money while doing it). Carl Barth, who sold piano-fortes before the war from his store on Whitehall between Alabama and Hunter, set up a drum-making establishment that made hundreds of brass and kettle drums for the army's regimental bands.

Army footgear was another significant product of Atlanta's wartime industries. With the steam tannery at Orme and Simpson Streets working as a departmental shoe factory beginning in March 1863, Major Cunningham produced thousands of pairs of shoes—over 3,200 in his first month of operation alone. When leather supplies were sufficient, only the want of shoemakers held him back. Adequately manned and supplied, the shoe factory could turn out 500 pairs a day. Private firms assisted. Advertising in late 1862 was the Confederate Shoe Blacking Manufacturing Company on Whitehall Street.[22]

---

[22] James Michael Russell, *Atlanta, 1847–1890: City Building in the Old South and the New* (Baton Rouge: Louisiana State University Press, 1988) 103–104; "Editors Appeal" (Wright advertisement), *Memphis Appeal*, 2 November 1863; G. W. Cunningham to William Preston Johnston, 9 April 1863, *OR*, vol. 23, pt. 2, pp. 767–69; Singer, "Confederate Atlanta," 102, 165; *Williams' Atlanta Directory*, 42 ("Barth & Nicolai, Dealer in Piano-Fortes"); Bowlby,

With all of these supplies being produced and accumulated, Atlanta became a major military storage center for all kinds of goods, especially foodstuffs. In April 1863, the Confederate Commissary Department, headed by Major James F. Cummings from his offices on Whitehall, had as many as eighteen warehouses throughout the city, all packed with an enormous quantity of food for the army: 45,000 pounds of dried beef, 4.75 million pounds of bacon and bulk pork, 1,700 barrels of flour and 2,500 barrels of lard. Most of these warehouses were leased, but at least one two-story structure was built by the government at Peachtree and Houston. The landowner, Frank Rice, was in late 1861 offered Confederate bonds in payment. Rice balked, preferring gold; the government refused, and confiscated the land anyway. Other Atlanta merchants found the commissary department to be a reasonable purchaser of their goods. James Stewart's Greenwood Mills ground flour on Marietta Street out near the city limits. The flour was baked into hardtack, the soldiers' legendary cracker, at the "Government Bakery" at Bridge and Marietta, operated by F. M. Jack and T. M. Bryson, as well as doubtless other bakeries in the city.[23]

"Role of Atlanta," 46 (Barth's drum shop); "Autobiography of Kate Hester Robson," typescript, MSS 291F, Atlanta History Center; Grant map, "Sketch of Atlanta Defenses," *OR Atlas* ("Steam Tannery, Q.M. Department"); "Confederate Shoe Blacking Manufacturing Company," *Atlanta Intelligencer*, 7 December 1862.

Chad Morgan has commented tellingly on the number of Atlantans employed in the war effort: "Between the Arsenal and the Quartermaster Depot, nearly 9,000 Atlantans worked in state factories in 1863, or to put the number in context, only about 1,000 fewer than had lived in the city altogether before the war" (*Planters' Progress: Modernizing Confederate Georgia* [Gainesville: University Press of Florida, 2005] 39). My thanks go to Dr. Gordon Jones of the Atlanta History Center for pointing me to this study.

[23] J. F. Cummings to W. P. Johnston, 4 April 1863, *OR*, vol. 23, pt. 2, pp. 770–73; Garrett, *Atlanta and Environs*, 1:509; Mitchell, "Atlanta the Industrial Heart," 25; Wilbur G. Kurtz, interview with James Bell, 31 May 1935, notebook 11, 224, 236, Wilbur G. Kurtz Collection, Atlanta History Center.

Kurtz recorded more of young Bell's experience at Jack's Government Bakery: "In 1862 James and William Bell went to work in a Confederate Government bakery that stood at the south-west corner of Broad [then Bridge] and Marietta Sts. The two lads did a variety of work here—fired the ovens, 'peeled on' crackers, and delivered bread to local camps and hospitals" (notebook 13, 45). After an interview on 21 June 1935, Kurtz recorded Bell's recollection that the bakery turned out bread in loaves, which "was of good quality as long as the flour lasted—but the time came when rice flour and ground peas—pea meal—was used, which wasn't so good" (notebook 10, 236, Wilbur G. Kurtz Collection, Atlanta History Center).

F. M. Jack advertised himself as a baker and candy manufacturer on Whitehall Street in the *Atlanta Southern Confederacy*, 28 March 1862. Kurtz notebook 12 (p. 247) contains his transcription of a military service exemption granted by the Georgia State Militia, 23 May 1864, to one C. L. Jack, worker at "the Government Bakery." Kurtz obtained the document from Mrs. John R. Marsh (*nee* Margaret Mitchell), in July 1937, who in turn had borrowed it

Confederate soldiers' rations relied upon meat as well as hardtack. As early as February 1862, F. R. Shackelford sought permission from the city council to construct a facility "for the purpose of curing meat belonging to our government." This Confederate smoke house was eventually set up at Alabama and Loyd Streets. Indeed, as it developed into a Confederate commissary depot, Atlanta became a major meat-packing and salting center. Major Cummings, viewed by Commissary General Lucius B. Northrop in Richmond as "without doubt a man of extraordinary efficiency," in April 1863 alone sent to the Army of Tennessee over a million pounds of bacon and 100,000 pounds of cured beef, as well as 900 head of cattle. This dual means of subsistence, in-the-barrel and on-the-hoof, suggested soldiers' dissatisfaction with both. After cattle were brought to the army by rail (usually from Florida) to Atlanta, commissary agents slaughtered the beeves, pickled the cuts in brine, and sent them on to the army. But the men found the processed meat unpalatable save after boiling; as General Johnston himself complained in February 1864, the men "therefore throw away the greater part of this except when pressed by hunger." Johnston therefore ordered live cattle to be brought by rail to his army for fresher slaughter, but this transit operation involved so many train cars that rolling stock could not be had for the army's other supplies. Moreover, once arrived at the front lines after several days without food or water, the cattle were often found to be emaciated. In the end, General Johnston came back around to accepting meat already butchered and brined in Atlanta. This proved only to be the less objectionable of two bad options. But in Atlanta, meat-packing meant good business for Alvin K. Seago, whose salt dealership offices were at Forsyth and Mitchell. In addition to his company's contract with the state to bring salt from southwestern Virginia to Atlanta for distribution to Georgia's civilians, Seago also sold to Major Cummings's commissary department—and in good quantity, too, for a 500-pound steer or cow required usually 1 1/4 bushels of salt for adequate preservation.

The corralling, slaughtering, and processing of so many cattle brought their own problems. Slaughterhouses and pens in Atlanta, frequently on the west and south side of town, were not only smelly nuisances but also public health hazards. The Fulton County Grand Jury brought indictments against owners of the worst stockyards on Whitehall and McDonough streets. Yet cattle, horses, and mules were not the only offenders when it came to public offensiveness:

---

from its owner, Telamon Cuyler. With this knowledge, Kurtz made a point of including "Jack's Bakery C.S.A." in his famed painting, *Atlanta in 1864*, which gives an aerial view of what downtown Atlanta might have looked like before the Yankees came (*Civil War Times Illustrated* 3/4 [July 1964]: 30). Recently, Kurtz's aerial image, whose original is possessed by the Atlanta History Center, has been reproduced in Wendy Hamand Venet, ed., *Sam Richards's Civil War Diary: A Chronicle of the Atlanta Home Front* (Athens: University of Georgia Press, 2009), and also in Wortman, *The Bonfire*, 144.

Atlanta's people and their trash were. Growing numbers of inhabitants all produced their share of waste and garbage, which strained the city's public waste collection services, obviously reduced in wartime. In its issue of 2 July 1864, the editors of the *Intelligencer* finally addressed the public sewage issue in its most blatant manifestation, that of the foul smell permeating large parts of the city. Trying to make light of an ugly subject, the paper observed that "in numerous places there are scents as though the triple distilled extract of the quintessence of stink was being brewed there." Editors complained of residents' backyards as "perfect seethpools of filth and nastiness." Uncleaned city gutters were "nuisances and abominations." Among the worst places of all were the gutters along the railroad crossing at Whitehall Street. The *Intelligencer* exclaimed that there "even the rats have become disgusted with the filth and stench that has accumulated beneath those horrible planks and abandoned the neighborhood." The editors asked the city's sanitary board to "nose out these festering spots...and abate their malignance and dangerous, poisonous exhalations." Then, as if to add comic hyperbole: "For fear that some of our city guardians may not understand that last big word, and that they may not have access to a lexicon—sometimes called a dictionary, we inform them that its definition is unhealthy, sickness breeding stink; stinking stink-k-k-k."[24]

While the city attended to its municipal issues, the Confederate army defending it attended to its needs as well. Besides meat, the army needed other goods, too, especially medicines and spirits. The Confederate Medical Department maintained a laboratory in Atlanta, supervised by Dr. George S. Blackie, for research in indigenous plants as medicinal sources. For corn whiskey, which army surgeons administered as a stimulant for exhausted men and as sedative for surgical patients, Commissary Major Cummings in February 1864 had contracts out for 3,000 gallons a month. Calvin W. Hunnicutt's drugstore downtown at Decatur and Peachtree streets purveyed both whiskey and vinegar. A large distiller, High, Lewis, and Company, became a major supplier to the military, producing thousands of gallons a year.[25]

---

[24] Atlanta City Council minutes, 21 February 1862, Atlanta History Center; Northrop to James A. Seddon, 12 January, 4 June 1863, *OR*, ser. 4, vol. 2, pp. 351, 574; Jeffrey N. Lash, *Destroyer of the Iron Horse: General Joseph E. Johnston and Confederate Rail Transport, 1861–1865* (Kent OH: Kent State University Press, 1991) 124–26; Bowlby,"Role of Atlanta," 40–41 (on Seago's salt business); Philip Secrist, "Life in Atlanta," *Civil War Times Illustrated*, 9/4 (July 1970): 31; "The City," Atlanta *Intelligencer*, 2 July 1864. I thank Professor Venet of Georgia State University for information on the Confederate smoke house.

[25] "Indigenous Remedies of the South," *Confederate States Medical & Surgical Journal* 1/7 (July 1864): 107; Frank R. Freemon, "Administration of the Medical Department of the Confederate States Army, 1861 to 1865," *Southern Medical Journal* 80/5 (May 1987): 634; James O. Breeden, "Medical Shortages and Confederate Medicine: A Retrospective Evaluation," *Southern Medical Journal* 86/9 (September 1993): 1042; Cummings to S. B. French, 12 February 1864, *OR*, ser. 4, vol. 3, p. 117; Singer, "Confederate Atlanta," 101, 139.

Atlanta was thus a vital manufacturing and munitions center, busy supply depot with numerous army warehouses, and important hospital and medical complex. Atlantans were quite aware that their city was doing much for the cause. "With the single exception of Richmond, no city in the Confederacy is doing more for the people than Atlanta," boasted the *Intelligencer* in late January 1863. With its many factories and commissary facilities, the paper asserted that no Southern city "is more devoted to the cause."

Atlanta's significance to the wartime Confederacy also strongly hinged on its railroads. By 1864, the convergence of four key lines into the city had already aided Confederate strategy in the western theater. The Atlanta & West Point Railroad was one of six Southern lines participating in the Confederacy's first great troop movement, that of Braxton Bragg's army from Tupelo, Mississippi, to Chattanooga in mid-1862. The Georgia Railroad from Augusta and the Macon & Western had helped bring Lieutenant General James Longstreet's corps, traveling from Virginia through the Carolinas in September 1863 to Atlanta; from there the Western & Atlantic had carried the infantry to North Georgia just in time to clinch victory for the Confederates at Chickamauga. After Missionary Ridge, with Johnston's Army of Tennessee refitting in Northwest Georgia, the W & A became logistical lifeline for the Confederate forces, keeping them supplied from the commissary, quartermaster, and ordnance complex in the Gate City.

The transport of arms, munitions, food, and other government supplies more than tested the efficiency of the Western & Atlantic; the incessant military traffic wreaked havoc with company scheduling of its trains. The W & A, able to run a prewar train 138 miles to Chattanooga in 8 1/2 hours, was taking four times that long in early 1864 to cover the 100-mile distance from Atlanta to Dalton, where the Army of Tennessee was spending the winter. In January 1864, with General Johnston complaining to Governor Brown that the state road was inadequate to his army's logistical demands, Confederate authorities affirmed that it would require seven trains of twelve cars each to bring 21,000 bushels of corn each day over the line from Atlanta to Dalton. All this assumed that the train car-space was to be had. Struggling to meet the needs of both army and civilian commerce, railroad companies had to sacrifice the latter. The W & A, Atlanta & West Point, and Macon & Western all raised rates on non-military freight. As early as May 1862, the A & WP announced that it would henceforth accept no private citizens' baggage for shipment (the company later relented). The railroads also indemnified themselves against liability for loss or damage of property—in Atlanta's crowded storehouses, priority was given to government goods, so that private baggage was set outside, many times without guard and vulnerable to theft.

Just as civilians' baggage gave way to military freight, so too did non-military passengers step aside. When they could find seats at all, civilians paid high prices, far higher than the 2 1/2 cents per mile that the several Georgia lines agreed to charge the government for soldiers. The railroads carried sick and wounded free of charge, along with bodies of the unfortunate dead (so long as they were suitably encoffined with odor-absorbing charcoal). Yankee prisoners with their guards were also transported at the railroads' expense to their destinations (in 1864 this usually meant to the officers' prison at Macon or, for enlisted men, farther on via the Southwestern Railroad to Andersonville). Obvious priority was given to ailing Confederate soldiers. The state legislature in 1862 called on all railroads to attach to every passenger train at least one specially furnished ambulance car. Sometimes, though, the inevitably heavy traffic after a battle meant additional suffering for the wounded. In early August 1864, by which time Confederate hospitals were strung out all along the rail line south of Atlanta, the Army of Tennessee's chief of staff Brigadier General Francis A. Shoup felt compelled to write the president of the Macon & Western company, complaining that trains loaded with maimed men sometimes took up to seventy hours to travel the 102 miles from Atlanta to Macon (covered in just seven hours before the war). Concern at delay was matched by medical officers' anxiety for their charges' safety, as bumpy train rides sometimes jolted patients from their tiered berths. When trains ran on tight schedules, too, there was little or no time to clean out boxcars in which, floored with straw and blankets, wounded or sick men were packed. Surgeon M. W. King expressed outrage in December 1863 when he had been forced to load patients into cars that "had recently been used in transporting cattle and horses, and had not been cleaned."[26]

It was Atlanta's importance as a railroad hub and supply center that brought the first Yankees near, indeed inside the city. Following their capture of Nashville, Union forces under Major General Don Carlos Buell slowly probed southward through middle Tennessee. Their objective lay just south of the Alabama line—the strategic Memphis & Charleston Railroad, the Confederacy's main east-west rail artery. Federal commander in the area, Brigadier General Ormsby Mitchel, aimed to capture Huntsville, a depot town on the railroad in northcentral Alabama, then move eastward along the road toward Chattanooga. To assist him in keeping the Rebel forces off guard, Mitchel turned to a civilian then in Union employ as a spy-of-sorts, one James Andrews. Andrews promised, if provided with a handful of soldiers, to slip behind Confederate lines, make his way toward Atlanta, steal a locomotive and race north on the Western & Atlantic, burning railroad bridges, wrecking track and fouling the Rebels' communications in North Georgia just as Mitchel marched on Huntsville. Andrews had already shown that it could be done, the first half anyway; in late March he and eight Union soldiers, dressed in plain clothes, had slipped into

---

[26] "The Business of Atlanta," *Atlanta Intelligencer,* 25 January 1863; Black, *Railroads of the Confederacy,* 182–83, 188–89, 196, 253; Singer, "Confederate Atlanta," 107, 144–45, 176–77; Bowlby, "Role of Atlanta," 6–8 (Gen. Shoup's complaint), 10–11, 13–14; Schroeder-Lein, *Confederate Hospitals on the Move,* 128–29.

Atlanta, long enough to register at the Trout House before making their way
back to Union lines.

On 6 April, General Mitchel allowed Andrews to proceed with his train
raid, with soldiers from his Ohio regiments to volunteer as Andrews'
accomplices. Disguised as civilians (their story, if confronted, was that they were
Kentuckians en route for Confederate enlistment), Andrews and his train thieves
got through Rebel lines and rendezvoused in Marietta on 11 April—the day, it
turned out, that Mitchel's troops entered Huntsville. The next morning, Andrews
and nineteen others boarded a northbound train, and rode it for 8 miles to Big
Shanty station (now Kennesaw). While the crew was at breakfast, they hijacked a
locomotive, tender, and three boxcars, then steamed north. Surprised railroad
officials figured out that it was a Yankee trick and organized pursuit. Seven
hours and 87 miles later, Andrews and his train-jackers were captured, out of
fuel and out of luck not 10 miles from the Tennessee line. They had not burned a
single bridge. (It was raining that day and their tinder was wet.) They had not
wrecked any long section of track, only removing two rails to slow their
pursuers. And while they had cut the telegraph wire several times, they failed to
prevent a message from going through to Chattanooga, from whence Southern
officers dispatched cavalry to intercept them. Altogether the Andrews Raid
contributed not one whit to General Mitchel's Union advance on Stevenson,
Alabama, which he occupied on 12 April.[27]

The boldness of the Yankee train thieves and the advance of Union forces in
North Alabama made Atlantans feel more vulnerable than at anytime previously
in the war. Like many communities facing collective fears, Atlantans found
expression for their anxiety by looking inward, worrying about dissidents and
traitors amongst them. Even before the Andrews Raid, there was talk in the city
about "spies." "We have been advised," warned the *Intelligencer* on 3 April, "that

---

[27] Kevin J. Weddle, "'Old Stars': Ormsby MacKnight Mitchel at the Gates of the
Confederacy," *Blue & Gray* 4/6 (July 1987): 27–28; Stan Cohen and James G. Bogle, *The
General & the Texas: A Pictorial History of the Andrews Raid, April 12, 1862* (Missoula MT:
Pictorial Histories Publishing Co., 1999); Charles O'Neill, *Wild Train: The Story of the
Andrews Raiders* (New York: Random House, 1956) 48, 52–56.

Russell S. Bonds, *Stealing the General: The Great Locomotive Chase and the First Medal of
Honor* (Yardley PA: Westholme Publishing, 2007), is the most recent and thorough account
of the Andrews Raid. The literature of the raid has credited one of the pursuers, Atlantan
William A. Fuller, as chiefly responsible for bringing about the failure of Andrews's
mission, but this conclusion rests largely on Fuller's zealous postbellum puffing of himself
and his often bitter quarrels with fellow Atlantan Anthony Murphy, who deserves every
bit as much credit in the successful running down of the Yankee engine thieves. See
Stephen Davis, "Joel Chandler Harris's Version of the Andrews Raid: Writing History to
Please the Participant," *Georgia Historical Quarterly* 74/1 (Spring 1990): 99–116; and Davis,
"The Conductor Versus the Foreman: William Fuller, Anthony Murphy, and the Pursuit of
the Andrews Raiders," *Atlanta History* 34/4 (Winter 1990–1991): 39–55.

spies of the enemy have been, and are still in Atlanta." The well-known presence of Northern natives among the city's citizenry, such as Connecticut-born William Markham, added to the fears of "suspicious characters" or "secret enemies." That some civilians, such as Vermonter Cyrena Stone and mulatto barber Robert Webster, visited Yankee patients in the city's hospitals or Yankee prisoners in the city jail distressed a good many folk, who rightly feared a secret cell of Union sympathizers in their midst.[28]

Editors of the *Intelligencer* were especially worried that Northern agents were apparently free to come and go in the city, possibly arranging secret deals for the transport of cotton northward, conniving to drive up the prices of commodities, and otherwise inflicting economic mayhem. For this reason as early as 22 March 1862, the newspaper called upon Governor Brown to declare martial law in the city. There ensued a public debate over the necessity of such a measure, a sometimes-heated discourse that revealed Atlantans' fears of Yankee activity in spring 1862. The *Intelligencer* intoned on 2 April, "Atlanta is now made Head Quarters for itinerant speculators, in gold, bank notes, Confederate Currency, meat and bread. It is, also, a point attractive to the spies of Buell's army, in Tennessee. In it, every day, may be seen men, who openly avow that they have been in Nashville, are just from there, and are going back again.... Martial Law, and an efficient Provost Martial are all absolutely necessary to put a stop to all this." Within a few days, Atlanta's two leading papers entered into a shouting match on the issue, with the *Southern Confederacy* opposing martial law, denying its necessity, and the *Intelligencer* repeating its argument that stricter regulatory measures were needed for the public good. Indeed, *Intelligencer* editors observed, Confederate authorities had in March invoked martial law for Richmond, New Orleans, and Mobile; the people of Charleston were actually calling for it as a safeguard against the Federal troops who had landed on the Carolina coast. But with Lieutenant Wright industriously establishing his arsenal in town, the populace sensed that Atlanta was becoming more militarily prominent, hence more vulnerable to espionage activities, even direct enemy attack.

The lurking of disguised engine thieves and the excitement of the locomotive chase on 12 April, well covered in both of the city's newspapers, spurred the *Intelligencer* further. Editors of the latter fairly puffed themselves with "I told you so" in their opinion column of 15 April, after Andrews and his cohorts had been rounded up.

---

[28] "Spies in Atlanta," *Atlanta Intelligencer,* 3 April 1862; Russell, *Atlanta, 1847–1890,* 95; Paul D. Lack, "Law and Disorder in Confederate Atlanta," *Georgia Historical Quarterly* 66/2 (Summer 1982): 173; Thomas G. Dyer, "Atlanta's Other Civil War Novel: Fictional Unionists in a Confederate City," *Georgia Historical Quarterly* 79/1 (Spring 1995): 159; Schroeder-Lein, *Confederate Hospitals on the Move,* 115; Dyer, *Secret Yankees,* 37, 83–84, 87–88.

We have warned the people of this; we have appealed to the authorities to look into this matter; we have advocated Martial Law to ensure our safety, and detect the rascals, as well as to rid our community of other evils.... We now repeat, that in our judgment, Martial Law is necessary for the security of both *person and property* in Atlanta. We confidently believe that our city has been and is daily being visited by spies and emissaries of the Lincoln government—that the public property here is endangered—and as a consequence private property will share its fate.

Other area papers soon joined in the editorial fray. The *Intelligencer* informed its readers, for instance, that the *Milledgeville Southern Union* in late April had sided with it in calling for martial law in Atlanta.[29]

As if disguised Yankee agents were not bad enough, there was the threat of Yankee armies themselves. One citizen wrote the *Southern Confederacy* in late April, direfully predicting that Federal forces would advance on Atlanta before the end of the year, and recommending that city authorities organize a home guard for emergency defense. Coincidentally, to sustain the prediction, Mitchel's Union division in Northeast Alabama launched a demonstration on 28 April against Bridgeport, a town located just 25 miles west of Chattanooga. The Andrews raiders, incarcerated in Chattanooga, were moved as a precaution to Atlanta on 2 May. An ugly mob gathered at the passenger depot, shouting out that the train thieves should all be hanged. (The raiders were taken to Madison, Georgia, for a few days' safekeeping before being returned to Atlanta.)[30]

To quiet the hubbub over security in the city, or at least to channel it to worthwhile purposes, in early May Mayor James M. Calhoun called a public meeting at city hall. There the state of Atlanta's defensive capacity was reviewed, and all men currently exempt from military service were encouraged to form reserve guard units. Still, fears of Yankee spies made some Atlantans yearn for militarily imposed order. After a fire in the city consumed a stock of government meat supplies, William C. Humphreys, an Atlanta butcher, wrote President

---

[29] "Shipment of Cotton to Tennessee," *Atlanta Intelligencer*, 22 March 1862 ("Let Governor Brown...declare *Martial Law* over Atlanta"); "Martial Law," *Atlanta Intelligencer*, 2 April; "The Confederacy on Reason," *Atlanta Intelligencer*, 9 April; "'How It Works,'" *Atlanta Intelligencer*, 10 April; "The 'Confederacy' and the Extortioners," *Atlanta Intelligencer*, 13 April; "Lincoln's Spies, Thieves, and Bridge Burners," *Atlanta Intelligencer*, 15 April; "Martial Law," *Atlanta Intelligencer*, 23 April; "Martial Law," *Atlanta Intelligencer*, 24 April; William M. Robinson, *Justice in Grey: A History of the Judicial System of the Confederate States of America* (Cambridge: Harvard University Press, 1941) 390–94.

[30] "Important Suggestions," *Atlanta Southern Confederacy*, 24 April 1862; Singer, "Confederate Atlanta," 122, 127; O'Neill, *Wild Train*, 240, 242–43; Bonds, *Stealing the General*, 220–21.

Davis on 15 May, adding a private citizen's appeal for martial law to be declared.[31]

By law, only the president could issue a proclamation suspending the writ of habeas corpus and instituting martial law. At the time, Jefferson Davis was exercising this privilege quite sparingly, only in areas threatened by enemy approach. For example, in late April the Confederate commander for Georgia and South Carolina, Major General John C. Pemberton, appealed to have martial law declared in the cities of Savannah and Augusta, as well as for the coastal area surrounding Charleston. The president authorized it for the Carolina coast, but balked at its necessity in Georgia. While the mayor and city council of Augusta favored martial law, and even Georgia's Governor Brown (usually an outspoken defender of civil liberties) expressed no objection, the mayor and aldermen of Savannah opposed suspension of the writ for their city, despite the Yankees' recent capture of Fort Pulaski, a dozen miles downriver. As a consequence, Davis disapproved the measure in both Savannah and Augusta. Atlanta seemed in less danger still than either of those places, so the Confederate chief executive probably gave very little consideration to martial law for the Gate City.[32]

As a step in that direction, however, Brigadier General Alexander R. Lawton, commander of the District of Georgia, declared Atlanta to be a "military post" on 14 May 1862. By this announcement, authorities were given special powers "for the purpose of guarding the government stores, to preserve order in and around Atlanta, and for the protection of all loyal citizens, and the punishment of all disorderly conduct." Specifically, around-the-clock guards and patrols would watch over the commissary and quartermaster stores and ordnance facilities; sentinels in the railroad yards could arrest "all suspicious persons"; cotton, hay, and other combustibles would have to be removed from stocks of government supplies; no vendor could sell liquor to an officer or soldier without permission; and military personnel were prevented from loitering in the city—the same went for "free persons of color" after 9:00 P.M.

Charged with enforcing these rules as post commander was Major George Washington Lee, an Atlantan in somewhat bad odor among his fellow townspeople. Illiterate and a barkeeper to boot (at the Senate Saloon, on Decatur between Peachtree and Pryor), Lee nonetheless managed to raise a company of soldiers in response to the Confederate government's first call for troops. Lee's

---

[31] Singer, "Confederate Atlanta," 127; William C. Humphreys to Davis, 15 May 1862, cited in Lynda Lasswell Crist, Mary Seaton Dix, and Kenneth H. Williams, eds., *The Papers of Jefferson Davis*, 12 vols. to date (Baton Rouge: Louisiana State University Press, 1971–) 8:177.

[32] Pemberton to Davis, 24 April 1862; Pemberton to Samuel Cooper, 29 April; Gen. Order 33, 1 May; Robert H. Mayo to Davis, 19 April; Joseph E. Brown to R. E. Lee, 6 May; Pemberton to Lee, 8 May; Lee to Pemberton, 9 May, *OR*, vol. 14, pp. 478–79, 486, 489, 492, 495.

reputation, however, preceded him, such that Governor Brown would not accept either him or his company of recruits. The Confederate War Department did, however, and sent Lee to Florida with a captain's commission. In mid-March 1861, before Fort Sumter, he presented himself and his men to Brigadier General Braxton Bragg, then commanding Southern forces at Pensacola, Florida. Bragg was not impressed, as he expressed in a letter of complaint to his superiors, characterizing Lee as "a man without education or character—you will observe he never signs his own name." Soon, however, Lee was accused of stealing his men's clothing allowance; under arrest he resigned and slunk back to Atlanta. There, Bragg disapprovingly noted, "by misrepresentation and downright falsehood, and by evading and misconstruing orders," he raised a force of some 500 home guards, cadged a major's rank, and thus stood in line to receive the post commandery as Atlanta's provost marshal in May 1862.

General Bragg, soon in charge of a military department that included Atlanta, concluded that Lee's administration was "destructive of discipline and efficiency," especially as Lee apparently winked at the exemption of able-bodied men from army service and was guilty of "expenditures most lavish." To achieve greater public order in Atlanta—specifically, as one communiqué stated, "to secure the safety of the hospitals, public stores, railroad communication, the discipline of the troops *in transitu,* and to collect deserters and absentees along the railroad and guard against espionage on the part of the enemy"—Bragg on his own authority declared martial law in and around the city on 11 August 1862. (The *Intelligencer,* at long last vindicated, expressed editorial approval.) Bragg used his new authority to try to get rid of Lee, even appealing to the War Department that he be brought to trial. In the meantime, the general sought to circumvent Lee's authority by appointing Mayor Calhoun "civil governor" of the city. This extraordinary step, however, excited civil officials' contempt for martial law—even the *Intelligencer* opined that Bragg had overstepped his authority. With no less than Confederate Vice President Alexander H. Stephens weighing in against Bragg, the legitimacy of a civil governorship and the necessity of martial law, the measure was revoked by the War Department on 12 September for the reason that Bragg had exercised a privilege accorded by law only to the president. Martial law had prevailed in Atlanta all of one month and a day.[33]

---

[33] William A. Richards, "'We Live Under a Constitution': Confederate Martial Law in Atlanta," *Atlanta History* 33/2 (Summer 1989): 28–34; *Williams' Atlanta Directory,* 95, 113 (on Guild and Lee's "Senate Saloon"); Samuel Cooper to Bragg, 19 March 1861, *OR,* vol. 1, p. 451; Bragg to Joseph E. Johnston, 2 March 1863, *OR,* vol. 23, pt. 2, pp. 656–57; J. A. Campbell to Samuel Jones, 27 October 1862, *OR,* vol. 16, pt. 2, p. 980; Special Order 148, 11 August 1862, *OR,* vol. 16, pt. 2, p. 754; "Martial Law," *Atlanta Intelligencer,* 14 August 1862; G. W. Randolph to Bragg, 12 August 1862, *OR,* ser. 2, vol. 4, p. 844; James E. Slaughter to J. M. Calhoun, 16 August 1862, Calhoun Family Papers, 1834–1960, MSS 50, Atlanta History Center; Garrett, *Atlanta and Environs,* 1:525–28; General Order 66, 12 September 1862, *OR,* ser. 4, vol. 2, p. 83.

The threat of Yankees very much remained, nonetheless. On 10 June 1862, the *Intelligencer* brought front-page news to Atlantans that Federal forces had shelled Chattanooga, little more than 100 miles away. At that time Atlanta's jail still confined the engine thieves and bridge burners captured two months before—at least, those who were left. Through the randomness of military justice, Andrews and seven train raiders were convicted of spying and sentenced to death. Andrews was hanged on 7 June, the seven others on 18 June near the City Cemetery. The rest remained incarcerated without formal trial. The escape of eight of them on 16 October 1862 alarmed city residents, and did nothing to enhance Provost Marshal Lee's standing in the eyes of Confederate authorities. Possibly for that reason, the next time Atlanta received a batch of distinguished Yankee prisoners (Colonel Abel D. Streight and other officers, captured near Rome, Georgia, in a failed Union cavalry raid, May 1863), the Federals were imprisoned on the second floor of city hall, with a ring of guards surrounding the building. At some point, the military authorities converted a downtown building that had been used as a barracks into a prison for captured Yankees. It stood on Peachtree, four or five blocks north of the railroad.[34]

---

[34] *Atlanta Intelligencer,* 10 June 1862; James G. Bogle, "The Great Locomotive Chase or the Andrews Raid," *Blue & Gray* 4/6 (July 1987): 53; G. W. Lee to Clifton H. Smith, 18 November 1862, *OR,* vol. 10, pt. 1, p. 639; Wilbur G. Kurtz, notebook 6, 37, Wilbur G. Kurtz Collection, Atlanta History Center (on Streight's men confined at city hall, based on Kurtz's interview with William Fort Williams, 19 May 1931).

On the downtown prison for Union prisoners, see *Memphis Appeal,* 18 May 1864: "PRISONERS.—About twenty-five *blue* looking miscegenationists arrived yesterday, and were sent to the barracks." "Prison" is a building on the west side of Peachtree marked for destruction on an unlabeled map accompanying the "Plan of Destruction" submitted to Col. William Cogswell, with structures designated for demolition by the 33rd Massachusetts (William Cogswell Collection, MSS 212, Phillips Library, Peabody Essex Museum, Salem MA). The map does not strictly conform to Vincent's, so it is difficult to place the barracks prison. It was on Peachtree, possibly in the area of Cain and Harris Streets. A Federal officer, Capt. Lewis Carter of the 9th (US) Tennessee, reported that after his capture in September 1863 he was "lodged in the barracks at Atlanta," and even forced to wear a leg iron with ball and chain (probably as punishment for being a "Tennessee Tory"). Carter stated that the prison was three blocks from a blacksmith shop, where his irons were fixed upon his left leg—the shop could therefore have been William Roach's blacksmith shop, located at Peachtree and Bridge (statement of Capt. Lewis L. Carter, 6 December 1863, *OR,* vol. 31, pt. 3, pp. 347–48; *Williams' Atlanta Directory,* 130). The barracks/prison yard was bounded apparently by a not-too-tall fence. After Capt. Carter succeeded in breaking his shackles on the night of 15 November, he was able to climb over the walls. Evidently during his two-month confinement, Carter had been visited in prison by Atlanta's Unionist civilians; he was harbored by them for nine days, when he made his way out of the city to Union lines (Carter statement, 348). A group of East Tennesseans with Unionist loyalties in Atlanta may have also helped other Federal officers escape (Dyer, *Secret Yankees,* 89).

Indeed, it was Streight's raid that jarred Atlantans into realizing that the time had come for serious measures to protect their city against Union soldiers on the outside, not merely secret Yankees inside. Much more than Andrews's rather flimsy scheme, the Streight cavalry raid was intended to send a strong Federal column of 2,000 mounted infantry through Northern Alabama and into Northern Georgia. Their mission was to strike and cut the Western & Atlantic Railroad south of Dalton, then make their way back to friendly lines the best way they could. Breaking the railroad would impede the flow of Rebel reinforcements, ammunition, and supplies to Bragg's army in middle Tennessee, just as the Union forces south of Nashville geared up for their spring offensive. Such was the raiders' intent. But setting out from Eastport, Mississippi, on 21 April, Colonel Streight never even reached the Georgia state line. Pursued doggedly by Confederate Brigadier General Bedford Forrest and his cavalrymen, Streight surrendered his worn out and broken-down troopers on 3 May near Cedar Bluff, Alabama, 20 miles west of Rome.

Rome itself was only 60 miles from Atlanta—a fact that did not escape the residents of the Gate City. The mayor and councilmen, meeting on 8 May 1863, formally expressed their gratitude by adopting a resolution that effused both exaltation of Forrest and contempt for the Yankees he had captured.

> Whereas our barbarous enemies lately fitted out and sent forward an expedition of brigands to invade North West Georgia to plunder and devastate the Country, burn up and destroy our foundries, work shops, manufactories and railroads, and especially to visit Atlanta and destroy Government stores, the enterprise and wealth of the place and leave it in ruins, which brutal intention of our foes was most happily prevented by the unparalleled energy of Gen. Bedford Forrest and the valor of the unconquerable men under this command....

The text ran on, closing with the city council and citizens of Atlanta extending their warmest hospitality to the general anytime he should visit the city.[35]

The specter of Yankee raids provoked more talk of civil defense than ever before. Mayor Calhoun called a special meeting of the council on 4 May to

---

After his capture in July 1864, Union Col. Francis T. Sherman recorded in his diary that he was "put in confinement in Atlanta in an enclosure of half an acre with a dirty barrack building as a lodging place" (C. Knight Aldrich, ed., *Quest for a Star: The Civil War Letters and Diaries of Colonel Francis T. Sherman of the 88th Illinois* [Knoxville: University of Tennessee Press, 1999] 7 July 1864).

[35] J. A. Garfield to A. D. Streight, 8 April 1863; report of W. S. Rosecrans, 9 May 1863, *OR*, vol. 23, pt. 1, pp. 281–82; Brian Steel Wills, *A Battle from the Start: The Life of Nathan Bedford Forrest* (New York: HarperCollins, 1992) 110–19; Atlanta City Council Minutes, 8 May 1863, Atlanta History Center.

organize volunteer patrols outside the city "against the approaches of the enemy"; the mayor would even provide horses at his expense. Four days later, "in view of the fact that the Yankee vandals have been making raids into our country and even threatening this City and vicinity," the city council urged all fit men to form military companies ready to be called up in emergencies. Civilians vocationally exempt from the army responded. Firemen of the Tallulah Company 3 organized as cavalry by mid-May (then asked the city for help in procuring horses and equipment). A proclamation from the city council on 29 May urged further military enrollment, specifying that the names of all eligible men identified as shirkers should be printed in the daily newspapers. Such pronouncements had their effect. The city's policemen, though not more than thirty in number, organized their unit in late July. The "Independent State Road Guards," made up of Western & Atlantic employees, formed on 3 August, with William Fuller, one of Andrews's pursuers the year before, appointed as captain. Georgia Railroad workers formed their guards unit the next month, as did some 115 workers at Colonel Wright's ordnance plant at the Race Track.[36]

Organization of these local defense companies helped ease the worries of Major Lee, who retained command of the military post in Atlanta in spite of his past performance. A few weeks after Streight's raid, Lee wrote the Confederate congressman representing the city, Lucius J. Gartrell, affirming the obvious lesson of the Yankees' recent foray: "They know as well as I do that the State road is a vital artery, and Atlanta the largest depot of supplies of the Confederate States, and they also know that to burn and destroy these would be almost to 'break the backbone of the rebellion.'" Unless Atlantans organized themselves more effectively for quick reaction to an enemy strike, Lee warned, "500 Yankees in a dash would destroy all before effectual resistance would be made." Congressman Gartrell endorsed Lee's concerns in a letter to Secretary of War James A. Seddon in Richmond on 22 May: "there is a great deal of apprehension for the safety of Atlanta and the railroad leading to Chattanooga."

This apprehension brought the city fathers to talk openly of a subject they could hitherto ignore: the need to fortify Atlanta against enemy attack. At the city council meeting of 22 May, Alexander M. Wallace—distinguished citizen, banker, former captain of the Atlanta Grays, now colonel—addressed the group, urging the construction of fortifications at the Chattahoochee to help prevent enemy crossings of the river. The councilmen agreed, and resolved that Wallace and another longtime Atlantan, Lemuel P. Grant (now serving as captain in the CS Engineer Bureau, with headquarters in the city) should conduct a survey of the terrain west of the city, bringing back recommendations on what should be done. When the *Southern Confederacy* reported the council's vote a couple of days

---

[36] Garrett, *Atlanta and Environs*, 1:530, 547–48, 550; Atlanta City Council Minutes, 4, 8, 22, 29 May 1863, Atlanta History Center; Lack, "Law and Civil Disorder in Confederate Atlanta," 187.

later, and Grant's and Wallace's proposed work, Atlantans were made to realize that their location in the Deep South, once thought impenetrable by Yankee armies, was now vulnerable and ultimately even in danger.

Military events reinforced that impression. In Tennessee, Union forces' advance in late June 1863 forced Bragg to order a retreat of his of army southeastward from Shelbyville through Tullahoma, and eventually, by the end of the first week in July, to Chattanooga. The Confederate concentration at Chattanooga and the certainty of an enemy advance toward it led authorities in Richmond to assume responsibility for the protection of Atlanta, which would eventually become the target of any further Yankee incursion. Thus when Captain Grant undertook his military survey west of Atlanta and of the Chattahoochee crossings, it was not under city government suggestion, but under orders from Colonel Jeremy F. Gilmer, chief of Confederate engineers in Richmond, issued 16 July 1863. "I desire you to examine carefully with a view to a proper system of defense, the approaches to & vicinity of, Atlanta," wrote Colonel Gilmer, impressing upon Grant, "this is an important duty confided to you & your earnest & prompt attention is requested." The order implied that lines of defensive works were needed not only at the Chattahoochee, but also around the city of Atlanta itself—a significant, ominous acknowledgement. Because of the importance of Grant's assignment, Gilmer wanted to promote him to lieutenant colonel, but Grant declined in view of his "private obligations"— meaning probably his business and real estate dealings in Atlanta. Increased rank would bring increased responsibilities; Captain Grant was happy with things as they were.[37]

As the War Department focused on Atlanta, its attention too was drawn to the by-now widespread dissatisfaction with George Washington Lee as provost

---

[37] Lee to Gartrell, 20 May 1863; and Gartrell to Seddon, 22 May, *OR*, vol. 52, pt. 2, pp. 476–77; *Williams' Atlanta Directory*, 143 (on Wallace); Atlanta City Council Minutes, 22 May 1863, Atlanta History Center; "Council Proceedings," *Atlanta Southern Confederacy*, 24 May 1863; Robert Selph Henry, *"First with the Most" Forrest* (Indianapolis: Bobbs-Merrill Company, 1944) 164–68; J. F. Gilmer to L. P. Grant, 23 June 1863 (box 7, folder 4) and 16 July (folder 5), Grant Papers, Atlanta History Center.

Some students have mistakenly inferred that the Confederate loss of Vicksburg surrendered on 4 July 1863, was the impetus to defensive preparations at Atlanta. See [Stephens Mitchell], "Colonel L.P. Grant and the Defenses of Atlanta," *Atlanta Historical Bulletin* 1/6 (February 1932): 33; Garrett, *Atlanta and Environs*, 1:567; and Singer, "Confederate Atlanta," 208. On the other hand, Wilbur Kurtz sought to call attention to the city council's vote of May 1863 after the Streight raid as the impetus to the Atlanta fortifications ("Forts to Defend Atlanta," *Atlanta Journal*, 24 May 1941). Allen P. Julian ("Atlanta's Defenses," *Civil War Times Illustrated* 3/4 [July 1964]: 23) also recognizes the Yankee cavalry raid as Atlanta's motivation to self-defense. Marc Wortman is a recent chronicler who gets it right in stating that "even before the fall of Vicksburg," Captain Grant received his orders to begin planning the fortifications of Atlanta (*The Bonfire*, 183).

marshal in the city. With Atlanta's male citizenry stepping forth to form local guards units, Major Lee seemed incapable of directing the activity. "At present all is in confusion," wrote Atlantan George G. Hull, superintendent of the Atlanta & West Point Railroad, in his letter to chief engineer Gilmer of 9 July. Lee's problem was that "he cannot, on account of his social position, command public confidence and respect sufficiently to insure [sic] the enrollment of the better portion of the citizens." In Lee's place, Hull urged the appointment of the efficient arsenal commander, Moses H. Wright. "Major Wright is the only officer here who is competent to the details of the job of putting this town in a state of defense. If he is appointed, it will at once convince our people that something serious is to be done, and they will go into it with enthusiasm. In fact, there is a general cry for him." Hull's recommendation, seconded by Major General Gustavus W. Smith of the Georgia Militia and Colonel Isaac M. St. John of the Nitre and Mining Bureau (in Atlanta at the time), won over Colonel Gilmer. Ordnance chief Gorgas, already an admirer of Wright's efficiency, added his support. At Gilmer's and Gorgas's urging, therefore, the War Department on 16 July 1863 conferred upon Wright his promotion to colonel, along with orders to take charge of the defenses of the city as well as the local troops organizing to protect it.

Colonel Wright did his job. He ended Major Lee's loose practice of issuing passes, and assured the citizenry of greater order. He also gave up trying to work with Lee. "I have tried in vain to learn from him his orders, &c.," Wright complained, "but for the life of me I can get nothing from him. I want to get at the bottom and commence the cleaning." Eventually he had Lee shoved to the Conscript Bureau and out of authority in the city; Maj. J.K. McCall took command of the Post of Atlanta. Finally able to "commence the cleaning," Colonel Wright organized the city's defense volunteers. By early April 1864, these numbered at least 500 effectives (some 750 by muster-roll): workers detailed to the Atlanta arsenal, Naval Works, and the quartermaster department; railroad employees; plus men exempted through other work, disability and age, both young and old—eight companies and a battalion altogether. Competently led, reasonably disciplined, and drilled weekly, Wright's force represented a creditable home-defense garrison.[38]

With Colonel Wright organizing Atlanta's defenders, Captain Grant laid out Atlanta's defenses. On 22 July 1863, Grant informed Richmond of his plans to begin surveying the country west of Atlanta, particularly the Chattahoochee River crossings north and west of the city. Within a couple of days, Grant was

---

[38] G. G. Hull to Gilmer, 9 July 1863; Gilmer and Gorgas to Samuel Cooper, 14 July; Samuel W. Melton to Wright, 16 July, *OR*, vol. 23, pt. 2, pp. 909–10, 914; Wright to W. W. Mackall, 20 August 1863, *OR*, vol. 30, pt. 4, p. 520; "City Military Directory," *Atlanta Intelligencer*, 11 May 1864 (showing "Major J.K. McCall, Commanding Post"), 4; M. H. Wright to M. J. Wright, 2 April 1864, *OR*, vol. 32, pt. 3, pp. 740–41.

procuring shovels, picks, and axes for his workmen; within two weeks he had begun fortifying the river ferries and had come up with his plan for works around the city. To Colonel Gilmer in Richmond on 4 August he proposed that Atlanta be completely ringed with "a cordon of enclosed works, within supporting distance of each other": twelve to fifteen strong forts, sited specially for artillery and connected by infantry entrenchments in a perimeter "between 10 and 12 miles in extent." Grant acknowledged that his planned fortifications would prove "somewhat embarrassing" in their vastness, as their construction would involve "an expenditure second only to the defense of Richmond." Once authorized to proceed, Captain Grant proposed to launch his program of construction after he had finished building small redoubts at the river crossings.

Gilmer readily approved all this, promising Grant any and all funding he would need for tools and the hiring of slave labor. In his reply, dated 11 August 1863, he advised Grant that the twelve to fifteen earthen forts should be connected by lines of rifle pits, with ditches, felled timber or other obstructions in front of them to impede an infantry charge. Gilmer added the rather dark suggestion that Grant's proposed perimeter should be "far enough from the town to prevent the enemy coming within bombarding distance." Captain Grant kept his superiors informed of his progress: 17 August, small works at the ferries nearly complete and three forts outside Atlanta under construction; 24 August, "we need Negro labor" (for each field hand, Grant was paying slaveholders $25 a month, with food, shelter, and medical care provided by the government); 15 September, "the defenses of Atlanta are progressing satisfactorily." Engineers were siting their batteries at commanding positions, regardless of civilians' property interest. That meant fields, orchards and gardens were dug up; barns and other outhouses, and even homes might be expropriated and torn down. Grant was forced to come to terms with the landowners, as he acknowledged to Richmond in late September: "In constructing works of defense around Atlanta, private property is necessarily damaged—in some cases seriously, in other cases slightly. Shall compensation be allowed?" (Grant was advised to record the extent of damages, but suspend reimbursement until Congress had allocated funding.)[39]

The most extensive property damage resulted from clearing away fields of fire in front of the trench lines. Gilmer stipulated to Colonel Wright, who was helping Grant supervise the fortifications project, that "in order to make the works...effective, the timber must be cut down in front of the lines for a distance

---

[39] L. P. Grant to J. F. Gilmer, 22 July, 17 August 1863; to George Arnold, 24 July 1863; to John W. Hurt, 24 August 1863; to A. L. Rives, 28 September 1863, in Grant Letterbook, 1862–1865, box 7, folder 1, Lemuel P. Grant Papers, Atlanta History Center; Grant to Gilmer, 4 August 1863, quoted in Julian, "Atlanta's Defenses," 24; Gilmer to Grant, 11 August 1863, *OR*, vol. 30, pt. 4, p. 489; Rives to Grant, 15 October 1863, box 7, folder 4, Lemuel P. Grant Papers, Atlanta History Center.

of, say, 900 to 1,000 cubic yards, and the cutting should be continuous." In receiving these instructions, Grant could only reply that "the destruction of forest will be great"—perhaps he was thinking of his own property, into some of which he had drawn defensive lines southeast of the city.

By late October, Grant had nearly completed his encirclement of Atlanta with "redoubts on prominent eminences connected by rifle pits." The redoubts, or artillery forts, numbered more than Grant had originally forecast, seventeen. The earthworks of thirteen of them had been finished, each with embrasures for five cannon, and an exterior trench that could be filled with abatis or debris to impede scalers. Inside wood planking—not yet laid in—would provide both gun platforms and wall revetments. Lumber for these purposes had to be procured from afar because the timber in front of the batteries had not begun to be felled (Grant was sending out officers to oversee shipment of 2-inch planks and was looking for axes, too). The connecting rifle pits were almost done.[40]

When measured or judged for distance, L. P. Grant's perimeter of defensive works ran nearly 10 miles. Despite this considerable length, it was still too close to the city. With Atlanta's antebellum suburbs having spread beyond the 1-mile city limits, the Confederate engineers' lines obtruded upon many people's homes and yards. There would as a consequence be costly civilian demands for compensation of damaged property. Anticipating these, Gilmer (recently promoted to major general) specified to Colonel Wright that each claim should carry two appraisals, one by an officer and the other by an independent assessor chosen by the property owner.

Aside from the cost to the government, however, the layout of Captain Grant's line invited military concerns. Though chief engineer Gilmer had enjoined Grant to make sure his line was flung sufficiently far to prevent enemy artillery fire from reaching the city, it was obvious that Grant had not done so. Both topographical features and garrisoning requirements—a defensive perimeter too extensive could not be adequately manned—required the Confederate engineers to site their line so close-in that when enemy forces approached much of Atlanta would actually be well within artillery range, at least for rifled guns. According to the US Army's standard ordnance tables, the Federals' two most common rifled guns, the 10-pounder Parrott and the 3-inch rifle, could with a 1-pound powder charge hurl their shells over a mile at 5 degrees elevation, some 3,000 yards at 10 degrees, and well over 2 miles at 15 degrees. The Confederates' defense line northwest of the city was ironically (given that this would be the likely direction of the enemy approach from the Chattahoochee) the very sector closest to the edge of the city. Indeed, more of

---

[40] Gilmer to M. H. Wright, 21 October 1863, *OR*, vol. 31, pt. 3, p. 575; Grant to Gilmer, 30 October; to R. P. Rowley, 4 November; to W. J. C. Nichols, 8 November; and to George Arnold, 16 November 1863, Grant Letterbook, Lemuel P. Grant Papers, Atlanta History Center; Garrett, *Atlanta and Environs*, 1:568.

Grant's earthworks in this area lay actually within the 1-mile city limits. The informal names given to Confederate forts surrounding the city, although they were formally designated by alphabetical letters, further suggested their urban impingement, as some were associated with Atlanta streets. In a rough sketch by Grant of his line, Batteries A, B, and C were each referred to as Whitehall; H and J carried the names Mills and Hunnicutt, thoroughfares of north Atlanta. Battery O, east of the city, was the Rolling Mill redoubt. Only south of town did the fortifications extend more than a half a mile away from the city limits. And this was the sector least likely to be tested by enemy forces, presumably approaching from the northwest.[41]

In Atlanta, Colonel Wright was aware of the defensive lines' dangerous closeness to the northwestern quadrant of the city. In October 1863, he was apparently in communication with General Gilmer about "exterior lines" that would require more funds, more tools, axes, etc. Gilmer gave the go-ahead for the work in a letter to Wright dated 21 October, which Wright then gave to Captain Grant. Within two weeks, Grant could report back to General Gilmer that he had selected five "eminences...[with] rounded or conical summits" northwest of Atlanta, hilltops suitable as battery positions (one of them was on Ephraim and Ellen Ponder's property). But construction of these would have to await the future; there was much work yet to be done on the initial defenses.

In the first week of December 1863, Gilmer came to Atlanta and spent several days inspecting Grant's line, progress of construction, and topography of the area. Gilmer, wrote Grant afterward, "seemed to be well satisfied with the efforts to defend Atlanta." Colonel Wright also kept commanders of the Army of Tennessee abreast of the construction. By then General Bragg's forces had been maneuvered out of Chattanooga, won a smart victory in North Georgia at Chickamauga, and suffered a disastrous defeat at Missionary Ridge. The army, now under command of General Joseph E. Johnston, was quartered at Dalton when Wright reported on 19 December that "defenses [are] all laid out and pretty well advanced." The Yankee army was also kept informed of Atlanta's defenses, through such statements as that given by a Federal officer who had escaped from the city after some two months' confinement. In early December, at Chattanooga, US Captain Lewis Carter reported on what he had seen. Rifle pits

---

[41] Gilmer to Wright, 21 October 1863, *OR*, vol. 31, pt. 5, p. 575; Robert J. Fryman, "Fortifying the Landscape: An Archaeological Study of Military Engineering and the Atlanta Campaign," in *Archaeological Perspectives on the American Civil War*, ed. Clarence P. Greier and Stephen R. Potter, 54–55 (Gainesville: University Press of Florida, 2000); "Table of approximate ranges, &c., for rifled guns in use in the armies of the United States, in 1861–'62," *Instruction for Heavy Artillery: Prepared by a Board of Officers, for the Use of the Army of the United States* (Washington, DC: Government Printing Office, 1862) 244–46; James C. Hazlett, "The 3-inch Ordnance Rifle," *Civil War Times Illustrated* 7/8 (December 1968): 35; untitled map, oversized folder 1, Lemuel P. Grant Papers, Atlanta History Center.

surrounded Atlanta, but were "very poor." Earthworks at the Chattahoochee River crossings actually impressed him as being much stronger than those in the main defenses. "They have also felled trees all around the city," observed Carter, "which I think is the greatest obstruction."[42]

With Union forces in Chattanooga, Southerners could well assume that the Yankees would be on the march in a spring offensive, and that they would be aiming for Atlanta. Captain Grant and Colonel Wright could therefore not afford to be idle during the winter months of 1863/1864. Grant had officers in South Georgia procuring wood planking for the batteries and revetments; he kept slaves, leased from owners all over the state, hard at work. He never seemed, however, to have enough laborers; in March 1864 he wrote his superiors in Richmond, seeking additional authority to impress slaves. "With 200 additional hands," Grant wrote on 28 March, "I can complete the works decided upon around the city in the space of two months."[43]

The Confederate high command paid increasingly close attention to the engineers' progress. General Johnston came to Atlanta from Dalton to conduct a personal inspection of Grant's line on 13 March; Grant accompanied the commanding general, along with Colonel Wright, explaining all that had been done, and what there was yet to do. Two weeks later, orders came down from Richmond, directing Grant "to make a thorough inspection" of his defenses, and to submit a report of their "character and condition...and the number of troops required to man them." Colonel Wright added his own request for the same information on 31 March. Everyone, it seems, wanted to know the estimated number of soldiers needed to defend Atlanta once they got within Grant's earthworks. No one—to judge from the existing records at least—asked General Johnston why he was looking so far to his rear, when the campaign in Northwest Georgia had not even begun.

On 12 April, Grant submitted to Colonel Wright an elaborate map of the city's defensive works that, in his accompanying letter, he said measured just under 10 1/2 miles, completely encircling the city. "To fully man this line," Grant estimated, "will require Fifty five thousand (55,000) troops." This was a felicitously chosen estimate, as Johnston's army at Dalton at the time numbered about that many men present for duty. The 10.4-mile line by then included a southeastern salient, not included in Grant's description of October–November

[42] Gilmer to Wright, 21 October 1863, *OR*, vol. 31, pt. 3, p. 575; Grant to Gilmer, 30 October 1863; to A. L. Rives, 7, 10 December 1863, Grant Letterbook, Lemuel P. Grant Papers, Atlanta History Center; untitled map, Lemuel P. Grant Papers, Atlanta History Center; Wright to G. W. Brent, 19 December 1863; Carter statement, 6 December 1863, *OR*, vol. 31, pt. 3, pp. 347–48, 848.

[43] Grant to M. I. Nichols, 12 January 1864; to John S. Blalock, 27 February; to A. L. Rives, 8 March; and to J. J. Clark, 28 March 1864, Grant Letterbook, Lemuel P. Grant Papers, Atlanta History Center.

1863, which had been constructed to take in some commanding ground. This pocket held two additional batteries, which raised the number of forts ringing Atlanta to nineteen (designated as A–U). In addition were the five batteries northwest of the city, intended to push the Confederate fortifications farther away from downtown; they were not yet connected with rifle pits. All of this work had severely scarred Atlanta's suburban landscape, and ruined much property—houses, sheds, yards, fields, and forests. Grant estimated in mid-May that landowners affected by his fortifying had suffered losses totaling a quarter million dollars; the civilians would surely have set a higher figure.[44]

Atlanta was thus in spring 1864 one of the South's most formidably fortified cities. The ring of earthworks and forts signified the importance that Atlanta's munitions factories, army warehouses, military hospitals, and bustling railroad facilities held for the beleaguered Confederacy. Indeed, as Southerners awaited the enemy offensives, probably only Richmond and Washington were more heavily protected by entrenchments and embrasures. The fortifications of the Confederacy's capital city and the South's Gate City would both be tested in the coming months. In Virginia, Robert E. Lee faced Ulysses S. Grant, brought from the west. In Georgia, Joseph E. Johnston faced William T. Sherman, also brought eastward to command the Union forces gathered around Chattanooga. S. Dexter Niles, editor of the *Atlanta Reveille,* recognized the challenges in his issue of 21 April: "The enemy will doubtless advance on Dalton at the same time they make a demonstration on Richmond, endeavoring thereby to prevent us from concentrating our forces." But the editor was cheerful. "Our prospects for a glorious termination of our struggle for independence were never brighter than they are today," he beamed. "If our people sustain themselves and their reputation for gallantry and endurance as well in this campaign as they have in the past none need have any fears of the result."[45]

With the Yankees a hundred miles away, Atlantans would soon have the opportunity to test their gallantry and endurance.

---

[44] A. W. Harris to Grant, 12 March 1864; Marcus J. Wright to Grant, 29 March, box 7, folder 5; Grant to Moses H. Wright, 12 April; to A. L. Rives, 17 May, Grant Letterbook, Lemuel P. Grant Papers, Atlanta History Center; Albert Castel, *Decision in the West: The Atlanta Campaign of 1864* (Lawrence: University Press of Kansas, 1992) 111 (54,500 as Johnston's "present for duty," 30 April); Grant map, "Sketch of Atlanta Defenses," *OR Atlas.*

[45] Reed, *History of Atlanta,* 185 (Niles as editor of the *Reveille*); "Old Newspapers; Relics of the War," *Atlanta Constitution,* 20 July 1898 (quoting the *Reveille* of 21 April 1864).

3

THE YANKEES APPROACH, MAY–JULY 1864

No matter with what determination the enemy may come, they will meet with a determination and an energy on our part that will be sufficient to counteract and overcome all the efforts they may make to reduce our people to submission. Never, no never, will the free-born sons of the South, the children of the sun, consent to be ruled by the hateful and hated Yankee. Sooner far will they welcome death for themselves, their wives and little ones, than be subject to a race so destitute of all the better and more ennobling traits of humanity. From the indications in every direction, we are fully satisfied that the Great Ruler of the universe is delivering us from the power and wrath of our cruel foes, who have, for some good purpose, been permitted to harass and vex our people for so long a time.[1]

With this boastful, saber-rattling and right-invoking declaration, editor John H. Steele of the *Intelligencer*, in his column of 11 May 1864, sounded the alarm to Atlantans that the Yankees were coming. And indeed they were. Opening their campaign on 4 May from their base south of Chattanooga, Sherman's Union forces advanced against Johnston's defensive line at Rocky Face Ridge north of Dalton and—an omen of things to come—soon found a way to outflank the Confederates' position. Johnston's army retreated toward Resaca on the night of 12 May. Then, after several days' hard fighting at Resaca, another Federal flanking maneuver forced Johnston to retreat again, this time across the Oostanaula River the night of 15 May.[2]

Atlantans reacted with predictable concern; some even began to voice pessimism about Confederate prospects. At one church service on Sunday, 15 May, the congregation heard the minister's usual prayer for victory, but the clergyman added a petition that if "our city should meet the fate that others had recently," the people should "be resigned" to their fate. "I find that very many people think it probable that this place may be occupied by the Yankees very soon," wrote Louise Pittman on 18 May to her father John Neal, wealthy Atlanta

---

[1] Editorial, *Atlanta Intelligencer*, 11 May 1864.
[2] Stephen Davis, *Atlanta Will Fall: Sherman, Joe Johnston and the Heavy Yankee Battalions* (Wilmington DE: Scholarly Resources, 2001) 37–42, 45–50.

merchant.[3] Editor Steele of the *Intelligencer* tried to calm his readers with soothing assurances of General Johnston's sagacity, the Army of Tennessee's indomitability, and the shortsightedness of the public grousers. The paper on 14 May observed that "the Ravens...on the street...have begun to croak.... There is a knot of them on the corner shaking their heads, with long faces and restless eyes." "We feel confident," intoned an editorial column the next day, "that there is no reason for any misgivings or forebodings as to the situation of General Johnston's army.... There is nothing in the situation to create any alarm in the result. Therefore, we say be of good cheer and wait." Several days later, though, after Johnston had retreated through Calhoun and given up Adairsville, the *Intelligencer* addressed the pessimists in a column titled "Long Faces."

> We are stopped daily on the street almost at every step, by people who anxiously enquire the news. A large number of these *quid nuces* wear the longest faces they can put on and their dark or pallid looks would lead one unacquainted with them to suppose they had lost their dearest and best friend or perhaps a whole family of friends. They croak in our ears a most dismal, raven cry. Some of them say to us, "Why do you publish such flattering opinions about the situation? You know as well as I do that Johnston is falling back, and that Atlanta is threatened, you are misleading people by holding out to them hopes which will be dashed to the ground. It looks mighty black for us up there. Johnston's been outgeneraled, and we are losing ground that we never will get back."

Editor Steele's advice for these ravens and croakers was two-fold: either leave town or "forget business awhile and advance as a shield between the enemy and your homes."[4]

Civil authorities were urging the latter as well. From the capital at Milledgeville Governor Brown on 18 May ordered certain state employees, previously exempt from conscription, to report for duty in Atlanta. Five days later Mayor Calhoun issued his own proclamation, calling on all men in Atlanta capable of military service to report to the city marshal's office at noon on 26 May, to be armed, organized, and turned over to military authorities for duty. The *Appeal* urged full and fast compliance. "Atlanta will never be taken by our ruthless invaders if the people, and especially our male population, will do their whole duty in the present emergency," editorialized the paper on 24 May. "Let them rather obey promptly the proclamation of the mayor...and all will yet be well." The mayor's proclamation realistically addressed those men who were not

---

[3] Thomas G. Dyer, *Secret Yankees: The Union Circle in Confederate Atlanta* (Baltimore: Johns Hopkins University Press, 1999) 165; Louisa Pittman to John Neal, 18 May 1864, in Andrew Jackson Neal Letters, box 1, folder 7, #218, Emory University.

[4] "The Situation," *Atlanta Intelligencer*, 14 May 1864; "From the Front," *Atlanta Intelligencer*, 15 May; "Long Faces," *Atlanta Intelligencer*, 19 May.

willing to serve: "All male citizens who are not ready to defend their homes and families are requested to leave the city at their earliest convenience, as their presence embarrasses the authorities and tends to the demoralization of others."[5]

Actually, some Atlantans had already begun to take flight, and not always southward. Dr. Henry Huntington, physician and dentist, had thus far escaped conscription by his profession and age; a Northerner (having moved to Atlanta just before the war), he harbored no Confederate sympathies. Now, with the crisis in North Georgia, Huntington feared being drafted all the more. So on 7 May he slipped out of town, heading northward, eventually through to Union lines. His wife Martha and three children stayed behind until their house, a block south of city hall, could be sold, when they, too, would escape.[6]

The Yankees' steady, seemingly unstoppable advance brought the war front ever nearer to Atlanta. By 24 May, Johnston had retreated across the Etowah River, and the opposing armies faced each other west of Marietta, toward Dallas. With the battlefront just 25 miles away, and the "long faces" in Atlanta getting longer, more townsfolk determined to flee. "This has been a day of wild excitement," wrote Cyrena Stone on 24 May; her house lay in the city's eastern suburbs just inside the corporate limits.

> From early morning until now—engines have screamed—trains thundered along; wagons laden with government stores, refugees, negroes and household stuff, have rattled out of town. Every possible conveyance is bought, borrowed, begged or stolen. Such packing up & leaving of those, who but a short time ago said with such great boasting & assurance, that Johnston would never fall back here, & allow the Yankees to step a foot on Georgia's soil—is perfectly marvelous to behold. One is amazed in witnessing these wonderful changes. Now there are fears & trembling—& some who leave their pleasant homes—know not where to go: many who have been refugeeing all the way from Nashville—sojourning first at one place, then at another—are preparing for another flight. While some say they have "run from the Yankees long enough, and are going to stay here & abide their fate." It is painful to see poor families—who can barely live where they are—frightened at the reported doings of the terrible foe—fleeing with the rest—sometimes only taking

---

[5] Joseph H. Parks, *Joseph E. Brown of Georgia* (Baton Rouge: Louisiana State University Press, 1977) 89; Franklin M. Garrett, *Atlanta and Environs: A Chronicle of Its People and Events*, 2 vols. (New York: Lewis Historical Publishing Co., 1954) 1:589; "The Front," *Memphis Appeal*, 24 May 1864 (also quoted in B. G. Ellis, *The Moving Appeal: Mr. McClanahan, Mrs. Dill, and the Civil War's Great Newspaper Run* [Macon GA: Mercer University Press, 2003] 294); Lee Kennett, *Marching through Georgia: The Story of Soldiers and Civilians during Sherman's Campaign* (New York: HarperCollins, 1995) 118.

[6] Ben Kremenak, ed., "Escape from Atlanta: The Huntington Memoir," *Civil War History* 11/2 (June 1965): 162–65; Dyer, *Secret Yankees*, 170–72.

half of their little all, in the fright. No home to go to—no money to procure one—but the *Yankees* are coming, & they must go somewhere!⁷

Townspeople could see for themselves what was happening. Outside the suburbs, Captain Grant kept his teams of slave laborers strengthening the trenches, forts, and obstructions, as if in sure knowledge that the Yankees would get this far. The mayor's call to arms on 23 May increased concerns, as men mustered and organized in city hall park. "I hope they will not be needed," wrote storekeeper Lewis Lawshe of the local guards. Feeling much the same way was Samuel Richards, who maintained a newspaperman's exemption from military service as printer of *The Soldier's Friend*, a religious periodical published in town for circulation in the army (which he had co-bought with his brother Jabez specifically to dodge the draft). Wrote Richards, "I trust we may never be called into action, I hate the sight of a musket." Nevertheless, Richards and other printers on 24 May formed the Atlanta Press Volunteers, electing Albert C. Roberts, editor of the *Southern Confederacy*, as their captain. On 3 June, the Atlanta Press Volunteers were ordered to assemble in front of the *Appeal* office to receive their equipment, and in the weeks ahead had to report from time to time for drill, as well as have their vocational status attested to in the county court.

Even a passle of refugees in the city formed their own unit, unimaginatively named the Atlanta Guards. There were indeed plenty of refugees in town, and not just from other states. Sherman's invasion had driven hundreds of folk from North Georgia into Atlanta, as sometimes whole towns depopulated. When the Yankees entered Calhoun, the street was strewn with papers, but nary a soul could be seen. At Kingston, only one family stayed. At Cassville, which emptied in hurried anticipation of a battle on 19 May, a Union officer found in one house "a full coffee pot and only part of the cups filled, some plates filled and others empty, a few chairs overturned and the doors open." Federal troops marching into Rome, northwest Georgia's biggest city, saw only a small group of blacks and a solitary white boy.

A lawyer living in Rome, Charles H. Smith (medically discharged from the army in 1863), was also an avocational newspaper columnist who wrote funny columns for local papers in the dialect of poorly educated plain folk, the customary coin of antebellum frontier humorists. Over his pen name of "Bill Arp," Smith contributed an account of the flight of the Romans during the night of 16 May for Atlanta's *Southern Confederacy*. Himself one of the Roman

---

⁷ Dyer, *Secret Yankees*, 309. Professor Dyer reprints Mrs. Stone's diary in its entirety (283–328); typescript copy of the "Miss Abby" diary reposes in the University of Georgia Hargrett Rare Book and Manuscript Library, MSS 1000. It was Dyer who identified Mrs. Cyrena Bailey Stone as "Miss Abby," pseudonymic author of this diary. See Thomas G. Dyer, "Atlanta's Other Civil War Novel: Fictional Unionists in a Confederate City," *Georgia Historical Quarterly* 79/1 (Spring 1995): 164–66, as well as "In Search of Miss Abby," appendix A in *Secret Yankees*, 270–82.

refugees—or "runagees," as Arp termed them—Smith made his way to Atlanta and penned this account:

> ...although the commandin Genrul asshoored us that Rome wer to be held at every hazerd, and that on to-morrer the big battle wer to be fout, and the fowl invaders hurled all howlin and bleedin to the shores of the Ohio, yet it transpired sumhow that on choosdy night the military evakuashun of our sitty was preemptorly ordered.... suddently, in the twinkling of an eye, a frend aroused us from our slumber, and put a new fase on the "sityashun." Genrul Johnson was retreatin, and the blue nosed Yankees wer to pollute our sacred sile next mornin. Then cum the tug of war. With hot and feverish haist we started out in serch of transportashun, but nary transport kould be had. Time honerd frendship, past favors shown, everlastin gratytood, numerous small and luvly children, konfederit kurrency, new isshoos, bank bills, blak bottels, and all influenses wer urged and used to secure a corner in a kar—but nary korner—too late—too late—the pressure for time was fearful and tremengious—the steddy klok moved on—no Joshuy about to lengthen out the night—no rollin stok, no steer, no mule. With reluctant and hasty steps we prepared to make our exit by that overland line which rale rodes do not kontrol, nor A.Q.M's impress.
>
> With our families and a little clothin we krossed the Etowah bridg in a dump cart about the broke of day on Wensday, the 17th of May.... By and by the brite rays of the mornin sun dispersed the hevvy fog which like a pall of deth had over spred all natur. Then were xhibited to our afflikted gaze a hiway krowded with waggins and teems, kattle and hogs, niggers and dogs, wimmen and childern, all movin in disheveled haist to parts unknown. Mules were brayin, kattle wer lowin, hogs wer squeelin, sheap wer blatin, childern wer kryin, wagginers wer kussin, whips wer poppin, and hosses stallin, but still the grand karavan moved on. Everybody was kontinualy lookin behind and drivin befo – everybody wanted to kno everything, but nobody knu nothin.

And such it was, wherever the Yankee armies came close. On 21 May, for example, the Confederate army's closing of the hospitals and removal of supplies from Marietta caused a public stampede from that town southward, across the Chattahoochee. The people all poured into Atlanta.[8]

---

[8] Lewis Lawshe, diary, 23 May, "From an Old Diary, Which Was Kept by Mr. Lewis Lawshe During the Civil War," photocopy of undated newspaper clipping [ca. 1898], 113, Edda Cole Scrapbook, MSS 267, Atlanta History Center; Wendy Hamand Venet, ed., *Sam Richards's Civil War Diary: A Chronicle of the Atlanta Home Front* (Athens: University of Georgia Press, 2009) 190–91, 193, 225 (entries of 3, 21 August 1863, 29 May 1864); "Atlanta

More and more wounded also entered into the city by train, overwhelmed the hospitals, and sprawled over the depot, into hotels and homes. Under direction from the Executive Aid Committee, citizens attended the Car Shed, meeting the trains in round-the-clock shifts. Lewis Lawshe was one of the volunteers, as he recorded his diary for one Sunday in late May, "Took my turn again for twenty-four hours at the carshed." ("The people of Atlanta style the passenger depot the car shed," commented the *Memphis Appeal* about that time, "but why, no one can tell.") Kate Cumming, Confederate nurse, saw one afternoon in mid-May how three long trains filled and topped with wounded were met by women and old men dispensing food and water. Soldiers who could walk made their way across the street to the Gate City Hospital, which in late 1863 had been designated by CS medical officers as the city's Receiving and Distributing facility. The "R & D" hospital was not for long-term care, but exclusively for registering patients, then sending them on to other hospitals, either in town or farther south by train. Some soldiers, too weak to walk, never entered the Gate City, but lay around the Car Shed, sometimes on cots (sometimes not). Miss Cumming saw soldiers "lying all over the platform of the depot, preferring to remain there, so as to be ready for the train which would take them to other places." Many ill or hurt soldiers were forced to lie out in the open anyway, as the army's "R & D" hospital was almost always overcrowded. Surgeon-in-Charge George D. Pursley complained to his superiors on 31 May, "I am compelled to receive all sick and wounded sent here, varying from 200 to 400, 500, and 600 daily with a hospital of only 250 capacity." As a result, ailing patients could be found everywhere. Kate Cumming encountered a wounded soldier lying in the hall of the Trout House, Atlanta's finest hotel. As always, citizens opened their homes. Mrs. George Hull, wife of the superintendent of the A & WP Railroad, cared for several wounded men in her house on Peachtree Street, even as she rolled bandages and baked biscuits for other patients in town. To lessen the medical crowding, city hall was rechristened on 9 June as Brown Hospital (named for the Governor), though not without a murmur of protest from the city council. Intended primarily for the care of Georgia troops, and with

---

Press Volunteers," *Atlanta Intelligencer*, 28 May 1864; "ATTENTION, PRESS VOLUNTEERS!," Atlanta *Appeal*, 3 June; Henry T. Malone, "Atlanta Journalism during the Confederacy," *Georgia Historical Quarterly* 37/3 (September 1953): 217; sworn statements of Jabez J. Richards (editor, *The Soldier's Friend*), James N. Ells (editor, *Baptist Banner*), John H. Steele (editor, *Atlanta Intelligencer*), and John C. Whitner (editor, *Atlanta Register*), 19, 23, 25, 31 May 1864, transcribed from original by Wilbur G. Kurtz, notebook 12, 48, 55–57, Wilbur G. Kurtz Collection, Atlanta History Center; Kennett, *Marching through Georgia*, 89–90; David P. Parker, *Alias Bill Arp: Charles Henry Smith and the South's "Goodly Heritage"* (Athens: University of Georgia Press, 1991) 8, 15–16, 58–59; [Charles Smith], *Bill Arp's Peace Papers* (New York: G. W. Carleton & Co., 1873) 67–69 (the column is reprinted, without dialect, in [Charles Smith], *Bill Arp, So Called. A Side Show of the Southern Side of the War* [New York: Metropolitan Record Office, 1866] 84–92); Castel, *Decision in the West*, 212.

400 beds, soon even this facility was full, with ailing patients at times overflowing onto the surrounding city park, which after a battle could be seen to be "filled with tents." Inside Brown Hospital, there was the usual gruesome mix of mortality and morbidity, of which one laborer attempted to make light as he wandered the wards calling out, "Anybody dead here? Anybody about to die?"[9]

More disturbing than the flood of refugees and sick or maimed men from the front, however, were the actual sounds of nearby battle. Mary Mallard, wife of the minister of Atlanta's Central Presbyterian Church, heard them on 25 May, when Johnston's and Sherman's forces were slugging it out near New Hope Church. The ominous thud of far-off artillery, never before heard in the city, created "a commotion," in the words of one newspaper report. "Waverly," a reporter for the *Appeal*, recorded the sensation in town on 25 May, with at least a little humor. "The sunny side of Whitehall...seems to be in a peripatetic condition, blockaded with guards and jammed with bales and boxes of merchandise. Surely you are not expecting a visit from Sherman, or any other distinguished foreigner? Why, I found half a dozen ladies of my acquaintance packing their preserves in bandboxes and their bonnets in butter kegs, out of downright confusion, they said; four old gentlemen locked themselves in their patent safes (for safe keeping, I suppose) where they will have to be dug out with pike and mattock, as they drew the keys and keyholes in after them.... " "Shadow," correspondent for the *Mobile Register & Advertiser* was in Atlanta on 25 May, and set down more dourly his impressions of "the condition of Atlanta at this moment." "Shadow"—Henry Watterson, veteran newspaperman then serving on General Johnston's staff—spoke of the city as being

> demoralized utterly; confused, bewildered; a whole city like one moving household, hurried, up-torn, panic-stricken. The scenes of sordid fear are abject in the extreme.... The Express office is thronged with anxious faces. The cars move out with heavy loads of spoil and merchandise. The order

[9] "From an Old Diary" (Lewis Lawshe's), 29 May, Edda Cole Scrapbook, Atlanta History Center; "The Passenger Depot," *Memphis Appeal,* 7 May 1864; Harwell, ed., *Kate,* 198–99, 201; Stephen Davis, "Another Look at Civil War Medical Care: Atlanta's Confederate Hospitals," *Journal of the Medical Association of Georgia* 88/2 (April 1999): 14–15, 18; Robert Scott Davis, Jr., ed., *Requiem for a Lost City: A Memoir of Civil War Atlanta and the Old South* (Macon GA: Mercer University Press, 1999) 90 (on cots at the R & D); Pursley to Dr. S. H. Stout, 31 May 1864, in Frank R. Freemon, "The Medical Support System for the Confederate Army of Tennessee During the Georgia Campaign, May–September 1864," *Tennessee Historical Quarterly* 52/1 (Spring 1993): 46; A. A. Hoehling, *Last Train from Atlanta* (New York: Thomas Yoseloff, 1958) 24–25; Special Order No. 389, Headquarters Georgia Militia, Atlanta, 9 June 1864, transcribed from original in Wilbur G. Kurtz, notebook 12, 56, Wilbur G. Kurtz Collection, Atlanta History Center; Atlanta City Council Minutes, meeting of 10 June, Atlanta History Center; "City Park," *Memphis Appeal,* 2 July 1864, Kennett, *Marching through Georgia,* 116.

of the Mayor calling everybody to the trenches is fast depopulating the principal thoroughfares. Wagons block up every way.... All is tumult, consternation.

Then, in a disturbing, even shocking admission of doubt and pessimism, "Shadow" acknowledged, "I observe my own feeling on the subject and I think Atlanta will fall."

"Shadow"/Watterson's gloomy opinion brought instant rebuttal. The Mobile paper that published his column itself confessed that "Shadow" seemed "slightly demoralized," but the *Atlanta Intelligencer* went further. "Vivid imagination," "hyperbolic assumptions" and panic of the very kind he thought he saw in Atlanta were behind "Shadow's" writing, the *Intelligencer* declared. Other Atlantans agreed, such as Mary Mallard, who wrote her mother that "Shadow's" was "a most absurd piece": "He describes the confusion and consternation of the citizens in a most exaggerated manner, and represents the whole population in a state of consternation and all moving off. The whole piece is a falsehood, for no such thing as a panic had ever existed here at all. Some few persons have moved away, and others have sent away articles of value and such things as could not be removed in haste; and this is the extent of the panic."[10]

More cannon fire was heard on 27 May, when the two armies engaged at Pickett's Mill, near Dallas. When Mrs. Stone, who harbored secret Unionist feelings, that day heard "the faintest echo of booming guns," the experience was gratifying, even exhilarating. For most Atlantans, though, the approaching battle sounds only fed the general sense of alarm. "For several days past some of our citizens have heard the report of the Artillery at *the front,*" recorded Samuel Richards in his diary on 29 May. The cannon-sounds jostled nerves, and even more townsfolk packed up their gear to leave. "A number of persons have left here," wrote Mrs. Mallard on 27 May, "though I do not think there has been

---

[10] Mary S. Mallard to Mary Jones, 27 May, 3 June 1864, in Robert Manson Myers, ed., *The Children of Pride: A True Story of Georgia and the Civil War* (New Haven: Yale University Press, 1972) 1174, 1176; Castel, *Decision in the West,* 226 (quoting *Memphis Appeal* of 27 May); "Letter from Waverly," *Memphis Appeal,* 25 May; "Shadow," "Letter from Atlanta," *Mobile Register and Advertiser,* 29 May 1864; *Atlanta Intelligencer,* 1 June 1864.

A generation ago J. Cutler Andrews guessed that "Shadow" may have been Henry Watterson (*The South Reports the Civil War,* 574). Barbara Ellis and Stephen J. Dick prove it in "'Who Was "Shadow"?' The Computer Knows: Applying Grammar-Program Statistics in Content Analyses to Solve Mysteries about Authorship," *Journalism & Mass Communication Quarterly* 73/4 (Winter 1996): 947–62. Dr. Ellis also confirms the fact in *The Moving Appeal.*

Watterson was only twenty-two when he took the editor's position at the *Chattanooga Rebel,* August 1862. With that paper, he developed widespread notoriety for strong opinions, including his frequent criticisms of Confederate General Braxton Bragg. Bragg's anger ultimately forced Watterson's resignation from the paper (Joseph Frazier Wall, *Henry Watterson, Reconstructed Rebel* [New York: Oxford University Press, 1956] 38–44).

anything like a panic." The minister's wife had sent away her carpets, sewing machine, winter clothing, and husband's books to relatives in Augusta; she herself was ready to pack and leave town with the servants. The *Intelligencer* on 1 June acknowledged that, yes, "occasionally we can hear the booming of artillery," and yes, "all is bustle here," as relief committees care for the troops, and "officers, soldiers, commissary and quartermasters' men crowd the streets." But was there widespread panic? No, assured the editors; the drays, carts, and wagons rattling about were mostly "engaged in the public service," not hauling away refugees and their goods. Citizens "seem all engaged actively in some pursuit," but "in only a few cases, have we noticed any preparation on the part of any of them to leave for parts more distant from the enemy." Nevertheless, the *Intelligencer* cautioned those folk living between the Yankees and the city to "have their arrangements affected by which to secure a rapid retreat if it should occur that our army retires before the advance of the enemy." Throughout Northwest Georgia, Sherman's "bluebellies" had plundered and foraged, stripping the land clean of supplies. They would surely do the same as they approached Atlanta. "It is a fixed fact," warned the paper, "that if the cerulean abdomens besiege our city, no family, no people can live securely anywhere near them."[11]

With newspapermen disagreeing among themselves as to what constituted a civil panic in the face of the Yankees' approach, Atlantans could measure the crisis by the official attention being given to the city's defenses. No one, apparently, doubted that Atlanta's fortifications would eventually be put to use. On 30 May, for instance, Captain Grant, the fortifications engineer, received a message to come immediately to meet with new post commandant Brigadier General Marcus J. Wright at his headquarters at Bridge and Marietta; Wright was then consulting with Major General Henry C. Wayne of the state troops on how the defenses would be manned. The importance of the meeting is suggested by the fact that Sherman's armies at the time were a mere 30 miles north of Atlanta, with only one more major river barrier (the Chattahoochee) blocking them. At that time the nineteen artillery forts in Captain Grant's defensive perimeter remained largely empty of gunnery, as it was expected that the Army of Tennessee's field pieces would fill the embrasures. But some bigger cannon were

---

[11] Dyer, *Secret Yankees,* 311 ("Miss Abby," diary, 27 May 1864); Venet, ed., *Sam Richards's Civil War Diary,* 225 (29 May); Mary Mallard to Mary Jones, 27 May 1864, in Myers, ed., *Children of Pride,* 1174–75; *Atlanta Intelligencer,* 1, 5 June 1864 ("cerulean abdomens").

The Atlanta press's derogations of Yankee soldiers included several terms derived from the theme of "blue belly." For instance, in addition to the "cerulean abdomens" above, the *Memphis Appeal* noticed the "eleven azure-stomached miscegenators" arriving in the city as prisoners on 7 June; a few days earlier, the paper had referred to other captured Federals merely as "a fresh importation of fourteen sorry looking miscegenators" (*Memphis Appeal,* 4, 7 June).

specially ordered. Sent from a Confederate gunboat moored on the Apalachicola River in northwest Florida on 28 May were four 32-pounders and a big 9-inch Dahlgren. Arriving sometime in June after a lengthy railroad trek, the 9-incher required three days for work crews to put it into position. This immense gun would clearly outweigh any field piece in Sherman's army. Four-and-a-half tons in heft, the Dahlgren, with a 10-pound charge, could send a 64-pound shell a mile or more.[12]

As the Yankees approached the city and Johnston's army gave ground before the enemy at an alarming pace, the people of Atlanta, including the city fathers, looked everywhere for help, even heavenward. In its weekly meeting of 3 June, the city council unanimously adopted the motion of Councilman Dr. Chapman Powell, proclaiming the following Friday, 10 June, as a day of "fasting, humiliation and prayer," with encouragement for businesses to close. "Let the merchant close his doors, let the laborer intermit his toil," called the *Knoxville Register*; the paper suggested that "the people who are more immediately exposed to the present invasion should most earnestly seek the Divine Succor." Dutifully Samuel Richards attended church on the appointed day; Mrs. Mallard, the minister's wife, went to the same service, which was held conjointly by the Baptists, Methodists, and Presbyterians. Among the speakers was a Texas colonel from General Patrick Cleburne's division. Richards observed that the officer spoke "quite encouragingly"; Mrs. Mallard called the service "deeply solemn and interesting."[13]

---

[12] Maj. Lauren L. Butler to L. P. Grant, 30 May 1864, box 7, folder 5, Lemuel P. Grant Papers, Atlanta History Center; Wilbur Kurtz, notebook 13, 73 (location of Wright's HQ), Wilbur G. Kurtz Collection, Atlanta History Center; Maxine Turner, *Navy Gray: A Story of the Confederate Navy on the Chattahoochee and Apalachicola Rivers* (Tuscaloosa: University of Alabama Press, 1988) 70, 205; Wallace P. Reed, *History of Atlanta, Georgia, with Illustrations and Biographical Sketches of Some of Its Prominent Men and Pioneers* (Syracuse NY: D. Mason & Co., 1889) 191 ("three days to drag it to its position"); Edwin Olmstead, Wayne E. Stark, and Spencer C. Tucker, *The Big Guns: Civil War Siege, Seacoast, and Naval Cannon* (Alexandria Bay NY: Museum Restoration Service, 1977) 87.

Brig. Gen. Marcus J. Wright succeeded Col. J. K. McCall as commander of the post in Atlanta by the end of May. His headquarters were in the Brumby building, a two-story brick structure on the northeast corner of Bridge and Marietta streets. Two Atlanta physicians, Drs. James Alexander and William Shelby, had previously held offices there. James Bell recalled that the post commandery moved into the building after the doctors had departed (Kurtz, interview with Bell, 21 June 1935, notebook 10, 236, Wilbur G. Kurtz Collection, Atlanta History Center).

[13] Atlanta City Council Minutes (meeting of 3 June), Atlanta History Center; "To-Morrow," *Memphis Appeal*, 9 June 1864; "The Call to Prayer," *Knoxville Register*, 10 June 1864, quoted in Frank Moore, ed., *The Rebellion Record: A Diary of American Events*, 11 vols. (New York: G. P. Putnam, 1861–1863; D. Van Nostrand, 1864–1868) 11:527; Venet, ed., *Sam Richards's Civil War Diary*, 225 (10 June 1864); Mary Mallard to Mary Jones, 11 June 1864, in Myers, ed., *Children of Pride*, 1181. The officer preaching that Sunday, named by Richards as

By that time, spring 1864, Atlanta had seen yet another church added to its downtown houses of worship. The Reverend Charles T. Quintard, Episcopalian, was serving in Atlanta as chaplain-at-large for Johnston's army, tendering as well various medical services to the city hospitals (Quintard had taken his MD degree in 1847). Quintard observed that St. Philips, the sole Episcopal church, proved unable to accommodate all the communicants among the city's new refugee population. He therefore won permission from the Right Reverend Stephen Elliott, Episcopal bishop of Georgia, to start a new congregation. For a while, these faithful worshipped in the Methodist church at Garnett and Forsyth streets in the city's southwest quadrant. Meantime their church was being built on Walton Street, three blocks northwest of the Car Shed. Lumber and nails were donated, and Southern soldiers helped in the work; accordingly there arose a frame structure looking more like a schoolhouse than anything else (Chaplain Quintard termed its simplicity "somewhat 'Confederate' in style"). It was large enough, though, for eighty-eight pews and double aisles, leading to a 10-feet-by-12-feet chancel, "handsomely furnished" (Doctor Quintard's words) by donations from other parishes in the diocese, and was thus ready for its consecration by Bishop Elliott on 22 April 1864 as St. Luke's Episcopal Church.

"The little refugee church," as it was called, held a notable funeral two months later, for no less than Lieutenant General Leonidas Polk, corps commander in Johnston's army and Episcopal bishop of Louisiana. After Polk was killed by a Union shell on 14 June at Pine Mountain, his remains were brought into Atlanta and, in a flag-and-flower-bedecked casket, were placed on view the next day at St. Luke's. Thousands of soldiers and citizens shuffled quietly past, till at noon Doctor Quintard conducted services and delivered an eloquent eulogy. Then Polk's remains were placed inside a metal coffin and borne to the rail depot by a distinguished team of pallbearers: Major General G. W. Smith, Brigadier General Daniel Ruggles, Brigadier General Marcus J. Wright, Brigadier General A. W. Reynolds, Colonel Benjamin S. Ewell, and Colonel R. A. Crawford. With New Orleans under Yankee rule, Augusta, Georgia, was chosen as the bishop's temporary place of burial. A car on the eastbound train was specially furnished in carpeting, upon which the sarcophagus, decorated in white roses, was placed with Polk's saber and side arms. In Augusta, the bishop-general received yet another funeral, attended by no less than Lieutenant General James Longstreet (recovering from wounds suffered at the Wilderness that May). Bishop Stephen Elliott presided over the interment at St. Paul's

---

"a Col Wilkes," was Franklin C. Wilkes, commanding a regiment of dismounted Texas cavalrymen in Granbury's brigade of Cleburne's division (US War Department, *The War of the Rebellion: A Compilation of the Official Records of the Union and Confederate Armies,* 128 vols. [Washington, DC: Government Printing Office, 1880–1901] vol. 38, pt. 3, p. 639 [hereafter *OR* and all references will be to series 1 unless indicated]).

Church after a lengthy sermon, in which Elliott besought the Almighty to deliver "justice and vengeance" upon Polk's murderers.[14]

But God's vengeance would not halt the Yankees. By 10 June Sherman had given up slugging it out along the New Hope Church-Pickett's Mill line and maneuvered eastward, back close to the Western & Atlantic Railroad, once again forcing Johnston to take up a new position northwest of Marietta. That day Johnston wired Colonel Moses Wright in Atlanta to divert engineers and slave laborers from their work around the city to strengthening the fortifications on the north bank of the Chattahoochee—an ominous hint of Johnston's expectation of further retreating. Nonetheless, the *Intelligencer* continued in its mission of bucking up the public morale. Even though the paper on 5 June had broached the possibility that the "cerulean abdomens" might besiege the city, the editors on 7 June exhorted, "Let there be not even the *'shadow'* of a panic here!"—its use of italics a deliberate poke at that needlessly despondent correspondent for the Mobile paper. Yet the very next day the *Intelligencer*, acknowledging Sherman's success thus far as masterful strategist, predicted that soon the battlefront would be at the banks of the Chattahoochee River. There was no cause for worry even then, assured the *Intelligencer*; at such a point Sherman's room for maneuver would disappear and the Yankees would be handed the decisive repulse they so richly deserved. The *Atlanta Confederacy* was just as sanguine. "Atlanta was not, is not, and will not be in danger," the editors affirmed. The situation was especially bright when one considered that in Virginia "we are constantly punishing Grant." If both Johnston and Lee could in fact hold fast on their respective fronts, "the Yankees will abandon both magnificent failures before another Fourth of July celebration is held in New England."

A sharp and smarting repulse was in truth delivered to Sherman's forces in the battle of Kennesaw Mountain, 27 June, though the Southerners' victory was by no means decisive. Realizing this, it was General Johnston himself who on the day after the battle wrote his friend Texas senator Louis T. Wigfall, recommending that his daughters, then residing in Atlanta with Mrs. Johnston, move off to a safer point. "You expose your children to risk," Johnston warned. The two Wigfall girls obligingly boarded one of the hospital trains bound for Macon. As Louise Wigfall, one of the senator's daughters wrote from Macon,

---

[14] Sam Davis Elliott, ed., *Doctor Quintard, Chaplain C.S.A. and Second Bishop of Tennessee: The Memoir and Civil War Diary of Charles Todd Quintard* (Baton Rouge: Louisiana State University Press, 2003) 83–87; Wilbur G. Kurtz, "St. Luke's Baptized by War," *Atlanta Journal Magazine*, 3 July 1932, 5; [Wilbur G. Kurtz], "How St. Luke's Was Built," *Atlanta Journal Magazine*, 6 October 1935; Davis, ed., *Requiem for a Lost City*, 114–15; *Funeral Services at the Burial of the Right Rev. Leonidas Polk, D.D.* (Columbia SC: Evans & Cogswell, 1864) 26 (original document at Emory University); "Obsequies of Lieut.-Gen. Polk," *Memphis Appeal*, 16 June 1864.

"Mrs. Johnston will remain till the last moment practicable, and then, in case of a rush to the cars, she has her carriage in which she can come."

Other Atlantans were similarly ready to go, even if they did not want to go just yet. Lieutenant David P. McCorkle, superintendent of the Atlanta Naval Ordnance Works, wrote on 25 June, "Have all surplus stores packed & ready to move. I hope Joseph [General Johnston] will give me time to save everything." Civilians echoed the naval lieutenant. "A good many persons are packed up who expect to leave if there is any danger of the enemy capturing the city," wrote young Augusta "Gussie" Clayton, daughter of the wealthy William Wirt Clayton (who resided at Marietta and Spring). Speaking of her sister, Gussie continued, "Sallie and I packed some bed clothes and curtains and mother had the carpets taken up and fixed, so they could be carried off, but we have done nothing further. If there is any danger we will go immediately to Augusta, tho' I sincerely hope we will not have to....."[15]

Others chose not to wait. When the armies got to Kennesaw Mountain, Mayor Calhoun sent off his wife and two sons to the family place at Thomaston, in Middle Georgia. With them went slaves, belongings and as much livestock as could be conveniently herded. The mayor himself chose to stay in town, in fulfillment of his public duties.

These discreet evacuations continued while the city's numerous factories and shops, for which Atlanta was so renowned, continued to smoke and clank. On 22 June, one J. Milton Glass, a civilian secretly employed by the Federals as a spy, was in Atlanta for three hours. "The time I could look around in Atlanta," he reported afterward to Union officers, "I noticed that the Government shops and manufactories were at work as usual."[16] But already some of the munitions machinery had been packed up and sent off. In late May Colonel Moses Wright at the Atlanta arsenal began removing surplus machinery to Macon and Augusta

---

[15] Richard M. McMurry, *The Road Past Kennesaw: The Atlanta Campaign of 1864* (Washington, DC: US Department of the Interior, 1972) 23–29; "The Situation—Army of Tennessee," *Atlanta Intelligencer*, 5, 7, 8 June 1864; Atlanta *Confederacy*, 9 June, quoted in *Mobile Register and Advertiser*, 11 June; W. W. Mackall to M. H. Wright, 10 June, *OR*, vol. 38, pt. 4, p. 767; Johnston to Wigfall, 28 June, quoted in Alvy L. King, *Louis T. Wigfall, Southern Fire-Eater* (Baton Rouge: Louisiana State University Press, 1970) 197; Mrs. D. Giraud Wright [Louise Wigfall], *A Southern Girl in '61: The War-Time Memories of a Confederate Senator's Daughter* (New York: Doubleday, Page & Company, 1905) 178–79; Turner, *Navy Gray*, 205; Hoehling, *Last Train from Atlanta*, 24 (" great deal of excitement"); Davis, ed., *Requiem for a Lost City*, 89n33.

[16] E. C. Bruffey, "Atlantan Tells of Siege of City—Pat Calhoun Gives Vivid Description of Time When Whitehall Street was Mass of Ruins," *Atlanta Constitution*, 10 October 1919; "Reminiscences of Patrick H. Calhoun," *Atlanta Historical Bulletin* 1/6 (January 1932): 43–44; statement of J. M. Glass, 24 June 1864, *OR*, vol. 38, pt. 4, p. 584; Wilbur G. Kurtz, "A Federal Spy in Atlanta," *Atlanta Constitution Magazine*, 8 June 1930, 5–6.

"in view of the proximity of the enemy to this place." These shipments were slight and gradual, though, as Wright intended both to continue his operations in the city and not, as he put it, "to create any uneasiness with the people here." As of 3 July, Wright's workers were turning out 30,000 rounds of .57-caliber rifle cartridges daily; on 4 July, the arsenal was about to deliver 400 rounds of 20-pounder Parrott artillery ammunition to Johnston's army.

On 5 July, however, General Johnston—having retreated the night before to his already-prepared line of fortifications on the north bank of the Chattahoochee—issued orders that the hospitals and munitions works in Atlanta be evacuated. Colonel Gorgas, ordnance chief in Richmond, reinforced these instructions with his telegram of 7 July to Colonel Wright: "Send the bulk of machinery & stores to Augusta & to Columbia, S.C. send workmen in same direction when it becomes necessary." At once officers of the various service branches scrambled to obtain space on railroad cars. Wright's subordinates saw to the loading up of arsenal machinery, only to learn that quartermaster officers were giving priority to hospital equipment. Dr. A. J. Foard, medical director for Johnston's army, called for Atlanta's hospitals—patients, bunks, personnel—to be put on the train and to be reestablished at points southward. As a result, the hospitals at the medical college, fair grounds, female institute, and Empire House were soon closed, as were other facilities that had moved into town with Sherman's advance, such as Foard's and Gilmer's Hospitals. The fair grounds, Empire and institute facilities were reopened in Vineville, north of Macon. Dr. Willis Westmoreland had the Medical College Hospital set up in Milner, near Barnesville, by 25 July. Not all patients could be safely moved, of course; weak and ailing soldiers were kept behind at the medical college and female institute, according to Dr. Ira L. Gunter, surgeon serving at the Gate City Hotel/Receiving & Distributing Hospital. For the rest of the campaign, the "R & D" remained the center of Confederate medical activity in the city.

The flight of the hospitals tied up Atlanta's railway facilities. Frustrated, Wright appealed to Johnston's chief of staff, General Mackall, protesting that "our valuable machinery, guns & other ordnance stores" were certainly of greater value than a bunch of "bunks and old Hospital furniture." Eventually Wright's percussion cap machines got off to Macon. Wright himself with other equipment relocated in Augusta, leaving Atlanta on or about 10 July. Meanwhile Lieutenant McCorkle, in charge of the naval ordnance works, was also busy and encountering the same problems with the railroads. Even though he had packed up his surplus stores by 25 June, McCorkle had a terrible time securing rail transport after the evacuation order came in early July. By the 8 July he had packed up all his lathes, planes, and steam hammer; he was in the midst of moving the boilers and engines but, he complained, "to crown all, they have given an order to move the hospitals, and I can not get cars enough to move." Within a matter of days, though, McCorkle's naval works, especially the gun carriage shop, were at Augusta, reestablishing operation. Valuable machinery of the Atlanta Rolling Mill, of course, went as well, making its circuitous way to Columbia, South Carolina. By 10 July, a correspondent for the *Montgomery Advertiser* reported that "Atlanta has been stripped of public stores and works."[17]

Smaller shops, too, shut down and packed up. C. J. Christopher, the sword-maker, for instance, transported his shop to Macon, where by late July he had reopened at an old dye house on Cotton Avenue. All the bustle of these evacuations further agitated the populace. "A day of excitement at Decatur," wrote Benjamin Hunter in his diary on 7 July. "Orders have been issued for the removal of all the Atlanta Hospitals, Commissary, and Quartermaster stores, and the general impression is that Atlanta will be given up without a fight," Hunter observed; "the people here packed up, amid confusion and bustle, yet none can leave in consequence of the Government having exclusive control of the railroads." Even the *Southern Confederacy,* generally upbeat about the public mood, published a report that "there is a little uneasiness manifested on the part of the civilians." Contributing to the general fear was the *Intelligencer* itself, whose editorial column of 7 July for the first time spoke of the possibility that the

---

[17] Col. M. H. Wright to Col. G. W. Rains, 25 May 1864, quoted in Kennett, *Marching through Georgia,* 120; Lt. Col. H. Oladowski to Brig. Gen. William W. Mackall, 4 July 1864, *OR,* vol. 38, pt, 5, p. 864; Col. Josiah Gorgas to Wright, 7 July, quoted in John M. Murphy and Howard Michael Madaus, *Confederate Rifles & Muskets: Infantry Small Arms Manufactured in the Southern Confederacy, 1861–1865* (Newport Beach CA: Graphic Publisher, 1996) 68; Wright to Mackall, 7 July, quoted in Jeffrey N. Lash, *Destroyer of the Iron Horse: General Joseph E. Johnston and Confederate Rail Transport, 1861–1865* (Kent OH: Kent State University Press, 1991) 148–50; Glenna R. Schroeder-Lein, *Confederate Hospitals on the Move: Samuel H. Stout and the Army of Tennessee* (Columbia: University of South Carolina Press, 1994) 138; Freemon, "Medical Support System," 46, 49; Davis, "Another Look at Civil War Medical Care," 21; Ira Lawson Gunter to wife, 6 July 1864, in Carolyn Latimer and Nancy Lee, eds., *Civil War Letters Written by Elder Ira Lawson Gunter, M.D.* (McDonough GA: self-published, 1993) 40 (my thanks to Dr. Jim W. Latimer of Jonesboro GA for this source); Mallet, "Work of the Ordnance Bureau," 14; Wright to Rains, 11 July 1864, "Letters Sent Atlanta Arsenal," Records of Ordnance Establishments; McCorkle to Cmdr. Catesby Ap R. Jones, 25 June 1864, quoted in Turner, *Navy Gray,* 205; and to Jones, 8 [July] 1864, US Navy Department, *Official Records of the Union and Confederate Navies in the War of the Rebellion,* 31 vols. (Washington, DC: Government Printing Office, 1894–1922) vol. 21, p. 901(hereafter *ORN*); a misprint gives the date of this letter as 8 June, though it is manifestly 8 July, as supported by Admiral Franklin Buchanan to Jones, 13 July ("McCorkle is moving everything from Atlanta," *ORN,* vol. 21, p. 906); Tom Henderson Wells, *The Confederate Navy: A Study in Organization* (University: University of Alabama Press, 1971) 53; William N. Still, Jr., *Confederate Shipbuilding* (Columbia: University of South Carolina Press, 1987) 45; "Letter from 'Ora,'" 10 July, *Montgomery Advertiser,* 12 July 1864.

City cemetery records support the date of the Confederates' medical evacuation of Atlanta. The mortality lists of soldiers who died at the Fair Grounds and other hospitals in the city have their last entries dated 4 and 5 July ("List of Confederate Soldiers Buried at Oakland," Atlanta History Center).

city could fall. In such an event, neither the Army of Tennessee nor its commander should be blamed, counseled the paper; instead, the public outcry should be directed against the Confederacy's chief executive, Jefferson Davis. "Should Atlanta fall, fearful indeed will be the responsibility"; if it be shown that the president did not do enough to support Johnston, struggling against Sherman's superior forces, "upon him must rest the responsibility of its fall into the hands of the enemy." The *Southern Confederacy* also broached the unpleasant subject: "if Atlanta should fall, the campaign…is not at an end." The paper sought to shore up its readers by reminding them that even if Sherman's forces won possession of Atlanta, they would be in the Deep South, vulnerable to raids and counterattack. "Atlanta may be captured—and so may Sherman!" the paper exclaimed. As if following the *Intelligencer* and *Southern Confederacy*, the *Appeal* also considered the prospect of Atlanta's fall, but did so in the same positive light. "Should Sherman succeed in taking Atlanta," the editors asserted that the Yankees would not be able long to hold the place. Reinforcements would rally and the Confederate army would counterattack; at the least, Sherman's long, tenuous rail line to Nashville would be raided and cut. "Let us then acquiesce in the military necessity," concluded the *Appeal*, "which may for the time being…subject us to the temporary rule of our despised and hated invaders. Even if Atlanta must be given up, …we feel that Sherman is a whipped man the day he enters the town."

Save for the secret Northern sympathizers in the city and, of course, the bulk of the enslaved African Americans who saw their chances of escape and freedom increase daily with Sherman's advances, everyone registered the dread on their faces. On 8 July, the *Intelligencer* observed, "There is a deep earnestness visible on the faces of our people." The latter paper commended Atlanta's civilians for their "calm and deliberate" packing up and removal of selves and belongings. In fact, suggested the editors, "we think it advisable for those, who can go quietly and without getting confused and excited, to go to those country places where they will not be subject to molestation [by the Yankees] again." After all, if the army stationed itself in the city, manning its fortifications against the enemy, "almost all the houses will be required for army quarters," and the citizenry will be a drain on military subsistence. As if they needed further encouragement, more civilians packed up. One of them was Mary Mallard. "We had hoped to have remained longer in Atlanta," she wrote a friend, "but when the order came to remove all hospitals in a few hours," she and her husband decided on 7 July to load their furniture onto a train car they had obtained. They left the next afternoon. Nineteen-year-old Sallie Clayton and her sister Caroline were among the other departing Atlantans that day; they were put on the train for Montgomery (Gussie was too sick to leave). The commotion of so many citizens leaving did not go unnoticed to the Confederate soldiers charged with defending the fast-depopulating city. "Most all the places of business in and around Atlanta are shut off and the inhabitants are leaving in large numbers," wrote Bernard C. Wagner of the 5th Georgia Cavalry on 8 July to his cousin Emmie. "Every train of cars that are in the city are as full as they can be."

The signs of civilians fleeing were for everyone to see—even Yankees. Colonel Frank Sherman, a Federal staff officer captured on 7 July while on recon, was passing through downtown on 8 July, en route to the officers' prison at Macon. He recorded in his diary that day the simple observation, "Citizens are leaving." One of them was Lewis Lawshe, who packed up his one-horse wagon on the morning of 9 July and headed off to Butler County with "three negroes, a cow and a calf, a yearling, a dog and the most valuable stuff I could pack into my wagon." A few days later he would return for "two more loads of stuff."[18]

With so many departing citizens expressing their fear for the fate of the city, Albert Roberts, editor of the *Southern Confederacy*, devoted his column of 9 July to an assessment of the situation. To be sure, he could not deny that Atlanta lay in "imminent peril." And the withdrawal of the machinery and military stores was indeed "ominous." Yet the Confederate defense of Atlanta was aided by several factors, chiefly that the Yankees still had to cross the Chattahoochee. Roberts placed much confidence in General Johnston's ability to contest the enemy at any of his possible crossing-points. At the same time, the editor added ominously, "if he cannot make a successful battle, or hold the enemy in check along the Chattahoochee, he cannot anywhere below it, and the only temporary check would in that event be the capture of Atlanta, purposely thrown at the feet of the rapturous invader to stay his appetite for conquest." Roberts would have been even more pessimistic had he known all the facts. The very day before, 8 July, Union infantry had crossed the Chattahoochee River downstream from Roswell. The river town was the site of a textile mill that made Confederate uniforms. Sherman ordered the workers, some 400 young women, to be put on trains and sent north in exile.[19]

---

[18] *Atlanta Intelligencer*, 4 August 1864 (Christopher announcement); Benjamin T. Hunter, diary, 7 July 1864, typescript, MSS 179f, Atlanta History Center; "The Front" (7 July, 12 midnight), *Atlanta Southern Confederacy*, 8 July 1864; "The Situation—the Responsibility," *Atlanta Intelligencer*, 7 July; "Invasion Is Not Subjugation," *Atlanta Southern Confederacy*, [8 July], quoted in Macon *Telegraph*, 11 July; "Richmond and Atlanta," *Memphis Appeal*, 8 July (quoted in *Macon Telegraph*, 11 July); *Atlanta Intelligencer*, 8 July 1864 ("there is a deep earnestness visible on the faces of our people"); Mary Mallard to Laura Buttolph, 18 July 1864, in Myers, ed., *Children of Pride*, 1191; Davis, ed., *Requiem for a Lost City*, 118–19; Timothy Daiss, ed., *In the Saddle: Exploits of the 5th Georgia Cavalry during the Civil War* (Atglen PA: Schiffer Military History, [2004]) 46; Aldrich, ed., *Quest for a Star*, 125; "From an Old Diary" (Lewis Lawshe's), Edda Cole Scrapbook, Atlanta History Center.

[19] "The Defense of Atlanta," *Atlanta Southern Confederacy*, 9 July; Michael D. Hitt, *Charged with Treason: Ordeal of 400 mill workers during Military Operations in Roswell, Georgia, 1864–1865* (Monroe NY: Library Research Associates, 1992) 22–23; Ruth Beaumont Cook, *North Across the River: A Civil War Trail of Tears* (Birmingham AL: Crane Hill Publishers, 1999) 88–89. Edwin Woodworth, a soldier in the 125th Ohio, wrote home, "we had a chanse

The Federals' river-crossing forced General Johnston to retreat across the Chattahoochee on the night of 9 July. The Army of Tennessee had now given up the last major river barrier to Sherman's armies, and was redeploying in an entrenched line just 3 or 4 miles from downtown south of Peachtree Creek, a tributary flowing into the Chattahoochee southwest of Atlanta. The next morning, the effect of the news was dramatic. Shopowners and merchants scurried to rid themselves of inventory at any price; several auctions a day, as advertised in the press, offered goods at drastically cut rates. "I can give you no idea of the excitement in Atlanta," wrote the correspondent for a Mobile newspaper.

> Everybody seems to be hurrying off, and especially the women. Wagons loaded with household furniture, and everything else that can be packed upon them, crowd every street, and women, old and young, and children innumerable, are hurrying to and fro, leading pet lambs, deer, and other little household objects of affection, as though they intend to save all they could. Every train of cars is loaded to its utmost capacity, and there is no grumbling about seats, for even the fair ones are but too glad to get even a standing place on a box car. The excitement beats anything I ever saw.[20]

Amid the excitement, and possibly contributing to it, came another of Governor Brown's proclamations issued from Milledgeville on 9 July, calling for more men at the front. This one urged every man—really, every adolescent sixteen and seventeen and senescent from fifty to fifty-five—to report to Major General Gustavus W. Smith of the Georgia Militia in Atlanta. The proclamation was reprinted by papers across the state, and the governor added to its impact by himself going to Atlanta. The *Appeal* of 13 July mentioned that Brown was in the city, working hard to bring forward state troops to augment General Johnston's forces. By the end of the month Smith counted some 5,000 "effective" militiamen with him, although the term "effective" was a virtual joke. Many feared that old men and boys "armed in great part with flint-lock muskets, ordinary rifles, and

---

to see som of the georgia wimen there was [about 400] factories girls and we had a fine time with them there was some of them was very good looking" (Woodworth to mother, 14 July 1864, MSS 645, box 2, folder 19, Atlanta History Center). Sherman also sent workers from another textile mill, the Sweetwater Factory west of Atlanta, via train to Louisville KY. See Carole E. Scott, "Total War Comes to New Manchester," *Blue & Gray* 12/2 (December 1994): 22. Lewis C. Russell relates the reminiscence of eighty-six-year-old S. H. Causey, how he and his mother, a Sweetwater Factory worker, exiled to Indianapolis after Sherman's banishment ("Georgia Towns Moved in War," *Atlanta Journal Magazine*, 28 February 1932).

[20] Stephen Davis, "The Battle for Atlanta. Actions from July 10 to September 2, 1864," *Blue & Gray*, 6/6 (August 1989): 9; Davis, *Atlanta Will Fall*, 100–101; Ralph Benjamin Singer, "Confederate Atlanta" (Ph.D. diss., University of Georgia, 1973) 247; "Atlanta Correspondent of Mobile News," quoted in *New York Times*, 7 August 1864.

shot guns" would not hold their ground against Sherman's veterans. Yet despite the need for manpower, certain exemptions continued among Atlanta's civilians, such as firemen and newspapermen working in the city. The city council was particularly solicitous for the former, as evidenced by the resolution it passed asking Confederate authorities not to conscript firemen "for the reason [as handwritten in the council minutes book] of their invaluable Servises to both private & public interests in cases of fire in the distruction of property."

One of those Atlanta males exempted was Samuel Richards, who recorded in his diary on Sunday, 10 July: "This has been a sad day in our city, for it has been quite evident for some days past that there is a great probability of Atlanta falling into the hands of the enemy and the city has been in a complete swarm all day and for several days. All the Govt stores and Hospitals are ordered away and of course the citizens are alarmed and many have left and others are leaving." Richards and his wife Sallie saw some friends off, but they decided "to stay at home, Yankees or no Yankees. We hear and read terrible tales of them, but I don't think they are as bad as they are said to be." Richards suspected he and his wife would have plenty of company, as "we hear of a good many who are going to remain in the city if the enemy gets possession." That ominous phrase was the talk among Atlantans, as when over dinner that same Sunday evening a Confederate officer, Colonel Taylor Beatty, encouraged his friends, the Cohens, not to flee to Augusta yet: "Stay at least a few days longer, as I think we will hold this place at least a week—if the enemy succeed in getting at it all."[21]

Many did not share the colonel's confidence. In the week after Johnston's retreat across the river, Richard Peters put his family and valuable property on the train to Augusta, where they moved into the home of John P. King. J. C. Moore, a civilian in the secret employ of the Union army as a "scout," slipped in and out of Atlanta, bringing news to the Federals of all the fugacious folk. On 11 July, he reported to Brigadier General Thomas J. Wood, a division commander in the IV Corps, that refugeeing civilians "in great numbers, taking the Negroes, &c." were leaving the city, following the "good deal of machinery" that the authorities had removed to Augusta and other safer parts. Three days later Moore reported again: "the inhabitants of Atlanta are still leaving, going farther south, and the town is pretty well cleaned out. All the valuable property, such as machinery and army stores, has been removed," to the point that "only a small

---

[21] Joseph E. Brown to the Reserved Militia of Georgia, 9 July 1864, *OR*, vol. 52, pt. 2, pp. 688–91; *Augusta Chronicle & Sentinel*, 14 July 1864 (quoting *Appeal*, 13 July); Gustavus W. Smith, "The Georgia Militia about Atlanta," in Robert Underwood Johnson and Clarence Clough Buel, eds., *Battles and Leaders of the Civil War*, 4 vols. (New York: Century Co., 1888) 4:332, 334; Atlanta City Council Minutes (meeting of 22 April 1864), Atlanta History Center; Venet, ed., *Sam Richards's Civil War Diary*, 226–27 (10 July 1864); Hoehling, *Last Train from Atlanta*, 65.

supply of subsistence" was being kept in Atlanta for the army and remaining residents.

Even the Atlanta City Council caved. On 11 July, in a call meeting prompted by the excitement about town, the councilmen succumbed to the prevalent pessimism in passing two resolutions: first, empowering Mayor Calhoun to use his judgment as to when the city records and other valuable papers should be dispatched to safety; and second, authorizing the street superintendent "to send the City Mules out of reach of the invading enemy" whenever he thought proper. Altogether, the evident mood about the city was depressing. Lieutenant W. L. Trask, a Confederate staff officer, visited Atlanta on 12 July and "found it nearly deserted. Government workshops all removed, Newspapers (except the Appeal) all gone."

This was not quite true, for the *Register* remained in Atlanta as of 12 July. The *Intelligencer* and *Southern Confederacy,* the city's two major dailies, had indeed gone. The *Intelligencer* staff, unnerved by Johnston's crossing of the Chattahoochee and the citizens' exodus, turned out its last issue on 10 July before boarding the train for Macon, settling in with one of the city's papers, the *Messenger* at Cherry and Third streets and resuming publication within two weeks. The *Confederacy* left for Macon, too, probably after its issue of 10 July. By the end of the month, it also was back in operation, though turning out a smaller extra as its daily issue. At the same time, the *Confederacy's* editor, Albert Roberts stayed in Atlanta, reporting news from the city.[22]

People began to wonder when the *Appeal* would leave. On 11 July, an *Appeal* "special" correspondent, writing as "Estrangero," reported that soldiers in Johnston's army were pleased to see the paper's afternoon edition that day, after the *Intelligencer* and *Confederacy* had left. "I suppose I have been asked one thousand times during the day whether the Appeal had run or not," the correspondent reported. "On my replying that it was the intention to remain and publish a paper as long as they would keep the pestiferous Yankees out of the composing and press rooms," the reporter stated that soldiers eagerly pledged to do so. The editors themselves soon addressed the question, "when is the *Appeal* going to leave Atlanta," by affirming that it would "remain in Atlanta issuing two regular editions each day, until the evening and the morning of the last day of its occupation by the army of Tennessee. We feel it to be our duty to stay here and do all in our power to aid the army by words of exhortation and

---

[22] Royce Shingleton, *Richard Peters: Champion of the New South* (Macon GA: Mercer University Press, 1985) 105; Brig. Gen. Thomas J. Wood to Lt. Col. J. S. Fullerton, 11, 14 July 1864, *OR*, vol. 38, pt. 5, pp. 116, 138; Atlanta City Council Minutes, 11 July; W. L. Trask, war journal, 13 August, microfilm, Emory University and typescript at Kennesaw Mountain National Battlefield Park; "The Newspapers," *Augusta Chronicle & Sentinel,* 27 July ("the first number of the Intelligencer was issued on Saturday last"); "The Southern Confederacy," *Macon Telegraph,* 19 July.

encouragement, and to rally the people of Georgia." There was a little fibbing here, for proprietor and chief editor John R. McClanahan was already planning to remove his heavy, expensive Hoe press to Montgomery when things got a little hotter. "Shadow" (Henry Watterson) reported, in a column written in Atlanta on 12 July that the *Appeal*, "which is considered a bird of ill omen, is pluming its wings to descend like a raven upon the unoffending capital of Alabama." But for the time being, the *Appeal* continued to publish in Atlanta, through the second and into the third week of July, under McClanahan's direction.

This determination, backed by the paper's two years of migration from Memphis, made the migratory pattern of the *Appeal* itself a subject of public conversation. The editors of the *Montgomery Advertiser* speculated that Atlanta must be "safe yet," so long as the *Appeal* was still there. "It will be recollected by those who have kept count of the various migrations of that sterling newspaper, that when Memphis fell the *Appeal* had an office ready to set up at Grenada, Mississippi; that as soon as Grenada was threatened it removed to Jackson; when Jackson fell it went to Atlanta." The *Advertiser* was therefore quite pleased that the *Appeal* had promised to remain in Atlanta as long as the city remained in Confederate hands. Soldiers of the Army of Tennessee were just as pleased, as the *Appeal* had become the main editorial voice in the city after the *Intelligencer* left. Sometimes bellicosely optimistic, sometimes peculiarly reserved, the paper issued its judgments from day to day as the Yankee hordes lay just beyond the gates of Atlanta. In a column printed 13 July, the *Appeal* noted that Governor Brown was once more in the city, urging the state militia forward to the front. "The governor believes that he is able, with the reserve forces of Georgia, to hold Atlanta, even though the policy of the government might lead them to abandon it." The editor added, somewhat lamely, "we see no reason why Atlanta should not be defended." Then, a day or two later, McClanahan assumed a hortatory if not exclamatory style in his call for all able-bodied men to get to the front lines.

> By the affection you bear your wives, daughters, mothers and sisters, and your tender regard for their chastity, comfort and peace; by your love for all that is pure and good; by all your hopes and desires; by every emotion that can actuate man to do and dare, the crisis demands that you should be at your post.... Meet the foe on the threshold of your State, and contest every inch of ground with him. If Atlanta must fall, make it prove a Moscow to the invader. If retreat you must let the trophies the enemy secures be the ashes of your houses and cities, and the smoking ruins of your property all that greets his approach. Come to that resolve and the enemy is yours.

Adding to the palpable tension within the city was the sudden appearance, on the morning of 13 July, of a distinguished visitor from Richmond—no less than General Braxton Bragg, former commander of the Army of Tennessee and now President Davis's chief military adviser. Bragg's arrival by train, and his almost immediate trip by carriage to General Johnston's headquarters, became a news story in itself. In its daily telegraphic report to subscribing papers, the Confederate Press Association office in Atlanta reported tersely, "Gen. Bragg arrived here this morning. Supposed with a view of conference." Henry Watterson, writing as "Grape" for an Augusta paper, attempted to allay suspicions that Bragg's visit might reflect anxiety in Richmond over the position of Johnston's army: "General Bragg has arrived. He had been sent out, it is understood, upon a tour of general inspection, and has visited this department merely by the way, and without any special purpose." Such assurances, however, became less convincing the longer Bragg stayed in the city (until 15 July) and the more he was seen in conference with Johnston (twice) and his corps commanders, lieutenant generals William J. Hardee, John B. Hood, A. Peter Stewart, and Major General Joseph Wheeler. "Ora," correspondent for the *Montgomery Advertiser*, acknowledged that "the presence of Gen. Bragg here at this time has caused a great deal of speculation." Like "Grape" and others, "Ora" explained that "his mission from Richmond…has been simply that of holding a conference" with Johnston. Then the reporter unwittingly signaled the apprehensions of many at the time: "It is not supposed for a moment that either the President or Gen. Bragg would attempt to interfere with the plans of Gen. Johnston." "Ora" would be proven wrong.

In the week after Johnston's army crossed the Chattahoochee, the Yankees seemed to have halted, lulling Atlantans' fears of an immediate attack. Sherman was actually busy, moving his troops across the river, rebuilding bridges that the Southerners had destroyed, strengthening his hold on the south bank, and allowing his soldiers to rest and refit. But the overall impression shared by the remaining residents of Atlanta during 10–16 July was that of sitzkrieg. "To-day has been the dullest of the campaign," wrote a correspondent of the *Appeal* on 16 July, "scarcely a shot being fired.… [neither Confederate infantry nor cavalry] has been troubled by any movements of significance for some time. Affairs here are as dull and monotonous as the siege of Charleston, and will remain so until one or the other [Sherman or Johnston] becomes disposed to assume the offensive."[23]

---

[23] Correspondence of "Estrangero," 11 July 1864, *Montgomery Advertiser*, 15 July; Ellis, *The Moving Appeal*, 305; "The Appeal remains to the last," *Mobile Register & Advertiser*, 16 July; "Shadow," "Our Army Correspondence," 12 July, *Mobile Register & Advertiser*, 17 July (and quoted in J. Cutler Andrews, *The South Reports the Civil War* [Princeton: Princeton University Press, 1970] 455); "Atlanta Safe Yet," *Montgomery Advertiser*, 15 July; "Governor Brown," *Memphis Appeal*, 13 July, quoted in *Augusta Chronicle & Sentinel*, 14 July; *Memphis Appeal*, n.d., quoted in Ellis, *The Moving Appeal*, 310–11 (from *Montgomery Daily Mail*, 16 July); "Telegraphic," *Augusta Chronicle & Sentinel*, 13 July; "Grape," "Letter from the Georgia Front," *Augusta Constitutionalist*, 16 July; "Ora," 14 July, in *Montgomery Advertiser*, 16 July; "Correspondence of the Appeal," 16 July, quoted in *New York Times*, 29 July.

At that time Johnston's forces held an entrenched line, running east-west little more than a mile south of Peachtree Creek. While Confederate soldiers manned this outer line, Captain Grant, Colonel Wright, engineers from the Army of Tennessee and hundreds, maybe thousands of hired slaves continued to work on the fortifications around Atlanta. Their work-pace, of course, had quickened as Sherman got closer to Atlanta. The labor had been redirected for awhile in mid-June, when General Johnston ordered that engineers and slaves turn from the defensive perimeter around Atlanta to strengthening the lines of works on both north and south banks of the Chattahoochee. Colonel Wright scrambled for the laborers he needed. Having just sent some slaves back to their Gwinnett County farm on 16 June, he was forced to recall them: "an emergency has arisen which requires the return of the negroes from your County to the work of Defences in this vicinity." In the city itself, Confederate officers continued to impress slaves. According to one newspaper report, the impressments could be rather abrupt as when, allegedly, "negro drivers were taken from carriages, and wood wagons and drays, leaving the vehicles in the street." The *Intelligencer* filed a protest with General Johnston after impressment officers took away the hired blacks who worked the paper's press. Army headquarters issued notices that the need for impressed labor was only temporary, and would be properly conducted. Meanwhile, the *Appeal* of 25 June encouraged citizens to donate their slave laborers cheerfully, at least dutifully. "Let every one who has a negro and can spare him, send him to the front to build fortifications.... No one should murmur or complain."

Milton Glass, the Northern spy, was in Atlanta on the morning of 22 June, and attested to seeing some 500 blacks at work digging cannon positions on the river and solidifying the main fortifications encircling Atlanta. These latter, Glass reported, were "well built"—earthen artillery forts with parapets 10 feet high connected with "strong and well-built rifle pits." Slaves were still hard at work two weeks later when, on 3 July, Glass again reported, "General Johnston had ordered out every negro to work on the fortifications." The line around the city was impressive. Each artillery position had plank flooring, and interior walls were held in place by boards. The parapets were buttressed by sandbags and fascine (huge wicker baskets filled with dirt). Outside the forts and trench lines were dug-out ditches or moats. Rows of wooden palisades, some 12 to 14 feet high, were occasionally set in front of the works to block the advance of enemy infantry. The planks themselves, wrote an officer, were spaced just far enough apart "to permit the infantry fire, if carefully delivered, to pass freely through, but not sufficient to permit a person to pass through." Beyond that and extending across the field of fire were various obstacles, ugly things for infantry having to confront them, but dignified by French names from the Napoleonic era. *Abatis* meant felled trees with branches entwined with tangles of cut brush. *Chevaux-de-frise*, "horses of Friseland" or Dutch horse, was the name for logs

86

driven through with rows of sharpened stakes pointed toward the expected enemy approach so as to impede charging infantrymen.[24]

Aware of the strength of Atlanta's defenses, General Sherman had no intention to run up against them. He had already, on 6 July, announced his plan to chief of staff H. W. Halleck in Washington: "Instead of attacking Atlanta direct, or any of its forts," Sherman declared, "I propose to make a circuit, destroying its railroads." One of these railroads, the Western & Atlantic, was already serving as Sherman's main supply line. The other three, however, served the Rebels. By blocking and destroying these rail arteries, Sherman intended to cut off supplies to the Confederate army in Atlanta and force it either to evacuate the city or to come out from its entrenchments and attack against heavy odds. Either way, Sherman expected to pressure the Rebels to give up Atlanta. At no point, however, did the Federal commander envision a siege of Atlanta—with *siege* defined as a full encirclement of the enemy-held city. Despite his numerical advantage, Sherman knew he did not have enough infantry to completely surround Atlanta and its fortifications. More important, Sherman did not need to besiege the place; it was enough to cut the Rebels' railroads, which could be done by cavalry raids, infantry marches and trench line extensions. Hence, the most that the Federals achieved during summer 1864 was a *semi*-siege of the Confederate city (which, as we shall see, proved enough for the Yankees to capture it).

The first step in Sherman's plan had been to get across the Chattahoochee River, the last major obstacle before Atlanta. This the Federals had begun to do on 8–9 July, getting across three infantry divisions and cavalry at upriver crossings beyond the Confederate right flank, forcing Johnston to retreat across the Chattahoochee on the night of 9 July. "We now commence the real game for Atlanta," wrote Sherman. "I expect pretty sharp practice, but I think we have the advantage and propose to keep it."

Sherman had several reasons for his optimism: he had retained the initiative since the opening of the campaign; he possessed an efficient supply and transport system that kept his men fed and equipped; and his buoyant morale was shared by his confident, even sunny troops. But most important of all was his numerical superiority. Sherman reported his strength on 30 June as over 106,070, including 88,000 infantry, 12,000 cavalry and almost 6,000 artillerymen.

---

[24] Brig. Gen. W. W. Mackall to Col. M. H. Wright, 10 June 1864, *OR*, vol. 38, pt. 4, p. 767; Capt. L. P. Grant to —, 8 June; and Grant to J. R. Bracewell, 16 June 1864, Grant Letterbook, Lemuel P. Grant Papers, Atlanta History Center; "The Impressment," *Memphis Appeal*, 22 June 1864; "A Prophecy—Shall It Be Fulfilled?," *Memphis Appeal*, 25 June 1864; statements of J. M. Glass, 24 June and 3 July 1864, *OR*, vol. 38, pt. 4, p. 584 and pt. 5, p. 32; "Forts to Defend Atlanta, " *Atlanta Journal*, 25 May 1941, 6; "Atlanta Fort Restored," *Atlanta Constitution Sunday Magazine*, 2 May 1937; report of Capt. Orlando M. Poe, 8 October 1865, *OR*, vol. 38, pt. 1, pp. 131–32.

Some of these troops were in the rear, protecting the Federals' supply line, and thousands more were not available for combat—in the hospitals, or detailed to various non-front-line tasks—but clearly Sherman held strength in numbers against the 59,000 Confederate officers and men, of all arms, listed as present for duty 10 July in Johnston's army.

The Union forces were organized as three armies. Largest by far was that of the Cumberland, led by Major General George H. Thomas (some 59,000 troops in three corps, the IV, XIV, and XX). The Army of the Tennessee, under Major General James B. McPherson, consisted of the XV, XVI, and XVII Corps (32,000). And Major General John M. Schofield's XXIII Corps (15,000 men) bore the name of the Army of the Ohio. All three of Sherman's army commanders were experienced, capable leaders. Thomas was the heralded "Rock of Chickamauga"; McPherson had fought with Sherman for a year and a half, and had excelled in the Vicksburg Campaign. Schofield had commanded the Union Department of Missouri before being brought east to beef up Sherman's "army group," technically known as the Military Division of the Mississippi.[25]

By 17 July, about half of Sherman's infantry had gotten across the Chattahoochee; they had crossed rather leisurely, thanks to the passivity of General Johnston. That morning, Sherman started moving. In keeping with his overall plan to cut Atlanta's rail lines, Sherman determined that his first objective would be the cutting of the Georgia Railroad to Augusta. At dawn all three armies were on the march, with McPherson's XV, XVI, and XVII Corps headed for Decatur, through which the railway ran. By nightfall of 17 July, all seven army corps had crossed the Chattahoochee, and most of them were aligned on Nancy Creek, a tributary just 8 miles north of downtown, flowing into Peachtree Creek. The next day, Thomas's army crossed Nancy Creek and pushed another mile or so against stiffening resistance from Rebel cavalry, supported by artillery and even infantry. Major General Oliver O. Howard's IV Corps made its way to Buck Head, a crossroads store where years earlier a slain buck's head had been mounted. Schofield's two divisions also advanced; of McPherson's army, the XV Corps actually crossed the north fork of Peachtree Creek. The real gains, though, were achieved farther to the east. Brigadier General Kenner Garrard's cavalry division, aided by one of McPherson's infantry brigades, succeeded in reaching the Georgia Railroad at Stone Mountain Depot, 13 miles east of Atlanta. After driving off Rebel cavalry, the Federals destroyed 2 or 3 miles of track.[26]

---

[25] Sherman to Halleck, 6, 11 July 1864, *OR*, vol. 38, pt. 5, pp. 66, 114; "Abstract from returns showing the effective strength of the army in the field under Maj. Gen. William T. Sherman," 30 June 1864, *OR*, vol. 38, pt. 1, pp. 115–16; "Abstract from returns of the Army of Tennessee," 10 July 1864, *OR*, vol. 38, pt. 3, p. 679; Davis, *Atlanta Will Fall*, 90 (62,700 Confederates present for duty on 30 June, against Sherman's 106,000).

[26] Special Field Order 35, 14 July 1864, *OR*, vol. 38, pt. 5, p. 143; Garrett, *Atlanta and Environs*, 1:160 (on Buckhead), 594, 608 (Wilbur G. Kurtz, maps "Military Operations June

Sherman's initial objective, the cutting of the Georgia Railroad, was thus achieved by 19 July. The Union commander might have wondered what the Rebels were up to, and why they were not more vigorously trying to check his progress. Atlantans, too, might well have worried what their defending army was doing to push the Yankees back. The *Appeal* voiced this concern in a column on "Sherman's Position." The Yankee army was so far from its base at Louisville, and so vulnerably deep into Confederate territory, that it offered General Johnston a great "opportunity for destroying or annihilating" it. Indeed, opined the *Appeal*, "if something is not now done…, we shall think there is a sad want of combination and cooperation among our military leaders."

The *Appeal* was onto something: there was very much a "sad want of combination and cooperation" among Confederate leaders. On the night of 17 July, General Johnston received a telegram from Richmond stating that as he had failed to arrest the enemy advance into Georgia, and expressed no confidence that he would be able to defeat or repel Sherman, he was being relieved of command. Lieutenant General John B. Hood, one of the three corps commanders in the army, had been promoted and was ordered to take over from Johnston.[27]

News of this sort travels fast. Major Charles W. Hubner, chief of the telegraph corps at the army's telegraph office in the Gate City Hotel at the corner of Pryor and Alabama, received the telegram from Richmond sometime that evening. It is possible that even before the message was transcribed—with the machinery of the time, the dots and dashes were printed on paper tape—its import had already been taken to the streets by excited staffers. It is even more probable that before Major Hubner arrived at Johnston's headquarters at the Dexter Niles house, 3 miles northwest of the Car Shed on the Marietta road, about 10 P.M., downtown residents had heard the story. Samuel Richards, who lived three blocks away from the telegraph office at Washington and Peters, got the dramatic news in time to enter it into his diary entry for that Sunday night, after his customary notice of the day's worship service: "All of a sudden Gen Johnston has been *relieved* of the command of the Army and Gen Hood or 'Old Pegleg' as the soldiers style him placed in command, so that there is thought to

---

22–July 17, 1864" and "July 17–19, 1864"); Garrard to McPherson, 19 July, *OR*, vol. 38, pt. 2, p. 808; Maj. Gen. John A. Logan to Col. W. T. Clark, 18 July, *OR*, vol. 38, pt. 5, pp. 176–77; Castel, *Decision in the West*, 365; David Evans, *Sherman's Horsemen: Union Cavalry Operations in the Atlanta Campaign* (Bloomington: Indiana University Press, 1996) 80.

[27] "Sherman's Position," *Memphis Appeal* (n.d.), quoted in *New York Times*, 20 July 1864. The most thorough explanation of why Johnston was relieved, and of the agonizing process by which President Davis reached the decision on 17 July, is still Thomas Lawrence Connelly, *Autumn of Glory: The Army of Tennessee, 1862–1865* (Baton Rouge: Louisiana State University Press, 1967) 391–421. See also Castel, *Decision in the West*, 352–58, and Davis, *Atlanta Will Fall*, 102–17 (including the Confederate Cabinet's unanimous decision to relieve Johnston on 14 July).

be a prospect for a fight before Atlanta is given up, as Hood is said to be a fighting man, if he *has* only one leg."[28]

Given the fleetness of the news, and its obvious bearing on the defense of the city, most Atlantans had probably already heard at least the outlines of the story when the *Appeal* hit the streets on the afternoon of 18 July. The issue carried Johnston's formal farewell to his troops, which also appeared in the telegraphic news column wired from Atlanta that day to other papers. The *Appeal* editor was cautious: "as to the motives or reasons that have influenced the President to make this change, which falls with startling effect upon the army and country, we are of course ignorant, and into which it would at this time be both imprudent and unprofitable to inquire."

A number of Confederates, though, particularly the higher-ranking ones, were in on "the motives or reasons" for the command change. Lieutenant Andrew Jackson Neal, son of prominent Atlanta businessman John Neal and serving in the Marion Light Artillery (attached to Hardee's corps) heard a remarkably well-informed and quite accurate account from "one of Cheathams Brigadiers who is an old friend and schoolmate at the University of Virginia and at the Lebanon Law School" (Confederate Brigadier General John C. Carter). Writing to his father from "the Field Near Chattahoochee," 20 July, Neal laid out the story.

> President Davis has been wanting Johnston to give battle ever since he crossed the Etowah and thinks he could have afforded it at Dallas and New Hope. Johnston would not divulge his plans to the President but told him he intended to fight at the first opportunity. As soon as Johnston

---

[28] Mary Hubner Walker, *Charles W. Hubner: Poet Laureate of the South* (Atlanta: Cherokee Publishing Company, 1976) 27, 31; Charles W. Hubner, "Some Recollections of Atlanta During 1864," *Atlanta Historical Bulletin* I/2 (January 1928): 6; Wilbur G. Kurtz, notes from interview of Charles W. Hubner, 2 April 1927, notebook 3, 101, Wilbur G. Kurtz Collection, Atlanta History Center; Ella Mae Thornton, "Mr. S.P. Richards," *Atlanta Historical Bulletin* 3/12 (December 1937): 74; Venet, ed., *Sam Richards's Civil War Diary*, 227 (17 July); Wilbur G. Kurtz, "At the Dexter Niles House," *Atlanta Constitution Sunday Magazine*, 28 September 1930, 5, 20.

Russell S. Bonds recently claimed that Major Hubner's telegraph office was located out of town, across the Marietta road from the Niles house, General Johnston's headquarters (Russell S. Bonds, *War Like the Thunderbolt: The Battle and Burning of Atlanta* [Yardley PA: Westholme Publishing, 2009] 65). This is not sustained by Hubner's "Some Recollections," which Bonds cites as his source. Indeed, Hubner writes, "our headquarters were in the old American Hotel, which stood on the corner of Alabama and Pryor Streets" ("Some Recollections," 6). This would have been the downtown Gate City Hotel, which stood at Alabama and Pryor, across from the Car Shed; it assumed the name American Hotel after the war (Garrett, *Atlanta and Environs*, 1:282). See also [Garrett and Kurtz], "Key to Map," 14 ("No. 64.—South-east corner Alabama and Pryor Sts. Site of Hospital and Signal Corps Hdqrs. C.S.A., 1864"), *Atlanta Historical Bulletin* 8 (September 1934): 14.

crossed the Chattahoochee it was resolved to relieve him from command of the Army. Hood was placed at the head because Hardee had refused command at Dalton last winter and the President was incensed at it. The change was very unexpected in the army and deeply regretted, but I cannot regard it as a calamity.

It was the *Appeal*'s issue of 18 July that alerted General Sherman that the Rebel army in front of him had a new commander. The next morning, one of the Northern spies floating about Atlanta brought out the previous evening's *Appeal* and took it to Major General Grenville M. Dodge, commander of the XVI Corps. Dodge sent the paper to General McPherson, who in turn routed it on to Sherman. By noon General Howard's IV Corps pickets had also picked up from prisoners word of the supersedure. Howard rushed the story to headquarters; Sherman confirmed it, telling Howard he had read Johnston's farewell address in the paper sent in by Dodge. Later that afternoon General Thomas had also gotten the *Appeal* and further corroborated the transfer of Rebel army command to Hood.[29]

Sherman formed a gradual impression of what the news meant. When the *Appeal* came in on 19 July, Sherman asked Schofield about Hood; the XXIII Corps commander had graduated from West Point with him. "Bold even to rashness" was the assessment. Sherman further assumed that the firing of Johnston was by Jeff Davis's order. Altogether, the news must have impressed him that the days of sitzkrieg were over.[30]

Apprised of goings-on in the Rebel army, Sherman also had a pretty clear idea of the citizenry's evacuation. Moore, the spy, brought a report from inside the city that allowed Union brigadier general Thomas Wood to relate on 14 July, "the inhabitants are still leaving, going farther south, and the town is pretty well cleaned out." About the same time, Confederate general Braxton Bragg fed Richmond authorities the same impression of Atlanta. Before he left town 15 July, he wired, "nearly all available stores and machinery are removed, and the people have mostly evacuated the town." Civil authority likewise evaporated as the police force melted away and the courts ceased to function. The city council held its last meeting on 18 July, when the fathers voted to have the fire

---

[29] *Memphis Appeal,* 18 July 1864, quoted in *New York Times,* 29 July; "From the Army of Tennessee. Change of Commanders. Gen. Johnston's Farewell Address. Gen. Hood's Address," telegraphic column, Atlanta, 18 July, in *Augusta Chronicle & Sentinel,* 20 July 1864; Lt. Andrew J. Neal to "Pa," 20 July, Andrew Jackson Neal Letters, Emory University; report of General Dodge, 25 November 1864, *OR,* vol. 38, pt. 3, p. 383; Maj. Gen. O. O. Howard to Sherman, 19 July, and Sherman to Howard, 19 July (midnight), *OR,* vol. 38, pt. 5, p. 188; Thomas to Sherman, 19 July, *OR,* vol. 38, pt. 5, pp. 184–85.

[30] Castel, *Decision in the West,* 367; William T. Sherman, *Memoirs of General William T. Sherman,* 2 vols. (New York: D. Appleton and Company, 1875) 2:72; Sherman to Thomas, 19 July, *OR,* vol. 38, pt. 5, p. 183.

department "select two of the Most Superior Fire Engines and have them removed from the City for safety in case of Atlanta's being occupied for a time by the enemy."[31]

Removal of the water-engines could not have been timed more infelicitously, as a severe fire broke out on the night of 19 July. Actually, when smoke began to issue from the three-story Connally Building (formerly Holland House building, northeast corner of Alabama and Whitehall streets), about eleven o'clock that night, it was more the lack of firemen, rather than of machinery, that handicapped firefighting efforts. As the *Atlanta Appeal* later noted, the number of firefighters in the city had shrunk when mechanics and other skilled workers were sent away with their machinery. To make matters worse, the water supply gave out after a half hour. Firemen and other onlookers could only watch as flames consumed the Connally Building and damaged a nearby building owned by John Beach. Along with them went the businesses inside, such as L. S. Mead's drugstore, the bookbinderies of R. J. Maynard and James P. Mason, and James McPherson's bookstore. As for the cause of the blaze, speculation centered on the insidious work of "incendiaries," deliberate arsonists out to collect insurance or even to steal loot as storefronts went up in smoke. (The *Appeal* commented disappointingly of "men, in the garb of soldiers and firemen" making off with property during the night.)

The fire also prompted one of the city's last two papers to leave. According to the *Appeal*, the flames destroyed "several cases of type, stands and an imposing stone" of the *Knoxville Register*, which until 19 July had been pluckily issuing dailies from its second-floor quarters on east Whitehall. The fire apparently persuaded the *Register* to move its operations out of town to Augusta, where it did not resume operations for at least another month. The *Appeal* thus remained the lone journalistic voice in Atlanta. Sherman, across the lines, commented on the paper's tenacity: "all newspapers have quit Atlanta except the Memphis Appeal. That, I suppose, is tired of moving...and wants to be left alone." Unshaken by the citizens' flight, the change in the Confederate army's high command, and the prevailing worries about the city's possible fall, the *Appeal* continued to bellow defiance against the Yankees. It also expressed its support for General Hood. Indeed, as opposed to Johnston, who had acquired a reputation for Fabian reluctance to combat the enemy, Hood was in fact popularly associated with "Stonewall" Jackson, whose battlefield victories had already earned for him a legendary status in the wartime South. Declared the *Appeal*:

---

[31] Gen. Thomas J. Wood to Col. J. S. Fullerton, 14 July 1864, *OR*, vol. 38, pt. 5, p. 138; Bragg to Davis, 15 July, *OR*, vol. 38, pt. 5, p. 881; Singer, "Confederate Atlanta," 256; Atlanta City Council Minutes, 18 July, Atlanta History Center.

Croakers, who three days ago were deploring the military strategy of Johnston, which lost us so much territory, are now lamenting the change, which substitutes Hood for our Fabius. Hood is too well known to be distrusted, and our whole army comprehends the necessity for the tenure of this city. Atlanta and its [railroad] connections are worth a battle.... If Atlanta were surrendered without a struggle, a howl of dismal satisfaction and of fiendlike joy would shake the capital of the North.... The greatest battle of the war will probably be fought in the vicinity of Atlanta. Its result determines that of the pending Northern Presidential election. If we are victorious, the Peace party will triumph: Lincoln's administration is a failure, and peace and Southern independence are the immediate results.... It is time perhaps that Stonewall Jacksonism had usurped the place of caution and strategy.... This war must end and the final battle be fought. Why not here, and even now, as well as at a later period?... God defends the right. His hand is the buckler and shield of the soldier who bravely maintains a cause as ours. True to ourselves, to justice and right, and we must triumph.[32]

The *Appeal*'s saber-rattling sentiment meant nothing to Sherman, who continued to hold the upper hand as his forces drew closer to Atlanta. By nightfall of 19 July, four of the nine divisions in Thomas's Army of the Cumberland had crossed Peachtree Creek in the face of resisting Rebel cavalry. Almost 3 miles southeast of the left of Thomas's lines—a gap that caused Sherman considerable concern—Schofield's troops camped at Judge James

---

[32] "Destructive Fire in Atlanta," *Memphis Appeal,* quoted in *Augusta Chronicle & Sentinel,* 24 July 1864; Sherman to Maj. Gen. George H. Thomas, 15 July, *OR,* vol. 38, pt. 5, p. 144; *Memphis Appeal,* [20 July], quoted in *New York Times,* 29 July 1864.

The *Register* may have stayed in Atlanta awhile after the Connally fire; the *New York Times* of 4 August quotes an *Atlanta Register* column of 26 July. On 19 August, the *Augusta Constitutionalist* noted that the transplanted Knoxville/Atlanta *Register* "will resume publication in this city in a few days." The *Constitutionalist* of 30 August congratulated the *Register* for its first number printed in Augusta on the 29th; and on 2 September observed that the *Register* "is in full blast."

After the war, the Connally Building fire gave rise to a local legend that the conflagration of 19 July had occurred during the actual bombardment of the city, 20 July–25 August. "During the Battle of Atlanta, July, 1864," as the *Atlanta Journal* mistakenly attested, "two of Sherman's men got through the Confederate lines and set fire to the building on the property to indicate the center of the city for the Union guns." When the proprietor, Dr. E. L. Connally died in 1930, the newspaper obituary commented that "in July, 1864, during the siege of Atlanta, the wooden building on the site, known even then as the Connally Building, was fired by spies from Sherman's army to mark the business center of Atlanta for bombardment" (*Romances of Atlanta Real Estate, Reprinted from the Atlanta Journal* [Atlanta: Sharp-Boylston Co., 1927] 37; "Dr. E.L. Connally, Beloved Physician and Leader of Atlanta Progress, Passes," *Atlanta Journal,* 17 March 1930).

Paden's plantation, now the site of Emory University. McPherson's three corps, having taken Decatur while Garrard's cavalry continued wrecking the Georgia Railroad, ended the day south and west of the town. More good news came in that night, when Sherman learned that a Union cavalry raid led by Major General Lovell Rousseau had succeeded in cutting the Atlanta-Montgomery rail connection near Opelika, Alabama. This reduced Atlanta's railroad supply system to one line, the Macon & Western.[33]

Sherman was determined to maintain his momentum. "The whole army will move on Atlanta by the most direct roads tomorrow, July 20, beginning at 5 a.m.," he ordered. That meant that Thomas's Army of the Cumberland would complete its crossing of Peachtree Creek and continue bearing down on Atlanta from the north. Schofield's XXIII Corps would approach from the northeast (via today's Briarcliff Road). And McPherson's Army of the Tennessee would continue its advance on the city from the east, tearing up the railroad as it progressed. Aware that Hood might launch an attack, he instructed Thomas, Schofield, and McPherson to "accept battle on anything like fair terms," although he suspected that any such blow would fall upon McPherson and Schofield, the weaker armies and the ones destroying Hood's eastward rail linkage. In fact, after receiving Thomas's assurance that Howard's IV Corps could by morning be in a position to aid a possibly embattled Schofield, Sherman rather liked the prospect of a pitched battle east of town. As he wrote Thomas, "with McPherson, Howard, and Schofield, I would have ample to fight the whole of Hood's army, leaving you to walk into Atlanta, capturing guns and everything."

What if Hood did not attack, though? The Union commander's plans for 20 July took in that eventuality, as well: "...but if the army reach within cannon-range of the city without receiving artillery or musketry fire he will halt, form a strong line, with batteries in position, and await orders. If fired on from the forts or buildings of Atlanta no consideration must be paid to the fact that they are occupied by families, but the place must be cannonaded without the formality of a demand." Sherman, in other words, as part of his vise on the Rebels, planned to

---

[33] Wilbur G. Kurtz, map and key, "Embattled Atlanta," *Atlanta Constitution*, 20 July 1930, 12–13; Davis, *Atlanta Will Fall*, 131–32; Castel, *Decision in the West*, 368 ("Good for Rousseau!" Sherman exclaimed); Evans, *Sherman's Horsemen*, 166. Dr. Evans calculates that Rousseau's horsemen wrecked 26 miles of track in east central Alabama, which the Confederates never repaired.

Sherman was insistent upon the thorough destruction of the Rebel railroads, and gave his cavalrymen particular orders on how to do it, as to Brigadier General Garrard, 20 July: "I want you to put your whole strength at this, and to do it quick and well...it is a matter of vital importance and must be attempted with great vigor. The importance of it will justify the loss of quarter of your command. Be prepared with axes, hatchets, and bars to tear up sections of track and make bonfires. When the rails are red hot they must be twisted. Burning will do for bridges and culverts, but not for ordinary track. Let the work be well done" (*OR*, vol. 38, pt. 5, p. 209).

use an artillery bombardment of Atlanta: not just the suburban homes and farm buildings that lay perilously close to the Confederate defensive perimeter, but the very heart of the city, with its stores, former factories, railroad depots, and intermingled residences, still inhabited by thousands of civilians. "My belief," Sherman wrote General Thomas on the evening of 19 July, "is we can approach from the east with certainty of getting within cannon reach of the town, in which case it cannot be held."[34]

[34] Sherman's Special Field Order 39, 19 July 1864, *OR,* vol. 38, pt. 5, p. 193; Sherman to Thomas, 19 July, *OR,* vol. 38, pt. 5, pp. 185–86; Castel, *Decision in the West,* 367–68.

4

SHERMAN'S SHELLING, 20 JULY–25 AUGUST

When General Sherman issued orders on 19 July 1864, that Atlanta "be cannonaded without the formality of a demand," he based his directive on two assumptions and one strong historical precedent.

The first assumption he voiced in a telegram to General Halleck on 20 July: "by the Atlanta papers we learned that...most of the newspapers and people have left Atlanta," implying that there were few civilians remaining in town. Sherman was only partly correct. Many Atlantans had departed the city in large numbers during May and June; probably less than half of the 17,000–20,000 people living in Atlanta before the campaign began remained after mid-July. More continued to leave after that, with big battles fought just outside the city and with Yankee shells fired into it. Yet many stayed. As late as 23 August the *Atlanta Intelligencer* guessed that one thousand families were left in the city, which would have meant (by the editorialist's math) four thousand individuals.

By some informed guesswork, then, we can estimate that at least 5,000 noncombatants—mostly women, children and the elderly—were living in Atlanta when Federal artillery began its bombardment of the city. One scholar, Mary Elizabeth Massey, has described the reasons for civilians staying inside a bombarded city: "primarily people who were too poor to flee, who had nowhere to go, or who for some reason did not want to leave and were willing to adjust to the [Federals'] occupation [if the city fell]. Some of these were refugees who had settled in Atlanta and who had decided that they had nothing to gain by running again."

General Sherman was shrewd enough to know that while "most of the...people have left Atlanta," innocent women and children likely remained in the city. Choosing to ignore them, the Northern commander was at least unconsciously if not deliberately deluding himself regarding the loss of life among noncombatants that his bombardment would cause.[1]

---

[1] Special Field Order 39, 19 July 1864, US War Department, *The War of the Rebellion: A Compilation of the Official Records of the Union and Confederate Armies,* 128 vols. (Washington, DC: Government Printing Office, 1880–1901) vol. 38, pt. 5, p. 193 (hereafter *OR* and all references will be to series 1 unless otherwise indicated); Sherman to Halleck, 20 July, *OR*, vol. 38, pt. 5, p. 195; "The Poor in Atlanta," *Atlanta Intelligencer*, 23 August; Mary Elizabeth Massey, *Refugee Life in the Confederacy* (Baton Rouge: Louisiana State University, 1964) 212 (on why civilians stayed in a bombarded Atlanta). Russell S. Bonds has more recently enumerated the categories of noncombatants who endured the Yankee shelling: "those

Sherman's second assumption lay in his statement to Thomas on 19 July, that if his artillery could get within range of Atlanta, "it cannot be held." Here, too, Sherman's thinking was faulty, as military history—not to mention his own soldierly experience—afforded few, if any instances of artillery bombardments alone bringing about the surrender of armed cities (as opposed to infantry siege tactics, denial of food and supplies to surrounded garrisons, etc.).

General Sherman should have remembered his own experience with city-shelling from the summer before. After the fall of Vicksburg, Grant sent Sherman to Jackson, Mississippi, to drive off the Rebel army that Joe Johnston had assembled there. In mid-July 1863 Sherman laid semi-siege to Johnston's position. Without trying to surround the Rebel forces, Sherman harassed and bloodied them in several ways: constant skirmishing along the front; occasional infantry sorties to test Johnston's lines and advance his own; cavalry raids into the enemy rear threatening Johnston's flow of supplies; and cannonading not only of the Rebels' trenches but, behind them, the city of Jackson itself. Union guns fired nearly 3,000 shells into town on 12 July 1863. On 14 July, Sherman ordered his rifled artillery to send a round into the city every five minutes. The Federal commander seemed proud of the work of his artillery when he wrote that "with plenty of ammunition I can make the town too hot to hold [Johnston]." In the end, the Confederates did indeed evacuate Jackson. But when they left, 17 July, it was not merely because Sherman's shelling had made the town "too hot"; Johnston had been cowed by Sherman's superior numbers, aggressive tactics, and unrelenting determination—in other words, the same combination of strengths that Sherman brought to Georgia in 1864, when he again faced Joe Johnston. Sherman was too smart to assume that only his bombardment of the city of Jackson had compelled Johnston's evacuation. Yet just as he had done at Jackson, Sherman would also predict to General Halleck on 7 August 1864 that he would "make the inside of Atlanta too hot to be endured." Here again, he would overestimate the power of an artillery barrage by itself to bring about the abandonment by Confederate forces of a partially populated city. Sherman may simply have intended to make downtown Atlanta a punishable hell for its inhabitants, one that was "too hot to be endured," but only simplistically could he make the claim that his bombardment would bring about the Rebels' evacuation of the city.[2]

---

with civic or other duties; those caring for the wounded or sick or old or very young; those with businesses or property they wanted to protect; those too poor or too frightened to leave; those with Union feeling; those with nowhere else to go" (Russell S. Bonds, *War Like the Thunderbolt: The Battle and Burning of Atlanta* [Yardley PA: Westholme Publishing, 2009] 213).

[2] Sherman to Thomas, 19 July, *OR*, vol. 38, pt. 5, pp. 185–86; Edwin C. Bearss, *The Siege of Jackson July 10–17, 1863* (Baltimore: Gateway Press, 1981) 84–89; Stephen Davis, *Atlanta Will Fall: Sherman, Joe Johnston and the Heavy Yankee Battalions* (Wilmington DE:

As for Sherman's strong historical precedent, American military history afforded plentiful instances of commanders deliberately ordering artillery fire upon civilian-occupied residences and commercial areas. As early as 1745, in King George's War, American colonial militia fired cannon into the town of Louisbourg, Nova Scotia. In early 1776, during the Revolutionary War, colonial artillery fired on British-held Boston; the 157 rounds directed on the city and its defenses on the night of 4 March were considered at the time a heavy barrage. Later, in October 1781, Washington himself pulled the first lanyard in the patriots' bombardment of Yorktown, as American and French shells damaged buildings and started fires in the city. The British did the same; General Sir Henry Clinton had cannonballs and red-hot shot fired upon the city of Charleston in April 1780 as his troops besieged the city. In the War of 1812, British troops did not have to bombard Washington; disorganized American troops in August 1814 gave it up too quickly. Later, in the Mexican War, Captain R. E. Lee directed General Winfield Scott's artillery in a cannonade of Vera Cruz—some 2,500 shells fired over three days in March 1847—on the garrison, buildings and civilian populace of the city.[3]

Sherman thus had abundant precedents in ordering his artillery to open fire on Atlanta. At the same time, military convention up to the time of the American Civil War generally prescribed no bombardment of a civilian populace without some warning, or the offer of suitable time for noncombatants' evacuation. In his orders of 19 July, Sherman deliberately contravened this practice when he directed that "the place must be cannonaded without the formality of a demand." Yet by spring 1864, the gentlemanly notion of fair warning before a city-bombardment had undergone a transformative weakening during the war. In its first two years, both sides observed a certain respect for civilian lives before shelling a town. In May 1862, Union naval captain S. Phillips Lee, commanding a gunboat flotilla on the Mississippi River, sent into Vicksburg a note demanding surrender of the town; then, when refused, Lee offered the mayor twenty-four hours to "remove the women and children beyond the range of our guns" before he opened an artillery bombardment. Prior to cannonading the Yankee garrison holding the US arsenal in Harpers Ferry, Virginia, in September 1862, Confederate major general Thomas J. Jackson sent in a demand for surrender and flag of truce to get the noncombatants out of town. Two months later, Union major general Edwin V. Sumner called upon the mayor of Fredericksburg, Virginia, to give up the city, warning that if refused his guns would open fire—

Scholarly Resources, 2001) 5–7; Sherman to Grant, 14 July 1863, and to Halleck, 7 August 1864, *OR,* vol. 24, pt. 2, p. 524; vol. 38, pt. 5, p. 408.

    [3] Fairfax Downey, *Sound of the Guns: The Story of American Artillery from the Ancient and Honorable Company to the Atom Cannon and Guided Missile* (New York: David McKay Company, 1955) 10, 36, 59, 106–107; Robert Leckie, *The Wars of America* (New York: HarperCollins, 1992) 198, 289.

but that they would grant sixteen hours "for removal from the city of women and children, the sick and wounded and aged, &c." In the end, on 11 December 1862, the Federals bombarded Fredericksburg, their 140 cannon raining several thousand shells into the Confederate city. Though most of the citizenry had evacuated, some Fredericksburghers huddled in their cellars as shot and shells riddled the town. Two civilians were killed in the barrage, but most damage was structural. One house was pocked with ninety-eight cannonball holes; the Episcopal Church steeple alone suffered twenty hits.

Other Union commanders ordered the bombardment of Southern cities as well. In August 1863, Union brigadier general Quincy A. Gillmore outside of Charleston, South Carolina, demanded that Confederate authorities evacuate Fort Sumter; if he received no response in four hours, he would begin shelling the city. By the time Gillmore's ultimatum reached Confederate General G. T. Beauregard, Union artillerymen had already begun fire. An indignant Beauregard protested the bombardment:

> Among nations not barbarous the usages of war prescribe that when a city is about to be attacked timely notice shall be given by the attacking commander, in order that noncombatants may have an opportunity for withdrawing beyond its limits. Generally the time allowed is from one to three days; that is, time for a withdrawal, in good faith, of at least the women and children. You, sir, give only four hours, knowing that your notice, under existing circumstances, could not reach me.... It would appear, sir, that despairing of reducing these works, you now resort to the novel measure of turning your guns against the old men, the women and children, and the hospitals of a sleeping city, an act of inexcusable barbarity...that you actually did open fire and throw a number of the most destructive missiles ever used in war into the midst of a city taken unawares, and filled with sleeping women and children, will give you a "bad eminence" in history, even in the history of this war.

In his reply, General Gillmore disputed Beauregard's charge that he had violated the "usages of civilized warfare." Especially significant to Gillmore, as he reminded the Confederate commander, was that Charleston lay under no siege (when defined as complete encirclement of a fortified place): "I will...call your attention to the well-established principle, that the commander of a place attacked, but not invested, having its avenues of escape open and practicable, has no right to expect any notice of an intended bombardment, other than that which is given by the threatening attitude of his adversary." Thus justified, Gillmore continued his bombardment of Charleston. Among the Union artillery was a huge 8-inch Parrott rifled cannon known as the "Swamp Angel," which fired from its emplacement on Morris Island 175-pound shells (some filled with "Greek fire," an incendiary fluid) a full 4 1/2 miles into the city. This made Gillmore's the longest-range bombardment of the war, so long-range that

Northern cannoneers aimed the "Swamp Angel" by compass-reading taken on the steeple of St. Michael's Episcopal Church. Other Morris Island batteries joined in Gillmore's bombardment, which waxed and waned for a year and half till Confederates evacuated Charleston in February 1865. During the period 11,000 to 22,000 shells rained down, destroying the lower portion of the city and forcing its inhabitants to flee. Charleston thus earned the sad honor of having endured the longest bombardment of any city in the American Civil War.[4]

Though even Gillmore had given a few hours' notice, from time to time Union forces had opened an artillery fire on civilian-inhabited places without formal notice of intent. As early as mid-November 1861, President Davis, in a message to Congress, complained that in the first months of the war Northern forces "have bombarded undefended villages without giving notice to women and children to enable them to escape" (although Davis did not identify specific instances). President Lincoln apparently approved of the bombardment of Southern cities. In late May 1862, when General George McClellan's Union army approached within sight of Richmond's church steeples, Lincoln wrote McClellan "Can you get near enough to throw shells into the city?" (McClellan never did.) Two weeks later, in June 1862 at Chattanooga, Union cannoneers under Brigadier General James S. Negley, engaging Confederate batteries in a three-hour artillery duel, fired a number of rounds into the city without warning to its citizenry. (A Federal officer reported, "our shells did terrible execution in the town, completely destroying many buildings, among others their commissary depot.") Thus as the war continued, and became progressively harder, there were at least a few instances of hostile artillery not giving "customary" notice of intention to bombard civilian-occupied areas. In spring 1863, the US Adjutant General's Office in Washington, with help from the legal

---

[4] Lee to Mayor L. Lindsay, 21 May 1862, *OR*, vol. 15, p. 13; Peter F. Walker, *Vicksburg: A People at War, 1861–1865* (Chapel Hill: University of North Carolina Press, 1960) 90–92; Jackson's orders, 14 September 1862, *OR*, vol. 19, pt. 2, p. 607; E. V. Sumner to mayor and common council of Fredericksburg, 21 November 1862, *OR*, vol. 21, p. 783; Edward J. Stackpole, *Drama on the Rappahannock: The Fredericksburg Campaign* (Harrisburg PA: Stackpole Company, 1957) 94; Thomas Rice, "Fredericksburg Under Fire: All the Imps of Hell Let Loose," *Civil War Times Illustrated* 22/4 (June 1983): 10–13; Gillmore-Beauregard correspondence, 21–22 August 1863, *OR*, vol. 28, pt. 2, pp. 57–60; E. Milby Burton, *The Siege of Charleston, 1861–1865* (Columbia: University of South Carolina Press, 1970) 251–52; Stephen R. Wise, *Gate of Hell: Campaign for Charleston Harbor, 1863* (Columbia: University of South Carolina Press, 1994) 169–72; James Goldy, "The Swamp Angel," *Civil War Times Illustrated* 28/2 (April 1989): 23–27; W. Chris Phelps, *The Bombardment of Charleston, 1863–1865* (Gretna LA: Pelican Publishing Co., 2002) 32–33, 151.

Roger Pinckney rightly uses the term "total war" in describing the Yankees' use of the Swamp Angel against the civilians of Charleston, as the big gun's shells were intended as much to wound and kill people as to destroy their property (Roger Pinckney, "Iron Angel of Death," *Civil War Times Illustrated* 38/5 [October 1999]: 66).

scholar Francis Lieber, issued a document that excused Federal officers from sending any warning at all of a proposed shelling. Through General Orders 100, dated 24 April 1863, "Instructions for the Government Armies of the United States in the Field" (which were approved by President Lincoln), the US War Department directed that "commanders, whenever admissible, [should] inform the enemy of their intention to bombard a place, so that the noncombatants, and especially the women and children, may be removed before the bombardment commences. *But it is no infraction of the common law of war to omit thus to inform the enemy. Surprise may be a necessity"* [italics added].

It is doubtful that Union field commanders paid any great attention to General Orders 100 or any similar document. Probably without having even read it, Major General Ulysses S. Grant in mid-May 1863 gave no warning to Confederate authorities at Vicksburg as he ordered his artillery and the river gunboats to open fire on Rebel fortifications and the town, when his army began its siege of the city. Typical of the orders given to Union gunners were these instructions, by Rear-Admiral David D. Porter to the commander of the gunboat *Benton*: "by shifting your 40-pounder to the bow, you can easily throw shell into the town. The object is to throw shell about the courthouse, if possible." In the ensuing bombardment of Vicksburg, intermittently continued until the surrender of the Confederate army garrison on 4 July, buildings throughout town were destroyed and probably five to ten Vicksburghers were killed (more wounded). In the month and a half of shelling, Grant's and Porter's batteries fired close to 75,000 rounds into the city (naval vessels alone fired 22,000). Commanding the XV Corps in Grant's army at the time, Major General W. T. Sherman participated in and directed part of the cannonading of the civilians and town. A Northern correspondent took particular note of Sherman's zest for the work, reporting in *Harper's Weekly* that "General Sherman seems to have a determined propensity to carry on the…war in a manner most offensive to the rebels. The last instance of his beneficence is a continued shelling of the 'Virgin City of Vicksburg'!"

On the other hand, the old rules were sometimes followed. When his cavalry approached Carlisle, Pennsylvania on the evening of 1 July 1863, Confederate major general "Jeb" Stuart sent in a demand for the surrender of the Northern garrison, threatening to bombard the town. The Southern officer bearing Stuart's note advised the Union commander, Major General William F. "Baldy" Smith, to evacuate the women and children. Smith saltily refused: "Shell away and be damned!" Stuart's artillery opened on the town, sending panicked civilians to their cellars. After a half hour the Confederate gunners ceased fire, and Stuart sent in another surrender demand. Smith again refused, and the Southern artillery resumed firing, well into the night. The shelling ended when Stuart led his troopers away to join General Lee's army at Gettysburg. Years later one of Stuart's officers, General Fitzhugh Lee, recalled that the Southerners had gone by the book: "it must be borne in mind that Carlisle was occupied by troops

& their commander refused to surrender it. Of course there was nothing left but to fight for it."

But such attention to protocol waned as the war went on. A year later Grant, promoted to lieutenant general, had gone to Virginia and taken overall command of Union operations against R. E. Lee's tough Rebel army. In mid-June 1864, with the opposing forces focused on Petersburg, south of Richmond, Grant—again, without warning—ordered the direct bombardment of the city. The artillery fire had been underway but a few days when Major General George G. Meade, commander of the Army of the Potomac (but serving under Grant's authority), wrote one of his corps commanders, "unless there is some military object other than mere annoyance of the enemy, I would prefer not shelling the town." The corps commander, Major General David Birney, replied, "shelling the town seems to compel the enemy to cease firing." Soon came the opinion of the army's chief of staff, Major General Andrew A. Humphreys, that "shelling the town to stop the firing of the enemy's batteries is a legitimate military operation, and may be resorted to whenever necessary." Humphreys's opinion provided further rationale—besides the US War Department's general orders of April 1863 and the simple fact that unannounced city-shellings had become the norm by this, the war's third year—for the Federals' continued bombardment of Petersburg. From mid-June 1864 until General R. E. Lee's army evacuated the city in early April 1865, Petersburg endured periodic Union artillery fire. The heaviest projectiles of any Civil War bombardment rained down on Petersburg and Lee's lines, including 220-pound shells fired from a huge 13-inch seacoast mortar nicknamed "the Dictator," which was mounted on a railroad flatcar. At the end of the war, a surveyor reported that more than 800 buildings in the town had been struck by whole projectiles; even more structures were damaged by shell fragments. In the northeast part of the city, nineteen out of every twenty buildings showed some sign of shellfire. (Despite this extensive structural damage, fewer than a half-dozen civilians were killed during the ten-month barrage.)[5]

---

[5] Gillmore to Beauregard, 22 August 1863, *OR*, vol. 28, pt. 2, p. 60; Davis to Congress, 18 November 1861, in Lynda Lasswell Crist, Mary Seaton Dix, and Kenneth H. Williams, eds., *The Papers of Jefferson Davis*, 12 vols. to date (Baton Rouge: Louisiana State University Press, 1971–) 7:416; Stephen W. Sears, *To the Gates of Richmond: The Peninsula Campaign* (New York: Ticknor & Fields, 1992) 110; Lincoln to McClellan, 26 May 1862. The Collected Works of Abraham Lincoln, 5:240; Brig. Gen. James S. Negley to "Gov." Andrew Johnson, 12 June 1862, and report of Col. H. A. Hambright, 8 June, *OR*, vol. 10, pt. 1, pp. 920–21; General Order 100, 24 April 1863, *OR*, ser. 3, vol. 3, p. 150; Walker, *Vicksburg*, 164–67, 203n4; Earl Schenck Miers, *The Web of Victory: Grant at Vicksburg* (New York: Alfred A. Knopf, 1955) 226–28; Porter to Lt.-Cmdr. James A. Greer, 19 May 1863, US Navy Department, *Official Records of the Union and Confederate Navies in the War of the Rebellion*, 31 vols. (Washington, DC: Government Printing Office, 1894–1922) vol. 25, p. 18 (hereafter *ORN*); *Harper's Weekly Magazine*, 16 May 1863, quoted in Walker, *Vicksburg*, 167; Eric J. Wittenberg, "The Shelling of Carlisle," *Blue & Gray* 24/2 (Summer 2007): 41–46; Meade to Birney, Birney

to Meade, and Humphreys to Birney, 20 June 1864, *OR,* vol. 40, pt. 2, p. 239; Noah Andre Trudeau, *The Last Citadel: Petersburg, Virginia, June 1864–April 1865* (Boston: Little, Brown and Company, 1991) 91–97, 422; James G. Scott and Edward A. Wyatt IV, *Petersburg's Story: A History* (Petersburg VA: Titmust Optical Company, 1960) 217–21. I thank Chris Calkins for providing me with this important source.

The shift in Northern officers' attitudes regarding bombardment of Southern cities parallels the hardening of Federal war practices from 1862 to 1864. Mark Grimsley describes the transition of Union policy from "conciliation" to "hard war" in *The Hard Hand of War: Union Military Policy toward Southern Civilians, 1861–1865* (New York: Cambridge University Press, 1995) 75-88. This and other scholarship has overturned the idea of the Civil War as a "total war"; see in particular Mark E. Neely, Jr., "Was the Civil War a Total War?," *Civil War History* 37/1 (March 1991): 5–28. Joseph Glatthaar, "Sherman's Army and Total War: Attitudes on Destruction in the Savannah and Carolinas Campaigns," *Atlanta Historical Bulletin* 29/1 [Spring 1985]: 41–52, is an example of the older perspective on "total" war.

In summer 1862, when many Northerners, both military and civilian, began to realize that harsher measures against the Rebels had become necessary, Sherman not only participated in the transition to "hard war," but by his rhetoric helped to lead the way. In July 1862, the US Congress called for the expropriation of Rebel property, including slaves (Steven V. Ash, *When the Yankees Came: Conflict and Chaos in the Occupied South, 1861–1865* [Chapel Hill: University of North Carolina Press, 1995] 150–51). That summer Union major general John Pope in Virginia ordered his troops to live off the land, issuing vouchers only to loyal citizens (Daniel E. Sutherland, "Abraham Lincoln, John Pope, and the Origins of Total War," *Journal of Military History* 56/4 [October 1992]: 577–78). The war grew harder, faster in the western theater. In Alabama, on 2 May 1862, after his brigade had occupied the town of Athens, Union colonel John Turchin announced he would shut his eyes for two hours so his men could pillage the people's stores and homes. Later Turchin justified the sack of Athens by saying, "I have tried to teach the rebels that treason to the Union was a terrible crime" (Roy Morris, Jr., "The Sack of Athens," *Civil War Times Illustrated* 24/10 [February 1986]: 26–31).

In this new, hard war, Rebels' property thus became a legitimate war aim of Union forces. But the deliberate killing of Rebels themselves—the distinction between hard war (against property) and total war (against people), was very distinct, and the latter was firmly off-limits—except in the mind of William T. Sherman. In July 1862, as military governor of Memphis, he had become so angry at guerrilla marauding that Sherman ordered the burning of Randolph, Tennessee, in reprisal (Clay Mountcastle, *Punitive War: Confederate Guerrillas and Union Reprisals* [Lawrence: University Press of Kansas, 2009] 75–76). As the "logical" next step, Sherman began to envision the murder of Southern civilians as a necessity to end the war more quickly. "The war will soon assume a turn to extermination," he wrote his wife Ellen on 31 July, "not of soldiers alone, that is the least part of the trouble, but the People" (Brooks D. Simpson and Jean V. Berlin, eds., *Sherman's Civil War: Selected Correspondence of William T. Sherman, 1860–1865* [Chapel Hill: University of North Carolina Press, 1999] 261).

To be sure, there was an obvious difference between Sherman's bark and his bite, but the dangerous element of the former is that whenever he wrote such outrageous statements, Sherman knew that he was making an outrageous place in history for himself—

Sherman's bombardment of Atlanta, which began just a month after Grant's guns turned on Petersburg, thus had numerous predecessors, if not justifiers. If Sherman needed further context, he could have compared his situation, north of Atlanta in July 1864, with Quincy Gillmore's south of Charleston in August 1863. Gillmore reminded General Beauregard that Charleston lay under no siege, and as such its people needed no extensive warning of impending bombardment. In other words, Charlestonians knew the Yankees were coming, and could have gotten out anytime. On the evening of 19 July, Atlantans could see Sherman's armies threatening the city in the same way, but at a distance. The closest Union force, Wood's division of the IV Corps, was 3 3/4 miles north of downtown, and fully 2 miles outside the Confederates' fortified perimeter. Schofield and McPherson were farther, 3 miles from the city's main defensive line. Moreover, the Federals' 7-mile arced line to the north and northeast of the city left open not only the major rail line out of the city to East Point, but all of Atlanta's southbound wagon roads free for traffic. The city was therefore certainly not invested, and most of its avenues of escape out and supply in, to use Gillmore's words, were very much open and practicable. Sherman, to use his later words,

---

and he did not care. Thus in June 1864 he asserted to Secretary of War Stanton, "there is a class of people, men, women, and children, who must be killed or banished before you can hope for peace and order" (Sherman to Stanton, 21 June 1864, *OR*, vol. 39, part 2, p. 132). The civilians remaining in Atlanta as Sherman's armies approached would have fit both categories, Rebel noncombatants too bold and defiant to flee the city, and therefore needing to be killed or banished from their homes by a general artillery bombardment of the city.

Mark Grimsley has pointed out that the US army did in fact adopt a policy of total war—not against Southern civilians in the Civil War, but against the Plains Native Americans in the decades afterward ("'Rebels' and 'Redskins': U.S. Military Conduct toward White Southerners and Native Americans in Comparative Perspective," in *Civilians in the Path of War*, ed. Mark Grimsley and Clifford J. Rogers [Lincoln: University of Nebraska Press, 2002] 137–61). It should be noted that when the United States army waged a war of extermination against the Native Americans, William T. Sherman was its general-in-chief, with the result that he was thus finally able to carry out the killing of noncombatants that he had talked about during the Civil War. "We must act with vindictive earnestness against the Sioux," he wrote in December 1866, "even to their extermination, men, women, and children. Nothing less will reach the root of the case." Quoting this statement, Evan S. Connell comments, "If one word of this extraordinary telegram is altered it reads like a message from Eichmann to Hitler" (Connell, *Son of the Morning Star: Custer and the Little Bighorn* [San Francisco: North Point Press, 1984] 132).

Connell is not alone in perceiving a theoretical link between Sherman's rhetoric and wartime atrocities. The point is the basis of James Reston, Jr.'s *Sherman's March and Vietnam* (New York: MacMillan Publishing Co., 1969). More recently, John A. Tures, who teaches at LaGrange College in Georgia, argues that Sherman's policies against Southern civilians and Plains Native Americans set precedent for the notorious abuses by US service personnel at Abu Ghraib prison in Iraq (Tures, "Civilians Were Sherman's Targets," *Atlanta Journal-Constitution*, 18 July 2004).

thus had "the books" on his side when he ordered no warning of his proposed city-shelling.

Further, from Milton Glass's and J. C. Moore's spy-reports on Atlanta's trenchworks, the Union commander probably knew that suburban homes mixed indiscriminately with the Rebel army's fortified lines. Confederates confirmed it. "My position was chosen near a new and beautiful residence on the Atlanta and Decatur road," wrote Captain Thomas J. Key, commander of an Arkansas battery in Hardee's corps on 19 July. "This residence, nearly completed and newly painted, was constructed in the Gothic style. It contained about ten rooms and looked as fresh as a young bride. Since the line of battle runs within fifty paces of this palace, all the adornments are already destroyed, and if the Yankees attack us here they will doubtless burn it with their shells." Then, too, if sharpshooters positioned themselves in such houses, the structures would become immediate targets for artillery. Both sides did it. Just the month before, for instance, near Kennesaw Mountain, after Union marksmen began firing from the York house on the Burnt Hickory road, Confederate gunners bore on the place with "hot shot," cannonballs deliberately heated to start fires.[6]

This kind of propinquity (civilian houses close to trench lines) and mixed identity (residences as snipers' nests) obviously invited the cannonading of at least suburban homes. For this reason alone Sherman foresaw the inevitability of citizens' homes becoming military targets—hence his orders for a bombardment of the city altogether if the Rebels fired on his forces "from the forts or buildings of Atlanta."

There was little doubt that the Rebels would do so. On 20 July, Confederate cavalrymen, with some infantry support, had been contesting the Union advance for the past four days; as Sherman's forces got closer to the Rebel lines they encountered more intense fire. And get closer they did. While Thomas's army completed its crossing of Peachtree Creek on the morning of 20 July and extended its left (Major General David S. Stanley's division) so as to connect with Schofield, McPherson's three corps were marching along the Atlanta–Decatur roads. Major General John A. Logan's XV Corps and Major General Frank P. Blair's XVII Corps struck Wheeler's cavalrymen east of the city. Digging in, using artillery, the Southerners fought hard, but heavily outnumbered, were forced back from position to position. At one point Union brigadier general Walter Q. Gresham, commanding Blair's advance division, ventured too close to his skirmish line and caught a minie ball in his lower left leg. "It's too bad, Gresham," Blair later said. "I was racing John Logan to get into Atlanta and you

[6] Davis, *Atlanta Will Fall*, 132 (map, situation, 19 July); Wirt Armistead Cate, ed., *Two Soldiers: The Campaign Diaries of Thomas J. Key, C.S.A., December 7, 1863–May 17, 1865 and Robert J. Campbell, U.S.A. January 1, 1864–July 21, 1864* (Chapel Hill: University of North Carolina Press, 1938) 90; Wilbur G. Kurtz, "Fort Hood and the Ponders House," *Atlanta Constitution Magazine*, 1 June 1930, 14.

go and get shot." For his part, even at the cautious rate of a mile every three hours, Logan made such headway that by noon his troops, pushing toward town, had gotten roughly to where today's Whitefoord Avenue intersects Boulevard. The day was hot and clear; already Union troops could see the chimneys and church steeples downtown, 2 1/2 miles away. Around one o'clock, the gunners in Captain Francis DeGress' Battery H, 1st Illinois Light Artillery, after unlimbering on a hill (at Whitefoord and Hosea Williams Drive), trained their 20-pounder Parrott rifles. "At 1 o'clock fired three shells into Atlanta at a distance of two miles and a half," DeGress later reported, adding proudly, "the first ones of the war." General Logan, in the friendly rivalry against the XVII Corps that Frank Blair had mentioned that morning, was clearly pleased that the "honor" of the first city-bound shells went to his gunners: "several of his [DeGress's] shots were observed by the signal officer of the corps to strike some buildings in the town. These were acknowledged to be the first shots from the army which had entered the city of Atlanta."[7]

The Federal shells exploded downtown. According to a reporter from the *Macon Telegraph*, on the afternoon of 20 July one shell struck the W & A depot; two others hit the Female Institute Hospital at Collins and Ellis; "and several others fell in different parts of the city." Other witnesses reported differently on where the shells exploded. The Right Reverend Henry C. Lay, Episcopal bishop of Arkansas, happened on 20 July to be staying at the home of Mr. and Mrs. William Solomon, just across the street from city hall square. "On the 20th affairs began to look very serious—all the roads and streets were filled with the wagons hastening at double quick to the rear," Lay wrote his wife. "At midday they [the Federals] were very close. A shell came whizzing and fell on the square next to me—and soon others fell not far from the depot."[8]

---

[7] Wilbur G. Kurtz, "Walter Q. Gresham at Atlanta," *Atlanta Constitution Magazine*, 24 August 1930, 21; Wilbur G. Kurtz, "Map showing positions of the 17th Corps during afternoon & evening of July 20th, 1864," accompanying Kurtz, "Gresham at Atlanta," *Atlanta Constitution Magazine*, 24 August 1930; Albert Castel, *Decision in the West: The Atlanta Campaign of 1864* (Lawrence: University Press of Kansas, 1992) 371; DeGress's report, 1 September 1864, *OR*, vol. 38, pt. 3, p. 265; report of Maj. Gen. John A. Logan, 13 September, *OR*, vol. 38, pt. 3, p. 102.

Among Sherman's troops word spread that their commander had followed the old protocols. "It is reported," wrote Illinois Pvt. James Snell in his diary "that Sherman has ordered the citizens and noncombatants of Atlanta to leave, or take the consequences!" (James P. Snell, diary, 21 July 1864, Illinois Historical Society, copy courtesy Dr. Albert Castel, Columbus OH).

[8] "From the Front," *Macon Telegraph*, 22 July 1864 (also quoted in *Augusta Chronicle & Sentinel*, 23 July); Bishop Lay to wife, 18, 22 July 1864, in Henry Champlin Lay Papers, 1841–1885, MSS418, Southern Historical Collection, University of North Carolina at Chapel Hill; Wilbur G. Kurtz map, "Environs of the present State Capitol and City Hall, Atlanta, Ga.," *Atlanta Historical Bulletin* 8/30 (October 1945): 32 (on location of Solomon house).

These first Northern shells apparently inflicted no casualties. Dr. George Peddy, writing from an "Infirmry in Atlanta" on 21 July told his wife that "a few shells were thrown into Atlanta yesterday," but mentioned no victims. The first newspaper reports of the shelling of 20 July also made no reference to anyone hurt. On 22 July, the *Macon Telegraph* reported that "quite a number" of refugees had come down on the train from Atlanta to get away from the bombardment. They told of the shelling of the 20th, and where the first shells had exploded, but gave no word of civilian casualties. Correspondent Felix de Fontaine, writing from Atlanta on the evening of 22 July and the following morning, recorded that despite the numerous enemy shells being hurled into the city, he had heard of "many narrow escapes made, but I hear as yet of no loss of life."[9]

This journalistic silence, plus the assumption that the press would have dramatically headlined the tragedy of any civilian maimed or murdered by Sherman's first artillery explosives, leads one to discredit one of the Atlanta Campaign's well-known legends. Not until a quarter-century after the war did Atlantan Er Lawshe claim to have witnessed the explosion of the very first Union projectile, and that it had killed a child. The *Atlanta Constitution* first published Lawshe's recollection in a column that was reprinted in the *Kennesaw Gazette*, 15 October 1888, under the title, "The First Shell Fired into Atlanta."

> In a conversation with Mr. Er Lawshe the other day, early history and war history were subjects under discussion…. Mr. Lawshe stated he distinctly remembered seeing the shell strike the ground at the intersection of Ellis and Ivy Streets. There were near the intersection at the time a man, a woman and a child, and when the cloud of dust and smoke, raised by the falling and bursting of the shell, had partly cleared away, it was seen that the child was seriously, if not fatally, wounded. It proved afterwards to be fatally. Mr. Lawshe was standing at the intersection of Peachtree and Ellis Streets, and distinctly saw the shell fall and heard it explode. He also remembers, with equal distinctiveness, that the explosion occurred about 2:30 p.m., of July 20, 1864…. Two other shells came into Atlanta the same afternoon, one of which fell near the Atlanta Medical college, and the other near the Washington Hall, now the Markham House, and both about six o'clock.

To Lawshe's "distinct" remembrance of Sherman's first shell and its young victim, the *Constitution* added corroboration: "Colonel Sam Williams… remembers, with equal distinctness, that there were three shells fired into Atlanta

---

[9] George Peddy Cuttino, ed., *Saddle Bag and Spinning Wheel, Being the Civil War Letters of George W. Peddy, M.D., Surgeon, 56th Georgia Volunteer Regiment, C.S.A. and his Wife Kate Featherston Peddy* (Macon GA: Mercer University Press, 1981) 268; "From the Front" and "Refugees," *Macon Telegraph*, 22 July 1864; "F.G. de F.," "From the Army of Tennessee" (Atlanta, 23 July, 10 A.M.), *Savannah Republican*, 27 July.

on the afternoon of July 20 and that the first one fired killed a child." Notwithstanding the allegers' certainty, and the newspaper's obliging credulity, the Lawshe/Williams recollection must be judged as false. To be sure, both men were probably in Atlanta in July 1864. Two years before the war Lawshe's downtown jewelry store stood on Whitehall between Alabama and Hunter; his residence was listed in the city directory as on Peachtree between Ellis and Cain. Lieutenant Colonel S. C. Williams commanded artillery in Stewart's Corps during the Atlanta Campaign. But their failure to come forth with their story for over two decades, the absence of other witnesses to this alleged first shell at Ellis and Ivy, and the failure of anyone during the bombardment to attempt to name the alleged child victim and its grieving parents, all dismiss the Lawshe/Williams recollection.

Wallace Reed, author of the first postbellum history of Atlanta (1889), however, fully accepted his townsmen's story. Reed worked for the *Constitution* and in his city history related the same particulars as the newspaper column: "The first shell fell at the intersection of East Ellis and Ivy Streets, where it exploded and killed a little child which was with its parents at the time. The shell was seen to fall by Mr. Er Lawshe, and the fact is confirmed by Colonel Samuel Williams, who at the time was in command of a regiment of artillery confronting Sherman's army to the eastward of the city. Two other shells fell later in the afternoon of the same day." A few years later, in 1895, other Atlantans repeated the story. When the United Confederate Veterans came to town in their annual reunion, a local committee prepared a pamphlet and map showing wartime sites that the aging soldiers could visit. Site 33 was the "Corner Ellis and Ivy, point where first shell fell, killing a child, July 20th." A few years after that another Atlantan, Thomas H. Martin, repeated the Lawshe legend in his history of the city. In October 1919, when the UCV was again meeting in Atlanta, *Constitution* writer E. C. Bruffey composed a lengthy history of the siege of Atlanta, including mention of "the first shell" whose "explosion killed a child."

As with all folklore, repeated retellings allowed narrators to embellish their material, adding new bits to the story, changing others. Thus did Martin have the first Northern shell fall on the morning of 20 July, not the afternoon. Paul W. Miller, in his history of Atlanta (1947), became the first writer to identify the slain child as "a little girl" (although, as we have seen, the original *Constitution* article mentions only a "child"). Surely the most vivid colorist, however, is A. A. Hoehling, whose *Last Train from Atlanta* (1958) may be said to have brought local history—several Atlantans' recollections, perpetuated by fellow Atlantans—to the national stage.

> Shortly before noon, Er Lawshe, of Atlanta, was crossing Ivy and East Ellis streets, past the home of H. Muhlenbrink.... The day had become humid. Lawshe mopped his brow as he hurried along, noticing as he did so a small girl and her parents walking by [Frank] Rice's place, on

the northwest corner, directly opposite him. He did not recognize the trio and assumed them to be refugees.

Suddenly, there was a rattle and whish of air just over his head. In the next instant, he was deafened and stunned by an explosion and enveloped in a choking cloud of dust. When he could see again, the child was in the middle of the intersection, lying on her face, in a welling puddle of blood. Her mother and father, dazed, were struggling to their feet.

Lawshe gasped, finding it difficult to believe the first shell had fallen on Atlanta, and that he had been but yards away from it. When he reached the little girl's side, he could see she was dead.

Other citizens were hastening towards the intersection of Ivy and East Ellis, attracted by the blast and the brown cloud of dust and smoke now slowly dissipating over the rooftops.

Without trying to name the slain child (here again, assumed to be a little girl) or her parents, and without finding the names of the Atlantans "hastening" to the scene of the tragedy, Hoehling accepts and embellishes the old Lawshe legend. He even dedicated his book "To the memory of the little girl who fell at the corner of Ivy and East Ellis streets, July 20, 1864."[10] This kind of drama is effective (and may have been a clever marketing ploy for his book). Since Hoehling, the little girl's death by the first Union shell has been accepted by almost every major writer on the Atlanta Campaign, scholarly and popular alike: Clauss (1965), Carter (1973), Bailey (1985) [not content with the original fable, Bailey states that the little girl was walking her dog with her parents when she was "killed instantly"]; McDonough and Jones (1987), Cannan (1991), even Castel (1992) and Kennett (1995). The tide may be turning. Recently, fellow Atlantan

---

[10] *Atlanta Constitution*, n.d., "The First Shell Fired into Atlanta," reprinted in *Kennesaw Gazette*, 15 October 1888; *Williams' Atlanta Directory*, 112 (Lawshe's jewelry store and residence); *OR*, vol. 38, pt. 3, p. 667 (on Lt. Col. Williams); Wallace P. Reed, *History of Atlanta, Georgia, with Illustrations and Biographical Sketches of Some of Its Prominent Men and Pioneers* (Syracuse NY: D. Mason & Co., 1889) 175; "Battles of Atlanta. Short Sketch of the Battles Around, Siege, Evacuation and Destruction of Atlanta, Ga., 1864...prepared under the direction of the Committee of the Atlanta Camp, United Confederate Veterans" (Atlanta: n.p., 1895) 10; Thomas H. Martin, *Atlanta and Its Builders: A Comprehensive History of the Gate City of the South*, 2 vols. (Atlanta: Century Memorial Publishing Company, 1902) 1:499; E. C. Bruffey, "The Siege of Atlanta—and Afterwards," *Atlanta Constitution Magazine*, 5 October 1919; Paul W. Miller, ed., *Atlanta Capital of the South* (New York: Oliver Durrell, 1947) 17; A. A. Hoehling, *Last Train from Atlanta* (New York: Thomas Yoseloff, 1958) [5], 113.

Russell S. Bonds (2009) agrees with me that the legend of the little girl most likely was a postwar fabrication.[11]

Whether or not Sherman's first shells killed anybody, they surely provoked a general commotion. If only three, maybe half a dozen, artillery shots fell into downtown on 20 July, the effect among the citizenry was still immediate. A Confederate officer, Captain J. P. Austin, was downtown that afternoon. He remembered later finding

> the city in a wild state of excitement. Citizens were running in every direction. Terror-stricken women and children went screaming about the streets seeking some avenue of escape from hissing, bursting shells, as they sped on their mission of death and destruction. Perfect pandemonium reigned near the union depot. Trunks, bedclothing and wearing apparel were scattered in every direction. People were striving in every conceivable way to get out of town with their effects.

Austin may have embroidered this scene when he published his recollections a generation after the war (as a postwar Atlantan, he used the later name "Union Depot" for the wartime Car Shed). Nonetheless, it cannot be denied that the shells that fell upon the city on the first day of the Yankees' bombardment had a decided effect upon Atlanta's citizenry. Some Confederates, later captured, reported to Federals that their shells on 20 July produced "great consternation" within the city. A soldier in the 9th Tennessee, Van Buren Oldham, fighting with Cheatham's division, recorded in his diary for 21 July that the "few citizens left behind are woefully scared."[12]

The fear among the citizens on the afternoon of 20 July was due not only to the first Yankee shells inside the city, but heavy battle just outside of it. Around 4 o'clock that afternoon, the loudest sounds yet to be heard boomed through the city: General Hood was attacking Thomas's Army of the Cumberland north of the city, near Peachtree Creek. Wagons bringing in wounded from the field that

---

[11] Errol MacGregor Clauss, "The Atlanta Campaign, 18 July–2 September 1864 (Ph.D. diss., Emory University, 1965) 72; Samuel Carter III, *The Siege of Atlanta, 1864* (New York: St. Martin's Press, 1973) 200–201; Ronald H. Bailey, *Battles for Atlanta: Sherman Moves East* (Alexandria VA: Time-Life Books, 1985) 95; James Lee McDonough and James Pickett Jones, *War So Terrible: Sherman and Atlanta* (New York: W. W. Norton & Company, 1987) 209; John Cannan, *The Atlanta Campaign, May–November 1864* (Conshohocken PA: Combined Books, 1991) 114; Castel, *Decision in the West*, 378; Lee Kennett, *Marching through Georgia: The Story of Soldiers and Civilians during Sherman's Campaign* (New York: HarperCollins, 1995) 125; Bonds, *War Like the Thunderbolt*, 434–35.

[12] J. P. Austin to parents, in Austin, *The Blue & Gray* (Atlanta: Franklin Publishing Co., 1899) 131; endorsement of Maj. Gen. J. M. Palmer to report of Brig. Gen. J. C. Davis and Thomas to Sherman, 21 July 1864, *OR*, vol. 38, pt. 5, pp. 213, 217; Christopher Losson, *Tennessee's Forgotten Warriors: Frank Cheatham and His Confederate Division* (Knoxville: University of Tennessee Press, 1989) 186.

evening further shook or sickened the populace. Sorting out what happened, straining to learn which side won, Atlanta's citizenry leaped upon every rumor or scrap of news from the battlefront. After nightfall, the story on the day's battle at Peachtree Creek must have taken the somber tone expressed in two Confederates' communiqués: "10 P.M. We have had some sharp fighting on the lines today resulting I fear in no good to us. I had heard of some successes but most places we failed to accomplish anything" (Lieutenant A. J. Neal to his father); "11 p.m. At 3 o'clock to-day a portion of Hardee's and Stewart's corps drove the enemy into his breast-works, but did not gain possession of them. Our loss slight" (General J. B. Hood to Secretary Seddon).

From the swirl of hearsay, the *Appeal* tried to make sense of the battle, but its printed account gave readers the same mix of disconnected anecdote, unconfirmed rumor and patriotic bravado they could have gotten at the street corners. "General Hood determined to attack their left, and Stewart's and Hardee's corps were ordered to advance upon them. The order to advance was received by the men with the wildest enthusiasm, and no sooner was the order given than the men swept forward with a yell such as only a Confederate can give," the *Appeal* recounted, "and the enemy's skirmishers were soon encountered and driven back upon the main line, where temporary works had been erected. Our men never faltered but dashed forward through the leaden rain and drove the enemy in disorder from the works, capturing a number of prisoners. The Yankees were driven back over a mile.... Our loss is small." The *Appeal* story, based on the best sources it could muster, was nonetheless inaccurate in surveying the battle and its outcome. Thomas's troops had no earthworks along much of their defensive line, and though the Southerners pushed the Federals back in places, they failed to drive the enemy from the battlefield. At the end of the day, Confederates had had to withdraw back into their outer trench line. Hood's attack at Peachtree Creek had been repulsed, with Confederate casualties numbering about 2,500 killed, wounded, and missing; Federal losses totaled roughly 1,900.[13]

On 21 July, burial parties under arranged truce roamed the battlefield, interring the slain of both sides in shallow graves, and searching for wounded who had not been retrieved from the field. A Michigan soldier chanced upon a Rebel who proved to be a woman. "She was shot in the breast & through the thy & was still alive & as gritty as any reb I ever saw"; she was taken to a US field hospital. Interring their comrades, burial crews tried to mark soldiers' identities. "We buried the dead in the rear of the line where they fought," wrote Sergeant Rice C. Bull of the 123rd New York. "Where it was known, a headboard was

---

[13] A. J. Neal to "Pa," 20 July 1864, box 1, folder 6, Andrew Jackson Neal Letters, Emory University; Hood to J. A. Seddon, 20 July, *OR*, vol. 38, pt. 5, p. 894; *Memphis Appeal*, quoted in *Augusta Chronicle & Sentinel*, 23 July 1864; Castel, *Decision in the West*, 375–81; Davis, *Atlanta Will Fall*, 135.

placed with name of the dead and his Company and Regiment." Confederates did the same for their fallen comrades. After the battle, a Northern cavalryman remarked upon "a graveyard of a Mississippi brigade into which they had gathered their fallen, burying the men of each regiment in a row, in separate graves, and marking the number of the regiment on a piece of board." Yet in burying enemy soldiers, both sides paid far less attention to dignity; commonly most bodies were laid in shallow pits, side by side in long lines, with only a thin covering of dirt over them. Unfortunately, this eventually washed away. A week and a half after the battle of 20 July, Union horsemen rode through the area of the graves. "Most of the Confederate dead," observed Lieutenant William Doyle of Indiana, "were partially exposed from the rains, they having been barely covered with earth. In many instances no trench was dug at all, when the body lay on a hillside. Then they dug earth from the upper side and threw upon it." Several weeks later the situation was even worse, as noted by a Federal whose regiment marched over the battlefield one night in late August: "notwithstanding more than a month's time had gone by since the fighting of that sanguinary battle, the stench, as borne to us by the midnight air, was awfully offensive, almost strangling to us."[14]

Such was the eventual effluvia of the battlefield of Peachtree Creek. Thomas's lines remained static on 21 July, as Federals strengthened their positions with earthworks. Confederates fortified, too, north of the city. Aware that he would soon have to withdraw from Johnston's outer line of works, Hood had his chief engineer, Colonel Stephen Presstman, hard at work strengthening the northernmost sections of the city's perimeter of defenses all day on 21 July. General Johnston had begun some of this work after retreating across the Chattahoochee and manning his outer line on 10 July; Johnston had ordered the five artillery forts sited by Captain Grant northwest of the city to be connected by trenchlines in a new salient. The Yankee spy, Moore, had attested to seeing CS engineers direct slaves digging the works a week earlier. By 21 July, this labor was still incomplete. Hood ordered it rushed, as he planned for his army that night to abandon its outer lines and withdraw into the city's defensive perimeter. Furthermore, to the northeast Hood and Presstman found that the line established by Captain Grant and apparently approved by General Johnston was "not only too close to the city and located upon too low ground, but was totally inadequate for the purpose designed." Hood therefore ordered "an entirely new line, and upon more elevated ground" staked out and hurriedly dug—a new

[14] Castel, *Decision in the West*, 385; K. Jack Bauer, ed., *Soldiering: The Civil War Diary of Rice C. Bull, 123rd New York Volunteer Infantry* (San Rafael CA: Presidio Press, 1978) 152; David Evans, *Sherman's Horsemen: Union Cavalry Operations in the Atlanta Campaign* (Bloomington: Indiana University Press, 1996) 216; William Henry Newlin, comp., *A History of the Seventy-Third Regiment of Illinois Infantry Volunteers* (Springfield IL: Regimental Reunion Association, 1890) 341.

northeastern salient adding hundreds of feet of entrenchments and two artillery forts to Captain Grant's original perimeter. This eleventh-hour construction, 10–22 July, lengthened Grant's original 10.5-mile perimeter to more than 12.

The Confederates' earthwork-building dislocated more suburban Atlantans. The family of Jeremiah Huff was living on the Marietta Road, close to the Niles house, when Confederate officers came. "After laying off a line of battle between the 'big house' and the thirty foot-away log kitchen," young Sarah Huff recalled, they "commanded my weeping mother to leave immediately." The family packed up hurriedly and carried its goods into town. Sarah's father Jeremiah was in the army serving in Virginia, so Sarah's mother had to oversee the move. In the commotion she lost a good deal of farm property, as she bitterly recorded:

> I move to town the most of my stuff though I had to leve lots. They staked off the battle line across my garden then betwene my house and kitchen they told me I had better get away from there if I wanted to save any thing and that Evening, too, for our boys would [be] back there that night. I had sent part of my stuff to Town so I took 2 more loads and left. I lost both my cows and calves. The calves our soldiers killed one night. I tell you they took my crop and stock—only my mules I have got them yet. I never got more than $200 for it all. I couldnt get any wheat thrashed so I lost that or most of it. They took my oats. I had to carry a few in my house to save any of them to feed my mules with.

With the army's engineering activity very evident, other Atlantans began to worry that their land, too, like the Huffs', might be expropriated. George G. Hull, superintendent of the Atlanta & West Point Railroad, whose house cornered on Cain and Peachtree, was out of town when he received a dispatch saying the army's trench line was being dug through his yard. This proved to be a false alarm; the Hulls' two-story frame house and gardens were well within the city limits, and away from the Grant-Presstman fortifications.[15]

Not so fortunate was Mrs. Ellen Ponder, whose two-story white stucco home, elegantly landscaped with boxwood and hedge-apple trees, was sited on high ground along the Marietta Road, 1 ½ miles out from the center of town.

---

[15] J. B. Hood, *Advance and Retreat: Personal Experiences in the United States and Confederate States Armies* (New Orleans: Hood Orphan Memorial Fund, 1880) 173–74; report of Gen. Thomas J. Wood, 14 July 1864, *OR,* vol. 38, pt. 5, p. 138; Sarah Huff, *My Eighty Years in Atlanta* (Atlanta: n.p., 1937) 22; E. M. A. Huff to "Mr. Henry," 12 September 1864, in Wilbur G. Kurtz, notebook 11, 79, Wilbur G. Kurtz Collection, Atlanta History Center; McDonough and Jones, *War So Terrible,* 273 ("Lieutenant Jeremiah Huff, serving in Virginia"); *Williams' Atlanta Directory,* 105; "From Atlanta" (*re* "G. Hull, Esq."), *Augusta Chronicle & Sentinel,* 24 July; Lucy Baldwin, typescript autobiography, MS 849, University of North Carolina at Chapel Hill.

Mrs. Ponder herself—divorced several years from Ephraim, the planter and slave trader—had refugeed to the south, so no one inhabited the house when Confederate engineers and work crews came to strengthen the nearby artillery fort, dubbed at some point Fort Hood. The house itself, brick and plaster, stood indomitably amid the fervent work, but the frame dependencies around it, which Mr. Ponder had built on his grounds, were more vulnerable. Workmen stripped the boards away, and fitted them into their parapets, or stuck them in the ground out in no-man's-land as palisade protection from infantry sorties.[16]

Having just won a smart defensive victory at Peachtree Creek, Sherman was of no mind to attack Hood's obviously elaborate fortifications. He did, however, want McPherson's army to continue advancing on the city from the east, while Thomas fortified his line south of Peachtree Creek and extended his left toward a connection with Schofield, whose corps was also advancing in on the city from the northeast. "Good results will flow from your pressing hard," Sherman wrote McPherson on the night of 20 July. Sherman's desire to shell the town was also evident in his prodding of McPherson. Several hours later, at 1:00 A.M. that night, he then sent another message: "I deem it necessary that you should gain ground so that your artillery can reach the town easily." McPherson had his troops east of the city ready to move early. Around 7:00 A.M. Union artillery opened on Wheeler's cavalry, dug in on a "bald" hill south of the Georgia Railroad. General Blair ordered a division of infantrymen to charge and take the position, which they did. (In so doing they bestowed to the hill the name of their commander, Brigadier General Mortimer Leggett—although not much today is left of Leggett's Hill, cut away and bisected at Moreland Avenue by Interstate Highway 20.) By 9:00 A.M., the Rebels were driven back and the place was secure. The Federals began digging in, and as Confederates had done in building their works, Northern soldiers stripped wood planking from houses and sheds to shore up their earthen parapets. Henry Spear, who owned a farm on Leggett's Hill, had his house torn down; Yankees used its timbers in their trenches.

Leggett quickly had a battery of artillery stationed on the hill, which was about 2 1/4 miles from the center of the city. "Before 9 a.m. of that day I had a battery in position and threw shells into Atlanta," Leggett reported. His superior officer, Frank Blair, proudly echoed the accomplishment, knowing that the commanding general would be pleased: "before 9 a.m. of the 21st General Leggett had placed a battery in position on the hill and threw shell into Atlanta." Like the shells fired by DeGress's battery into the city on 20 July, these too evidently inflicted no casualties. That evening, "Orion" wrote for the *Macon*

---

[16] Kurtz, "Fort Hood and the Ponders House," 5, 14; Franklin M. Garrett, *Atlanta and Environs: A Chronicle of Its People and Events,* 2 vols. (New York: Lewis Historical Publishing Co., 1954) 1:511–12; Wilbur Kurtz, notebook 5, 93 (Kurtz's exploration of the Ponder house site, April 1931), Wilbur G. Kurtz Collection, Atlanta History Center.

Telegraph, "There has been several shells of the enemy burst near the Female College, but did no damage."

If Captain DeGress claimed distinction for having commanded the first battery to bombard Atlanta on 20 July, "honors" for the second Union battery to do so the next day probably go to the 3rd Ohio Light Artillery, four 20-pounder Parrott rifled guns, commanded by Lieutenant John Sullivan. It would have taken rifled cannon, not smoothbores, to hit Atlanta from Bald Hill, and of the two rifled batteries assigned to Leggett's division, the 20-pounders had the longer range. (The other, Captain Marcus Elliott's 1st Michigan Light, had 3-inch ordnance rifles.) With a 2-pound charge of gunpowder and its barrel elevated at fifteen degrees, one of these Parrott guns (named for Captain Robert Parrott, US ordnance officer) could fire an 18 1/2-pound exploding shell theoretically 4,500 yards, or 2 1/2 miles.[17]

Because of their greater range and accuracy, the rifled cannon of Sherman's artillery as a rule shelled Atlanta; smoothbore guns did not have sufficient range. Predominantly, the 254 field pieces with which Sherman and his chief of artillery, Brigadier General William F. Barry, began the campaign were of four types: 3-inch rifled guns, 10- and 20-pounder Parrott rifles, and 12-pounder smoothbore Napoleons (named for French Emperor Napoleon III, who had taken an interest in development of the gun in the 1850s). Among Union ordnance, there were a few more categories of cannon, such as 12- and 24-pounder howitzers, but Sherman's artillery included only a few such guns. Grouped in batteries of four to six cannon each—within each battery, two guns were termed a "section"—

---

[17] Castel, *Decision in the West,* 383–84; Sherman to McPherson, and McPherson to Sherman, 21 July 1864, *OR,* vol. 38, pt. 5, pp. 218–19; reports of Maj. Gen. Frank P. Blair, Jr., and of General Leggett, 25 July, *OR,* vol. 38, pt. 3, pp. 544, 564; Kurtz interview with James Bell, 21 June 1935, notebook 10, 236 (on the fate of Henry Spear's house), Wilbur G. Kurtz Collection, Atlanta History Center; "Orion" (7 P.M., 21 July, Atlanta), *Macon Telegraph,* 23 July; organization of Sherman's forces, Atlanta Campaign, *OR,* vol. 38, pt. 1, p. 109; report of Capt. Andrew Hickenlooper, 31 July, *OR,* vol. 38, pt. 3, p. 58 (on composition of Leggett's three batteries); "Table of approximate ranges, &c., for rifled guns in use in the armies of the United States in 1861–'62," *Instruction for Heavy Artillery: Prepared by a Board of Officers, for the Use of the Army of the United States* (Washington, DC: Government Printing Office, 1862) 243, 246.

On this basis, Dr. Castel errs in stating that on the morning of 21 July, Leggett placed "a howitzer battery on the crest" of his hill to begin "lobbing shells into Atlanta" (*Decision in the West,* 384). The 24-pounder howitzers of Battery D, 1st Illinois Light Artillery, smoothbores, had the shortest range of the three types of cannon in the batteries attached to Leggett's division, and were manifestly incapable of the work. Castel, drawing from the statement of Lt. Col. Gilbert D. Munson of General Leggett's staff that "McCallister's big howitzers" helped clear the Rebels from Bald Hill, mistakenly infers that the same howitzers opened on the city (Gilbert D. Munson, "Battle of Atlanta," in Sydney C. Kerksis, ed., *The Atlanta Papers* [Dayton OH: Press of Morningside Bookshop, 1980] 416).

General Barry's fifty batteries were apportioned among Sherman's three armies: 24 batteries with 130 guns to Thomas's Army of the Cumberland, 19 batteries (96 cannon) for McPherson's Army of the Tennessee, and 7 batteries (28 guns) for Schofield's Army of the Ohio. In the fighting around Atlanta in July and August, the smoothbore Napoleons and howitzers would be used on the front lines to pound the Rebel fortifications, shell Hood's troops, and knock out enemy batteries. The 3-inch and Parrott rifled guns could do this, too, but they alone had the range to bombard the city. This distinction is useful in identifying the Union batteries that inflicted so much damage to the city of Atlanta during Sherman's thirty-seven-day bombardment from 20 July to 25 August.[18]

While some of McPherson's artillery east of Atlanta got within range of downtown, other Union batteries opened fire on the outer Rebel works north and northeast of the city. The IV Corps divisions of David Stanley and Thomas Wood made progress 21 July against Rebel skirmishers as the Federals pushed toward the northeast salient of the outer Confederate line. Doing so, their artillery was given opportunity for exercise. Lieutenant Lyman White, commanding Bridges's Illinois battery of 3-inch rifles in Wood's division, brought his cannon into position on a hill commanding a portion of the Southern works. The Union guns opened fire and, in White's words, "were successful in silencing a very troublesome line of rebel skirmishers and in badly shattering their works."

Federal artillery firing on Confederate fortifications meant that Northern shells began exploding around the civilian homes near those fortifications. Mrs. Cyrena Stone discovered the discomfort of coming within range of gunfire. Her house, just inside the eastern circle of city limits, lay close to the outer Confederate line. By 19 July, all of her neighbors had gone, some into the city, others to points farther removed from the war-zone. Cyrena decided to stay in

---

[18] Report of Brig. Gen. William F. Barry, 10 September 1864, *OR,* vol. 38, pt. 1, pp. 120–21; L. Van Loan Naisawald, *Grape and Canister: The Story of the Field Artillery of the Army of the Potomac, 1861–1865* (New York: Oxford University Press, 1960) 537–52; Fairfax Downey, *Storming the Gateway: Chattanooga, 1863* (New York: David McKay Company, 1960) 45–55.

For more background on cannon used by Sherman in his bombardment of Atlanta, see Fairfax Downey, "Field and Siege Pieces," *Civil War History* 2/2 (June 1956): 65–74; L. Van Loan Naisawald, "Field Artillery in the War," *Civil War Times* 3/3 (June 1961): 4–7, 24; James C. Hazlett, "The Parrott Rifles," *Civil War Times Illustrated* 5/7 (November 1966): 27–33; John Selby, *Stonewall Jackson as Military Commander* (London: B. T. Batsfords, 1968) 222–28 ("Jackson's Artillery"); James C. Hazlett, "The 3-inch Ordnance Rifle," *Civil War Times Illustrated* 7/8 (December 1968): 30–36; Dean S. Thomas, *Cannons: An Introduction to Civil War Artillery* (Gettysburg: Thomas Publications, 1985); Wayne Austerman, "Case Shot and Canister: Field Artillery in the Civil War," *Civil War Times Illustrated* 26/5 (September 1987): 16–29, 43–48; and Harold L. Peterson, *Round Shot and Rammers* (Harrisburg PA: Stackpole Books, 1969) 92–95.

her home with her servants, at least to protect it against the Confederate soldiers who were milling about. Besides, she had another motive. Cyrena and her husband Amherst, both Vermont-born emigrants to Atlanta in 1853, were among the city's most ardent Unionists. Amherst had already left the city for New York to escape conscription but had not been able to get his wife out of the South. Cyrena remained at their home in east Atlanta, comforted by the circle of Unionist friends who shared her hope of Northern deliverance. With the war-front nearing the city, she hoped someday to see triumphant Federal troops liberating her from Rebel rule.

Mrs. Stone kept a diary, recording her secret feelings of being "alone on a hill"; she entered an incident of 21 July, when a Confederate officer came to her door and asked for a room, as he was ill.

> I asked in return—if he would protect us.
>
> "Certainly madam, as long as we remain here." So he seated himself under a tree, allowing no soldier to enter the house or garden. He was a kind hearted Christian man, & seemed to deprecate the war; spoke of his own family with tears, and said he could pity others left unprotected. He thought I was wise in not "running from the Yankees," & said if all who refugeed had remained in their homes, they would have saved themselves immense losses & suffering.
>
> We were getting accustomed to the continued roaring of cannons and rattle of musketry, surrounding us with the fiery guerdon of War; but at noon, a horrid whizzing screaming thing came flying through the air, and burst with a loud explosion above us. Rushing into the Col's room where he was reposing, and the servants following perfectly *pale* with affright, I cried out—"O Col! What was *that?*"
>
> "It is a *shell* madam. I beg of you to be calm. I think there is no danger here—you are safer than you would be in town. The enemy are only trying the range of their guns." So we left the soldier to his slumbers, which were not disturbed by any thing so slight as a few *shells*. But not long—for here came another & another screaming through the air, & the poor Col was again appealed to.
>
> "I beg of you madam, be calm, & put your trust in God. He alone can protect us." I tried to trust—but be *calm*—when these murderous things

Later that evening of 21 July, Mrs. Stone was further rattled when an excited slave rushed in, announcing that the Confederate troops nearby were withdrawing from their works back into the main defensive perimeter around the city. With the prospect of her property being swept up in battle, Cyrena packed what she could, and moved in with a friend closer into the city. Her house would not survive.[19]

On his side of the lines, General Sherman was quite pleased at the progress made by McPherson on 21 July, particularly in capturing the bald hill. "From this hill," Sherman wrote that evening, "he has an easy range of the town. We will try the effect of shelling to-morrow." For the morrow, the 22d, Sherman ordered McPherson's, Schofield's and Howard's units to "open a careful artillery fire on the town of Atlanta, directing their shots so as to produce the best effect." Judging by his report on the night of 21 July to General Halleck in Washington, Sherman believed that his artillery bombardment of the city would have a strategic, campaign-ending effect:

> To-day we have gained important positions, so that Generals McPherson and Schofield, on the east, have batteries in position that will easily reach the heart of the city, and General Howard, on the north, also has advanced his lines about two miles, being within easy cannon-range of the buildings in Atlanta.... The city seems to have a line all around it, at an average distance from the center of town of one mile and one half, but our shot passing over this line will destroy the town, and I doubt if General Hood will stand a bombardment; still he has fought hard at all points all day. I will open on the town from the east and northeast tomorrow....[20]

By such statements, Sherman seemed at least as determined to destroy the buildings of Atlanta as he was in defeating the enemy army.

With McPherson already in advantageous position east of town, the two other Federal armies would also get closer. By 4:00 A.M. on 22 July, Sherman learned that the Rebels had withdrawn from their outer works. Excited, he jumped to the conclusion that Hood might be withdrawing from Atlanta altogether. At daylight, however, riding with General Schofield, Sherman saw the Rebels strongly fortified in front of him within their main perimeter of works. Snapping back to the realization that the enemy was very much in control of the city, he therefore ordered Thomas to "press down close from the north and use artillery freely, converging in the town."

Thomas moved forward. On the extreme right of Sherman's line, Major General John M. Palmer's XIV Corps was able to advance northwest and west of

---

[19] Wilbur G. Kurtz, map and key, "Embattled Atlanta," *Atlanta Constitution*, 20 July 1930, 12–13; report of Lt. Lyman A. White, 9 September 1864, *OR*, vol. 38, pt. 1, p. 496; Thomas G. Dyer, *Secret Yankees: The Union Circle in Confederate Atlanta* (Baltimore: Johns Hopkins University Press, 1999) 116, 155–57, 175–77, 181, 322–23 ("Miss Abby," diary, 19 and 21 July 1864).

[20] Sherman to Thomas, 21 July, and Special Field Order 40, 21 July 1864, *OR*, vol. 38, pt. 5, pp. 212, 222; Sherman to Halleck, 21 July, *OR*, vol. 38, pt. 5, p. 211.

Atlanta. Palmer's 2nd Division commander, coincidentally named Jefferson
Davis, reported that on the morning of 22 July he moved his troops to west side
of the Marietta road, and took position on the Turner's Ferry Road, which he
fortified. The Federals' new positions north of the city brought their artillery
within range of downtown, which meant that 22 July saw a significant increase
in the volume of Yankee artillery fire upon the city. "My batteries bore upon the
city from these works with great ease," General Davis reported. One of his
battery commanders was Captain Charles M. Barnett of Battery I, 2nd Illinois
Light Artillery, who took his four 3-inch rifled guns from Peachtree Creek to a
new position much closer to the city. "22d, marched about five miles...; went
into position on the west of town and threw a few shells into it." Another battery
was Captain Otho F. Morgan's 7th Indiana. He too on 22 July led his four 3-inch
rifles into position, "where we remained twelve days. Fired at intervals during
this time, directing most of our shots at the city and the rebel works in front." To
the left of the XIV Corps, Hooker's XX Corps advanced 2 miles from south of
Peachtree Creek, where it had been engaged in the battle of 20 July, to a new line
running from the Western & Atlantic Railroad eastward, roughly along today's
10th Street and 1/2 to 3/4 mile from the Rebel works. Brigadier General John
Geary, commanding Hooker's 2nd Division, recorded that on 22 July his men
marched over and through the Rebels' abandoned outer line, and took up new
position "on a cleared ridge half a mile east of Howell's Mill road." Geary
estimated it was 2 miles from the center of Atlanta. Despite skirmishing and
artillery dueling with the enemy in their works, maybe a thousand yards away,
he took satisfaction that the "shells from our guns" during the day and into the
night were "being thrown far into the city."

When the infantry dug in, so did the artillery. Sergeant Rice C. Bull, of the
123rd New York (in Williams's 1st Division, XX Corps), recorded in his diary
that to the right of his regimental front during 22–23 July, "a large redoubt was
being built to be equipped with siege guns." For several decades after the war,
Atlantans were able to mark the Yankees' gun positions. The embrasure
observed by Sergeant Bull may have been the earthwork observed in 1895 on a
hill between the railroad and Howell Mill Road, when R. M. Clayton mapped the
Atlanta area's wartime sites for Confederate veterans about to reunite in the city
(the battery site is today 10th Street at Brady Avenue, near the railroad).[21] It is

---

[21] Castel, *Decision in the West,* 389, 392; Sherman to Thomas, 22 July 1864, *OR,* vol. 38,
pt. 5, p. 223; report of Bvt. Maj. Gen. Jefferson C. Davis, [-] September 1864, *OR,* vol. 38, pt.
1, p. 635; report of Capt. Charles M. Barnett, 6 September, *OR,* vol. 38, pt. 1, p. 830; report of
Capt. Otho F. Morgan, 6 September, *OR,* vol. 38, pt. 1, p. 832; report of Brig. Gen. John W.
Geary, 15 September, *OR,* vol. 38, pt. 2, p. 142; Bauer, ed., *Soldiering,* 154; "Map Showing
Battle Fields of July 20, 22 & 28, 1864" in "Battles of Atlanta," UCV pamphlet (original
document at Atlanta History Center).

further likely that the guns occupying this position belonged to Captain Arnold Sutermeister's 11th Indiana Battery, four 20-pounder Parrott rifles and two 24-pounder howitzers; Sutermeister's battery was designated the siege artillery for the XX Corps. A few days into the bombardment, Southern newspaper reports mentioned shells from "twenty-pounder Parrott guns on the line of the Western & Atlantic Railroad." Other Federal batteries deployed farther to the east along the XX Corps lines. One was Captain Charles E. Winegar's Battery I, 1st New York Light Artillery, with six 3-inch rifles. On the morning of 22 July, the unit began deploying on the line of the 1st Division, XX Corps, taking some enemy artillery fire and returning it. Next to it, Battery M of the 1st New York Light (Captain John D. Woodbury) fell into line. As one of Woodbury's gunners put it, "Charley Winegar's battery is rite side of us, and he is well." Then, as part of John Geary's 2nd Division, Lieutenant Henry Bundy's 13th New York Light Battery took position. "All these guns occupied revetted embrasures in the breast-works," one Union officer recorded, meaning that in the line of entrenchments, each cannon was protected by a wall of stacked logs shoring up the earthen parapet.

A few of these Federal battery positions can be marked on today's map of Atlanta. Wilbur G. Kurtz in the 1930s found "heavy entrenchments" in a then-wooded section near 11th Street and Kontz Avenue; the earthworks included artillery embrasures. Another Union battery position was noted in 1934 as "at or very near the present 13th Street entrance to Piedmont Park." In the 1950s, Allen P. Julian called attention to these Federal artillery positions in a motor-tour text he prepared for the Peachtree Creek battlefield area. Driving north on the downtown expressway in the heart of the city, at the 10th Street overpass, Julian noted, "A Union battery was on wooded hill just beyond overpass. This battery duelled with Confederate batteries.... also fired on downtown targets. Another Union battery was on high ground to our right. Union 20th Corps occupied this line." Modern Atlantans' knowledge of the positions occupied by Union artillery—in this case, the area encompassed today by the Turner Broadcasting Corporation complex—adds tangible detail to our narrative of how the Yankees shelled the city's people and buildings.[22]

The map of war sites was made by R. M. Clayton, with help from E. P. Howell and other Confederate veterans. The "Federal Battery on hill between Railroad and Howell's Mill road" is site 28 on the Clayton map. The battery site is also noted by Franklin M. Garrett and Wilbur G. Kurtz in their key to accompany I. U. Kauffman's 1934 map of Atlanta: "No. 117—Site of a Federal Battery in 1864. High ground between W. & A.R.R. and Howell Mill Rd. About present intersection of Brady Ave. and 10th St., N.W."

[22] Report of Capt. Arnold Sutermeister, 14 September 1864, *OR,* vol. 38, pt. 2, p. 488; "Telegraphic," 25 July 1864, in *Mobile Register and Advertiser,* 27 July; report of Brig. Gen. Alpheus S. Williams, 12 September, *OR,* vol. 38, pt. 2, p. 27 (on Winegar's 3-inch guns); William C. Niesen, "'The Consequences of Grandeur': A Union Soldier Writes of the Atlanta Campaign," *Atlanta History* 33/3 (Fall 1989): 11; report of Col. Horace Boughton, 10

In their advance of 22 July, soldiers of the Union XX Corps encountered what may be considered Civil War Atlanta's suburban sprawl. Marching south of Peachtree Creek, still well outside the city limits, Federals began to see the urban outskirts. "By noon," wrote Sergeant Bull of the 123rd New York, "we had gone two miles and there was every indication we were approaching a town. There were many houses, lumber mills, a tannery and other factories and some places of business where power was used." These places of business and residence were now in the war zone and would consequently suffer in the coming days.

Sherman's lines north of the city continued east of the XX, with IV Corps infantry also taking up new positions on 22 July. "All the artillery was placed in position and intrenched," recorded the IV Corps artillery commander, Captain Lyman Bridges. Bridges's Illinois Light Battery, 3-inch rifles, managed to fire "occasional shells into the city" that day. The IV Corps's left connected with the right of the XXIII as Sherman's lines constricted in the general advance of 22 July. Here, too, Federal artillery was able to draw closer to the city. As General Schofield wrote, "Early in the morning we advanced and took up position on front of the Howard house, intrenched, and established batteries, preparatory to operations against the town." (The "Howard house" was actually that of Augustus F. Hurt, which Sherman used as his headquarters 22 July; it is located at the site of today's Carter Center.) One of Schofield's division commanders, Brigadier General Milo S. Hascall, recorded that early in the morning of 22 July, upon word of the Rebels' withdrawal into their main works, "batteries were ordered to be established as soon as possible, to begin shelling of the city." One of Hascall's batteries, the 19th Ohio, did just that. "July 22, moved in front of Atlanta," recorded battery commander Captain Joseph C. Shields, who after his unit had moved into line and dug in, noted that his 10-pounder Parrotts "fired 187 rounds into Atlanta" that day.[23]

September, *OR,* vol. 38, pt. 2, p. 93; undated map, box 39 (oversized), folder 5, Wilbur G. Kurtz Collection, Atlanta History Center; [Garrett and Kurtz], "Key to Map," 22; [Allen P. Julian], "Tour of the Peachtree Creek Battle Field Area," typescript, box 26, folder 6, Wilbur G. Kurtz Collection, Atlanta History Center.

[23] Bauer, ed., *Soldiering,* 152–53; report of Capt. Lyman Bridges, 9 September 1864, *OR,* vol. 38, pt. 1, p. 484; W. B. Hazen, *A Narrative of Military Service* (Boston: Ticknor Company, 1885) 273; report of Maj. Gen. John M. Schofield, 10 September, *OR,* vol. 38, pt. 2, p. 516; A. F. Hurt to Wilbur G. Kurtz, 18 September 1913, in Hurt Family Papers, box 103, folder 7N, Alabama Department of Archives and History; Kurtz, "The Augustus F. Hurt House," *Atlanta Constitution Sunday Magazine,* 22 June 1930, 5–6; report of Brig. Gen. Milo S. Hascall, 10 September, *OR,* vol. 38, pt. 2, p. 572; report of Capt. Joseph C. Shields, 9 September, *OR,* vol. 38, pt. 2, p. 673.

In 1895, R. M. Clayton and the Confederate veterans marking extant sites noted "Federal Battery near Copenhill," which was the location of the Augustus Hurt house. The Howard/Hurt confusion arose in summer 1864, when with the Augustus Hurt family

With General Sherman looking forward to seeing what McPherson's batteries on the bald hill could do—the commanding general had told Thomas at 11:00 A.M. of 22 July that "our battery on this [left] flank will open about 1 P.M."— General McPherson was eager to get his artillery into action. Sherman and Schofield were at the Augustus Hurt house when McPherson rode up to say that from Mortimer Leggett's hill he could see the "high smoke-stack of a large foundry in Atlanta"— the Rolling Mill, now idle and empty of its machinery. McPherson announced he was having batteries dug in atop the hill from which, as Sherman recalled the conversation, "he intended to knock down that foundry, and otherwise to damage the buildings inside of Atlanta."[24]

At least one of McPherson's batteries got off a few rounds into the city late that morning. Lieutenant Richard S. Tuthill, in Battery H, 1st Michigan Light Artillery (attached to Leggett's division, XVII Corps), remembered having "finished my noonday bean-soup, hard-tack and coffee" when he heard artillery fire from the city, which by orders had to be answered. So Tuthill dropped his pen and paper from the letter he was writing, and "ran up to the guns to direct the firing of my section.... We threw quite a number of shots into the city," before he, and every other soldiers in Leggett's division—in McPherson's whole

---

absent, two different tenants moved into the house. One, a Dr. Schon, apparently lived in it up to the time of the Federals' arrival (at least one map in the *Official Records Atlas* [plate 60, map 2] shows the "Schon" house). Then a neighbor, Thomas C. Howard, wartime city postmaster, moved into the Hurt house, which was called "Tacoma" (Wilbur G. Kurtz, "The Augustus F. Hurt House," 6; "Sherman Made Howard Farm Headquarters," *Atlanta Constitution*, 10 December 1948; Kurtz notebook 22, 250, Atlanta History Center). Kurtz learned that the name of the Copenhill area (today's Carter Center) derived from its three postwar real estate developers: Coker, Pennington, and Hill (notebook 3, 96–97, Wilbur G. Kurtz Collection, Atlanta History Center).

[24] Sherman to Thomas, 22 July (11 A.M.), *OR*, vol. 38, pt. 5, p. 223; William T. Sherman, *Memoirs of General William T. Sherman*, 2 vols. (New York: D. Appleton and Company, 1875) 2:75–76; Wilbur G. Kurtz, "McPherson's Last Ride," *Atlanta Constitution Magazine*, 29 June 1930, 9.

Shelby Foote seems to have embellished upon Sherman's remembrance of this conversation before the "Howard" house on the morning of 22 July, implying that the bombardment of the city began with McPherson's request for permission to bombard the foundry smokestacks: "Sherman readily assented to the shelling of the city, and ordered it to begin as soon as the guns were in position" (Shelby Foote, *The Civil War: A Narrative*, 3 vols. [New York: Random House, 1958–1974] 3:480). Foote thus overlooks Sherman's earlier orders for the bombardment of Atlanta, as well as contemporary reports of the first Union artillery shells falling on 20–21 July; he also gets a detail wrong. "What he wanted was permission to open fire with a battery of long-range 32-pounders on a foundry whose tall smokestack he could see" (479); in all of the 254 cannon with Sherman's three armies, there were no 32-pounders (*OR*, vol. 38, pt. 1, p. 120).

army, for that matter—had their attention drawn to the sounds of gunfire suddenly erupting sometime after noon.[25]

The Confederates were attacking again, just two days after the battle at Peachtree Creek. With McPherson's left flank unprotected and "in the air"—Sherman had sent Kenner Garrard's horsemen off to destroy more of the Georgia Railroad—Hood determined upon a surprise flank attack on 22 July. His battle plan was ambitious. Lieutenant General William J. Hardee's corps was to abandon its trench lines north of the city, march through town during the night of 21 July, head south then swing back northeast, positioning itself at daylight to strike McPherson's left flank and rear. Two divisions of Wheeler's cavalry would accompany the movement, then ride east in a quick raid upon McPherson's wagon train at Decatur. If all went well, the Yankee Army of the Tennessee would be rolled up and crushed while Hood's remaining troops and militia, manning the defenses, held Thomas and Schofield at bay.

Hood's flank attack east of the Atlanta, 22 July (commonly known as "the battle of Atlanta" for want of a more specific name, although a few historians have begun naming it the "battle of Bald Hill") resulted in some significant Confederate gains. That morning McPherson had been jittery about his airy left flank, and had ordered some precautions against just such a Confederate surprise, which struck the Union lines around noon. McPherson's repositioning of a XVI Corps infantry divison, Brigadier General Thomas Sweeny's, blunted the Rebels' initial assault. Nevertheless, after some initial repulses, the Confederates pushed the Yankees back, taking a division-length of enemy works before being halted at Leggett's/Bald Hill. Hood also launched a second supporting assault around 4:00 P.M., sending his former corps (now under Major General Frank Cheatham) against McPherson's right flank near the Georgia Railroad. This attack achieved temporary success, breaking the XV Corps line, but here too the Southerners were forced back. At the end of the day, the Confederates withdrew to their lines, having inflicted some 4,000 casualties (including General McPherson killed, when he rode into an enemy skirmish line in the battle's opening minutes), against 5,500 killed, wounded and missing of their own. Moreover, Hood's men were able to bring back with them twelve captured cannon. Captain Francis DeGress's battery, which had fired the first shots into the city two days before, was also nearly captured. Placed near the two-story brick house of George M. Troup Hurt (Augustus's brother), DeGress's guns were overrun by Cheatham's infantry. Counterattacking Federals reclaimed them before the Confederates could wheel them off.[26]

---

[25] Richard S. Tuthill, "An Artilleryman's Recollections of the Battle of Atlanta," in Kerksis, comp., *The Atlanta Papers*, 438–39.

[26] Davis, *Atlanta Will Fall*, 138–39, 147; Castel, *Decision in the West*, 413–14 (on Sherman's having done nothing to contribute to the Northern victory on 22 July). Actually, if Sherman had had his way, McPherson's army might have been defeated. Early that

Hood's plan for his attack of 22 July had hinged on Hardee's infantry corps marching from their positions north of the city to the southeast of it. On the night of 21 July, thousands of Confederate soldiers slogged through downtown—their route taking them down Peachtree past the Car Shed, left on Hunter and south on McDonough. The sight absolutely unnerved civilian residents, who logically jumped to the conclusion that Hood was evacuating Atlanta. "All last night our

---

morning McPherson had received a handwritten note from Sherman: "Instead of sending Dodge to your left, I wish you would put his whole corps at work destroying absolutely the railroad back to and including Decatur. I want that road absolutely and completely destroyed; every tie burned and every rail twisted" (William E. Strong, "The Death of General James B. McPherson," in Kerksis, comp., *The Atlanta Papers,* 515). Of course, it was McPherson's disregard for this instruction (perhaps because it was Sherman's "wish" rather than order) that allowed Dodge's XVI Corps to meet Hood's flank attack and save the day. Sherman's note later came into possession of the Georgia Department of Archives and History (Robert McKee, "New Sherman Letter Shows General's Iron Will," *Atlanta Journal,* 24 January 1956).

Hood's haul of captured artillery, twelve cannon (enough to fill three Confederate batteries) was unusually rich by Civil War battle standards. (In Lee's greatest victory of the war, Chancellorsville, the Confederates captured fourteen Union guns [report of Brig. Gen. Henry J. Hunt, 1 August 1863, *OR,* vol. 25, pt. 1, p. 253]). Half of the guns captured by Hood's troops east of Atlanta were 3-inch ordnance rifles, belonging to Battery F, 2nd US Artillery; the battery, according to a member of the headquarters staff, 2nd Division, XVI Corps, had been "sent off to the front to take an advanced position; took the wrong road, got lost, and ran on to the rebels" (Snell, diary, 23 July, Illinois Historical Society). The other six guns were 12-pounder Napoleons, of Battery A, 1st Illinois and Battery F, 2nd Illinois (reports of Capt. Andrew Hickenlooper, 31 July 1864; Lt. George Echte, 6 September; and Lt. Lemuel Smith, 2 August, *OR,* vol. 38, pt. 3, pp. 58–59, 262, 539). A month later, four of the guns of Battery F, 2nd US were recaptured by Union troops at Jonesboro, 1 September (Snell, diary, 1 September, Illinois Historical Society).

The fighting around the Troup Hurt House, with Brig. Gen. Arthur Manigault's brigade of South Carolinians crowded around DeGress's battery firing behind cotton bales, is among the highlights of the mural known in Atlanta as the Cyclorama. The artists (German panoramists plus Theodore Davis) who painted the Cyclorama a generation after the war saw no Hurt house as they studied the battlefield of July 1864, for the structure was destroyed shortly after the battle. Local historian Kurtz is probably right in complaining, therefore, that the artists erroneously painted it too tall, its brick of the wrong color, and situated too near the railroad for a country manor (Wilbur G. Kurtz, "At the Troup Hurt House," *Atlanta Constitution Sunday Magazine,* 25 January 1931, 4). Another criticism could point out the addition of cotton bales to the scene. No member of Manigault's brigade attested to cotton bales at the Troup Hurt house; the artists probably indulged in a bit of romance including them (my thanks to Dr. Jones of the Atlanta History Center for this observation). In his recent study of the battle of Atlanta, Gary Ecelbarger mistakenly claims, "Manigault's troops lined behind haystacks at the Troup Hurt house"; anyone who has been to the Cyclorama knows that they are *cotton* bales (Ecelbarger, *The Day Dixie Died: The Battle of Atlanta* [New York: St. Martin's Press, 2010] 228).

city was in a complete hubbub with army wagons and soldiers and marauders as though the whole army was passing through," recorded Sam Richards in his diary. "Everybody thought the army was running and everybody wanted to run, too—and they did," commented Lieutenant W. L. Trask, one of General Hardee's staff officers. "The citizens became alarmed at the prospect and hurriedly packed up such things as they could carry and began to leave the city in every direction," Trask wrote. "Every available means of transportation was called into service. Roads leading southward were thronged with fugitives all night—the greatest alarm prevailed." Lieutenant Trask further recorded that the soldiers were under the same impression: "everyone thought we were retreating again." Under that misconception and therefore given to abandon, Confederates helped themselves in their march through downtown. Taking advantage of the fact that "many houses were left wide open with furniture, carpets, bedding, tableware of every description, scattered everywhere and the occupants gone," Trask noted, "the soldiers plundered and robbed indescriminately." Wheeler's cavalrymen, exercising their characteristic, notorious lack of discipline, were particularly active in the looting of stores and shops. To Trask, it was another of Wheeler's cavalry raids, only this time upon "the principal stores in the city...[the horsemen] gutted them completely—clothing of all kinds—rations of every description—cigars, tobacco, and whiskey were gobbled up and carried off."

"I saw a sight this morning that I never saw before and never wish to see again," wrote Robert Patrick of the 4th Louisiana Infantry. "A lot of cavalry, said to be the 7th Alabama Regiment, went all over the business part of the city breaking open the doors as they came to them, and robbing every house of whatever it contained, carrying away with them such things as they desired and throwing such as they did not like into the streets. They had sacks tied to their saddles and seemed to have come prepared for the business, and all through the day [22 July] cavalrymen would be seen with their horses literally piled up and almost concealed by the plunder they had on them." Lieutenant Trask saw this disgraceful flaunting of loot, too: "all over the army to-day can be seen fancy ornaments, brass and porcelain door knobs, small bells and other items decorating the harness of the horses and mules." Some of Hardee's infantry, marching through town past midnight, joined in the free-for-all, as there were no proprietors on hand to defend their Whitehall shops. One Confederate on the march remembered "those tall dwellings remained as close and silent as convents." This of course invited more plundering. James Bell, a lad of thirteen whose family lived at Marietta and Walton streets, watched soldiers break into Jennings and Harris' Cigar and Tobacco store. ("Next morning," Trask rather ruefully observed, "nearly every man in the Army had a cigar stuck in his mouth.") Even stationery went. Samuel and Jabez Richards's book and music store, on Whitehall between Alabama and Hunter, was on the Confederates' direct line of march and accordingly suffered. "A lot of cavalry robbers broke into the stores and stole everything that they took a fancy to. They stripped our store of the paper and other stationery that we had there, and about thirty dollars in money," as Sam Richards discovered the next day. Lieutenant Andrew J. Neal rode through Atlanta on 22 July, disheartened at what he saw: "It really makes me sad to witness the ruin and desertion of the place. The soldiers have broken open many stores and scattered things over the streets promiscuously. There is the same noise and bustle on White Hall but instead of thrift and industry and prosperity it is hurried scramble to get away fleeing from the wrath to come."[27]

Among those fleeing on 22 July was John McClanahan of the *Memphis Appeal*; the publisher and his staff packed up their big Hoe press and print equipment onto wagons and headed for Montgomery, Alabama. Sam Richards, one of several thousand civilians who had resolved to stick it out, recorded in his diary on 22 July, "Today our last newspaper departed, the 'Appeal' also the Postoffice, and every other establishment and individual that intended to go." The paper's departure was lamented in the Confederate press. "Even the Memphis Appeal, 'the last of a long line' of papers, has pulled up stakes and moved to the rear," reported the *Columbus Times*. "For information respecting affairs around Atlanta, we must henceforth depend upon telegraphic and verbal reports—a very unsafe reliance, as experience has often demonstrated."

Fortunately, the *Times*'s prediction was not fulfilled, as the *Appeal* did not quit Atlanta altogether so much as reduce its operations. The newspaper's editor, John B. Dumble, stayed behind in the city, and with the help of Isaac B. Pilgrim, shop foreman for the *Intelligencer*, continued to print one-page broadsides each afternoon on a hand press in the Franklin Printing House on Alabama Street. In one of these, Dumble rather meekly explained that "it was our purpose to continue the regular publication until the issue as to Atlanta was decided, but the

---

[27] Wilbur G. Kurtz, "Map of Atlanta as of 1938 Showing the Field and Fortified Lines of the Confederate Forces, Together with Those of the Federal Armies—Also the Fields of the Three Major Engagements, During the Summer of 1864," Atlanta Chamber of Commerce, 1938, FF 148, T2, folder 2 (on Hardee's route through the city), Wilbur G. Kurtz Collection, Atlanta History Center; Wendy Hamand Venet, ed., *Sam Richards's Civil War Diary: A Chronicle of the Atlanta Home Front* (Athens: University of Georgia Press, 2009) 228 (22 July); Trask, journal, 24 July 1864, Kennesaw Mountain National Battlefield Park; F. Jay Taylor, ed., *Reluctant Rebel: The Secret Diary of Robert Patrick, 1861–1865* (Baton Rouge: Louisiana State University Press, 1959) 200; Nathaniel Cheairs Hughes, Jr., *The Civil War Memoir of Philip Daingerfield Stephenson, D.D.* (Conway AR: University of Central Arkansas Press, 1995) 216; Wilbur G. Kurtz interview of James Bell, 28 June 1935, notebook 10, p. 252, and notebook 13, p. 59, Wilbur G. Kurtz Collection, Atlanta History Center; *Williams' Atlanta Directory*, 130 (on location of Richards's store); A. J. Neal to "Ma," 23 July 1864, Andrew Jackson Neal Letters, Emory University.

The Confederate press later reported that General Hood cracked down on the worst looters. "Five of the ringleaders have been shot, and eighty others are in arrest for trial," reported the *Montgomery Advertiser* (5 August) based on correspondents' reports from Atlanta.

turn of events has prevented this." Nevertheless, he pledged to issue a broadside every day henceforth. And this he did. Although actual copies of the *Appeal Extra* are hard to find today, they made their way to other Southern cities, where newspaper editors widely reprinted the *Appeal's* news columns. The reports, daily printed under the title of "The City," thus serve as among the best sources of information from Atlanta during the Yankees' bombardment.

As Sherman's shelling increased in late July, the passenger depot downtown became a scene of massive confusion as people tried to get aboard trains leaving the city. One Atlanta woman boarding a crowded car, remembering afterward how "people were frightened almost to death, and didn't know where to go or what to do, but they were just going somewhere." When trains ran out of room, citizens commandeered wagons, carriages, and transport of any kind to carry off their prized belongings. "I can give you no idea of the excitement in Atlanta," wrote a correspondent for the *Mobile News.* "Everybody seems to be hurrying off, and especially the women. Wagons loaded with household furniture and everything else that can be packed upon them crowd every street, and women old and young and children innumerable are hurrying to and fro. Every train of cars is loaded to its utmost capacity. The excitement beats anything I ever saw."

Some could find humor in the situation, terrifying as it was. After fleeing Rome as a "runagee," Charles Smith/"Bill Arp" made his way with family to Atlanta. By 3 June, he had joined a law practice in town; the *Appeal* of that date noted that "Chas. H. Smith, Esq., better known as 'Bill Arp,' attorney and counselor-at-law, has opened an office in this city, with Col. J.W.H. Underwood." A few weeks later he also signed on as assistant editor of the *Knoxville Register.* In July he was on hand to witness the panicky flight of the civilians, and of course was able to parlay the mass confusion into a comic story.

About this time the fust big shells kommensed skatterin their unfeelin kontents among the sububs of that devoted sitty. Then cum the big paniks.... All sorts of peepul seemed movin in all sorts of ways, with an akselerated moshun. They ganed ground on their shadders as they leened forwerd on the run, and their legs grew longer at evry step.... Kars was the all-in-all.... The passenger depo was throngd with ankshus seekers of transportashun. "Wont you let these boxes go as bagidge?" "No, madam, its onpossible." Just then sumbodys family trunk as big as a niter buro was shoved in, and the poor woman got desprite.

"All I've got ain't as hevvy as that," sed she, "and I am a poor wider, and my husband was killed in the army. I've got five little children, and my things hav got to go." We took up her boxes and shoved em in. Another good woman axed very anxshusly for the Makon trane. "There it is, madam," sed I. She shuke her hed mournfully and remarked, "You

127

are mistakin, sur, don't you see the injine is hedded rite up the State Road towards the Yankees? I shant take any trane with the injine at that end of it. No, sur, that ain't the Makon trane."

Evry where was hurryin to and fro at a lively tune. I went into a doktors shop, and found my friend packin up vials and pisen, and copavy, and sich like. Varyous xsited indivijuals cum in, looked at a big map on the wall, and pointed out the roads to McDoner and Etonton, and soon their propoased lines of travil wer esily and gresily visible from the impreshun of perspirin fingers. An old skeleton with one leg was swinging from the selin, lookin like a mournful emblem of the fate of the trubbled sitty. "You are goin to leave him to stan gard, Doktor?" sed I. "I suppose I will," sed he; "got no transportashun for him." "Take the screw out of his scull," sed I, "and give him a krutch, and he'll travel; all flesh is a movin, and I think the boans will katch the kontagion soon."

By and by the shells fell as thick as Guvener Brown's proklama-shuns, causin a more speedy lokomoshun in the xsiled throng who hurrid by the dore.... All day and all nite long the iron hosses were snortin to the ekoin breeze. Trane atter trane of goods and chattels moved down the rode, leavin hundreds of ankshus fases waitin their return. There was no method in this madness. All kinds of plunder was tumbuld in promiskuously. A huge parler mirrer, sum 6 foot by 8, all bound in ilegant gold, with a barass buzzard a spreddin his wings on the top, was sot up at the end of the kar, and reflekted a butiful assortment of parler furnichure to match, sich as pots and kittles, baskets and bags, barrels and kegs, bacon and bedsteds, all piled up together.

Smith himself caught the "kontagion," as he too, with family, eventually left Atlanta for safer parts while the Yankees' shelling and semi-siege ensued.[28]

---

[28] B. G. Ellis, *The Moving Appeal: Mr. McClanahan, Mrs. Dill, and the Civil War's Great Newspaper Run* (Macon GA: Mercer University Press, 2003) 313; "J.W.M." (Joseph W. Miller), "September 2," *Cincinnati Commercial,* 13 September 1864 ("the Franklin Printing House where the Memphis Appeal has been printed"); *Columbus Times,* 26 July (quoted by *Mobile Register and Advertiser,* 31 July); "The Appeal," *Macon Telegraph,* 4 August; Aaron M. Boom, ed., "Testimony of Margaret Ketcham Ward on Civil War Times In Georgia," *Georgia Historical Quarterly* 39/3 (September 1955): 377; "Atlanta Correspondent of the Mobile News," "Getting Out of Atlanta" (undated), *New York Times,* 7 August (quoted also in Foote, *The Civil War,* 3:491–92; and in Castel, *Decision in the West,* 341); "Local Intelligence," *Memphis Appeal,* 3 June 1864; "Editorial Accession," *Atlanta Intelligencer,* 25 June; [Charles Smith], *Bill Arp's Peace Papers,* 74–80; Anne M. Christie, "Civil War Humor: Bill Arp," *Civil War History* 2/3 (September 1956): 113–14.

The big battle of 22 July showed what happened when suburban houses found themselves on a battlefield; the Troup Hurt house (where Manigault's Confederate brigade briefly seized DeGress's battery and withstood a Union counterattack) obviously suffered damage. Other houses also came under direct fire on 22 July. During the engagement Union sharpshooters took roost in the house of "Spanish Jim" Brown, firing at Confederate artillerymen posted near the City Cemetery. The Southern gunners of Captain E. P. Howell's battery retaliated by firing hot shot. Soon the Brown home was ablaze. North of the cemetery, Lucius Gartrell's house on Decatur Street took a Union shell that might have been a wide miss at Howell's battery. It might too have come from a sharp-eyed artillery spotter if he had noticed that atop the Gartrell home stood a Confederate officer watching the battle. Either way, the enemy missile struck the house and exploded, driving out the Rebel, Charles B. Howry. "You may be certain," Howry recalled after the war, "that I lost no time in descending to the comparative safety of the ground."

The day after the battle east of Atlanta (like the day after the battle fought south of Peachtree Creek) soldiers of both armies looked for wounded and buried the dead under flag of truce. Federals took their injured to field hospitals in the rear; Confederates carried their wounded back into town, where all but the gravest cases were boarded on trains headed for hospitals to the south. In the burial process, as always, soldiers of both armies gave less attention to the slain of the enemy; these unfortunates always got the shallowest ditches. In front of the XV Corps line a fence rail was stuck in the ground, casually labeled in charcoaled letters, "24 Rebs." Some corpses, however, remained on the battlefield unattended. As one US officer put it, "we cook and eat, talk and laugh with the enemy's dead lying all around us as though they were so many logs." A. W. Reese, a Union surgeon, did not share in this disregard for the dead. He was in fact horrified by the "windrows and piles" of slain Rebel soldiers lying in front of the Federal battle lines, "mangled, torn, and battered by balls in every conceivable manner and shape." On 24 July, Confederate Lieutenant Trask recorded that "many of the dead still lie unburied, their bodies festering and rotting in the burning sun." There were even wounded men still on the battlefield. "This evening I helped to remove twenty horribly mangled Yankees, by General Hardee's order," Trask wrote. "They had lain where they fell for forty eight hours, without assistance; their wounds were fly blown and their condition was terrible. We carried them to our hospital."[29]

---

[29] Kurtz interview with J. W. McWilliams, 11 October 1930, notebook 6, 186, Wilbur G. Kurtz Collection, Atlanta History Center; "Veterans Here During Battle of Atlanta Back for Reunion," *Atlanta Constitution,* 8 October 1919; Castel, *Decision in the West,* 415–16; Dyer, *Secret Yankees,* 182–83, 193; Trask, journal, 24 July, Kennesaw Mountain National Battlefield Park.

Even during the engagement on the afternoon of 22 July, Sherman reminded his officers to keep shelling the city. He specifically called for the artillery of Thomas's army, on the northern outskirts, to "open upon Atlanta at the same hour," 3:00 P.M., with the shorter-range smoothbores to pound the enemy forts. Though preoccupied with their attack east of the city, Confederates took note; Lieutenant Trask observed that "while the battle was going on the enemy commenced shelling Atlanta with long range guns." The Southern cannoneers fired back. "The enemy is replying to our artillery fire with much spirit," wrote Thomas.

In his orders to all three armies for 23 July, Sherman called for the bombardment to be continued: "Good batteries will be constructed for the artillery and a steady fire be kept up on the city of Atlanta." From Sherman's headquarters, orders were passed down through Generals Thomas and Hooker to Captain Sutermeister of the 11th Indiana Battery, directing him to fire one shot every five minutes. With his section of howitzers covering the Marietta road and his 20-pounders to their right, Sutermeister fired a few rounds at the three Rebel forts in his front, whereupon "the bombardment of the city was ordered to commence.... The fire was directed mostly toward the center of town and the railroad shops." Artillery in the XIV, XX, IV, and XXIII Corps all opened fire on downtown Atlanta that day. In Hascall's division of Schofield's corps, gunners fired a round every fifteen minutes into the city. Major General O. O. Howard, commanding the IV Corps, ordered his rifled batteries to open upon Atlanta at 2:00 that afternoon. Captain Lyman Bridges's Illinois battery of 3-inch rifles did so, "getting some replies from the enemy's batteries," as one Federal officer noted. Bridges's guns, probably sited near today's Piedmont Avenue and 8th Street, kept firing through the night at a deliberate rate; according to the battery commander, every three minutes from 6:00 P.M. to 6:00 A.M., and every five minutes from 6:00 in the morning to 8:00 P.M. of 24 July. This "occasional" shelling, if maintained on schedule, would have added up to more than 400 rounds fired by Bridges's battery alone.

The nocturnal bombardment—the first in Sherman's shelling—allowed the Federals to see their handiwork. J. C. Van Duzer, Sherman's chief telegrapher, working well into the night of 23 July sending off his commander's usual day-end reports to Washington, recorded at 11:00 P.M., "as I write our heavy artillery is at work, and large fires are burning in Atlanta." But van Duzer mistook the cause of the conflagrations, which he "supposed to be the enemy destroying stores preparatory to evacuating."

Obviously Hood's soldiers were not setting fires in downtown Atlanta; Sherman's cannoneers were. Moreover, Federals were aware that civilians were still in the city, undergoing a lethal artillery bombardment. Corporal Leander S. Davis, of Battery M, 1st New York Light (attached to the XX Corps), wrote his wife Susan in the early morning of 23 July: "Some of our artillery pieces from our battery is within a mild and a half from Atlanta. We don't want to shell the town if they will give it up without for there is great many woman and children in it from the surrounding country that are taking refuge in the city for safety." Charles Harding Cox, with the 70th Indiana positioned north of the city, on 23 July went so far as to write his sister that although the Federal artillery was within easy range of downtown, orders forbade firing into the city, at least for the moment: "Non Combatants will receive timely notice when the shelling comes off." Cox, of course, was wrong; Union cannon had been shelling downtown Atlanta, not just the Rebel fortifications, for seventy-two hours. Later that day, Corporal Davis acknowledged this in a postscript to Susan, "we are shelling the town with 20-pound parrots." He imagined how the Rebels, both uniformed and not, were reacting to the shellfire: "it don't suit them pretty much."

Davis was correct. Even the hardened veterans of Hood's army, dug into their ditches and protected by parapets, found the Yankee cannonading at least annoying, if not life-threatening. But in their time-honored way, soldiers found ways of making light of the danger. A Kentuckian, Johnny Green, later set down in his memoirs an incident under date of 23 July. Green's buddy, Jim Bemis, had been given a Scott novel, *The Heart of Midlothian,* by a local woman as her gift. In work-breaks from strengthening their entrenchments, Green and his comrades shared the pleasure of reading aloud from the romantic tale.

> He & I would sit in the rifle pits with the enemies shells flying over us & read this charming story. Sometimes the bursting shells would make so much noise that the person reading aloud would be interrupted by a request "Read that over again; the blamed fool yanks made so much noise I did not hear that sentence."
>
> One day the yanks tried to take a hill in our front.... We opened both artillery & infantry on them & drove them back. This interrupted our reading so much that Jim Beamis said, "The 'Dag Gone Yanks' have no soul for literature."

Reminiscing Rebs could even make light of coming under shellfire from Sherman's bombardment of Atlanta. James C. Nisbet, colonel of the 66th Georgia, recalled how he and others were in the city in mid-July, leisurely "lying about on the streets and sidewalks," noticing how "the fine residences had been hastily abandoned, the owners leaving their *lares and penates* behind in their hasty flight." One lanky Confederate was walking about, snacking on hardtack and "oblivious to bursting shells," when he heard a voice calling from the trees: "Give poor Polly a cracker!" It turned out that an escaped parrot was calling for food. "Gee Whilkens, boys," said the soldier, "damned if the world hain't coming to an end! Even the birds are talking and begging for bread." "Give poor Polly a cracker," came the plea again, but the Reb refused. "I'm sorry for you, but you go to hell!" he shouted at the bird. "This is the first cracker I've seen for two days!"[30]

The increased Yankee bombardment of 22–23 July brought forth a broader, more detailed reporting from Southern newspapers. On the night of 22 July, Felix de Fontaine wrote his column for the *Savannah Republican*. He mentioned that General Hood's forces had withdrawn from their outer line north of the city, and that the enemy had advanced to new positions, and "planting their guns, commenced to throw shell among the women and children." And while some residents remained, the city gave every appearance of having been evacuated; it was "a mere shell of its former self." Among the civilians not yet left, de Fontaine observed, "every face wore a look of despondency." Scared by the Yankee artillery fire, noncombatants were still trying to get out of town. "Shells were dropping in the streets," de Fontaine observed, "and sad groups of women and children, with a temporary supply of provisions, were wending their way to the woods."

The next morning de Fontaine was again reporting from downtown. "Shells are thrown freely and frequently into the city," he wrote at 10:00 A.M. of 23 July, "and I find it inconvenient to write a letter under their inspiration." DeFontaine reported that the city's buildings were beginning to show the effects of bombardment—"several houses have been badly damaged"—but he could not yet report any casualties. "Many narrow escapes made," he wrote, "but I hear as yet of no loss of life." That afternoon, however, the Savannah reporter, as well as other correspondents, began hearing of the first Atlanta civilians wounded and killed. Observing that "a missile explodes every five minutes within these precincts," de Fontaine noted that the Yankee cannonfire was becoming so timed, regulated, and intense as to merit a scientific term, "ferruginous conchology"—a creative derivative from the Latin, roughly meaning "iron-plated shell-study":

---

[30] Fullerton, journal, *OR*, vol. 38, pt. 1, p. 908 (12:30 P.M., 22 July); Howard to Stanley, 22 July (12:30 P.M.), *OR*, vol. 38, pt. 5, pp. 225–26; Trask, journal, 24 July; Thomas to Sherman, 22 July, *OR*, vol. 38, pt. 5, p. 224; L. M. Dayton, Special Field Order 41, 22 July, *OR*, vol. 38, pt. 5, p. 233; report of Capt. Arnold Sutermeister, 14 September, *OR*, vol. 38, pt. 2, p. 488; report of Brig. Gen. Milo S. Hascall, 10 September, *OR*, vol. 38, pt. 2, p. 572; report of Capt. Lyman Bridges, 9 September, *OR*, vol. 38, pt. 1, p. 484; Hazen, *Narrative of Military Service*, 273; report of Lt. Lyman A. White, 9 September, *OR*, vol. 38, pt. 1, p. 496; J. C. Van Duzer to Maj. T. T. Eckert, 23 July, *OR*, vol. 38, pt. 5, p. 239; Niesen, "'Consequences of Grandeur,'" 10; Lorna Lutes Sylvester, ed., "'Gone for a Soldier': The Civil War Letters of Charles Harding Cox," *Indiana Magazine of History* 48/3 (September 1972): 211–12; A. D. Kirwan, ed., *Johnny Green of the Orphan Brigade: The Journal of a Confederate Soldier* (Lexington: University of Kentucky Press, 1956) 150; James Cooper Nisbet, *Four Years on the Firing Line*, ed. Bell Irvin Wiley (Jackson TN: McCowat-Mercer Press, 1963) 211.

Since about noon to-day the citizens have enjoyed the privilege, for the first time on a systematic scale, of studying the science of ferruginous conchology. The enemy have three batteries in play, and the Parrott shells intrude everywhere. A mother and child have been killed, a few persons and mules wounded, and a number of houses damaged. One three-inch visitor entered a bag of corn while being carried on the back of a man, and then exploded, scattering the contents in every direction. The porter was only slightly injured.

De Fontaine concluded his column by noting that services of the mail and express office were "interrupted and uncertain. Public stores and machinery are gone." "Confederate," writing from Atlanta 23 July for the *Columbus Sun,* corroborated de Fontaine's dispiriting observations: "The post office [on Whitehall, between Alabama and the railroad] has been removed. No private messages can be sent by telegraph.... Everything movable of any value has been carried to a place of safety. The city is almost entirely abandoned by the citizens and it presents a sad and gloomy appearance."

One citizen who had not abandoned the city was Samuel P. Richards, who owned and operated a book and stationery store on Whitehall Street and a grocery store east of downtown on Decatur Street. Through his exemption as a publisher of a newspaper, *The Soldiers Friend,* Richards was able to stay in Atlanta even as it underwent Yankee shelling. "We have had a considerable taste of the beauties of bombardment today," Sam recorded in his diary on Saturday night, 23 July.

The enemy have thrown a great many shells into the city and scared the women and children and *some* of the *men* pretty badly. One shell fell in the street just below our house [on Washington, four blocks south of the Car Shed, in the city's southwest quadrant].... My wife and children had to put their beds on the floor behind the chimney to be secure from shells which were thrown into the city all night long. No more fell near our house however, and but little damage was done anywhere.[31]

---

[31] "F. G. de F.," "From the Army of Tennessee" (Atlanta, 22 July [night] and 23 July [10 A.M. and night]), *Savannah Republican,* 27 July, 4 August; "Confederate" (Atlanta, 23 July) in *Columbus Sun,* 28 July; Frank J. Byrne, "Rebellion and Retail: A Tale of Two Merchants in Confederate Atlanta," *Georgia Historical Quarterly* 79/1 (Spring 1995): 44–48; Ella Mae Thornton, "Mr. S.P. Richards," *Atlanta Historical Bulletin* 3/12 (December 1937): 74; Venet, ed., *Sam Richards's Civil War Diary,* 228 (23 July).

Information on the site of the wartime city post office is in Wilbur G. Kurtz, interview with William Fort Williams, July 1933, notebook 22, 253, Wilbur G. Kurtz Collection, Atlanta History Center. "Williams said: The war-time Post Office, Atlanta, stood on Whitehall Street—the east side of it—between Alabama St. and the railroad, on what is now the approach to the Whitehall-Peachtree Viaduct. It was in a frame building standing

Despite the increasing volume of shellfire, reports of civilian casualties remained few. The city's residents were becoming enured to the shell detonations, even demonstrating nonchalance under fire. On the morning of 24 July, Captain Thomas Key, the Confederate artilleryman, rode into town on an errand and was impressed by the residents' bold indifference to danger. "While I was in Atlanta shells were bursting among the houses," Key wrote in his diary, "and ladies were walking the streets apparently unconcerned, though there were few people there." Amidst their stresses and fears, civilians staying in the city also began worrying about their supply of food. Surplus commissary stores had been evacuated, along with important machinery and hospitals, earlier in the month, and in the bombarded city ordinary commerce had been virtually halted. One distressed resident was Julia Davidson, who lived in the city's northwest suburbs not far from the gas works. With her husband away in the army, she had children to feed, and found it difficult. "There is not a bit of provisions in the city," she complained on 21 July; "all the flour meal & bacon have been run off." Both civilians and soldiers in Atlanta were fed by supplies brought in by rail and wagon. The Confederates' transport service kept food sufficient to allay Mrs. Davidson's fear of outright starvation ("what are we to do who have to remain—*starve to death*," she had written). Still, the supply was certainly not plentiful. Confederate Lieutenant Trask recorded in his diary on 28 July that "our own rations of meal and bacon...are already about as low in quantity as they can well get to keep us from downright starvation," but so long as the trains kept coming in, soldiers and civilians would have at least a skimpy sustenance. For some Confederates, this was not enough, so they resorted to thievery to supplement their rations. Trask recorded disagreeably on 25 July that he had spent the day "on duty protecting a man's cornpatch and hen roost to keep them from being plundered by the soldiers. Our troops rob friend or foe of everything edible when not well guarded."

Among basic needs for those enduring the Federal bombardment—after food—came shelter. The almost constant bombardment, and the promise of no relief from it, had a predictable effect upon the more faint-hearted of the citizenry. More people left town, some even seeking safety among the very Federals who were blasting their city. Corporal Leander Davis, whose battery was posted north of town, commented "there are thirty women came into our lines yesterday for protection." Davis took a rather malign satisfaction at what the Northern guns were doing, including the setting of fires downtown. "I guess we fired the city last nite with our shell. The battery fired a shot evry ten minutes and are at it yet," Davis wrote on 24 July. "They say we are tearing the city pretty

---

on the ground lower than the then grade of the street, so that the public entered the building on its second floor. Howard [the postmaster] also operated a grocery at this time."

bad with our shell, but we hain't commenced to shell it yet. Wait till we open fifty pieces of artillery on them. See what they think then."[32]

Corporal Davis probably underestimated the number of Union field pieces firing along Sherman's lines by 24 July. General Geary wrote his wife that day, "the roar of several hundred pieces of artillery is incessant night and day." Union artillerymen directed their fire not only upon the city, but also the Rebel works. At times Confederate cannoneers answered the enemy fire, and occasionally the exchange of salvos developed into a hot artillery duel. During the night of 23 July, men of the 20th Connecticut (3rd Brigade, Geary's 2nd division) performed fatigue duty, building a six-gun redoubt in their second line. In the morning, a battery of 20-pounder Parrotts occupied the work, and soon the Federal gunners began engaging the Rebel batteries dug in a half-mile distant. "In the morning the Rebels tried their metal on the new redoubt," recorded a Connecticut soldier; one shot came perilously close to a Union artilleryman, knocking the sponge staff from his hands.

Our gunners sighted their pieces upon a single embrasure in the Rebel redoubt, and just as the smoke belched from its embrasure, the order was given, and six shells went whizzing from the muzzles of the twenty-pounders, every one striking the point aimed at. The smoke cleared away, and by the aid of a field glass, the Rebel gun was seen dismounted, and a big hole where was an embrasure. The Rebels filled up the place with sand bags and there was one less gun to annoy us. "Wonder if they were satisfied with that," says the captain of our battery, "or will they want to wake us up again? If they do let them try it on." But not another shot came from the redoubt during the day. Evidently they wanted our twenty-pounders "to let them alone."[33]

The two sides engaged not only in brisk artillery fire, but also infantry skirmishes that at times became severe. After entering in his journal for 24 July— "we have been firing shell and shot from our guns into Atlanta during the whole day, and the enemy replies with his guns from the works around the city"—a Union IV Corps staff officer recorded "considerable skirmishing to-day and

---

[32] Cate, ed., *Two Soldiers*, 99–100; Davidson to "My Dear Johnny," 21 July, in Jane Bonner Peacock, ed., "A Wartime Story: The Davidson Letters, 1862–1865," *Atlanta Historical Bulletin* 19/1 (Spring 1975): 94; *Macon Confederate*, 13 July, quoted in Columbus *Enquirer*, 15 July ("but little quartermaster or commissary stores now remain in Atlanta, all having been removed to safer and more secure points in the rear"); Trask, journal, entries of 25, 28 July, Kennesaw Mountain National Battlefield Park; Niesen, "'The Consequences of Grandeur,'" 10.

[33] Geary to "My Dearest Mary," 24 July 1864, William Alan Blair, ed., *A Politician Goes to War: The Civil War Letters of John White Geary* (University Park: Pennsylvania State University Press, 1995) 189; John W. Storrs, *The "Twentieth Connecticut": A Regimental History* (Ansonia CT: Press of the "Naugatuck Valley Sentinel," 1886) 140.

artillery firing from both sides" (25 July); "skirmishing and artillery firing during the greater part of the morning" (26 July); "the usual amount of skirmishing and more artillery fire than usual" (later that night). Rebel sharpshooters took their toll on Yankee arillerymen. Sergeant Frederick Smith of Battery I, 1st New York Light, positioned with the XX Corps north of the city, recorded several casualties: Lieutenant Frank Henchen, shot in the head, 27 July (dead within the hour); George Baer, wounded 5 August; and Louis Vetteron, 13 August, etc. Some Confederate riflemen took advantage of buildings still standing close to their lines, ascended their upper stories, and used the perches as sniper nests. On 23 July, Captain John Woodbury's four Napoleons fired over fifty rounds upon such buildings occupied by Rebel sharpshooters. Against some of these, Union infantry were sent out the next day in sorties to roust out the enemy. Woodbury's battery supported one of these dashes, as the captain later related. "July 24...a detail of infantry was made to destroy buildings occupied by the enemy. Battery M kept up a fire to cover the movement, expending fifty rounds." Elsewhere on the XX Corps front, Union infantrymen of the 3rd Wisconsin (Brigadier General Thomas H. Ruger's brigade, Alpheus Williams's division) found themselves subjected to an irritating musketry from Rebel pickets posted behind houses situated out in no-man's land. "The enemy's sharpshooters were close enough to keep dropping their bullets incessantly into our camp. It was at first rather annoying to have them come pattering around whenever anyone moved," wrote Captain Julian Hinkley of Company E, but eventually he and his comrades got accustomed to the enemy rifle-fire. Nevertheless, on 27 July generals Williams and Ruger, "crooching under the works and taking squints" at the enemy sharpshooters, according to Private William Wallace of the 3rd Wisconsin, resolved to drive them off, and ordered the 13th New Jersey to do so. The Jerseymen equipped themselves with turpentine and torches, and sallied forth from their lines through a ravine. Wisconsan Wallace recorded the episode. While Union artillery fired to distract the Rebels, "the Jersey boys pounced right onto the Johnies," killing and wounding many and capturing three dozen. They then set fire to the buildings that had protected the enemy sharpshooters; Wallace observed that "the planters' homes was in ashes in a short time, negro huts included. We all sat watching the whole maneuver, and it was done good."

One building in particular on the XX Corps front drew heavy Union cannonfire. After Rebel riflemen took position in the second-floor rooms of the Ponder house, near Fort Hood, and started firing at the Yankees, General Geary ordered artillery to open up on the big, white-stucco-covered house. Charley Winegar's six 3-inch rifles did so, as Captain Winegar related: "On the morning of the 24th were ordered to open on a large stone house in our front and burn it, if possible. Although every projectile thrown struck the building, it proved impossible to communicate fire to it; distance, about 1,050 yards.... Ammunition expended, seventy-two rounds." Unable to destroy the house, or even to keep Rebels sharpshooters out of it, Union gunners kept firing at the Ponder place throughout Sherman's semi-siege of Atlanta. (Winegar's battery alone fired thirty rounds at the house on 3 August.) Afterward, scavengers reportedly found almost a ton of Northern shot and shell in the house.[34]

Besides those in the suburbs, buildings downtown continued to suffer damage. Press reports occasionally mentioned specific structures hit. "Grape" (Henry Watterson), writing for the *Augusta Constitutionalist*, claimed he was talking with an officer downtown when a shell went through the roof of Dr. Quintard's Episcopal church on Walton Street, and another through the now vacant office of the *Southern Confederacy*. "The Atlanta Hotel, the Washington Hall and the Methodist Church, and dwellings adjacent, all bear the marks of recent visitations of round shot and shell," Watterson noted. At the same time, Confederate newspapers paid more attention to the growing reports of civilian casualties in the city. Felix de Fontaine had reported for the *Savannah Republican* that "a mother and child have been killed" as early as 23 July. "I learn that one woman and two children [were] killed," reported "J.T.G." in the *Columbus Enquirer*, 24 July; "these are the only casualties that I have heard of in the city since the fighting commenced in front of it." A report sent on 25 July for the *Macon Telegraph* also mentioned that "a lady was wounded and a child killed by a shell on Saturday [23 July]." Alexander St. Clair Abrams, signing himself "St. Clair," reported for the *Telegraph* from Atlanta on 26 July that so far casualties numbered two women and a child dead, and another child severely wounded by the shells. "Grape" gave a similar report on 26 July: "the casualties in the city [have been] comparatively insignificant. Several members of a family up town

---

[34] Lt. Col. J. S. Fullerton, journal, 24–26 July 1864, *OR*, vol. 38, pt. 1, p. 910; Cyrus Kingsbury Remington, *A Record of Battery I, First N.Y. Light Artillery Vols. Otherwise Known as Wiedrich's Battery during the War of the Rebellion, 1861–65* (Buffalo NY: Press of the Courier Company, 1891) 116; report of Capt. John D. Woodbury, 13 September, *OR*, vol. 38, pt. 2, p. 479; Clauss, "The Atlanta Campaign," 190–91 (Hinkley of the 3rd Wisconsin); John O. Holzhueter, ed., "William Wallace's Civil War Letters: The Atlanta Campaign," *Wisconsin Magazine of History* 57 (Winter 1973–1974): 103; report of Capt. Charles E. Winegar, 7 September, *OR*, vol. 38, pt. 2, p. 476; Kurtz, "Fort Hood and the Ponders House," 14 ("nearly a ton of shot and shell was found in the house").

Wilbur Kurtz pinpointed the site of some of Geary's artillery at Curran St. and 10th (notebook 6, 93, Wilbur G. Kurtz Collection, Atlanta History Center). In 1935 Kurtz even interviewed an elderly Atlantan, James Bell, who recalled the Ponder house coming under fire. Kurtz recorded that Bell, a lad of fifteen at the time, "was in the house during siege; wandered out there boy-like.... Was in house talking to some private soldiers when a red headed captain poked his head in the door and ordered them all out, since shells had begun to drop in the vicinity. Years later Bell related this incident to Capt. [Robert L.] Barry, "'Did you say the captain was red headed?' asked Barry. 'Yes,' replied Bell. 'Well that red headed captain was myself!' admitted Barry, 'for I recall the incident of ordering some men out of the Ponder house, and so you were there too, eh?'" (notebook 10, 222, Wilbur G. Kurtz Collection, Atlanta History Center).

were wounded by fragments of an exploded shell, and one little child was killed." Writing from Atlanta for the *Telegraph* at 6:00 A.M. of 26 July, "W.P.H." noted that "wonderful to say, only one or two persons have been hurt." The correspondent was able to name two victims: "Mrs. Weaver," was wounded, the same shell killing her child in her arms." That day the *Mobile Register and Advertiser* also tried to tally the victims to date: "The casualties from the shells have been two white women, one white child, and one white man killed. One white woman wounded, one negro man killed and another wounded. The child was killed in the mother's arms, and she was also wounded by the same missile."

These accounts suggest that newspaper reporters were largely dealing with hearsay, but repetition of it confirms that at least some civilians were indeed being killed and wounded by the Northern bombardment. Moreover, two casualties seem to have been the unfortunate Mrs. Weaver (as identified by "W.P.H.") and child, the former wounded and the latter killed on Saturday, 23 July (as best as we can make out); they represent the first partially identified shell-victims in Atlanta. Nevertheless people about town were talking about the incident. Julia Davidson, writing her husband on 26 July, mentioned that she had heard of four people killed by enemy projectiles. Besides a soldier and two teamsters, Mrs. Davidson had learned that "a little child was killed in its mothers arms & her face was much injured with splinters." But as with most city-stories spread by word-of-mouth, this one became embellished, even distorted. Thus "J.A.B.," writing from Atlanta 28 July for the *Columbus Sun,* reported, "I was informed by a gentleman that a lady and her babe was killed by a shell a few days ago while lying in her bed asleep and the babe in her arms." Presumably he was referring to Mrs. Weaver and her child. With seven "Weavers" in the 1859 city directory, the names of the wounded mother and slain child might only be guessed, save for the letter of Marcus A. Bell, owner of the Calico House on Collins Street. Writing his wife (then at Elberton) from home on 11 August, Bell reported that "Mrs. Weaver, on Walton street, was in her kitchen with her child near by and the shell ripped through the walls and tore her child to pieces." Of course, Bell was probably repeating what he had only heard. But the several references to Mrs. Weaver's child, plus Bell's placing the family on Walton Street, lead one to infer from the city's prewar directory that an early death-victim of Sherman's shelling was the daughter of John M. Weaver, engineer, who lived on Walton between Spring and Duncan streets.[35]

[35] "Grape," "The Siege of Atlanta" (Atlanta, 26 July), *Augusta Constitutionalist,* 29 July 1864; J. Cutler Andrews, *The South Reports the Civil War* (Princeton: Princeton University Press, 1970) 551 (on Henry Watterson as "Grape"); "F.G. de F.," "From the Army of Tennessee" (23 July), *Savannah Republican,* 4 August; "J.T.G.," "From Our Correspondent with General Hood's Army," *Columbus Enquirer,* 30 July; "For the Daily Telegraph," *Macon Telegraph,* 27 July; "St. Clair," "Special Correspondence of the Telegraph" (Atlanta, 26 July), *Macon Telegraph,* 28 July; "W.P.H.," "From the Front," *Macon Telegraph,* 27 July; "Wounded

Not even a week into Sherman's bombardment, Atlantans remaining in the city were nonetheless finding safe havens within it. On 24 July, after a Northern shell had nearly killed two servants' children living in his backyard, William Clayton moved his family from their house at Marietta and Spring into the sturdy stone Georgia Bank building farther downtown at Peachtree and the railroad. Sallie, Clayton's nine-year-old daughter, later remembered "the shells came from the Marietta side of the town at the time," and thus understood the need to move her family's quarters. Similarly Julia Davidson knew even before the Yankees started firing that her small house in northwest Atlanta would be in jeopardy; her husband had warned her in early June, "if our Army has to fall back to Atlanta to Ditches around town you would have to leave for the shells would reach our House." Shortly after the cannonade started she accordingly moved with her children and two servants from her home near the Winship Iron Works farther into town (hurriedly, apparently, and amidst shellfire, as she complained, "we lost our chickens as the shelling was so severe we could not go back for them"). Their new residence was a bigger house at Marietta and Bridge Streets, apparently offered them by a friend, one Doctor Holmes Sells, whose house next door had a cellar—very useful when the Yankee shells started dropping. "The side fronting the street is entirely underground. The partitions are all of brick," Mrs. Davidson described approvingly. As a result, she and her family had slept there three nights, 23–25 July, when the Northern cannon were intensifying their fire; "the first night the Dr's family and all of us piled up in one room." While preparing meals for her children ("we cook at home principally"), Julia wrote that sometimes they "have to run from an unfinished meal to seek shelter." On Sunday evening, 24 July, the enemy guns seemed to quiet before darkness, so the Davidsons' hosts had retired to their usual bedroom. But when the shells started exploding around 10:00 P.M., "the Dr & wife came downstairs again"; even Julia's mother ran over from a house nearby to seek shelter in Doctor Sells's basement.

Meanwhile Davidson reported that some Atlantans were digging underground shelters against the Yankee shells: "A good many have had *bomb proofs* made. Miss Chattie is going to have one made in the ditch along the railroad" (the W & A, one block west of the Davidson's and Sells's lodgings). At

---

by the Enemy Shells in Atlanta," *Mobile Register and Advertiser,* 3 August; Julia Davidson to "My Dear Husband," 26 July, Peacock, ed., "A Wartime Story," 96; "J.A.B." (writing from Fayetteville GA, 28 July), *Columbus Sun,* 4 August; Pyromis H. Bell, "Bombardment of Atlanta Described by Letter Written Amid Falling Shells," *Atlanta Constitution,* 8 October 1919 (Marcus A. Bell to wife, 11 August 1864); *Williams' Atlanta Directory,* 143 (the Weavers on Walton).

Though printed almost a century ago, Marcus Bell's letter has not been previously cited in the literature. That it only now comes to light reinforces the view that the scholarship of Atlanta's Civil War bombardment is still formative—a good thing for future students and buffs.

the same time, as Julia related, those homeowners with basements or cellars did not have to dig, but could descend to their bottom floors when the bombarding began. And as the case with Dr. Sells, fortunate folk with safe places opened them to friends and neighbors, even strangers. A correspondent for the *Macon Telegraph* arrived in Atlanta on Sunday, 24 July, and found downtown so deserted, "with the exception of a few families," that walking about the streets he could find no one from whom he could request a place to spend the night. At last a resident of Decatur Street, one J. C. Harrington, opened his home, and the newspaperman was shown the cellar (the only part of the house being inhabited), where five women and two men besides his host shared space as refuge from the 20-pounder shells bursting outside. Like other reporters in Atlanta at the time, this one related what he had heard, that "a lady was wounded and a child killed by a shell on Saturday"—the Weavers, tragic victims on 23 July. Unlike others, though, he was able to describe his own close call with a Yankee shell. After dinner, everyone in the household gathered on the piazza,

> ...seated ourselves, and were conversing on the state of affairs in and around Atlanta when suddenly Mr. Harrington exclaimed, "Look there!" Immediately we looked in the direction Mr. H. was pointing. It was a shell making its way directly towards us. It was then so near that I had only time to stoop to avoid being struck. Passing about 12 inches over the heads of the ladies, who were sitting opposite me, it exploded about six inches immediately over my head. Had I not lowered my body, I would certainly have been struck by the missile, as sparks from the burning fuse flew in my face. A fragment of the shell made its way through the opened (front) door-way, near which I was sitting, grazing Mr. Rendleman's shoulder—who, by this time, with the ladies, had entered the passage-way—and striking the floor, glanced and lodged in the corner of the passage-way, between the rear door and the partition. Then there was a general skedaddling for the cellar, where the ladies thought best to remain. My escape was miraculous—indeed the escape of all was a miracle.

Everywhere residents faced the same dangers. "The shells have fallen all around us," Julia Davidson wrote her husband on 26 July. "The house just below has been damaged considerably & the family in it. The Dr premises have been struck twice. he found one shell on top of the house not exploded having bounded there from the ground. The other passed through the front yard to the corner of house cutting off an arbor vitea." In the indiscriminate path of Yankee shells, any and all things could be cut up, even houses of worship. "The Wesley

Chapel is nearly ruined," Mrs. Davidson despaired, "& many other buildings considerably damaged."[36]

Just in time to report these events in its hometown, the *Atlanta Intelligencer* resumed publishing in Macon on 23 July, printing the articles and correspondence of its writers and staff members still in the bombarded city. These correspondents, as well as those filing reports for newspapers in Augusta, Savannah, Columbus, and elsewhere, made frequent use of the Southern Express office (south side of Alabama Street, opposite the passenger depot), from which they dispatched their handwritten articles onboard the trains.[37] One of these, an *Intelligencer* column published on 24 July, indicated that the enemy shells had thus far not inflicted many casualties: "A large number of shells constantly continue to visit every nook and cranny of the city, though thus far the smallest amount of damage to life has been effected by their explosions." Another *Intelligencer* column, printed on 26 July, represented one of the first long reports from Atlanta on the Yankee cannonade, and was widely reprinted, even in the *New York Times.* The article, entitled "The Position in Georgia," cited the first civilian deaths from hostile bombardment, as well as damage to urban stores and residences, with even a few lighter anecdotes of the enemy shellfire.

The enemy continues to perpetrate his practical jokes in the neighborhood of Atlanta. He amuses himself by shooting shot and shell over the entire surface of the city, so that no spot is sacred or safe. Many buildings have been torn and defaced by the missiles, but they will only remain as honorable scars to exhibit in future the gratifying fact that

---

[36] Robert Scott Davis, Jr., ed., *Requiem for a Lost City: A Memoir of Civil War Atlanta and the Old South* (Macon GA: Mercer University Press, 1999) 127–28, 175–76; Peacock, ed., "A Wartime Story," 96 (Julia Davidson to "My Dear Husband," 26 July); "For the Daily Telegraph" (Atlanta, 25 July), *Macon Telegraph,* 27 July.

[37] *Atlanta Intelligencer,* 24 July, quoted in *Columbus Enquirer,* 30 July 1864; "The Newspapers," *Augusta Chronicle & Sentinel,* 27 July ("The first number of the Intelligencer was issued on Saturday last [23 July]"). The resumption of operation by the *Intelligencer* was commented on approvingly by the *Augusta Constitutionalist* of 28 July ("the Atlanta Intelligencer has again resumed publication, presenting the same neat appearance, and containing its usual amount of interesting news and general information"). The *Columbus Enquirer* also congratulated the newly relocated *Intelligencer*: "This enterprising and valuable paper has been removed to Macon, and its publication resumes there. It now comes to us in its full proportions and unaltered in any respect save the locality of its publication" ("The Atlanta Intelligencer," *Columbus Enquirer,* 30 July).
On correspondents' use of the Southern Express Office as means of sending articles out to their respective newspapers, see "Outline," "Special Correspondence of the Times" (Atlanta, 26 August), *Columbus Times,* 29 August. "Outline" expressed thanks to Mr. Hurlburt and the staff of the express office for "their many kind favors" and "courtesy to the Press," especially when "shells are falling around it constantly."

Atlanta was defended even if it was destroyed in the effort. A great many women and children remain in its limits, and are exposed to the enemy's fire. They however do not seem to be much disturbed by their dangerous position, for the women walk the streets as indifferently, even more so than the soldiers do, and the children make a business of picking up the fragments of the impotent shells, to keep for playthings, or perhaps for sale as relics.

Several persons have been killed and wounded by these explosions. On Friday [22 July], a white man and a mule were killed and two negroes wounded on the street before Franklin Printing Office [Pryor and Alabama Streets]. On the same day [when the City Cemetery came under Union artillery fire during the battle of Atlanta] whilst the sexton was engaged in burying the body of one of Mr. Crew's family, the enemy furiously shelled the funeral party whilst it remained in the cemetery. No one was hurt but the monuments and grave stones were very much broken. This must have been exceedingly delightful amusement for the people who are trying to teach us Christianity and recover us from barbarism by effective force measures.

A great many houses on Peachtree street have been completely torn to pieces by the destructive shots that rained on it. This being the most prominent portion of the city and plainly exposed to view, the enemy has easy and accurate range of the place.

On Saturday [the 23d] a soldier was walking in the passenger depot with a sack of corn on his back. A shell entered the sack and exploded, without injury to the man. A friend remarked to us—that shell went against the *grain*—dreadful![38]

The Confederate Press Association's telegraphic news also issued brief daily reports on the enemy cannonade. "Most of the shells came from the twenty-pounder Parrott guns on the line of the Western & Atlantic Railroad," announced the wire statement of 25 July, "with occasional missiles from another gun east of the city." The press association also raised the issue of bombardment protocol, whether the Federals were obliged to have given advance notice to Atlantans that their city was about to be shelled: by implication from the CPA, they were. "No notice of intention to shell the city was given to enable women and children to be removed to a place of safety," read the "Telegraphic" column of 25 July. In the first week of the Federal bombardment, Atlantans were apparently talking about the conventions of warfare, and whether Sherman had violated them. For his part, General Hood seems to have given the matter little

[38] "The Position in Georgia," *Atlanta Intelligencer* (undated), in *Macon Telegraph*, 26 July 1864; also reprinted (undated) in *Augusta Constitutionalist*, 29 July; and as "Shelling Atlanta" (identified as from the *Atlanta Intelligencer* of 26 July), *New York Times*, 16 August.

thought. In his telegraphed reports to Richmond, he only occasionally referred to the enemy's bombardment: "All quiet to-day except skirmishing, and the enemy occasionally throwing shell into the city" (23 July); "all has been quiet to-day except a little picket-firing and occasional shells thrown into the city" (24 July). Nevertheless some in the Confederate ranks expressed resentment that the Yankees had refused to follow the (presumed) rules of warfare; a rumor was going around that Sherman warned Hood of a bombardment only after it had begun. Artillery Captain Key entered into his diary for 24 July, "It is said that Sherman has notified General Hood that tomorrow he will shell the city of Atlanta, and for the noncombatants to be removed. This notice was sent after he had been shelling the women and children for five days [20–24 July], and to cover his cruel and ungentlemanly conduct, for I saw the effect of his cannon balls several days prior to this." At the same time, Alexander St. Clair Abrams, writing as "St. Clair" for the *Macon Telegraph* on 26 July, took a position that favored Sherman when he wrote,

> The Yankees have been amusing themselves for several days past by shelling the railroad, and, as a natural consequence, many buildings have been struck. I regret to say that two women and a child have been killed by the shells, and another child severely wounded. Nevertheless, this shelling by the enemy is not contrary to the usages of war. I was told by a distinguished officer on yesterday morning that whenever a city is only partially invested and the attacking party is close enough to shell it, no formal notice for noncombatants to leave is necessary; for there being ingress and egress, it is expected that all who do not belong to the defenders will promptly leave. If this is correct, and I have no reason to doubt it, Sherman is only acting up to the "code," and cannot be censured.

Abrams's statement was charitable toward the enemy in two ways: it excused the Yankees from violating the "usages of war," and viewed their bombardment of downtown buildings in connection with their "shelling the railroad." Others made the same connection. So many Northern shells were falling downtown, townsfolk reckoned that Sherman's target was the passenger depot and the surrounding rail yards at the center of the city. "Shelling the city still kept up with long range guns," recorded a Confederate soldier in his diary on 25 July. "Many shell have fallen near the railroad depot and the Trout House and several buildings have been struck and damaged." The Yankees were apparently trying to disrupt train traffic, and sometimes the Federal artillery fire did indeed get in the way of army supply workers. Confederate commissary officer Benedict J. Semmes wrote his wife Jorantha ("Eo") on 25 July that the rail depot where he distributed stores had been under fire for thirty hours: "Without intermission the shells struck all over, around, & everywhere but one teamster was killed and one wounded. On my representing the condition of Depot and that the enemy had the exact range Genl Hood ordered us with the trains of cars a little out of the range." Yet he was even then writing his letter in a railway car with enemy shells still bursting nearby.

And the Yankees' bombardment showed no sign of cessation. "W.P.H.," writing for the *Macon Telegraph* from Atlanta on the morning of 26 July, claimed that from Friday, 22 July, to 4:00 P.M. on 25 July, Yankee artillery had fired a 20-pound Parrott shell every ten minutes into the city. He believed at least 200 buildings had been struck, including residences (a shell exploded in John Lovejoy's living room) and churches (a dozen hits on Wesley Chapel and its parsonage). The Methodist church was definitely in range of the enemy cannon, but so too was the Car Shed, "and they peg away night and day, making line shots in the direction of the State R.R. bridge" [the pedestrian overpass two blocks west of the depot]. This "pegging away" became more and more the subject of commentary among people who had to endure it. A correspondent for the *Macon Telegraph*, writing from Atlanta on 25 July, described his experience debarking the train the afternoon before: "The first thing that greeted my ears on stepping off the cars was a shell which came whizzing past about forty feet away above me; I began to think then that Atlanta was quite a hot place to be in. In a few moments came another, and another, which was then kept up at intervals of every two minutes for about a quarter of an hour, after arrival."

On the other side, Federals also held that their artillerists' target was the downtown rail complex. Some claimed to have witnessed General Sherman himself aiming a gun at the depot. "Gen Sherman is here at the battery to-day," recorded John Storrs of the 20th Connecticut on 25 July, "and sights the first gun leveled against the city, aiming to strike the railroad depot. The fuse was too long; the next is shortened, and the shell explodes near the desired point. From that time the trains are no longer heard coming into the city of Atlanta. The battery is directed to continue the fire, and night and day for several days a shell goes screaming over into the city every five minutes."

While some on both sides thus believed that General Sherman wanted his cannon to aim for the railroad complex at the center of Atlanta, the Federal commander issued no such orders in the first weeks of the bombardment. Nevertheless, Union gunners aimed for the area, as when Captain Sutermeister trained his field pieces "mostly toward the center of town and the railroad shops." Smoke and whistle-shrieks announced to all when a train was moving downtown. The Yankees could clearly hear them. "The cars were running out and in of Atlanta last night," recorded Illinois Private James Snell in his diary, 21 July; "the whistle has been heard as often as a dozen times an hour. 7 P.M. Even now, while I write, the 'toot-toot!' sounds in my ears." The commotion seemed to be a signal for the Yankee gunners. Fannie Beers, working as a nurse in Newnan, had reason to travel to Atlanta and did so on a train while the city was under bombardment. "The whistle of the engine was a signal to the enemy, who at once began to shell the depot," she recalled. It was obvious that the Union cannoneers had found their range. "J.T.G.," writing for the *Columbus Enquirer*, stated that on the night of 27 July enemy artillery, bearing "directly upon the depot and vicinity," fired a shell a minute. Yet there was no reportable damage to the rail facilities. Indeed, the continued functioning of Atlanta's railroads throughout the bombardment proved to be a key factor in the Confederates' defense of the city. Some residents thought General Hood even ordered locomotives to blow their whistles, to indicate to the Yankees that train-traffic was proceeding unabated during the semi-siege, with supplies and reinforcements coming into the city. It was said that some Atlantans asked Hood to rescind his alleged order for the train whistles, so that the passenger depot would be made less of an enemy shell-target. On the other hand, according to a Northern reporter writing after the fall of the city, Confederate prisoners reported that "ordnance and commissary stores were brought into the city at night," presumably because the locomotive engines' black smoke would be obscured to Yankee observers eyeing train traffic into town.

Sometimes the Union artillery fire seemed scheduled, with residents downtown able to time the intervals between shells. Captain Semmes wrote home on 25 July that "the enemy continue their wanton shelling of the city—one battery of 20 pound Parrott guns in particular, fires regularly every 3 minutes day & night into the very heart of the city." Other times the enemy fire seemed sporadic, and occasionally it ceased altogether. Confederate Captain Tom Key recorded on 26 July, "this morning unusual quiet prevails along the entire line, and I am anticipating a terrible bombardment from the untiring Yanks. No doubt the few remaining ladies and children in the city are in great and unpleasant suspense." Key was right. On the same day Julia Davidson wrote her husband Johnny that even though "there was no shelling last night & none so far today," and that she was using the period of calm "to get as much work as possible done," nevertheless the uncertainty of when the bombardment would resume made even "the little respite" a time of much stress. "Oh we have been in great dread and anxiety," she wrote. "God grant it may cease."[39]

---

[39] "Telegraphic," Atlanta, 25 July, 1864 in *Augusta Chronicle & Sentinel*, 27 July, and *Mobile Register and Advertiser*, 27 July; Hood to J. A. Seddon, 23–24 July, *OR*, vol. 38, pt. 5, pp. 903, 906; Cate, ed., *Two Soldiers*, 100–101; "St. Clair," "Special Correspondence of the Telegraph" (Atlanta, 26 July), Macon *Telegraph*, 28 July; "B.J.S." to wife, Atlanta, 25 July, Benedict Joseph Semmes Papers, 1848–1865, MSS 2333, University of North Carolina, Chapel Hill; Trask, journal, 25 July, Kennesaw Mountain National Battlefield Park; "W.P.H.," "For the Telegraph" (Atlanta, 25 July) and "From the Front" (Atlanta, 26 July), *Macon Telegraph*, 27 July; Storrs, *The "Twentieth Connecticut,"* 141; Sutermeister report, *OR*, vol. 38, pt. 2, p. 488; Snell, diary, 21 July, Illinois Historical Society; Fannie A. Beers, *Memories: A Record of Personal Experience and Adventure during Four Years of War* (Philadelphia: J. B. Lippincott Co., 1889) 165; "J.T.G.," "From Our Correspondent with General Hood's Army" (Atlanta, 30 July), *Columbus Enquirer*, 7 August; "J.E.H.," "From Sherman's Army [A Deferred Letter]" (Atlanta, 21 September), *New York Tribune*, 9

It did not. On 27 July even more Union batteries got into action, including Captain George W. Spencer's Battery M, 1st Illinois Light, with its four 3-inch rifled guns. Though it had taken position in the line of Newton's 2nd Division, IV Corps, Spencer's battery did not open fire until 27 July. It shelled the city intermittently from then on in varying frequency (e.g., on 29 July, "opened fire on Atlanta by order of Captain Bridges, firing one shot a minute during the day"). Spencer's guns were located in Atlanta's northeast quadrant, between Peachtree Road and the Augustus Hurt house—evidently part of the Union artillery that residents termed firing from "east of the city."

It was on 27 July that the other Hurt house—Troup Hurt's, the brick structure that had been damaged in the battle east of Atlanta on 22 July —met its fate, caught up in the tactical movement of Union forces. Now that the Georgia Railroad had been "secured"—meaning destroyed by his infantry and cavalry, with rails pulled up, twisted over fires and bent around trees, and with key trestle bridges burned for miles running eastward from Atlanta—Sherman was prepared to move against Hood's remaining supply line, the one extending southwest from the city. On 23 July, Sherman informed his chief engineer, Captain Orlando M. Poe, of his plans. As Poe phrased them, "he would attempt to reach the enemy's line of railroad communication, at or near East Point, the junction of the roads from West Point and Macon to Atlanta. It is about six miles southwest of Atlanta. This movement he hoped would either result in a general engagement, with the chances greatly in our favor, or in the evacuation of Atlanta." In short, the Army of the Tennessee (now commanded by Major General O. O. Howard, following McPherson's death), then east of Atlanta, would swing around the city in rear of Thomas's lines, then extend them west of town, heading for East Point, moving gradually toward the Macon and West Point railroad. Schofield's XXIII Corps would for awhile become the new left flank of the army group, and Sherman instructed Poe to draw up a defensive line that could be held, one that terminated close enough to the Georgia Railroad so that the Federals could still control it. The withdrawal of the XV, XVI, and XVII Corps began in the early hours of 27 July. In the reconfigured Union lines, the Troup Hurt house north of the railway, once behind XV Corps trenches, now lay out in no man's land, a possible haven for advancing Rebel skirmishers. Thus Sherman's orders to Schofield that day: "If you don't occupy that brick house as an outpost, burn it." By 9 P.M. that night Schofield gave his response: "The brick house you refer to was burned this evening."

In the Union military correspondence, the George M. Troup Hurt house was never named as such, only "the brick house"; afterward Federals called it the "burnt brick house" or the "burnt house on the railroad." There were soon

---

November (on Southern supply trains entering the city at night); Hoehling, *Last Train from Atlanta*, 199 (on Atlantans' belief that Hood ordered train whistles blown); Peacock, ed., "A Wartime Story," 95–97.

more burnt houses in the area. When a Union reconnaissance by one of Schofield's brigades on 28 July pushed back the Confederate skirmish line, the Southerners withdrew to their main works, determined to leave no refuge for Yankee sharpshooters. Union Colonel David Cameron, in charge of the recon, reported, "four large dwellings have been burned by them to-day as they fell back." Thus did Atlanta's suburban homes continue to be casualties of war. Confederate Captain Key commented on the fate that placed "many costly and beautiful residences near where the work of death is being carried on." He, too, noted on 28 July that "at dark several large houses were in flames in front of Hardee's lines, fired because they furnish a rendezvous for the Yankee pickets." The burned homes, trapped like the "brick house" between warring armies, went unidentified, but their loss would have been devastating to the owners. Years later, Dr. J. W. Hurt, a son of Troup Hurt, bitterly complained that after the fighting in east Atlanta, his father's proud home "was never anything but a pile of brick bats after that." In 1929, the indefatigable researcher Wilbur G. Kurtz was able to find "traces of brick footings in the front yard," and hence to mark the house's location in his comprehensive map of war sites in Atlanta as of 1938.[40]

The skirmishing in Schofield's sector, the new Union left, was trivial compared to the big battle fought on Sherman's right as the Army of the Tennessee marched around and behind the XXIII, IV, XX, and XIV Corps to the west of Atlanta. Just hours after Howard's army began its march early in the morning of 27 July, Hood knew of it, and determined to strike the enemy and block his further advance. His plan called for a flank attack, but as so often happened, the battle of Ezra Church (28 July), showcased futile and bloody Confederate frontal charges. The Southerners' lopsided casualties—CS 3,000 to US 600—demonstrated the by-then well-known understanding in both armies that infantry frontal attacks on prepared enemy defenses would not work. But Sherman got the message: the Rebels were wise to his strategy, and would contest every foot of ground as the Yankees pushed toward the remaining

---

[40] Report of Capt. George W. Spencer, 7 September 1864, OR, vol. 38, pt. 1, p. 493; report of Capt. O. M. Poe, 8 October 1865, OR, vol. 38, pt. 1, p. 132; Davis, Atlanta Will Fall, 149–50; Sherman to Schofield and Schofield to Sherman, 27 July, OR, vol. 38, pt. 5, p. 275; Col. David Cameron to Major Wells, 28 July, OR, vol. 38, pt. 5, p. 288; Cate, ed., Two Soldiers, 102–103 (27–28 July); OR, vol. 38, pt. 5, pp. 286–87, 293, 598, 612 (references to the "brick house"); Wilbur G. Kurtz's notes of conversation, 21 April 1927, with Dr. J. W. Hurt, notebook 3, 241, Wilbur G. Kurtz Collection, Atlanta History Center; Kurtz, "At the Troup Hurt House," 4; Kurtz, "Map of Atlanta as of 1938" (the Troup Hurt house is marked as site 37 on today's DeGress Avenue), Wilbur G. Kurtz Collection, Atlanta History Center.

Within just a few days of McPherson's death in the battle of Atlanta, Sherman had recommended Howard as his successor. Washington approved the promotion 27 July. Joe Hooker, believing himself entitled to army command, angrily left the next day. Alpheus Williams assumes temporary command (Castel, Decision in the West, 419, 422).

Confederate rail line. Building on positions taken by Lee's corps that night, Hood ordered a line of works (dubbed by Kurtz the "railway defense line") constructed beyond the city's fortified perimeter, extending southwest to protect the railroad toward East Point. Sherman responded in kind, drawing Schofield's army corps from northeast of the city over to the sector, extending the Union right, trying unsuccessfully to overlap the lengthening Confederate left. Adding to Sherman's frustration was the failure of a Union cavalry raid against the Macon and Western. Two mounted columns, under Major General George Stoneman and Brigadier General Edward McCook, set out on 27 July. McCook tore up possibly 2 miles of track near Lovejoy's, which was repaired in just a few days. (Stoneman's column never even reached the M & W.) Confederate cavalry punished both columns; General Stoneman himself was captured. This tactical situation remained much the same throughout most of August: both sides stretching their lines southwestward, Sherman trying to break the railroad somewhere, Hood thwarting him. The digging and fortifying meant that more of Atlanta's suburban landscape was laid waste. On 31 July, for example, General Shoup, Hood's chief of staff, directed Major General Frank Cheatham, whose division held lines north of the city, to "fell the timber, large and small, in your front…the object being to form an impassable abatis."[41]

While the two armies jockeyed for control of the all-important railway, the Union bombardment continued. Major James A. Connolly, staff officer in an Illinois regiment with the XIV Corps, wrote his wife on the evening of 27 July, "we can shell the city at our pleasure, and a bright light in that direction tonight, indicates that some of our shells have fallen among inflammable substances." Sherman himself sometimes ordered nighttime firing into the city, as he did on 28 July: two of Thomas's 20-pounder Parrott batteries and one of Schofield's were to "keep up fire on Atlanta all night, each battery throwing a shot every fifteen minutes." Not surprisingly, that evening "large fires were seen in the direction of Atlanta," according to a soldier in the 15th Ohio. Inside the city, structures that shells did not ignite were punched and battered. Hugh Black, a Confederate from Florida, wrote his wife on 28 July that Atlanta was "riddled with shot and shell." Federal officers picked up occasional reports of this damage, as when the Union "scout" J. C. Moore slipped out of the city and told Brigadier General Thomas J. Wood that "our shells fall into the town and annoy them very much, though they have inflicted no great loss." The notion that his bombardment was not achieving anything did not deter General Sherman, as the

---

[41] Davis, *Atlanta Will Fall*, 150–56; F. A. Shoup to Cheatham, 31 July, *OR*, vol. 38, pt. 5, p. 935. The fate of the Methodist chapel that gave its name to the battle west of Atlanta on 28 July shows what often happened to buildings caught in the middle of a battlefield. "Ezra Church….is obliterated," wrote Pvt. James P. Snell of the 52nd Illinois in his diary, "'wiped out' by army operations, but it was standing on the 28th July" (Snell, diary, Illinois Historical Society).

Federals' cannonade showed no signs of abating. On 29 July, Winegar's New York battery alone fired 106 rounds on Atlanta, one every five minutes. More batteries got into action west of the city. DeGress's 20-pounder Parrott battery, having swung around with the rest of Howard's army on 27 July, was in new position by 31 July, "firing at the rebel forts and city." Brigadier General Elliott Rice, commanding a brigade in the XVI Corps, was quite pleased with his new front, which was "in plain sight of Atlanta, and from it shot and shell were constantly thrown into the doomed city."[42]

Sherman's personal interest in the artillery-destruction of the Rebel city before him was unmistakable. To each of his three army commanders, he issued orders on 1 August: "You may fire from ten to fifteen shots from every gun you have in position into Atlanta that will reach any of its houses. Fire slowly and with deliberation between 4 P.M. and dark. I have inquired into our reserve [ammunition] supply and the occasion will warrant the expenditure." Among the cannon within range of Atlanta were those of Brigadier General John M. Corse's 2nd Division, XVI Corps. One of Corse's soldiers, Illinois private James Snell, recorded in his diary entry of 1 August that the Federal artillerists were following Sherman's orders precisely, firing fifteen rounds from each piece beginning around 5 o'clock. Corse reported that day that his 3-inch rifles could "shell the center of the city of Atlanta with tolerable accuracy." Battery commanders in the XX Corps were just as scrupulous in following the orders handed down to them. The 1st New York Light (Lieutenant Winegar's battery) fired sixty rounds at intervals of five minutes, which meant ten rounds apiece for each of the six 3-inchers—the minimum expenditure called for in Sherman's directive. The IV Corps guns were also active that afternoon. "At 5 P.M. all of our artillery opened fire upon Atlanta and kept it up until dusk," recorded Lieutenant Colonel J. S. Fullerton (assistant adjutant general, IV Corps) in his journal.[43]

Damage to Atlanta's buildings was not confined to downtown; suburban houses continued to suffer, and not just from shellfire. Sometimes they were

---

[42] Paul M. Angle, *Three Years in the Army of the Cumberland: The Letters and Diary of Major James A. Connolly* (Bloomington: Indiana University Press, 1959) 245; Sherman to Thomas and Schofield, 28 July 1864, *OR*, vol. 38, pt. 5, pp. 280, 285; Alexis Cope, *The Fifteenth Ohio Volunteers and Its Campaigns 1861–1865* (Columbus OH: Edward T. Miller Co., 1916) 532; Robert Gibbons, "Life at the Crossroads of the Confederacy: Atlanta, 1861–1865," *Atlanta Historical Journal* 23/2 (Summer 1979): 46; Brig. Gen. Thomas J. Wood to Lt. Col. J. S. Fullerton, 29 July, *OR*, vol. 38, pt. 5, p. 282; report of Capt. Charles E. Winegar, 7 September, *OR*, vol. 38, pt. 2, p. 476; report of Capt. Francis DeGress, 1 September, *OR*, vol. 38, pt. 3, p. 265; report of Brig. Gen. Elliott W. Rice, 11 September, *OR*, vol. 38, pt. 3, p. 423.

[43] Sherman to Schofield and Howard, 1 August 1864, *OR*, vol. 38, pt. 5, pp. 324–25; Snell, diary, 1 August, Illinois Historical Society; Brig. Gen. John M. Corse to Capt. John W. Barnes, 1 August, *OR*, vol. 38, pt. 5, p. 326; report of Capt. Charles E. Winegar, 7 September, *OR*, vol. 38, pt. 2, p. 476; Fullerton, journal, 1 August, *OR*, vol. 38, pt. 1, p. 912.

turned on by soldiers (of both sides) who simply needed wood. "S.D.L." reported to his paper, the *Columbus Sun,* that Confederate soldiers had taken the planking from many houses near the fortifications, and fixed the wood over their trenches as shelter from the summer sun and rain. Houses southwest of the city were stripped of their planking when the armies extended their trench lines along the railroad to East Point. Decades after the war W.W. Heren, who as a boy lived in the area of Cascade Road, remembered how his family moved in with relatives to the south when the battle lines came near. Afterward, they returned to find the home destroyed. "When we came back the house had been leveled to the foundations," Heren recalled, "soldiers tore it down and used the timbers in making breastworks." After Schofield's corps marched from northeast of the city around to the army group's right flank (beginning on 1 August), soldiers of the IV Corps stretched their lines to cover the front. Captain Ira Read of the 101st Ohio was among them, taking new position with his regiment. "In our front there was standing a very fine house surrounded by a beautiful grove," he wrote his aunt, "but the house was soon stripped of every board almost and only the skeleton left standing. I hope the owner will think he has got his rights when he sees it. Boards are above par in the army, to use for beds and 'shanties.'" Soldiers stripped away wooden walls not only for their shelters, but also for their forts; boards were useful in revetting entrenchments. As the Federal IV Corps moved its lines on 1 August, members of the 15th Ohio, according to one, marched past a house which had served as the very headquarters of the division, "stacked arms and began tearing down the buildings," carrying the wood to where they began digging their trenches and "building a line of works with timbers."

In the area northeast of the city was the house of Augustus Hurt, where Sherman had headquartered during the battle of 22 July. Already the house of August's brother Troup had been burned, a victim of its situation in no-man's land. The Augustus Hurt house also went down, not by intentional torching so much as gradual deconstruction during the Yankees' semi-siege. Located behind Federal lines, the fine two-story frame structure offered wood aplenty for Northern soldiers seeking planking for their camps and kindling for their campfires. The house was literally picked apart. Later, Augustus Hurt returned to this property, and found nothing. Hurt blamed the Yankees: "the house was afterwards torn down by the soldiers and shacks were built of the same." Hurt added that he even saw "hinges and locks and pieces of marble mantels scattered at many places where the soldiers built fires." Decades later, Hurt's son reported that "the old house was not burned," but dismantled piecemeal. "I remember distinctly seeing parts of it scattered all through the woods over towards the Georgia road and down toward Kirkwood." Moreover, he had been told by his father that the Yankees had stolen the fine furniture, including the mahogany dining room suite.[44]

Thus the architectural landscape outside of Atlanta bore the scars of war as much as the shelled districts inside the city. More importantly, civilian casualties of the bombardment continued to be the talk of the town, even though Confederate soldiers and residents remained unclear as to their number. Reports in the newspapers were anecdotal. The Confederate Press Association's telegraphic report of 30 July noted merely that "a lady on the train" was killed that morning by a shell. The *Memphis Appeal* of 2 August reported "the killing of an old lady residing in a little house at the extreme north end of Marietta street." During the night of 3 August, "one young lady was killed by a shell," the press association stated. In its issue of 5 August, the *Appeal* told how the city had the previous afternoon and evening "received more than the usual attention of the enemy's batteries," and that "one young lady and a gentleman and his little daughter" had been killed by shell fragments; on 6 August it announced that another unnamed "lady was struck yesterday and her foot severely cut." "Rover," a writer for the *Augusta Chronicle and Sentinel,* gave a tally less dire on 3 August, when he noted that thus far "four casualties only have occurred. An old lady was killed in her bed, on the north end of Marietta street; one teamster was killed and another wounded, near the Macon depot; and a negro boy killed." His point, though, was the same as other correspondents; despite the presence of noncombatants under hundreds of enemy shells, "little personal injury has resulted." Confederate soldiers at the front picked up on these stories, and credited them, as did W. L. Trask of General Hardee's staff, who wrote on 4 August, "one or two women, and children, and an old man with his daughter have been killed but little other damage has been sustained so far."

The "old man and his daughter" were Joseph F. Warner and his daughter Elizabeth, both killed on the night of 3 August. Much more than the press report

---

[44] "S.D.L.," "Correspondence of the Daily Sun" (Atlanta, 20 August), *Columbus Sun,* 25 August 1864; "Dodging Federal Shells," *Atlanta Journal Sunday Magazine,* 12 October 1930 (Heren recollections); Richard B. Harwell, ed., "The Campaign from Chattanooga to Atlanta as Seen by a Federal Soldier," *Georgia Historical Quarterly* 25/3 (1941): 274; Cope, *Fifteenth Ohio Volunteers,* 533; Edge to Logan, 23 August, *OR,* vol. 38, pt. 5, p. 642; Augustus F. Hurt to Wilbur G. Kurtz, 13 April 1918, in Wilbur G. Kurtz, notebook 6, 107, Wilbur G. Kurtz Collection, Atlanta History Center; A. F. Hurt to Kurtz, 18 September 1913, as copied by Kurtz in notebook 3, 241, Wilbur G. Kurtz Collection, Atlanta History Center; Kurtz, "The Augustus F. Hurt House," 6 ("it was literally torn apart to build shacks, and to feed the voracious camp fires of the thousands of federal soldiers who swarmed about"); "Kurtz Article Is Given Praise by Old Atlantan," *Atlanta Constitution,* 24 June 1930, 4. Kurtz in 1913 located Augustus Hurt's daughter, who was living in an Atlanta suburb. To his question about her father's house, Mrs. Annie Vary wrote, "My dear old father Mr. Augustus F. Hurt now 84 years of age will never forget & forgive the destruction of the beautiful place" (Wilbur G. Kurtz, notebook 7, 12, Wilbur G. Kurtz Collection, Atlanta History Center).

the week before of the alleged wounding of "Mrs. Weaver" and the death of her unnamed child, the slaying of the two Warners made significant news. From it we have the most substantial evidence of the Federal bombardment's civilian victims. Joseph Warner, aged about forty-two, and his young daughter Elizabeth had lived near the then-named Fowler and Rhodes Streets in the northwest suburbs, two blocks from the city gas works—Warner was superintendent of the company. People immediately started talking and writing about their tragic deaths. On 4 August, a former neighbor (Mrs. Davidson, who was thinking about moving from her borrowed lodgings back to her own residence) was writing to her husband: "Mr. Warner who you know lives in the white house on the corner above our house & his little daughter Lizzie whom you have seen at our house were both killed in bed. A shell passing through the house.... *oh it is dreadful.* I was up at home today & went in to see Mr. W- and Lizzy. The house is injured very much & the mattress was ruined. The flour is all on the floor." Based on stories evidently shared among the townsfolk, the *Appeal* published a short article, "Death of Mr. Warner and Daughter," which recounted the grisly details: "We learn that Mr. W. and his daughter, aged about ten years, were occupying the same bed, when they were struck by a solid shot, thrown by the enemy about 11 o'clock Wednesday night [August 3]. The little girl was literally cut in two, and died instantly. Mr. W. had both legs shot off near the body. He lived about two hours, and was able to give some directions about his family and affairs. The community has suffered a great loss in his decease." The dramatic story of the Warners' deaths was retold in the *Knoxville Register,* this time under the title of "Sherman's Murders." "Confederate," writing for the *Columbus Sun* from Atlanta on 5 August, also identified the Warners as shell-victims: "The enemy for two days have been shelling the city, from battery on the Marietta road. Three persons were killed night before last. Mr. Warner and daughter ten years old killed in bed, the latter being cut in two and died instantly; the former had both his legs cut from his body, lived some hours."

The *Chattanooga Rebel* slightly embellished the story, according to the *Columbus Sun,* which paraphrased it: "On Wednesday night in Atlanta, says the Rebel a shell penetrated the dwelling of Mr. Warner, formerly superintendent of the gas works, striking him and cutting off both his legs above the knee, killing him instantly. The same shell struck his little daughter, aged seven years, tearing out her bowels. The shell did not explode." With so many people talking about the gruesome event, public conversation could itself be a journalistic source. In a column written in Atlanta on 4 August, I. B. Pilgrim wrote, "a shell struck the house of Mr. Warner, Superintendent of the Atlanta Gas Works, killing him and his only child. This happened on Wednesday night [3 August]. I was told of this by Mr. Markham." Days later Samuel Richards included the story in his Sunday diary entry for 7 August, as he distilled the week's events: "Last Wednesday night...a gentleman and his little girl, ten years of age were both killed in bed by the same shell last week, and several others have lost their lives.... "

Indeed, among Atlanta's Civil War bombardment victims, the deaths of Joseph and Elizabeth Warner are the most extensively documented. In addition to all of the notices in Confederate newspapers, the Northern press covered it as well. A month and a half after the event, when Sherman's forces occupied the city, a reporter for the *New York Tribune*, "J.E.H." (John E. Hayes, according to J. Cutler Andrews) wrote a long column, "From Sherman's Army," dated from Atlanta, 21 September (not printed in the *Tribune* until 9 November). Hayes encountered two Atlantans who had been sharing the Warner household during the bombardment and who had witnessed the tragedy of that August night; they told him their story. Hayes took it down so meticulously, with such detail and drama, that it deserves to be printed in full.

THE "WARNER FAMILY" CALAMITY.

On the night of the 3d of August a desultory fire was kept up upon the city of Atlanta for the purpose of disturbing as much as possible the repose of the enemy, and to embarrass him in obtaining his supplies from the railroad, for prisoners reported that the ordnance and commissary stores were brought into the city at night. At 11 o'clock that night a twenty-pounder shell from one of our batteries struck the dwelling of Mr. Joseph E. Warner, a loyal citizen of Atlanta, and a native of Philadelphia, tearing through the kitchen, passing thence through the dining room, and making its fearful exit through the floor of Mr. Warner's bed-chamber, instantly killing his little daughter "Lizzie," a sweet and interesting child of seven years, and severing both legs from Mr. Warner's body. At the time the house was struck, Michael Campbell, one of Mr. Warner's workmen, and Emeline Campbell, his wife, housekeeper for Mr. Warner, were sleeping in an adjoining apartment, not more than fifteen feet from the spot where the shell entered.

THE ROOM OF DEATH.

The delicate little spread whose fleecy folds had but a few moments before enveloped the idol of a doting loyal father's heart, was torn into shreds and dripping with human gore. Michael, the ever-faithful servant, of whom I shall have more to say anon, approached the cot, slowly and with a heavy heart, gently turned down the ragged bed-spread, and while removing the splinters of wood and mortar, great God! What a sickening sight greeted their eyes! The delicate little creature was completely disemboweled, and as he stooped to pick up the debris on the floor, he found her entrails mingled with the rubbish.

Hearing a few groans, Michael got up and in the dark groped his way to Mr. Warner's room. Opening the door a dense volume of dust nearly stiffled him, while from out the dark room arose Mr. Warner's voice, who cried, "Michael get a light quick, for I am killed by a shell." A candle was quickly brought, but so suffocating was the dust caused by the destruction of the walls, that it was impossible to discover the outlines of the ghostly picture for several minutes. Opening the windows the dust faded gradually away, revealing one of the most appalling spectacles that the human mind could possibly conceive. Upon a little cot in one corner of the room lay the lacerated remains of "Little Lizzie," as she was familiarly called, her innocent features illumined even in the somber shadows of death into a childish heavenly smile, while her soft blue eyes were raised to heaven as if pleading to her Savior for mercy. Over her shoulders nestled her flaxen hair, clotted with her young life's blood, while one of the dainty hands besmeared with blood, was raised as if to part from off her forehead a stray lock which had stealthily curled over her left eye.

DEATH OF MR. WARNER.

A few feet from this revolting sight lay the mangled body of the father, both legs lacerated in a shocking manner, while the blood flowed in streams over the floor and down the walls, from out his gaping wounds. With the assistance of his wife, Michael bound up the shattered limbs, hoping to stop the flow of blood, but this he was unable to do. Three male neighbors were summoned for aid; but, arriving at the house, the frightful scene was unendurable, and one of the men fainted and reeled to the floor, while the remaining two were palsied with horror, and could render no assistance. It mattered but little, for, excruciating as was the torture of Mr. Warner, he was so injured that all human skill with its puny efforts, could but prolong his hours of misery and suffering. For two long hours the struggle between life and death lasted, during which time Mr. Warner gave Michael instructions in regard to his orphan child, a little boy of four years, who is now residing in Alexandria, Va., with its aunt. His last words, "Good bye, God bless you," were addressed to his loyal and faithful Michael, who with his wife braved every danger while endeavoring to soothe the dying moments of their generous employer; for even while death held high carnival that starless night within that stricken dwelling, the midnight air without rang, and the streets of the deserted city reverberated, with the demoniac shriek of the savage shells, as they seethed and tore through the heavens, on their errands of death and desolation.

Occasionally, by way of horrible variety, a solid shot would whistle, hiss, and hum, as it shot through the tops of the trees surrounding the house of death, scattering the branches upon the lonely roof, reminding one of the sound of the dull, heavy clods of earth as they strike upon the fragile coffin that holds the clay tenement from out of which a loved spirit has flown. What a night of horrors was spent within that afflicted mansion, no one save the two brave inmates can ever tell, but Mr. and Mrs. Campbell describe it as terrific, as though all the imps of diabolism were reveling in blood.

MR. WARNER A LOYAL MAN—THE ADVENTURES AND SUFFERINGS THAT ARE DEMANDED OF LOYALISTS SOUTH.

The sentiments of Mr. Warner were known to be of the strongest Union character, and from the beginning of the accursed Rebellion which cost him his life and that of his innocent child, he was closely watched and suspected by the Rebel community. Mr. Warner arrived in Atlanta in 1860 to accept the position of Superintendent of the city Gas Works, an office which he continued to hold up to the time of his death. The supply of coal having been exhausted in the early part of June, the gas works were obliged to stop operations, leaving the city in total darkness for nearly three months. Our forces held the Etowah region, from whence the coal was drawn to supply the city. This provoked the bitter Rebels, who started the report that "Warner, the Yankee," had purposely neglected to lay in a large quantity of coal sufficient to meet such an emergency as then threatened the rebellious city. This falsehood was rumored from house to house, until it finally assumed a serious aspect, for besides the personal menaces, Mr. Warner's Union friends ascertained that the Rebel authorities had resolved to wreak their spite and personal hatred against Mr. Warner by forcing him into the Rebel ranks.

Being then without any particular occupation, and no hope of his obtaining any situation in Government employ, he was admonished once more to escape, if possible, into our lines. Such an espionage was kept up around his house, that there was no chance to elude the vigilant Rebels, and Mr. Warner, aided by his Michael, began to prepare a hiding-place within his dwelling, to evade the conscript hunters. After forty-eight hours hard labor, day and night, they succeeded in boarding up an old well, about twenty feet beneath the surface of the ground. Removing the bricks from one side of the well, undermining operations began, and on the morning of the third day a tunnel eighteen feet long, three feet wide, and five feet in height, was completed and ready for immediate occupation. While engaged in constructing this subterranean abode, the shells were bursting in every direction, and once or twice Mr. Warner had narrow escapes from "Gov. Brown's Pets," who were scouting and spying at every house. A few nights spent in this cavern convinced Mr. Warner that certain death awaited him and his little daughter "Lizzie" if they continued longer to inhabit the tunnel, for the miasma and dampness was very heavy, so much so that after remaining in its gloomy recesses two hours, the moisture would hang like drops of perspiration from every portion of the body. To remedy this evil, Michael set to work alone and constructed another place of refuge, beneath the floor of Mr. Warner's bedroom.

A trap-door was cut, large enough to freely admit the passage of a man's body and a wall of six or eight thicknesses of stone and brick was then made, forming a sort of casket. At night and during most of the day, particularly when there was any danger of Rebel emissaries, Mr. Warner was hustled into this curious retreat by Michael. Michael and his wife acted as sentinels, and by certain signals gave notice of the approach of the enemy. The trap-door was concealed from view by placing a bedstead over it and a piece of oil-cloth. Holes were bored in the floor, through which water and air was passed to Mr.Warner, while he could easily hear every word that was spoken in the room. Many times, while crouching in his citadel, Mr. Warner heard the footsteps of his persecutors and listened to their threatening insolence.

ANOTHER HIDING PLACE.

Almost constant confinement in this narrow cell cramped Mr. Warner, and it became quite painful for him to sit, or stand erect, after several hours imprisonment. To remedy this, Michael set to work once more to develop his ingenuity for another place of intombment. A brick cellar was prepared which would afford protection from the shells as well as the Rebel scout. Into this new bastile Mr. Warner and his little daughter were led by their two faithful custodians. Mrs. Campbell was relieved of all suspicion by her sex, and upon her devolved the duty of preparing the food for her precious captives. No little shrewdness was required to perform this duty in order to escape detection, for often at meal hours the Rebel spies would suddenly present themselves day after day, expecting to ascertain by close scrutiny how many meals were prepared. Woman's artful cunning proved too much for man's curiosity and as the rhyme runs,

"Woman, when she will, depend on it.
And when she won't, she won't, and there's an end on it."

Several searches were made in Mr. Warner's house, but Michael and his wife rendering their *valuable* assistance the investigations failed to accomplish much, beyond pretty good proof that Mr. Warner was not at his home. The many visits of these desperadoes induced Michael to hide all Mrs. Warner's valuables, which he did by removing several bricks from the cellar, and placing in a glass jar a watch, some gold and silver specie, jewelry belonging to the late Mrs. Warner, who died in 1860, together with a quantity of table silver. These were hid beyond the reach of these plunderers, and it will shortly be seen that this foresight was Providential, for the bandits were ransacking the house a few days after the valuables were concealed, helping themselves to whatever they pleased.

FURTHER PROOF BY TWO LOYAL EYE WITNESSES THAT "CONFEDERATE" TROOPS ARE THE GALLANT KNIGHTS OF CHIVALRY.

On the 4th of August, while the hearse was standing at the door of the late Mr. Warner's house, waiting to receive the remains of Mr. Warner and his daughter, to convey them to the city cemetery, a gang of Gen. Pat. Cleburne's assassins made their appearance and at once began an indiscriminate plunder. The mind naturally revolts at the bare thought of such a scene. The mangled bodies could not touch a chord of pity within such stony hearts, and in spite of all pitiable pleadings of Mr. Farnmouth, Martin Neilson, Edward Mercy, the three loyalist neighbors who came to assist in last rites of christian burial, the monsters gutted the house of death, and when Mrs. Campbell remonstrated against such infamous conduct one of the "Confederates," with a terrible oath levelled his musket at her head. It should not be forgotten that while these heartless villains pursued their crime, the shells were exploding through the city, and the citizens were ensconsed in their caves to escape the perils of the bombardment.

THE TABLEAUS OF HORRORS.

It was a dreadful picture to witness the departure of the hearse with the two bodies from the tenantless house, while the Rebels were engaged in their work of robbery and destruction. Slowly the little unpretending cortege moved down Marietta st. toward the Atlanta Cemetery, while in front of it, in the rear of it, to the right, and to the left, the solid shot and shell were falling and bursting, each moment threatening to hurl both the driver of the hearse and the three funeral attendants into eternity.

The grave-yard was finally reached in safety, and two loyal bodies were mingled with the dust that filled a patriot's grave.

From Hayes's story in the *Tribune*, one could infer that Michael Campbell, "one of Mr. Warner's workmen," was a servant, possibly African American ("his loyal and faithful Michael"). More probably Michael was not a slave at all, but an employed groundskeeper. Furthermore, despite Hayes's references to Michael's wife, there was no "Mrs. Emeline Campbell" at all, according to a century-old source that has recently come to light. Emily E. Molineaux was a thirty-five-year-old divorcee living in Atlanta during the bombardment with her eight-year-old son. Her reminiscences were published in 1902 under the wordy title, *Lifetime Recollections: An Interesting Narrative of Life in the Southern States before and during the Civil War, with Incidents of the Bombardment of Atlanta by the Union forces, the*

Author Being Then a Resident of That City. From Molineaux's memoir, we learn that she was the woman living at the Warners' home in August 1864, whom Haynes mistook or misrepresented as Michael Campbell's wife, but who with him was the reporter's other eyewitness to the two tragic deaths.

Mrs. Molineaux and her son had come to Atlanta in summer 1863, refugees from Tennessee. They were apparently living in an unoccupied cooper's shop downtown when Joseph Warner came upon them and offered his home in return for Emily's service as caregiver for his eight-year-old daughter, Elizabeth (his wife had died "a short time ago"). Thus did the Molineauxs become tenants in the Warner household, a nice "cottage of six or seven rooms," in which too lived one Michael Campbell. Mrs. Molineaux states that he had been a sergeant in the Confederate army, but had been discharged "because of age and feebleness." Warner now employed him as gardener and caretaker of his property. The gas works superintendent himself had secured exemption from military service thus far—he was one of Atlanta's "secret Yankees," with Unionist loyalties—but now the Confederate conscription officers were after him. Emily confirms Hayes's story of how Michael built for Warner a hiding-place against the Rebels, and how she helped alert him when they approached the house. She also tells of the abandoned well in which Michael dug them a "bomb-proof" against the Yankee shells; they descended into this cavern by hook and ladder. "I felt thankful that our lives were secure for at least a short time," she relates, "although the terrific explosions of the shells above our heads shook the whole foundation, and it seemed at times as though the earth would cave in on us and send us to the bottom of the well, and bury us there."

The well-cave was a damp place, and little Lizzie fell sick. One night, to comfort her, the father took her into his bedroom. Emily was awakened by the sound of groaning. She and Michael rushed to the Warners' room: there they saw everything smashed by a big 20-pound shell, unexploded. Elizabeth was dead. Her father's body was mangled, his legs severed. Three neighbors ran in and, horrified, just as quickly fled. To Emily, Joseph whispered, "I shall not live. I shall soon be with Susy in heaven." After dictating his will, within fifteen minutes, he too was dead.

Emily and Michael saw to the Warners' funerals. Despite the notability of Joseph Warner, the attention to the circumstances of his and his daughter's deaths in the Southern press, and the report by the Northern correspondent Hayes that they were buried in the City Cemetery (now Oakland), their burial places cannot be confirmed. Although the sexton, Green A. Pilgrim, stayed in Atlanta throughout the bombardment, City Cemetery interment records break off in June 1864, not resuming until early 1865.

In fact, residents continued to inter their dead in the cemetery during the bombardment, sometimes under hectic circumstances. After the war, old Atlantans talked about funerals conducted under shellfire. In the 1930s, Lucian Lamar Knight related the story of how a hearse bearing the body of "the son of one of the best known citizens" was rattled by a shell explosion; the frightened driver fled and the solemn procession stalled until a replacement was found. "It was not a good time for burials. One hesitated to attend the funeral of his best friend. It is said that mourners were always in a hurry, and that hearses flew to the cemetery as if they were on the race-track." Atlantans Thomas and Sarah Dye lost their young son to illness while the battle of Peachtree Creek raged to the north. Mrs. Dye, helped by an African American servant, buried the lad in the family plot at the City Cemetery. After the war the Dyes placed the headstone for John Morgan Dye; it stands today in Oakland, noting his date of death, 20 July 1864. Another interment came just a day later. After James Crew's brother-in-law Griffin Killian died of his wound from Peachtree Creek, the family on 21 July buried him in the city graveyard, according to Mrs. Crew's diary, "amidst the shells that were falling in the cemetery."

One well-recorded event involved the death and burial of fifteen-year-old Augusta ("Gussie") Clayton, daughter of wealthy William Wirt Clayton. Typhoid fever raged in Atlanta in summer 1864, and Gussie succumbed to it in the early morning of 22 July. The bombardment was then so heavy that the family could not take Gussie from their home on Marietta Street across town to the cemetery, so they buried her in their backyard garden. Several days later her father wrote of the interment: "she now reposes in our garden where we had to lay her for the present on account of the incessant shelling of the City by our cruel, barbarous and ruthless enemy." Wartime Atlantans talked about Augusta Clayton's garden-burial for years. Recalling her eighty years in Atlanta, Mollie Smith remembered the "young lady who...had to be buried in the garden, because her family could not take her to the cemetery." Years later the Claytons moved Augusta's remains from their backyard to Oakland. The Claytons' may not have been the only such instance; during the bombardment other burials may have taken place in private yards or other spaces throughout the city.[45]

---

[45] "Telegraphic," 30 July, 4 August 1864, in *Augusta Chronicle & Sentinel*, 2, 5 August; "The Army News," *Memphis Appeal*, 2 August, quoted in *Atlanta Intelligencer*, 4 August; "The City," *Memphis Appeal*, 5, 6 August, quoted in *Atlanta Intelligencer*, 6, 9 August; "Rover," "Special Correspondence" (Atlanta, 3 August), in *Augusta Chronicle & Sentinel*, 7 August; Trask, journal, 4 August, Kennesaw Mountain National Battlefield Park; Peacock, ed., "A Wartime Story," 99; "Death of Mr. Warner and Daughter," *Memphis Appeal* (n.d.), *Augusta Constitutionalist*, 10 August; "Sherman's Murders," quoted in *Richmond Sentinel*, 22 August, attributing to the *Atlanta Register* (also quoted in *Mobile Register and Advertiser*, 13 August); "Confederate" (Atlanta, 5 August), *Columbus Sun*, 9 August; "Effects of the Bombardment," *Columbus Sun*, 10 August; Isaac B. Pilgrim, "The Houses Shelled in Atlanta" (Atlanta, 4 August), *Atlanta Intelligencer*, 6 August; Venet, ed., *Sam Richards's Civil War Diary*, 230 (7 August); "J.E.H.," "From Sherman's Army [A Deferred Letter]" (Atlanta, 21 September), *New York Tribune*, 9 November; J. Cutler Andrews, *The North Reports the Civil War* (Pittsburgh: University of Pittsburgh Press, 1955) 754 (on Haynes' identity); Emily E. Molineaux, *Lifetime Recollections: An Interesting Narrative of Life in the Southern States before*

Sarah Huff and Mollie Smith were girls in Atlanta during the war years; they set down their recollections decades later. On the other hand, perhaps the youngest contemporaneous chronicler of the Union bombardment was Carrie Berry, a nine-year-old living with her family on Fairlie Street, near Walton, one block from St. Luke's Episcopal Church. Her father, architectural contractor Maxwell R. Berry, had supervised the construction of the Catholic Church of the Immaculate Conception, Trinity Methodist, and First Presbyterian churches. He encouraged his daughter to keep a diary during the summer's drama. Carrie started writing on 1 August: "We can hear the canons and muskets very plane, but the shells we dread. One has busted under the dining room which frightened us very much. One passed through the smoke-house and a piece hit the top of the house and fell through, but we were at Auntie Markham's, so none of us were hurt. We stay very close in the cellar when they are shelling." (Carrie's aunt, Amanda Berry Markham, was wife of prominent Unionist William Markham, who lived on Alabama Street a few blocks away.) The little girl's short

---

and during the Civil War, with Incidents of the Bombardment of Atlanta by the Union forces, the Author Being Then a Resident of that City (San Francisco: C. W. Gordon, 1902) 29–36; conversation with Franklin Garrett, 13 April 1989 (on Warner's possible burial site; Garrett's necrology at the Atlanta History Center has no listing for J. F. Warner); Wilbur G. Kurtz, "Persons Removed from Atlanta by Gen. W.T. Sherman, September 4, 1864," *Atlanta Historical Bulletin* 1/6 (February 1932): 27 (on Green Pilgrim's staying in city); Kent Moore, "Atlanta's Pride and Problem," *Atlanta Historical Bulletin* 20/2 (Summer 1976): 23–24; Robert E. Zaworski, *Headstones of Heroes: The Restoration and History of Confederate Graves in Atlanta's Oakland Cemetery* (Paducah KY: Turner Publishing Co., 1998) 7 ("the last…burials recorded were June 19, 1864"); Lucian Lamar Knight, *History of Fulton County Georgia* (Atlanta: A. H. Cawston, 1930) 101; Cathy J. Kaemmerlen, *The Historic Oakland Cemetery of Atlanta: Speaking Stones* (Charleston SC: History Press, 2007) 87–88; conversation with Ruth Middleton, Historic Oakland Foundation, 8 March 2012 (on John Dye's gravesite); T. D. Killian, "James R. Crew," *Atlanta Historical Bulletin* 1/6 (January 1932): 11; Davis, ed., *Requiem for a Lost City*, 88n28, 175; Huff, *My Eighty Years*, 45 ("typhoid fever was raging in Atlanta during the siege"); Mollie Smith, "Dodging Shells in Atlanta," *Atlanta Journal Magazine*, 24 March 1929; Lollie Bell Wylie, "Interesting Sketches of Pioneer Women," *Atlanta Journal*, 8 May 1910 (Mrs. M.B. Torbett's recollection of Augusta Clayton's reburial).

Emily Molineaux's memoir has recently (2008) been reprinted by Read Books. I express my sincere gratitude to Sue VerHoef, archivist at the Atlanta History Center, for putting me onto this important source. A rare copy of the original reposes in the Georgia Room collection of Willet Memorial Library, Wesleyan College in Macon; I thank Sybil McNeil, library director, for making it available to me. Marc Wortman makes use of Molineaux in *The Bonfire: The Siege and Burning of Atlanta* (New York: Public Affairs, 2009) 294; as does Bonds in *War Like the Thunderbolt*, 221.

For reference to the Warner's deaths see also James H. Tate, *Keeper of the Flame: The Story of the Atlanta Gas Light Company, 1856–1985* (Atlanta: Atlanta Gas Light Company, 1985) 13. Warner is also cited in "Mr. Davis," "History of the Atlanta Gas Light Company" (undated typescript, Wilbur G. Kurtz Collection, box 29, folder 9, Atlanta History Center).

but descriptive diary entries give a virtually day-by-day bombardment report, one of the very few we have.

—"Aug. 1.... we thought we would not have any shelling today...but before night we had to run to the cellar.
—"Aug. 2.... We have not been shelled much today....
–"Aug. 3.... This was my birthday. I was ten years old, but I did not have a cake times are too hard....
—"Aug. 4.... The shells have ben flying all day and we have stayed in the cellar....
—"Aug. 5.... In the evening we had to run to Auntie's and get in the cellar. We did not feel safe in our cellar. They fell so thick and fast."

Another important eyewitness to the shelling was Isaac B. Pilgrim, foreman of the *Intelligencer* who had stayed in the city; he composed frequent columns and put them on the train to Macon for printing in his relocated paper. Pilgrim was a longtime resident of Atlanta—he appears in the 1859 directory as "printer," boarding two blocks south of city hall. As a newspaper employee, he had secured exemption from conscription and in mid-1863 was also listed as secretary of the Atlanta Fire Company, demonstrating the need of exempted men to serve in multiple capacities in the wartime city. He thus knew it well. On 6 August, the *Intelligencer* printed a particularly long and detailed article by Pilgrim, one of the best accounts of city damage after two weeks of Yankee bombardment. "Mr. Pilgrim made a complete tour of the city," his editors began the column, "and being an old resident of the city and perfectly acquainted with it, he has reported to us accurately the damage he discovered."

Pilgrim dated his column from Atlanta, 4 August, but it is evident he had spent much time beforehand in surveying the city and recording his observations. "Thursday, August 4th, is the fifteenth day that the city has been shelled," he began, informing his readers that he would attempt not only to catalog buildings struck by the Northern projectiles, but also verify casualties among the residents and dispel some of the hearsay sweeping the city for the past several weeks.

"There are a great many houses which have been struck and damaged, which I was unable to visit," Pilgrim announced. As a good reporter, he acknowledged when he was reporting word-of-mouth, as when he wrote "the residence of Mr. John Flynn [at Bridge Street and the railroad] was struck with two or three shells and damaged a great deal. I did not see this house, and know only by hearsay." From the level of detail in his report, it was clear, however, that he had visited many areas of the city. By far the hardest hit area was its northwest quadrant, west of Peachtree and north of the railroad (in contrast, he reported not one shell-hit in the entire southeastern part of the city). Marietta Street had numerous buildings visibly damaged. Pilgrim walked the eight or nine blocks from Peachtree to its outer reaches, and concluded, "there is not a house on Marietta street to the Gas Works but what has been struck." Near Foundry Street, "all the houses in the rear of Winship's foundry have been injured by the shell and shot more or less." "Passing up Marietta street" towards downtown he identified a number of buildings hit: Christian Kontz's, T. V. Rhodes's at Duncan, the Lafayette House, Charles Nort's ("a shell passed through Mr. Norte's house, coming out in the piazza, tearing up the floor considerably"). Also Judge Basil Overby's at Marietta and Spring streets, the First Presbyterian Church (one shell, Thursday morning), the homes of Dr. Westmoreland, John W. Duncan, Sion Robson, Mrs. William Underwood (at Cone Street), and Colonel Bleckley (at Bridge Street) "were all damaged more or less."

At Peachtree and Marietta, Thomas Kile's grocery store building "had a shell to explode in a room, which entered from the roof, but doing little damage. The building next to Kile's had a shell to strike the roof and pass out at the gable end." In the small Cherokee block northeast of Marietta and Peachtree, "every building on it was struck in several places, doing considerable damage." Two blocks north at Peachtree and Houston, "five shells passed through the Wesley Chapel from the rear of the building, and three from the front, one going through ten seats. The church is horribly mutilated. The Parsonage is considerably damaged, some four balls having struck it." Across the street from the Methodist chapel, Pilgrim saw that Judge William Ezzard's home "has one end near the roof battered to pieces; the house of Dr. and Mrs. Bartley Smith has one corner torn off, and the kitchen is riddled. The damage is heavy." On the other hand, damage to the commissary building near Peachtree and Houston was slight; it had been hit by only one shell. Walking north, Pilgrim observed, "about every third house on Peachtree has been struck and damaged more or less." Between Houston and Ellis, "a shell bursted at the window of Joseph Winship's residence, breaking the glass and otherwise damaging the house."

Other places on Spring, Luckie, and Bridge streets also showed signs of shellfire. Among them were the Spring Street houses of Major Shackelford (struck in the roof) and John Peel, which had "five shells to strike it, one exploding inside, besides seven or eight to cut down the shade trees in the yard, tear up the fencing and yard, making a wreck of the whole premises." Running parallel to and a block north of Marietta, Walton Street evidenced repeated strikes, including St. Luke's Episcopal Church at Walton and Forsyth. Pilgrim cataloged all of this damage matter-of-factly:

> A shell struck the brick house on Walton street, occupied by Dr. Goodman, exploding in a room.
> The house in which the Rev. J.S. Wilson resides, on Walton Street, was struck by a solid shot but the damage is slight.

The residence of Mr. John Weaver, on Walton street was struck by two shots, one passing through the cellar, the other through the parlor, tearing piano and furniture up.

Two houses owned by Mr. Weaver, near Walton Spring were struck by solid shot.

A brick edifice on Walton street, owned by Mr. Smith, had a shell to pass through from the roof into the cellar, and exploded.

The house on Walton street occupied by Mrs. Frank Grubb, was struck by a shot which tore off one side of the house.

In contrast, buildings in Atlanta's northeastern quarter were less frequently struck, but Pilgrim recounted the damage, especially along the three streets paralleling east of Peachtree—Ivy, Collins, and Calhoun. At Peachtree's southern end, near Decatur Street, several buildings had been hit: Dr. Harrison Westmoreland's house as well as Mrs. Cooley's and Mrs. Anderson's boarding houses. Heading north, in the area crossed by Wheat, Houston, Ellis and Cain streets, Pilgrim saw more evidence of the bombardment.

Three shells struck the Female College, only one doing any material damage, it struck the belfry, tearing about half of it away [east side of Collins, between Ellis and Cain]....

On Ivy Street, in the neighborhood where Col. Wallace and Mr. John Glenn resided [between Wheat and Houston], several houses were struck. I did not learn the names of the owners or the amount of the damage....

One ball struck the African church, on Collins street.

Mrs. Henderson's house, on the corner Church and Collins streets, was struck by two shells, one bursting inside, and damaging it considerably.

John McGhee's house had a shell to burst in a room where his lady was cutting up meat, without hurting her, but making several holes in the walls.

John Butler, on Collins street, had a shell through his house, bursting on the inside and four falling in his garden.

A shell passed through Mr. Down's house on Collins street, carrying away the back piazza.

Mrs. Schuatt's house on Collins street had a ball to pass through the roof, from gable to gable.

Mark. A. Bell's [Marcus Aurelius Bell's "Calico"] house, on Collins street, was struck without penetrating.

Mr. Willis' house, on Calhoun street, was struck by two shells.

> The house formerly occupied by Mrs. William Barnes had a shell to pass through the roof, two feather beds, a bolster, and out under the house, without exploding.

Closer to the city's center, the various railroad facilities, public buildings, and businesses on Whitehall Street suffered greater damage. On the Western & Atlantic roundhouse Pilgrim counted twenty perforations; to its rear, Mrs. A. D. Rhodes's residence was also hit, but without much harm. The W & A freight depot had three or four hits. The Concert Hall, at the railroad and Peachtree, had three holes in it. Despite the talk that the Yankees were targeting the railroad depot at the center of town, Pilgrim attested to the randomness of the Federal artillery's effects. Pilgrim reported, "I examined the Car Shed, but could not find but one hole in it." Just across the street, the Trout House also showed one shell-hit, but this one "exploded in a room, tearing it up considerably." A block south, at Whitehall and Alabama,

> only a piece of shell went into the old Intelligencer building, but did not as much as leave its impress, as it passed inside an open window, and lodged on the floor harmless.... Two shells exploded in the store of Mr. Kantrawitch, on Whitehall street, tearing everything into ribbons.... Rawson's house, on the corner of Whitehall and Hunter streets, was struck, knocking out a window and bursting in a room. Wood's Jewelry store, on Whitehall street, has been hit in front. Mrs. Valentino's store was hit on the roof, scattering the shingles in every direction.

To the south of State Square, the twelve-block area bounded by Alabama, Forsyth, Peters, and Washington streets had a number of private homes, and these too had been struck: Mr. Hackett's house on Pryor, Kilby's ("only a hole in the building") and L.B. Davis's at Peters and Forsyth ("two shells...one in the garret, the other in the cellar. Damage slight"). On Mitchell Street, "one shell struck the fine residence of Mr. John Neal," without inflicting much damage; a shell passed under the floor of Mrs. Durham's without harm; and a printer with the *Intelligencer*, J. M. P. Calvo, "had a solid shot to pass through his house, thence through the dining table, which was set for supper and on into the ground. The family were all in the front porch when this happened. No one hurt."

Talking with homeowners about their bombardment ordeals led invariably to Isaac Pilgrim's hearing about casualties: "one shell bursted in Peter Hage's house wounding a child of Mrs. Callahan, and Mrs. Flake, and Mrs. Coons.... A shell struck the house of Mr. Warren, on Pryor street, next door to Hunter, on Thursday evening on the end, scattering the splinters in every direction, wounding one lady very severely on the right arm." As he had done with the city's structural damage, Pilgrim tried to tote up Atlanta's human loss. Altogether, he could name or report only ten civilians killed or wounded, a surprisingly low number given the volume of enemy cannonfire. Atlantans had learned to cope with the enemy shells by constructing subterranean shelters, or improvising other safe places. "A great many persons in the city have pits dug in their yards, and bomb proofs made, where they stay during the severest of the shelling." Even huddled in basements for safety, some found their shelter insufficient. In one house located at Hunter and Loyd Streets, a shell "passed into the cellar and exploded amidst the family, wounding Dr. Gates' wife and child." Pilgrim reported other casualties as he heard them, including the deaths of Mr. Warner and his child on Wednesday night, 3 August. Another fatality that evening occurred at a house on Peachtree Street, where a woman was killed by a shell "while she was ironing out some clothing. The lady's name is Smith. She was a refugee from Rome. The shell struck her in the breast, tearing her and mutilating her person very badly. A gentleman informed me of this who was trying to make arrangements for her burial." One reported fatality occurred on 31 July: "On Sunday, a militia man picked up a 24-pounder fuse shell, which fell near where he was stationed, without exploding, and was pecking away on it with a rock, to get the powder out, when it bursted, killing him instantly."

At the same time, the *Intelligencer's* foreman shrewdly discerned that some talk of casualties was exaggeration. "I hear of a great many persons being killed," he wrote, "though I cannot trace them to any person who actually knows it to be a fact. On my arrival I learned that a lady had been killed by a shell. I called on the lady's sister, who is an acquaintance of mine, and she informed me that it was news to her as her sister was in the city of Macon." Perhaps for this reason, Pilgrim did not mention the wounding of Mrs. John Weaver and the death of her child on or around 23 July even though he reported the Weavers' home being struck by two shots.

Throughout the bombardment, the *Intelligencer* reported other city news, probably also from Pilgrim. Signing himself only as "P.," the correspondent wrote from Atlanta on 4 August, "the enemy threw about thirty shell into the heart of the city yesterday evening, without doing much damage. From Tuesday [2 August] at 12 M., until Wednesday, at 1 o'clock, no shells were thrown into the city. An occasional shell came over into our midst during last night." "P."/Pilgrim related that a visitor to Atlanta who had last seen it in the third week of July ("before the army fell back on this place") "is astonished at the great change that has been effected"; the city was badly torn up, trade was at a standstill, the population depleted. But "P." expressed a more optimistic outlook. For one thing, civilians had ceased to exhibit the terror that was so visible in the first days of the bombardment. Indeed, they had become so accustomed to the Yankee cannonade that it was for them now almost a commonplace ("I notice women and children walking about the streets as though there was no army within a hundred miles of the city"). Moreover, despite some of the "big yarns" he had heard about Atlanta having been deserted by its citizenry, "I notice, too, in perambulating the town, that about two-thirds of the residences of the city are occupied by families, and several of them the oldest inhabitants of the place." In fact, "P." reeled off the names of "some of our most substantial and influential citizens" still residing in Atlanta: "J.E. Williams, Dr. J.S. Denny, Markham, Muhlinbrink, A.S. Myres, David Mayer, W. Herring, A. Austell, the three Lynches, John, James and Peter and many others."

Others also noticed that Atlanta still held a good number of women and children, all enduring the Yankee barrage. On the night of 3 August, Captain Tom Key was riding through downtown when "a 20 pound shell burst across my path, and I had just passed the spot when a solid shot swept across the road just in my rear. The residences on both sides of the street were occupied by women and children." Other observers, however, emphasized the depopulation that Sherman's shelling had brought about. "Almost all citizens has left Atlanta," wrote Dr. George Peddy of the 56th Georgia on 2 August. "It is now a dreary looking place and is greeted occasionally by a shell from the enemy." With fewer people about, the good news was that there were fewer casualties from the enemy's shells. "I have heard of but one being injured by them," Dr. Peddy recorded, "and that was a lady." Eyewitness reports were thus conflicting; no one knew just how many people were left in the city, and how many were being hit. Whether of high station or low, however, all civilians still in Atlanta underwent the same dangers of the enemy shells. While residents cursed the Yankees, a reporter for the *Augusta Chronicle & Sentinel* noticed that they were getting used to the ordeal, "many of them, even women and children, looking on with as much sangfroid as could the oldest veterans." "They begin to act," he concluded, "as if even living in a city that was being shelled was 'nothing when one gets used to it.'"[46]

---

[46] Carrie Berry, diary, 1–5 August 1864, MSS 29f, Atlanta History Center; Michael Rose, *Historic Photos of Atlanta* (Nashville: Turner Publishing Company, 2007) 92 (on Maxwell Berry as contractor); Hoehling, *Last Train from Atlanta*, 206 (on location of Berry home); Dyer, *Secret Yankees*, 187 (on Markham home); *Williams' Atlanta Directory*, 126 (on Pilgrim); list of employees of *Atlanta Intelligencer* exempted by Georgia Militia from service, 23 May 1864, in Wilbur G. Kurtz, notebook 12, 56, Wilbur G. Kurtz Collection, Atlanta History Center; "Attention, Atlanta Fire Company," *Atlanta Intelligencer*, 20 August 1863; Isaac B. Pilgrim, "The Houses Shelled in Atlanta" (Atlanta, 4 August), *Atlanta Intelligencer*, 6 August 1864; "P.," "For the Intelligencer" (Atlanta, 4 August), *Atlanta Intelligencer*, 6 August; Cate, ed., *Two Soldiers*, 107–108 (3 August); Cuttino, ed., *Saddle Bag and Spinning Wheel*, 271; "Letter from the Georgia Front" (Atlanta, 3 August), *Augusta Chronicle & Sentinel*, 7 August.

The diary of Carrie Berry (1854–1921), which she maintained for a year and a half, is frequently quoted in the literature. Excerpts from 1 August 1864 to 14 February 1865 are printed as an appendix in James Marten, ed., *Children and Youth during the Civil War Era* (New York: New York University Press, 2012) 227–33. Parts of the diary have been made into a children's book as well: Christy Steele and Anne Todd, eds., *A Confederate Girl: The*

Still the Yankees kept up their cannonade. On 5 August, Major General David Stanley (recently placed in charge of the IV Corps) ordered all his batteries to fire into Atlanta once every quarter-hour from noon to sundown. Federal signal officers, with field glasses from high places, tried to observe the effect of the shelling. In the XX Corps sector on the Union left, spotters at the Augustus Hurt house saw "some of our shells burst over city" (5 August) and "shells from the Twentieth Corps burst near the center of the city" (6 August). On 7 August, a signal officer saw that a "dense volume of smoke arose out of the city this evening for a few minutes near tall brick smoke stack." With the bombardment in its third week, Atlantans pondered the Yankees' purpose in shelling. A reporter for the *Atlanta Confederacy*, writing from the city under date of 10 August, confirmed what all the townfolk knew. "We captured a prisoner the other day who belonged to one of their batteries," the correspondent commented. "He told us that Sherman rode up to his battery in person and instructed the gunners 'not to fire at the fortifications but to rake the city.'" This deliberate targeting of civilians and their property by the Yankees' commanding general was at least censurable (or worse). "He knows that all machinery and public works have been removed, so he can't have that for an excuse, as the Yankees did at Charleston," the reporter concluded, "and he is also aware that our army is in his front, and the city only occupied by hospitals and the women and children who can't get away.[47]

Sherman may or may not have known the true state of Atlanta and its remaining inhabitants. More likely he simply did not care, as he directed that even more damage be inflicted on the Rebel city. As of 7 August, he had extended his right beyond Utoy Creek, just 2 miles from East Point, the key rail junction. But Hood's army lay entrenched in front of him guarding the railroad, and the Rebels seemed able to extend their railway defense line faster than Sherman was able to flank it. Moreover, they held it strongly. Union attacks testing the Rebel works at Utoy Creek failed 5–7 August, with US losses close to a thousand men and Confederate casualties in the low hundreds. "The nature of the ground, with its artificial defenses," Sherman explained to Halleck, "makes it too difficult to assault, and to reach the Macon road by a farther extension will be extra hazardous"—his line was already 10 miles long. Sherman nevertheless was sticking to his goal, that of cutting Hood's last railroad supply line. Lovell Rousseau's cavalry raiding through east central Alabama in July had already cut the railway to Montgomery; Southerners were unable to repair the two dozen

---

Diary of Carrie Berry, 1864 (Mankato MN: Blue Earth Books, 2000). A lifelong Atlantan, Berry married William M. Crumley. She is buried in Oakland Cemetery.

[47] Report of Capt. Lyman Bridges, 9 September 1864, *OR*, vol. 38, pt. 1, p. 485; Burch Foraker and Alfred F. Berry to Capt. Charles R. Case, 5, 6 August, *OR*, vol. 38, pt. 5, pp. 373, 394; W. W. Hopkins to A. K. Taylor, 7 August, *OR*, vol. 38, pt. 5, p. 413; "Correspondence Atlanta Confederacy. From the Front." *Columbus Enquirer*, 14 August.

miles of wrecked tracks, so the southwest rail line out of Atlanta was now inoperable (as Sherman told Schofield on 8 August, "the railroad you see is the West Point road, which the enemy does not use"). Thus Hood's last link to the outside was the Macon & Western, running out of Atlanta via East Point and southward to Macon.

While Sherman contemplated his next move against the Macon road, he decided to intensify his cannonade of the city. "I do not deem it prudent to extend more to the right," he wired Halleck on the night of the 7th, "but will push forward daily by parallels, and make the inside of Atlanta too hot to be endured"—echoes of Sherman's own words before Jackson, Mississippi, the summer before. To enforce his will upon the hapless city, on 8 August he spotted a hill in front of Corse's division west of the city, south of Proctor's Creek, from which his guns could fire more advantageously ("it would make sad havoc of Atlanta"). He added, "I would like to get a good battery as near it as possible that will reach the heart of Atlanta and reduce it to ruins, and to keep up a fire that will prevent wagon supply trains from coming into town." But he was not merely seeking to interdict Rebel wagon traffic. To Halleck he ominously telegraphed, "I have sent to Chattanooga for two 30-pounder Parrotts, with which we can pick out almost any house in the town.... One thing is certain, whether we get inside of Atlanta, or not, it will be a used-up community by the time we are done with it."[48]

Sherman placed Thomas in charge of the heavier bombardment, directing him on 7 August to "telegraph to Chattanooga and have two 30-pounder Parrotts sent down on the cars, with 1,000 shells and ammunition. Put them into your best position, and knock down the buildings of the town." That very night Thomas reported that the big cannon had been ordered down on express train and that he would begin finding a site for them on the morrow. In the process, Sherman's request for two guns was parlayed into four of them. Moreover, the

---

[48] Davis, *Atlanta Will Fall,* 149, 156–57; Sherman to Halleck, 7, 9, 13 August 1864, *OR,* vol. 38, pt. 5, pp. 408, 434, 482; to Schofield, 8 August, and to Howard, 8 August, *OR,* vol. 38, pt. 5, pp. 423, 428–29.

Sherman would have become acquainted with 30-pounder Parrotts during Grant's shelling of Vicksburg the previous year. The gun was proving its worth in Gillmore's then-ongoing bombardment of Charleston. There one 30-pounder Parrott fired 4,606 shells before bursting; the first 2,164 of these rounds were fired at five-minute intervals. With a distance of 6,600 yards from the gun on Cummings Point to the nearest part of Charleston, 4,253 shells were seen to have reached the city; the rest fell short or exploded prematurely (Warren Ripley, *Artillery and Ammunition of the Civil War* [New York: Promontory Press, 1970] 114–15).

The barrel (or "tube," as artillerists called it) of a 30-pounder Parrott cannon is mounted on the grounds of the Atlanta History Center. The heavy piece was bought by famed Civil War relic collector Beverly DuBose in the 1960s and subsequently donated to the Center. My thanks go to Melanie Stephan of the AHC for this background.

cannon dispatched from Chattanooga were not 30-pounder Parrotts, but 4.5-inch "siege & garrison rifles." The difference was slight; both were mounted on wheeled carriages for mobility, and both could throw an iron missile weighing 30 pounds over 3,000 yards—well within range of Thomas's batteries bearing on the city.[49]

General Thomas, his chief of artillery Brigadier General John M. Brannan, and Captain Poe, the engineer, worked on 8 August to find the best site for the heavy rifles. Sherman was clearly anxious for their earliest arrival, and wrote Thomas, "Let me know if the 4 1/2-inch guns have come and where you will place them." The commanding general spent that day on Howard's front west of the city, and thought he had found a good position for heavy guns near Proctor's Creek, "giving a plain view of the very heart of the town." Thomas replied that he had also selected "a very good point for them" on the left of Geary's XX Corps division, "and half a mile nearer than any other position.... The position selected enfilades White Hall street, upon which is General Hood's headquarters, and the battery is being built to-night." The guns themselves were reported to have left Chattanooga that morning, and were expected to arrive on 9 August.

Three of the big cannon did arrive as promised, but not before Sherman had begun expressing even more anticipation, if not excitement, at the prospect of seeing them at work. To Thomas he wrote, "send me word when the 4 1/2-inch guns come, as I want to come over and watch the effect of a few of the first shots." Thomas asked for patience. By dark three of the four cannon had arrived, but their ammunition was still behind. Thomas had to explain that the battery for the guns had been constructed, and he expected the ammo to come tomorrow. Captain Arnold Sutermeister of the 11th Indiana Battery was attached to Thomas's headquarters, and served under his personal supervision; Sutermeister took charge of the three guns and saw them into position. The site was in front of Geary's third brigade (Colonel David Ireland's), described as 1 1/2 miles to the left of the Marietta road, "500 yards from Buck Head road" (Peachtree) and a half-mile east of Howell Mill Road. The embrasures themselves were more elaborate than usual. A curious New York infantryman later got permission to "take a stroll from camp" and see the big guns he had been hearing. "They looked large to me," Sergeant Rice Bull recorded in his diary. "It required quite a large force to man the redoubt, which was strongly built, with heavy iron doors in front that closed when the guns were not in action. These siege guns were only used to shell the city."[50]

[49] Sherman to Halleck, 7 August 1864, *OR*, vol. 38, pt. 5, p. 408; Sherman to Thomas and Thomas to Sherman, 7 August, *OR*, vol. 38, pt. 5, p. 412; Ripley, *Artillery and Ammunition of the Civil War*, 114, 165–66, 370, 374.

[50] Report of Capt. Orlando M. Poe, 8 October 1865, *OR*, vol. 38, pt. 1, p. 134; Sherman to Thomas, 8, 9 August 1864, *OR*, vol. 38, pt. 5, p. 419, 435; Thomas to Sherman, 8, 9 August, *OR*, vol. 38, pt. 5, p. 419, 436; report of Brig. Gen. John M. Brannan, 14 September, *OR*, vol.

Thanks to the scrupulous research of Wilbur G. Kurtz, who trekked Atlanta in the 1920s and '30s before urban sprawl obliterated many war-vestiges, we know the location of Sutermeister's siege gun battery: roughly along today's 11th Street at Plum and Cherry, in the vicinity of Georgia Tech. Kurtz was walking the area 29 December 1928, when he found earthworks denoting three distinct artillery embrasures. In his placement of Civil War sites onto the map of Atlanta as of March 1930, Kurtz took pains to ink in these three gun sites behind the line of trenches held by the XX Corps, 22 July–25 August; he repeated the placement of the three sites on another map drawn in 1938. Kurtz astutely made the connection that the embrasures held Sherman's 4 1/2-inch siege cannon. Writing in 1932 about the Federal batteries between the city's 8th and 11th streets, Kurtz wrote "three large gun-pits are still visible near Home Park School, where the four and one-half inch rifled guns of the Federal Twentieth Corps were planted."[51]

Sherman planned for a big bombardment of the city, bigger than anything before, and hoped the 4 1/2-inchers could participate in it. To Thomas on 9 August he instructed, "Get your guns well into position, and the moment the ammunition comes, let them open slowly, and with great precision, making all parts of the town unsafe. Guns of that caliber with good shells have a better effect than any I ever used." Disappointed at the delay in getting his siege artillery into action, Sherman nevertheless called for a general bombardment of the city on 9 August, specifying a heavier volume of fire than previously

---

38, pt. 1, p. 184; report of Capt. Arnold Sutermeister, 14 September, *OR*, vol. 38, pt. 2, p. 489–90; report of Col. Henry A. Barnum, 7 September, *OR*, vol. 38, pt. 2, p. 303; report of Brig. Gen. John W. Geary, 15 September, *OR*, vol. 38, pt. 2, p. 142; Bauer, ed., *Soldiering*, 163.

The three siege guns apparently were borne from Chattanooga on flat open-air platform cars, as they were visible to soldiers manning a hilltop battery overlooking the railroad bridge on the Etowah River ("Etowah Bridge, Tuesday, August 9. Rainy day.... No news. Heavy artillery, caissons and carriages going to the front in large numbers [Jenkin Lloyd Jones, *An Artilleryman's Diary* (Madison: Wisconsin History Commission, 1914) 237–38]).

[51] Wilbur G. Kurtz, sketched map, notebook 3, 150, Wilbur G. Kurtz Collection, Atlanta History Center; Wilbur G. Kurtz, map and key, "Embattled Atlanta," *Atlanta Constitution*, 20 July 1930, 12–13; and "Map of Atlanta as of 1938," Wilbur G. Kurtz Collection, Atlanta History Center. Kurtz's hand-drawn map of December 1928 in his notebook shows Union trenches and "3 gun sites" north of 10th St. at "Prolongation of Cherry St" and "will be Plum St." Kurtz returned to them in November 1929 to confirm their location. On a sketched map of the area of Kontz Ave. and 11th St., Kurtz also highlighted the three gun embrasures (box 39 [oversized], folder 5, "maps"). He also found earthworks south of 10th St., east of Fowler (notebook 3, 79–80, 83–88, Wilbur G. Kurtz Collection, Atlanta History Center).

Neither Kurtz's "Embattled Atlanta" nor his "Map of Atlanta as of 1938" contains any reference that the three ink-dots are positions of the Federals' 4.5-inch siege cannon; the connection is made only in Kurtz's notebooks.

ordered. "All the batteries that can reach the buildings of Atlanta will fire steadily on the town," read his orders, "using during the day about fifty rounds per gun, shell and solid shot." The Federal commander, however, suggested that his artillerists concentrate on the city's north side. To Howard, whose Army of the Tennessee occupied the Union lines west of Atlanta, Sherman advised, "there is little use of your firing from the right of your line, as that [the southern] end of town is of little depth or importance." At the same time, one of Sherman's purposes with the barrage involved Schofield's forces, to the right (south) of Howard's sector: "The enemy's cavalry manifests activity on our right, threatening to cross Utoy Creek to General Schofield's rear," Sherman wrote Thomas on the night of 8 August. "I want him [Schofield] to-morrow to develop well the enemy's flank, which I believe is along the south fork of Utoy Creek, covering East Point. To enable him to do this I want a general cannonading to-morrow, the 4 1/2-inch guns included, if they come in time." Sherman was ostensibly linking the general shelling ordered for 9 August to Schofield's infantry probes on his right flank, also ordered that day. Yet he did not call for a bombardment of the Rebel infantry lines, which would have been a true diversionary tactic. It is thus apparent that in ordering a bombardment of the city and its remaining inhabitants, Sherman was only half-heartedly seeking a tactical military diversion. For days, he had expressed his desire for a huge shelling of Atlanta; now he was going to get it.

And he did. The Union artillery opened fire about 10:00 A.M. on 9 August and continued for five or six hours. Fifty rounds per gun meant that six-gun units such as Battery I, 1st New York Light, fired 300 rounds, as Captain Winegar recorded, "in direction of railroad depot, at an interval of two and a half minutes." Federals perched in trees and other high places observed the effect of the heavy cannonade. "The lookouts report great commotion in Atlanta," read one report, "and that our shells burst immediately over all parts of the town." With all of Geary's division artillery firing its fifty rounds, one lookout, W. W. Hopkins, climbed a tree near the general's headquarters to see the effect. "Shells exploded over the city and in it, judging from the sound," Hopkins observed, even noting "a small piece was knocked off top of brick smoke-stack in town." Lieutenant Hopkins noted that the Federal artillery pounded not only the city, but the Rebel works. "The most noticeable effect of the shelling was in front of General Geary's division at a fort and house," he recorded. "This fort was struck; also the works near it, and the house had a large hole knocked in it besides being riddled." In all likelihood, Hopkins was referring to the Ponder house, situated near the Confederate lines and the northwest salient anchored by Fort Hood.

That night, with evident satisfaction, General Sherman wired Halleck in Washington, "I threw into Atlanta about 3,000 solid shot and shell to-day." If firing fifty rounds each, Sherman's shell-count would have involved sixty of his cannon, at least ten batteries. General John Geary thought even more had been involved in the day's work. "Yesterday was a day of continuous cannonading," he wrote his wife Mary on 10 August, "from 100 pieces on our side, from morning to night, inflicting terrible damage upon the houses and public edifices in the doomed city." By Geary's estimation, a hundred cannon each firing fifty rounds meant that fully 5,000 Union artillery projectiles were fired on Atlanta in that six- or seven-hour period on 9 August. That meant a minimum (at 10 pounds per projectile) of 25 tons of metal thrown into the city. General Geary offered to his wife a further comment on the bombardment: "I cannot tell how many lives were lost but the casualties among the enemy must have been numerous."[52]

In fact, no one could verify the number of civilians or soldiers killed and wounded in the cannonade of 9 August, which proved to be the heaviest day of Yankee shellfire during Sherman's bombardment. As usual, newspapermen inside the city did their best to report on what they had heard or in rare cases had actually witnessed. The *Appeal* of 8 August acknowledged the difficulty of verifying the various rumors circulating the city: "we have a report of three casualties having occurred, but on investigation conclude it is without foundation." The Confederate Press Association report in the *Intelligencer* accurately described the barrage of 9 August as the "heaviest shelling of the city yet," with "many buildings being struck." But the column only reported that "one citizen was killed and a child was wounded"—although it could not offer their names. The *Appeal* concurred that it was "the most furious cannonading of the siege of Atlanta."

> The amount of Federal spite vented against the city yesterday far exceeded any demonstration our enemies have yet made. His batteries opened about eleven o'clock A.M., and were continually at work until after four P.M. During the time many hundred shots fell into the city and suburbs. Of course many buildings were struck, and strange to say, most of these were private residences. The damage to the business part of the

---

[52] Sherman to Thomas, 8, 9 August 1864, *OR*, vol. 38, pt. 5, pp. 418, 431, 436; Sherman to Howard, 8 August, *OR*, vol. 38, pt. 5, p. 429; Lt. Col. J. S. Fullerton, journal, *OR*, vol. 38, pt. 1, pp. 917–18; report of Capt. Charles E. Winegar, 7 September, *OR*, vol. 38, pt. 2, p. 476; Geary's report, *OR*, vol. 38, pt. 2, p. 143; W. W. Hopkins to A. K. Taylor, 9 August, *OR*, vol. 38, pt. 5, p. 437; Sherman to Halleck, 9 August, *OR*, vol. 38, pt. 5, p. 434; Blair, ed., *A Politician Goes to War*, 194 (Geary to "My Dearest Mary," 10 August).

The number of Union cannon taking part in the heavy bombardment of 9 August cannot be documented. If perhaps only 80 percent of the over 100 rifled cannon in Sherman's three armies (chiefly 3-inch ordnance guns, 10- and 20-pounder Parrotts) were in range for shelling the city, and each fired the 50 rounds ordered by Sherman, an estimated 4,250 rounds would have fallen on Atlanta on 9 August. Estimates of 3,000–5,000 shells fired that day are therefore reasonable. Hoehling quotes Union soldier Andy Rose's statement that "100 guns had fired fifty shells each at Atlanta" on 9 August—the same number of rounds estimated by General Geary (*Last Train from Atlanta*, 282).

city was slight. But two casualties have been reported. A gentleman in the outskirts of the city had both legs taken off by a shell, while sitting on his doorstep, and died before a surgeon could be procured. The other was a child, who was severely bruised by a lump of earth set in motion by a shot.

The heavy shelling further convinced Atlantans that the Yankees aimed to wreck their city, and to kill or maim the people inside of it. Confederate artillery officer Lieutenant Andrew J. Neal, whose battery was posted in the Confederate lines northwest of town, described the enemy gunners' routine: "Almost all the shells they throw into the City come screaming just above our heads. Generally they commence on this fort and throw around it shells and then elevate their guns and send the balance into the city." The Federals' fire was having its effect, Neal observed; "in some parts of town every house has been struck a dozen times." Another artilleryman, Private Phil Stephenson, also refused to fall for the Yankees' line that they were only firing at the Rebel fortifications. "True, our lines were close into the city," he wrote, "but veteran soldiers like Sherman's knew how to fire accurately." "Nay," concluded Stephenson, "it was designed, part of a cold blooded policy of war on women and children and property." The *Appeal* of 10 August addressed this obvious design as another instance of Northern criminality.

> Many of the Yankee prisoners captured since the practice of shelling the city has been going on, protest most vehemently that their guns are not directed against the place, and assert that the shells that daily visit us are fired at our batteries, but miss the mark at which directed. This is all sheer humbug. The Yankee gunners are better marksmen than these assertions would give them credit for, and that the act of shelling the city is a purposed one there can be no doubt. The unwarrantable practice— unwarrantable because no notice has ever been given—can not be excused by any such shallow pretences. The whole procedure is a result of Federal spleen at the success of resistance to their plans, and they have doubtless determined to destroy what they no doubt begin to conclude that they cannot possess.[53]

---

[53] "The Immediate Front," *Memphis Appeal*, 8 August 1864, quoted in *Columbus Times*, 12 August; "Latest from Atlanta," *Atlanta Intelligencer*, 11 August; "The Immediate Front," *Memphis Appeal*, 10 August, *Columbus Times*, 13 August; Neal to "Ella," 4 August, Andrew Jackson Neal Letters, Emory University; Hughes, ed., *Civil War Memoir of Philip Stephenson*, 230.

In counting civilian casualties of the Union cannonade on 9 August, secondary accounts are as vague as Confederate newspapers' and at times more misleading. Wallace Reed's *History of Atlanta* (1889) alludes only to "that red day in August, when all the fires of hell, and all the thunders of the universe seemed to be blazing and roaring over Atlanta"—

As if a personal target of the "Federal spleen," one occupant of Atlanta who definitely came under Yankee shellfire on 9 August was no less than General Hood himself. As General Thomas indicated to Sherman, Union spies in the city kept him informed of the location of Hood's headquarters; on 8 August he knew it was in a house on Whitehall Street. Actually the general had stayed at several different residences since taking over from Joe Johnston on 18 July. During 19–21 July, Hood was at the Alexander F. Luckie home, on Peachtree just south of Prescott Street. At the time, he would have been in the city's northern suburbs, just inside the Confederates' main line of fortifications. Then, with the abandonment of the city's outer line and the army's withdrawal into the main works, the general apparently moved eight blocks south, where on the evening of 21 July his headquarters were said to be at Austin Leyden's house, on Peachtree between Ellis and Cain.[54]

After watching the battle of Atlanta, 22 July, from the home of James E. Williams near the City Cemetery, that night Hood established new headquarters at the home of his friend John S. Thrasher, general manager of the Confederate Press Association. The autumn before Thrasher had opened his house on Whitehall Street to Hood as a place for him to convalesce after his severe

---

but he never gives the date of that "red day." "It was on this day of horrors that the destruction of human life was greatest among the citizens," Reed asserts, as he counts six deaths from enemy projectiles—although he includes among them Mr. Warner and his daughter, whom we know to have been slain on the night of 3 August (Reed, *History of Atlanta*, 191). Local writer William Key quotes Reed extensively, but guesses that the "red day" occurred on 10 August (William Key, *The Battle of Atlanta and the Georgia Campaign* [New York: Twayne Publishers, 1958] 69). Samuel Carter omits the two Warners in his death-toll for August 9, but claims that an unnamed family of six died when a shell struck their "bombproof" shelter (*The Siege of Atlanta*, 284). In his Time-Life volume, Ronald H. Bailey writes, "on August 9, Federal gunners poured more than 5,000 shells into the city. On that day at least six civilians [unnamed by Bailey], including women and children, died in the bombardment," thus returning to Wallace Reed's "red day" death count of a century before, but adding no details or even corroboration (Bailey, *Battles for Atlanta*, 139).

[54] Thomas to Sherman, 8 August 1864, *OR*, vol. 38, pt. 5, p. 419; [Garrett and Kurtz], "Key to Map" (site 151); Russell K. Brown, *To the Manner Born: The Life of Gen. William H.T. Walker* (Athens: University of Georgia Press, 1994) 263 (Hood's headquarters at Leyden house); "Here Are Some Last Farewell Views of the Old Leyden House," *Atlanta Journal*, 23 February 1913.

The Leyden house became the site of one of Atlanta's principal department stores. In 1939, Davison's commissioned Wilbur G. Kurtz to draw the house with Confederate officers and citizens standing in front. Kurtz's illustration was the basis of a Davison's advertisement, which ran in the *Atlanta Journal*'s "Gone With the Wind" Souvenir Edition of 15 December 1939, the day of the movie's premiere in Atlanta. "Just up the Street from Us Lived Scarlett and Aunt Pittypat," the ad's headline beamed, informing readers that "on the very spot of our store was a historical landmark of the Old South—the Leyden House" (*Atlanta Journal*, 15 December 1939).

wounding and leg amputation at Chickamauga. Thrasher's Whitehall home was south of the city's busy central business and railroad complex. On the night of 22 July, Lieutenant Thomas B. Mackall (cousin and aide-de-camp to Brigadier General William W. Mackall, chief of staff for Johnston and Hood up to 24 July), recorded in his diary that the new army command center was established at "Thrasher house—suburbs of Atlanta."[55]

---

[55] Wilbur G. Kurtz, notebook 7, 43 (citing one Richard Fickett as source for Hood at Williams house, 22 July), Wilbur G. Kurtz Collection, Atlanta History Center; Richard M. McMurry, *John Bell Hood and the War for Southern Independence* (Lexington: University Press of Kentucky, 1982) 82; "Serenade to General Hood," *Memphis Appeal,* 5 November 1863 ("the residence of Col. J.S. Thrasher on Whitehall Street"); Richard M. McMurry, ed., "The Mackall Journal and Its Antecedents," 22–23 July ("Thrasher House-suburbs of Atlanta"), unpublished typescript of Lt. Thomas B. Mackall's diary, Earl Greg Swem Library, College of William and Mary, Williamsburg, Virginia. I am indebted to Dr. McMurry for lending me his edited transcription of Lt. Mackall's diary. This important source has too long been overlooked by historians of the Atlanta Campaign.

Dr. McMurry's newspaper sources, cited above, are important in identifying Hood's headquarters as the home of John S. Thrasher, on Whitehall Street. John Sidney Thrasher, originally of Galveston, was a newspaperman who moved to Atlanta in April 1863 when he established the headquarters of the new Confederate Press Association (Andrews, *The South Reports the Civil War,* 56). The Confederate Press Association's "Telegraphic" columns routinely identify "J.S. Thrasher" as the head of the CPA. No picture of J. S. Thrasher's house has come to light, but "Outline," a correspondent for the *Columbus Times,* described it: "Gen. Hood's quarters, in the pretty gothic cottage formerly occupied by Col. J.S. Thrasher, would scarcely be distinguished by a stranger, if he failed to observe the little headquarters' battle-flag, which falls lazily around the white staff at the gate" (*Columbus Times,* 27 August 1864).

The "Thrasher House" used by General Hood has sometimes been erroneously linked to John *James* Thrasher, longtime Atlanta businessman, known as "Cousin John." ("John J. Thrasher, trader" is listed in *Williams' 1859 Directory.*) Garrett mistakenly claims that during August 1864 John J. Thrasher's home "had a distinguished tenant, General John B. Hood," and that the general stayed at Thrasher's estate, situated on today's Ashby Street at West End Avenue (*Atlanta and Environs,* 1:207). (The place, called "Homestead," was built in 1857; see Huff, *My Eighty Years,* 62; and Laureita Fancher, "Historic Home May Be Razed," *Atlanta Journal Sunday Magazine,* 21 December 1930, 2.) Local writer William R. Scaife accepts the idea that Hood's headquarters were at "Cousin John's," and in his map of "Civil War Atlanta" marks "HOMESTEAD Hood's Headquarters July 27 & 28" at its Ashby Street location. But as thus located, the site is shown to be *outside* of the Confederate fortifications—a very unlikely place for army HQ to be (Scaife, *The Campaign for Atlanta* [Saline MI: McNaughton & Gunn, 1993] f.p. 130).

On "Cousin" John J. Thrasher, see David E. Sumner, "Everybody's Cousin: John J. Thrasher Was One of Atlanta's Founders and Most Colorful Figures," *Georgia Historical Quarterly* 84/2 (Summer 2000): 295–307. For his help in sorting out the two Thrashers, I wish to thank Leighton Wingate of Seattle, who at the time of this writing is at work at the

It was here that Hood came under Union bombardment. "Cannonading has been going on all day," wrote Confederate Captain Key on 29 July; "while I was at General Hood's, shells were exploding near his headquarters." J. Milton Glass, the Northern spy in Atlanta, kept his superiors informed of the Rebel commanding general's HQ site, possibly in the knowledge that they might direct cannon fire toward it. On 3 August Glass reported that "General Hood's headquarters is in White Hall street, near Rodgers tannery." That would set the Hood HQ/Thrasher house between Garnett Street and Grenville's alley, fully four blocks south of the Car Shed and central railroad sector. The area would still have been within range of Union guns north and west of the city. General Thomas had made a point of telling Sherman that he had chosen a position for the soon-to-arrive siege artillery that could enfilade Whitehall.[56]

The 4 1/2-inch siege cannon were not able to participate in the general bombardment ordered by Sherman on 9 August, but Hood's headquarters in southwest Atlanta clearly came under fire of the Federals' Parrotts and 3-inch rifles. Visitors to the army command center that day documented their discomfort when the Yankee shells began exploding nearby. The Right Reverend Henry C. Lay, Episcopal bishop of Arkansas, happened to be visiting Hood's HQ with Chaplain Charles T. Quintard when the shelling started. "[August] 9 with Dr. Quintard came to Atlanta—were invited to Head Qrs. where I am the guest of General Shoup, Chief of Staff. Shells are exploding all around Head Qrs (at Thrasher's House)," Bishop Lay recorded laconically in his diary, "and it is proposed to move them." Describing his visit with Bishop Lay that day, Chaplain Quintard was a little more candid: "The city was being shelled by the Federals, and some of the shells fell very thickly about the General's headquarters. I thought the locality seemed very unhealthy, but as the General and his staff did not seem in the least disturbed, Bishop Lay and I concluded that everything was going on all right according to the art of war and we stood it with the best of them." Word circulated through the army that its leader was enduring the same dangers and life-threats as the men. "Town shelled heavily last evening," entered W.L. Trask, of General Hardee's staff, into his diary for August 10; "Hood's quarters came in for a large share of the shelling."[57]

University of Washington on a dissertation about John Sidney Thrasher, the CPA, and Confederate newspapers.

[56] Cate, ed., *Two Soldiers*, 105; Ed. C. Denig to Brig. Gen. W. D. Whipple, 3 August 1864, *OR*, vol. 38, pt. 5, p. 348; Francis F. McKinney, *Education in Violence: The Life of George H. Thomas and the History of the Army of the Cumberland* (Detroit: Wayne State University Press, 1961) 358 (on Thomas's selection of siege artillery site "from which it could enfilade the street in which Hood had his headquarters").

[57] "Excerpts from Diary of Bishop Henry C. Lay," (typescript, prepared in 1947, of the Lay diary, University of North Carolina), box 26, folder 4, Wilbur G. Kurtz Collection, Atlanta History Center; Arthur Howard Noll, ed., *Doctor Quintard Chaplain C.S.A. and Second Bishop of Tennessee Being His Story of the War (1861–1865)* (Sewanee TN: University

After the Yankee bombardment of 9 August (when Bishop Lay wrote "it is proposed to move them"), General Hood and his staff relocated their headquarters still farther out Whitehall Street, even more southwesterly and into the suburbs. On 12 August, the "scout" Milton Glass reported that Hood's headquarters were now "where White Hall street intersects Faith's alley." This new location was another three or four blocks south of the city center—farther still from the Union artillery's apparent emphasis. Postbellum Atlantans had clear recollections of this site, and together their remembrances help us pinpoint where Hood spent the last few weeks of the Atlanta Campaign. In 1895, marking wartime points about the city, ex-Confederates recorded the southeast corner of Whitehall and Hood Streets as the army commander's headquarters sometime during summer 1864 (the city had so named the street after the general). Other Atlantans, such as former Confederate Major Charles W. Hubner, also remembered that Hood had his headquarters in a house at Whitehall and Hood (in 1864, it was Rawson Street, or Faith's Alley). Hubner, in charge of the army telegraphic service (located in the Gate City Hotel, at the corner of Alabama and Pryor Streets) remembered, though without giving a date, that "it was somewhat disconcerting to me, when a fragment of a shell which had burst in front of the building, came through the window where I sat recording messages, and ripped off the page opposite to the one upon which I was writing, and I was relieved when orders came to move the office out on Whitehall Street, opposite General Hood's headquarters, which were then on the corner of Whitehall and what is now known as Hood Street." In 1897, George W. Adair, who had edited the *Atlanta Southern Confederacy*, claimed that it was he who had Hood Street so named; during the war he had been on Hood's staff, and had spent much time at the headquarters of the general, "who was camped right where Hood Street now runs into Whitehall." A fifteen-year-old at the time, James Bell, later recalled that Hood (possibly because of the heat) pitched a tent in the backyard of the large two-story white frame house, rather than occupy it. Major Hubner remembered that Hood was still at "the corner of Whitehall and what is now Hood Street" when the fateful dispatch arrived from General Hardee announcing his defeat at Jonesboro on 31 August. For years, however, no one could recall the name of the house that Hood occupied through much of August 1864. Finally, armed with images such as the *Frank Leslie's Illustrated Newspaper* woodcut of "headquarters of the Rebel General Hood, Now Occupied by Col. H. A. Barnum," the local historian Wilbur G. Kurtz by 1950 had established Hood's headquarters as the

---

Press, 1905) 100; Trask, journal, 10 August 1864, Kennesaw Mountain National Battlefield Park.

Bishop Quintard's memoir and Civil War diary are now republished, edited by Sam Davis Elliott, as *Doctor Quintard, Chaplain C.S.A. and Second Bishop of Tennessee: The Memoir and Civil War Diary of Charles Todd Quintard* (Baton Rouge: Louisiana State University Press, 2003).

house of L. Windsor Smith. Smith had been an early Atlanta landowner, for whom by the time of his death in 1861 Windsor Street in the southwest suburbs had been named.[58]

Throughout his correspondence during the semi-siege, Sherman never called for his artillery to target Hood. But he did want the center of the city thoroughly battered. As we have seen, on 7 August Sherman had decided to spend some days in "knocking Atlanta" before he made another tactical move in pursuit of his overall plan, which was to take the city by cutting off the Rebel army's last rail line. "I want to expend 4,000 heavy rifle-shots on the town before doing anything new, and then will be prepared to act quick," Sherman told General Howard on 10 August. He wanted especially that day to see his 4 1/2-inch siege rifles in action. "I am going this morning to General Thomas' front to watch the effect of the new battery of 4 1/2 -inch guns," he wrote Howard. He made clear that his artillerists' target was not the enemy's fortified lines, but the interior of the city—the very "heart of Atlanta," as he wrote Grant. For the first time, Sherman on 10 August singled out the downtown Car Shed for his gunners. To General Thomas he expressed hope that a 4 1/2-inch gun could be placed so as to "demolish the big engine-house." By this time, the Union commander had even more succumbed to the fiction that he was not targeting civilians. "Most of the people are gone," he wrote to his wife; Atlanta "is now simply a big fort." Under this mistaken impression, it made sense to Sherman to pour on the artillery fire with even greater intensity. From spy reports, he knew that the important machinery and military supplies had been removed, but he entertained the notion that somehow these remained. "Keep up a steady, persistent fire on Atlanta with the 4 1/2-inch guns and 20-pounder Parrotts," he wrote Thomas on 10 August; "I think those guns will make Atlanta of less value to them as a large machine-shop and depot of supplies. The inhabitants, of course, have got out." The same message went to General Howard, whose Army

---

[58] "Statement of J. Milton Glass (Scout)," 12 August 1864, *OR,* vol. 38, pt. 5, p. 477; "Battles of Atlanta," UCV pamphlet, 10: "20. Site of Headquarters of General John B. Hood during the movements around Atlanta"; Kurtz notes on interview with Maj. Charles W. Hubner, 2 April 1927, notebook 3, 101, Wilbur G. Kurtz Papers, Atlanta History Center; Hubner, "Some Recollections," 5; "Gov. Harris at the Close of the War," *Confederate Veteran* 5/8 (August 1897): 403 (Adair's recollection of Hood's HQ); notes from James Bell interview, 24 June 1935, notebook 12, 107, Wilbur G. Kurtz Papers, Atlanta History Center; "What James Bell told me about the Siege of Atlanta," box 34, folder 13; "Some Unpublished Glimpses of General John B. Hood," Kurtz manuscript, read at the Southern Historical Association annual meeting, Atlanta, 11 November 1950, box 33, folder 6 ("Local historians know that after the battle of July 22d, General Hood set up headquarters at the Windsor Smith house, on the southeast corner of Whitehall and Hood streets," 8), Wilbur G. Kurtz Papers, Atlanta History Center; Garrett, *Atlanta and Environs,* 1:625; "Headquarters of the Rebel General Hood, Now Occupied by Col. H. A. Barnum, 3rd Brigade, 2d Division," *Frank Leslie's Illustrated Newspaper,* 29 October 1864.

of the Tennessee artillery was also bombarding the city from the west. Sherman even urged Howard to order a night bombardment, as if that had some military advantage more than sheer pyrotechnic effect: "Can't you get your 20-pounders tonight...and put them to work? The moon is light enough, and night is better than day for artillery." To make perfectly clear his wishes, he added to Howard, "Let us destroy Atlanta and make it a desolation."[59]

With Sherman obviously impatient for the big siege rifles to get into action—"I don't hear the 4 1/2-inch guns," he complained to Thomas on 10 August—finally they did. That day the engineers finished work on the earthwork embrasures in Geary's front. General Geary himself oversaw the construction. "Today I have been busy in superintending the erection of a battery in which I will place 6 forty pounders, with a view to the bombardment of the city," he wrote his wife on 10 August. "I assure you I will awake her up when I get them ready." The three 4 1/2-inchers (not the six 40-pounders Geary boasted of) finally belched forth between 4:00 P.M. or 5:00 P.M. "The 4 1/2-inch guns have been firing every five minutes since 5 P.M.," Thomas answered. "I will order them to increase.... The shells...burst beautifully." Sherman was satisfied in the knowledge that he had plenty of ammunition on hand for his artillery's new firepower. "We are now cannonading with 4 1/2-inch rifle bolts, and have 4,000 of them on hand," he wrote Schofield that afternoon, adding in a message to Howard that he intended to continue "until the ammunition is used up." On 11 August, General Geary again wrote home to Mary, "The battery of heavy guns placed in my lines, was opened yesterday, and during the night a gun was fired every five minutes. It was fearful to listen to the crashing of the shell through the houses as if they were so many eggshells."[60]

The fourth big gun arrived late on 10 August and was transferred from General Thomas's army to General Howard's—some said Thomas grumbled at having to do so. It was deployed west of town on the afternoon of 11 August in the lines of the XVI Corps, Brigadier General John M. Corse's division near Proctor's Creek (now the area of Maddox Park, west of Ashby Street). Private James Snell, on the headquarters staff of the division, saw the big cannon being hauled by a team of a dozen horses. Railroad iron accompanied it; Snell figured the bars were for a gun platform. The 4 1/2-incher, manned by a detachment of Battery F, 2nd US Artillery, began shelling the city that afternoon. With the other

---

[59] Sherman to Howard, 10 August 1864, *OR,* vol. 38, pt. 5, pp. 452–53; to Grant, 10 August, *OR,* vol. 38, pt. 5, p. 447; to Thomas, 10 August, *OR,* vol. 38, pt. 5, pp. 448–49; M. A. DeWolfe Howe, ed., *Home Letters of General Sherman* (New York: Charles Scribner's Sons, 1909) 306.

[60] Sherman to Thomas, 10 August 1864, *OR,* vol. 38, pt. 5, p. 448; Geary's report, *OR,* vol. 38, pt. 2, p. 143; Blair, ed., *A Politician Goes to War,* 194–95 (Geary to wife, 10, 11 August); Thomas to Sherman, 10 August, *OR,* vol. 38, pt. 5, p. 448; Sherman to Schofield and to Howard, 10 August, *OR,* vol. 38, pt. 5, pp. 450, 454.

three, its rate of fire was maintained around the clock every five minutes during daylight and every fifteen minutes at night.[61]

Sherman on 11 August told General Schofield that he would not be over to see him, as "I want to watch the effect of the heavy bombardment." He was pleased with what he saw. That night he wired Washington, "all well here. I am knocking Atlanta with 4 1/2-inch rifle-shells." The four siege rifles went through their ammunition quickly. Firing around-the-clock since about 5:00 P.M., 10 August, Thomas's 3 cannon within 3 days used up well over half of the 4,000 shells that had come down with the cannons. The gun on Corse's front, firing from 5:00 P.M. on 11 August, also expended several hundred rounds in its first forty-eight hours. Thomas therefore told Sherman on 12 August that he was having to order another thousand rounds.

Besides a new and heavier caliber of gun bearing down on Atlanta and its people, 10th August brought another new element to the Yankee cannonade: the deliberate heating of shot to start fires in the city. This incendiary technique was not used often in Sherman's bombardment, as "hot shot" usually meant the solid iron cannonballs customarily fired by smoothbore cannon—which in most cases were positioned in Sherman's lines too far to be able to reach Atlanta's buildings. Nevertheless Captain Cullen Bradley's 6th Ohio Battery of six 12-pounder Napoleon guns, attached to the IV Corps north of the city, apparently was the first to fire hot shot. On the 10th, Bradley recorded that his men "erected temporary furnace for heating shot and threw six shot into the city, also four shell filled with port fire." Portfire, sometimes called "Greek fire," was a flammable composition of niter and sulfur; it took the place of gunpowder in the shell. Upon impact, if the iron shell broke open, the igneous fluid could spread fire and flame. The problem was that "Greek fire" shells often exploded in the cannon tubes, and were considered unreliable. General Quincy Gillmore's gunners tried firing them on the city of Charleston in August 1863 from the "Swamp Angel," and had most detonate prematurely. As result, heated round shot were considered more reliable. Word of Captain Bradley's hot-shot trial

---

[61] Brannan to Sherman, 11 August 1864, *OR*, vol. 38, pt. 5, p. 457; McKinney, *Education in Violence*, 353; report of Maj. Thomas W. Osborn, 16 September 1864, *OR*, vol. 38, pt. 3, p. 60; Corse's report, *OR*, vol. 38, pt. 3, p. 411; Snell, diary, 58, Illinois Historical Society.

The fifty-three officers and men of Battery F, 2nd US Artillery were available for duty with the newly arrived siege rifle on General Corse's front; all six of their guns had been captured in the battle of 22 July (*OR*, vol. 38, pt. 3, pp. 58, 519, 539).

For more on the 4.5-inch rifle, see Craig Swain, "Yankee Super Gun," *Civil War Times* 49/4 (August 2011): 49–51. Swain concludes that the big siege guns "remain little more than a footnote to history. They've fallen behind in memory..." I wrote to the editors of *CWTI*, suggesting that Swain's statement "will surprise Atlantans, who remember that Sherman used these big guns against our city in August 1864." The magazine published my letter in its next (October) issue, under "Atlantans Will Never Forget."

made its way to IV Corps headquarters, as that evening Lieutenant Colonel Fullerton, the assistant adjutant gneral, entered into his journal, "we threw a few red-hot shot from the batteries in General Wood's front to-day into Atlanta." An Ohio infantryman, Wilbur F. Hinman, recalled seeing the work of Captain Bradley's gunners: "The men of the Sixth battery constructed a furnace for heating shot, the material therefore being supplied by an old brick chimney. One afternoon in the early part of August, they put a lot of twelve-pound shot into the furnace, brought them to a red heat, and in the evening threw them over into Atlanta. A large fire was soon seen, which, according to the statements of rebel pickets the next morning, was caused by the shot." Hinman added, "It is scarcely necessary to say that the battery boys did not undertake the experiment of heating shells" (which were powder-filled and would explode when heated).[62]

But Sherman wanted more than incendiary effect, even calling for "more rapidity of firing" from his artillery chief, General Brannan. During this time, besides the 4 1/2-inch siege guns, the rest of the Union cannon capable of reaching the city maintained their bombardment. "The shelling goes on almost constantly," reported "C-," writing to the *Intelligencer* from the city on 12 August; "to-day they are screaming and bursting over the Post office corner, but doing no damage." Two 20-pounder Parrotts in Sutermeister's Indiana battery had been fired so repeatedly that they burst at their muzzles on 12 August, and had to be replaced. The next day saw no let-up. "By order of Major-General Sherman," Geary recorded that day, "all the artillery bearing upon the city was directed to open and continue a regular fire upon it during the afternoon and night." Captain Charles Winegar's battery of 3-inch rifles fired every 2 1/2 minutes through the night. The shelling of that Saturday (13 August) was particularly fierce, noted the *Appeal.* Bishop Henry Lay, still in the city, tried to have tea at a friend's but "was driven away by the furious shelling. Two balls went through the house after I left." Captain Benedict Semmes described the nighttime bombardment of 13–14 August in a letter to his wife almost as if it were a fireworks display—albeit with the threat of danger.

[62] Sherman to Schofield, 11 August 1864, *OR*, vol. 38, pt. 5, p. 465; Sherman to Stanton, 11 August, *OR*, vol. 38, pt. 5, p. 456; Thomas to Sherman, 12 August, *OR*, vol. 38, pt. 5, pp. 472–73; report of Capt. Cullen Bradley, 6 September, *OR*, vol. 38, pt. 1, p. 504; Francis A. Lord, "'Greek Fire' Enflamed Beauregard at Charleston," *Civil War Times* 2/8 (December 1960) 9; J. S. Fullerton, journal, *OR*, vol. 38, pt. 1, p. 917; Wilbur F. Hinman, *The Story of the Sherman Brigade* (Alliance OH: Wilbur F. Hinman, 1897) 582.

Captain Bradley's report, cited above, is printed in the *Official Records* as having some "daily details omitted." I thank Michael Meier, Military Reference Branch of the National Archives, for providing me with a full copy of Bradley's handwritten report, showing use of hot shot on the city of Atlanta, 15–16 August.

...last Saturday night commencing about 8 oclock and continuing until after sunrise Sunday morning they kept up a furious fire. Over 2000 shells were thrown into the city and it was really a beautiful sight to see so many shells coursing through the air at the same time, looking precisely like meteors or shooting stars. About midnight the fire was so hot at my quarters that I had to get up and vacate to another point 100 yards distant but after awhile I returned, the shells being as thick there as at my quarters. No one could sleep however and most every one spent the night out of doors.

Even without the use of hot shot or portfire, the Union artillery fire caused blazes downtown. "Rover" (for the *Augusta Chronicle & Sentinel*) described one outbreak on the night of 12 August. The Northern cannon fired so many rounds, "at times a half-dozen fuse shells could be seen in the air at the same time." Around midnight one of these projectiles struck a wooden building downtown and apparently ignited some cotton inside. The flames spread even as firefighters rushed to the scene. "Rover" believed that the enemy directed further shots toward the light they could see from the burning buildings, as "for a couple of hours his missiles fell thick and fast in the area." The firemen nevertheless stood their ground, but in spite of their efforts five structures were destroyed. On the next night, that of 13 August, some Federals could see fires again blazing in the city, thanks to signal stations having been set up in trees; in the IV Corps, there was an observation post for each division. Other Northern watchmen were so close that they heard fire bells ringing downtown; by that sound Captain Alexis Cope of the 15th Ohio concluded that "our guns were doing some execution." "About 11 P.M. a large fire broke out in the center of the city," General Geary wrote, "bells and cries of 'fire' were plainly audible. The fire became larger and continued until daylight." For those Northerners still doubting, the audible cries from downtown confirmed that there were still innocent noncombatants in Atlanta. "My brigade officer of the day," wrote Union colonel I. M. Kirby, "says that he could distinctly hear loud cries from women and children, as if praying &c. There is now [midnight, 13/14 August] quite a fire burning in the town." In addition to their own distant observations, the Federals got occasional reports on the extent of damage from inside the city. The Yankee spy Milton Glass attested that "a large block of buildings" near the corner of Marietta and Wadley streets had been destroyed; among them Glass mentioned a cotton storeroom and a big drug store.

Writing from Atlanta on 14 August, a correspondent for the *Mobile Register and Advertiser* gave the particulars of the fire downtown the previous night.

About midnight a shell entered the frame storehouse of Biggers & Co., Marietta street, between Peach Tree and Church, setting fire the loose cotton. The flames spread rapidly and the building was soon in flames.

The bell rang and engine No. 3 replied promptly. The enemy immediately concentrated his fire on that point. The firemen nobly stood their ground despite the rain of shell, and succeeded in saving the large warehouse of Kyle & Co. The other buildings on the square were consumed.

"Engine No. 3" meant the Tallulah Fire Co. No. 3, one of the four that the city had at the time of the war. Members of the company were volunteers whose service exempted them from military duty, but at times like these, the firemen's work was as dangerous as that on the front lines—struggling heroically to extinguish fires while under artillery fire. The number of firefighters in Atlanta in the first years of the war may have risen to 500, especially as word spread that firemen avoided conscription. Yet the approach of Sherman's armies would have reduced that number when men went forth to serve in the infantry trenches, departed with evacuated munitions machinery, or fled with their families in the summer's mass exodus. The city council's decision on 18 July to send two of the best fire pumps away for safekeeping, and the drying out of downtown water cisterns during the bombardment made the remaining firefighters' task no easier. Encountering these difficulties, the blaze-battlers received high praise in the *Intelligencer*'s article on the fires of 13/14 August.

We have had quite a still time from the shells of the enemy until about 9 o'clock to-night, when the shells commenced falling in nearly every part of the city, striking many houses, and doing considerable damage. About 12 o'clock two shells struck Dr. [Stephen T.] Biggers' house on Marietta street, setting it on fire, destroying it; also Dr. J.F. Alexander's brick house adjoining, the house on the east side of Dr. H's [Daniel O. C. Heery's], and several other small houses adjacent to those buildings. Mr. Kile's large brick building, at the corner of the angle of the square, was saved only by the energy of Fire Company No. 3, which was on the spot soon after the first broke out, and worked with but little help and more energy than I have ever seen firemen work before— several citizens assisting them. The other Fire Companies could not get help enough to keep their engines at work. No. 1 went to the cistern but could not get help to work on the brakes so they assisted No. 3, and succeeded in saving all the buildings fronting on Peachtree street. The wooden house that Mr. Buice did business in caught fire two or three times, but it was put out and saved. While the fire was progressing, the shells of the enemy fell every half minute in and about us all the time the houses were burning. Solid shot were also fired, falling near the brakes, but the firemen continued to work as though utterly regardless of them. I do not think a man left the place until the fire was extinguished. I have but little idea of the loss.... The shelling continued after the fire, without any intermission until 3 o'clock this Sunday morning....

Atlanta, it seems, is to be fired and battered to the ground, if it cannot be captured by Sherman. To the Fire Battalion which so nobly did their duty on Saturday night, great credit is due. We know most of them personally, and a braver set of men never lived. To them it seems is entrusted now all the guard duty of the city, as well as to protect it from fire. Verily they have the post of danger as well as of honor. May the fortunes of war soon relieve them of the danger, and may they live long to enjoy the honor they have already won!

Even though it appeared that the Yankees aimed their artillery toward the vicinity of the blazes, no firefighter was hurt during the night of 13 August. Neither was anyone else, according to the *Mobile Register & Advertiser* correspondent: "not a citizen was injured, the women and children having sought safety in bomb proofs." Other papers nevertheless reported at least a few casualties. The *Appeal* counted one: "an officer had been spending the evening with some friends in the city, when just as he was starting for camp he was struck in the leg by a whole shell, rendering amputation above the knee necessary. He is doing well." This officer may have been the same cited by an Atlanta correspondent of the *Richmond Enquirer,* "Cedric," who stated that in the heavy bombardment on the night of 13 August, a Captain H. M. Pollard of General C. L. Stevenson's staff "was conversing with a lady on her porch when a shell struck him, shattering his leg below the knee and severely wounding the lady." Captain Pollard was engaging in one the favorite pastimes of the men in Hood's army: getting passes into town and making social calls. "We soldiers would visit the young ladies and family groups known to us," recalled Phil Stephenson (a mere nineteen-year-old in the artillery service). On one of these outings, a friend of his, one Lieutenant Sam Anderson, became another shell-casualty: Anderson "lost his leg while standing on a balcony talking to some girls."

On the whole, however, the low number of bombardment casualties among the people in Atlanta was noteworthy. After the fiery night of 13 August, in which Benedict Semmes believed the Yankees fired 2,000 shells, Semmes wrote that the casualties were but one soldier killed "and several women and children killed and wounded." Servicemen escaped injury from the downtown shelling, Semmes noted, because they were usually at their front-line posts rather than in the city. The *Appeal* also observed, "the escape of our citizens is remarkable, when it is considered they were subject to an incessant fire from five different batteries for a period of ten hours." The *Intelligencer* concurred: "The wonder is that so few of the citizens have been hurt. There are a great many still in the place, but they confine themselves to their premises."[63]

The citizens' escape from death or injury during the bombardment had really ceased to be a wonder, given everyone's knowledge of how basements and "bomb proofs" were being used extensively in the city. "The Yankees throw shells into the City every day," wrote Private Colin Dunlop of the 6th Texas to his sister on 13 August; "most of the familyes have caves to go into...." "Mentor" wrote for the *Columbus Sun* that "every citizen has a bomb proof in his yard"; soldiers even helped civilians dig their shelters. "Mentor," himself a soldier, assisted one family in the construction of their dugout "till my hands were well blistered but felt well paid when dinner time came." Without a bombproof, Cyrena Stone endured the bombardment with friends whose house offered a cellar for safety. On 11 August, when shells started exploding, everyone ran downstairs. Mrs. Stone was unharmed, but an adult and a child were badly wounded by flying fragments; the house itself was struck by five 30-pound projectiles. In another incident, Edgar L. Ivy, a grandson of Hardy Ivy, remembered years after the war that "I stayed in James L. Wiley's cellar all during the shelling of the town," presumably because his parents' home (Ellis Street, between Collins and Calhoun) was unsafe. Another Atlanta boy, John Horton, was not only too young for the army, but too small (he was called "Toad" when he worked at the Atlanta Arsenal); he recalled carrying food to families in bombproof dugouts during the bombardment. Still another Atlantan, Mollie Smith, remembered that one morning,

...a neighbor's family came to our house seeking shelter, saying their home had been struck by a shell and that much damage had been done. Because our house was built of brick, people thought we were proof against the shells, but we soon found we were badly mistaken. We moved

[63] Sherman to Brannan, 12 August, *OR*, vol. 38, pt. 5, p. 472; "C," "Editor of the Intelligencer" (Atlanta, 12 August), *Atlanta Intelligencer*, 14 August; Geary's report, 15 September 1864, *OR*, vol. 38, pt. 2, p. 143; report of Capt. Charles E. Winegar, 7 September, *OR*, vol. 38, pt. 2, p. 476; "The Immediate Front," *Memphis Appeal*, 14 August, quoted in *Columbus Enquirer*, 17 August; Lay, diary, entry of 13 August, University of North Carolina; Semmes to wife, 21 August, Semmes Papers, University of North Carolina (quoted also in Hoehling, *Last Train from Atlanta*, 348); "Rover," "From the Georgia Front" (Atlanta, 13 August), *Augusta Chronicle & Sentinel*, 19 August; Capt. Lyman Bridges's report, 9 September, *OR*, vol. 38, pt. 1, p. 485; Cope, *Fifteenth Ohio Volunteers*, 540; Col. I. M. Kirby to Maj. W. H. Sinclair, 13 August, *OR*, vol. 38, pt. 5, p. 484; Milton Glass report of fire, 13–14 August, *OR*, vol. 38, pt. 5, p. 580; report from Atlanta, 14 August, *Mobile Register and Advertiser*, 16 August; Reed, *History of Atlanta*, 67–68; "Fire in Atlanta—Shelling of the City," *Atlanta Intelligencer*, 16 August; "Cedric," "From Atlanta" (18 August), *Richmond Enquirer*, 30 August; Hughes, ed., *Civil War Memoir of Philip Daingerfield Stephenson*, 231; "The Immediate Front," *Memphis Appeal*, 15 August; "Atlanta," *Atlanta Intelligencer*, 13 August.

some bedding into the basement and slept there at night. Other friends came in during the day and wanted to stay with us, feeling we were secure. About midnight two soldiers asked permission to bring over a sick lady who was in a small wooden building just across the street from us. It was pouring down rain, and of course we could not refuse to give shelter. We did not know who she was, but we ministered to her wants until daylight. The men came for her, took her away, and the house she left was almost destroyed by shells.

Another late-in-life recollection came from John Henderson, who in 1895 remembered that "one night a shell entered our home at the corner of Jenkins and Collins Sts. It went through one end of the wall, and then on through the floor and into the cellar where it entered the brick wall and exploded. Part of the plastering fell on my wife and a young lady who were in bed...." This close call sent everyone flying out of the house, Henderson added. "They made their toilet in the street and fled for safety to Mr. Poplin's bomb proof on Decatur St., accompanied by Dr. D'Alvigny and his wife."

Atlantans' shell shelters were the subject of frequent comment. "The citizens have excavated holes in their yards and covered them with timbers upon which they throw dirt," wrote Captain Key in his diary on 4 August, "and when the shelling begins they resort to these for safety." Noble Williams described these in his turn-of-the-century reminiscence:

> Most of the citizens constructed on their premises what were known as bombproofs, which were holes dug in the earth eight or ten feet deep, and of a desirable length to suit the builder, covered overhead with heavy beams, which contained a covering of boards or tin to keep out the rain, and then covered them with earth from three to five feet dep. The entrance to the small door was dug out in the shape of a letter L, and many persons' lives were preserved by using them as a shield.

Yet long stays in bombproofs could be boring, tedious, and unhealthy. Such dark, dank places, according to another reminiscing Atlantan, gave rise to "much sickness." At the same time, residents learned that any form of shelter was better than none. For those without cellars or dug-outs, sometimes even ravines would do, once one knew the direction of the enemy cannonfire. "Several families took refuge in a very large culvert on Houston St. near Fort St. [in the city's northeast quadrant]," remembered John Henderson; "they laid planks on the rocks, letting the water run under them, and staid there until they were forced to leave by the bursting of the shells in the culvert." On 12 August, Episcopal Bishop Henry Lay entered into his diary that he had visited that afternoon the headquarters of Major General Henry Clayton (division commander in Stephen D. Lee's corps), only to find that "he had left the house, owing to the shelling and was camped in a ravine near by."

With some parts of the city seeming safer at times than others, civilians moved about. After having moved closer downtown to take advantage of a friend's house (Mr. Parrott's) with a cellar next door (Dr. Sells's), Julia Davidson on 4 August wrote her husband that it was not working out: "Well we have concluded to return to our own house.... I do not like much to go for I do not feel as secure there as I do in Dr. Sells' basement but we are not satisfied here. you know two sets of children do not get along well together that is not the worst. you know Mr. P's disposition & it is impossible to keep the children quite in this large house & *many other things* fret him." Mrs. Davidson had begun moving a load of belongings back to her own house, when her mother expressed her worries that they

> had made a bad move & the fightin alarmed her & if they should shell much over there we would be very much exposed. Dr Sells told her she was very foolish indeed to go so close to the line & advised her to abandon the idea. so this morning she had the load brought back & we are going to look for a house with a good basement so we will not be running back & forth so much & will be imposing on no one. as it is now we are compelled to cook over here. shells or no shells & then run for safety to Dr. Sells basement. & I fear he is becoming tired of so many children. perhaps we will go to Sasseens house.... to tell you the truth we know not what to do. We would get away if we could....[64]

Heedless of the civilians' plight inside Atlanta, Union artillerymen continued their nighttime pyrotechnics. From an observation station near General Geary's headquarters, Captain W. W. Hopkins sent in notice on 14 August that "the shells fired from the heavy guns, with but few exceptions, exploded in the city." With considerable understatement, Corporal Salma Morton of the 65th Ohio wrote his wife, "I tell you they make the thing pretty warm for them in town." That night General Geary recorded that "shortly after dark another large fire broke out in the city, lasting about three hours." On 15 August, Geary wrote his wife Mary, "Even at this very moment, more than 50 cannon are being fired upon the doomed city of Atlanta. This continues night and day, without intermission. Fires are frequent and of nightly occurrence in the

---

[64] Colin Dunlop to sister, 13 August 1864, Colin Dunlop Letters, typescript, MSS 96F, Atlanta History Center; "Mentor," "Letter from Atlanta" (17 August), *Columbus Sun,* 21 August; Dyer, *Secret Yankees,* 186; "Old and Lonesome, Siege Survivor Longs to Gossip with Atlantans," *Atlanta Constitution,* 6 July 1937; "Boy Arsenal Worker Now Hunting Friends in Siege of Atlanta," *Atlanta Constitution,* 29 May 1931; Smith, "Dodging Shells"; John Henderson to William L. Calhoun, 6 August 1895, Calhoun Family Papers, Atlanta History Center; Cate, ed., *Two Soldiers,* 108; Noble C. Williams, *Echoes from the Battlefield; or, Southern Life During the War* (Atlanta: Franklin Printing Co., 1902) 33; Lay, diary, 11 August, University of North Carolina; Peacock, ed., "A Wartime Story," 99–102.

city." General Geary, from whose front so much of the heavy Union artillery was destroying Atlanta, seemed to enjoy the nighttime spectacle. A staff officer, Captain David Conyngham, recalled that one evening, "the scene at night was sublimely grand and terrific! The din of artillery rang on the night air. In front of General Geary's headquarters was a prominent hill, from which we had a splendid view of the tragedy enacting before us. One night I sat there with the general and staff, and several other officers, while a group of men sat near us enjoying the scene, and speculating on the effects of the shells."[65]

Conyngham, Geary, and the other Northern officers viewing the "sublimely grand and terrific" nighttime bombardments recorded very few worries about the fate of the noncombatants enduring them. Indeed, like General Sherman, many Federals preferred to consider how the once-bustling population of Atlanta had disappeared, and in this estimation they received some support from the people inside. Julia Davidson wrote on 4 August that "the city is almost deserted. You rarely see a lady on the street except when they cease shelling which they do sometimes." Most invisible of all were African Americans. Many slaveowners who left the city took their servants with them, or sent them away (as did Mayor Calhoun when he dispatched his wife and children to south Georgia). In addition, an indeterminate number of blacks doubtless took advantage of the Federal army's proximity, and the general confusion, to escape. ("Our servants all ran away except 'Uncle Dick' and Mammy," recorded Lucy Harvie Hull, a resident of Peachtree Street, on 10 August.) Even more a minority were Atlanta's free blacks, who had numbered a mere twenty-three in the census of 1860. One of those who actually stayed in the city during summer 1864 was the barber, Solomon Luckie. He was listed in Williams's *Atlanta Directory, City Guide, and Business Mirror, 1859* as "LUCKEY'S SOLOMON. Barber Shop and Bathing Saloon, ss Decatur b Whitehall and Pryor, Atlanta Hotel Bldg."

Luckie was apparently affluent enough before the war to be photographed— young, handsome, with flamboyant bow tie and dark suit (his picture is in the Atlanta History Center archives). Yet artillery makes no social distinction; Solomon Luckie is said to have lost his life to a Federal shell-blast in August, though the date is unclear. In their regular reporting of bombardment casualties, Confederate newspapers do not mention Luckie (throughout the summer they only occasionally mention "a negro" victim). As in the case of the apocryphal "little girl" allegedly slain on 20 July, here again we seem to have only postbellum reminiscences, published in the *Atlanta Constitution* or *Journal*

---

[65] Capt. W. W. Hopkins to Capt. A. K. Taylor, 14 August 1864, *OR*, vol. 38, pt. 5, p. 492; Paul Taylor, *Orlando M. Poe: Civil War General and Great Lakes Engineer* (Kent OH: Kent University Press, 2009) 174 (Morton to wife, 14 August); Geary's report, 15 September, *OR*, vol. 38, pt. 2, p. 143; Blair, ed., *A Politician Goes to War*, 196 (Geary to wife, 15 August); David P. Conyngham, *Sherman's March Through the South* (New York: Sheldon & Co., 1865) 192.

two decades after the war. Wallace Reed includes Luckie among the casualties of the barrage on a "red day in August," although neglecting to note that he was a free man of color:

> Sol Luckie, a well-known barber, was standing on the James's Bank corner, on Whitehall and Alabama, when a shell struck a lamp-post, ricocheted and exploded. A fragment struck Luckie and knocked him down. Mr. Tom Crusselle and one or two other citizens picked up the unfortunate man and carried him into a store. He was then taken to the Atlanta Medical College, where Dr. D'Alvigney amputated his leg. The poor fellow was put the under the influence of morphine, but he never rallied from the shock, and died in a few hours.

Reed, who worked for the *Constitution* and who had access to its published columns, almost certainly got his story about Crusselle and Luckie from the newspaper, which for decades printed articles about the war. Crusselle, who lived in Atlanta until his death in 1890, was giving reminiscent interviews in the papers such as "Atlanta Pioneers. The Builder of the First House Talks." A. A. Hoehling, whose *Last Train from Atlanta* (1958) did so much to popularize the probably false story of the death of "the little girl," quotes Reed and the Crusselle-Luckie account, but also adds something new.

> Captain E.C. Murphy, commanding the 1st Volunteer Fire Department, was on Whitehall Street at Alabama when the shell hit.
> "All of a sudden," he wrote, "there came a moaning overhead and a shell hit crack in the middle of Alabama Street. It ricocheted off the street and came straight at me. It hit a lamp post, blip! And down I fell flat on my stomach. Right behind me was an old negro man (Luckie) and the shell pieces, went right over my head with a sucking noise and...to him. When I got up he was lying there covered with blood. Johnny Magee and I wrapped him up in a horse blanket and took him to a little hospital shack."

Hoehling gives no specific note for Murphy's recollection, only citing in his bibliography the Atlanta Public Library, "for the amazing completeness of the files, which furnished an eyewitness account of the death of Sol Luckie, the barber, beside the lamp post." If the eyewitness were Captain Murphy—he was known in town as having been "struck by another bit of the shell [that mortally wounded Luckie] but escaped serious injury"—it seems his story changed. In another version related in a history of Atlanta firemen, Sol Luckie had stepped out of his barber shop when a shell bounced down Alabama Street, struck the gas light post, and exploded.

A large piece of the projectile struck Luckie just below the knee, severing his leg completely. Captain Edward C. Murphy, of Atlanta Fire Company No. 1 and Johnny Magee, who was on his way to report in at the fire hall, happened by in his buggy. He stopped his horse and removing a blanket from the rear of the rig, rushed to the fallen Negro, wrapped him in the blanket and placed him in the buggy and rushed him to the Medical College where Doctor D'Alvigny operated and amputated the stump above the knee, but the old man died of shock and loss of blood.

Unfortunately, today, fifty years after Hoehling's research, the Atlanta Public Library no longer seems to have the alleged "eyewitness account" of Sol Luckie's tragedy (either Tom Crusselle's or E. C. Murphy's postbellum reminiscence), even in its Georgia History/Genealogy Collection. Closer examination of Atlanta newspaper files may yet turn it up, but the published evidence ends here.

The story of Sol Luckie's death might be dismissed by historians of Atlanta's bombardment, given its elusive detail and thin bibliography: Wallace Reed (writing a quarter-century later) and local newspaper articles with "eyewitness" accounts (possibly by Tom Crusselle or E. C. Murphy cited by later writers but yet to be fully researched). Still, there remain two distinctive facts: Sol Luckie is known to have been a resident of wartime Atlanta (as opposed to the unnamable "little girl"); and the lamppost, from which the fatal Northern shell is said to have ricocheted, survived far longer than Sol Luckie. The post was one of the city's original fifty gaslit ornamental street lamps ordered by the mayor in 1855 and first illuminated that Christmas Day by the newly established Atlanta Gas Light Company. After it was knocked down (and broken into three pieces) by a Union shell, it was stored in city hall until, by resolution of the city council in 1880, it was returned to its original site, Whitehall and Alabama streets. At its metal base was the obvious hole made by the Yankee shell. Several decades later, in October 1919, as the United Confederate Veterans held a reunion in the city, the Atlanta National Bank, which stood behind the post, put a sign on it welcoming the veterans and noting that "this lamp post, shot down from this spot August 15, 1864, was replaced by the city and remains one of the few standing relics of your brave fight to save Atlanta. Its battle scars—note the holes—tell of the intensity of that fight." Pasting a newspaper article about the plaque into one of his meticulously kept scrapbooks, historian Wilbur Kurtz noted, "this is the first time I've noticed a date [15 August] given to the affair of the shell."

The date of the Sol Luckie incident (Reed's "red day in August")—possibly 9 August, maybe 15 August —has been lost. We know more about the shell-pocked lamppost. While the UCV members met in Atlanta in 1919, the Atlanta Chapter of the United Daughters of the Confederacy placed a bronze plaque on the post, not mentioning Sol Luckie, Tom Crusselle, or Edward Murphy, but honoring the memory of Atlantan Andrew J. West, former Confederate officer in the Army of Tennessee, who had always wanted some kind of marker on the lamppost. Worse, the little plaque states that "the damage at the base of this post was caused by a shell during the War Between the States, Battle of Atlanta, July 22, 1864"—thus rendering Wallace Reed's "red day in August" into a red day in July.

Twenty years later another metal plaque was added to the lamppost at Whitehall and Alabama, this time on 14 December 1939, amid all the hoopla surrounding the premiere of *Gone With the Wind.* Dedication of the plaque, which was again conceived by Daughters of the Confederacy, designated the post and its light as the "Eternal Flame of the Confederacy." On hand for the ceremonies were Mayor William B. Hartsfield and Carl Wolf, president of Atlanta Gas Light, which reinstalled the gas line and donated the fuel for the lamp's perpetual burning, as well as Ann Rutherford, the actress in Selznick's movie who played one of the secondary roles, "Carreen." Dignitaries from the UDC and the Gate City Guard gave speeches; the old guardsmen looked on, bearskin hats and all. At the conclusion, a high school band played "Dixie."

The shell-scarred lamppost has suffered the usual plight of historical artifacts caught in a busy city. It was taken down for viaduct construction in the 1920s; in 1949 the "Eternal Flame" plaque was stolen and had to be replaced by the gas company (the newspaper noted that the new plaque "will be soldered in place [and] will be as theft-proof as possible"). Then a bus hit the post in the 1950s, forcing its repair. More recently it came down for MARTA construction, but was restored and relit on 15 September 1982. It was finally moved to Underground Atlanta, where it stands today below the Alabama and Peachtree entrance, at its original site. A sign points out, "This gas lamp is one of the 50 street lights erected by the Atlanta Gas Light Company in 1856. It stood at this location when Atlanta was shelled by Union forces during the Civil War. Notice the hole in its base where it was struck by a cannonball." The lamppost still bears the 1919 bronze plate honoring Andrew West, a white real estate developer and UCV dignitary, as well as the plaque from 1939 commemorating "the eternal flame of the Confederacy." (It still burns.) Yet nowhere is Solomon Luckie mentioned. Even the helpful sign at the lamppost placed by Underground Atlanta fails to mention that probably antebellum Atlanta's most notable free African-American citizen was mortally wounded near it. Thus Luckie, one of Atlanta's uncounted civilian casualties from the Federal armies' bombardment, has vanished. Even Franklin Garrett, Atlanta's necrologist, could only guess that he was buried in Oakland; without headstone or cemetery records, no one will ever know where Luckie's grave may be.[66]

---

[66] Peacock, ed., "A Wartime Story," 101; Hoehling, *Last Train from Atlanta,* 130 ("a shell burst in the street and narrowly missed Major A.J. West" in Atlanta, 22 July); 280–81 (Captain Murphy on Luckie's death), 286 (Hulls' servants running away), 552 (crediting the

Atlanta Public Library for "an eyewitness account of the death of Sol Luckie"); *Williams' Atlanta Directory*, 115; Reed, *History of Atlanta*, 191–92; "Atlanta Pioneers" (undated newspaper clipping, probably *Atlanta Constitution* or *Journal*, 1880s, copy courtesy of Mr. and Mrs. Thomas A. Crusselle of Atlanta); Mary Davis, "Shell-Scarred Lamp Post Relic of Atlanta War Days," *Atlanta Constitution*, 5 August 1928; Steve B. Campbell, "History of Atlanta Volunteer Fire Companies, 1846–1882," typescript on microfilm, n.d., Atlanta History Center; "Mr. Davis," "History of the Atlanta Gas Light Company," Wilbur G. Kurtz Collection, Atlanta History Center; Tate, *Keeper of the Flame*, 12; "Old Lamp Post, Relic of Battle of Atlanta, Attracts Attention," *Atlanta Constitution*, 8 October 1919; "Andrew West Sought Marker For Lamp Post," *Atlanta Constitution*, 1 September 1942; "Eternal Flame to the Confederacy Dedication Ceremony, Atlanta, Georgia, December 14, 1939," program pamphlet, box 15, folder 1, Wilbur G. Kurtz Collection, Atlanta History Center; Wilbur G. Kurtz, notes on the dedication, notebook 12, 75, Wilbur G. Kurtz Collection, Atlanta History Center; Margaret Shannon, "New Plaque Slated for 'Eternal Flame,'" *Atlanta Journal*, 25 April 1949; "'Eternal Light' Flickers as Bus Hits Lamppost," *Atlanta Journal-Constitution*, 29 January 1956; "Historic Sites and Markers in Underground Atlanta," Underground Atlanta flyer, ca. February 1995; conversation with Franklin Garrett, 7 April 1989 (on Luckie's burial place).

Writing in the 1890s, Joel Chandler Harris told the story of one "freakish" shell in the Federal bombardment of Atlanta, referring to its African American casualty (although he did not name Solomon Luckie) and the shell-pocked lamppost.

One of the missiles (to mention one instance out of many) went tumbling down Alabama Street, turned into Whitehall, following the grade, and rolled through the iron lamp-post that stands in front of the old James's Bank building. It was moving along so leisurely that a negro lounging near the corner tried to stop it with his foot. He was carried off with a broken leg. The lamp-post stands there to this day, having been thoughtfully preserved as a relic that might be of interest, and if you give it a careful glance as you pass, you'll see the jagged hole grinning at you with open-mouthed familiarity. (Joel Chandler Harris, *Tales of the Home Folks in Peace and War* [Boston: Houghton, Mifflin, 1898] 215–16, 253–54.)

(Harris's text was first published as two stories, "A Baby in the Siege," and "The Baby's Fortune" in *Scribner's Magazine*, April and November 1896. For this information my thanks go to Anne A. Salter, director, Philip Weltner Library, Oglethorpe University.)

If Solomon Luckie's name is at times lost in the literature, so is his race. Wallace Reed had led the way in calling him "a well-known barber." Subsequent local accounts drawing on Reed's *History of Atlanta* repeated the omission. One example is "Sherman's Shells Burst on Streets Where Vets Unite," *Atlanta Journal*, 5 October 1919: "a barber standing on the corner of Whitehall and Alabama streets was struck by a fragment of shell as it ricocheted off a lamp post."

In a recent visit to Underground Atlanta, I for a brief moment thought that finally someone had remembered Sol Luckie. Across the plaza from the shell-pocked lamppost I saw a thrift store with a sign out front: "Sal Lucky Bamboo Plan & Atlanta Tshirt."

Though I couldn't figure out what the "Bamboo Plan" was, I was excited at the thought that a local vendor was remembering the free African American barber, even if he

Nor are there medical records to confirm Luckie's amputative surgery, as Atlanta's medical care system had largely disappeared with the removal of most army hospital facilities after 10 July. Left to care for the sick and wounded of Hood's army there was only the "receiving and distributing" hospital, located near the Car Shed downtown in the Gate City Hotel, which treated men only for the purposes of putting them on trains headed for other Confederate hospitals away from Atlanta. Even though the army's Medical College Hospital had been transferred to Milner, 50 miles south of Atlanta, the Medical College building itself continued to serve as a hospital. "P." (probably Isaac Pilgrim) wrote for the *Atlanta Intelligencer* on 4 August that wounded Union prisoners were being treated at the Medical College, adding that "the Yankees hit it occasionally" with their projectiles. It was here that shell-struck civilians were also brought and treated by the small number of Atlanta physicians still in the city. These included Drs. Thomas S. Denny (whose prewar office was on Peachtree), Stephen T. Biggers (Decatur St., between Ivy and Collins), and Noel D'Alvigny. (The latter was listed in the 1859 city directory merely as "Dalvena ———, phys. Rooms e s Collins b Gilmer and Wheat.") Dr. D'Alvigny's work during the bombardment was remembered by Atlantans. Then-thirteen-year-old Anton Kontz much later recalled having been slightly wounded by a shell, and treated on the sidewalk by the good doctor. Confederate medical officers commended D'Alvigny, though he apparently remained a private physician in Atlanta and not a contract surgeon with the army. "Dr. D'Alvigny is attending to the wounded," wrote Dr. A. J. Foard (medical director for the Army of Tennessee) to Dr. S. H. Stout (army hospital director) on 16 August, complimenting him as "a competent man" and a good candidate for duty with the service. Besides physicians, other Atlantans also tried to help as they could, including women who volunteered for the hospital wards. Mrs. John Henderson made a point of visiting the Medical College hospital twice a day, although she occasionally had to take cover from the shells; a whizzing fragment once tore off a piece of her dress.[67]

---

couldn't get his name right. So I went inside and asked about the sign. The shop owner pointed to a potted plant: "Lucky bamboo." What? I asked again. "Lucky Bamboo." Walking out, I finally got it: the store sign had lost a couple of letters, as it was meant to read "SALE LUCKY BAMBOO PLANT ATLANTA TSHIRT." Disappointed, I concluded that after all these years, Atlanta's noted black shell-victim is still unheralded.

[67] Stephen Davis, "Another Look at Civil War Medical Care: Atlanta's Confederate Hospitals," *Journal of the Medical Association of Georgia* 88/2 (April 1999): 21; "P.," "Ed. Intelligencer" (Atlanta, 4 August), *Atlanta Intelligencer,* 6 August 1864; *Williams' Atlanta Directory,* 47, 71, 75; Lamar Q. Ball, "Monument of Service Left City in Long Life of Anton Louis Kontz," *Atlanta Constitution,* 24 January 1937; A. J. Foard to S. H. Stout, 16 August 1864, Samuel Hollingsworth Stout Papers, MSS 274, box 2, folder 16, Emory University; Henderson to Calhoun, 6 August 1895, Calhoun Family Papers, Atlanta History Center.

Doctors Denny and Biggers's presence in the city during the bombardment is substantiated by a list of 705 adults who, after staying in Atlanta during the Federals'

And the bombardment continued. Sherman had told Thomas on 10 August to have his "4 1/2-inch and 20-pounder guns…hammer away [while] I will think of the next move." At that time, the Federal commander was thinking of how to cut Hood's last railroad, the Macon & Western, into the city. With his lines stretched halfway around the city, Sherman telegraphed General Grant on 10 August, "I cannot extend more without making my lines too weak"—as it was, Sherman sought reinforcements just to replace the regiments being mustered out that summer at the end of their enlistment terms. More important, he had grown impatient with the halting progress being made on his far right flank near East Point. As General Schofield's troops probed and felt closer to the railroad, Hood's Confederates seemed able to parry each Federal movement; "the enemy can build parapets faster than we can march," Sherman exasperatingly concluded. "Our movements are all too slow to be productive of good results," he wrote Schofield on 11 August; "it does seem to me with an enemy besieged we should be a little more enterprising." Indeed, Sherman complained, "we all know that the enemy holds us by inferior force…it seems we are more besieged than they."

Actually, about the time Sherman wrote of Hood's inferior force in the second week of August, the enemy force he faced was striving to be less inferior. After his three costly repulses of 20–28 July, and with his army locked in a trench-war not unlike that being faced by General Lee in Virginia, John Bell Hood sought to reinforce his ranks. Rather than call on Richmond for more troops (which he knew could not come), Hood drew front-line reinforcements from within his own army. Medical officers cleared the hospitals of malingerers; previously detailed workers had their noncombatant status revoked; couriers, orderlies, cooks, and teamsters were reassigned, and all were armed with muskets and ordered into the trenches. Enslaved African Americans were impressed for army service, especially as teamsters. Even artillery crews, customarily of seven men per gun, were reduced when one gunner was ordered to take up a musket. Newspaper appeals for absentees to return, widely published throughout the region, also helped. As a result, the Army of Tennessee's effective strength, about 51,000 on 10 July, stood at a respectable 44,500 at the end of the month, even after the three big battles of the month. In the returns of 10 August, the number of effectives even increased slightly. Governor Brown assisted with more vigorous forwarding of state militiamen to the front lines at Atlanta. "Our Army have been strengthened by the Militia and reinforcements," wrote artilleryman Andrew Neal on 4 August to his sister Ella from his battery's position before the city. "Besides these all the bands cook details extra artillery men drivers and dead heads have been brought to the front

---

shelling, were forcibly expelled from the city by Sherman's order on 4 September (Wilbur G. Kurtz, "Persons Removed from Atlanta by General W. T. Sherman, September 4, 1864, *Atlanta Historical Bulletin* 1/6 [January 1932]: 27,30).

and given muskets." Lieutenant Neal evinced optimism for the army's prospects. "Very few people think the enemy will get any nearer to Atlanta," he reasoned, although he could not escape the observation that "they have ruined its value to us in a great measure."[68]

With his gradual encroachment upon the Macon & Western stalled, Sherman developed a new grand tactical approach. He explained it to Grant as early as 10 August: "in order to destroy effectually his communications I may have to leave a corps at the railroad bridge, well intrenched, and cut loose with the balance and make a desolating circle around Atlanta." By the morning of 13 August, Sherman had his mind set upon a huge infantry raid. He planned to leave one of his seven corps entrenched at the Chattahoochee to guard the W & A; then, with the rest, at least 60,000 men, to abandon the lines occupied since 22 July and march southward, aiming for the M & W 15 or 20 miles south of Atlanta. The overall Federal strategy conformed to the plan Sherman announced when his armies first crossed the Chattahoochee: either Hood would have to come out of his fortifications and attack, or the Federals would gain control of the Rebels' last supply line, forcing Hood to give up the city. Either way, Atlanta would have to fall.

General Sherman had his plans for this operation drawn up, but he suspended the army's movement when he learned that Confederate cavalry on 10 August had launched a raid against his railway line to Chattanooga. Indeed, General Hood had sent Joe Wheeler and half of the Confederate army's cavalry, about 5,000 horsemen, behind Sherman's lines to destroy the Western & Atlantic rail line supplying the Union army. This gave Sherman the idea on 14 August to launch a cavalry raid of his own against the Macon & Western, in effect giving his horsemen a chance to accomplish what he originally intended his infantry to do. Thus Sherman postponed his "grand movement by the right flank" as 4,000 Union cavalrymen, under Brigadier General Judson Kilpatrick, set out on 18 August to cut the railroad at Jonesboro.[69]

"You understand of course," Sherman wrote General Thomas on the morning of 18 August, "that I have suspended the movement contemplated for

---

[68] Sherman to Thomas, 10 August 1864, *OR*, vol. 38, pt. 5, p. 448; to Grant, 10 August, *OR*, vol. 38, pt. 5, p. 447; to Schofield, 11 August, *OR*, vol. 38, pt. 5, pp. 459, 464; Davis, *Atlanta Will Fall*, 160–67; *OR*, vol. 38, pt. 3, pp. 637, 681; Neal to "Ella," 4 August 1864, Neal Collection, Emory University.

An example of the Union regiments mustering out of Sherman's forces, after three years of Union service, was the 32nd Indiana. See Joseph R. Reinhart, trans. and ed., *August Willich's Gallant Dutchmen: Civil War Letters from the 32nd Indiana Infantry* (Kent OH: Kent State University Press, 2006) 176.

[69] Sherman to Grant, 10 August 1864; and to Halleck, 13 August, *OR*, vol. 38, pt. 5, pp. 447, 482; Special Order 57, 16 August, *OR*, vol. 38, pt. 5, p. 546; Davis, *Atlanta Will Fall*, 174; Sherman's report, 15 September, *OR*, vol. 38, pt. 1, p. 79; Sherman to Kilpatrick, 14 August, *OR*, vol. 38, pt. 5, p. 493.

to-night until General Kilpatrick tries his hand. Keep the big guns going and damage Atlanta all that is possible." Union artillery (and not just the big guns) kept up the bombardment of Atlanta in the third week of August, as Sherman awaited the results of Kilpatrick's cavalry raid on the railroad. The clear weather seemed to invite nocturnal firing. "We are now having moonlight nights," wrote one Federal on the evening of 15 August, "therefore we have some pretty sharp fighting at nights." "Thundering away around Atlanta," he added, "they seem to be a little boisterous tonight." "J.T.G." reported from Atlanta on 16 August that "for four nights the enemy have continued to fire regularly, at intervals of every five minutes, upon the city, with their heaviest guns, prisoners say 32-pound Parrotts." "Saturday night [13 August] the house of Dr. Biggers was fired by the explosion of a shell among a few bales of cotton, and was burned to the ground. Sunday night a fire originated on McDonough street, from a similar cause; a large frame dwelling on Whitehall street was fired and burned on Monday night; last night [15 August] two large houses on Whitehall street were burned to the ground...." Fortunately, "J.T.G." reported that he had not heard of any casualties from all of this shellfire.

During this time, the Federals seemed content to let their artillery do all the fighting. One brigade commander in the XX Corps recorded that during 19–25 August, "excepting the bombardment of the city by the artillery, hostilities almost entirely ceased." Union artillery kept up its fire not only on the city, but also on the Rebel works and the soldiers in them. In his diary entry for 18 August, Confederate Major General Samuel French, whose division held the lines west of town, recorded, "The Yankees must be angry...they raised—well—(I begin it with a 'w') and never ceased until 2 P.M., and they threw not less than two thousand shot at us." Union shells sometimes landed first on the Confederate entrenchments, then rolled toward the rear, barraging Southern soldiers' camps and officers' quarters. French acknowledged that such heavy shell fire made his headquarters, the home of Joseph B. Jennings, "anything but a pleasant residence." Once, so many Yankee shells exploded around and over French's house that a visitor, Lieutenant General Peter Stewart, delayed his departure; even the veteran officer deemed it "dangerous to leave." (The house itself got at least one shell-perforation.)

Meanwhile, in the daily artillery exchanges Confederate cannoneers were able to get in some licks of their own. General French had twenty-five pieces of artillery in his front (including the four 32-pounder rifled guns sent by the CSA Navy) that annoyed the Federals in their camps. Grenville Dodge's XVI Corps was among the targeted Yankees. "The rebs have been quite saucy today," Private James Snell of the 52d Illinois recorded in his diary on 30 July. Snell recorded five men in the 7th Indiana Battery killed by just one shell. Other explosions wounded men, killed horses, cut trees, and eventually forced General Dodge to move his headquarters a half mile farther to the rear.

Snell commented particularly on 64-pound shells thrown "so thick around us, as to endanger our Hd. Qrs. and the lives of everybody near them." He recorded that the Federals called the Rebels' big 64-pounder Dahlgren gun the "Growler"; its big shells made such a loud noise that the Yankees could yell out warnings: "Look out for that cart-wheel!" "There comes an anchor!" or "Look out for that blacksmith's shop!" One of them fell in among the soldiers' tents near General Wood's headquarters, but failed to explode. Captain David Conyngham admitted that it nonetheless "made a regular fuss and a scare, kicking up a whole lot of puddle; in fact, conducting itself like a miniature volcano." The big shellgun's projectiles took their share of casualties among the Yankees. A New York private, in a letter written home in mid-August, recalled that from the time the XX Corps dug in on 22 July, "every little while they sent over sum sixty five pounders...and killed James Biling and took a leg off one other and wounded one or two others you can bet it made a pretty big mess." The Confederates' Dahlgren gun would in turn doubtless have become a target of Union artillerists, though the *Official Records* contain no correspondence to confirm this. Lieutenant Ralsa Rice, whose 125th Ohio occupied part of the IV Corps line north of the city, thought that a Federal battery of six rifled cannon near his position directed its fire "to silence the rebel siege gun." The Yankees might have been successful in knocking the cannon out of action. The unidentified New York private quoted above noted on 16 August that "we have got that old fellow still at least they have not shot it this way for a few days." The 64-pounder was apparently dislodged by Union cannon; if so, it would have been too heavy to be remounted during the constant artillery exchanges of mid-August. After the fall of the city, Lieutenant Rice returned to the fortifications north of Atlanta and found that "the enemy's large siege gun was dismounted and lay in a ditch."[70]

---

[70] Sherman to Thomas, 18 August 1864, *OR*, vol. 38, pt. 5, pp. 572–73; "Harry" to ___, "Before Atlanta Georgia Monday night August 15th 1864" (unidentified Union soldier's letter), Beverly DuBose Collection, MSS 1020, Atlanta History Center (thanks to Melanie Stephan for this source); "J.T.G.," "From Our Correspondent with General Hood's Army" (Atlanta, 16 August), *Columbus Enquirer,* 20 August; report of Col. Horace Boughton, 10 September, *OR,* vol. 38, pt. 2, p. 94; Samuel G. French, *Two Wars: An Autobiography of Gen. Samuel G. French, An Officer in the Armies of the United States and the Confederate States, A Graduate from the U.S. Military Academy, West Point, 1843* (Nashville: Confederate Veteran, 1901) 220–21; Wilbur Kurtz, notebook 9, 99 (on Joseph Jennings's house as French's headquarters), Wilbur G. Kurtz Collection, Atlanta History Center; French's report, 6 December 1864, *OR,* vol. 38, pt. 3, p. 904; Snell, diary, 30 July, 4 August, Illinois Historical Society; "From Gen. Sherman," *New York Times,* 27 August; Conyngham, *Sherman's March through the South,* 200; "Camp near Atlanta" (unidentified Union soldier's letter), 16 August, MSS 2355, Georgia Historical Society, Savannah (typescript copy compliments of Dr. Todd Groce); Ralsa C. Rice, *Yankee Tigers: Through the Civil War with the 125th Ohio,* ed.

Like the troops in the trenches under artillery fire, inside the city Atlantans endured the bombardment with continued reliance upon their subterranean shelters. "We have been in the cellar all day," Carrie Berry recorded in her diary 6 August. Martha Huntington, sharing the two-story home of another family during the siege, remembered after the war how she and her children took shelter in the house basement: when "the shells came thicker and faster...we would waken the children, drag our mattresses with us, go down onto the lower floor and try to rest." "We all, black and white, huddled into it like frightened sheep," she confessed. "C-," writing for the *Intelligencer* from Atlanta on 12 August, reported an incident from 7 August, when a bomb-proof helped a family avoid becoming cannon-casualties.

> A family of six persons had taken refuge in a cellar, and were preparing their morning meal, when a shell penetrated the wall, about two feet from the ground outside, passed through the ceiling, struck the opposite wall, from which it rebounded back to the ceiling, and then exploded, scattering its own fragments and those of the ceiling in all directions; yet, strange to say, no one present was even touched. Nearly all who inhabit houses on the back streets are digging caves in their gardens. One of these, on Peachtree street, I saw, and which was skillfully constructed. An excavation is dug about eight feet deep and three feet wide, proceeding in a westerly direction; it then turns at right angles and proceeds four feet, when it again makes another right angle west, where it is made large enough to accommodate ten persons. A roof of timber and earth six feet thick covers the whole. A shell coming in at the entrance and exploding

Richard A. Baumgartner and Larry M. Strayer (Huntington WV: Blue Acorn Press, 1992) 135, 140.

We know that a 9-inch Confederate Dahlgren naval shellgun was sent to Atlanta on 28 May 1864 from the *CSS Chattahoochee*, then docked at Fort Gadsden, Florida, on the Apalachicola River (Turner, *Navy Gray*, 196, 205). But after its arrival by rail, probably sometime in June, we are not sure of where it was positioned in the Confederate fortifications north of the city. Three contemporary sources place the 64-pounder smoothbore at or near Fort Hood, the Confederate salient northwest of the city (now the Georgia Tech campus). 1) Union general Geary specifies that on 28 July the Rebel artillery fired "64-pound shells" from "heavy guns recently mounted in a fort near the railroad and close to Mrs. Ponder's house" (Geary report, 15 September 1864, *OR*, vol. 38, pt. 2, p. 142). 2) Union artilleryman Capt. Arnold Sutermeister wrote that after taking position in the lines north of Atlanta near the Marietta road (which abutted the west face of Fort Hood) his guns came under fire from "the forts...on our right...with 12-pounders and one 64-pounder rifled gun (Sutermeister report, 14 September 1864, *OR*, vol. 38, pt. 2, p. 488). 3) "J.T.G.," probably a Southern soldier doubling as a correspondent for the *Columbus Enquirer*, reported that "upon the north side of the city and near the state road (the Western & Atlantic, less than 700 feet from Fort Hood) we have planted a...64 pounder" ("From Our Correspondent," *Columbus Enquirer*, 9 August 1864).

cannot injure any of the inmates as the fragments must all strike the clay bank opposite.

A correspondent for the *Jackson Mississippian* offered another description of "bomb-proofs."

These are excavations in the soil, and roofed with heavy logs, over which is heaped the loose earth to the height of a young Ararat. These little mounds may be seen all over the city. The garden to almost every house which does not boast a cellar is now supplied with its artificial "bomb-proof." They are perfectly secure against the metal-storm, and many of them are quite comfortably furnished with beds and chairs and other furniture. Women and children are huddled together in them for hours at a time, and when the city is furiously shelled at night the whole community may be said to be under ground. Especially is this the case when the moon is unusually bright and the shells cannot be marked by their fiery trail.

The heavy shelling of 9 August apparently persuaded more Atlantans to dig in. On 10 August, Marcus Bell, serving on the staff of Major General Howell Cobb at Macon, returned home on furlough (having sent his wife and two children to Elberton) and was sitting in his "Calico House" when he saw his neighbor's wife, Della Pittman, overseeing the digging of a "big cave" in the backyard of their home on Collins Street. Another family pitched in, and after completion Bell reported the shelter was "full of women and children." "You go over the city," Bell wrote his wife on 11 August, "and everywhere during the shelling you see poor and rich men, women and children now and then poke their heads out of the little doors of those dens."

Outside the city to the southwest, as Hood's railway defense line of entrenchments was extended toward East Point, expansion of the war zone meant that more civilian families outside of the city also came under hostile fire. When their households fell close to the battle lines or within no man's land, noncombatants in the countryside did what noncombatants did in the city: they dug in. After Brigadier General Jacob Cox's division of Schofield's XXIII Corps advanced into the area of today's Cascade and Campbellton roads on 7 August, General Cox came upon a bombproof shelter at the home of Joseph Willis. Cox learned that several of Willis's relatives with their families had dug a shelter against the bombardment big enough to accommodate them all—twenty-six in number. Writing home on 11 August, he described what he had seen.

They excavated a sort of a cellar just in rear of the house, on the hillside, digging it deep enough to make a room fifteen feet square by six feet high. This was covered over with a roof of timbers, and over that they piled earth several feet thick, covering the whole with pine boughs, to keep the earth from washing.

In their bomb-proof four families are now living, and I never felt more pity than when, day before yesterday, I looked down into the pit, and saw there, in the gloom made visible by a candle burning while it was broad day above, women sitting on the floor of loose boards, resting against each other, haggard and wan, trying to sleep away the days of terror, while innocent-looking children, 4 or 5 years old, clustered around the air-hole, looking up with pale faces and great staring eyes.... they cling to home because they have nowhere else to go, and they hope we may soon pass on and leave them in comparative peace again.[71]

Besides finding shelter, finding food also preoccupied Atlantans during Sherman's shelling. The Federal semi-siege left open not only the Macon & Western Railroad but also wagon roads leading southward from the city. Daily wagon trains thus brought in provisions. Most supplies, to be sure, went to Hood's soldiers, but some nourished the civilian populace, albeit not abundantly. Samuel Richards commented in his diary 1 August, "it is to be hoped the contest will not be prolonged indefinitely for there is nothing much to be had to eat in Atlanta though if we keep the R.R. we will not quite starve, I trust." To supplement this pinched availability, some families were able to draw upon their gardens or animals. Richards noted that his family's garden was providing so much corn, tomatoes, and butter beans that he was able to give some away. Henry Watterson ("Grape"), though, noted the uncertainty of family gardens as a

---

[71] Carrie Berry, diary, entry of 6 August, Atlanta History Center; Ben Kremenak, ed., "Escape from Atlanta: The Huntington Memoir," *Civil War History* 11/2 (June 1965): 166–67; "C-," "Editor of the Intelligencer," *Atlanta Intelligencer,* 14 August; "Position of Affairs Before Atlanta. From the *Richmond Examiner,* September 1" (quoting the *Jackson Mississippian*), in *New York Tribune,* 5 September; Bell, "Bombardment of Atlanta"; Bell, "The Calico House," 31; Jacob Dolson Cox, *Military Reminiscences of the Civil War,* 2 vols. (New York: C. Scribner's Sons, 1900) 2:303–304; Wilbur G. Kurtz, "Dugout Home in Atlanta," *Atlanta Journal Magazine,* 10 July 1932, 3, 27.

Kurtz's newspaper article on the Willis family dug-out is arguably the most detailed account in the literature concerning an actual civilian bombproof in the Atlanta Campaign. In May 1932 in southwest Atlanta, he interviewed sixty-five-year-old Elizabeth Herren, daughter of Joseph Willis, the dug-out builder. Born a year after the war ended, she had heard her family's stories and told Kurtz how the bombproof had been built and sited it for Kurtz off today's Cascade Road. She could even remember the names of twenty-one occupants of the bombproof in which they lived for three weeks (7 August–ca. 25 August). We are fortunate that Kurtz acted when he did. Two months after his interview with Mrs. Herren, she was kicked by a cow and broke her hip. After two months, she died of complications. Without Kurtz's meticulous notes (notebook 9, 89–90) and his subsequent article, the story of the Willis bombproof would never have been recorded.

means of sustenance, particularly for the poorer families. "Few of them made any preparation for a siege," he wrote on 13 August, "and the little produced by the truck patches within the city is rapidly disappearing before the rapacity of a great circle of nocturnal thieves." Watterson criticized these food-robbers by adding, "these rogues do not confine their operations to dwellings which have been abandoned, but wander with pertinacious effrontery into every aperture which promises plunder." Still, some gardeners raised enough produce to put some on sale. In his report of 4 August on bombardment damage, Isaac Pilgrim wrote that on that morning some thirty people had gathered in the market house near Bridge Street and were "marketing" when a shell exploded inside. "Strange to say, no one was hurt," he noted. "James Parker and Robert McMaster, who were attending to their respective stalls, were knocked down, but no injury was done them, except the fright they received." There was reportedly one grocery store open in downtown in early August, but its supply of goods was always uncertain.

First priority for supplies coming into the city, of course, was the army. "Rover" reported from Atlanta on 8 August:

> So far as meal and meat are concerned the fighting men of the army are well fed. Rations of beef and bacon are alternated. The cooking is done by details in the rear, and distributed along the trenches at night. It is to be regretted more vegetables have not been forwarded, as they might be. There is plenty in the country, but little reaches here—barely sufficient to supply the hospitals. This is not as it should be. The people of Georgia owe more than this to their defenders.

Commissary Captain Benedict Semmes cast the supply situation a little more positively in a letter written 12 August: the Yankees kept bombarding Atlanta and pressing their lines around the city, "though we are not by any means *besieged*." In fact, Semmes noted "plenty of rations &c on hand and our road well guarded."

Thus soldiers and civilians alike in Atlanta made do for food as best they could. A newspaperman writing for the *Intelligencer* on 14 August commented that of sustenance "there…is, but very little in the city, and, since the 22d July last, there has been scarcely any provisions for sale here." The food supply, dependent upon train and wagon into the city from Macon, fluctuated. In mid-August the *Appeal* observed, "the commerce of Atlanta is just now principally confined to the watermelon and apple trade, and the arrival of each train causes many transactions for a short space of time thereafter." Prices were high; $5–$25 for a melon, "according to the anxiety of the purchaser"; even "very inferior" apples ran $50 a bushel. As always in a supply-and-demand economy, prices rose and fell with the availability of goods. This gave opportunity to the ever-cursed "speculators," as "Rover" reported from Atlanta on 17 August.

We are beginning to witness the opening of a little trade in the City, principally, as it should be, in the provision line. Flour and meal has been coming in pretty freely—the former retailing at $250 per barrel, and the latter at $15 per bushel. But little bacon is brought in. I observe, however, that some of the butchers are in regular attendance upon market every morning, and what is a little remarkable, prices are much lower than before the siege began. Beef, mutton and fresh pork then sold at from three to five dollars a pound, whereas now it is retailed at from one to three dollars a pound, and the average quality is full as good. Thus many will be enabled to eke out their scanty supply of bacon. No vegetables are to be seen in market, and but few anywhere—all the fine gardens in the city and vicinity having been plundered by the soldiers. Whiskey, watermelon and goober speculators are also making their appearance, and it must be admitted that the fabulous prices demanded for these articles will soon deplete a full purse if the owner indulges in them. The soldiers, however, curse but buy at every opportunity, while the trader pockets the cash and laughs in his sleeve.

The *Appeal* of 23 August observed that "we judge there is enough [food] to meet the wants of our greatly reduced population," but added that "the prices of some articles are high, speculators holding all there is upon the market, but as a general thing our market is now but little ahead of those of other cities."[72]

With all of the market-pinching forces at work during Sherman's semi-siege in summer 1864, the real news was that even at its peak intensity the Federal bombardment failed to diminish the flow of food into Atlanta for Hood's army. Union observers watched closely for signs of traffic, and carefully recorded what they saw, especially reinforcements or supplies for the Rebels.

Signal officer reports 5.10 pm. three trains of cars loaded with troops just arrived at Atlanta. No. 1, four passenger and seven freight cars; No. 2, thirteen freight cars; No. 3, seventeen freight cars, full outside and inside. (12 August) Three trains of cars arrived at Atlanta during the day: No. 1, of four platform and two box-cars, used as a construction train; No. 2, of four passenger and five freight cars; No. 3,

---

[72] Venet, ed., *Sam Richards's Civil War Diary*, 229 (entry of 1 August 1864); "Grape," "From Atlanta" (3 August), *Augusta Constitutionalist*, 10 August [see also "Distress in Atlanta," *Columbus Sun*, 14 August]; "The Houses Shelled in Atlanta," *Atlanta Intelligencer*, 6 August; Castel, *Decision in the West*, 464 ("only one grocery store"); "Rover," "Letter from the Georgia Front" (Atlanta, 8 August), *Augusta Chronicle & Sentinel*, 12 August; "B.J.S." to wife, 12 August, Semmes Papers, University of North Carolina; "Fire in Atlanta—Shelling of the City," *Atlanta Intelligencer*, 16 August; "Rover," "Letter from the Georgia Front" (Atlanta, 17 August), *Chronicle & Sentinel*, 21 August; "The Immediate Front," *Memphis Appeal*, 23 August, quoted in *Atlanta Intelligencer*, 26 August.

of fifteen freight cars, doors closed; could not see with what loaded, or whether loaded or not. Train ran slow; engine appeared to be working hard. [14 August)]

At 10.40 A.M. one passenger and one freight train left Atlanta apparently empty. At 5.10 P.M. one train of cars, three passenger, one baggage, and five freight cars, apparently the same train that left town at 10.40 A.M., arrived; also a train of eighteen cars, five of them loaded with white sacks. The rest of the train appeared to be empty. Green corn was hauled in and issued to the rebel troops in their works this P.M. [15 August]

The Northern spy, Milton Glass, reported on 18 August after visiting several Southern camps that the Rebels "appear to have plenty of rations and forage from day to day, but there is no supply on hand; supplies are all brought from Macon." As always, it depended upon from whom you heard as to whether the men in the ranks were happy with what they got to eat. A staff officer in Ferguson's cavalry brigade wrote home on 15 August, "for the last twenty days we have enjoyed a respite from the fighting, have been lazying in a good camp, with tolerable fare and little or no work to do, and are growing fat." This was from an officer, and one in the cavalry at that (with liberty to conduct "foraging" expeditions on his own). The infantrymen in the trenches may have had more to grumble about. A Confederate deserter, Captain J. B. Jordan of the 36th Alabama, told his captors on 14 August that rations were issued to the troops two or three days at a time, consisting of bacon, cornbread, and sometimes beef. They were, to be sure, skimpy; Jordan had "often seen his men eat a day's supply at a meal and then not be satisfied." Yet by these standards Hood's men certainly fared no worse than, say, Lee's soldiers in the trenches before Petersburg about the same time or, for that matter, Rebels in other theaters of the war where Confederates' rickety railway system determined the availability of rations at the front.

Having even a harder time than the soldiers were the poor people in the city, unable to get out; now, in hard times, the indigent probably represented a higher proportion of Atlanta's population than ever before. "The poor in Atlanta are said to be suffering for something to eat," lamented the *Columbus Sun*, 3 August. "Nothing can be brought there. Their condition is indeed deplorable." "All the poorer people here 'draw' rations," recorded Marcus Bell on 11August; "the people wander about in distress." Even the men in Hood's army felt they were better off than the impoverished in town, so some soldiers gave up their rations, scanty as they were. On 26 July, Cheatham's entire division gave up its day's issue for "the indigent families of Atlanta." A correspondent for the *Chattanooga Rebel*, writing from the army on 2 August reported, "I had the pleasure of a visit to General Carter's Brigade the other day. It was *fast-day* with the boys. They had made a donation of their rations for that day to the poor of Atlanta. I was told that other brigades had done likewise.... "

In addition to the fast-day dole-outs from the army, the needy in Atlanta also got provisions from the civil authorities still in the city. "There are not stores in town," wrote Colin Dunlop to his mother from the "trenches near Atlanta" on 17 August; "government issues rations to the poor." By the third week in August, the situation had gotten so bad that some were even asking whether the indigent population could be transported out of the city. The *Intelligencer* of 23 August reported that the chairman of the "Committee in Atlanta to deal out rations to the Poor" had written a state official, passing on the opinion of an unnamed Confederate general that "the poor had all better be removed to some point where they can be better *fed*...than in Atlanta." The said officer estimated that there were "one thousand families, averaging, say, four to the family" still in town. If the Macon & Western Railroad were cut—all well informed Confederates knew that this was Sherman's design—General Hood could not feed both the army and the civilian population. As it was, "the shelling is so heavy and constant that we cannot get grinding of corn done."

The *Intelligencer* credited General Hood with doing all he could to "ameliorate the condition of the poor who are still in Atlanta, and who have not the means to leave that city, or other home, or place of refuge to flee to." At the same time, with the city government virtually collapsed, and the state handicapped by military exigency, the *Intelligencer* could only appeal to public philanthropy.

> We publish the foregoing in order to suggest that relief be sent to the poor of Atlanta, especially by those who are able and are refugees from it. There was a time when the people of Atlanta nobly and generously gave to other suffering communities. Will not other communities now help the poor of that city? Send them meal and bacon—if only a bushel of the one, and a side or shoulder of the other, many from different sections of the State thus contributing will do great good. Living in cellars, bombproofs and caves, let them at least have bread and meat![73]

Despite their privations and dangers during the barrage, Atlantans managed to eke out some social life. Organized gatherings sometimes took place, such as a ball held at the Medical College on the night of 12 August. Social calls

---

[73] Howard to Sherman, 12 August, and Lt. Samuel Edge to General Logan, 14–15 August, *OR*, vol. 38, pt. 5, pp. 480, 501, 512–13; statement of Milton Glass, 18 August, *OR*, vol. 38, pt. 5, p. 580; Capt. William L. Nugent to "Nellie," 15 August 15 1864, in William N. Cash and Lucy Somerville Nugent, eds., *My Dear Nellie: The Civil War Letters of William L. Nugent to Eleanor Smith Nugent* (Jackson: University Press of Mississippi, 1977) 200 ("we...are growing fat"); statement of Captain Jordan, 14 August, *OR*, vol. 38, pt. 5, p. 495; *Columbus Sun*, 3 August (on "the poor in Atlanta"); Bell, "Bombardment of Atlanta"; Losson, *Tennessee's Forgotten Warriors*, 186; "Special Correspondence of the Rebel" (Atlanta, 2 August), *Columbus Times*, 4 August; Colin Dunlop to mother, 17 August, Colin Dunlop Letters, Atlanta History Center; "The Poor in Atlanta," *Atlanta Intelligencer*, 23 August.

on friends and neighbors, as always, relieved the tedium. Samuel Richards and his family spent one evening at Sidney Root's home; when a regimental band from the army serenaded the group, Root asked them in for cakes and whiskey. Sometimes visits were for other than social reasons. Marcus Bell was sitting on his front porch on the morning of 12 August, observing "slow but constant shelling" when an explosion nearby sent several ladies running into his house, heading for the back porch. They evidently did not stop to exchange pleasantries with their host.

People came together, too, to worship—that is, when their churches were open. None held services on 24 July, according to Sam Richards, who noted in his diary that day, "no church in the city open." The next Sunday, 31 July, Richards recorded that services were only held at the Catholic cathedral, as "not a Protestant Church was open." Part of the reason was that a number of clergymen had left the city, although residents at times were unsure just who remained. "All the ministers have forsaken their posts except the Catholic," wrote Sam Richards on 1 August; "the Episcopal minister I think is here but the Church is under repair." Reverend Andrew F. Freeman was rector of St. Philip's Episcopal; he was staying 2 miles from the city's center with friends, the Ormonds, who had "a cave," according to Confederate Colin Dunlop, writing to his sister from the "trenches near Atlanta" on 13 August. Dunlop added that "Mr. Freeman & the Catholic Priest are the only Clergy in Town." Father Thomas O'Reilly of the Catholic Church of the Immaculate Conception was indeed still in town, refusing to abandon his parishioners throughout the bombardment. Private Philip Stephenson of the Washington Artillery described O'Reilly as "a handsome young Irishman fond of the good things of this life"; Stephenson enjoyed a visit with him at his parsonage one afternoon when he got a pass into town.

For a time, services at Trinity Methodist were held only because a chaplain in Hood's army conducted them; the church pastor, the Reverend Harwell Parks, had fled the city with his family. But on Sunday, 7 August, Confederate Captain Key noticed the enemy fired no shells into the city that Sabbath morning— another minister, the Reverend Atticus Haygood, conducted the service and preached the sermon. Sam Richards worshiped at Trinity that morning; it was his first time at church in three weeks. Maxwell Berry also took his daughter to Trinity on 7 August; "It is the first time I have ben to Church in a month," wrote Carrie in her diary. On the following Sabbath, 14 August, Bishop Lay himself gave the sermon at St. Philip's, which had reopened its doors. The Episcopal church was also open on 21 August; the usually Methodist Sam Richards attended the services despite the rainy weather.

Nonetheless Marcus Bell recorded on 11 August that "church going here has almost ceased." Besides absence of clergy, another cause of the inactivity was that the places of worship themselves at times had come under bombardment. Atlanta historian Wilbur Kurtz reasoned that "since most of the shells fell in the downtown section, it is obvious that the Second Baptist and Central Presbyterian

Church spires, together with the city hall tower, afforded the Federal gunners range-finding objects." "The spire of the Central Presbyterian Church was struck by a shell," wrote Kurtz (even though city hall across the street underwent no damage). Other churches also suffered. By 4 August, the Methodist Wesley Chapel was described by Isaac Pilgrim as "horribly mutilated" by eight shells which had struck it. St. Luke's, the Episcopal church organized that spring, bore evidence of the Yankees' indiscriminate cannonading. On 10 August, Bishop Lay and Chaplain Quintard visited the building, having heard of its damage. "We looked in wonder at the sight that met our eyes upon our entering the sacred edifice," recorded Quintard. "One of the largest shells had torn through the side of the building and struck the prayer desk on which the large Bible happened to be lying. The prayer desk was broken and the Bible fell under it and upon the shell so as apparently to smother it and prevent its exploding. I lifted up the Bible and removed the shell and gathered up all the prayer books I could find for the soldiers in the camps." St. Luke's never saw another worship service after mid-August. Yankee fires would destroy the church three months later.[74]

As with churchgoing, social life in the shelled city depended upon people being able to get out from their places of shelter; seeing others required a certain measure of cautious ambulation about town. To do so, some rules-of-thumb developed, such as staying away from the Car Shed area when locomotives

---

[74] "Special Correspondence," *Atlanta Intelligencer,* 18 August 1864 (on the Medical College ball); Bell, "Bombardment of Atlanta"; Venet, ed., *Sam Richards's Civil War Diary,* 229–32 (1, 7, 14, and 21 August); Audria B. Gray, "History of the Cathedral Parish of St. Philip's in the City and Diocese of Atlanta," *Atlanta Historical Bulletin* 1/4 (December 1930): 6 (on Father Freeman); Colin Dunlop to sister, 13 August, Colin Dunlop Letters, Atlanta History Center; Hughes, ed., *Civil War Memoir of Philip Stephenson,* 230; Ralph Benjamin Singer, "Confederate Atlanta" (Ph.D. diss., University of Georgia, 1973) 257 (on the army chaplain at Trinity Methodist); "History of Trinity Methodist Church, 1853–1867," *Atlanta Historical Bulletin* 3/15 (October 1938): 287; Cate, ed., *Two Soldiers,* 106; Carrie Berry, diary, entry for 7 August, Atlanta History Center; Lay, diary, 14 August, University of North Carolina; Wilbur G. Kurtz, "Shells for Dinner," *Atlanta Journal Magazine,* 7 September 1941, 9; "The Houses Shelled in Atlanta," *Atlanta Intelligencer,* 6 August 1864, 2; Elliott, ed., *Doctor Quintard,* 88; Alex M. Hitz, "The Origin and Distinction Between the Two Protestant Episcopal Churches Known as St. Luke's Church, Atlanta," *Georgia Historical Quarterly* 34/1 (March 1950): 4.

After the war, Dr. Quintard, then Episcopal bishop of Tennessee, wrote of the big shell that crashed into St. Luke's and how the Bible's falling on it seemed as if angels had "placed it just on top of the terrible monster" to prevent if from exploding (Charles Todd Quintard, *Nellie Peters' Handkerchief and What It Saw: A Story of the War,* ed. Arthur Howard Noll [Sewanee: University Press, 1907]). Quintard's pamphlet centers on the handkerchief of Richard Peters's daughter Nellie, which she had dropped at St. Luke's during the funeral in summer 1864 for her eleven-month-old brother. Quintard found it in his visit to the church of 10 August and returned it to its owner. A copy of the pamphlet is in the Nellie Peters Black Papers, MSS 32F, Atlanta History Center.

approached with their pillars of smoke visible to the Yankees. Furthermore, while no civilian claimed to be so nimble as literally to dodge shells, one could at least hear them coming and thus take precautions. Some noncombatants, like veteran soldiers in the trenches, could identify projectiles from their sounds— percussion shells were said to have a short, shrill whistle. To his wife, Captain B. J. Semmes described what could be heard: "some of the shells make a noise like a rail road train flying through the air, and are called 'through to Macon' or 'Augusta' as they go screaming over head. They are only dangerous when they burst before reaching us or when striking a building. Others sing 'flibberty gibbety' in a very loud and fearful manner as they are whirled along, and others again make a hissing noise and explode only on striking some object." At night if the moon were not too bright, people could see the shells arc through the air; "we could tell when they were coming over at night by the burning fuse," recalled one resident, Thomas H. Jeffries, a boy of ten at the time. Then too, the Yankee gunners' fire patterns helped. After their move into the Georgia Bank building, Caroline Clayton, wife of William and mother of Sallie, fed her family by preparing meals at their Marietta Street home, and hurriedly carrying them the six blocks to the bank. She learned to make this transit during the bombardment by timing the intervals, frequently five minutes, between the enemy batteries' salvoes. The populace was further favored when enemy shells failed to explode. Wallace Reed, writing in the 1880s based on recollections of wartime Atlantans, offered that "most of the shells had percussion caps, and, as fully as three fourths of them had struck the wrong end, they failed to explode." Decades later, these undetonated Yankee visitors would appear in Atlantans' gardens and beneath buildings, sometimes creating furor with their long-delayed explosions.[75]

After a while, everyone realized that the southern half of the city was the safest area from the enemy shellfire. On 1 August, writing from his home four blocks south of the Car Shed, Samuel Richards entered into his diary, "We have had shelling semi-occasionally but thus far none of the deadly missiles have reached our house and we could look upon them at a safe distance with composure." On the other hand, the Richards bookstore on Whitehall, closer into

---

[75] Carter, *Siege of Atlanta,* 242, 267; B. J. Semmes to wife, 21 August 1864, Semmes Papers, University of North Carolina; Cooper, *Official History of Fulton County,* 175; Davis, ed., *Requiem for a Lost City,* 128; Reed, *History of Atlanta,* 183.

On the failure of Union shells to detonate on contact during the war, see "West End Thinks Japs Are Here When Civil War Shell Explodes," *Atlanta Journal,* 22 April 1942, which relates how a long-buried shell exploded as Mrs. Annie Milam was burning trash in her garden on Peeples Street. As recently as August 1994, construction crews digging under the former Rich's store downtown found a Federal shell, which the police bomb squad took away for safe detonation (WSB-TV news, 26 August 1994; Bill Hendrick, "Treasure beneath Rich's Revealed in Bits, Pieces," *Atlanta Constitution,* 30 August 1994; and Hendrick, "Digging into Downtown's History, *Atlanta Constitution,* 24 December 1994).

the city, had had a shell pierce its cornice and descend into the Beach & Root building opposite. Isaac Pilgrim, updating his column printed in the *Intelligencer* 6 August, a week later added a few more structures damaged by Northern shells. The home of Judge C. H. Strong, near the Baptist Church, had been injured. A shell had passed through the window of Washington Hall and exploded in the bar room, "doing considerable damage." Beach & Root's store was hit (as Richards had noted), and Herring & Son's on Whitehall had a projectile explode inside. Two Ivy Street residences, of E. B. Walker and Colonel A. M. Wallace, were struck, the former greatly damaged. Eventually, however, Pilgrim gave up: "It is impossible to enumerate all the buildings that have been struck either by shells or fragments." Occasionally a notable home was singled out for mention, as when the *Intelligencer* of 14 August noted, "the handsome residences of Mr. William Solomon and of Judge Lyon…have both been shelled by the enemy—the residence of the former being severely injured." Pilgrim concluded that most of the damage was on the city's north side. "You can find evidences of the enemy's barbarity in almost every house or lot in the city, except in the Southern and Southeastern portion." Some Atlantans accordingly shifted their lodgings to those quarters. After Mrs. Callender Bell was wounded in the left shoulder by a projectile, the Bells moved from their residence on Marietta at Walton to a vacant house on McDonough Street between Fulton and Richardson, six blocks south of city hall. Yet even in the southwest part of the city, folk could not feel perfectly safe. On the night of 3 August, Samuel Richards noted, "the horrid missiles of destruction whizzed *past* our house and discomposed us considerably. Heretofore they had fallen short, but now we cannot tell at what moment they may strike us again." Richards kept an eye on his store downtown, where Northern shells fell more heavily. "Upon entering our store today I was puzzled at finding the stove tumbled down and moved forward six feet," he wrote,

> …but the rubbish around and the side of the *flue* in the wall told that a shell had "dropped in" but where it had made its entrance I could not discover until I went upstairs and then the mystery was explained. The shell had entered the roof and passing through five partitions of wood and plaster had pierced the side wall into the flue, and its force being expended it *dropped* in the flue to the store below and there exploded, doing the mischief before spoken of. I found the butt end of the shell. The diameter of which is four inches and weighs 3 1/4 lbs. The length was probably ten or twelve inches and the entire weight 16 or 20 lbs. I hope no more such visitors will enter our premises.[76]

---

[76] Venet, ed., *Sam Richards' Civil War Diary*, 229–31 (1 and 7 August 1864); [Isaac B. Pilgrim], "Atlanta," *Atlanta Intelligencer*, 14 August; "Atlanta," *Atlanta Intelligencer*, 13 August (also in *Savannah Republican*, 15 August); Wilbur G. Kurtz, "Interview with James

Atlantans would long remember their close encounters with Sherman's shells. In the early 1900s, the *Atlanta Journal* ran an occasional column in its Sunday "ladies' section" on "pioneer women," early settlers of Atlanta still around to spin their memories. Martha Powell, daughter of one of the Atlanta area's first physicians, Dr. Chapman Powell, was interviewed in 1912 at the age of eighty-three. She had a vivid recollection of the wartime bombardment and how it forced her to flee the city: "My husband and I took our children in our arms and left the house as General Sherman's army began shelling the town. I shall never forget that night of terror as we were escaping." Mrs. Powell and family joined her father, who was refugeeing in Newton County.

In her interview of July 1909, Cornelia Venable recalled the dugout shelter in which she, husband, mother, and childen huddled during the bombardment. "There was just enough room in the bomb-proof for the children to lie down," she said, "and we had to sit up and sleep at their feet." She remembered that one morning she and her son made an errand-visit to their house, and had a close call with one of Sherman's messengers. "As William and I were leaving the house that morning, a shell came tearing through the roof, exploding directly over our head, and scattering shot about us. It did not take us long to return to our place of safety in the pit." The Venables resolutely stuck it out until a Northern shell killed two neighbors. "It was not until that incident," she declared, that they decided to move to a dwelling on the south side of town. "There we put our mattresses on the floor," and forty-five years afterward, she still remembered how once in safer shelter, "I slept the sweetest sleep I ever enjoyed in my life."

Lollie Belle Wylie, historian of the Atlanta Women's Pioneer Society, conducted most of these interviews, and transcribed them into articles for the *Journal.* Wylie talked with Lucy Pittman Ivy in June 1909. Four decades after the war, Ivy still remembered that during the bombardment her family had to get up before sunrise, cook their meals for the day, then retire into the basement of A. C. Wyly's building on Peachtree Street. Though the name of Jennie Smith does not appear in other wartime stories of shell-casualties, Ivy related her death vividly.

One of the saddest incidents of the war was the killing of Miss Jennie Smith, of Acworth. During the siege of Atlanta she was on a visit to her aunt, Mrs. Roberts. Early one morning, when the shelling began, Miss Smith and Mrs. Roberts ran to the cellar, where they hoped to find protection. Nearly there, Miss Smith remembered something she desired to carry with her, and ran back for it. Just as she was starting again for the cellar, a shell struck the house, tearing a hole in the side, and killing Miss Smith instantly.... Next morning Mr. Ivy and Mr. Willingham took the remains out to Oakland cemetery and dug the grave and buried her.

Bell—June 21st-1935," notebook 10, 234; "What James Bell told me about the Siege of Atlanta," box 34, folder 13, Wilbur G. Kurtz Collection, Atlanta History Center.

Lucy Caldwell Kicklighter, whose family had settled in Atlanta in 1853, with their home located downtown near the Car Shed, recalled scenes from the bombardment. "I will never forget the first shell I heard," she told Wylie; "it is impossible to describe to any one who has never heard the whizzing and bursting of these shells the terror the sound carries." She took shelter in a neighbor's bomb-proof, in which the owner had laid out a carpet and a few chairs. Other "pioneer women" shared vignettes of the barrage. Mrs. Alfred Austell recalled that her husband dug a bomb-proof in their back yard: a deep, large, square hole, filled with straw, and topped by heavy logs and timber as roof. Mrs. M. B. Torbett told Wylie of how her girlhood home on Marietta Street had been in the Northern cannons' line of fire, and took seventeen separate hits during the bombardment. Her father, Hamilton Goode, fashioned an embankment of railroad crossties in front of the house to protect the basement in which the family sought shelter. The place was big enough for Mr. Goode to invite neighbors. Because the shelling usually started at 6 A.M., and lasted till dark, Mrs. Torbett remembered preparing meals during the night, then sitting in the cellar all day. Forty-five years later, she could detail her own frightening shell encounter. Out for fresh air during a lull in the barrage, "I was suddenly startled by the bursting of a stray shell on Spring street, and one of the pieces falling between my knees, cut through my dress and just missed wounding me severely."

Other Atlanta women also put their memories in print. Mary Hubner recorded a story passed through her family about the Whitneys, who lived near the Medical College about Calhoun and Wheat. Mary Frances ("Miss Frank," the eldest daughter and a musician) was entertaining some Confederate soldiers in the parlor when "a fragment of a shell went through an upper room, entered a wardrobe, cut a dress apart, passed through the floor, chipped a piece from the edge of the piano upon whose keys Miss Frank was playing, and lodged in the floor. 'Oh, that's nothing but a shell. Let's finish our song,' one of the soldiers said. So the music was resumed." Another Atlantan, Mollie Smith, remembered when a projectile from the Federals' 4 1/2-inch guns came calling.

> Just as the family seated themselves at the breakfast table, a thirty-two pound shell struck the house. It hit the room above the dining room, and the brick wall amounted to nothing in the way of protection. The shell made an opening of some three feet in the wall, tearing into atoms the door leading into the hall. It passed into the opposite room and exploded near the piano, wrenching off one leg and carrying it to the opposite side of the room, where it turned it upside down.
>
> One end of the sofa was torn to pieces, every pane of glass broken in the windows and the blinds smashed. Pieces of shell penetrated to a closet in an adjoining room and tore some clothing. Other pieces went through the floor, and the bedclothes caught on fire. The house was so

filled with smoke that we thought it was blazing. Some soldiers who were camped near us rushed in and took part of our things out into the street, where they stayed all day. The shelling was so great that my father could not have them put back until night.

In 1931, William Fort Williams, son of the postwar Mayor James E. Williams, recalled to Wilbur Kurtz about his living on the west side of Washington Street, across from city hall and next to Central Presbyterian Church. The family was nursing a sick cavalryman upstairs when a shell crashed through the roof, leaving a big hole and unnerving the soldier. Williams recalled that the same projectile had struck the spire of the church next door.

There were other tales. In the 1920s, at the death of Mrs. J. W. Wade, her obituary in the city papers told the story of how "during the War Between the States, Mrs. Wade was in her kitchen preparing broth for wounded soldiers when a shell struck a corner of the house near which she was standing. Other shells destroyed trees in the vicinity of her home." Another Atlanta family that stayed in the city throughout the bombardment was Mary Edwardy and her three children. Edward Edwardy, her husband (a Hungarian who had emigrated to New York, ca. 1850), had moved to Georgia by 1859 and owned a grocery on Whitehall between Hunter and Alabama streets. He returned to New York before Sherman's armies neared Atlanta. The wife and kids then lived in the family's grocery store "seeking refuge in the cellar when the shelling got dangerous," as Frederick Edwardy, then five, told Wilbur Kurtz years later. Other children remembered the trauma of war-events. Anton Kontz, thirteen years old, lived at 82 Marietta Street in the large, three-story brick house built by his parents, Christian and Elizabeth. Playing in the street, Anton heard a shell whine too late to duck; the blast killed his dog and slightly wounded him in the chest. Crying, trudging home with the dead animal in his wagon, Anton was met by Dr. D'Alvigny. The doctor treated the boy's wound with tape from his satchel and sent him home, where Anton sorrowfully buried his pup.

For years after the war, buildings in Atlanta also gave testimony to the shelling of summer 1864. When the home of Dr. W. S. Armstrong, at 82 E. Hunter Street, was about to be torn down years after the war, a window sill bore a "shell wound" that caused wary workmen to dig about for a possible unexploded projectile. At the demolition of the Austin Leyden house on Peachtree in 1913, the *Journal* rehashed a story of how during the bombardment a shell had entered the house at its northwest corner, plunging inside but failing to explode. Henry Grady, a frequent visitor, opined on the unwelcome lodger, saying it had "paused to reflect" in its course. Residents of the John Collier home, at the corner of Nelson and Chapel streets, were not only able to tell the story of the Union shell which tore into their house (but did not detonate); years later they could produce the thing.[77]

While postwar memories attest to the dramatic impact of the Union bombardment upon Atlanta's residents, truest impressions of course come from those who wrote them down at the time. Invaluable in this regard are the diarists Sam Richards and Carrie Berry. "Our cruel foe had the grace to cease from shelling us on the Sabbath, at least he has not done so yet," wrote Richards on Sunday, 7 August, in his customary end-of-the-week entry. Young Carrie dutifully entered a comment, albeit briefer, each day.

"We have not had many shells to day." (8 August)
"We have had to stay in the cellar all day the shells have ben falling so thick around the house. Two have fallen in the garden, but none of us

---

[77] Isabelle Ormond Thomas, "Pioneer Woman Tells Interesting Story of Early Days in Atlanta," *Atlanta Journal,* 24 November 1912; Lollie Belle Wylie, "Interesting Sketches of Pioneer Women" (Mrs. Cornelia Venable), *Atlanta Journal,* 1 August 1909; Wylie, "Interesting Sketches" (Mrs. Lucy P. Ivy), *Atlanta Journal,* 20 June 1909; Wylie, "Interesting Sketches" (Mrs. C. J. Kicklighter), *Atlanta Journal* 13, June 1909; "Mrs. Alfred Austell," typescript recollections, box 1, folder 30, Atlanta Women's Pioneer Society Collection, MSS 391, Atlanta History Center; Wylie, "Interesting Sketches" (Mrs. M. B.Torbett), *Atlanta Journal,* 8 May 1910; Mary Hubner Walker, *Charles W. Hubner: Poet Laureate of the South* (Atlanta: Cherokee Publishing Company, 1976) 52–53; Smith, "Dodging Shells"; Kurtz's notes on interview with William Fort Williams, 19 May 1931, notebook 6, 39, Kurtz Collection, Atlanta History Center; "Mrs. Wade, 102, Who Saw Atlanta Rise from Ruins, Dies at Grandson's Home," undated newspaper clipping [ca. September 1927], notebook 3, 200; Wilbur G. Kurtz, notes from interview with Frederick W. Edwardy, 16 October 1937, notebook 6, 39, Wilbur G. Kurtz Collection, Atlanta History Center; Ball, "Monument of Service"; Wilbur Kurtz, notebook 10, 5 (on Armstrong house), Wilbur G. Kurtz Collection, Atlanta History Center; "Here Are Some Last Farewell Views of the Old Leyden House"; Thomas H. Martin, *Atlanta and Its Builders: A Comprehensive History of the Gate City of the South,* 2 vols. (Atlanta: Century Memorial Publishing Company, 1902) 500 (Collier residence photograph).

Not all late-in-life Atlantans' memories of the war are reliable. In one of Lollie Wylie's columns, printed in the *Atlanta Journal* in 1909, Mrs. Eugenia Morgan spoke of the Yankees' entrance into the city, a visit of Confederate officers ("they were sanguine and in good spirits"), and the typhoid death of Augusta Clayton as if they had all occurred on the same day. Nevertheless, Morgan, well advanced in years, possessed the seniority to tell Miss Wylie, "the moonlight doesn't shine now like it did then." Her remark sounds like Mark Twain's observation from the 1880s that Southerners dated things from before and after the war. Twain was in New Orleans when he overheard the conversation between a young New Yorker and an old black woman. The Yankee observed, "What a wonderful moon you have down here!" The woman sighed and responded, "Ah, bless yo' heart, honey, you ought to seen dat moon befo' de waw!" (Twain, *Life on the Mississippi* [New York: Harper & Brothers, 1911] 338).

were hurt. Cousin Henry Beatty came in and wanted us to move, he thought that we were in danger, but we will try it a little longer." (9 August)

"We have had but few shells to day." (10 August)

"We had to go in the cellar often out of the shells. How I wish the federals would quit shelling us so that we could get out and get some fresh air." (11 August)

"...we have not had so much wirk to do so I have ben knitting on my stocking." (12 August)

"We have had a very quiet day to day.... We fear that we will have shells to night. We can hear muskets so plane." (13 August)

"Sure enough we had shells in abundance last night. We averaged one every moment during the night. We expected every one would come through and hurt some of us but to our joy nothing on the lot was hurt. They have ben throwing them at us all day to day but they have not ben dangerous. Papa has ben at work all day making the cellar safe. Now we feel like we could stay at home in safety. I dislike to stay in the cellar so close but our soldiers have to stay in ditches." (14 August)

On 15 August, young Miss Berry recorded once more how it felt to be under bombardment: "After breakfast Zuie and I were standing on the platform between the house and dining room and a very large shell filled with balls fell by the garden gate and bursted. The peices flew in every direction. Two peices went in the dining room. It made a very large hole in the garden and threw the dirt all over the yard. I never was so frightened in my life. Zuie was as pale as a corpse and I expect I was too. It did not take us long to fly to the cellar."[78]

Carrie and Zuie were lucky; others were not, as the casualties continued. "Car," a correspondent from the *Augusta Constitutionalist*, wrote from Atlanta on 16 August that in the heavy shelling of the previous night, "5,000 shells were thrown into town. They came at the rate of from six to ten a minute for eight or ten hours. Capt. Blair, of the 4th Alabama, was killed, and a Lieutenant of the 56th Tennessee had his leg shot away. A lady on Peachtree street was badly wounded, also a child and two negro servants." "Car" even named one of his journalistic colleagues as a shell-victim: "I learn among the other casualties that of Henry Waterson, late of the Confederacy, wounded by a fragment." (Of course, "Car" was wrong, as Watterson, writing for the Mobile, Augusta, and other papers, would surely have mentioned his own wounding.) The telegraphic news column of 17 August, wired by the Confederate Press Association from Atlanta to its subscribers, mentioned that a citizen had been killed in the "slow fire kept up all night" of 16 August. The *Appeal* on 18 August spoke of another

[78] Venet, ed., *Sam Richards' Civil War Diary*, 230 (7 August 1864); Carrie Berry, diary, entries for 8–15 August, Atlanta History Center.

civilian's death, that of a railroad employee, but could not offer his name. The industrious Isaac Pilgrim learned his identity: one Francis Hale of the Western & Atlantic's woodshop, struck by a shell in the shoulder on the morning of 17 August. He left a wife and five small children behind. Pilgrim also named the injured from a shell explosion in the candle factory, where a dozen women and children were seeking shelter: a Mrs. George, Mrs. Welch, Mrs. John Weaver, and Mrs. Stanley, all slightly wounded. Moreover, Pilgrim was able to relate a shell-blast incident he had apparently witnessed himself. Like other newspapermen, Pilgrim used the Express Office (south side of Alabama Street, opposite the Car Shed) to write his columns before sending them off. So when he told of "a negro in the Express Office today" (17 August), Pilgrim must have been there to describe how the black man received his wound, rolling an unexploded shell "over the floor and touching the powder as it rolled out with a match, when it exploded, tearing a large hole in his side, a gash on the side of his neck, and cut his leg below the knee. It was thought that the powder was out of the shell. It is strange that there were several persons in the office at the time, but none were hurt but the negro." On the other hand, for most of the cannon casualties he reported, Isaac Pilgrim was as reliant upon what he had heard (and not what he had seen) as any other reporter in barrage-struck Atlanta. "There has been several persons wounded in the city to-day by fragments of shells," he wrote on 18 August, "but I have been unable to learn their names." Even Unionist Atlantans, harboring their secret loyalties while awaiting the arrival of Sherman's armies, fell victim to the Northern shells. William Dyer, a railroad worker who thought of sneaking his family into Union lines, waited too long. On 20 August, standing in his yard, he was killed by a Yankee shell. His wife Amy and three small sons attested to the tragedy in their affidavit to the postwar Southern Claims Commission, which collected the testimony of Unionist Southerners. As a sworn statement, Mrs. Dyer's deposition is indeed strong evidence identifying William Dyer as a civilian casualty of Sherman's shelling.

The *Appeal* on 19 August related an incident of the previous afternoon: "a sixty-four pound shell entered a house occupied by a refugee, a Mr. Gibbs, and exploded in a room where his family had just gotten to welcome a soldier friend, who had called upon them. The soldier had his leg torn off, and died from loss of blood before medical aid could be procured, and a little child was killed by splinters. Two ladies in the room were also injured." This column, probably based on secondhand hearing but faithfully recorded by the *Appeal*'s correspondent, suggests the weaknesses of contemporary Confederate newsreporting of the Union bombardment of Atlanta: technical details could be misstated. None of Sherman's artillery, including the 4 1/2-inch siege rifles brought in early August, could fire any projectile heavier than 32 pounds. (The heaviest shell fired during the artillery exchanges of July–August 1864 was that of the Confederates' 9-inch naval Dahlgren.) The 64-pound heft of the Northern shell in the *Appeal* story is therefore erroneous.

In a city where people's talk of shell-casualties formed the main body of reportable news for journalists, hearsay sometimes also led to differing versions of the same incident. The telegraphic report of 23 August mentioned that on the previous evening "a lady was killed near the Express Office last evening by a shell, and a soldier lost a leg"—sounding much like "the soldier [who] had his leg torn off" in the *Appeal* story of the 19 August. The *Appeal* identified the victim as a Mrs. Cook, slain on Marietta Street, and added that another woman was wounded on Peachtree. Efforts to name victims further suggested the newspapermen's conscientiousness, but rarely led to specific identities, as when "S.D.L." claimed that on 19 August "a soldier in town was killed by a shell and a Mrs. Baldwin had both feet badly injured."

In the various correspondents' multiple tellings, sometimes the details got mixed up. For example, the *Augusta Chronicle & Sentinel* published a column, dated 19 August from Atlanta, stating that "a forty-two pounder Sawyer shell exploded in the house of Mr. Peters, killing Capt. Garrison of the 14th Texas Cavalry, and two children, and wounding several ladies." (Never mind that a 42-pound projectile was not in Sherman's arsenal.) When the *Intelligencer* published the story of the 42-pounder Sawyer shell that killed Captain Garrison and the two children (filed from Atlanta, dated 22 August), the incident was said to have occurred that morning (not on 19 August) and it was in a house on Peters Street, not the house of Mr. Peters. Such slips of pen or of memory add to the difficulties faced by the historian attempting to tally the toll of civilians killed and wounded in Sherman's bombardment of Atlanta.[79]

But there is no shortage of hearsay. Henry Watterson ("Shadow") reported on 22 August that a woman had been recently killed and several persons hurt; all went unnamed. Isaac Pilgrim, writing on 23 August, reported another alleged occurrence. "I have not heard of but one accident, since my last letter, and that was a lady, who had the nipple of her breast taken off by a fragment of shell, and

---

[79] "Car," "From Atlanta," *Augusta Constitutionalist,* 20 August 1864; "Telegraphic" (Atlanta, 17 August), *Atlanta Intelligencer,* 18 August; "The Immediate Front," *Memphis Appeal,* 18 August, quoted in *Mobile Register and Advertiser,* 23 August; "MIRGLIP," "Special Correspondence" (Atlanta, 17 August), *Atlanta Intelligencer,* 19 August; PILGRIM, "Special Correspondence" (Atlanta, 18 August), *Atlanta Intelligencer,* 20 August; Dyer, *Secret Yankees,* 187; "The City," *Memphis Appeal,* 19 August, in *Atlanta Intelligencer,* 24 August; "Late from Atlanta" (telegraphic report, 23 August), *Atlanta Intelligencer,* 24 August; "The Immediate Front" (*Memphis Appeal,* 23 August), *Atlanta Intelligencer,* 26 August; "S.D.L.," "Correspondence of the Daily Sun" (Atlanta, 20 August), *Columbus Sun,* 25 August; "From Atlanta" (19 August), *Augusta Chronicle & Sentinel,* 23 August; "From Atlanta" (22 August), *Atlanta Intelligencer,* 23 August.

Richard Peters's biographer Royce Shingleton accepts the version of the Sawyer shell story that has it crashing into Peters's home on Forsyth Street and notes that Peters's decision to leave Atlanta in mid-August "perhaps saved his life" (*Richard Peters: Champion of the New South* [Macon GA: Mercer University Press, 1985] 112n29).

her right leg bruised; otherwise she was unhurt." That same day "Rover" wrote that casualties for the previous twenty-four hours were two women killed and one soldier and a boy severely wounded. Confederate soldiers heard some of these stories, and noted them, as did Captain Tom Key in his diary: "A lady was killed yesterday by a cannon ball." In his *Intelligencer* column of the twenty-fourth, "B." noted that a Mr. Kennedy had been slightly wounded in the arm by a shell piece or flying brick. On 24 August "Shadow" did a rare thing: he wrote that he had actually seen "a poor woman killed this morning on Alabama street" by a Northern shell. But, as usual, he could not offer her name. Captain Key recorded in his diary entry of 25 August, "I was told that one shell killed six ladies in the same room," but such an incident does not appear in the newspaper reports. On the other hand, recorded in detail was the explosion of a big shell in the basement of the First Presbyterian Church near Spring and Marietta on the night of 24 August. According to the telegraphic report of the next morning, although several families were sheltered there, only one serious casualty was reported, an unnamed man whose arm was severed by a fragment. "Outline" described the incident for the *Columbus Times*:

> On Wednesday night a large 42-pound shell entered the Presbyterian Church, on Marietta street, and after passing through the pulpit exploded in the basement, or Sunday school room. Several families in the vicinity, having taken refuge there, were more or less stunned and injured by the explosion, and one man had his right arm taken off. The scene in the room was frightful—it was after midnight, and all the inmates were sleeping peacefully, perfectly confident of security. Mothers caught up their children hurriedly and rushed frantically into the streets screaming, though without any definite purpose in view, save that of escaping for the time from the scene which had struck such terror into their souls—and there, out upon the open streets, they stood crouching, with their little families clinging around them, and knowing not where to fly for safety. Shell after shell in rapid succession came screaming through the air, and as the light of each terrific explosion—like lightning flashes—quivered over them, the figure of one pale-faced mother could be described, with bare outstretched arms, vainly hoping to shield her little ones from the falling fragments. Oh! The heartless cruelty of the foe! Oh! The mighty depths of a mother's love!

Despite the harrowing Union bombardment, Henry Watterson inclined to the poetic when he wrote his column on 24 August as "Grape" for the *Augusta Constitutionalist:* "Affairs in the city remain in their usual condition. Shells all night, shells all day, shells for breakfast, dinner and tea, shells—'For all hours and all sort of weather.'" Borrowing on "one of our older bards," "Grape" expressed his wish: "Tell me ye winged winds, / That round my pathway roar— / Is there not / Some favored spot / Where Yankees shell no more."[80]

But the Yankees were indeed shelling more. General Dodge, XVI Corps commander, recorded on 18 August that his signal officer reported excellent work by his batteries, "doing considerable damage." Sherman was pleased by the work of his guns; on the afternoon of 18 August he observed that shells from a 10-pounder Parrott battery west of the city went particularly deep into downtown. And the Yankees kept it up. "August 19, at 3.30 A.M.," wrote Colonel Ario Pardee of the XX Corps, "all the batteries of the corps bearing on the city opened fire, firing fourteen rounds per gun." An Ohio infantryman noted in his diary that Union batteries opening early that morning "sent a tornado of shells over the enemy." Sherman was evidently looking for results, including flame and smoke inside the Rebel city. On the night of 19 August he noted that his early morning bombardment had started a heavy fire visible at daylight; continued cannonading through the day had made another blaze visible around three in the afternoon. The flames continued into the night. On 20 August, Chauncey Cooke of the 25th Wisconsin wrote his family, describing "the red sky over Atlanta every night which we boys look at until we fall asleep. It is the light from burning buildings, set on fire by our cannon."[81]

For some Atlantans, the fear and stresses of the bombardment became just too much. Sarah Huff, eight years old at the time, later recalled how the rock-walled basement of the Peters flour mill provided her family and neighbors a place of safety during the bombardment. But life could still be perilous, even with this shelter, and even on the east side of the city ("they haven't throwed many shells down on this side of town like they have on the Marietta side," recorded Sarah's mother in a letter of 21 August). "I hope we will get away from

---

[80] "Shadow," "Our Army Correspondence" (Atlanta, 23 August), *Mobile Register & Advertiser*, 27 August; PILGRIM, "Special Correspondence," *Atlanta Intelligencer*, 26 August; "Rover," "Special Correspondence" (Atlanta, 23 August), *Augusta Chronicle & Sentinel*, 28 August; Cate, ed., *Two Soldiers*, 120; "B.," "Atlanta Correspondence" (24 August), *Atlanta Intelligencer*, 27 August; "Shadow," "Letter from Atlanta" (24 August), *Mobile Register & Advertiser*, 28 August; "Telegraphic" (25 August), *Atlanta Intelligencer*, 26 August; "Outline," "Special Correspondence of the Times" (Atlanta, 26 August), *Columbus Times*, 29 August; "Grape," "From Atlanta" (23 August), *Augusta Constitutionalist*, 28 August. Wilbur G. Kurtz uses Watterson's line as his article's title: "Shells for Dinner," *Atlanta Journal Magazine*, 9 September 1941, 9.

[81] Dodge to Lt. Col. William T. Clark, 18 August 1864, *OR*, vol. 38, pt. 5, p. 587; Sherman to Thomas, 18 August, *OR*, vol. 38, pt. 5, p. 573; report of Col. Ario Pardee, Jr., 10 September, *OR*, vol. 38, pt. 2, p. 160; Charles T. Clark, *Opdycke Tigers 125th O.V.I.: A History of the Regiment and of the Campaigns and Battles of the Army of the Cumberland* (Columbus OH: Spahr & Glenn, 1895) 302; Sherman to Schofield, 19 August, *OR*, vol. 38, pt. 5, p. 602; Chauncy H. Cooke, "Letters of a Badger Boy in Blue: The Atlanta Campaign," *Wisconsin Magazine of History* 5 (1921–1922): 95.

here soon for 'tis dangerous to stay here," Ellen Huff wrote her mother on 21 August.

> none of the shells has hit a house neare mine yet, but I feel bad though for fear they mite. Tel Effey, Irvin Hudson's House has been hit 4 or 5 times and they are yet at home. The Yank's brest works is in plain view, every one that passes the street they throw shells at them so Irvin is afraid to try to move out, they have a pit to stay in.

With his family endangered—"the shells come whistleing over and around us every day and night," Ellen wrote—Lieutenant Jeremiah Huff returned home on furlough from Lee's army, saw to the loading up of family and possessions and on 24 August left town for Covington. That same day, the *Intelligencer* in Macon carried a report from Atlanta: "The city is very desolate. There are few people remaining who could get away.... The streets are deserted, the homes desolate and abandoned except by the casual denizens."

Those "big guns"—the 4 1/2-inch rifles—that Sherman had ordered to keep firing (while he awaited results from Kilpatrick's raid against the Macon & Western) very much did so, to such an extent that they again depleted their ammunition supply and had to be restocked; Thomas assured Sherman on 18 August that he had ordered up another thousand shells so they could keep firing. More important, the siege guns began to show signs of wear-and-tear from their around-the-clock operation. For instance, the gun on General Corse's front west of the city was replaced on 23 August after 1,080 firings because its vent had become enlarged. Among the three siege rifles with Geary's division, Captain Sutermeister found two of them unserviceable after ten days' work; all three were replaced on 22 August. Nevertheless, General Barry, Sherman's artillery chief, at the end of the campaign concluded that the 4 1/2-inch siege guns had more than met expectations "in accuracy, range, and certainty of flight and explosion." Sherman's soldiers took a certain pride in the big guns' work. When the siege cannon roared, sending another 30-pound shell screaming toward Atlanta, Federals told one another, "There goes the Atlanta Express!"[82]

Finally, after waiting for days, General Sherman got the disappointing news that Kilpatrick's cavalry (sent out on 18 August) had inflicted only slight damage to the Macon & Western Railroad south of Atlanta. Despite the

---

[82] Huff, *My Eighty Years,* 25; E. M. A. Huff to E. Huff, 21 August 1864, and to "Mr. Henry," 12 September, in Wilbur G. Kurtz, notebook 11, 81–82, Wilbur G. Kurtz Collection, Atlanta History Center; "B.," "Intelligencer" (Atlanta, 24 August), *Atlanta Intelligencer,* 27 August; Thomas to Sherman, 18 August, *OR,* vol. 38, pt. 5, p. 571; Corse's report, 8 September, *OR,* vol. 38, pt. 3, p. 411; Osborn's report, 16 September, *OR,* vol. 38, pt. 3, 60; Sutermeister's report, *OR,* vol. 38, pt. 2, p. 489; Barry's report, 10 September, *OR,* vol. 38, pt. 1, p. 121; David Evans, "The Atlanta Campaign," *Civil War Times Illustrated* 28/4 (Summer 1989): 56.

cavalryman's claim upon his return 22 August that he had destroyed enough track to keep Hood's supply line down for ten days, it was actually out of operation for only two. Union signal officers in fact had spotted a train entering Atlanta from Macon on the afternoon of 22 August, even before Kilpatrick reported to Sherman's headquarters. The next day, Sherman therefore ordered Thomas, Schofield, and Howard to have their armies (minus the XX corps, which would guard the W & A bridge across the Chattahoochee) ready to execute the "grand movement" he had originally proposed on 13 August, then suspended. All were to get moving early in the morning of 26 August.[83]

As the Federals secretly prepared their movement, their artillery continued to fire on the city. Sam Richards observed that on 20 August enemy shells had arced near his home on the southside for the third time during the bombardment; a fragment fell into his backyard. As a result, he had the pit in his cellar dug 3 feet deeper, and placed dirt-filled boxes as a barricade in front of it. The day before, the Richards downtown bookstore had another ferruginous visitor; it burst as it passed through the floor and "tore up the latter pretty badly." "The wily Yanks did not let the citizens or soldiers in Atlanta sleep much last night," recorded Captain Key in his diary, 23 August. "They kept their 20 pound Parrotts throwing shells into the heart of the city the live-long night. Whether anyone was killed I have not heard." Sutermeister's 4 1/2-inch siege guns on Geary's front also hit their licks till the last. After the replacement of his three cannon on 22 August, the captain recorded, "with good effect the fire was again kept up till the morning of 25 August, causing fires in town every night." "Rover" counted three fires in town during the night of 23 August and into the next day: a house north of the W & A workshops, a warehouse between Pryor and Whitehall, and a lard oil factory. The *Intelligencer's* faithful correspondent in the city, Isaac Pilgrim, wrote up the first blaze: "the dwelling house of Mr. Daniel Flake, near the State road shop, was consumed by fire, destroying nearly everything...." From his lines Confederate General French noted that the Yankees were once more shooting fire-starting projectiles into Atlanta. "The enemy fired hot shot on the city all last night," he wrote in his diary on 24 August, "and to-day they set on fire some cotton, and burned a few houses."

Others noted the fire early on 24 August. "Early this morning I heard the fire bells calling up the frightened denizens of the city to witness the destruction of their property," wrote Captain Key. Charitably, he added, "whether the fire originated from the enemy's shells or from accident I cannot say." Of course it was the Yankee shells, as the newspapers made clear. "McDaniel's ware-house on Hunter street between Pryor and Whitehall, was destroyed by fire this morning at 6 o'clock," reported the Confederate Press Association in its telegraphic report from Atlanta on 24 August. "Five hundred bales of cotton

---

[83] Davis, *Atlanta Will Fall*, 174–75; Edge to Logan, 22 August, *OR*, vol. 38, pt. 5, p. 631; Sherman to Thomas, Howard, and Schofield, 23 August, *OR*, pt. 5, pp. 639, 641–42.

were consumed. The City Fire Battalion was promptly on hand and checked the spread of the conflagration under a heavy fire from the enemy's batteries. A small frame building near the State Railroad Shops was also burned last night. Both buildings were fired by shells." Union artillery started another fire on the afternoon of that same day, as "Rover" noted, in the warehouse and lard factory on Alabama Street near the railroad. "Outline," writing for the *Columbus Times,* supposed that the fire-igniting projectiles contained "Greek fire." "B." (probably William D. Barr, who also wrote as "B." for the *Appeal*), described the damage in a column for the *Intelligencer* written from Atlanta on 24 August.

> At about 4 o'clock a shell exploded in the Holland warehouse on Alabama street, (less known as the Lard Oil factory) and set fire to 120 bales cotton, destroying the warehouse with its contents, Mr. Hancock's two buildings in the rear of Mrs. Immell's and Mr. R.M. Clark's, on Alabama street. Mrs. Immell's house had some furniture in it which was all burned. Mr. Clark's house, formerly occupied by M. Jackson, had but very little in it, all destroyed.

Pilgrim lauded the city's firefighters who were still at their posts:

> This evening about four o'clock, the warehouse at the junction of Alabama street with the Macon & Western Railroad, was observed to be on fire. It was but a few seconds before the flames spread.... the fire was checked by our gallant firemen from spreading in the direction of Whitehall street. One house near the railroad engine house was consumed. It is impossible to calculate the loss at the present time. The shells were flying thick and fast around the burning buildings, but the firemen stood to their posts without flinching. Too much praise cannot be bestowed upon the Atlanta Firemen.

Nonetheless, the frequent shell-ignited conflagrations caused some in the city to worry that the heroic firefighters were being asked to do more than they really could. Writing about the McDaniel and Holland warehouse fires, which burned up cotton and "a large quantity of tobacco," "B."/Barr reported that "citizens, soldiers and negroes" helped the firemen in combating the blazes, out of neighborly spirit. The dried-out water cisterns downtown did not help the firefighting efforts, but these were reportedly soon to be refilled. Of greater concern was the paucity of the firefighters themselves. The *Intelligencer* judged that in late August there were no more than 70 or 80 firemen in town, out of a paper departmental strength of 300. "So many firemen have left the city," Barr observed, "we have hardly enough to work any one engine, and a portion of them being on guard could not leave their posts." The city's provost marshal, however, had affirmed that battling the Yankee-caused blazes was the firemen's paramount duty, not standing guard at posts in the city. "If this be true," commented the reporter, "I have no doubt it will have but a good effect, as the

firemen who are left will have more interest in saving the property of citizens."
"B." / Barr then offered another suggestion.

> As strange as it may appear for good loyal citizens to have cotton stored
> away in Atlanta, it is nevertheless true. I learn this evening that there is
> some in the Express office and almost 300 bales in houses on Whitehall.
> Why is it not ordered out by the authorities and not left here to endanger
> the city? All the fires we have had have been caused by shells exploding
> near cotton. And if the city is to fall who will be benefited by the cotton
> and tobacco left in the city?

Yankee observers, perched in their tree-high buzzard roosts, continued to
watch their artillery comrades' handiwork and report what they saw. Lieutenant
Colonel Joseph S. Fullerton, IV Corps assistant adjutant general, recorded in his
journal on 24 August, "5 P.M. signal officer reports…that at present there is a
large fire near the business part of the city; that it has been burning for two
hours, and that our shells burst just at the fire." Passed through the ranks, the
news that Union cannon were burning up Atlanta on 24 August made its course
all the way to Washington before the end of the day. Although Sherman knew he
would be giving up his semi-siege in a few days, this last chance to punish
Atlanta's innocent civilians and inert buildings seemed worth reporting to the
War Department. The several messages that day worked their way up the chain
of command:

> [Lieutenant Samuel A. Edge, chief acting signal officer, to Major
> General John A. Logan]
> At 11:30 A.M. I discovered a column of smoke rising from Atlanta. I
> examined it closely, but could not determine from what it originated.
> The fire emitted black smoke for a space of five minutes, then white
> smoke, something like steam. Heated air could be seen to rise in thick
> white clouds. It was still burning at dark…. The smoke appeared like
> that of burning grain…. [After 6 P.M.] Two more large fires occurred,
> one in the evening and the other at about dark; appeared to be large
> buildings of some kind.

> [Captain W. W. Hopkins to Brigadier General A. S. Williams]
> …at least three houses, two frame and one brick, were destroyed by
> the fire in Atlanta this afternoon. Our shells burst in the city to right and
> left of brick stack.

> [Major General O. O. Howard to Major General W. T. Sherman]
> A fire seems to be raging in Atlanta, direction 10 degrees south of
> east from my tree. Can see heated air rising in dense column; seems to
> be spreading; town is filled with smoke. I have directed my heavy guns

to fire on the town.... 3.30 P.M.—Fire reported spreading in Atlanta. 4 P.M.—It broke out in rear of large block.... Signal report 6 P.M. says: ...the fire is still burning and spreading.

[Sherman to Major General Henry W. Halleck]
Heavy fires in Atlanta all day, caused by our artillery.[84]

Conflagrations in mid- to late August were so common, particularly at night, that Federal soldiers could no longer deny that their cannon were causing them. Such denial, however, had been possible in the first days of the bombardment. On 23 July, Captain John C. Van Duzer (Sherman's telegraph superintendent) had wired to Major T. T. Eckert in Washington, "large fires are burning in Atlanta, supposed to be the enemy destroying stores preparatory to evacuating." That reasoning eventually became impossible. Union corporal Leander Davis saw the same fires as Van Duzer and saw a different cause: "I guess we fired the city last nite with our shell." Evidence of the bombardment accumulated when Yankee papers reported Atlanta's bombardment. "Silent," writing for the *New York Times* from "near Atlanta," 18 August, related that

> some heavy guns have been placed in position recently, which are throwing shell to a damaging effect into the heart of the city. The explosion can be plainly heard from our lines. Bundy's battery (13th New York) has been making a target of one very fine house, until now it presents a very highly ventilated appearance. For the last three nights there has been quite an extensive conflagration in the city; one evening the firebells could be distinctly heard. We have reports of the buildings on one street being entirely consumed.

---

[84] Venet, ed., *Sam Richards's Civil War Diary*, 232 (21 and 27 August); Cate, ed., *Two Soldiers*, 119–20; Sutermeister's report, 14 September 1864, *OR*, vol. 38, pt. 2, p. 489; "Rover," "Letters from the Georgia Front" (Atlanta, 24 August), Augusta *Chronicle & Sentinel*, 28 August; Pilgrim, "For the Intelligencer. Special Correspondence. Atlanta, August 24, 1864," *Atlanta Intelligencer*, 26 August; French, *Two Wars*, 221; "From Atlanta" (24 August), *Atlanta Intelligencer*, 25 August; "Outline," "Special Correspondence of the Times" (Atlanta, 26 August), *Columbus Times*, 29 August; "B.," "Atlanta Correspondence" (24 August), *Atlanta Intelligencer*, 27 August; Andrews, *The South Reports the Civil War*, 548 (William D. Barr as "B."); "Our Atlanta Friends," *Atlanta Intelligencer*, 2 September; "Interesting Sketches of Pioneer Women: Mrs. Frank P. Rice," *Atlanta Journal*, 6 June 1909 (Mrs. Rice's recollection that firefighters battled the flames of the Holland cotton warehouse/lard oil factory while shells fell and burst in the city); Fullerton, journal, 24 August, *OR*, vol. 38, pt. 1, p. 925; Edge to Logan; Hopkins to Williams; Howard to Sherman and Sherman to Halleck, all 24 August, *OR*, vol. 38, pt. 5, pp. 649, 651, 655–57.

Northern readers learned more of Atlanta's travail when their newspapers reprinted columns from the Southern press, following the journalistic practice of both sides during the war. For instance, the *New York Tribune* reprinted the column from the *Columbus Times* about the alleged 42-pound shell that crashed into the Presbyterian church on 22 August.

Yet occasional evasiveness regarding the bombardment of Atlanta could still be seen in the Northern press. Some papers occasionally played word-games with their readers to suggest that maybe the fires were not raging, and if they were, maybe they were not being caused by Union artillery. "Chickamauga" reported from Atlanta on 29 July for the *New York Times* that "the whole heavens were illuminated last night for hours in the direction of Atlanta, and a large fire, it is supposed, must have been raging." "Epsilon," writing on 1 August, hedged a bit in stating, "very many large fires have been seen in Atlanta since our advent to our present position, caused, it is presumed, by our shells, which are being constantly thrown into it." "It is supposed" and "it is presumed" were phrases evasive enough to have distracted Northern readers from an awareness that Sherman's gunners were deliberately setting fires in Atlanta, destroying buildings on direct orders from their commanding general, and endangering civilians, if not killing them outright. Another guilt-assuaging tactic, following Sherman's lead in his private correspondence, was to deny the presence of civilians altogether. A correspondent for the *Cincinnati Commercial* reported on 4 August, "The city is now almost evacuated, and scarcely a family remains." Another journalistic device was to suggest that even if Atlanta still housed noncombatant residents, as a "modern Sodom" (the *Commercial* reporter's term) the city merited a punishing barrage of its unholy people and their damned buildings.

A particularly effective pictorial trick was to show the Rebels' fortified lines as closely intertwined with the city's downtown areas; presumably aiming for the enemy entrenchments Union artillerists could not avoid hitting noncombatants' houses. A big map printed on the front page of the *New York Herald* on 5 August hilariously depicted the Confederate lines five or more blocks within the corporate limits circle. The map was based on that drawn by Federal topographical engineers in July. To be sure, the city layout was impeccably reproduced from Vincent's map of 1853—to the point of referring to Atlanta hotels (Thompson's, Loyd's) that had long ceased operation by 1864. And the circle of city limits was also accurately drawn: two blocks north of Alexander, at Hunnicutt; to the east, beyond Yonge Street and the Georgia Railroad. Sherman's engineers did not draw in the opposing armies' lines of fortifications. These seem to have been added by the *Herald*'s wood engravers, who drew the Rebel works so obviously wrong that their intent must have been deliberate. In the *Herald* map the Confederates' northernmost point, Battery K, is sited at Baker and Peachtree, almost 3/4 of a mile south of where it actually was (today on the Fox Theatre hill). But Northern readers would not have known better, and only wondered why the Rebels had so stupidly laid out their works within the very city they were charged to defend.[85]

Another Northern justification of Sherman's bombardment lay in the implication that inside Atlanta, the Rebels' huge complex of war industry was still in operation, thus deserving Sherman's artillery fire. A long article, "The Rebel Government Works at Atlanta," appeared in the *New York Times*, 13 August (reprinted from the *Nashville Times*), describing the rolling mill as producer of iron plating for a number of Confederate armored warships; "this fact alone renders a good point for destruction." (The *Times* did not mention that the rolling mill was no longer in operation, its heavy machinery long since removed from Atlanta.) The Spiller & Burr pistol factory was also noted. "This work has given employment to nearly three hundred hands," the writer comments, neglecting to mention that the Spiller & Burr pistol factory had transferred to Macon by mid-February 1864. Similarly the government arsenal and Winship's foundry were implied still to be in operation. The former "has been in vigorous operation" since its establishment early in the war; the latter "has filled some of the largest Government contracts, and kept in constant employment a large number of hands."

Finally, even when forced to admit that Atlanta still housed a number of civilians, and that Union shells were burning up their homes and stores, Northern newspapermen could find the ultimate exoneration of General Sherman for his city-shelling: blame it on the Rebels themselves. Writing from Atlanta on 25 August, "Huguenot" told of the many secret Unionists who were escaping the city and entering Sherman's lines. "They are justly indignant at the Confederate Generals for placing their troops so close to their homes," thus subjecting suburban residents to gunfire. "Huguenot" claimed that some

---

[85] J. C. Van Duzer to Maj. T. T. Eckert, 23 July 1864, *OR*, vol. 38, pt. 5, pp. 239; Niesen, "'The Consequences of Grandeur,'" 10; "Silent," "From Gen. Sherman's army" ("near Atlanta," 18 August), *New York Times*, 1 September; "Atlanta During the Siege," *Columbus Times*, quoted in *New York Tribune*, 6 September; "Chickamauga," "The Army Before Atlanta" (29 July), *New York Times*, 10 August; "Epsilon," "General Sherman's Army" (Chattanooga, 1 August), *New York Times*, 9 August; "Confronting Atlanta" (4 August), correspondence of the *Cincinnati Commercial* in *New York Times*, 14 August; map, "Atlanta. From Vincent's Subdivision Map, published by the City Council. Drawn and printed at Topl. Engr. Office, Hd. Qrs. A.C., in the field, July 25th 1864," William J. Miller, *Great Maps of the Civil War* (Nashville TN: Rutledge Hill Press, 2004) 38; map, "The City of Atlanta. The Defensive Works of the Rebel Army at Atlanta and the Position of Sherman's Lines on July 27," *New York Herald*, 5 August.

The *New York Herald*'s improbable map of Atlanta's fortifications well inside the city limits is reproduced in Hoehling, *Last Train from Atlanta*, with the caption "this map was prepared by Sherman's engineers." From there it has been redrawn by Theodore R. Miller for publication in Samuel Carter's history of the campaign, thus further perpetuating the Yankees' joke (*The Siege of Atlanta*, 186).

Unionist Atlantans even blamed the Rebel generals for Northern shells falling downtown. "Our shells by day and by night crash through the city, destroying life and property," "Huguenot" noted. "It is a well-known fact that a large majority of the population of Atlanta was composed of men of Northern extraction.... There were a thousand Northern men in the machine shops and founderies, many of whom were forcibly detained.... The military authorities actually draw upon their homes and families our destructive fire...[as] if to punish them for a want of heart in the Confederate cause." By this admittedly tenuous reasoning, "rebel Generals" through their "sinister motives" actually conspired to cause Sherman's artillery to fire down upon Northern-sympathizing civilians still in the city.[86]

After a bombardment of over a month, the Union cannon fell silent. The Confederate Press Association's telegraphic report from Atlanta on 25 August noted that "for some cause the Federal batteries are silent this morning." Young Carrie Berry was doubtless relieved to write that night, "we had no shells all day." Samuel Richards also recorded, "on Thursday [25 August] the shelling ceased altogether." The next day, 26 August, Confederate Captain Key recorded in his diary, "the significant thing is that for twenty-four hours they have ceased throwing shells into the city." Yet others reported some Union shelling of the city on the night of 25 August. "Shadow"/Watterson wrote on 26 August that "last night Marietta Street was knocked into a cocked hat." The Confederate Press Association's telegraphic report out of Atlanta on 26 August reported at least "three shells fired from the right last night." An Augusta paper cited the *Macon Confederate* of 28 August as source for the statement of a passenger from Atlanta that "not a shell had been thrown into the city since Thursday night last" (25 August). "Shadow," the CPA, and *Confederate* thus confirm 25 August as the probable day of the last Federal shellfire into Atlanta.

The Northern cannonade into town late on 25 August would have come from Howard's Army of the Tennessee ("the right," as mentioned in the news telegraphic report), which kept position west of the city while Thomas's army north of it began Sherman's "grand movement" to cut the Macon railroad once and for all on the night of 25 August. Howard's bombardment would thus have been intended to cover the withdrawal of Thomas's army from its lines. With his siege guns withdrawn from their positions, their embrasures filled with brush, all surplus wagons sent back across the Chattahoochee, and his troops supplied for a fifteen-day march, Thomas swung around from the north, leaving the XX Corps behind. He was soon joined by Howard's Army of the Tennessee, and eventually by Schofield's XXIII Corps (which withdrew at noon on 28 August).

---

[86] "The Rebel Government Works at Atlanta," *New York Times,* 13 August; Matthew W. Norman, *Colonel Burton's Spiller & Burr Revolver,* 58; "Huguenot," "The Last Great Movement Foreshadowed" (Atlanta, 25 August), *New York Times,* 5 September.

All six Union infantry corps headed toward Jonesboro to cut the Rebels' railway lines—the event that Sherman believed would end the campaign.

Sherman's bombardment of Atlanta, begun 20 July, thus ended with the last cannon firing late on 25 August. On the next morning Confederate pickets learned that the Yankees had abandoned their trenches north and northwest of the city. While General Hood and his officers pondered the meaning of the sudden development, both soldiers and civilians explored the former enemy encampments. "Shadow"/Henry Watterson reported on the quantities of flour, bacon, and meal left behind. Captain Robert M. Gill of the 41st Mississippi wrote his wife Betty, "I was among the first that mounted their works and saw many of the boys pick up from 1 lb. to 12 lbs. bacon. I got a fine lot of roasting years and a big mess of beans, the first I have had this year." Captain Trask noted the same wonderful abundance in his diary: "Several Sutler stores were left full of nice things, and to-day our troops are feasting on sardines and lobsters, canned fruit of every kind, candies, cake and raisins, besides many other good things their stomachs had long been strangers to." Southerners roaming about the enemy lines made other observations. "Rover," reporting for his Augusta paper, thought the Yankee soldiers' encampments were so orderly and clean of debris that he suggested CS officers should take hints from them in the future when laying out Southern soldiers' quarters. On the other hand, Captain George Mercer of the 57th Georgia found the enemy lines "badly policed and very filthy." General French, wandering about the area formerly held by the Yankees in his front, recorded finding "the brick furnace where they made 'shot red hot' to fire day and night at intervals to burn the city." Some shot were still hot. French watched black children, intent upon selling them to Southern ordnance officers in town, get their fingers burned trying to pick them up. Young Sarah Huff was among a group of curious Atlantans inspecting the abandoned enemy camps near Marietta Street. She remembered coming upon one of the Union observation posts, "where strips of plank had been nailed, ladder-fashion, in the tall pine trees, from which with the aid of a spy glass, the men could see all over the city." A reporter for the *Appeal* commented on the enemy's artillery positions: "the batteries bearing upon the city were not so formidable in appearance, but they occupied positions from which almost every building of prominence was visible, and afforded the artillerists the most desirable targets." Others, perambulating the area previously occupied by the enemy, noted the Yankees' property destruction behind their lines. A correspondent for the *Augusta Chronicle & Sentinel* reported, "All the houses vacated between the deserted Yankee fortifications and the Chattahoochie have been demolished." The same reporter stated that in the Yankee camps was found "a sentence scribbled on a blazed tree"—perhaps a note tacked to the trunk, or maybe carved into the wood itself: "Not being able to drive the rebels out of their works we leave them ours."[87]

So the Yankee shelling of Atlanta and its people was over. A surgeon in town, Dr. Josiah Flournoy, wrote on 28 August, "the Yankees stopped shooting at the city last Friday [the 26th] & a good many of the citizens here are returning." Henry Watterson ("Shadow" of the *Mobile Register and Advertiser*) expressed his relief: "there are no more Parrotts, no more Napoleons to worry our dreams, no more schrappnels to fright us when we wake." Like his fellow journalist Felix de Fontaine (who had earlier confessed that with so many shells exploding in the city he had found it "inconvenient to write a letter under their inspiration"), "Shadow" proudly asserted, "I write you with a hand as firm as that of old John Hancock. Note the change in my penmanship. But yesterday, and it was hurried, misshapen. To-day it is full, clear, legible. Give thanks to God, oh Printer, and rejoice with Atlanta, people of Mobile!"

During the thirty-seven days of bombardment, Confederate newspaper writers had been vociferous in their denunciations of Sherman, the Yankees, and their fiendish fusillade. The complaints and criticisms covered a range of Yankee barbarities. A telegraphic column from the press association within the first several days of the cannonade protested that Sherman had given no notice of his intent to shell the city, which would have allowed women and children to evacuate: "This barbarous violation of the usages of civilized warfare only

---

[87] "Telegraphic," *Atlanta Intelligencer*, 26 August; Carrie Berry, diary, 25 August, Atlanta History Center; Venet, ed., *Sam Richards's Civil War Diary*, 232 (27 August); Cate, ed., *Two Soldiers*, 121; "Shadow," "Letter from Atlanta" (26 August), *Mobile Register & Advertiser*, 30 August; "Telegraphic" column, "Atlanta, August 26," *Macon Telegraph*, 27 August, and *Augusta Chronicle & Sentinel*, 27 August; "From the Front," *Augusta Constitutionalist*, 30 August (citing *Macon Confederate* of 28 August); Castel, *Decision in the West*, 485; Davis, *Atlanta Will Fall*, 175–91; Bell I. Wiley, "A Story of 3 Southern Officers," *Civil War Times Illustrated* 3/1 (April 1964): 34 (Captain Gill); W. L. Trask, journal, 26 August, Kennesaw Mountain National Battlefield Park; "Rover," "Letter from the Georgia Front" (Atlanta, 27 August), *Augusta Chronicle & Sentinel*, 31 August; Scott Walker, *Hell's Broke Loose in Georgia: Survival in a Civil War Regiment* (Athens: University of Georgia Press, 2005) 173 (Mercer, diary, 29 August); French, *Two Wars*, 221; Huff, "Dodging Shells in Atlanta"; "The Immediate Front," *Memphis Appeal*, 27 August, quoted in *Mobile Register & Advertiser*, 1 September; "From the Front," *Augusta Chronicle & Sentinel*, 31 August.

My conclusion that 25 August was the last day of the Union shelling is based on re-examination of "Shadow's" claim on 26 August ("last night Marietta street was knocked into a cocked hat"), the CPA report from Atlanta, the *Confederate* column and Dr. Flournoy's letter of 28 August (recently discovered with the help of the Atlanta History Center's Sue Verhoef). In the course of my study, I had earlier thought that the bombardment ended on 24 August; see my "'A Very Barbarous Mode of Carrying on War,'" *Georgia Historical Quarterly* 79/1 (Spring 1995): 84 and "How Many Civilians Died in Sherman's Bombardment of Atlanta?" 45/4 *Atlanta History* (2003): 17. Russell Bonds astutely notes this in *War Like the Thunderbolt*, 452.

enabled him to murder a few noncombatants." Some writers would not forgive this lack of chivalry. "Rover," from Atlanta on 3 August, reported, "since the first shot was thrown at the city, over a week ago, Sherman has not failed to send in a few of his unwelcome missiles daily. Altogether many hundred have fallen in our midst. Your readers are aware, ere this, that the work was commenced without any notification to noncombatants to leave, and they will not be surprised to learn that up to this writing he has observed the same barbarous silence, while his malignant work goes on." The *Appeal*, in a column reprinted in the *Intelligencer* of 9 August, also blamed Sherman for not giving notice to the city's people. The editorialist accused the Yankees of targeting the very innocents in the city itself, noting that the Northern barrage harmed neither the army nor government property, its rightful targets: "Neither are exposed to his annoying missiles, this contingency having been fortunately provided against. It is only the few citizens left who are endangered, and these were not satisfied to leave. The rules of civilized war demanded that notice should be given, but these have been disregarded." "As we have an unchristian enemy to deal with, some retaliatory measures should be adopted," the *Appeal* argued, and asked whether the several thousand enemy prisoners captured in the recent campaigning might be quartered in those parts of Atlanta most heavily shelled. "Could not captured Yankees share the dangers to which our women and children are exposed by their inhuman leader? Cannot the suggestion be acted upon?" the editors asked. They were doubtlessly getting their idea from Charleston, where Confederates temporarily quartered Union POWs in the shelled city. Nevertheless, the suggestion was not acted upon by General Hood or the Confederate authorities.[88]

The nature of the "unchristian enemy," whose national war aims trumpeted liberty and morality while Northern cannon bombed and blasted innocent civilians, raised the issue of Yankee hypocrisy (a favorite theme of Confederate propagandists). In late July, the *Intelligencer* recounted the story of the Crews family undergoing Federal shellfire while innocently trying to bury a loved one in the City Cemetery. The paper concluded with a jab at Yankee deceit: "no one was hurt, but the monuments and gravestones were very much broken. This must have been exceedingly delightful amusement for the people who are trying

[88] Dr. Josiah A. Flournoy to Anna, 28 August 1864, typescript, folder 1, Winship-Flournoy Papers, MSS 209, Atlanta History Center; "Shadow," "Letter from Atlanta" (28 August), *Mobile Register & Advertiser*, 1 September; "F.G.F." (Atlanta, 23 July), *Mobile Register & Advertiser*, 4 August; "Telegraphic Reports of the Press Association. Yankees Shelling the City. No Notice Given to Noncombatants. Gen. Hood's Address to the Troops," (Atlanta, 25 July), *Augusta Chronicle & Sentinel*, 27 July; "Rover," "Letter from the Georgia Front" (Atlanta, 3 August), *Augusta Chronicle & Sentinel*, 7 August; *Memphis Appeal*, quoted in *Atlanta Intelligencer*, 9 August; Phelps, *The Bombardment of Charleston*, 102–105 (on Federal prisoners housed in the shelled city; see also Mauriel Phillips Joslyn, *Immortal Captives: The Story of the Six Hundred Confederate Officers and the United States Prisoner of War Policy* [Shippensburg PA: White Mane Publishing Co., 1996] 17–40).

to teach us Christianity and recover us from barbarism by effective force measures." The same sarcasm toward the self-righteous enemy was voiced elsewhere. After attempting a tally of civilian casualties in the first days of the bombardment, the *Mobile Register & Advertiser* concluded, "noble warfare. The Yanks in this fight seem determined to illustrate how far they can distance savages in mere barbarity." At the same time, the *Macon Telegraph* of 2 August offered the judgment that "there is no use in indulging in invectives against the barbarity of Sherman."

On 13 August, after reminding readers of the horrible shell-deaths of the Warners, the father and daughter killed in their bed, the *Knoxville Register* asserted that they should be called "Sherman's Murders."

> We call these murders, though the murderer will be treated with the utmost courtesy when he falls into our hands. He knows that all this fire upon a position in the rear of our army will not drive them from their lines, and it is only to gratify his own diabolical propensities that he keeps up this bombardment on unarmed people. What a retribution is in store for the people who are carrying out this hellish work! The whole world will laugh at their calamity and laugh when their fear cometh.

In its "Immediate Front" column of 16 August, the *Appeal* noted that the Yankees had not been shelling the city for the past twenty-four hours, and wondered whether Sherman "has become ashamed of the practice of shelling defenceless women and children." Others saw no reason to assume that the Yankees had renounced their vengeful ways. Indeed, the Confederate Press Association telegraphic report of 15 August hurled a harsh accusation of hypocrisy at the Northerners who allegedly were trying to instruct Southerners on the ways of civilized people. Noting that some shells had been thrown into the city, the CPA observed that "[s]ome of them had Scriptural quotations in Hebrew pasted on them." Southerners were particularly incensed when Sherman's troops tried to deny what their artillery was doing. Recounting the bombardment of Saturday night, 13 August, in which "seven to nine batteries played upon every part of the city, shooting high over our works and right into the heart of the city," Captain B. J. Semmes bristled, "yet the Yankee prisoners when charged with it swear they are *shooting at our lines*." Henry Watterson as "Shadow" related an event in which a resident of the city mocked the Yankees' attempt to deny their city-shelling.

> A few days ago a party of ladies obtained passes to cross the lines into the enemy's country. They made their exit through our pickets and were permitted by the officer of the day on the other side to approach the Yankee outposts, where they were detained all day and then informed that they could not go through and must return. In the course of a conversation between one of the ladies and a Yankee officer he asked her

why she wished to leave Atlanta? "Because," she replied, "it is unsafe." The Federal feigned surprise. "How so?" The lady, in turn, raised her brows as she answered, "You know very well a city under bombardment is not very secure from danger." "But Atlanta is not under bombardment—we have never thrown a shell. Our shots are directed entirely at the works." The lady was a little indignant. "You must be a poor marksman, then," said she, "for your balls fall in the heart of the city, killing innocent women and children, who cannot get away." The officer who made this denial was an artillerist. Shells from the battery with which he is connected fall, night and day, all over the populous quarters of the town. He never wastes them upon the commons. He never cuts them for the works. His motive is murder; and when he spoke as above, he willfully lied.—He is a black-hearted assassin, and so is the entire gang in our front. I saw a poor woman killed this morning on Alabama street, and every now and then distressing accounts reach me of the havoc of the shells among those indigent persons whose poverty forces them to remain at home. What a miserable set of villains, they, who pretend to observe the Sabbath by a cessation of fire, and begin to murder innocent citizens with the first ray of Monday's light!

"Lavengro" in the *Augusta Constitutionalist* added his opinion on Yankee "observance" of the Sabbath. "What a commentary upon this cruel depravity is their cessation of fire on Sunday out of respect to the day of the Lord!" he exclaimed. "The miserable, puritan hypocrites! No sooner does the dawn of Monday proclaim the beginning of a new week, than they open with fresh energy their work of murder. But they add insult to injury, when with the cant of the devil upon their lips, they deny that their shots are directed towards the town." "Lavengro" further protested the Yankee cannonade for its military purposelessness, and its base intent upon the mere killing of harmless civilians.

The shelling still goes on. "The murder of the innocents"—bids fair to be one of the most poignant tragedies of modern times—night and day it is unabated, one continuous explosion of forty pound spherical case balls.

Can you imagine anything more brutal than the bombardment of a city, crowded with poor people, who are unable to get away, and are forced by their poverty to remain and suffer? Bear in mind that this bombardment is not pretended even by the enemy to bear upon the military situation one bullet's weight. There are no stores to destroy; the soldiers are all in the trenches, and the thousands of shells thrown into harmless dwellings cannot possibly effect the reduction of the city. The motive is one of petty spite, the spite of cowards, who dare not attack our lines and wreak their disappointment upon women and children.

While "Shadow" and "Lavengro" railed against the denials of Federal officers, in the Southern press it was Sherman who received the harshest accusations for the shelling of Atlanta. Isaac Pilgrim on 23 August commented that the enemy batteries "make it very unsafe for the women and children to remain in the city. …there [are] a great many yet, but no soldiers, and it seems to be Sherman's intention to kill as many noncombatants as possible. I understand that he has been officially notified that there were no troops in the city, only noncombatants, and women and children, still he persists in shelling us." The *Intelligencer* in its morning issue of Wednesday, 24 August, was much harsher.

Impotent to attack and carry the stronghold, the Yankee General has devoted his entire attention and energies to reducing the place to ruin by siege, into an uninhabitable place. This, and this only seems to be the expectation of the enemy, for if every building is pulverised into dust by the vindictive machinery of the foe, yet still will the site of Atlanta remain to show that a Southern General and an invincible Southern host of armed soldiers, defended it *successfully* against the most despicable nation on earth.… What boots it that he destroys and ruins the exterior of one of the fairest cities of the South? Not a jot of advantage is gained except to gratify the bent of his malicious and spiteful vindictive policy.

In Augusta, the *Chronicle & Sentinel* expressed its outrage at reports that Sherman "now denies that he has been aiming to shell Atlanta, pretending that he has only been firing at our defences!" It was a "miserable and cowardly pretence," the paper contended, after Sherman had "thrown his shells for weeks, by night and by day, at the habitations of that devoted city, slaughtering hapless women and children with a ruthlessness that would disgrace a demon." The paper offered, however, a fanciful vision of accounts finally being settled with Sherman. It could happen that "the ghosts of his murdered victims" could eventually haunt the Yankee general, reproaching him for his crimes. In such a vision, "the vengeance of an outraged people may blanch his cheek, and smite his craven heart with deadly fear."[89]

---

[89] "From the Front" (*Atlanta Intelligencer*, n.d.), *Augusta Chronicle & Sentinel*, 28 July; "Wounded by the Enemy's Shells in Atlanta," *Mobile Register & Advertiser*, 3 August; "Shelling Atlanta," *Macon Telegraph*, 2 August; "Sherman's Murders," no date, quoted as from the *Atlanta Register* in the *Mobile Register & Advertiser*, 13 August and in the *Richmond Sentinel*, 22 August; "The Immediate Front. Atlanta *Appeal*, 16th," *Columbus Enquirer*, 19 August; telegraphic report, Atlanta, 15 August, *Augusta Chronicle & Sentinel*, 16 August; B. J. Semmes to wife, 21 August, Semmes Papers, University of North Carolina; "Shadow," "Letter from Atlanta" (24 August), *Mobile Register & Advertiser*, 28 August; "Lavengro," "From Atlanta" (23 August), *Augusta Constitutionalist*, 28 August; Pilgrim, "Special Correspondence," *Atlanta Intelligencer*, 25 August; "The Position," *Atlanta Intelligencer*, 24 August; "The Georgia Front," *Augusta Chronicle & Sentinel*, 24 August.

One of the most brutal denunciations of Sherman came from the pen of Henry Watterson, writing from Atlanta on 26 August as "Grape" for the *Augusta Constitutionalist*:

> The vandals in front of us having failed to take the city by fair means, and in open combat are resorting to the last expedient of a baffled, unprincipled, and disconsolate bully—that of its destruction by fire. Within the last four and twenty hours as many as nine buildings have touched the ground, and are now visible only in smouldering walls and charred ruins. During these conflagrations the Yankee batteries played vigorously upon the fire-battalion. They obtained the range by the clouds of smoke and flame and had nothing more noble to do than to drop their shells in among the humane noncombatants at their work of charity, and the frightened and houseless women and children fleeing from the wrath of the two fierce and consuming enemies. Can anything be more typical of the desperation of the ruffians who came here under the illusion of winning an easy victory, or the infamy of the universal Yankee nation? It is a perfect symbol of the fear of the intolerable wretch who commands them. Sherman, who said that the waistcoat of God Almighty was not big enough to make him a coat, supports his pretentions to the character indicated by this blasphemy in every conceivable way, and rolls up mountain upon mountain of guilt every hour that he inspires the breath of life. Of all the Yankee Generals he is the poorest, the vainest, the meanest. He is without honor as a man, or conscience as a human being. His wit, by which he sets great store, is that of a Dutch dissenting class leader, his wisdom that of a circus clown, his temper that of Meg Merriles, his honesty that of Ananias and Sapphira, his ambition that of Beast Butler, and his appearance and manners those of Uriah Heep. His fate will be upon the earth wreck and ruin, the exposure of his littleness and puppiness, the disgrace of his military pretensions and the discomfiture of all his schemes; in the world to come—though I judged not lest I be judged—you can imagine what awards will be assigned to a villain, who not content with insulting the purity of womanhood and assailing the innocence of children, points his blasphemous tongue like a hissing adder in the face of his Maker. Ugh! what a disgust the thing inspires! Scorn him honest men of all lands! Cast him out as an odious reptile incapable of good, potent only for evil! A paltry villain, a currish knave, the very Fawkes of society, the situs cates of war, a dull sharper, a cheat and shame upon the name of soldier, the very embodiment of an ill-begotten, ill-bred and destined caterpillar, clinging only to sloth and

mildew, climbing no higher than the scum of a rank and putrid atmosphere.[90]

Alas for "Grape" and all other Confederate detesters of Sherman, the "dull sharper" won. As we know, the Federals' "movement round Atlanta by the south," as Sherman termed it, was the decisive maneuver of the Atlanta Campaign's last stages. General Hood, with his army stretched from Atlanta to Jonesboro, 15 miles to the south, was unable to guard the Macon & Western at all points. (The city's fortifications were held by just one corps plus the militia; according to the *Appeal* of 30 August, some Atlantans even began "expressing fears that a portion of our lines around the city are not sufficiently manned to protect us against raids.") Hood consequently had no troops to prevent Federal infantry from cutting the railroad mid-afternoon of 31 August below Rough and Ready, some 6 miles above Jonesboro. A major Confederate attack that afternoon at Jonesboro failed to drive off the Yankees. Even worse, the Confederate infantry there did not know that the railroad had already been broken to the

---

[90] "Grape," "Trying to Burn Atlanta—Vandalism Gone Mad—Sherman the Viper…" (Atlanta, 26 August), *Augusta Constitutionalist,* 28 August.

A century after all this Southern invective against Sherman for his bombardment of Atlanta, scholars have offered their cooler perspective. Dr. Castel reasonably concludes that Atlanta as a fortified and garrisoned city was "a legitimate target of bombardment." Still, Sherman "deserves to be criticized for not having offered to allow the city's civilians an opportunity to leave." But Castel also adds that "Hood is equally at fault for not having requested such permission" (*Decision in the West,* 489).

A stronger justification of Sherman's shelling comes from Professor McPherson, formerly of Princeton. As the quintessential Yankee scholar, he notes that "factories, rail facilities, warehouses and other military targets—including artillery emplacements—were scattered among residential areas of Atlanta" (James M. McPherson, *Battle Cry of Freedom: The Civil War Era* [New York: Oxford University Press, 1988] 755n8). By this premise, McPherson exculpates Sherman for shelling Atlanta's houses with the same reasoning that the Allies used to justify their "strategic bombing" of German cities during World War II. In *A History of Bombing,* Sven Lindqvist states that in 1940 the British leadership worked through this rationale:

> Churchill's decision to begin to bomb Germany originally applied only to military targets, which included, however…targets that often lay in the center of large cities. On June 20, 1940, the definition of "military targets" was expanded to include industrial targets, which meant that the workers' homes adjacent to those industries also became targets.… According to Churchill's statement of October 30, he wanted to maintain the rule that targets should always be military. But at the same time, "the civilian population around the target areas must be made to feel the weight of war."

Lindqvist adds, "Churchill was most likely not unaware that his wording echoed General Sherman's famous promise that he would let the American South feel 'the hard hand of war' by burning their cities" (Sven Lindqvist, *A History of Bombing,* trans. Linda Haverty Rugg [New York: New Press, 2001] 83–84).

north, and that their bloodletting was purposeless. On the morning of 1 September, with his supply line at last cut, Hood was forced to order the evacuation of Atlanta. Confederate troops abandoned the city during the night of 1 September, blowing up trains and supplies that could not be removed. Federal troops entered Atlanta the next morning, 2 September. General Sherman wired the news to Washington: "Atlanta is ours, and fairly won."[91]

Thus the campaign ended in Union victory. So we may ask ourselves, to what degree had the Federals' thirty-seven day bombardment of the city contributed to Sherman's success? The answer, both strategically and tactically, is that it had not.

Sherman was too smart and too experienced to believe what he had written to George Thomas on 19 July, that if he could get "within cannon reach of the town…it cannot be held"—in other words, that an artillery bombardment of Atlanta and its civilian populace would alone cause Hood to evacuate the city. His experience in Jackson, Mississippi, the year before had shown that a bombardment of a semi-besieged enemy city might contribute to its downfall, but only in conjunction with constant infantry sorties and skirmishing, artillery barrage of the enemy's entrenchments, gradual envelopment of their lines, and cavalry raids to the flank and rear threatening their supply routes. Such a combination had unnerved Joe Johnston in mid-July 1863. Sherman knew that it would take at least this combination to beat the lion-hearted Hood in July 1864.

Sherman's chief engineer, Captain Orlando Poe, writing more than a year later, recalled a conversation he had had on 23 July with the commanding general: "from him I learned that no assault would be made at present, neither did he desire anything like regular siege operations, but….that he would attempt to reach the enemy's line of railroad communication, at or near East Point…. This movement he hoped would either result in a general engagement, with the chances greatly in our favor, or in the evacuation of Atlanta." Poe's remembrance may have reflected the way the campaign eventually unfolded instead of what Sherman reportedly told him on 23 July, but the strategy by which Sherman took Atlanta was clear. Though he had superior troop strength, Sherman did not use it in frontal attacks against the Rebels in their strong defensive fortifications. At the same time, Sherman did not have sufficient numerical strength to completely encircle the city's 12-mile perimeter of works and starve Hood's army out by conventional siege. Rather, while keeping up a daily skirmishing against and cannonading of Hood's troops in their trenches, he extended his lines two-thirds around the city in a semi-siege to cut its railroads. He interdicted and wrecked the railroads leading into Atlanta from Augusta and Montgomery by which the Confederates received their supplies. Then, in late August he finally succeeded

---

[91] Sherman to Halleck, 24 August 1864, *OR*, vol. 38, pt. 5, p. 649; "The Front," *Macon Telegraph*, 1 September (quoting *Memphis Appeal*, 30 August); Davis, *Atlanta Will Fall*, 200; Sherman to Halleck, 3 September, *OR*, vol. 38, pt. 5, p. 777.

in cutting the Macon railroad to the south, Hood's last link. By this plan and its execution, the Federals had beaten the Rebels and captured Atlanta. But nowhere in this campaign narrative does the Union bombardment of the city—its inert buildings and innocent civilians—appear as decisive, even influential in the final result. It is even plausible that the Federals could have taken the city without subjecting its people and buildings to a deadly, grinding barrage.

On the other hand, from his frequent expressions of personal interest in the shelling, and his commitment of considerable resources to it, Sherman evidently believed that an artillery bombardment of the town might help with several tactical objectives. First, he hoped that his bombardment would hinder, even if it could not totally obstruct, the Confederates' supply system. On 8 August, Sherman directed his artillery "to keep up a fire that will prevent wagon supply trains from coming into town"; two days later he hoped that the rifled 4 1/2-inch siege cannon west of town could be placed so as to "demolish the big engine-house." Artillery Captain Sutermeister recorded after the campaign that his fire "was directed mostly toward the center of town and the railroad shops." Union infantryman John Storrs, seeing Sherman at a battery near his regimental front, wrote that the commanding general even sighted a cannon "aiming to strike the railroad depot." The downtown Car Shed was in fact occasionally hit, as reported by Confederate newspaper correspondents, although it was not put out of action, much less demolished. Isaac Pilgrim found "but one hole in it" as of 4 August, after 2 1/2 weeks of enemy shellfire; "B.," writing from Atlanta 24 August, reported "the shells are falling around the car shed now very frequently, several striking it." At least once a train engine was actually hit. The Western & Atlantic locomotive *Swiftsure* was firing up in the Car Shed when a Union shell struck its front center-plate, crashing through and hitting the front of the boiler behind it. Fortunately, the shell did not explode. Still, it "knocked out some of the flues, damaging the engine considerably," "B." reported.

Thus even at its peak intensity the Federal bombardment failed to diminish the flow of food and munitions into Atlanta for Hood's army, both by rail car and wagon. "Rover" on 8 August observed for the *Augusta Chronicle & Sentinel* that "Sherman's malicious practice of shelling" did not prevent "the presence of hundreds of wagons, ambulances, etc., continually going and coming," a bustling traffic which the correspondent termed "only such as is incident to the taking care of and supplying such a vast army." Days later the same correspondent was even more positive. "Supplies for the army, so far as meal and meat are concerned, continue to arrive punctually," wrote "Rover" on 13 August, "and it is frequently a subject of remark that the commissary department was never more vigilant in the performance of its important duties. I am not posted as to who is at the head of this branch of the service at present, not being a hanger on, but somebody deserves honorable mention."

Indeed, as we have seen during August, Northern signal officers, posted in their high, pine-tree perches, routinely spotted and reported the comings and goings of supply-laden trains into Atlanta. We have also seen how the spy Milton Glass observed that Rebels appeared sufficiently nourished from the rations brought in from Macon. Captain Nugent in Ferguson's cavalry wrote home in mid-August that he was even growing fat during the armies' static operations. Privates in the trenches, of course, always grumble, as Captain Jordan related about his hungry soldiers. Yet Hood's supply system, in the end, continued to function despite the Yankee torrent of iron thrown into the city.[92]

Another purpose of the bombardment, as Sherman himself said, was to reduce the value of the city's war capacity. "I think those guns will make Atlanta of less value to them as a large machine-shop and depot of supplies," the Federal commander wrote Thomas on 10 August. He wanted the Rebel stronghold to be "a used-up community" whether he won it or not; hence he had counseled Howard, "let us destroy Atlanta and make it a desolation." At the same time, as we have seen, from his spy reports and captured newspapers Sherman knew that the Rebels had removed by mid-July at least their most precious ordnance equipment, if not all of it, as well as their hospitals and supply stores. From the frequent reports of the city's forlorn, depopulated appearance, the Federals would also have concluded that Atlanta's factories and military goods shops had ceased operation, if only for want of the customary labor force, which fled with the panicked citizenry or was drafted into service in the trenches. Thus Sherman had actually devalued Atlanta as a war manufactory and depot by the time his armies had crossed the Chattahoochee and approached the city, well before his artillery fired upon it. His cannonfire wrecked buildings that once held Atlanta's vaunted munitions capacity, but it did not wreck that capacity itself.[93]

Sherman might have hoped that the Union bombardment served a third, far less significant tactical purpose when it diverted attention from the Federal army's movements. As we have seen, Sherman ordered especially heavy cannonading on 9 August, fifty rounds per gun, during which time Schofield was instructed to probe the Rebels' left flank near East Point; he similarly

---

[92] Sherman to Thomas, 19 July 1864, *OR,* vol. 38, pt. 5, p. 185; Poe's report, 8 October 1865, *OR,* vol. 38, pt. 1, p. 132; Sherman to Howard, 8 August, *OR,* vol. 38, pt. 5, p. 429; and to Thomas, 10 August, *OR,* vol. 38, pt. 5, p. 449; Sutermeister's report, 14 September, *OR,* vol. 38, pt. 2, p. 488; Storrs, *"The Twentieth Connecticut,"* 141; "The Houses Shelled in Atlanta," *Atlanta Intelligencer,* 6 August; "B.," "Atlanta Correspondence" (24 August), *Atlanta Intelligencer,* 27 August; *Kennesaw Gazette,* 1 May 1887 (on shell strike to locomotive *Swiftsure,* as transcribed into Wilbur G. Kurtz, notebook 22, 242, Wilbur G. Kurtz Collection, Atlanta History Center); "Rover," "Letter from the Georgia Front" (Atlanta, 8 August) and "Rover," "From the Georgia Front" (13 August), *Augusta Chronicle & Sentinel,* 12 and 19 August.

[93] Sherman to Thomas, 10 August 1864, *OR,* vol. 38, pt. 5, p. 448; to Halleck, 7 August, *OR,* vol. 38, pt. 5, p. 409; to Howard, 10 August, *OR,* vol. 38, pt. 5, p. 452. Albert Castel observes that by the time of its capture, "without its factories and shops, long since transferred to safety elsewhere, the city is just an 'empty shell'" (*Decision in the West,* 546).

ordered a sustained city-shelling 18 August as Kilpatrick set out on his cavalry raid against the enemy-held railroad. But as we know, Schofield's probe to the right failed, same as Kilpatrick's cavalry raid. If Sherman hoped that his barrage of the downtown area would help his tactical flanking moves against Hood's army, he found himself repeatedly mistaken.

At the same time, if diversion were their purpose, the Federals would have created greater commotion amongst the Rebels by firing front-line cannon upon the enemy entrenchments, keeping the occupants huddled in their fortifications. To be sure, the Northern cannoneers did this too, usually causing Confederates to hunker down in their works. A Union officer recorded on 12 August, "our artillery annoys them severely, causing their troops to remain in the trenches." A Northern signal officer reported on 14 August his satisfaction that the fire of a battery on General Ward's front "exploded in front, above, and to the rear of the enemy's works.... The men in these works confined themselves closely all day to their bomb-proofs." Yet the Federal bombardment of the Confederate lines inflicted only slight casualties among the Southern troops, and achieved no measurable result. Sherman may have been aware of this; at least once he announced his preference of shelling downtown buildings than Rebel works. To General Howard on 10 August he wrote, "Hood is anxious to draw our fire from the town to their fort at White Hall, which is of no value to us."[94]

Similarly without result was Sherman's ostensible fourth purpose in bombarding Atlanta, subjecting General Hood himself to such a psyche-shattering shelling that he would lose his nerve and order an evacuation of Atlanta (as Johnston had done at Jackson the year before), or that he would commit under shell-stress a blunder of such significance as to lead to Sherman's seizure of the city. The Union commander had written on 21 July, "I doubt if General Hood will stand a bombardment." We have seen some evidence that Union officers were interested in the whereabouts of General Hood's headquarters, and that they may have wished to subject him and his staff to bombardment. "Cannonading has been going on all day," wrote Captain Thomas Key on 29 July; "while I was at General Hood's, shells were exploding near his headquarters." General Thomas informed Sherman on 8 August that he had selected a good artillery position which "enfilades White Hall street, upon which is General Hood's headquarters." Bishop Lay commented on the shells bursting around Hood's headquarters on 9 August, but as Chaplain Quintard added, "the General and his staff did not seem in the least disturbed." Lay indicated that Hood moved his HQ farther out Whitehall from the center of the city, but beyond this inconvenience, the Federal cannonade failed to realize Sherman's hopes. Indeed, during the days of the most intense bombardment, in the first half

[94] Van Duzer to Eckert, 12 August 1864, *OR,* vol. 38, pt. 5, p. 481; Capt. W. W. Hopkins to Capt. A. K. Taylor, 14 August, *OR,* vol. 38, pt. 5, p. 492; Sherman to Howard, 10 August, *OR,* vol. 38, pt. 5, p. 452.

of August, Hood proved to be his most resourceful in checking Sherman as the two armies lengthened their lines towards East Point. On 11 August, when he was directing and watching the destructive fire of his newly arrived 4 1/2-inch rifled guns, Sherman expressed his unhappiness that General Schofield seemed stymied by Hood in the movement of the Union right against the railroad at East Point. That day he confided to Schofield, "I feel mortified that he holds us in check by the aid of his militia." The Northern commander's mortification would have increased had he known that soldiers in his ranks were saying the same thing. An infantryman in the 20th Connecticut remembered after the war that during the first two weeks of August "there was so little progress made in the siege that the idea became prevalent among the men of the Union army that 'Uncle Billy had got his match this time' and was going to back out of the attempt to take Atlanta." Of course, Sherman did no such thing. But the point is that it was only after the bombardment had ended, in the last days of August, that Hood proved unable to counter Sherman's movement on the Macon & Western near Jonesboro and to prevent the fall of Atlanta. The shelling which Hood underwent, 20 July–25 August, failed to diminish his capacity to command, and thus in this way had no tactical effect upon the outcome of the Atlanta Campaign.[95]

As further evidence of Hood's imperviousness, if not nonchalance, to the enemy shelling of Atlanta is the fact that he issued no statements to the Confederate press that would have whipped up the already hostile journalistic feeling against the Yankees' bombardment. Throughout the campaign he made little mention of Sherman's shelling, referring to it only three times, briefly, in his telegraphic reports to Richmond during the semi-siege: "All quiet to-day except skirmishing, and the enemy occasionally throwing shell into the city" (to Secretary of War James A. Seddon, 23 July); "All has been quiet to-day except a little picket-firing and occasional shells thrown into the city" (to Secretary Seddon, 24 July); and finally "No important change in the past two days. Some skirmishing and a little shelling from the enemy" (to Seddon, 4 August). Hood's relative inattention to the enemy cannonade suggested that it was merely an unfortunate consequence of war. At the same time Confederate newspapers documenting the damage to Atlanta by Yankee shellfire credited the Southern commander at least with empathy toward Atlanta's civilians in their plight, even if he could do nothing about it. The *Macon Telegraph* of 2 August reported that Hood was aware of the many women and children still in the city; the general "informed us, on a recent visit to Atlanta, that he was anxious for all the women and children to leave the city, and would give every assistance in his power to

---

[95] Sherman to Halleck, 21 July 1864, *OR*, vol. 38, pt. 5, p. 211; Cate, ed., *Two Soldiers*, 105; Thomas to Sherman, 8 August, *OR*, vol. 38, pt. 5, p. 419; Lay, diary, 9 August, University of North Carolina; Elliott, ed., *Doctor Quintard*, 87; Sherman to Schofield, 11 August, *OR*, vol. 38, pt. 5, p. 461; Storrs, *The "Twentieth Connecticut,"* 142–43.

facilitate their so doing." That remained the extent of Hood's response. After the war he recalled the people's brave endurance of the bombardment; he could not remember "one word from their lips expressive of dissatisfaction or willingness to surrender."

Taking cue from General Hood and the people of Atlanta, Southern newspapers never called upon Confederate military or Atlanta's civil authorities to take some action to stop the bombardment of the city. Instead, it was a Northern newspaper that carried such a "story." Writing from Atlanta 25 August, *New York Times* correspondent B. C. Truman claimed that "a few days after we crossed the Chattahoochee River" (around mid-July), Mayor James Calhoun of Atlanta sent a letter to General Sherman "asking him not to destroy the city." Sherman allegedly replied that if his troops were not fired upon, "neither Atlanta nor its citizens should be molested. He also wrote the mayor, that if the reverse should occur he could not take the consequences." While Truman's statement had a pinch of substance—as in Sherman's message to his army commanders of 19 July ("if fired on...the place must be cannonaded without the formality of a demand")—no such letters between Calhoun and Sherman have ever been found, no other reference to such a correspondence was ever made in the press of either country, and the alleged correspondents themselves never gave any confirmation of Truman's story. Nevertheless, the *Times* column carried an even more dramatic declaration: after Sherman "kept his word" and unleashed his barrage upon Atlanta, "the Mayor appealed to Hood to stay the destruction of the city," to the point of even asking Hood to "withdraw his army and cease fighting over the shoulders of innocent and unprotected men and women." Truman claimed that after Hood refused to evacuate the city, Mayor Calhoun persisted in his plea, "and a correspondence, I have learned, is now going on between the two officials, in which a good deal of acerbity is displayed by both parties." The *Times* correspondent further wrote, "the entire population of Atlanta, as well as the Governor of the State, and many others, take sides with the Mayor," while the army and the Richmond authorities sided with Hood. Truman even cited an "excellent gentleman, named Magee, who left Atlanta the day before" as his source for his claim that "the correspondence between Hood and the Mayor is still being carried on." Truman's contention of a Sherman-Hood-Calhoun correspondence during the Union bombardment, however unfounded, contained two undisputed facts at the time of his writing, 25 August: "There are still quite a number of men, women and children, of all stations, within the limits of the city" and "There is a perfect range up Marietta and Peachtree streets for our guns, and...a large amount of property has been destroyed."[96]

---

[96] Hood to Seddon, 23, 24 July, 4 August 1864, *OR*, vol. 38, pt. 5, pp. 903, 906, 943; Sherman's Special Field Order 39, 19 July, *OR*, vol. 38, pt. 5, p. 193; "Shelling Atlanta," *Macon Telegraph*, 2 August; Hood, *Advance and Retreat*, 202–203; B. C. Truman, "Mayor

Just as General Hood never buckled under the city-shelling, among Hood's troops as a whole we have no evidence that the Union bombardment weakened morale or the spirit of resistance among soldiers in the Army of Tennessee. On the contrary, the Northern bombardment of Atlanta's innocents angered Southern soldiers just as much as it did civilians, in many cases steeling their resolve to endure and not give in to the Yankees. In his diary entry of 4 August, Captain Thomas Key vented his anger at an enemy who would imperil the lives of the innocent. "Every five minutes throughout the whole night one or two 20 pounder guns threw shells into the city, striking through houses and exploding amidst families, killing women and children. All day that same cruel piece of cowardice has gone on under the direction of the inhuman and ungentlemanly Sherman."A week or so later, Captain B. J. Semmes wrote his wife Jorantha, railing against "the murderous and vindictive Yankee guns" firing through the night. But he closed by assuring Jo, "we are confident of winning the campaign." In other words, the Yankees' bombardment was annoying, but not campaign-ending.[97]

Sherman thus apparently wanted his artillery fire on downtown Atlanta to achieve four tactical purposes: hinder and reduce the flow, by wagon or railroad, of supplies into the city; damage Atlanta's vaunted war-munitions industry; divert the Rebels' attention from specific Union troop movements; and demoralize or frighten Hood and his soldiers. Sherman never received information that these ends were being achieved by his bombardment because they were not. Captain Poe, Sherman's engineer, wrote home on 7 September, expressing strong opinion to his wife that the bombardment had done nothing to bring Union victory in the campaign. "You know I was opposed to shelling the place for it did no good at all, and only brought harm to unoffending people.... I venture to say that all the shelling we did, did not get us into the town a *single second* sooner than we would have got in anyhow. It was the movement of our army around to their rear that drove the rebels out, and not the burning & destruction of a few houses occupied by noncombatants instead of rebel soldiers, who were safely and snugly stowed away in their forts, where no shot could reach them." Four days later, Lieutenant Colonel Charles F. Morse, of the 2nd Massachusetts, wrote home with the same sentiment. "Our shells destroyed a great deal of property, but I am sorry now that a single one was thrown into the city, for I don't think they hastened the surrender by a day," he observed; "they did not harm the rebel army, the only casualties being twenty harmless old men, women and children, and two soldiers." General Stanley, the IV Corps's

---

Calhoun and Gen. Hood at Loggerheads—The City Under Our Guns—Damage Done by Our Shells—Hood's Communications—Miscellaneous" (Atlanta, 25 August), *New York Times*, 5 September.

[97] Cate, ed., *Two Soldiers*, 107–108; Semmes to wife, 12 August 1864, Semmes Papers, University of North Carolina.

commander, wrote in his memoirs that the entire barrage was "a waste of ammunition." Occasionally, historians agree. Francis McKinney, General Thomas's biographer, concludes that "the artillery bombardment contributed nothing to Sherman's plan for forcing Hood out of Atlanta."[98]

At the same time, the Federals' bombardment of the city seemed to serve psychological purposes for General Sherman himself. With his armies virtually stalemated, ca. 7–9 August, in their efforts to cut the Rebels' railway by extending their right flank, Sherman decided to intensify his bombardment of the city while he thought of his "next move." Thus the Federal commander satisfied himself that his artillery was at least doing something, even if his infantry were not. One might even speculate that bombarding the city gratified Sherman when he otherwise felt frustrated at his armies' inability to capture it. At least some Southerners thought so. The *Appeal* of 10 August editorialized on the enemy shelling: "the whole procedure is a result of Federal spleen at the successful resistance to their plans, and they have doubtless determined to destroy what they no doubt begin to conclude that they cannot possess." Confederate artillery Captain Thomas J. Key, after recording in his diary on 25 August that Yankee shells had destroyed an oil factory and several other buildings, added, "not brave enough or strong enough to drive Hood from Atlanta, Sherman is trying to burn the city."

The Federal commander clearly thought that cannonading the city and its occupants was important, as he repeatedly expressed in his writing.

—"Our shot passing over this line will destroy the town." (to Halleck, 21 July)
—"Use artillery freely, converging on the town." (to Thomas, 22 July)
—"Good batteries will be constructed for the artillery and a steady fire be kept up on the city of Atlanta." (Special Field Orders 41, 22 July)
—"Keep up fire on Atlanta all night, each battery throwing a shot every fifteen minutes." (to Thomas and Schofield, 28 July)

---

[98] Orlando M. Poe to wife, 7 September 1864, O. M. Poe Papers, box 2, Library of Congress; "Atlanta, Ga., September 11, 1864," Charles F. Morse, *Letters Written During the Civil War* (Charles F. Morse, 1898) 189; Castel, *Decision in the West* (Stanley quotation), 489; McKinney, *Education in Violence*, 358.

Poe's recent biographer comments on his letter to Eleanor of 7 September. "Poe had felt that the continuous, round-the-clock shelling of Atlanta had been pure overkill as the town held no real military value, and he told Sherman as much. In his opinion, the bombardment only brought harm to 'unoffending people' and did not help to get the Union army into Atlanta a single second sooner than they would have without it. Further, he mused that some of those buildings and warehouses destroyed by Yankee iron would have now been of valuable use for storing the various supplies an army needed to stockpile. He thought back to the campaign's original mission. Was it not the destruction of the Rebel army rather than the capture of Atlanta?" (Taylor, *Orlando M. Poe*, 181).

— "You may fire from ten to fifteen shots from every gun you have in position into Atlanta that will reach any of its houses." (to Schofield and Howard, 1 August)

—"Put [the siege rifles] into your best position, and knock down the buildings of the town." (to Thomas, 7 August)

—"All the batteries that can reach the buildings of Atlanta will fire steadily upon the town to-morrow, using during the day about fifty rounds per gun, shell and solid shot." (to Thomas, 8 August)

—"...let [your guns] open slowly, and with great precision, making all parts of the town unsafe." (to Thomas, 9 August)

—"Keep the big guns going and damage Atlanta all that is possible." (to Thomas, 18 August)

With these express orders, no one could delude himself that General Sherman had any intention other than to bombard downtown Atlanta. Union soldiers could not truthfully tell Atlanta's civilians that their shells striking downtown were mistakenly fired too high over the Confederate trench lines; New York Sgt. Rice Bull recorded that the 4 1/2-inch rifled siege cannon "were only used to shell the city." Moreover, Sherman's repeated and strong desire to see Atlanta destroyed suggested that he considered the physical city as a symbol of the Rebellion that had to be obliterated, much as the Rebellion itself had to be crushed. "They have sowed the wind & must reap the whirlwind," Sherman had written his wife Ellen the year before. He wanted it to be "a used-up community"; he wanted to "destroy Atlanta and make it a desolation," and to "reduce it to ruins." No other Federal commander involved in a sustained shelling of any Southern city during the Civil War expressed himself so vengefully against a bunch of buildings.[99]

At the same time, Sherman seemed heedless of the noncombatants in Atlanta who were endangered, injured, or killed by his artillery projectiles. Part of his attitude stemmed from his willful self-persuasion that "most of the People are gone & it is now simply a big Fort" (as he wrote to his wife, 2 August). "The inhabitants, of course, have got out," he told General Thomas on 10 August. Other Federals, however, knew this was not so. General John Geary wrote his

[99] Sherman to Thomas, 10 August 1864, *OR*, vol. 38, pt. 5, p. 448; "The Immediate Front," *Memphis Appeal,* 10 August, quoted in *Columbus Times*, 13 August; Cate, ed., *Two Soldiers,* 120; Sherman to Halleck, 21 July; to Thomas, 22 July; Special Field Order 41, 22 July; to Thomas and Schofield, 28 July and 1 August; to Thomas, 7–9 and 18 August, *OR,* vol. 38, pt. 5, pp. 211, 223, 233, 280, 285, 324–25, 412, 431, 436, 573; Bauer, ed., *Soldiering,* 163; Sherman to "Dearest Ellen," 27 June 1863, in Brooks D. Simpson and Jean V. Berlin, eds., *Sherman's Civil War: Selected Correspondence of William T. Sherman, 1860–1865* (Chapel Hill: University of North Carolina Press, 1999) 493; Sherman to Halleck, 7 August; to Howard, 10 August; to Thomas, 11 August, *OR*, vol. 38, pt. 5, pp. 409, 436, 456.

wife that in the fierce bombardment of "the doomed city" on 9 August, "I cannot tell how many lives were lost but the casualties among the enemy must have been numerous." Colonel I. M. Kirby several days later wrote that one of his officers thought he "could distinctly hear loud cries from women and children, as if praying &c" during one night's fiery shelling. On the other hand, Federal signal officers seemed intent on feeding their superiors information that could sustain the impression that Atlanta had been abandoned by its civilian residents. On 17 August, one outpost observer reported to his captain, "very few people to be seen in the city." This got to General Sherman very quickly, as within hours he pointed out to General Thomas, "your signal officer at the Howard house reports...but few people can be seen in the city...." Sherman's unusual message leads one to wonder if it was addressing concerns of General Thomas's about the bombardment of the city's residents.[100]

How many unoffending people were in fact killed or wounded by Northern artillery shells, 20 July–25 August? No one will ever know. Without cemetery interment figures, surgeons' patient care records, or other data, the historian must resort to contemporaries' estimations. And of even these there are few. Samuel Richards, the printer and downtown bookseller, wrote in his diary, 21 August, that since the start of the bombardment, "it is said that about twenty lives have been destroyed by these terrible missiles." Atlanta newspaperman Isaac Pilgrim, writing on 23 August near the end of the cannonade, recounted how he had "heard a prominent physician of the city say a few days ago that there had been one hundred and seven limbs amputated in the city since the shelling had commenced. This does not include any person in the service, but is exclusively among the citizens." The Confederate commissary officer B. Joseph Semmes evidently talked to the same physician, for he wrote to his wife from Atlanta on 25 August that the post hospital's surgeon had told him that he had performed 107 civilian amputations since the beginning of the bombardment.

Confederate newspapermen, our best source of information for what happened during the Northern artillery barrage, were more dependent upon

---

[100] Sherman to "Dearest Ellen," 2 August 1864, Simpson and Berlin, eds., *Sherman's Civil War*, 681; Sherman to Thomas, 10 August, *OR*, vol. 38, pt. 5, pp. 448–49; Blair, ed., *A Politician Goes to War*, 194 (Geary to Mary, 10 August); Col. I. M. Kirby to Maj. W. H. Sinclair, 13 August, *OR*, vol. 38, pt. 5, p. 484; Burton to Capt. Case, 17 August; Sherman to Thomas, 17 August, *OR*, vol. 38, pt. 5, pp. 549, 552.

Russell Bonds judges Sherman's intentional and personally ordered bombardment of Atlanta as "arguably...his most callous and deliberate destruction of civilian life and property," even in the context of his burning of Atlanta and the march to the sea. "Here, no one could argue that a fire spread unwittingly and got out of control, or that private soldiers had disobeyed their officers' orders or had gone too far in their foraging" (*War Like the Thunderbolt*, 212). In another recent book, Marc Wortman also dismisses Sherman's claim to General Thomas that "the inhabitants have, of course, got out": "he was being disingenuous" (*The Bonfire*, 289).

what they heard than what they were able to see. Their reports are consequently replete with alleged casualties, both killed and wounded, almost all of whom go unnamed. The exchanging and reprinting among Southern newspapers of correspondents' articles led to further blurring and loss of specific fact. Thus the *Richmond Sentinel* of 31 August, without naming its journalistic source, stated in a short column entitled, "Murder of the Innocents": "We learn that the sexton in Atlanta reports thirty children killed by the enemy's shells in that city." To be sure, Green Pilgrim, the City Cemetery sexton, was one of those civilians who stayed in the city throughout the bombardment (he is listed on the manifest of civilians forcibly expelled from Atlanta by Federal authorities after their capture of the city). But Pilgrim evidently kept no records of interment during the barrage, much less an itemization of children *versus* adults slain by the Yankee missiles.

Another effort to tabulate the number of civilians killed by Sherman's shells attempted a comprehensive estimation, but by all accounts was a gross exaggeration. Writing from Atlanta on 30 August, Henry Watterson/"Shadow" (in a column appearing in the *Mobile Register & Advertiser* of 3 September) reported, "the casualties during the bombardment are reported to be 691 wounded and 497 killed." (He also reported that as result of the bombardment, "at least 47 houses were destroyed by fire, involving a loss of five millions of dollars of property"—and this did not count the houses damaged but not burned down.) Watterson names no sources for his numbers. As for casualties he also does not specify if he is counting civilians or soldiers, and offers no comment on the disproportionately high ratio of killed to wounded (which should have been, based on the war's other surgical data, roughly one-to-four or five).

Nonetheless, "Shadow's" article was reprinted in the Southern press, and the estimate of 497 killed/691 wounded caused some journalistic jousting. A religious publication in Petersburg, Virginia, the *Christian Sun,* commented on "Shadow's" high number of casualties in Atlanta's month-and-a-half bombardment, compared to the estimated 16 killed/32 wounded after three months of Grant's shelling of Petersburg. The disparate numbers were picked up by another religious paper in Macon, the *Christian Index.* In an editorial, the *Index* suggested that Petersburghers' low casualties represented a special blessing from Providence. By contrast, the figure of 1,188 Atlantans dead and injured by Union shells indicated, the *Index* claimed, God's displeasure with the people of the Gate City: "Atlanta was a place noted for its covetousness and extortion—its eager pursuit of mammon and its forgetfulness of God.... during all the time Sherman was threatening the city, its citizens neglected to meet and pray, except for a *few days* only. They forgot God, and he gave them over to their enemies."

The *Index*'s accusation of Atlanta's wicked ways created an uproar. "An Atlanta Refugee" in Macon wrote a long letter to the *Intelligencer,* reminding everyone of Atlantans' faithful religious observances during the semi-siege, and their Christian charity to the city's refugees, etc. Besides, the numbers of

Atlanta's civilian bombardment casualties accepted by the Petersburg *Sun* and the *Christian Index* were all wrong and way too high, "Refugee" argued.

> An old and prominent citizen of Atlanta, whose duties as a member of a Relief Committee and of the Fire Battalion required him to remain in the city during the whole time it was shelled, states that from all the information which he was able to gather, the total number of persons injured by the firing of the enemy did not exceed 40 or 50, and that of these not more than 8 or 10 were instantly killed, or died from the effects of their wounds. How different from this number from the 1168 of the *Sun*, as brought to our notice by the *Index*. A number of the exiles from Atlanta confirm this statement of the small number of persons injured by the shelling of the city. The wonder is that so few were injured, and not so many were. If we do not boast that it was a special providence that thus protected the citizens of that city in the midst of shelling so furious as it is known to have been, we may at least question the right of the Editor to assert that it was an evidence of the Almighty's displeasure.

The *Intelligencer* chimed in, editorially blasting the *Christian Index* for its very unchristianlike commentary—and it laid in a scolding about Atlanta's alleged bombardment casualties:

> The *canard* that during the shelling of Atlanta 497 persons were killed and 691 wounded ought not to have deceived any journalist.... Its fact, upon which the Editor bases his assumptions, is groundless. In the bombardment of Atlanta, not more than 50 persons were killed and wounded—say 10 killed and 40 wounded. It is to us apparent, and we feel deeply and reverently grateful for it, that God's "special Providence" saved, rather than destroyed the hundreds of Atlanta's exposed inhabitants, upon and amidst whom the enemy's shells rained as it were over 40 days.

A little arithmetic further demolishes Watterson's surprisingly high casualty toll. Merely counting the civilian casualties reported from 22 July to 24 August by the Confederate press yields a toll of about 19 killed and between 24 and 34 wounded. This number is doubtless off; for example, newspapers made no mention of the mortal wounding of Solomon Luckie or the efforts of Dr. D'Alvigny to save his life. There is indeed only sketchy journalistic evidence of the work of surgeons caring for the shell-wounded in the city. Isaac Pilgrim and B. J. Semmes in late August attested to 107 civilian amputations during the barrage, but their source goes unnamed—and could have himself been a purveyor of the kind of hearsay that bedeviled the conscientious reporters who tried to chronicle the city under shellfire. For example, the aforementioned case of Pilgrim's attempts to verify a woman's death, only to hear from the lady's sister that "her sister was in the city of Macon."[101]

Thus at the end of the bombardment, the people still in Atlanta knew that many of their fellow citizens had been hurt or worse, but no one knew the exact number. Without any means of corroboration, some historians have accepted Samuel Richards's judgment of 21 August that "about twenty lives" were lost in the first month of the Union bombardment. This is the number that Federal Lieutenant Colonel Charles Morse heard upon his entrance to the city, and which he related in his letter home, 11 September ("twenty harmless old men, women and children, and two soldiers"). Other Atlantans, responding to all the street-corner tales of shell explosions and civilian casualties, may have floated a higher number of fatalities. After entering the city with the victorious Union columns, commissary officer Rufus Mead wrote home on 8 September how he had heard that despite all the bombproof shelters about town, "100 or so were killed nevertheless."

Yet the killing, however untolled, did not end with the cessation of Sherman's shelling, for casualties from unexploded Northern projectiles continued even after the Union cannon had ceased firing and rolled away in late August. Many of the Yankees' shells fired into the city had not exploded. "There are thousands of shells lying about the streets and yards," wrote "Outline" for the *Columbus Times* on 30 August. Sam Richards, viewing the damage to his Methodist church building, found an unexploded shell; it had "passed through the back of the seat in the choir close to Sallie's usual place." Some people could not resist collecting the projectiles and tinkering with them. This practice led to accidental detonations and tragedy. Two such incidents took place on Sunday, 28 August. An old man named Weaver had gathered a number of shells and was trying to extract the powder from one when it exploded, setting off the others. Miraculously, he was only slightly wounded. Two boys also accidentally detonated a projectile as they tried to get gunpowder from it. One had his leg broken in the blast, but the other was much more seriously wounded, with both hands blown off at the wrists and his legs damaged. Altogether, as the *Augusta Chronicle & Sentinel* for 31 August stated, these explosions after the Yankees' departure had resulted in "killing and wounding many citizens." A writer for the *Macon Telegraph* may have overstated the case in saying that on 28 August alone

---

[101] Venet, ed., *Sam Richards's Civil War Diary*, 232 (21 August 1864); PILGRIM, "For the Intelligencer. Special Correspondence," *Atlanta Intelligencer*, 25 August; "J." [Joe] to wife, 25 August, Semmes Papers (quoted also in Hoehling, *Last Train from Atlanta*, 365); "Murder of the Innocents," *Richmond Sentinel*, 31 August; Davis, "How Many Civilians Died in Sherman's Bombardment?," 4–23; "Shadow," "Our Army Correspondence" (Atlanta, 30 August), *Mobile Register & Advertiser*, 3 September; "An Atlanta Refugee," and "Atlanta Calumniated," *Atlanta Intelligencer*, 16 October 1864; [Isaac B. Pilgrim], "The Houses Shelled in Atlanta," *Atlanta Intelligencer*, 6 August.

"twelve or fifteen persons [were] killed or wounded in this hazardous business"; men and boys particularly had been "killed and mutilated in the effort to unscrew the powder and balls inclosed in these shells, and making merchandise of them." In view of such claims, one may estimate that Northern projectiles caused perhaps a half-dozen civilian fatalities from the time the shelling ended until the Yankees expelled most civilians from the city several weeks later.[102]

In the end, the Union barrage of Atlanta had been substantial, merely from the volume of ammunition expended. Sherman's 4 1/2-inch guns alone had thrown a total of 4,526 shells into the city, almost 75 tons of metal. The volume of fire from the Parrotts and the 3-inch rifles is not calculable for the 37 days of the city-shelling, but given Sherman's repeated and insistent demands, the number of shells fired would have reached at least 100,000 (5,000 on 9 August alone, as we have estimated). Similarly, the weight of those projectiles, close to 10 and 20 pounds each, leads one to conclude that at least 500 tons of Northern iron lay in and around downtown Atlanta by the end of the campaign.[103]

The Federal bombardment had damaged or destroyed countless buildings, as reported in the careful columns provided by Isaac B. Pilgrim and other on-the-scene reporters. Unfortunately, the Confederate evacuation and quickly ensuing Federal occupation of Atlanta prevented the kind of house-by-house detailing of the shell damage that General Beauregard called for in Charleston, just four and a half months after Gillmore's bombardment had begun. A Confederate officer's

---

[102] Venet, ed., *Sam Richards's Civil War Diary*, 232–33 (21 and 27 August); Morse, *Letters Written During the Civil War*, 189; Rufus Mead to "Folks at Home," 8 September, Rufus Mead, Jr. Papers, 1861–1865, Library of Congress; Reed, *History of Atlanta*, 183; "Outline," "Special Correspondence of the Times" (Atlanta, 30 August), *Columbus Times*, 1 September; "From the Front," *Augusta Chronicle & Sentinel*, 31 August; "From Atlanta—A New Movement," *Macon Telegraph*, 30 August.

Atlanta writers accepting Richards's estimate of "about twenty lives destroyed," 20 July–25 August include Garrett, *Atlanta and Environs*, 1:631; Franklin M. Garrett, "Civilian Life in Atlanta," *Civil War Times Illustrated* 3/4 (July 1964) 32; Secrist, "Life in Atlanta," 36; and Gibbons, "Life at the Crossroads of the Confederacy," 47. Dr. Albert Castel adds his scholarly authority to this literature in concluding, "probably Sam Richards comes much closer to the truth" than any other estimate (*Decision in the West*, 488). In my article of 2003 (cited above), after combing through Confederate newspaper sources, I come roughly to the same conclusion.

[103] Barry's report, 10 September 1864, *OR*, vol. 38, pt. 1, p. 123. Maj. Thomas W. Osborn, chief of artillery for the Army of the Tennessee, summarized the activity of the one 4 1/2-inch rifle that operated west of the city: "one 30 pound shell was dropped in the city every five minutes between sun rise and sun set and each fifteen minutes from sun set to sun rise" (Richard Harwell and Philip N. Racine, eds., *The Fiery Trail: A Union Officer's Account of Sherman's Last Campaigns* [Knoxville: University of Tennessee Press, 1986] 17). This single cannon fired 1,174 rounds during 11–25 August—17 1/2 tons of metal (Snell, diary, "Recapitulation of the operations of 2nd Div. 16th A.C.," 120, Illinois Historical Society).

report to Beauregard, dated 6 January 1864, was very specific: "126 buildings (including kitchens) had been struck by shells, about 85 much injured and 41 only slightly." But in Atlanta, aside from, say, Isaac Pilgrim's street-by-street report of early August or Watterson's estimate that "at least 47 houses were destroyed by fire," we have no conclusive tallying of individual structures damaged or burned down by the shelling.

The Northern cannonade had killed or wounded a number of civilians uncounted then and uncountable now, save for our guess that perhaps two dozen men, women and children were slain (including casualties caused by shell explosions after the Yankees had ceased firing), and at least several score more wounded. Again, we wish we had the kind of military report ordered by General Beauregard in Charleston: Major Henry Bryan, assistant inspector-general, counted five shell-deaths up to early January alone; he was able to name them and their tragic circumstances (although his sources of information may not have been more reliable than the hearsay in the Confederate press reports of Atlanta's bombardment). As for the siege and bombardment of Vicksburg, Professor Peter F. Walker estimates, "it appears that not more than five to ten persons died" in the Union barrage of 19 May–3 July 1863. As for Petersburg, victim of the other major Yankee city-shelling of the war, the literature has concluded that half a dozen civilians lost their lives. But journalistic sources will differ, such as the article in the *Petersburg Christian Sun*, in October 1864—just four months into Grant' s bombardment—when the paper counted 14 to 16 whites and blacks killed. Similarly in Atlanta, going against Richards' guess of a score of civilian shell-deaths, the *Intelligencer* offered a figure half that: "not more than 8 or 10 were instantly killed, or died from the effects of their wounds."

Thus we have it, or do not, based on our closest sources for Atlanta's bombardment. But a comparison of other Southern shelled cities is in order. Charleston claims the "distinction" of the longest bombardment of the war, beginning 22 August 1863 and ending when the Federals occupied the city in February 1865. Petersburg suffered the second-longest bombardment by the Yankees, 26 June 1864–2 April 1865, and was shelled with the heaviest projectiles (from the mortar dubbed "Dictator"). Charleston succumbed to the longest-*range* bombardment (across the harbor, from Northern cannon on Morris Island).[104]

---

[104] Maj. Henry Bryan report to General Beauregard, 6 January 1864, *OR*, vol. 28, pt. 1, p. 683; Pilgrim, "The Houses Shelled in Atlanta," *Atlanta Intelligencer*, 6 August; "Shadow," "Our Army Correspondence," *Mobile Register & Advertiser*, 3 September; Walker, *Vicksburg*, 203n4; Trudeau, *The Last Citadel*, 422; Scott and Wyatt, *Petersburg's Story*, 220 (on fewer than half a dozen civilian deaths); "Atlanta Calumniated," *Atlanta Intelligencer*, 16 October 1864 ("not more than 8 or 10" Atlantans killed or mortally wounded); Henry L. Abbot, *Siege Artillery in the Campaigns against Richmond* (New York: D. Van Nostrand, 1866) 176–77 (on 2 April 1865 as date of last firing on Petersburg by Union artillery, although Major Abbot does not state whether Confederate lines or Petersburg itself was the target).

In terms of statistics, Atlanta falls in among these unfortunate Southern cities, with a thirty-seven-day barrage and probably two dozen shell-deaths. Yet with Vicksburg, Charleston, and Petersburg, Atlanta also shares an unheralded but undeniable truth in the Civil War. Despite the intermittent intensity, and month-plus duration of Sherman's artillery bombardment, one must judge that the shelling produced no strategic benefit for Federal forces. Indeed, it achieved little tactical result as well, failing to affect or weaken the Confederates' ability to hold back Sherman throughout the campaign. At its end, Atlanta had fallen, but the Yankees' artillery shelling of our city had contributed nothing to their victory.

5

UNION OCCUPATION, 2 SEPTEMBER–16 NOVEMBER

September 1—This was a day of terror and a night of dread. About noon came the tidings of a severe fight on the Macon RR and that our forces were worsted and the city was to be evacuated at once. Then began a scramble among the inhabitants thereof to get away—others to procure supplies of food for their families. If there had been any doubt of the fact that Atlanta was about to be given up it would have been removed when they saw the depots of Government grain and food thrown open and the contents distributed among the citizens free gratis by the sackful and the cartload. The RR cars and engines were all run up to one place in order to be fired just as the army left. Five locomotives and 85 cars, Cousin Bill told me were to be burned. Mr West told me that the militia were ordered to be on hand to go out with the army, so I thought I would resign, as I was not bound to go. About midnight Mr West came to our back gate and called to me and told me that the Battalion had gone to McDonough and that he had backed out. I then went to the Macon depot with him and secured three sacks of meal. As we went down the Ammunition Train was fired and for half an hour or more an incessant discharge was kept up that jarred the ground and broke the glass in the windows around.[1]

So did Samuel Richards record the Confederate army's evacuation of Atlanta. Such an event is always chaotic, and civilian residents see the worst of it. Richards' realization that Southern forces were leaving Atlanta should have come as no surprise, for word had spread a day or two before that the city was in danger. "Rover," correspondent for the *Augusta Chronicle & Sentinel* and writing from Atlanta on 30 August, gave a remarkably clear description of the military situation then unfolding. While Sherman maintained some forces at the Chattahoochee, "his main strength" had destroyed long sections of the railroad to West Point and to Montgomery (already out of operation from the Yankee cavalry destruction a month earlier in east central Alabama) and was "advancing toward the Macon road in great force, in a direction that will probably strike

---

[1] Wendy Hamand Venet, ed., *Sam Richards's Civil War Diary: A Chronicle of the Atlanta Home Front* (Athens: University of Georgia Press, 2009) 233 (1 September 1864). This excerpt is quoted in full in Franklin M. Garrett, *Atlanta and Environs: A Chronicle of Its People and Events,* 2 vols. (New York: Lewis Historical Publishing Co., 1954) 1:636–37.

between Rough and Ready and Jonesboro.'" To meet the threat, "Rover" explained that General Hood's army was stretched from the Georgia Railroad east of the city and around it (Stewart's corps and the state militia) with Lee's and Hardee's corps extended from East Point to Jonesboro (the latter point was 15 miles south of the Car Shed by direct line, but 23 by rail; the Confederate defenses would have followed the railroad). "The point now threatened is the front of Hardee and Lee, as it is ascertained the enemy is slowly advancing upon them with well-appointed columns, by as many different routes." "Rover" presciently asked the key question: what would happen if the Yankees broke the railroad to Macon?

The next day brought the situation to crisis. Writing late Wednesday night, 31 August, "Rover" reported that around noon a train had left Atlanta,

> but about four o'clock it returned to the city, bringing intelligence that, having proceeded a short distance below Rough and Ready, it was stopped by some of our retreating cavalry, who reported the enemy occupying the road a short distance below.... in a very short time the engineer backed up the road, and soon reached the city. Shortly afterward...the intelligence was spread that the enemy...were in possession of the road near Rough and Ready, strongly fortified, and in a position from which there was no possibility of their being driven, unless...by the corps of Hardee and Lee.

"Rover" had it right. Yankees had indeed cut the railroad to Macon that afternoon below Rough and Ready, by rail about 14 miles south of the Car Shed. Major General Jacob Cox's Union division had come upon the M & W about 3:00 P.M., and after driving off the Rebel cavalry that had been contesting its advance, secured a lodgment on the road, soon reinforced by elements of Stanley's IV Corps. Hardee and Lee were engaged 6 miles to the south at Jonesboro, trying to drive off the enemy forces there, and hence were unable to counter the Federal road-break near Rough and Ready. Hardee and Lee's attacks at Jonesboro were easily repulsed. But the Confederates' defeat (and their casualties of 2,200 killed and wounded) had no impact on the Federals' interposition on the M & W, which was the campaign's decisive event.

General Hood learned that afternoon not only that the enemy had cut the railroad to Macon, but that a large amount of artillery ammunition he was trying to get out of town had not escaped. (Hood had already seen to the removal of the army's regular ordnance train, sending it south of the city to Hardee—who in fact later complained that "the immense subsistence and ordnance stores of the army" proved to be an onerous burden upon his corps's operations.) The reserve ordnance was considerable; Captain W. D. Humphries had made an invoice of it, according to Captain Charles Swett, one of the army's artillery inspectors, preparatory to sending it out of the city. "Rover" reported that the reserve ordnance train had set out from East Point in the afternoon, but had run into the

Yankees blocking the route near Rough and Ready, and was forced to return. Corroboration of the journalist's claim comes from the indefatigable local researcher Wilbur G. Kurtz, who in summer 1935 interviewed James Bell, wartime resident of the city. Seventy-one years before, Bell had been a fifteen-year-old Atlantan, working in the CS government bakery. Based on Bell's recollections, Kurtz in his inimitable style described how Hood on 31 August faced the threat of the Macon railroad being cut and tried to get the army's reserve ordnance out of the city.

> On the tracks of the Macon and Western R.R., southwest of the city, stood a large number of cars loaded with ammunition and arms. While it was known that Hardee's and Lee's corps would have an affair with Sherman's troops down Jonesboro way, it was not assumed that the Federals had destroyed—or would be permitted to destroy, any of the Macon + Western R.R.... It might be proper to further assume that General Hood fancied he could remove the loaded cars *before* the Federals reached the railroad.
>
> Be that as it may, two locomotives were coupled each to a string of ammunition cars and steamed boldly forth to Macon! The "General" and the "Missouri" were the engines.... Running blind, the two locomotives and their cars of high explosives passed East Point and so on, toward Rough and Ready and Macon. Extending from East Point to a mile and a half below Rough and Ready, a thin line of grey-clad men, composed partly of dismounted cavalrymen, gave what protection they could to the railroad. It was about 3 P.M. when the trains reached Rough and Ready and all seemed to be well until they ran a mile below and saw that the cavalrymen were being attacked by a Federal force.... This would never do; the engineer of the leading train hastily slacked up— stopped...and reversed. So did the other. They both backed their trains to Atlanta. The last exit had been closed![2]

---

[2] "Rover," "Letter from the Georgia Front" (Atlanta, 30 August 1864) and "A Day of Excitement and Rumors" (Atlanta, 10 P.M., 31 August), *Augusta Chronicle & Sentinel,* 6 September; "Railroads" (mileage from Atlanta to stations), *Barnwell's Atlanta City Directory and Stranger's Guide...for the Year 1867* (Atlanta: Intelligencer & Job Office, 1867) 109; Stephen Davis, *Atlanta Will Fall: Sherman, Joe Johnston and the Heavy Yankee Battalions* (Wilmington DE: Scholarly Resources, 2001) 185–87; Hardee's report, 5 April 1865, US War Department, *The War of the Rebellion: A Compilation of the Official Records of the Union and Confederate Armies,* 128 vols. (Washington, DC: Government Printing Office, 1880–1901) vol. 38, pt. 3, p. 701 (hereafter *OR* and all references will be to series 1 unless otherwise indicated); Capt. Charles Swett, remarks appended to "Abstract from inspection report of the light artillery, Army of Tennessee," 20 September 1864, *OR,* vol. 38, pt. 3, p. 684; Wilbur G. Kurtz, notes on interviews with James Bell, summer 1935 (Kurtz observed, "his memory was excellent") in notebook 12, 37, Wilbur G. Kurtz Collection, Atlanta History Center;

This was the dire news circulating the city on the morning of 1 September. "Rover"—who could have been Henry Watterson, Albert Roberts, or a few other newspaper reporters still in Atlanta—wrote that "early on the morning of the 1st" word had it that the Yankees were lodged on the railroad to Macon and that General Hood had no choice but to abandon the city. "Rover" explained how it happened, in the only extant Confederate newspaper source on the momentous evacuation.

> The removal of all the supplies and ammunition that the trans-portation facilities of the army would permit, commenced early Thursday [1 September], and was continued throughout the day. Large quantities of provisions were also distributed to the people, and at nightfall all on hand stored in the Georgia railroad warehouse, and cars on the track. Throughout the day, also, the several bodies of troops, as they were withdrawn from the defences and filed through the city, were permitted access to the public stores.—The rolling stock of the railroads, consisting of about one hundred cars and six engines, was concentrated near the rolling mill before dark, and by that hour all the troops had passed through, with the exception of the rear guard.... Previous to my leaving the telegraph office was also closed, and at dark the evacuation was completed....
>
> Of course great excitement prevailed throughout the day, but a moderate degree of good order obtained. A few licentious citizens and soldiers embraced the occasion to display the wickedness of their natures, but the great mass of both classes acted with the greatest decorum. The citizens who had suffered from the malice of the enemy during the bombardment, looked on sorrowingly, and indulged in conjectures as to what would be their fate when once in the enemy's power; while the troops filed through the streets, with a steady tread it is true, but nevertheless with sorrow depleted on their weather beaten faces.

"Rover" correctly captured the story of Atlanta's Confederate evacuation. Before noon on 1 September, army headquarters downtown had issued orders for the withdrawal of the three army divisions (Stewart's corps) still in the city, along with the Georgia militia, all heading out the McDonough road toward a junction with the rest of the army, Hardee's and Lee's corps. General Hood himself, having remained at his Atlanta headquarters, rode among the retreating

---

James G. Bogle, "The Western & Atlantic Railroad in the Campaign for Atlanta," in Theodore P. Savas and David A. Woodbury, eds., *The Campaign for Atlanta & Sherman's March to the Sea, Volumes I and II* (Campbell CA: Savas Woodbury Publishers, 1994) 335 (on the *General, Missouri*, and the effort to move the army ordnance out of town).

columns; much of his headquarters baggage had to be burned for want of wagons to haul it. Henry Watterson, at the general's HQ, managed to jot a letter to his fiancée, Rebecca: "We shall certainly evacuate the city tonight," he wrote: "I am well, I am constant. And I do not despair." Panicked civilians, dreading the Yankees' occupation of the city, attached themselves to the retreating Southern columns. In the hubbub, some slaves doubtless found their way out and into the Union lines. General Schofield reported that on the morning of 2 September "a negro who has just come in from Atlanta" confirmed the Rebel army's evacuation, "all the citizens joining in the flight."[3]

Besides "Rover," the exodus of Atlanta's fleeing residents was also reported by a Northern correspondent, Captain Joseph W. Miller, writing for the *Cincinnati Commercial*. Miller arrived in the city on the evening of 2 September, in time to ask about the Rebels' evacuation of the city.

> On the morning of the first orders were issued in Atlanta for an evacuation that night, and though confided at first to the army commanders alone, and to those citizens whose welfare they had especially at heart, it was blown over the city by the afternoon, and fell like a thunder-clap upon the unsuspecting inhabitants, who but a day or two ago had been hilarious over the withdrawal of Sherman. They thought him foiled, and put to a last trump of building railroads and, possibly, digging canals. Every vehicle in the city was brought into requisition by fugacious families. Negroes, free and bond alike, were arrested and started south on foot. Shopkeepers packed up their scanty wares, or found places where they concealed them. The confusion intensified as night came on, and I am told that the scene beggared description. The faces of most of the citizens wore a look of despair as they turned their backs upon their homes, from which they were driven so unexpectedly. The streets were cluttered with wagons, tottering under hasty, ill-adjusted loads; the sidewalks swarmed with two classes—the fugitives and the wreckers. For be it known that in the last hours of the rebel occupation of Atlanta, thousands of the lower classes, who proposed to remain, fell to plundering the abandoned houses and stores as soon as their owners disappeared. Staff officers dashed from point to point with gloomy faces, while drunken soldiers brawled along the

---

[3] "Rover," "The Evacuation of Atlanta" (Atlanta, 2 September), *Augusta Chronicle & Sentinel*, 6 September 1864 (see also "Rover Reports the Fall of Atlanta," J. Cutler Andrews, *The South Reports the Civil War* [Princeton: Princeton University Press, 1970] 461–62); Albert Castel, *Decision in the West: The Atlanta Campaign of 1864* (Lawrence: University Press of Kansas, 1992) 522–23; Thomas G. Dyer, *Secret Yankees: The Union Circle in Confederate Atlanta* (Baltimore: Johns Hopkins University Press, 1999) 188 (Watterson's letter, 1 September); Schofield to Sherman, 2 September, *OR*, vol. 38, pt. 5, p. 733.

banquettes, and cursed alike the citizens they encountered and the patrols that dragged them to their commands.

Before they left, Confederate soldiers threw open the army's commissary warehouse on Whitehall Street for civilians to enter and take whatever they wanted. "Some commissary stores were distributed to the citizens," recorded Brigadier General Francis A. Shoup, Hood's chief of staff, in considerable understatement. Major Charles Hubner later wrote that "the warehouse was filled with foodstuffs of all kinds, and for several hours a large crowd of women, children and men, were kept busy rolling away barrels of syrup, sugar, etc. Upon their shoulders they carried hams, side-meat and sacks of provisions, all of which had been indiscriminately distributed to the eager, hungry populace." Confederate commissary officer Joseph Semmes wrote home that fully 550,000 pounds of corn meal were given out to the civilians. That which was not taken was soon burned. Confederate Brigadier General Arthur Manigault later complained that there had been a "great amount of supplies, consisting of sugar, bacon, coffee, whiskey, shoes, and clothing of every description, that were given over to the flames and destroyed, whilst they had been under the impression that no such stores existed with the army." In the hurried evacuation, ordnance officers could not carry out boxes of rifles and ammunition, so the arms were dumped down wells in the city. Quartermaster's stores and medical supplies were also burned. Confederates charged with destroying the army's postal office downtown, with presumably thousands of letters unsent or undelivered (given the strains on the city's train traffic), applied their own solution to the task: they loaded a wagon with the mail and rode off toward Covington. Tearing envelopes open in search of cash, the soldiers threw the letters away, with the result (as one recalled) that "the Covington Road was paved with paper for a distance of ten miles."[4]

---

[4] "J.W.M." (Capt. Joseph W. Miller), "September 2," *Cincinnati Commercial,* 13 September (reprinted in Frank Moore, ed., *The Rebellion Record: A Diary of American Events,* 11 vols. [New York: G. P. Putnam, 1861–63; D. Van Nostrand, 1864–68] 11:documents 281); Shoup, journal, 1 September, *OR,* vol. 38, pt. 5, p. 695; Hubner, "Some Recollections," 6; Benedict J. Semmes to Jorantha Semmes, 4 September, quoted in Robert Scott Davis, Jr., ed., *Requiem for a Lost City: A Memoir of Civil War Atlanta and the Old South* (Macon GA: Mercer University Press, 1999) 17n26; R. Lockwood Tower, ed., *A Carolinian Goes to War: The Civil War Narrative of Arthur Middleton Manigault, Brigadier General, C.S.A.* (Columbia: University of South Carolina Press, 1983) 249; Lee Kennett, *Marching through Georgia: The Story of Soldiers and Civilians during Sherman's Campaign* (New York: HarperCollins, 1995) 199–200 ("paved with paper").

On the small arms dumped into wells in the city, Lee Kennett observes, "some of this ordnance was turned up in expressway excavations a century later," during construction of Atlanta's downtown freeways (*Marching through Georgia,* 199). Beverly DuBose, the renowned Atlanta Civil War relic collector, snatched up some of this century-old weaponry not for its sake, as he once told me, but for the wooden boxes storing it, stamped with the

Stewart's infantry began marching out of the city around five o'clock in the afternoon, according to General Shoup. They were able to bring out almost all of the army's light artillery, including twenty-eight field pieces belonging to the Georgia state forces. Confederate artillery Captain Charles Swett, charged with tallying the ordnance stores destroyed in the evacuation, reported ten field cannon (a 3-inch rifle, three 12-pounders and six 6-pounders) left behind, possibly in damaged condition. Also lost were eight big 32-pounder smoothbores sited on the line (according to a Northern newspaperman walking around the city later, these had been spiked). Parked in the rear and also abandoned were a 24-pounder cannon and five more 32-pounder tubes, unmounted. Somewhere among the lost ordnance, too, would have been the big 9-inch Dahlgren naval cannon north of the city. In their quick evacuation—conducted in just about twenty-four hours after Hood had learned that the enemy were on his last railroad—Confederates had no time to destroy any factories or munitions shops. Example was the Novelty Iron Works on Marietta Street. In late October 1864, James Ormond was able to write his business partner William McNaught that "up to the 20th inst all our property in Atlanta was unharmed."[5]

Criss-crossing orders always lead to foul-ups, as Confederate Major General Samuel French experienced in the frantic afternoon of 1 September. French, whose division was the last out of the city, had received orders that at 11:00 P.M. he was to spike the five heavy guns on his division-front. But French was surprised and chagrined to learn that under orders of the army chief of ordnance, Lieutenant Colonel J. M. Kennard, the five guns had been spiked and their carriages set afire prematurely at 5:00 P.M. This act, in broad daylight, and thus "a proclamation to the enemy in my front that we were evacuating the place," convinced French that amidst the hectic activity of an evacuation, "common sense is wanted." Worse, when the last of the army's infantry marched out that evening, General French also observed that some of the soldiers were drunk. These may have been the culprits who set fire to abandoned houses in the

---

name of the Confederate arsenal in Atlanta—which were by far the more valuable relics for his famed collection (conversation with Mr. Beverly DuBose, 3 May 1970).

[5] Captain Swett's report, 20 September 1864, *OR*, vol. 38, pt. 3, p. 684; "Letter from Marietta, September 4, 1864," for *Chattanooga Gazette, Atlanta Intelligencer*, 18 September (on heavy cannon having been spiked); Ormond to McNaught, 31 October 1864, box 3, folder 1, McNaught Papers, Atlanta History Center. (Ormond predicted ominously, "if they have to leave as is now imminent they will probably destroy everything as they go.")

The misconception that Confederates evacuating Atlanta on the afternoon of 1 September had enough time to set fire to factory and shop buildings leads to the miscaptioning of George Barnard's photograph of the shell-blasted Atlanta Lard Oil Factory in William C. Davis, ed., *The South Besieged: Volume Five of The Image of War 1861–1865*, 6 vols. (Garden City NY: Doubleday & Company, 1983) 5:293, which pictures "the Lard Oil Factory destroyed by Hood's retreating Confederates."

city; as one disgusted Confederate put it, the men had engaged in arson "for no other purpose than to satisfy their hellish desires."[6]

The last acts of demolition in the city were carried out that night by elements of Brigadier General Samuel W. Ferguson's cavalry and of the Georgia militia. Special targets, according to "Rover," were locomotives, train cars, and the rolling mill. To be added, very significantly, was the army's reserve artillery ordnance supply, which had remained in the city after its failed effort to escape. Confederate railroaders had brought the long train from East Point into town, through the Car Shed and a mile to the east, alongside the rolling mill (present-day site near Oakland Cemetery). Other locomotives and the dozens of freight cars unable to get out before the Yankees cut the Macon road were also packed onto the Georgia Railroad line. "Rover" had predicted the demolition on the night of 31 August, after the reserve ordnance trains had chugged back into town. "The amount of rolling stock thus concentrated here is large. A prominent railroad official informs me there are ninety-eight cars—mostly freight boxes—and six engines. Should the city fall their loss is inevitable."

"Rover" was right; Southern demolition crews on the afternoon of 1 September set to work destroying the locomotives. Two of the engines were the *General* and the *Missouri*, according to James Bell. The *Missouri* was run backward into its cars and smashed. After David Young, engineer of the *General*, refused to knock out the cylinder heads of his locomotive, he ran it backward into the *Missouri*, but not fast enough to do major damage. After that, soldiers began setting fire to the trains. L. A. Rumph, of the 8th Georgia Militia, recalled how his company was detailed for the demolition. The men poured five barrels of tar on the locomotives except the *General* (somehow spared) before setting the whole mess afire. Then they started blazes all around, burning hundreds of bales of cotton as well as the rolling mill building before they torched the ordnance-filled freight cars; as Rumph recalled, they then "ran for their lives." "The explosion consequent upon the firing of the ordnance train took place about two o'clock this morning," "Rover" wrote on the morning of 2 September, "and was heard and felt to a great distance." Young Carrie Berry recorded in her diary that she and her family did not get much sleep that night: "The Confederates had four engines and a long train of box cars filled with ammunition and set it on fire last night which caused a grate explosion which kept us all awake."

Everyone realized that the destruction of precious locomotives and rolling stock was a huge blow to the already rickety Southern transportation system; merely quantifying the disaster caused considerable public conversation. Sam

---

[6] Samuel G. French, *Two Wars: An Autobiography of Gen. Samuel G. French, An Officer in the Armies of the United States and the Confederate States, A Graduate from the U.S. Military Academy, West Point, 1843* (Nashville: Confederate Veteran, 1901) 222; W. P. Archer, quoted in Allen Phelps Julian, "Atlanta's Last Days in the Confederacy," *Atlanta Historical Bulletin* 11/2 (June 1966): 10 ("hellish desires").

Richards heard that five locomotives and eight-five cars had been destroyed. The Yankees also tried to estimate the Rebels' loss; a reporter for the *Cincinnati Commercial*, arriving in Atlanta on the first day of the occupation, put the number at seven locomotives and eight-three cars. Confederate authorities tried to tote up the extent of the calamity. Brigadier General Shoup put the loss at five locomotives and eight-one cars, figures eventually accepted by Richmond after a court of inquiry had investigated the large loss of ordnance in Hood's evacuation. Regardless of the details, the *Augusta Chronicle & Sentinel* was correct in its observation of 6 September: "a few more losses of this kind will pretty well use up our means of transportation."

In addition to all the railroad equipment, Confederates also lost the Army of Tennessee's entire ordnance reserve; ammunition had filled at least twenty-eight of the eighty-odd train cars blown up on the night of 1 September. According to Captain Swett's report, the inventory included over 12,000 shot and shell of various calibers, as well as another 43 boxes of ammo that were listed as damaged but possibly reparable. Sixteen gun carriages, caissons, or limbers were also not brought out, plus another seventy-nine damaged carriages, ammunition chests, limbers, caissons, or forges.

The explosion of the ordnance train lit up the night. George Adair, voluntary member of Hood's staff, had been placed in charge of a headquarters wagon, and was driving it out of the city. Joining him were Governor Isham Harris of Tennessee, Henry Watterson and his fellow journalist Albert Roberts ("John Happy" of the *Chattanooga Rebel*). He recalled the huge, fiery blaze that night: "On going up a big hill below Atlanta the fire was blazing so brightly I could count the hairs on the horse's tail by its light." This kind of hyperbole was shared by others in describing the huge ammo explosions. A woman living a half-mile away claimed that minie balls rained down on her house from the Confederates' ordnance detonations. It was a great story, regardless of its possible fabrication.[7]

---

[7] "Rover," "The Evacuation of Atlanta" and "A Day of Excitement and Rumors," *Augusta Chronicle & Sentinel,* 6 September 1864; Kurtz's transcription of Bell's reminiscence on the *Missouri* and *General,* notebook 13, 68, 70, Wilbur G. Kurtz Collection, Atlanta History Center; Wilbur Kurtz, notebook 22, 127–29 (naming also the *Etowah*), Wilbur G. Kurtz Collection, Atlanta History Center; Ellie Lou McKenzie, "Five Men Who Fought the War," *Atlanta Journal,* 2 November 1930 (quoted in Kennett, *Marching through Georgia,* 199); Carrie Berry, diary, entry of 2 September, Atlanta History Center; Venet, ed., *Sam Richards's Civil War Diary,* 233; Moore, ed., *Rebellion Record,* 11:documents 281 (*Cincinnati Commercial*); Brig. Gen. Francis A. Shoup, journal, 1 September, *OR,* vol. 38, pt. 3, p. 695; "Findings of the Court of Inquiry," 2 March 1865, *OR,* vol. 38, pt. 3, p. 992; Mary A. DeCredico, *Patriotism for Profit: Georgia's Urban Entrepreneurs and the Confederate War Effort* (Chapel Hill: University of North Carolina Press, 1990) 99 (quoting *Augusta Chronicle & Sentinel*); Swett's report, *OR,* vol. 38, pt. 3, pp. 685–86; Robert Adamson, "Isham G. Harris as Warrior and Fugitive," *Atlanta Constitution,* 1 August 1897 (reprinted as "Gov. Harris at the Close of the War,"

The sound of Hood's train-demolition on the night of 1 September alerted Sherman, 20 miles south of Atlanta with Howard's army near Jonesboro, that the city was being abandoned by the Rebels. By nightfall of 1 September, Sherman knew that his forces had cut the railroad below Atlanta, and that Hardee had been defeated in battle at Jonesboro. "That night I was so restless and impatient that I could not sleep," the general recalled, "and about midnight there arose toward Atlanta sounds of shells exploding, and other sound like that of musketry." He could not conclude whether they came from the Rebels blowing up their magazines, or from the XX corps engaging battle near the Chattahoochee. He heard more noise around 4:00 A.M., apparently closer. After daybreak rumors reached headquarters that the Rebels had evacuated the city; Sherman sent courier-message to General Slocum asking for confirmation. General Schofield, whose XXIII Corps was farther north than Sherman's position with Howard, sent in corroborating intelligence provided by Kenner Garrard's cavalry. Garrard had heard the explosions, and Schofield, too. "Very large fires were visible in the direction of Atlanta," General Schofield reported. "Brilliant flashes followed at regular intervals by loud explosions, far too loud for any artillery, and then by very rapid explosions of shells. The interval between the flash and explosion gave the distance to Atlanta. All the circumstances indicate the burning of magazine at Atlanta." The later explosions, around 4:00 A.M., seemed to come from East Point (from which place Confederates were also retreating). Schofield was convinced that the enemy had blown up their supplies and evacuated. "I cannot explain the phenomena of last night in any other way. No battle I have ever witnessed would begin to account for it." Later on 2 September, Sherman received a note written out by Slocum himself, under heading of Atlanta, stating that he had heard the explosions in the city and in the morning had moved a column forward. Finding the city abandoned by the enemy, his troops had occupied it.[8]

Confederate Veteran 5 [1897]:402); Paul Taylor, *Orlando M. Poe: Civil War General and Great Lakes Engineer* (Kent OH: Kent University Press, 2009) 178.

[8] William T. Sherman, *Memoirs of General William T. Sherman,* 2 vols. (New York: D. Appleton and Company, 1875) 2:107–108; Sherman to Thomas and to Schofield, 2 September (4 A.M.), *OR,* vol. 38, pt. 5, pp. 764, 772; Lt. M. J. Kelly to Slocum, 2 September, *OR,* vol. 38, pt. 5, pp. 767–68; Schofield to Sherman, 2 September (8 A.M.), *OR,* vol. 38, pt. 5, pp. 772–73.

Numerous Federal soldiers heard the explosions early in the morning of 2 September. One of the more colorful notices of them comes from the diary of Pvt. James P. Snell of the 52nd Illinois, who on that day wrote that he was in camp 2 miles north of Lovejoy's Station on the Macon railroad, below Jonesboro: "Last night I dreamed that I was married and *strange*! To a woman already married.... Before the conclusion of the joyful ceremonies I was suddenly awakened by a loud explosion, which continued for two hours I thought, and ending about half-past two or three o'clock this morning" (Snell, diary, 2 September, Illinois Historical Society). Wilbur G. Kurtz copied this passage into his

Slocum, commanding the XX Corps since 27 August after Hooker's resignation in late July, was still at the Chattahoochee River, 8 miles northwest of downtown, and heard the loud explosions the night of 1 September. Slocum had been in the practice of sending out reconnaissance columns each morning to ascertain enemy movements; this recon would have additional meaning, given the possibility that the Rebels had exploded stores or munitions downtown. Well before dawn, orders went out that each division would send forth a strong scouting force on its respective front. Brigadier General Alpheus S. Williams's 1st Division, in the center of Slocum's line, held the area of the railroad bridge across the Chattahoochee near Bolton. Williams had heard the loud, repeated explosions in the night, and knew something was up when orders came to send out the usual dawn patrol. He dispatched a column of three infantry regiments under Colonel Nirom Crane to march toward the city.

Brigadier General John W. Geary's 2nd Division held Slocum's left, and at Pace's Ferry on the river was the farthest north of Atlanta. Geary assembled a column of two regiments of infantry, parts of two more, plus twenty Pennsylvania cavalrymen; they marched out at 6:45 A.M. on the road from Pace's Ferry toward Howell's Mill. Lieutenant Colonel Thomas M. Walker, in charge of the column, picked up signs that Rebel cavalry had retreated several hours before, but his skirmishers encountered no enemy. The Federals crossed Peachtree Creek at Howell's Mill, the infantrymen making their way over the water on a big log. This took a while: when Walker reached the outskirts of Atlanta, he learned that the recon column of the 3rd Division had beaten him to the city.[9]

Brigadier General William T. Ward's division of the XX Corps held the right of Slocum's line at Turner's Ferry. Ward directed Colonel John Coburn to take 900 infantry, with a squadron or two of cavalry, and march toward the city. They set out from camps around 6:00 A.M., heading for the area where the corps had been entrenched 22 July–25 August. One of General Ward's staff officers, Captain Henry M. Scott, rode in the advance with the cavalry. Reaching the former Union lines, from a hilltop Scott could see Atlanta, but observed no Rebel troops anywhere. He sent a rider with the news to Colonel Coburn and rode on. Crossing the abandoned enemy lines northwest of the city, Scott's party saw a few Confederate cavalrymen retreating before them, and lit out in chase until they came upon a sizable body of enemy horsemen lined up astride Marietta

---

notebook from the typewritten copy of the Snell diary then in possession of John R. Peacock (notebook 21, 111,Wilbur G. Kurtz Collection, Atlanta History Center).

[9] Slocum's reports, 3 and 19 September 1864, *OR*, vol. 38, pt. 2, pp. 20–21; report of Brig. Gen. Alpheus S. Williams, 12 September, *OR*, vol. 38, pt. 2, p. 35; report of Col. Nirom Crane, 8 September, *OR*, vol. 38, pt. 2, p. 76; report of Brig. Gen. John W. Geary, 15 September, *OR*, vol. 38, pt. 2, p. 145; report of Lt. Col. Thomas M. Walker, 6 September, *OR*, vol. 38, pt. 2, p. 319.

Street, making menacing moves toward the flank while opening fire. Scott sent word back to Coburn, who would be bringing the infantry up, and withdrew his column to a safer position.

People still in the city apprehensively awaited the arrival of the Yankees; after the Confederates' departure, they also had to guard their property against vandalism. On the morning of 2 September, John Silvey left his residence on Walton Street and proceeded to his store two blocks away on Decatur near Peachtree; happily he found it undisturbed. But lawlessness was in the air. John Ficken, tobacco merchant, saw someone throw a rock into the window of his store on Whitehall Street, break in, and make off with some of his merchandise. Straggling Confederate soldiers were still helping themselves to goods from the government commissary, joined by some fifty destitute women and their children. Bridget Doyle, who ran a small store on Decatur Street, saw some drunken Southern cavalrymen and hovering women, apparently prostitutes. "I told them they were no gentlemen," Doyle recalled, whereupon they fired shots into the air, sending her scurrying back into her store.

Mayor James M. Calhoun recognized the benefit to the public order if Federal military control were quickly brought into the city. With Confederate authorities gone, he accepted the painful responsibility of formally surrendering Atlanta, seeking to safeguard the city's remaining citizenry and their property. Ferguson's cavalry brigade was still in town, charged with at least nominally contesting the enemy's entrance. After rising early and breakfasting, Calhoun met with Ferguson at his headquarters, asking that he withdraw from the city. The general politely refused, stating that his orders "were to defend the city to the last," as Mayor Calhoun recalled in an affidavit filed months later. He returned to his home near the courthouse. Around 11:00 A.M., Ferguson changed his mind and called for the mayor, announcing that he would contest the enemy advance no further; Calhoun could go and tell the Yankees. By that time, his troops had clashed with Scott's column (and possibly had spotted the stronger force of Coburn's infantry coming up behind). Either way, Ferguson had done his duty and there was no further use in imperiling the city's people or their property.

The mayor waited till Ferguson's cavalry column had passed him, heading south from the city, before he rode out Marietta Street, accompanied by a group of prominent citizens. They rode through the Confederate trenchlines carrying a white flag, and in what was once no-man's land encountered Captain Scott's column. "Going forward," Scott recalled, "I asked them what propositions they had to make."

One of them then made himself known as mayor, and said that he had come to surrender the city and ask protection for noncombatants and private property. In answer to further interrogatives he said that General

Ferguson's brigade was just retiring from the city, and that the general had agreed to withdraw without offering us resistance in order to insure [sic] the safety of noncombatants.

The mayor asked Scott if he were the officer in charge; Scott said no, and rode off to find Colonel Coburn, soon bringing him back. Calhoun later recorded what he said: "Col. Coburne, the fortune of war has placed Atlanta in your hands. As Mayor of the City I come to ask your protection for noncombatants and for private property." Coburn asked if the Rebel cavalry were still in the city, and was told by the mayor that they were leaving. Coburn recalled the exchange: "I replied that my force was moving into the city and that unless that force retired there would be a fight in which neither person nor property would be safe, and that if necessary I would burn the houses of citizens to dislodge the enemy; that I did not otherwise intend to injure persons or property of the citizens unless used against us."

Afterward Calhoun did not recall such belligerence from the Yankee colonel. Instead, he later attested that Coburn told him, "We did not come to make war upon noncombatants or on private property; *both shall be protected and respected by us*" (emphasis original). Calhoun further emphasized the importance he placed on preserving private property in the city by his choice of the citizens who accompanied him on the ride out Marietta Street. The mayor later stated only that "a number of citizens of Atlanta" went with him. Yet historian Thomas G. Dyer, working through Calhoun's other postwar statements, has established that it was a surprisingly large deputation of prominent Atlanta citizens who with the mayor faced the Yankees on the morning of 2 September: Alfred Austell, Thomas G. W. Crusselle, Julius Hayden, Thomas Kile, William Markham, E. E. Rawson, Robert Webster, and J. E. Williams—to a man, Union loyalists or (like Rawson) Northern natives who during the war years had tried to keep their sentiments secret, even under public and sometimes CS governmental suspicion. More, Robert Webster was a black man, a free barber like Solomon Luckie; he had won quiet acclaim among Atlanta's "secret Yankees" for tending to wounded Union prisoners. Calhoun's intent can be surmised: by bringing forth a delegation of Atlantans obviously sympathetic to Sherman's arrival, he was establishing a de facto city council that could work with Federal authorities in the best interests of the city's remaining populace.

Coburn remembered his roadside encounter with Mayor Calhoun as occurring around 11:00 A.M.; if Calhoun met with the retreating Ferguson at 11, it would have been later. The mayor even remembered Coburn confessing, "he had but few troops with him and did not come prepared that day to make any effort to take the City—merely came to reconnoiter it, but in a day or two they expected to take it." Calhoun then repeated that Ferguson's cavalry were leaving and that the Federals could at once enter the city without apprehension of violence. He wanted a quick establishment of Union authority to prevent further looting by the lawless elements. Coburn complied, and sending word to both generals Ward and Slocum, rode into Atlanta.[10]

As with all such events, things did not go as smoothly as the officers wanted. Some of Ferguson's cavalrymen still roamed downtown, seeking one last shot at the Yankees coming down Marietta Street. A decade after the war, Henry Ivy (who had lived in Atlanta since 1843) remembered seeing 75 to 100 Confederate cavalrymen aligned at the public square, under an officer's command and ready for action. John Henderson recalled that some of Ferguson's troopers fired a few rounds standing behind the granite columns of the Norcross building at Marietta and Peachtree. Another Atlantan, standing near Cone and Marietta, remembered the Southern horsemen riding by, wearing "large broad-brimmed slouch hats with large plumes attached." Their mission achieved— confirming that the Yankees were entering Atlanta, and taking a last few pot-shots at them, to boot—the Rebel riders took off southward. As they passed through the Car Shed, an observer noted the "buckety buckety" sound of the horses' hooves on the depot's wooden flooring. Off they vanished, down the McDonough road to catch up with the rest of the army.

Captain Scott was with the Union cavalry first riding into the city. "Notwithstanding the assurance of the mayor that resistance would not be offered us, we had scarcely entered the city before we were fired upon and a spirited skirmish ensued. I notified some of the citizens that we considered this as a violation of good faith, and that if the rebels continued to fire from behind houses they need expect no protection for persons or property, and that they had better communicate this fact to the enemy." In his report, Scott commended Mayor Calhoun for having ridden out to try to stop the Southern horsemen from firing, but noted that he had been unsuccessful, adding the mayor's complaint that he could not control the last Confederate cavalrymen, "that it was but a few drunken stragglers, and that they had come very near shooting him." Edward Rawson, who had ridden out with the mayor to meet the Federals, had the same experience. He later recounted that a couple of "rough necks" at Forsyth and Marietta streets drew revolvers and fired at the approaching Yankees. When he admonished them that the city had been surrendered, one of the roughnecks cursed Rawson and drew his pistol but did not fire. Meanwhile, in these several

---

[10] Report of Brig. Gen. William T. Ward, 5 September 1864, *OR*, vol. 38, pt. 2, p. 330; report of Col. John Coburn, 12 September, *OR*, vol. 38, pt. 2, p. 392; report of Capt. H. M. Scott, 3 September, *OR*, vol. 38, pt. 2, pp. 332–33; Dyer, *Secret Yankees*, 188–91; "Affidavit of James M. Calhoun, Mayor of Atlanta as to Facts in Regard to Surrender of Atlanta September 2, 1864," made to W. L. Calhoun, notary public, Fulton County, 31 July 1865, typescript, folder 7, Calhoun Family Papers, Atlanta History Center.

The mayor's handwritten affidavit was discovered among dusty papers in the basement of city hall in May 1931, according to Mayor William B. Hartsfield. See Hartsfield, "Document in Handwriting of Atlanta's War-Time Mayor Describes Formal Surrender of the City to Federal Army," *Atlanta Constitution Magazine,* 31 May 1931, 12.

lawless hours some people took advantage of the situation by breaking into businesses and homes in search of food or loot. Carrie Berry entered in her diary, "Every one has been trying to get all they could before the federals come.... They have been running with saques of meal, salt and tobacco. They did act rediculous breaking open stores and robbing them."

By then, probably after noon, the first Union infantry under Colonel Coburn marched into Atlanta. Coburn reported finding a few hundred small arms in city hall and capturing 123 prisoners, including sick and wounded Rebel soldiers left behind. The colonel also related how he and his troops continued to hear that morning and afternoon the "loud reports" of enemy ammunition exploding "among the ruins of the ruined shops and buildings." Confederates had apparently placed stores and supplies they could not carry away in structures that they set afire during the evacuation. After entering the city and looking about, Union General Geary concurred: "the rebels in their haste burned a large number of houses containing stores of various kinds." Colonel Coburn also counted sixteen pieces of artillery "left almost perfect" among the enemy fortifications. He furthermore described the reaction of those civilians who had not hurried away with the last columns of Hood's retreating army. "As we passed through the streets many of the citizens ran gladly out to meet us, welcoming us from the despotism of the Confederacy; others regarded us with apprehension and begged to be spared from robbery." On the other hand, a Northern newspaper correspondent, Captain Joseph W. Miller of the *Cincinnati Commercial* (and a staff officer in the XVII Corps), reported that the Northern soldiers were not greeted warmly: "...our troops entered the city with music and flags, marching proudly erect. The inhabitants looked on sullenly for the most part.... Some peered timidly from behind blinds; others ate their humble pie morosely and unflinchingly on the street corners; and, no doubt, some innocent old ladies were duly concealed in impracticable places, to avoid a fate which they flattered themselves was imminent." Other civilians welcomed the chance to make a quick buck. Edward Bartlett of the 150th New York recorded, "for the most part the inhabitants professed to be very glad to see our soldiers, and some of them brought out tobacco in large quantities, which was eagerly purchased by the men. Possibly these cash sales had something to do with the cordial welcome which they professed!"

In truth, among the people in the city were a fair number of Union sympathizers—loyalists who had stuck it out through the years of war, now to this happy hour of deliverance. After Ferguson's rowdy horsemen had sent her packing into her store, Bridget Doyle made her way downtown to halloo the Federal soldiers entering the city. She even hoped to spot her brother somewhere in the Union ranks. Correspondent Miller of the *Cincinnati Commercial* reported that some Union soldiers, formerly hospitalized in the city, now appeared before their entering comrades, albeit in Rebel clothing; Miller added that the garb had been provided the prisoners by furtive Union people in the city, who had routinely tried to help wounded Northern soldiers in the city's hospitals.[11]

As more regiments marched into the city, so too did XX Corps commander General Slocum, who entered later on 2 September and established his headquarters at the Trout House. Sometime that afternoon as well, Coburn called on Mayor Calhoun at his home and asked for a written statement of their verbal exchange that morning. Coburn claimed that he needed a formal, written surrender of the city addressed to his commander, Brigadier General Ward, and not himself. The mayor wrote out a brief document, and two officers attested. "Sir: The fortune of war has placed Atlanta in your hands. As mayor of the city I ask protection to noncombatants and private property." Given what subsequently happened to the city at the hands of the Yankees, Calhoun later regretted not including in his note the verbal assurance he had received that morning from Colonel Coburn, that the citizens and their property would be protected. "I will always regret my failure to give Gen'l Sherman notice of promise of protection," Calhoun later wrote—as if written pledges would be worth anything to Sherman once he took over the city.

Not surprisingly, there was some rivalry among Slocum's units as to which was first to enter the much-vaunted Rebel stronghold. Lieutenant Colonel Walker, leading the column from Geary's division, made a point of stating that after he encountered Colonel Coburn, the two officers agreed to enter the city simultaneously. Walker then claimed that two of his regiments, the 111th Pennsylvania Infantry and the 60th New York, were first to reach city hall, and first to raise their colors over the building. This allowed General Geary to state in a letter to his wife that the first Federal flag over the town hall was raised by men of his 2nd Division. But it was a near thing, acknowledged by Private Emory Sweetland of the 154th New York: "my division was the first (by about fifteen minutes to raise the flag in this, the commercial capital of the Confederacy." (A *New York Times* correspondent, "Sileus," sided with them, as he reported that men of the 60th and 111th raised the first Stars and Stripes over the city.) On the other hand, Colonel Coburn of Ward's 3rd Division could not resist the boast

---

[11] Dyer, *Secret Yankees*, 189–90 (Henry Ivy and Bridget Doyle); John Henderson to William L. Calhoun, 6 August 1895, box 1, folder 9, Calhoun Family Papers (also quoted in John Robert Smith, "The Day Atlanta Was Occupied," *Atlanta Historical Bulletin* 21/3 [Fall 1977]: 64); Wilbur G. Kurtz, notes of conversation with Eugene and Stephens Mitchell, 26 March 1931 (Eugene Mitchell's recollection of remembrances of George Stewart, wartime Atlantan), notebook 6, 92; notebook 10, 252 (James Bell's telling of the story about E. E. Rawson and the "rough necks"), Wilbur G. Kurtz Collection, Atlanta History Center; Scott's report, *OR*, vol. 38, pt. 2, p. 333; Carrie Berry, diary, 2 September, Atlanta History Center; Coburn's report, 12 September, *OR*, vol. 38, pt. 2, p. 393; Moore, ed., *Rebellion Record*, 11:documents 282 (Miller, *Cincinnati Commercial*); Edward O. Bartlett, *The "Dutchess County Regiment" (150th Regiment of New York State Volunteer Infantry* (Danbury CT: Danbury Medical Printing Co., 1907) 121, 123.

that it was his command that was "the first...of our army to enter the city." This allowed members of the 33d Indiana to claim rights as "the first Union troops to enter the city of Atlanta." Even some from Williams's 1st Division got into the act, as a member of the 5th Connecticut claimed after the war that it was his regiment that had "the honor of being the first Union regiment to march through the streets of the city of Atlanta." The 101st Illinois, also of Williams's division, argued as well that it had been first to enter Atlanta.

To John Potter of the 101st, all this arguing was a lot of "twaddle." He put a mature cast to the controversy with his judgment, "it is possible that, owing to the size of the place and the number of men marching on it, different commands may have gone into the city nearly simultaneously." Besides, he wondered why it was so important, when the honor of marching in first "is an empty one, for to enter a city whose defenders have fled from it is not worth contending for." True, indeed—though Potter made a point of stating that men of the 101st Illinois raised the second US flag over Atlanta. But in the end, every unit in the army shared in the glory, as headquarters instructed that on each regimental, battery, or corps flag was to be inscribed "Atlanta." In addition to the Union colors flying over city hall, someone raised the Stars and Stripes over the Franklin Printing house, the tall building on Alabama Street, from whose flagstaff, Potter added, "a few hours before, had floated the Confederate rag."[12]

Laurels for first-to-arrive and first-to-float-the-flag could be decided later. (A chaplain for the 22nd Wisconsin also claimed his regiment was first to march into the city, but someone forgot to bring the regimental colors.) The first order of business was to establish military rule. General Slocum assumed responsibility for preserving the peace in the now occupied city. Colonel William Cogswell's 2nd Massachusetts was ordered into downtown for provost guard. Until they got situated, a vacuum of authority existed in which some people saw their last

---

[12] Miller, "September 2," *Cincinnati Commercial* (on Slocum at Trout House); Calhoun affidavit, Calhoun Papers, Atlanta History Center; Walker's report, 6 September, *OR*, vol. 38, pt. 2, p. 320; Blair, ed., *A Politician Goes to War* (Geary to wife, 3 September); Mark H. Dunkelman, *Marching with Sherman: Through Georgia and the Carolinas with the 154th New York* (Baton Rouge: Louisiana State University Press, 2012) 20; "Sileus," "The Fall of Atlanta" (Trout House, 2 September), *New York Times*, 19 September; John R. McBride, *History of the Thirty-Third Indiana Veteran Volunteer Infantry* (Indianapolis: Wm. B. Burford, 1900) 138; Edwin E. Marvin, *The Fifth Regiment Connecticut Volunteers: A History Compiled from Diaries and Official Reports* (Hartford: Wiley, Waterman and Eaton, 1889) 335; John Potter, *Reminiscences of the Civil War in the United States* (Oskaloosa IA: Globe Presses, 1897) 101.

A slightly different version of the mayor's surrender note appears in Moore, ed., *Rebellion Record*. Here, *Cincinnati Commercial* correspondent Joseph Miller (who arrived in Atlanta late on 2 September) states that Calhoun, after meeting Coburn's party out on Marietta Street, invited several Union officers back to city hall, where he wrote out the surrender document addressed to General Ward (11:documents 282).

chance for plunder. Samuel Richards recorded in his diary that Union soldiers marched into the city around noon on 2 September, noting approvingly that "the private houses were not molested." But that was before he experienced a looting of his bookstore on Whitehall.

> I went down town to see armsful and baskets full of books and wall-paper going up the street in a continuous stream from our store and when I reached the store, the scene would have required the pencil of Hogarth to portray. Yankees, men, women, children and niggers were crowded into the store each one scrambling to get something to carry away, regardless, apparently, whether it was any thing they needed, and still more heedless of the fact that they were stealing! Such a state of utter confusion and disorder as presented itself to my eyes then, I little dreamed of two hours before when I left it all quiet and, as I thought, safe. The soldiers in their mad hunt for tobacco had probably broken upon the door and the rabble had then "pitched in" thinking it a "free fight".—At first I was so dismayed that I almost resolved to let them finish it, but finally I got them out and stood guard until after dark when I left it to its chances until morning....

The next morning Richards went to his store to pack what was left of his merchandise and carry it to his house on Washington Street. Borrowing a wagon and a mule—his had been stolen in the night—the bookseller completed his task that afternoon. He again encountered the confusing conduct of enemy troops entering an open city. "A number of books were *stolen* by the Yankees during the day before our eyes and that by men who *looked* like gentlemen! Of course their looks belied their character," Richards wrote disgustedly, but then had to add that indeed several Federal soldiers "took books and *paid* for them."

In charge of "the post of Atlanta"—meaning, the city, its remaining residents, and the Federal soldiers pouring into it Colonel Cogswell first rounded up the drunken stragglers who still roamed the city, looking for loot and making mischief. Captain Miller of the *Commercial* reported that "between one and two hundred stragglers, the majority of them very drunk, were fished from their hiding-places and placed under guard at the Court-house." Next was the obvious task of stopping the looting by civilians, which had been more sporadic than widespread. "I noticed on entering the city, some females walking leisurely homeward with armfuls of boxes, containing, doubtless, what might be ungallantly termed plunder," Miller wrote. "One shopkeeper says the confounded women have taken his salt."[13]

---

[13] Kennett, *Marching through Georgia*, 200 (22nd Wisconsin); report of Col. William Cogswell, 8 September 1864, *OR*, vol. 38, pt. 2, p. 66; Venet, ed., *Sam Richards's Civil War Diary*, 234 (2 September); Moore, ed., *Rebellion Record*, 11:documents 282–83 (Miller's column in the *Cincinnati Commercial*, 13 September).

Of course, the troops had their way, too. In the first hours of occupation, many Union soldiers considered the city fairly won and hence ready for the taking. Sergeant David Nichol entered the city with his Pennsylvania battery about 9:00 P.M. on 2 September. After parking their guns, the men lit out for loot. "The Boys had free access to the town," he wrote; "& I tell you they made use of their liberty. Every one was loadened down with plunder, the greater part Tobacco and cigars." "We then went in, every one for himself," recorded Sergeant L. V. B. Hubbard of the 20th Connecticut, openly acknowledging his happiness at the atmosphere of licentiousness. "After marching and fighting one hundred and forty days, with nothing in the way of food but the regular rations of hard tack and coffee, my thoughts turned on what might be a good chance to fill up with—the good things in the city. Why not? Had not a few of us full possession? But we must strike quick, before the main line came up." Hubbard and a few buddies ran into some inviting storefronts; soon he had a ham and bag of flour. He would have been satisfied, but he saw some other comrades robbing a jewelry store and making off with finer booty than he had. He concluded, "it was a good time to get a watch." So he stowed his edibles in an alleyway and ran to the jeweler's, only to find that it had already been cleaned out. He then went back to his alleyed stash, but found the ham and flour gone there, too. "By this time soldiers were getting very plenty," meaning that a lot of Yankees were running about downtown with visible signs of their plunder. Not to be outdone, Hubbard then entered a general goods store, and though the place had already been ransacked, he found a few boxes of matches. "By this time the troops began to arrive and foraging [his delicate term for robbery] was stopped." Hubbard's great regret was not that he had participated in the brief, wholesale plundering of Atlanta by Union soldiers on 2 September, but that he had made off with so little to show for it. "I returned to camp with only four boxes of matches and a plug of tobacco. This seems rather small when it is considered that I, with a very few others, were the first to enter the 'Gate City' of the south, and had full control for some time."

It was a good time to get a watch, indeed. That night, a Baptist minister's family shuddered within its downtown home; all neighbors had fled and they were by themselves on their block. Sure enough, around ten o'clock came the predatious Yankee caller. Cora Warren Beck, then twelve and the chronicler of this story, remembered that her father walked out to reason with the soldier, who demanded a watch. He proved to be an officer and a gentleman, and settled for a home-cooked meal. Others continued to look for free goods. Soon, certainly by daybreak of 3 September, what was left of Atlanta's downtown stores had been "cleaned out," in the words of Wisconsan William Wallace; a day or two after his regiment had marched in Wallace walked about the city and found nothing on hand that he could use. At one place Wallace observed that "there was a man about half crazy about '56 boxes of tobacco that the federals took this morning from me'"—though he did not specify if they were soldiers illicitly plundering, or Cogswell's provost guards operating under orders to confiscate all tobacco and cotton in the city. "Oh! I am ruined," he cried, leaving his store, doors flung wide open; there was nothing left for the taking. Wallace entered a cellar and found some men helping themselves to sacks of corn meal. He got a peck and found it made a pretty good porridge.

Within a day of entering the city, Federal provost guards had calmed everything down. Captain Henry Comey of the 2nd Massachusetts, serving under provost marshal Lieutenant Colonel Charles F. Morse, wrote home that he "did not sleep a wink" during the night of 2 September, "trying to protect the citizens and their properties from the depredations of the vandals in our army." Sergeant Rufus Mead, whose 5th Connecticut had marched in around noon of 2 September, recorded that in the free-for-all that day, "our soldiers as well as citizens and more especially darkies" engaged in pillaging. "Our boys helped themselves to tobacco," Mead acknowledged, adding, "in fact that was about all there was left." Writing his folks at home on 4 September, Mead credited Federal provost guards for stopping the pilfering; "the best of order prevails now." Indeed, Mead stated that while the "citizens themselves went in for their share along with our boys as long as they could," still, "all the citizens say our soldiers are not half so bad as the Rebs were when they found they were going." Word of the quick restoration of law and order travelled out of Atlanta to Macon, where those writing for the *Telegraph* on 6 September had to acknowledge that in their evacuation of the city, some evacuating Southern soldiers had been "guilty of serious excesses in the way of breaking and opening stores and private houses and helping them to the contents." The paper even gave slight credit to the Yankees, commenting that "up to latest accounts the Federals committed no violence."[14]

Soon Cogswell had three regiments downtown with which to keep order in the city (the 33rd Massachusetts entered 3 September with its band playing "Hail Columbia" and "Red, White and Blue"). He eventually quartered his own 2nd Massachusetts in the park around city hall; the 111th Pennsylvania encamped in the park area north of the Car Shed; and the 33rd Massachusetts settled in on

[14] Sgt. David Nichol to "Sister," 4 September, James P. Brady, comp., *Hurrah for the Artillery!: Knap's Independent Battery "E," Pennsylvania Light Artillery* (Gettysburg: Thomas Publications, 1992) 370; John W. Storrs, *The "Twentieth Connecticut": A Regimental History* (Ansonia CT: Press of the "Naugatuck Valley Sentinel," 1886) 262–63; Kennett, *Marching through Georgia*, 204 (Cora Beck); John O. Holzhueter, ed., "William Wallace's Civil War Letters: The Atlanta Campaign," *Wisconsin Magazine of History* 57/2 (Winter 1973–1974): 108–10; Lyman Richard Comey, ed., *A Legacy of Valor: The Memoirs and Letters of Captain Henry Newton Comey, 2nd Massachusetts Infantry* (Knoxville: University of Tennessee Press, 2004) 194; James A. Padgett, ed., "With Sherman through Georgia and the Carolinas: Letters of a Federal Soldier," *Georgia Historical Quarterly* 32/4 (1948): 310 (Rufus Mead to "Folks at Home," 4 September); "Enemy's Advance in Georgia," *Macon Telegraph*, 6 September.

McDonough Street, south of city hall. Until they could lay out their encampments and build their huts, the soldiers took "comfortable quarters in deserted buildings," as one wrote. The soldiers of these commands patrolled the streets, guarded prisoners, and stood watch on the stores of tobacco (500 pounds) and cotton (600 bales) that had fallen into their hands. On 5 September General Slocum ordered Colonel Cogswell to "seize all horses and mules in this city belonging to citizens" and turn them over to the XX Corps quartermaster. Various officers of the three regiments had other specific duties. For instance, Lieutenant Peter Sears of the 33rd Massachusetts was "street commissioner," responsible for the cleanliness of the city thoroughfares—no small task, given all the trash, debris, and even dead animals lying about from the Confederates' hurried exodus. Cogswell later made a point of recording that during the occupation, "Lieutenant Sears was engaged seven hours each day (Sunday excepted), with all the prisoners of the provost guard in sweeping the streets, carrying off the filth, and burying all dead and decaying matter within the limits of the fortifications." The colonel's rules for public discipline even included an order for Sundays, when he mandated all stores and public buildings be closed.[15]

Besides his civil administration of Atlanta, General Slocum also had to guard against the possibility, however remote, that the Confederates would launch some attack to regain the city. As a consequence, after they had entered Atlanta, soldiers of the XX Corps were deployed outside of it in the old Rebel entrenchments. Williams's division, sent forward on the afternoon of 2 September, was assigned to man the Rebel works to the northeast and east. As part of Williams's deployment, for instance, Colonel Ezra Carman's 13th New Jersey marched through town at 8:00 P.M. on 2 September, and promptly marched out to the enemy fortifications in the vicinity of the railroad to Augusta.

Once their units had found their places, some Union soldiers got a chance to stroll the city. On 3 September, Sergeant Rice Bull and his comrades of the 123rd New York were hungry, awaiting arrival of their brigade's supply wagons. Bull ventured off in search of a meal and received one "from a lusty colored woman who lived in a small cabin; gave her fifty cents and had a fine meal of fresh pork, sweet potatoes and 'Pones.'" Rice then walked about downtown. "It showed the effects of our bombardment," he noticed; "many business buildings and residences had been damaged. Quite a number had bomb-proofs in their yards for use when the shelling was brisk. During the last two weeks of our

---

[15] Andrew J. Boies, *Record of the Thirty-Third Massachusetts Volunteer Infantry from August 1862 to August 1865* (Fitchburg MA: Sentinel Printing Co., 1880) 89; Adin B. Underwood, *The Three Years' Service of the Thirty-Third Mass. Infantry Regiment, 1862–1865* (Boston: A. Williams & Co., 1881) 233; Cogswell's report, 26 December 1864, *OR*, vol. 39, pt. 1, pp. 650–52; Lt. Col. Henry W. Perkins to Colonel Cogswell, 5 September ("seize all horses and mules in this city belonging to citizens"), William Cogswell Collection, MSS 212, Phillips Library, Peabody Essex Museum, Salem MA.

investment our long-range guns destroyed much property." (This would have meant the 4.5-inchers firing from 10 August on.) Bull observed that "the railroad depot and shops and all buildings housing Confederate supplies as well as places where they manufactured ordnance stores were burned by the enemy when they evacuated the city. The ruins still smoked."

Regiments and brigades of Slocum's corps continued to march in for the next several days. Having started out from its lines in the afternoon of 2 September, the 3rd Wisconsin reached downtown around 10 o'clock that night after a brisk march that had the troops "swetting pretty freely," according to William Wallace of Company E. Coming up before a downtown hotel, the Wisconsans hailed a group of spectators. "One of the boys asked them what they had to eat lately," Wallace recorded; "the reply was: 20 pound parrott shells." Major John Higgins's 143rd New York Infantry got its marching orders on 3 September, proudly tramping through the city before going into camp northeast of it, manning the former Rebel entrenchments. Other regiments of the XX corps came into town on 4 September. Even when they could not be the first to enter, Federal units made a grand showing of their presence. Lieutenant Colonel Edward S. Salomon, 82nd Illinois, related the march of his regiment on 4 September: "To the great gratification of the soldiers we marched through the conquered city, with colors flying and bands playing, and occupied the works erected by our enemies, and from behind which they had sent so many deadly missiles into our ranks."[16]

One regiment's itinerary will tell the tale of many. Around noon on that Friday, 2 September, officers of the 154th New York, positioned at Pace's Ferry on the Chattahoochee, got their orders to march. By twilight, the New Yorkers

---

[16] Williams's report, 12 September 1864, *OR*, vol. 38, pt. 2, p. 35; report of Col. Ezra A. Carman, 6 September, *OR*, vol. 38, pt. 2, p. 72; K. Jack Bauer, ed., *Soldiering: The Civil War Diary of Rice C. Bull, 123rd New York Volunteer Infantry* (San Rafael CA: Presidio Press, 1978) 168; Holzhueter, ed., "William Wallace's Letters," 108; report of Maj. John Higgins, 15 September, *OR*, vol. 38, pt. 2, p. 108; report of Lt. Col. Edward S. Salomon, 15 September, *OR*, vol. 38, pt. 2, p. 101.

Anecdote of Northern troops entering Atlanta comes from a column printed in the *Atlanta Constitution* of 20 July 1898, during the 8th Annual Reunion of the United Confederate Veterans held in the city. One E. G. Stephens, former captain in the 13th Iowa, wrote to the newspaper before the reunion, enclosing a daguerreotype of a young infant he had picked up in the streets of Atlanta on 3 September 1864, when he and his regiment were marching into the city. On its back was written, "My little Sallie." He had kept it until, in 1898, knowing Confederate veterans were gathering in Atlanta, he sent it to the newspaper, asking for an inquiry as to its owner. The *Constitution* obediently had the photo rendered into a pen-and-ink sketch, published the drawing, related Captain Stephens' story, and asked if any of the returning veterans could claim the picture and so confirm paternal ties to its subject. There is no record that anyone did ("Photograph of 'Little Sallie' Found in Atlanta in September, 1864," *Atlanta Constitution*, 20 July 1898).

were passing through the Rebels' abandoned fortifications. Later, with the band of Geary's 2nd Division playing "Battle Cry of Freedom," the regiment marched through the center of the city. Some of Atlanta's secret Unionists waved their handkerchiefs in happy appreciation of their arrival. The regiment pitched camp that night a few blocks south of city hall. The next morning it marched through the Fairgrounds to the old Rebel works southeast of the city. On 4 September, the New Yorkers marched a half mile west, and settled in near the McDonough Road. They laid out their camp with streets, stripped a barn for timber to use in building huts, and roofed them with their tents. Second Brigade commander Colonel George Mindil moved into the fine brick home of James Ormond, on Washington Street south of the city limits. Other officers occupied houses left behind by their pro-Confederate owners. Commissary Sergeant Marcellus Darling and two other officers, for instance, enjoyed sleeping in a four-poster bed, storing their uniforms in an armoire, and reading novels from the owners' library.

Once in Atlanta, Union soldiers were thrilled at the sight of their hard-earned accomplishment. "When we reached Atlanta, we were of course in the best of spirits and marched through with great cheering," recorded New Yorker Sergeant Bull in his diary entry of Friday, 2 September. Though they were entering an arch-Rebel city, Federals noticed some Atlantans giving them a warm welcome. Brigadier General Alpheus Williams was leading a column of his division into the city on the night of 2 September when "I heard a window shoved up and a female voice cry out, 'Welcome!' I cried back, 'Thank you, and the more so as it is a rare sound down here.'" One Federal, George W. Baker of the 123rd New York, wrote home on 3 September about the "great many northern people" in Atlanta who greeted the entering Union troops. "The main body of the inhabitants are well pleased with our entry into their City," he told his mother. "As our Brigade entered the city," wrote a member of the 3rd Wisconsin, the 2nd Massachusetts band played "The Star-Spangled Banner" and "at about nine o'clock at night, many of the women brought out buckets of water for us to drink."

One of the civilians enjoying the sight of blue uniforms was Cyrena Stone, who stood on a street corner for several hours, waving a silk United States flag that she had stashed away for this very event. Some women welcomed the Yankees out of relief that the Southern soldiers who had robbed them were now gone. Captain Julian Hinkley of the 3rd Wisconsin recorded that the women "were very bitter against Hood's army, which they said had robbed them of everything that could be carried off." Others heard the same things—cries of joyous welcome, curses of the Rebel army. "Nickajack," writing for the *New York Times* on 3 September, noticed that "there are number of people here, real Yankees," who had been employed in Atlanta's factories and shops; he predicted that their Unionism, long suppressed, would soon come out. On the other hand, "Nickajack" was a little suspicious of some citizens who "assert with all due vigor their Union sentiments." The welcoming faces of folk on the sidewalk seemed "not quite earnest." Nevertheless he and the troops were glad to see anything approaching hospitality, "as we hope it will result in a complete return to the fold" of Unionist loyalty. After all, he charitably conceded, "they are only backsliders."

Some Northern soldiers kept a lookout for the black folk they expected to see in Atlanta. Captain Alfred Hough of the 19th US Infantry remembered that riding into the city he had found "but very few able bodied young men and what there were had been working in the Govt shops a good many foreigners, many poor people, and some of the upper class, but no negroes except old ones." Other Federals saw African Americans lining the sidewalks to hail their liberation. "Very few white people were in sight, but lots of Negroes watched us as we marched along," observed one. "To the best of our ability we sang, 'We will hang Jeff Davis on a sour apple tree.'" "The negroes…hailed our men as their deliverers sent of God," wrote a soldier of the 33rd Massachusetts. "'Bress de Lord,' they shouted…, 'de Yanks am come, yah! yah! yah!'"[17]

The soldiers were struck by the damage they saw in the city from their shellfire. "Many of the buildings were found to be much injured by our artillery," wrote Colonel Coburn, whose troops entered Atlanta around noon of 2 September. The next day, Union General Geary wrote home to his wife, "There is scarcely a house that does not exhibit in some degree the effects of the battle which so fearfully raged around it. Many of the best are utterly ruined, and many of the ornamental trees are cut down by our shells." A Connecticut infantryman noted in his diary on 2 September, "the whole city perforated with our shells." After a more extended walk about town a few days later, he added, "terrible destruction by shot and shell everywhere." Lieutenant George Baker of the 123rd New York observed, "on one side of the City most every house had a shell through it and some were completely riddled." He also commented on the shell-casualties: "a great good many inoffensive ones were killed as Hood never gave orders for the noncombatants to remove and they curse Hood beyond all

---

[17] Dunkelman, *Marching with Sherman*, 19–20, 24–25; Bauer, ed., *Soldiering*, 167; Milo M. Quaife, ed., *From the Cannon's Mouth: The Civil War Letters of General Alpheus S. Williams* (Detroit: Wayne State University Press, 1959) 341; Jack H. Lepa, *Breaking the Confederacy: The Georgia and Tennessee Campaigns of 1864* (Jefferson NC: McFarland & Co., 2005) 129 (Baker letter, 3 September); Edwin F. Bryant, *History of the Third Regiment Wisconsin Veteran Volunteer Infantry* (Madison: Veteran Association of the Regiment, 1891) 269; Kennett, *Marching through Georgia*, 200 (Sweetland to wife), 206 (Campbell's remark on houses as pigeon coops); Dyer, *Secret Yankees*, 193–94 (Cyrena Stone); Julian Wisner Hinkley, *Narrative of Service with the Third Wisconsin Infantry* (Madison: Wisconsin History Commission, 1912) 141–42; "Nickajack," "Occupation of the City" (Atlanta, 3 September), *New York Times*, 19 September; Robert G. Athearn, ed., *Soldier in the West: The Civil War Letters of Alfred Lacy Hough* (Philadelphia: University of Pennsylvania Press, 1957) 213–14; Underwood, *Thirty-Third Mass. Infantry Regiment*, 233.

account." (Here we see Northerners' evasion of responsibility for civilian deaths in the bombardment, already evident, come full circle: it was Hood who was responsible for the killing, not Sherman.)

Lieutenant Henry D. Stanley marched into the city with the 20th Connecticut on 4 September. The next day he recorded in his diary what he had seen.

> A few houses stood between the two lines and were perfectly riddled with balls and shell. They looked for all the world like a high coal screen. As we passed into the town the damage done by our shell became more and more apparent and some very fine residences were completely torn down by them. It seemed a pity to destroy so much property but they would not give up the city until it was ruined and they are to blame for the damage. Marietta Street suffered the most being in direct range, and every house *but one* was hit more or less times. That *one* was of brick a very fine building though the houses near it had been ruined. Strange to say not a shot had struck that. Of course no one lived in that part of the City. It would have been almost certain death. Some buildings had one side completely torn off by the bursting of a shell inside, others were destitute of a chimney, and all were without windows and had holes in them *every where*. As we proceeded into the city, the damage grew less as that part was more out of range than the rest or that part on Decatur St. only two or three buildings were burned but they were very large and valuable. We passed the Trout House in good style and came to that portion of the city which had been considered safe. The houses were most of them small and reminded one of the houses one sees so often in New England, though they did not have that comfortable cozy and inviting look that those do.

Private James Snell of the 52nd Illinois observed that the Federals' artillery fire "did great damage to the place, riddling and tearing down houses, and burning others to the ground. Marietta Street plainly showed the damage done by Welker's guns," a reference to Captain Frederick Welker, commanding artillery of Corse's division, XVI Corps. "The west, north-west, and north portions of the city were found to have been very much injured by our shells and solid shot," observed a member of the 73rd Illinois. After a walk along Marietta Street and its vicinity, an officer of the regiment entered into his diary, "the portion of the city we passed through was badly injured by shot and shell; some of the houses having as high as twenty holes through them." Captain Julian Hinkley of the 3rd Wisconsin wrote that "the effects of the Union bombardment could everywhere be seen in the city. Almost every house had the marks on it of shot and shell. One man showed me a dozen shells that had struck it in his garden." Allen Campbell, a Michigander, saw so many holes in residences, he wrote home that "it now looks as if each house was a pigeon coop." "But such houses!" exclaimed Sergeant George Cram of the 105th Illinois in a letter to home, "each one riddled and torn by our shells, here a tall chimney knocked down and there a portico carried away." Henry Neer, whose 25th Michigan Regiment was encamped outside of the city near Decatur, ambled around with his comrades on 13 September for hours: "The city shows rather a ragged appearance and many a sign of yankee artillery practice."

Benjamin C. Truman, a reporter for the *New York Times* travelling with Sherman's armies, estimated that 2/3 of the houses in the city had been hit by shells, and of these many were "demolished or burned." David Conyngham, correspondent for the *New York Herald,* had accompanied Sherman's army throughout the campaign (winning a captaincy on the staff of General Schofield). Conyngham entered the city soon after its fall and observed the shell damage.

> The city had suffered much from our projectiles. Several houses had been burned, and several fallen down. In some places the streets were blocked up with the rubbish. The suburbs were in ruins, and few houses escaped without being perforated.... Some shells had passed through the Trout House Hotel, kicking up a regular muss among beds and tables. One woman pointed out to me where a shell dashed through her house as she was sitting down to dinner. It upset the table and things, passed through the house, and killed her neighbor in the next house.

Of course, various observers will always see things differently. Examples are the conflicting views of Corporal Eli S. Richer, 102nd Illinois, and Colonel Emerson Opdycke, 125th Ohio. Corporal Richer wrote that "Atlanta has been a beautiful place. It is now invested with the desolation of a grave-yard. A large number of citizens are still there, but the west side is almost entirely deserted. Not a building in that portion of the city can be pointed out but what is more or less riddled and torn with shell." Colonel Opdycke saw things otherwise, perhaps based on different parts of the city he had observed. He and Brigadier General Luther Bradley, commander of the 3rd Brigade, 2nd Division, IV Corps, went out for a ride through town on 9 September; he agreed that Atlanta was "a beautiful city." But unlike others who emphasized the shell-shattered buildings, Opdycke contended that the Federal bombardment "did but little damage." "Many of the buildings have been perforated but a shot or shell will cut a neat hole through a brick wall, without doing much harm."[18]

---

[18] Coburn's report, 12 September 1864, *OR,* vol. 38, pt. 2, p. 393; Geary to wife, 3 September, Blair, ed., *A Politician Goes to War,* 199; Marvin, *Fifth Regiment Connecticut Volunteers,* 335–36; Taylor, *Orlando M. Poe,* 180 (Baker letter, 3 September); Henry D. Stanley, diary, 5 September, MSS 645, Atlanta History Center; Snell, diary, 9 September, Illinois Historical Society; William Henry Newlin, comp., *A History of the Seventy-Third Regiment of Illinois Infantry Volunteers* (Springfield IL: Regimental Reunion Association, 1890) 362, 366; Hinkley, *Third Wisconsin Infantry,* 142; Kennett, *Marching through Georgia,* 206

Other soldiers had to wait a few days more to get their tour of the city. Captain Ira Read of the 101st Ohio wrote his aunt about marching into the city on 8 September. "I wish you could see how our shot and shell have torn the houses to pieces," he described. "On some streets in the more exposed portions of town there is scarcely a house that is not riddled by the shell." Major Charles B. Loop (95th Illinois, XVII Corps) described to his wife what he saw in his visit downtown of 11 September: "the North Western portion of the city is very much torn to pieces by our shells. I traveled at least half a mile on one street when not a single building had escaped and many of them perforated like a honey comb while others were litterly torn to fragments by the bursting of the warlike missles: take it all in all Atlanta has had a taste of War that it will not soon forget and it will carry scars that will not be obliterated for generations to come." Alva Sinks of the 71st Ohio also saw the damage on the northside, as he wrote his father on 20 September: "The city is very large and many are the magnificent dwelling houses in it but the Major part of the Houses on the north side of the city are completely Riddled with shot & shell." Captain Thomas Speed wrote his parents on 13 September that Atlanta, "once a perfect gem of a city...is...now a ruin and desolation." It had become "a city of deserted houses and nothing more," representing "the very climax of what folly and war will accomplish." Dr. James C. Patten, assistant surgeon of the 58th Indiana, drew a lesson from the shell damage he witnessed in Atlanta. "I had often heard of the terrors of a bombardment of a crowded city but I never realized it before," he wrote. "Houses were shattered and torn in every shape that can be imagined, some utterly destroyed and some but little injured. Some had shells through the doors, some places the shells had burst inside of a house and torn it all to pieces." To Doctor Patten, the sight of what Atlantans had endured seemed to explain the "insane fury" of Rebel soldiers' fierce charges in battle. "I would not for a great deal have missed that ride through Atlanta. It almost paid me for the whole campaign."

The Federals occupying the city, of course, could not know how many Atlantans had been killed by their bombardment. Sergeant Newton Chaffee of the 154th New York wrote home on 13 September that he had heard of 200 women and children killed in the shelling. At the same time, the Yankees were

(Campbell's remark on houses as pigeon coops); Jennifer Cain Bohrnstedt, ed., *Soldiering with Sherman: Civil War Letters of George F. Cram* (DeKalb IL: Northern Illinois University Press, 2000) 147; Henry Neer, diary, 13 September, University of Michigan (copy courtesy of Albert Castel, Columbus OH); B. C. Truman, "Atlanta. How the City Was Captured" (Atlanta, 4 September), *New York Times,* 15 September; Conyngham, *Sherman's March through the South,* 218–19; Edward G. Longacre, ed., "From Atlanta to the Sea: The Civil War Letters of Corporal Eli S. Richer, 1862–1865," 146 (typescript courtesy of Dr. Castel); Glenn V. Longacre and John E. Haas, eds., *To Battle for God and the Right: The Civil War Letterbooks of Emerson Opdycke* (Urbana: University of Illinois Press, 2003) 223.

also curious about the dugout bombproofs that had protected so many Atlantans during the bombardment. Captain Alfred Hough wrote home to Mary on 18 September: "Almost every house has what we call a 'gopher hole' attached to it.... Many of these have been nicely fixed up with furniture and stores in them. The one in my yard has bunks fixed along the sides and is very comfortable." Lieutenant Edwin Weller of the 107th New York said the same: "it was quite a curiosity to visit those caves soon after we occupied the city and see with what taste and comfort they had arranged them for living in." Some garden bombproofs he saw were not only furnished, but floored and carpeted. "Almost every garden and yard around the city had its cave," observed Captain Conyngham. "They were sunk down with a winding entrance to them, so that pieces of shells could not go in. When dug deep enough, boards were placed on the top, and the earth piled upon them in a conical shape, and deep enough to withstand even a shell. Some of these caves, or bomb-proofs, were fifteen feet deep, and well covered." Some civilians, perhaps without homes of their own, dug their shelters not in backyards, but in railway culverts. Illinois Sergeant Cram noticed that "along each side of the railroad were holes in the bank where families had crawled in to escape our iron showers." Ohio Captain George W. Pepper also noticed the "gopher holes" dug into embankments alongside the railroads in town. "These holes were large enough, in many instances, for a fire-place or a stove, a table and beds," he recalled.[19]

Other Federals ranged farther out into the suburbs. William Wallace of the 3rd Wisconsin observed that "all the houses around the suberbs is clean gone and torn down by the rebels to make shelters for themselves." General Williams rode the entire perimeter of the enemy fortifications (correctly judging them to be at least 10 miles in circumference) and got a good look at them, close up and from the inside. Counting at places fully three and four lines of chevaux-de-frise and abatis, Williams concluded, "it seems fortunate that we did not attempt a direct attack." Private Laforest Dunham of the 129th Illinois agreed: "They had

---

[19] Harwell, ed., "Campaign from Chattanooga to Atlanta," 276 (Captain Read's letter); Frank Crawford, ed., "Your Charlie" (Letters of Maj. Charles Loop), *Civil War Times Illustrated* 31/6 (January–February 1993): 66, 68; Alva Sinks to "Father," 20 September 1864, MSS 732, Georgia Historical Society, Savannah (my thanks to Dr. Todd Groce, president, for pointing me to the Sinks letter, as well as to other sources in the Georgia Historical Society's abundant Civil War archives); Thomas Speed to "Parents," 13 September, Speed letterbook, Filson Club, Louisville KY (copy courtesy of Dr. Albert Castel); Robert G. Athearn, ed., "An Indiana Doctor Marches With Sherman: The Diary of James Comfort Patten," *Indiana Magazine of History* 49/4 (December 1953): 408, 410; Dunkelman, *Marching with Sherman*, 29; Athearn, ed., *Soldier in the West*, 213; Larry M. Strayer and Richard A. Baumgartner, eds., *Echoes of Battle: The Atlanta Campaign* (Huntington WV: Blue Acorn Press, 1991) 321 (on Weller); Conyngham, *Sherman's March Through Georgia*, 219; Bohrnstedt, ed., *Soldiering with Sherman*, 147; George W. Pepper, *Personal Recollections of Sherman's Campaigns in Georgia and the Carolinas* (Zanesville OH: Hugh Dunne, 1866) 171.

awful strong works. It would have ben impossible to have charged them and taken them." With something of an engineer's eye, Dunham observed how any Union infantry attack that breached the Rebel line might have ultimately failed: "even if we had taken them we could not have held them for they are in such shape that they would have had cross fire on ous from all directions." Sergeant John Wilkens of the 33rd Indiana went further after looking over the Confederate fortifications. "We had not the least idea of their being so strong," he wrote his sister on 5 September. "To think of charging them would be the idea of a lunatic." To make his point he drew a cross-section diagram of the Rebel line: abatis out front, then a line of palisades, rifle pits, two more palisades going up the slope, chevaux-de-frise, a huge pit 15 feet deep, and more palisades, topped by an artillery fort. "If you see how men could go over as many obstacles as these while under the continual fire of the enemies guns you can do better than I can."

Northern press correspondents added their impressions of the city, as did this reporter for the *Chattanooga Gazette,* whose story was posted from Marietta on 4 September.

Atlanta presents a frightful spectacle of dilapidation and the horrors of war. I traversed the dirty streets for two hours, noticing the deserted houses that had been perforated by our artillery. On the west side a dozen buildings, I suppose, had been fired by hot shot from our batteries and entirely consumed. The northern portion of the city, against which most of our guns were directed, tells a fearful tale; a story which is, however, very complimentary to Yankee artillerists. The walls of the buildings have been nearly razed to the ground, and what was once a magnificent stone front structure at the head of Peachtree street, is now the terror of a few remaining urchins, who tremble to approach it, for it is but a towering ruin, which threatens every moment to come down with a crash.

Writing from Atlanta on 5 September, "Huguenot" of the *New York Times* commented on all the round shot and unexploded shells that lay in the city's streets and cellars. But the Union cannonade had done its work. "The central portion of the city, located on Whitehall street, and about the depot, is very much destroyed by shells," he wrote. "Huguenot" could even tell from the damaged buildings that most of the shells had come from General Thomas's line north of town. Another *New York Times* correspondent, "Nickajack," noticed that among the downtown businesses pocked by Northern shells was one bearing the sign "Auction Sales of Negroes." "Nickajack" imagined that the Union cannon striking the offending building "was but uttering the condemnation of God and the civilized world, against the diabolical traffic." "It was like a thunderbolt from Heaven," he judged, "speaking for humanity, and carrying destruction to the accursed tenement wherein the dearest rights of man have often been violated."

In his column for the *Cincinnati Commercial*, Captain Joseph Miller observed, "hardly a house in Atlanta has escaped damage from the shells which, for over a month, have been hurled at it.... The majority of the roofs in the city are torn, and the walls scarred.... In the room where I slept last evening, the wall was garnished with a ragged orifice, made by a fragment of a shell, and in the adjoining apartment was a chair, partially demolished by the same irate messenger." Sergeant Rufus Mead recorded in his diary, 5 September, "got a pass & rode around town in the afternoon.... Found desolation on every hand all over town." In a letter home a few days later, Mead added details:

> I have been around the city somewhat and the destruction in the Northern & eastern portions is astonishing I knew our batteries threw over enormous quantity of shells but I couldnt think they were so effective.... The Macon Depot is in the centre of the city and has been a good target for all our batteries I should judge by the way things are splintered up. A large round house capable of holding 40 locomotives with a turntable in the centre is fairly riddled both by shells passing through and also by bursting inside, while wooden buildings near by are splintered ties slivered and rails broken by them. Shade trees a foot through are cut off. fences broken down in short every kind of mischief is done by those iron missiles.

Mead observed the ruins of the rolling mill east of town; "when the rebs left the mill was burnt in the general conflagration." At the site of the rolling mill, William Wallace of the 3rd Wisconsin saw "steam boilers, fly wheels, great piles of iron in various stages of manufacture," but of the mill building itself, only the chimneys stood. Illinois private Dunham also saw the wreckage, and saw "lots of plateing for gun boats that they could not get off"—evidence as much of the Confederacy's overtaxed railroad system as of Atlanta's industrial capacity.[20]

Captain Read of the 101st Ohio was amazed by the sight of the wreckage of the Rebels' ordnance train. "The most interesting sight," he wrote after a walk through the city, "is where they blew up the 81 carloads of ammunition. What a

---

[20] Holzhueter, ed., "William Wallace's Letters," 108–10; Quaife, *From the Cannon's Mouth,* 344; Arthur H. DeRosier, Jr., ed., *Through the South with a Union Soldier* (Johnson City TN: East Tennessee State University Research Advisory Council, 1969) 149–50 (Laforest Dunham to Mr. and Mrs. Simeon H. Dunham, 17 September 1864 ["They had awful strong works"; "never was a nice place"] and 22–23 September ["lots of plateing" and "an awful sight of propity"]); John A. Wilkens to sister, 5 September 1864, Wilkens Collection, Indiana Historical Society (copy courtesy of Dr. Albert Castel); "Letter from a Marietta correspondent of the Chattanooga Gazette," *Atlanta Intelligencer,* 18 September; "Huguenot," "Inside View of Atlanta" (Atlanta, 5 September), *New York Times,* 16 September; "Nickajack," "Occupation of the City," *New York Times,* 19 September; Moore, ed., *Rebellion Record,* 11:document 283 ("J.W.M.," "September 2," printed in the *Cincinnati Commercial,* 13 September); Mead, diary, 5 September, Rufus Mead, Jr. Papers, Library of Congress; Padgett, ed., "With Sherman through Georgia and the Carolinas," 310–11 (Mead to parents, 8 September).

scene! Load after load of shell and pieces of shell thickly strewing the grounds." "The locomotives were badly battered, and one of them thrown from the track; all of the woodwork was burned off the car-wheels," recorded W. H. Newlin of the 73rd Illinois; "the wheels were standing on a tieless track, surrounded by broken shells, huge solid shot, some one hundred-pounders, grape-shot, canister, and all manner or kind of ammunition used." Wisconsan Wallace was also struck by the scene. Burned cars, "all in ashes except the iron," showed evidence that some had been loaded with leather harnesses, but most often ammunition, "from a 100 pound shell to a rifle ball." The heat of the explosions had been so intense that Minie balls had melted. "Lead from melted bullets had settled in depressions and cooled in masses a foot in thickness," observed an Indianan. "It was very pleasant to see ammunition used this way by the rebels which had been intended for our destruction." Grape and canister "lay around the track like wheat around a threshing machine." Wallace saw also the big pond into which the Rebels had thrown whole boxes of artillery shells. He wrote home on 22 September "when they left heare they distroid an awful sight of propity. They had any amount of guns and ammunition of all kinds that they could not get away so they burnt it up."

Private Snell from Illinois recorded in his diary entry of 9 September similar impressions of the ordnance train wreckage. Snell apparently talked with citizens living in the city's eastern edges, and heard of casualties from the ammunition train.

> Many of the people were hurt during the progress of the seige, and by the explosion of the trains of ammunition, of which they were entirely ignorant, until the explosion occured. The noise was that of an earth-quake, and many of the people tumbled out of bed and rushed out in terror and confusion, thinking some great convulsion of nature was upon them. Those who were living near the railroad, where the cars stood on the track, were the worst sufferers—some lost their lives, and many were wounded. One lady had both legs taken off above the knees; another received severe wound in the side, from a fragment of a shell, other pieces of which killed a child, and crippled a man, in the same house.
>
> The cars were a complete wreck—nothing was left of them but the iron wheels, and many of them were broken by the explosion, or bent by the heat. The ammunition kept exploding all night, as fast as the flames reached the shell—scattering the bolts and timbers of the cars, along with the iron missiles, a long distance away.

Private Snell raises the possibility that the explosions of the Rolling Mill and ordnance train on the east side of the city may have caused more civilian casualties in Atlanta on the night 1 September. No confirmation, however, has come to light.

Some of the Yankees ambulating through the city were impressed by its overall appearance. An officer of the 2nd Massachusetts, Captain John Fox, gave a favorable report in a letter home: "Atlanta is a very pretty town, covering a large area and having the appearance of about half city and half country. It is more like [a] New England place than any place I have seen south. It is clean— the people stand well as far as education, wealth, and refinement go." Others did not take such favorable notice. "I suppose the city is a little larger than Jeffersonville, Ind.," sniffed Indianan John Wilkens in a letter home on 5 September; "there is not much taste displayed in their buildings." Another Hoosier, Doctor Patten of the 58th Indiana, thought Atlanta about the size of Evansville in his home state. Private Dunham, whose regiment marched into town on 17 September, wrote to his parents, "it is not as nice a city as I expected to find it. Our shells have riddled it considerable, but after all it never was a nice place." Similarly, Corporal Charles E. Smith of the 32nd Ohio recorded in his diary, "I was disappointed." At least Smith acknowledged that the Union artillery may have had something to do with it. "Instead of seeing a beautiful and handsome city, I saw a desolate cluster of houses, some of which were shattered with cannon shot. Others had been burned." Like Wilkens and Patten, Captain Poe, Sherman's chief engineer, could also not help but express some chauvinism in his letter to his wife, 7 September: "Atlanta is quite a town—is about the size of Dayton Ohio. It has something of the tumbledown look of all Southern towns, but still there are some fine residences, and more evidences of thrift than are usually met with south of Mason's & Dixon's line." Poe, too, observed the Northern shell damage, but only briefly: "The city, in some localities has been a good deal injured by our shot, and I learn that several women & children were killed."[21]

While most of the XX Corps marched out to their respective posts along the old Rebel line of works, general and staff officers chose finer places inside the city for quarters. General Slocum first took his rooms at the Trout House; despite its several shell perforations, the four-story brick hotel was still billed as the best in town (although *Commercial* reporter Miller found it to be "in no means in

---

[21] Harwell, ed., "Campaign from Chattanooga to Atlanta," 276; Newlin, *Seventy-Third Illinois*, 357; Samuel Merrill, *The Seventieth Indiana Volunteer Infantry* (Indianapolis: Bowen-Merrill Co., 1887) 167 ("lead from melted bullets"); Snell, diary, 9 September 1864, Illinois Historical Society; John A. Fox to "My Dear William," 15 September, copy courtesy of Wiley Sword, Suwanee GA, from original in his possession; Athearn, ed., "An Indiana Doctor," 410; George R. Cryder and Stanley R. Miller, comps., *A View from the Ranks: The Civil War Diaries of Corporal Charles E. Smith* (Delaware OH: Delaware County Historical Society, 1999) 442–43; Poe to "wife," 7 September, box 2, O. M. Poe Papers, Library of Congress.

thorough running order"). General Geary also checked into the Trout, as did other officers of the XX Corps, at least at first. General Thomas directed Slocum on 3 September to "permit no one to take quarters" among the city's private homes until authorized by General Sherman or himself. By 8 September, according to an Illinois soldier marching past it with his regiment, the Trout House was already being seen as "a loafing-place for '*Yankees*.'" Within a week, however, the Trout and any other city hotel trying to operate were shut down, in keeping with the commanding general's orders that there be no commerce in the city. Captain Thomas Speed rode in from Nashville on 11 September to assume duties with the army. Upon arrival in Atlanta he quickly found there was no hotel open; "I in company with 5 or six officers lugged my baggage into a large deserted store room, and slept until the sun waked me up."

High-ranking officers deserved better than a hotel (certainly a storeroom). On the first night of the Federals' occupation, 2 September, Lieutenant Colonel William Le Duc and several other Union officers took rooms "in the house of Judge Lyon," which evidently had civilian occupants. Le Duc had set up his desk downstairs when he heard singing and piano in the parlor; a lady was playing "Maryland, My Maryland," a favorite air among Confederates. Le Duc admonished the woman not to play the song. "I did not wish to sing it," the lady snapped; "your officers here insisted upon it!" Le Duc counseled them: "Gentlemen, you should have been more thoughtful. You know our troops are marching by this place, and, hearing a song like that, might throw a missile through the window endangering the lady's life." The music ended.

Post commander Cogswell and provost marshal Morse scouted downtown for choice residences to house the army's brass. Among his picks was "The Terraces," Edward E. Rawson's spacious home five blocks south of city hall, built upon a terraced hill. Conifers and topiary surrounded the estate, which occupied a full city block. On the morning of 3 September, as Mary Rawson recorded in her diary, "the provost marshal and several other officers" came knocking on her father's door, seeking permission to accommodate a general within the home. "This request Father told him it was impossible to comply with for where could we find another home of any kind," she wrote. The Rawsons won as the Federals backed down. "They finally gave up the idea of taking it from us and seemed much pleased with our old school house instead."[22]

---

[22] Moore, ed., *Rebellion Record,* 11:documents 282–83 ("J.W.M.," "September 2"); William D. Whipple to Slocum, 3 September 1864, *OR*, vol. 38, pt. 5, p. 781; Newlin, *Seventy-Third Illinois Infantry*, 356; Speed to parents, 13 September, Speed letterbook, Filson Club, Louisville, Kentucky; William G. Le Duc, *Recollections of a Civil War Quartermaster: The Autobiography of William G. Le Duc* (St. Paul MN: North Central Publishing Co., 1963) 127–28; Garrett, *Atlanta and Environs*, 1:431 (on "The Terraces"); Mary Rawson, diary, 3 September 1864, box 2, folder 4, Rawson-Collier-Harris Family Collection, MSS 36, Atlanta History Center.

On 4 September, Sherman was still near Lovejoy's Station, 25 miles south of Atlanta, with the bulk of the army group. He told General Halleck that he intended to stay a few days more "for effect" (meaning, so as not to give Hood the impression that he needed to hurry his several infantry corps into the safety of Atlanta's Rebel-built defenses), "and then will fall back and occupy Atlanta, giving my command some rest." Sherman finally arrived in Atlanta late on 7 September. It was obvious to all that the general was to be housed in one of Atlanta's finest houses, and engineer Captain Poe had personally selected it. On the southwest corner of Washington and Mitchell Streets, across from city hall, rose the two-and-a-half story home of the wealthy planter and merchant John Neal (the house in which Captain Le Duc had lodged on the night of 2 September). Fronted with Corinthian columns and mounted by a cupola with stained glass windows, the Neal home was one of the showcase residences of Atlanta. Better yet, toward the southside rather than the north, the Neal house had suffered little Federal shell damage. (Lieutenant Andy Neal, one of the homeowner's sons, had visited his family home in August and found it had only been struck twice by Yankee shells, once through the parlor, the other in his brother's bedroom.) Finally, best of all, the owners were gone. Earlier Neal had taken his family out of town for safer parts, selling his house to one Judge Richard Lyon of Albany. But Lyon never took possession, and did not even make good on his note. (Poe and Sherman nevertheless called the place "Judge Lyon's house.") Before his departure, Neal had arranged for James Mayson to move his girls' academy into the home, so as to keep it safer. Even the furnishings were in good order; prior to the Yankees' arrival, Mayson had the best part of the Neals' furniture stored into the parlor. A story circulated in the North that Sherman personally met with Mrs. Lyon, telling her that he wanted to occupy her house. As reported in the *New York Times*, the general added that "if she would leave her furniture he would take care of it and see that she got it all back." Of course, this interview could not have occurred, as neither Judge Lyon nor his wife was in Atlanta at the time. The story, though, conveyed a sense of Sherman's kindliness as well as his sternness; he "advised her not to stay at Griffin, Macon, Milledgeville or Augusta, as his army would soon hold those places, and subject her to further annoyance." Without occupants—neither Neals nor Lyons—the fine house on Washington Street was ready for General Sherman to move in.[23]

---

[23] Sherman to Halleck, 4 September 1864, *OR*, vol. 38, pt. 5, p. 792; to George W. Tyler, 7 September ("I am now writing in Atlanta"), *OR*, vol. 38, pt. 5, p. 822; Poe, diary, 7 September 1864 (on selecting the Neal house for Sherman), box 12, Poe Papers, Library of Congress; Garrett, *Atlanta and Environs*, 1:638–39 (on Neal house); Elinor Hillyer, "New City Hall Where Sherman Made Headquarters," *Atlanta Journal Magazine*, 4 September 1927, 11; Neal to "Ella," 4 August, Andrew Jackson Neal Letters, Emory University (also quoted in Samuel Carter III, *The Siege of Atlanta, 1864* [New York: St. Martin's Press, 1973] 275); "The Enemy in Atlanta," *Atlanta Intelligencer*, 15 September ("Sherman occupies as

Other prominent homes were occupied by Union officers. General Thomas moved into the Austin Leyden house, a large two-story edifice on the west side of Peachtree between Ellis and Cain (where Hood had spent a few days in July). During the bombardment, a Union shell had entered a front room but not exploded; damage to the structure was therefore slight. As with Edward Rawson's home, Union officers were apparently unsuccessful in their initial efforts to gain access. Major Leyden was in Virginia, serving with the artillery of Lee's army; his wife and daughter were the only occupants. Two generations after the war, the *Atlanta Constitution* told the story of when the Yankees arrived at the doorstep.

> It is said that Mrs. Leyden defied the federal officers to cross her threshold, and that she repelled them at their first sally; but that they returned, and by diplomacy and persistence gained entrance. Whereupon, it is said, Mrs. Leyden, in high dudgeon, bundled up her little daughter, Estelle, and departed with the baby and a basket of biscuits, finding her old negro coachman waiting for her at an appointed place near town with a rig and a team of black horses. So she refugeed in Athens, leaving the invaders in sole possession of the shot-battered house which their own guns had served to make uncomfortable.

General Slocum took up quarters at the two-story, yellow stucco house of Needom Angier—banker, insurance agent, and Union sympathizer—on Washington Street across from both city hall and the Neal home. Northern loyalists, of course, had an easier time giving up their homes to Federal lodgers than steel magnolias like Mrs. Leyden. Besides, the presence of a high-ranking boarder assured greater protection of the premises. When Lewis Scofield wrote Cogswell's provost marshal, Lieutenant Colonel Morse, seeking guarantee that his home on Peachtree would be protected, he offered it for government use— but asked that he and his family be allowed to stay on their property. Perhaps they did, but soon enough they were sharing it with Major General David Stanley.

Thanks to Northern photographer George N. Barnard, under employ of Captain Poe and the US army engineers, we have visual evidence of just how much Federal officers enjoyed their accommodations in Atlanta. Barnard, then at

---

Army Headquarters, Judge Lyon's house"); "This House Used by Gen. Sherman," *Atlanta Constitution,* 20 July 1898; "Southern News," *New York Times,* 2 October.

The Neal house is pictured as "Major-General Sherman's Headquarters, Atlanta" in *Frank Leslie's Illustrated Newspaper,* 29 October 1864. The same engraving was used by John Neal's granddaughter, Ella May Thornton, in a greeting card that she inscribed with verse: "My mother's home when the sky rained bullets. / And nothing was safe, from gold to pullets. / Come then the terror that whitened the hair, / With Sherman ensconced in my grandfather's chair" (*Atlanta Historical Society Newsletter,* December 1988).

Nashville, had been summoned to Atlanta by Poe on 4 September to photograph the Rebel works around the city as a complement to his reports. The photographer and his equipment were packed and on the train by 11 September, arriving in Atlanta a few days later. In the next two months, Barnard took over a hundred pictures of the city, the Union troops occupying it and the fortifications around it. An example is the view of Colonel Henry Barnum and his staff in front of the Windsor Smith house on Whitehall. Mindful that the place had once served as HQ for the Rebel commander, Barnum had the front of the house draped with a huge US flag.

When objecting Atlantans were "asked" to give up their homes to Union officers, tensions ran high. Mary Rawson recorded such an incident in her diary entry of 6 September.

> While we were at breakfast this morning Grand-father came and told us that Aunty had been ordered to leave her beautiful home to give place to a *Yankee colonel* who had given her only half a day to move all her property. O cruel soldier! Could you not be a little more lenient? Could you not allow her one day for this work? I concluded I would go with Father…. I found Miss Delia indignant at the thought of being driven from home. O she said I would not live among them and if I had had any idea of their coming I would have gone ere this. I went…to see Grand-ma. The house was all in confusion, occasioned by the bringing of Auntys furniture. Then I went to Auntys to see if I could not render some assistance and by constant running to and fro we succeeded in getting most of her valuables removed. But all this time the officers were there dictating as to what should be carried away and what should remain and continually repeating the injunction of haste, haste, forgetting that haste makes waste. Tongue cannot express her trouble in leaving she has no home to go to elsewhere.[24]

---

[24] "Here Are Some Last Farewell Views of the Old Leyden House," Michael Rose, *Atlanta: A Portrait of the Civil War* (Charleston SC: Arcadia Publishing, 1999) 113 (George N. Barnard photograph of Leyden house with Federal guards); Wilbur Kurtz, notebook 10, 64 (on Angier home), Wilbur G. Kurtz Collection, Atlanta History Center; Dyer, *Secret Yankees*, 197 (Scofield's request to stay in home); Keith F. Davis, *George N. Barnard: Photographer of Sherman's Campaign* (Kansas City MO: Hallmark Cards, Inc., 1990) 77–78; photograph, "Col. Henry A. Barnum and staff on front porch of the Windsor Smith house," Atlanta History Center Visual Arts, image 874 (also in Wilbur G. Kurtz Collection, box 55, folder 12, Atlanta History Center); Rawson, diary, 6 September 1864, Atlanta History Center.

Michael Rose, formerly director of archives and research services and now executive vice president of the Atlanta History Center, has studied Barnard's photographs closely. The picture of Barnum and officers on the Windsor porch demonstrates his observation that Barnard photographs keep surfacing; to my knowledge this one has not been published. Another view shows the same officers in the Smith house yard; in the

On 6 September, Lieutenant Colonel Morse recorded that he had established offices in city hall, "and quarters in an elegant house near by," the William Solomon residence, across Mitchell Street from City Hall Park. Morse shared the place with Colonel Cogswell, the post commandant. Morse called it "one of the finest houses of the city, opposite our camp, —Brussells carpet, elegant beds and other furniture." Morse added that "the family were very glad to have us occupy the house for their own protection"; the head of the household, William Solomon, was "a fine old man: he is seventy-two years old and in poor health." Other officers also got good places to stay. Lieutenant Colonel Willard Warner, inspector general of Thomas's army, got a big two-story domicile on the west side of Peachtree Street. For his quarters, Captain Orlando Poe selected for himself the home of Marcus Aurelius (Mark) Bell, the famed Calico House at the corner of Wheat and Collins. He occupied the place from 3 September to 10 November—virtually the first day of the Union army's occupation to the time when Poe began directing the destruction of the city's railroad complex before Sherman's army moved out toward Savannah.[25]

Captain John A. Fox, adjutant of the 2nd Massachusetts, wrote home on 15 September about the nice place he had cadged downtown: "We are lodging in a very elegant house that would have cost $30,000 North in peace times. The parlor has a $1,000 grand piano. We sleep on beds of down under mosquito nets, etc. In short, we are making up for lost time. The family consists of an old gentleman and his wife, a son about sixteen years old, and a very stunning little daughter of thirteen, whose winning ways make me wish I were ten years younger." One Federal soldier, Corporal Harvey Reid, wrote that he had found for himself a "small but not ill looking dwelling house" in southeast Atlanta. Sleeping among cotton sheets, waking to breakfast actually served on white china plates, with the

---

background is the white star pennant of Geary's division (Kirk Denkler, ed., *Voices of the Civil War: Atlanta* [Alexandria VA: Time-Life Books, 1995] 140). A woodcut of "Headquarters of the Rebel General Hood, now occupied by Col. H. A. Barnum, 3rd Brigade, 2nd Division, is in *Frank Leslie's Illustrated Newspaper,* 29 October 1864. Mary Rawson's "Aunt Delia" was Mrs. Sidney Root, whose house on South Collins Street is pictured in Frank J. Byrne, "Rebellion and Retail: A Tale of Two Merchants in Confederate Atlanta," *Georgia Historical Quarterly* 79/1 (Spring 1995): 54.

[25] Morse, *Letters,* 187–89; George Barnard photographs, "Inspector General's Office, Dept. & Army of the Cumberland, Atlanta, with groups of officers and soldiers," #90 and "The 'Calico House', Atlanta. Office of the Chief Engineer, Military Divn. Of the Mississippi," #95 as captioned in "List of War Photographs in the Collection of O.M.Poe," typescript, US Military Academy, West Point NY.

The Poe Collection list, a typewritten inventory of over 250 Barnard images taken in Nashville, Chattanooga, Atlanta, Savannah, and Charleston, is indispensable for identifying Barnard's photographs, which are now scattered among many repositories, chiefly the Military Academy and the Library of Congress. I am indebted to Keith Davis of Kansas City for a copy of it.

table covered in clean linen and himself seated in a fine cane chair, Reid pronounced the end of the campaign a gratifying one. Yet the taking of residents' houses did not always work out. Brigadier General Alpheus S. Williams, commanding Slocum's 1st Division, moved into a "very imposing-looking house" on the night of 2 September. After four months in the field, he was looking forward to a good night's sleep in "a very large room with a broad bed and white counterpane." But the room was stuffy and—worse—bedbugs "worked on me from head to foot." Sleeping on the ground during the campaign, he had never encountered such torment from the "wood-ticks, jiggers, and other festering biters that fill every atom of the dirt of this section." General Williams looked forward to pitching his tent in the yard.[26]

Once settled into the city, Federals noticed more of the civilians still in it. In his column on the fall of the city, John E. Hayes, special correspondent for the *New York Tribune*, cited Mayor Calhoun as source that perhaps 2,000–3,000 men, women and children remained as residents. Among these he had personally observed a number of foreigners, and more blacks than he had seen through North Georgia. Union soldiers quickly learned that a number of people in Atlanta harbored Unionist loyalties. An officer of the 73rd Illinois, Captain Kyger, recorded in his diary the story of Luther Faught, a Maine native who had come to Atlanta in 1857 and had become foreman in the Winship foundry. Walking about the city, Kyger came upon Faught's home at Marietta and Spring: "We observed many holes through the front of the house, which had been made by our shot and shell." Northern cannonballs notwithstanding, Faught seems to have kept his Unionist faith, claiming that he had tricked the Rebels when they ordered out the city's munitions works, and that he had saved the Winship machinery for Federal use. Faught even asserted, "it is now running for the

---

[26] Fox to William, 15 September, Wiley Sword personal collection, Suwanee GA; Frank L. Byrne, ed., *Uncommon Soldiers: Harvey Reid and the 22nd Wisconsin March with Sherman* (Knoxville: University of Tennessee Press, 2001) 185; Quaife, ed., *From the Cannon's Mouth,* 342.

Federal officers' occupation of many Atlanta residences gave rise to good stories, some of which are documentable. After Captain Grant, the Confederate engineer, left with Hood's army, his wife stayed in the city as long as she could. In mid-September she was forced to leave in Sherman's mass expulsion of the citizenry. The Grant house, an imposing two-story brick and stucco just outside the city limits, survived the Federal occupation, it was said, because Northern soldiers found inside an apron with the Masonic emblem (Rawson, diary, entry of 13 September 1864 [on Mrs. Grant "in a great deal of anxiety not knowing where to go], Atlanta History Center); William G. Le Duc, "Official account of the people sent south, their numbers and luggage, under Special Field Order No. 67, issued by Major-General W.T. Sherman, Atlanta Georgia, September 4, 1864," in *Memoirs of Gen. W.T. Sherman,* 2 vols., 4th ed. [New York: Charles L. Webster & Co., 1891] 2:552 [Mrs. L. Grant registering on 18 September for transport out of the city]; "Colonel Grant's Historic Home, Atlanta Battle Survivor, Sold," *Atlanta Journal,* 8 June 1941).

'*Yankees*'"—an ingratiatingly tall claim indeed, given the Confederates' evacuation of the city's war munitions apparatus in July, and the depopulation of the work force during the bombardment.

From the time they entered Atlanta, Federal authorities had wanted to identify those individuals of the remaining civilian population who could be counted upon as loyal. The task was made difficult when citizens, doubtless hoping for favored treatment at the hands of the city's new occupiers, said what they thought the Yankees would want to hear. Mayor Calhoun himself led the way, as Captain Henry Comey of the 2nd Massachusetts recorded in a letter of 3 September. "Today I dined with the Mayor of the city, a nephew of John C. Calhoun," Comey wrote; the mayor said that he "has always been opposed to seceding." Mayor Calhoun went on to tell the captain that in the presidential contest of 1860 he had opposed the Southern-rights Democrat, Breckinridge, to the point that he had been "one of the delegates in 1860...to the Bell and Everett Convention," a reference to the Constitutional Union Party convention that nominated the compromise candidates, John Bell of Tennessee and Edward Everett of Massachusetts. The captain was impressed, adding that among the townspeople, "many represent a strong Union sentiment, which I should think might be true, judging from appearances."

Other Federals made similar judgments. Within a day of the Union occupation, Lieutenant Colonel William Le Duc, quartermaster of the XX Corps, had met William Markham, whom he quickly recognized as a "loyal man." William Armor, another officer, walked parts of the city to "learn who were Union & who were not." Sometimes the encounters were accidental. The chaplain for a Union regiment came upon David Young, a minister and pharmacist who had been a friend of Atlanta's black community, and hence was judged as loyal. One Mary Wilkens presented herself to Colonel Le Duc, and told him how she had taken in a Northern spy in 1863, only to have her house hit repeatedly by Union shells; she was herself severely wounded by a fragment to her shoulder. Le Duc was obviously impressed by her sincerity, wrote it down at length, and sent it to General Sherman as an appeal for leniency. The commanding general complied, as Le Duc recorded, and "made good the loss of her house by our shells, and helped her in other ways."

Not surprisingly, skeptical Northern soldiers found some citizens' profession of Unionism a little hard to take. An Indianan wrote home that "the citizens were very glad to see us," noting that they were "mostly foreigners and not wishing to have anything to do with the war." He concluded, "of course we could not consider them as union men." Another Hoosier, Dr. Robert Bence of the 33rd Indiana, wrote home on 8 September that of the people he had met "all pretended to be loyal now," causing him to assert that he had "no faith in the Unionism of one fourth of them." Indianan Magnus Brucker, assistant for the 23rd Indiana, wrote to his wife on 18 September how he and his comrades were encountering multiple cases of instant and shallow conversion. "Hundreds of rebels come daily to our lines and declare that they were forced to fight against their old Union, in which they lived happily and had no complaints." Now, Brucker chuckled, "they are all cured of their deceit and recognize their wrong."

A case in point was that of John Boutelle and his family. He had formerly lived in New York state and could thus claim ties to the North. His wife Hannah Winship Boutelle asserted that she and her husband were Unionists, and that she and her daughters had fed and nursed wounded Federal prisoners of war. Dr. Henry Van Aernan, surgeon of the 154th New York, was unimpressed, as there was counter-evidence: that Boutelle had helped his brothers-in-law, the Winships, manufacture shot and shell for the Rebels; that as architect he helped build Atlanta's fortifications; and that his wife and daughters had assisted ailing Rebels, not Yankees, in the city's hospitals. Doctor Van Aernan thus had solid grounds to doubt the Boutelles' loyalty to the Union. With some satisfaction, he wrote home on 9 September, noting that the Boutelle house at Collins and Ellis Streets had been struck by multiple shells, and two family members had been wounded by fragments. The Boutelles, Van Aernan judged, "are pretty low now."

Eventually Federal officers hit upon a process for identifying loyalists that seemed to work well: a panel of verifiable Union men—Markham, James Dunning, and Thomas Crusselle—sat in judgment of all who wished to be regarded as loyal, and certified their truthfulness. At the same time, Northern soldiers occupying Atlanta had their own means of measuring residents' loyalties. Rufus Mead was pitching his tent in the yard of one family and on 4 September expressed his contentment in a letter home:

Now you'll find me in the S.E. part of town, or nearly out of it, under my 'fly,' in the dooryard of a good Union family.... I have made the acquaintance of the whole family even to the dog, who now lies in one corner of the tent as contented as can be, in fact he is a thorough going Union dog. The children are playing around as happy as any children can be, while the whole family appear as cheerful as any family I have seen, quite a contrast to the generality of the citizens we have met hitherto.[27]

---

[27] "From Our Special Correspondent," "Fall of Atlanta" (Atlanta, 4 September), *New York Tribune,* 15 September; J. Cutler Andrews, *The North Reports the Civil War* (Pittsburgh: University of Pittsburgh Press, 1955) 560 (on Hayes of the *New York Tribune*); Newlin, *Seventy-Third Illinois,* 365; Comey, ed., *Legacy of Valor,* 194–95; Dyer, *Secret Yankees,* 191–92 (Bence and Brucker), 194–96 (including Kyger's conversation with Luther Faught), 202; 358n39; Wilkens to sister, 5 September 1864, Indiana Historical Society; Dunkelman, *Marching with Sherman,* 22, 30; Padgett, ed., "With Sherman through Georgia and the Carolinas," 309 (Rufus Mead letter).

Despite its improbability, Faught's claim to have saved the Winship machinery for the Union cause made its way into the press. A correspondent of the *Chattanooga Gazette,* writing from Atlanta on 6 September, recorded that the plant machinery, somehow not

Thus in the first few days of the Federal occupation there grew a feeling of comity among Northern soldiers and many Atlanta civilians. John Hayes, the *New York Tribune* correspondent in the city, wrote on 4 September that the several thousand inhabitants were evidently committed to getting along with "Uncle Sam." Even those not avowedly Unionist took cue from Mayor Calhoun that the invaders must somehow be accommodated. The Yankees' maintenance of law and order and respect for private property impressed, if not surprised, many citizens. Once Cogswell and Morse got their administration in place, provost guards in the city looked out against theft and ruffian behavior toward civilians. Captain Julian Hinkley of the 3rd Wisconsin recalled how people in the city "were agreeably disappointed to find that the Yankees did not rob them of a thing." Those Atlantans "fortunate" enough to have Union officers boarding at their homes had an added measure of security. Even the *Macon Telegraph* had to comment, "refugees report general kind personal treatment from General Sherman and his officers. Whatever exceptions may have occurred, have been in violation of orders—instances of individual pilfering, which cannot always be prevented in an army, and in many cases have been detected and punished." In such an atmosphere of wary optimism, General Sherman's announcement that he intended to expel all civilians from the city came as a thunderbolt.

Even before he arrived in Atlanta, Sherman had decided what he would do with the people still living there: expel them. On 3 September, from Lovejoy's, he issued instructions to General Slocum, then settled in at the Trout House: all confiscated cotton was to be sent north to Nashville. Good buildings in the city were to be seized for the army's use, but not as quarters until so specified. Then came the real punch: "Advise the people to quit now. There can be no trade or commerce now until the war is over. Let Union families go to the North with their effects, and secesh families move on."

Sherman amplified his instructions in Special Field Orders 67, issued under date of 4 September: "The City of Atlanta being exclusively required for warlike purposes, will at once be vacated by all except the Armies of the United States and such civilian employees as may be retained by the proper Departments of Government." That day Sherman explained his purposes to General Halleck in Washington: "I propose to remove all the inhabitants of Atlanta, sending those committed to our cause to the rear, and the rebel families to the front." He would allow "no trade, manufactories, nor any citizens there at all." He was prepared for a popular outcry of protest. "If the people raise a howl against my barbarity and cruelty," he concluded, "I will answer that war is war, and not popularity seeking. If they want peace they and their relatives must stop war."

Sherman's purposes were both punitive and practical. First, in Union-occupied Atlanta, there would be no business activity, no way for civilians to

evacuated, "was left in complete running order.... This will be of considerable value and importance to the present occupants of the city" (*Atlanta Intelligencer,* 2 October).

290

earn a living. To enforce the fact, Southerners' principal cash crop, cotton, would be seized as US property; Sherman made a point of stressing that "all cotton is tainted with treason, and no title in it will be respected." Depriving people of their livelihood was only the first step in Sherman's tough plan; thrown out of work, next they would be thrown out of their houses. Expelling people from their homes would create massive psychological trauma for those affected and, when publicized, for all Southerners fearful of the same consequences at the hands of Yankee conquerors. Here Sherman was calculatedly cruel: he intended to remind the Southern populace of the hardships they would continue to suffer until they stopped fighting and begged for peace. But it would not only be the Rebels and secesh to suffer, as Northern sympathizers would be ejected from the city, too. This harshness to Atlanta's "secret Yankees," who had endured years of anxiety, fear, sometimes stigma and actual punishment, reflected another of Sherman's purposes: he wanted no responsibility for the well-being of any civilians, even the loyal Unionists. They could go north with their property, but they would go, same as the traitorous Rebels.

Finally, it became evident that Sherman planned to occupy Atlanta for quite a while, at least a month, and he wanted no noncombatant hangers-on. "I am not willing to have Atlanta encumbered by the families of our enemies," Sherman wrote Halleck on 9th: "I want it a pure Gibraltar, and will have it so by the 1st of October." In orders issued on 4 September, the commanding general laid out what lay ahead for his three armies, beginning with the occupation of Atlanta and its vicinity: Thomas's Army of the Cumberland would be stationed in and around the city proper, Howard's Army of the Tennessee at East Point, and Schofield's Army of the Ohio at Decatur. The officers and men would enjoy "a full month's rest," while they refitted and replenished clothing and so on. Then would come preparations for "a fine winter's campaign," details of which were not divulged. Sherman did not fear attack by Hood's army, which was then well south of Atlanta. The Rebels were too weak and without a supply base; Sherman's army group, far stronger numerically, now enjoyed the security of the very fortifications that the Rebels had themselves built.[28]

---

[28] "Fall of Atlanta," *New York Tribune,* 15 September 1864; Hinkley, *Third Wisconsin Infantry,* 142; "From Atlanta," *Macon Telegraph,* 17 September; Sherman to Slocum, 3 September, *OR,* vol. 38, pt. 5, p. 778; "Special Field Order 67. In the Field, Atlanta, Ga., September 4, 1864," printed broadside in Cogswell Collection, Peabody Essex Museum, Salem MA; Sherman to Halleck, 4 September, *OR,* vol. 38, pt. 5, p. 794, and 9 September, *OR,* ser. 2, vol. 7, p. 791; Special Field Order 64, 4 September, *OR,* vol. 38, pt. 5, p. 801 (on general quartering areas for the three armies, and "a fine winter's campaign").

There is a discrepancy in the dating of Sherman's Special Field Order 67. Usual citation is to *OR,* vol. 38, pt. 5, p. 837, which carries the date of 8 September. The Atlanta History Center has a handwritten, penciled copy of Special Field Order 67, clearly dated 8 September and signed by Sherman (it is at the time of this writing on display at the center's "The War in Our Backyards" exhibit). On the other hand, Lieutenant Colonel Le Duc's list

Thus situated, Sherman lost no time in implementing his new administrative policies. On 5 September, post commander Cogswell distributed printed circulars throughout the city, announcing what was in store for the populace.

> All families living in Atlanta, the male representatives of which are in the service of the Confederate States, or who have gone south, will leave the city within five days. They will be passed through the lines and will go south.
>
> All citizens from the North, not connected with the army, and who have not authority from Major-General Sherman, or Major-General Thomas to remain in the city, will leave within the time above mentioned. If found within the city after that date, they will be imprisoned.
>
> All male residents of this city, who do not register their names with the city Provost Marshal within five days and receive authority to remain here, will be imprisoned.

News of this magnitude registered slowly among people in disbelief. On the evening of 5 September, as recorded in her diary, young Mary Rawson noted that a family friend came in and announced that "Gen. Sherman had ordered all ladies whose husbands in 'Rebel service,' as he said, to leave the city in five days." The next day Mary family weighed the shocking news:

> We could be sent farther down in Dixey or we could attempt the ice and snow of the Northern winter. Father did not think the report at all reliable, but went to the provost marshal to inquire but on reaching the office the door was closed; and a notice was tacked on the door, saying

---

of citizens expelled, cited above, dates Special Field Order 67 as 4 September. Further, a printed broadside of the order over the name of "L.M.Dayton, Aide-de-Camp," is in Colonel Cogswell's papers at the Peabody Essex Museum and is unmistakably dated 4 September. Moreover, the *Atlanta Intelligencer* was able to print SFO 67, also clearly dated 4 September ("Sherman's Order of Exile," *Atlanta Intelligencer*, 15 September). The conflicting dates can be explained by this set of assumptions: that Sherman, near Jonesboro on the 4th, was in communication with Slocum by courier, and sent these orders; that they were printed in Atlanta by Federal staff officers, who carried a small printing press for this kind of document to be circulated; that in Sherman's absence the order was printed over the name of Capt. Lewis M. Dayton, Sherman's aide-de-camp. We can further surmise that SFOs were not official till signed by the commanding general. We know Sherman arrived in Atlanta late on 7 September ("I am now writing in Atlanta, [OR, vol. 38, pt. 5, p. 822]; "I am just this moment in" [vol. 39, pt. 2, p. 346]). Hence we can assume that he signed another copy of SFO 67 on 8 September, and that official version is the one in the *Official Records*. My thanks go to Rick Vespucci of the Atlanta History Center for helping me to resolve this problem.

that no-one would be admitted until the next day, he then called on Gen. Geary and asked him concerning the order but he had heard nothing of it so wearied out by walking and anxiety he returned home without any cheering news.

To better inform the populace, Lieutenant Colonel Morse issued on 6 September a broadside, giving everyone instructions on what they were to do in the coming days.

> I. All citizens who are to go South, in compliance with General Orders No. 3, Post Headquarters, will assemble in the Park of the City Hall at 9 A.M., September12, 1864. They will be allowed to take with them only the necessary wearing apparel, sufficient household furniture for their actual comfort, and subsistence enough to last them till they arrive inside the lines of the rebel army.
>
> II. All citizens to go North under same order, will apply at once at this office for passes. They will take with them only what they brought here.[29]

Like other Atlantans, the Rawsons were plunged into turmoil by the Northern army's proclamations. Having obtained no information at Colonel Morse's headquarters and having gotten none too from General Geary, on the morning of 7 September Edward Rawson made his way to Slocum's headquarters at Needom Angier's, then back to Cogswell's and Morse's offices.

---

[29] Cogswell's General Orders, 5 September 1864, and Morse's Notice, 6 September, are printed in "Sherman's Third Order of Exile," *Atlanta Intelligencer,* 18 September; Mary Rawson, diary, 6 September, Atlanta History Center.

Historians have not noticed that the Federals' eviction orders of 5 and 6 September were published in Confederate newspapers. For local awareness of them once again we are indebted to the conscientious research and note-taking of Wilbur G. Kurtz, who in the 1930s transcribed Cogswell's expulsion order of 5 September and Morse's notice of 6 September "from the original circulars in possession of a neighbor of mine" (notebook 12, 38–39, Wilbur G. Kurtz Collection, Atlanta History Center). The circulars do not appear in the *Official Records.* Kurtz quotes Cogswell's and Morse's eviction orders of 5–6 September in his article, "'Leave Atlanta Within Five Days,'" *Atlanta Journal Magazine,* 12 October 1941, 1. His wife Annie Laurie Fuller Kurtz also quotes them in full in her "Surrender of Atlanta—Evacuation of Its Citizens," *Atlanta Journal Magazine,* 12 January 1936.

Cogswell's General Order 3 is fully quoted in G. S. Bradley, *The Star Corps; or Notes of an Army Chaplain, during Sherman's Famous "March to the Sea"* (Milwaukee: Jermain and Brightman, 1865) 166. Lee Kennett's *Marching through Georgia* (1995) is the first scholarly history to quote the expulsion order of 5 September (p. 207), although he does not note his source. Russell S. Bonds also quotes the expulsion order (citing Bradley's *Star Corps*) in *War Like the Thunderbolt: The Battle and Burning of Atlanta* (Yardley PA: Westholme Publishing, 2009) 314.

There he evidently got one of the handbills that the provost marshal had printed up, announcing the planned expulsion of the people, for around noon he was able to read it to the family. Rawson worked hard to seek some kind of exemption from the order. Mary recorded that her father during the morning had again talked with General Geary and other Federal officers; from them he had gotten the impression that the expulsion orders pertained only "to those men who had in some way been in the Confederate service and that all others could remain quietly in their home." Such hopefulness, however, was soon shattered, as Mary recorded in her diary on Thursday, 8 September: "The order compelling all persons to evacuate the city was today plainly written out; we could not misunderstand it." In all likelihood the "plainly written order" was the notice that Mayor Calhoun had printed and distributed in the city, as he sought to add the force of his office to what everyone recognized was a miserable but unalterable situation.

Major-General Sherman instructs me to say to you that you must all leave Atlanta; that as many of you as want to go North can do so, and that as many as want to go South can do so, and that all can take with them their movable property, servants included, if they want to go, but that no force is to be used, and that he will furnish transportation for persons and property as far as Rough and Ready, from whence it is expected General Hood will assist in carrying it on. Like transportation will be furnished for people and property going North, and it is required that all things contemplated by this notice will be carried into execution as soon as possible.

All persons are requested to leave their names and number in their families with the undersigned as early as possible, that estimates may be made of the quantity of transportation required.

Another version of the mayor's announcement may have circulated, one that specified how African Americans still in the city would be treated in the planned expulsion. According to a text printed in the *Louisville Journal* on 14 September, Mayor Calhoun stated that "Negroes who wish to do so may go with their masters. Other male negroes will be put in Government employ. Negro women and children will be sent out of the lines." Additional information was at hand as well; Mary Rawson recorded that northbound Atlantans would apparently be given more time to make their arrangements: "All those whose husbands were in the service were to leave on Monday [12 September], while the remainder were given fifteen days to pack and leave." The Rawsons now knew they were going to have to leave; their only decision was whether it would be to the north or to the south. (They had friends and relatives in Southwest Georgia.) They ended up heading for Iowa.[30]

It was on 8 September, too, that the Berry household got confirmation of the Yankees' expulsion orders. The morning had started brightly enough, according to young Carrie in her diary. She was helping her mother with the ironing "when Papa came and told us that Gen. Sherman had ordered us to move. It broke all into our rangements." Of course it did; in fact, for the next several days the only topic Carrie wrote about was the prospect of her family being kicked out of their house.

> Fri. Sept. 9 We all commenced this morning for moving. We don't know how long we will get to stay here. We are all in so much trouble.
>
> Sat. Sept. 10. Every one I see seems sad. The citizens all think it is the most cruel thing to drive us from our home but I think it would be so funny to move. Mama seems so troubled she can't do any thing. Papa says he don't know where on earth to go.
>
> Sun. Sept. 11. We all have been trying to rest to day and feel contented. Mama went over to Aunt Healy this evening and she felt as sad as we.

Samuel Richards was another Atlantan trying to sort through the Yankees' instructions. He entered into his diary on 9 September: "We have had several days of great excitement, as it was understood that 'orders' had been, or were about to be, issued to the effect that *every* body not belonging to the army must leave the city going North or South as they saw fit, except the families of those men who had left the city before the Yankees came, and such *must go South*."[31]

The Federals at the time did not know how many civilians were then in or about the city, and thus could not gauge what kind of exodus General Sherman had ordered. John Hayes, the reporter for the *New York Tribune*, on 4 September cited Mayor Calhoun as his source for a guess of 2,000–3,000 people left. Two days later, however, another *Tribune* correspondent, "D.B.," guessed "about six thousand are here now." If so, this larger number might have included African Americans who, formerly enslaved but now suddenly freed by their masters' quick exodus, had logically wandered into the city held by their emancipators. Adding to the uncertainty, authorities did not know how many would opt to go south or go north. As announced in Lieutenant Colonel Morse's notice of 6 September, those going north would need a pass, and Morse's provost office was

---

[30] Rawson, diary, 6–8 September 1864, Atlanta History Center; Mayor Calhoun, notice, 8 September, *OR*, vol. 38, pt. 5, p. 838; "From Atlanta," *New York Times*, 16 September, reprinting from the *Louisville Journal*, 14 September.

[31] Carrie Berry, diary, 9–11 September 1864, Atlanta History Center; Venet, ed., *Sam Richards's Civil War Diary*, 235–36 (entry of 9 September).

soon overwhelmed with applicants. There was a second step to the process, as well, that applied to Atlantans deciding to go south into General Hood's lines: to secure help in transporting their possessions, one had to apply for a permit with the XX Corps chief quartermaster Lieutenant Colonel William Le Duc. Le Duc had entered the city on 2 September and spent a few nights at the Neal house until giving it over to the commanding general. He then moved into Richard Peters's fine residence at Mitchell and Forsyth Streets, and from its porch issued papers to applicants after the expulsion order went out. Le Duc performed his duties efficiently, although he did not agree with Sherman's order. When Charles Ewing, the general's aide, brought it to Le Duc, the latter said flatly, "Charley, tell Cump Sherman from me that this order won't read well in history." Le Duc later recorded the exchange.

> "All right," he answered, "I'll tell him, but it won't make any difference."
> "I know that, but I want him to know how others look at it."
> I saw Ewing again in the afternoon. "Did you tell Cump?"
> "Yes, and he said, 'You tell Bill Duc I care not a damn how others read it—I am making the history, and the citizens of this rebel town shan't eat the rations I need for my army. Tell him to turn them out."

And they would be turned out. Those heading south were to be transferred through the opposing armies' lines; Hood's forces were then around Lovejoy's Station, 25 miles south of Atlanta. To secure the Rebels' cooperation in the civilian exodus, on 7 September Sherman wrote Hood, stating his intentions. "I have deemed it to the interest of the United States that the citizens now residing in Atlanta should remove, those who prefer it to go South, and the rest North." He would provide food and transport to those northbound; he would help everyone else with the moving of their possessions "by cars...and also wagons" as far as Rough and Ready (by rail, 14 miles south of Atlanta; today the place is called Mountain View), where he proposed that Southern officers receive them under a truce, which could be arranged for a couple of days. Sherman asked Mayor Calhoun to choose two citizens for the delivery of his letter to the Rebels' headquarters (they would be James R. Crew, former city councilman, and James M. Ball, another civic leader).

Up to this point Hood had no inkling of the hubbub in Atlanta created by Sherman's expulsion order. Rather innocently on 8 September, he proposed an exchange of prisoners. (There were plenty of them at Andersonville, about to be removed to other camps at Millen, Georgia; Florence, South Carolina; or elsewhere.) Sherman got Hood's written offer that evening and quickly agreed, but only up to a point; he capped the exchange at 1800 or 2000 men, which was the number of Rebel POWs he had in Atlanta or in transit to Chattanooga.[32]

These crossing letters—Sherman to Hood, 7 September, on the expulsion of civilians, and Hood to Sherman, 8 September, on the exchange of prisoners— began two weeks of sometimes sharply worded correspondence between the two generals on both topics, totaling sixteen missives. The Hood-Sherman epistolary dueling of September 1864 adds a further measure of drama to the chronicle of the Atlanta Campaign, such that the five letters on the subject of the expulsion merit some detail.

Hood's reply to Sherman's announcement, 9 September. The pen duel started when, late on 8 September, Hood received Sherman's announcement of the forced expulsion of Atlanta's populace. He was outraged, and expressed his feeling in a reply of 9 September. "The unprecedented measure you propose transcends in studied and ingenious cruelty, all acts ever before brought to my attention in the dark history of war," Hood wrote. "In the name of God and humanity, I protest, believing that you will find that you are expelling from their homes and firesides the wives and children of a brave people." At the same time, Hood faced reality and conceded that he had no choice but to cooperate. He therefore agreed to have an officer at the Rough and Ready rail station available on 12 September to begin receiving the exiles. Hood also sent word to Mayor Calhoun, which would have been borne back to the city by Messrs. Crew and Ball: "I shall do all in my power to mitigate the terrible hardships and misery that must be brought upon your people by the extraordinary order of the Federal commander."

The language of indignation ("unprecedented measure"; "transcends in cruelty") allows for hyperbole, which Hood sought to employ in his letter of protest. Actually, Sherman's expulsion of Atlanta's civilians was not at all unprecedented. Nor did Sherman's order transcend earlier population expulsions in the Civil War; two earlier measures probably forced more noncombatants to leave their homes.

The first of these involved the people of New Orleans. After the city's fall in spring 1862, Major General Benjamin F. Butler ordered all civilians to take an oath of allegiance to the United States (or, for foreigners, a sworn oath of

---

[32] "Fall of Atlanta," *New York Tribune*, 15 September 1864; "D.B.," "How Atlanta Looks" (Atlanta, 6 September), *New York Tribune*, 19 September; Le Duc, *Recollections of a Civil War Quartermaster*, 127–29; Sherman to Hood, 7 September, *OR*, vol. 38, pt. 5, p. 822 (announcing the citizens' expulsion; also in vol. 39, pt. 2, pp. 414–15); Garrett, *Atlanta and Environs*, 1:104 (on Rough and Ready as today's Mountain View); Annie Laurie Fuller Kurtz, "Atlanta's Envoys to Sherman," *Atlanta Journal Magazine*, 7 January 1934 (particularly on Crew); Hood to Sherman and Sherman to Hood, 8 September, *OR*, ser. 2, vol. 7, p. 784; and Sherman to Halleck, 9 September, *OR*, vol. 38, pt. 5, p. 839 (on the exchange of prisoners).

neutrality). Within several months, all but some 4,000 individuals had taken the oaths; those who refused became "registered enemies." In spring 1863, Butler—reviled locally as "the Beast"—ordered these disloyalist New Orleanians to leave the city, but Major General Nathaniel Banks, who succeeded him as commander of New Orleans at that time cancelled the order. Banks then reversed himself and ordered all these "enemies" banished from the city. Those civilians who still refused to swear their loyalty were thus forced to leave; many made their way to Mobile. Thus, in the words of Mary Elizabeth Massey, authority on Civil War refugees, Banks won "the distinction of banishing from a single city more noncombatants than did any other Federal officer." Massey, however, does not number the people expelled from New Orleans, assumed to be several thousand. As we shall see, the people expelled from Atlanta by General Sherman also approached several thousand, but no precise number (especially of those who travelled north from the city) has been determined. This numerical uncertainty allows Massey to make the same claim for Sherman as she did for Banks: at Atlanta, Sherman "secured for himself the unique distinction of having been responsible for the single largest forced evacuation of an entire city during the Civil War."

Massey's terminology is important: "single city" places Nathaniel P. Banks at New Orleans and William T. Sherman at Atlanta in the same category. In a different one, for *multiple counties* instead of a single city, the largest forced depopulation of an area during the American Civil War was brought about by Union brigadier general Thomas Ewing's Order No. 11. In August 1863, Ewing sought to combat guerrilla operations in western Missouri by ordering all inhabitants of three counties, both loyal and disloyal, off their land within fifteen days. An estimated 20,000 people were affected by the order, but as in New Orleans and Atlanta, there is no exact count of the unfortunate folk actually forced from their fireplaces. Most scholars assume all 20,000—the prewar populations of Jackson, Bates, and Cass counties—were evacuated, but some people were allowed to stay; Ann Davis Niepman notes that perhaps 600 persons in Cass County remained of some 9,800 counted in the census of 1860. Nevertheless, Albert Castel rightly concludes that Ewing's expulsion order "was the most drastic and repressive military measure directed against civilians by the Union Army during the Civil War." Thomas Goodrich concurs, terming Ewing's General Order No. 11 "perhaps the harshest act of the U.S. government against its own people in American history."[33]

---

[33] Hood to Sherman, 9 September 1864, *OR*, vol. 39, pt. 2, p. 415; "From Atlanta," *New York Times,* 16 September, reprinting from the *Louisville Journal* of 14 September (Hood to Mayor Calhoun, undated); John D. Winters, *The Civil War in Louisiana* (Baton Rouge: Louisiana State University Press, 1963) 136; Mary Elizabeth Massey, *Refugee Life in the Confederacy* (Baton Rouge: Louisiana State University, 1964) 8, 209–10; Ann Davis Niepman, "General Order 11 and Border Warfare During the Civil War," *Missouri Historical Review*

The prisoner exchange: correspondence of 7–29 September. As the two generals corresponded over the expulsion issue in early September, they also discussed an exchange of prisoners; in this correspondence they managed to conduct themselves considerably more calmly than on the former subject. On 9 September, Sherman explained that he counted 1,810 officers and men as prisoners whom he would exchange, but stipulated that he would only accept in return Union soldiers of regiments in his army "who can resume their places at once"; he would not take any soldiers from the forces of Grant in Virginia, Canby in Alabama, etc. He suggested Rough and Ready as a point of exchange, the same area for the passage of city residents into the Southern lines. Eventually, as result of eleven letters over a period of three weeks, 2,600 US and CS prisoners were exchanged at Rough and Ready between 19 and 30 September: 1,128 Federals and 1,332 Confederates. The two sides observed the rules that had been arranged by exchange cartels earlier in the war (e.g., one colonel for fifteen privates, a captain for six, a sergeant for two, etc.), so that the number of "equivalents" totaled 2,047 CS privates and 2,045 US privates (for example, Confederate Brigadier General Daniel C. Govan counted for twenty privates when he was exchanged). The commanding generals even worked through a few side issues. To Sherman's insistence that he only receive US POWs who could be immediately returned to regiments in his army, Hood went along after initial objections. And Sherman kept to his word. Lieutenant Colonel Willard Warner, the Federal officer in charge of the exchange, even turned away 132 US soldiers who had been captured by Forrest in Mississippi and who did not belong to Sherman's armies; these unfortunates were taken back to Andersonville. In turn, Hood declined Sherman's offer of an exchange of close to a thousand noncombatant workingmen whom Sherman claimed to have apprehended in his occupation of Atlanta. "By your laws all men eligible for service are ipso facto soldiers," Sherman wrote, "they seem to have been detailed for railroad and shop duty.... I am satisfied they are fit subjects for exchange, and if you will

---

66/2 (January 1972): 205; Albert Castel, "Order No. 11 and the Civil War on the Border," *Missouri Historical Review* 57/4 (July 1963): 357; Charles R. Mink, "General Order 11: The Forced Evacuation of Civilians during the Civil War," *Military Affairs* 34/4 (December 1970): 132–36; Michael Fellman, *Inside War: The Guerrilla Conflict in Missouri during the American Civil War* (New York: Oxford University Press, 1989) 95; Thomas Goodrich, *Black Flag: Guerrilla Warfare on the Western Border, 1861–1865* (Bloomington: Indiana University Press, 1995) 100.

Hood's message to Calhoun ("I shall do all in my power to mitigate") does not appear in the *Official Records,* nor have I seen it printed elsewhere; it is also not in the mayor's papers at the Atlanta History Center (MSS 50, box 1). Nevertheless, it is plausible that Hood sent such a note, as Crew and Ball were carrying his reply to Sherman back to Calhoun. Moreover, the *Louisville Journal,* which published the note to the mayor, also included in its column of 14 September correctly quoted excerpts of Sherman's Special Field Order 67, 4 September, and Hood's letter to Sherman of 9 September.

release an equal number of our poor fellows at Anderson I will gather these together and send them as prisoners." Hood could not take them, however, without documentation of their alleged exemption from the army, so they were not made part of the exchange. The fate of these civilian men remains uncertain; it is plausible that they were sent away in the same manner that Sherman had earlier banished the female textile factory workers from New Manchester and Roswell, Georgia, sending them north by railroad.[34]

---

[34] The Hood-Sherman correspondence on POW exchange is in *OR,* ser. 2, vol. 7, pp. 784, 791–92; 799, 808, 822, 852, 858, 883, 891. Reports from the officers in charge of the exchange at Rough and Ready are in *OR,* ser. 2, vol. 7, pp. 851–52 (Confederate Lt. Col. Gustavus A. Henry, 20 September), and pp. 907–908 (Federal Lt. Col. Willard Warner, 1 October). On officers'/privates' equivalencies observed during the war, see Lonnie R. Speer, *Portals to Hell: Military Prisons of the Civil War* (Mechanicsburg PA: Stackpole Books, 1997) 102.

Union Maj. Gen. George Stoneman, captured east of Macon during his unsuccessful cavalry raid in late July, would have equaled thirty privates. The highest-ranking Federal captured during the war, Stoneman was being held at Charleston when on 17 September General Hood asked Richmond if he could include him in the prisoner exchange he had worked out with Sherman. After Secretary of War Seddon affirmed that "there is no such peculiar ground of offense by General George Stoneman as would exempt him from general exchange," Hood ordered Stoneman brought by train and passed through the lines at Rough and Ready (Hood to Bragg, 17 September; Seddon to Hood, 19 September; and Maj. J. E. Austin to Maj. Gen. Samuel Jones, 25 September, *OR,* ser. 2, vol. 7, pp. 837, 846, 879). In naming Stoneman as highest-ranking POW, I am not counting Union Maj. Gen. William B. Franklin, who was senior to Stoneman in date of promotion by eight months, and who was captured by Confederate cavalrymen in Maryland on 11 July 1864. He escaped within hours of his seizure, and never had to endure Rebel imprisonment (Virgil Carrington Jones, *Gray Ghosts and Rebel Raiders* [New York: Henry Holt & Co., 1956] 263–64).

Webb Garrison mentions the approximately 800–1,000 male laborers Sherman claims to have arrested in *Atlanta and the War* (Nashville TN: Rutledge Hill Press, 1992), but does not speculate on what happened to them; they "seem to have dropped from the record…an even more obscure riddle than that of the fate of the factory workers and their children transported to the North from Roswell" (207).

Federals imprisoned at Andersonville and exchanged were arriving in Sherman's lines by 28 September. Sgt. William Miller of the 75th Indiana recorded in his diary that day:

> Our wagon Train brought in Some of our Boys who have been prisoners and was exchanged. Some of them was Starved nearly to death. To look at the poor naked and Starveing men it makes my blood boil. Any Set of men who will deliberately Starve prisoners guilty of no crime but fighting for freedom when they have no way to protect themselves it seams to me there is no punishment severe enough on earth to do them Justice and if there is a Purgatory hereafter that is the place for them. The Prisoners tell some horable Stories of their cruel treatment. Their appearance confirms their Stories. (Jeffrey L. Patrick and Robert

Sherman's "kitchen sink" reply of 10 September. Hood's letter of 9 September, borne by Messrs. Crew and Ball, with its insults to Sherman and invocations to God, proved too much for the Union commander. In a long reply of 10 September, Sherman responded with all due verbal force. First, to get business out of the way, he enclosed a copy of the orders he had circulated that day, announcing that at Rough and Ready station and out to a 2 miles' radius, a truce would be in effect from dawn Monday, 12 September to dawn Thursday, 22 September, for the passage of Atlanta's civilians into Confederate lines. Each army would post in the vicinity a command of 100 men to maintain the white flag. US army wagons and ambulances directed by Federal quartermaster officers would bring the people and their baggage.

Sherman then launched into his lecture. He denied that his mass expulsion of Atlantans was unprecedented; he claimed that Joe Johnston had "removed the families all the way from Dalton" in the campaign of several months before. He also emphasized how Hood had hurt the people of Atlanta: "You, yourself, burned dwelling-houses along your parapet, and I have seen to-day fifty houses that you have rendered uninhabitable because they stood in the way of your forts and men." He even found a way to blame Hood for his bombardment of the city, conveniently forgetting his own repeated orders to his artillery. "You defended Atlanta on a line so close to town that every cannon shot and many musket shots from our line of investment that overshot their mark went into the habitations of women and children." Citing other examples—Hardee at Jonesboro, Johnston the summer before at Jackson—in which Confederate officers had presumably subjected Southern townspeople to hard war by investing their lines so close to towns, Sherman then offered to "challenge any fair man to judge which of us has the heart of pity for the families of a 'brave people'" (in throwing back Hood's phrasing, it is evident that Sherman was rankled by the Confederate commander's praise of the South's "brave people").

As for his expulsion order, Sherman made much of his claim that he was actually being kind to the city's civilians by removing them from the ordeal of a harsh military occupation. He further wondered why chivalrous Southerners would even want their women and children to remain in a city under Union occupation, subjecting them "to the rude barbarians who thus, as you say, violate

---

J. Willey, eds., *Fighting for Liberty and Right: The Civil War Diary of William Bluffton Miller, First Sergeant, Company K, Seventy-fifth Indiana Volunteer Infantry* [Knoxville: University of Tennessee Press, 2005] 257–58.)

Included in the prisoner exchange during September were not only enlisted men confined at Andersonville, but Union officers held in Macon. On 28 September, for instance, Colonel Henry and Colonel Warner at Rough and Ready exchanged 149 US officers and 473 CS privates, plus sixteen surgeons and four chaplains without equivalent ("Sherman in Georgia by the Right Reverend Henry C. Lay," *Atlantic Monthly* 149/2 [February 1932]: 167).

the laws of war." Having defended himself against Hood's accusations of cruelty, the Federal commander launched into new accusations of his own, in such a wide range of issues as figuratively to exclude only the kitchen sink. He blamed the South for having insulted the national flag, for having seized forts and arsenals, and for having started the war, all without provocation from the Federal government. He accused Southerners of having tried to coerce Kentucky and Missouri into secession. He charged them with having "falsified the vote of Louisiana" in the state referendum on secession in January 1861 (when Sherman was in Baton Rouge, watching the events unfold). He also charged Southerners with having "turned loose your privateers to plunder unarmed ships; expelled Union families by the thousands; burned their houses and declared by an act of your Congress the confiscation of all debts due Northern men for goods had and received." Sherman's purpose for engaging in this hot rhetoric is not clear, but it reflects the Union general's obvious anger and resentment as much at the Southern people and Confederate government as at Hood and his army. Moreover, the fact that he hurled so many charges at Hood in one sitting suggests that the Federal commander carried with him, at a moment's notice, a lot of resentments against the South. As a psychological clue to why Sherman so obviously wanted to punish Southern noncombatants in Atlanta with bombardment and eviction, this letter works as well as any other of Sherman's voluminous and much-quoted writings.

But he did not stop there. "Talk thus to the marines, but not to me, who have seen these things, and who will this day make as much sacrifice for the peace and honor of the South as the best born Southerner among you." (This would have proven hard for General Hood to take.) Finally, he asked the Confederate commander to keep God out of their argument: "In the name of common sense I ask you not to appeal to a just God in such a sacrilegious manner.... If we must be enemies, let us be men and fight it out, as we propose to do, and not deal in such hypocritical appeals to God and humanity. God will judge us in due time, and He will pronounce whether it be more humane to fight with a town full of women, and the families of 'a brave people' at our back, or to remove them in time to places of safety among their own friends and people."

The mayor's appeal to Sherman, 11 September. Around that time, Mayor Calhoun and two city councilmen weighed in with their own protest of Sherman's expulsion order. In a letter dated 11 September, Calhoun, Edward Rawson, and S. C. Wells pointed out that as the people of the city prepared to evacuate, the scenes had been "appalling and heart-rending." Poor pregnant women had no place to go; other women, their husbands away in the army, were giving birth in houses about to be abandoned; the sick and infirm faced eviction into the cold, cruel elements. Those without friends or relatives elsewhere faced an endless wandering. Everyone was wracked by the dilemma of deciding which of their possessions they should carry and which they would have to leave behind. Many found Rough and Ready no place at all to be dropped off by the

Federals and wondered just how far beyond that General Hood's wagons could be expected to bear them and their goods. And with so many North Georgians in the war zone having already left their homes for places southward and taken up housing elsewhere in the state and beyond, Calhoun, Rawson, and Wells asked where would Atlanta's evacuees, mostly women and children, find shelter? All the churches and outbuildings in cities such as Macon were already occupied. "How can they live through the winter in the woods? No shelter or subsistence, in the midst of strangers who know them not, and without the power to assist them much, if they were willing to do so"—such was the plight of Atlanta's helpless. The mayor and his fellow supplicants did not know how many people as yet were in the city, but they pledged that if left alone Atlantans would fend for themselves for several months without burdening the Northern forces. "In conclusion," they pleaded, "we must earnestly and solemnly petition you to reconsider this order, or modify it, and suffer this unfortunate people to remain at home and enjoy what little means they have."

Sherman refuses, 12 September. Of course Sherman said no, although he gave Mayor Calhoun the courtesy of a rather long-winded no.

1. "The use of Atlanta for warlike purposes is inconsistent with its character as a home for families. There will be no manufactures, commerce, or agriculture here for the maintenance of families, and sooner or later want will compel the inhabitants to go. Why not go now, when all the arrangements are completed for the transfer?"

2. The way he saw it, the people of Atlanta would have to suffer hardship for the good of the country (the United States, not the Confederate) and in the interest of peace. "We must have peace, not only at Atlanta but in all America. To secure this we must stop the war that now desolates our once happy and favored country." Atlantans would have to do their part by submitting to Federal authority, no matter how bitter the consequence; spreading out through the land and spreading word, they would communicate the Yankees' hard measures. Southern civilians would have to make a choice, as Sherman put it, whether they would be "those who desire a government and those who insist on war and its desolation."

3. Sherman acknowledged that "to stop war we must defeat the rebel armies," but he also believed that "to defeat these armies we must prepare the way to reach them in their recesses," a rather cryptic way of saying that Rebel soldiers must be made to feel responsible for the hardships suffered by their families.

4. Finally, Southerners had brought on this war, and now Southerners must suffer for it. "War is cruelty and you cannot refine it," Sherman wrote in some of his more memorable words. "You might as well appeal against the thunderstorm as against these terrible hardships of war, and the only way the people of Atlanta can hope once more to live in peace and quiet at home is to stop the war,

which can alone be done by admitting that it began in error and is perpetuated in pride."

As consolation (for what it mattered), Sherman closed by promising that when peace finally came, "you may call on me for anything. Then will I share with you the last cracker, and watch with you to shield your homes and families against danger from any quarter."[35]

Hood's history lesson and closing correspondence. With their appeal against the thunderstorm having failed, the mayor and citizens gave up. Only Hood continued to argue with Sherman. In Hood's reply of 12 September, an elaborate rejoinder to Sherman's "kitchen sink" letter of the 10th, Hood took on Sherman's accusations like an energetic debater. He denied that Johnston removed civilians as the Confederate army retreated through North Georgia; civilians panicked at the Yankees' coming, and fled on their own. Hood also claimed that neither he nor General Hardee expelled civilians from their homes, although he conceded that they both defended their positions before Atlanta and Jonesboro "at the expense of injury to the houses, an ordinary, proper, and justifiable act of war." Further, if there were any fault in conduct at Atlanta, Hood argued "it was your own, in not giving notice.... of your purpose to shell the town, which is usual in war among civilized nations." He refused to accept that Federal artillerymen had merely overshot the Rebel lines, sending their shells into the city because the Confederate works were too close to the urban edge. "There are a hundred thousand witnesses"—Hood was apparently counting Northerners as well as Southerners—"that you fired into the habitations of women and children for

---

[35] Sherman to Hood, 10 September 1864, *OR,* vol. 39, pt. 2, p. 416; Special Field Order 70, 10 September, *OR,* vol. 39, pt. 2, pp. 356–57; James M. Calhoun, E. E. Rawson, and S. C. Wells to Sherman, 11 September, *OR,* vol. 39, pt. 2, pp. 417–18; Sherman to Calhoun, Rawson, and Wells, 12 September, *OR,* vol. 39, pt. 2, p. 418–19.

Southern apologists have long noted Sherman's attempt, in his letter of the 10th, to pass off culpability for his bombardment of Atlanta and its noncombatants. Walter Brian Cisco has recently derided the Yankee general for "blaming the Confederate commander for his own deliberate shelling of civilians" (*War Crimes against Southern Civilians* [Gretna LA: Pelican Publishing Co., 2007] 111).

Scholars are well aware of Sherman's complicated ideas on war's hardships against civilians, and his role in creating them. Michael Walzer, in a recent study, offers the idea that in claiming that *war is hell* Sherman was providing a "doctrine, not description," that justified his actions, a protestation of innocence for command decisions he well knew would be severely criticized (Michael Walzer, *Just and Unjust Wars: A Moral Argument with Historical Illustrations* [New York: Basic Books, 2000] 32). Sherman biographer Michael Fellman agrees, astutely distinguishing between "total war," which Sherman did not practice, but *moral totalism* that Sherman not only practiced but perfected in his many written justifications of his banishment of Atlanta civilians and marches throughout Georgia and the Carolinas, which preyed on civilian's farms, crops, and livestock (*Citizen Sherman: A Life of William Tecumseh Sherman* [New York: Random House, 1995] 179).

weeks, firing far above and miles beyond my line of defense. I have too good an opinion, founded both upon observation and experience, of the skill of your artillerists to credit the insinuation that they for several weeks unintentionally fired too high for my modest field works, and slaughtered women and children by accident and want of skill."

Then, while claiming that as a Confederate general officer he had no responsibility to discuss the causes of the war and other such political matters as Sherman had raised, Hood refused to allow his enemy's contentions to go unchallenged, and delivered a history lesson of his own. Hood rejected the notion that the Confederacy had started the war and insisted that Southern commissioners had sought to *prevent* war. He contined, "You say we insulted your flag. The truth is" that Confederate forces only fired on Fort Sumter when US subjugation became evident. As for the seizure of forts and arsenals, it simply became necessary for the Confederates to forcibly gain possession of forts and arsenals that by rights were already theirs. Hood likewise dismissed Sherman's charge regarding Missouri and Kentucky: "You say that we tried to force Missouri and Kentucky into rebellion... The truth is" that the US government has used military repression to prevent the people of Kentucky and Missouri from the free exercise of their political will. Sherman's Louisiana argument fared no better in Hood's eyes since "Louisiana not only separated herself from your Government by nearly a unanimous vote," but had distinguished herself by the heroic conduct of her sons from Gettysburg to the Sabine. Hood was equally unimpressed with charges against the Confederate navy: "You say that we turned loose pirates to plunder your unarmed ships. The truth is when you robbed us of our part of the navy, we built and bought a few vessels, hoisted the flag of our country, and swept the seas."

The Confederate general was no more tolerant of Sherman's final two criticisms. Regarding the Rebel expulsion of Union families, Hood insisted that "not a single family has been expelled from the Confederate States, that I am aware of." Further, whatever financial assets may have been seized by the Confederacy were the property of those merchants who had loudly denounced Southerners as traitorous. (They had even been given plenty of time to leave with their assets.)

"Such are your accusations," Hood concluded, in something of a feeling of triumph, "and such are the facts known of all men to be true." But he closed with a return to the main issue, Sherman's expulsion order. Even "Beast" Butler had ordered out from New Orleans only those residents who would not swear loyalty to the United States, and acknowledged that his eviction was a punishment for their conduct. Here, Sherman was ordering all people out of Atlanta, pro-Union and well as pro-Confederate, regardless of their loyalty, and pronouncing it as a "kindness." Hood resented this as much as he did Sherman's pledge that he would work as arduously for the peace and honor of the South "as the best born Southerner among you." And finally, there was the Federal commander's taunt that they should "fight it out as men." Yes, Hood answered, "we will fight you." Then he announced, "I close this correspondence with you."

Sherman's last word, 14 September. But Sherman could not stand the thought of Hood's ending their correspondence; he had to have the last word. On the 14th, he wrote one more letter, resenting one more time the "unfair and improper terms" with which Hood had characterized Sherman's expulsion order, and defending himself one more time against the accusation that he had begun his bombardment of Atlanta without warning the populace. "I was not bound by the laws of war to give notice of the shelling of Atlanta, a 'fortified town' with magazines, arsenals, foundries, and public stores. You were bound to take notice. See the books. This is the conclusion of our correspondence, which I did not begin, and terminate with satisfaction."[36]

---

[36] Hood to Sherman, 12 September, *OR*, vol. 39, pt. 2, pp. 419–22; Sherman to Hood, 14 September, *OR*, vol. 39, pt. 2, p. 422.

Hood made a point in his letter of 12 September to affirm that despite the cruelty of Sherman's shelling of the city, "I made no complaint of your firing into Atlanta in any way you thought proper. I make none now...." After the war, however, Atlantans got the impression that at some point during the bombardment, 20 July–25 August, Hood had formally asked Sherman to stop his shelling of the city. No authoritative wartime source substantiates this idea. In their respective memoirs, both Sherman (1875) and Hood (posthumously, 1880) published in full their five starchy letters of 7–14 September 1864, concerning the bombardment and expulsion; they would surely have included in their reminiscences any other wartime correspondence on the subjects.

Yet postbellum Atlanta writers seem to have confused the dates of the September Hood-Sherman correspondence, embellished it a bit, blurred some details, and construed it to have occurred *during* the semi-siege of August. Their mistakes gave rise to a century of historiographical error. Wallace Reed, the *Constitution* writer, led the way in 1889 by stating that during the bombardment, Hood "wrote a long letter to General Sherman" protesting the shelling. Reed summarized Sherman's reply as "one of the strongest, sharpest and most brutal letters in our war literature," accusing Southerners of siting their fortifications too near the city. "After this remarkable correspondence the shelling went on more briskly than ever" (Wallace P. Reed, *History of Atlanta, Georgia, with Illustrations and Biographical Sketches of Some of Its Prominent Men and Pioneers* [Syracuse NY: D. Mason & Co., 1889] 193).

Several years later, Atlantan Isaac Avery also referred to Hood's "long letter to Gen. Sherman, against his firing into the city," and Sherman's reply as having been written during the bombardment. "The correspondence failed to stop the shelling" (Isaac W. Avery, "Atlanta. Its History and Advantages," in *City of Atlanta. A Descriptive, Historical and Industrial Review of the Gateway City of the South* [Louisville KY: Inter-State Publishing Company, 1892–1893] 26).

A decade later Thomas H. Martin, another Atlanta writer, also got the story wrong. "As soon as the Federals began to throw shells into the city, immediately after the battle of Atlanta, General Hood addressed a letter to General Sherman," protesting the bombardment (*Atlanta and Its Builders: A Comprehensive History of the Gate City of the South*, 2 vols. [Atlanta: Century Memorial Publishing Company, 1902] 1:498).

John Hornaday's history of the city, published in the 1920s, gives no date for when "General Hood...wrote a letter to General Sherman protesting [the bombardment] in the most vigorous terms," but implies that it was before the city fell (John R. Hornaday, *Atlanta: Yesterday, Today and Tomorrow* [n.p.: American Cities Book Company, 1922] 46–47). Lucian Lamar Knight's local history also avoids a specific date, but states, "while the shelling of Atlanta was in progress a vigorous protest was made by General Hood"; "seemingly the intervention was without any helpful result, for, after this extraordinary correspondence, the shelling went on, more briskly than ever." (Lucian Lamar Knight, *History of Fulton County Georgia* [Atlanta: A. H. Cawston, 1930] 102–103). Walter G. Cooper, *Official History of Fulton County* ([Atlanta]: History Commission, 1934) 174, repeats Reed's error.

Atlanta's renowned historian Franklin Garrett also errs in stating, "while the shelling of Atlanta was in progress, General Hood addressed several letters of protest to General Sherman"; his source was Martin's earlier local history (Garrett, *Atlanta and Environs,* 1:629). Bill Key, writer for the *Atlanta Journal-Constitution,* turned his articles into a slim volume in which he implied that after Sherman called for his big siege cannon in early August, Hood sent his "official protest" of the bombardment (William Key, *The Battle of Atlanta and the Georgia Campaign* [New York: Twayne Publishers, 1958] 68).

With such a full foundation of inaccuracy, subsequent writers could mistakenly assume that the Hood-Sherman correspondence occurred during the bombardment. "Despite the frequent letters of protest sent by Hood to Sherman concerning the shelling of civilians and their property, the rain of destruction continued" (Ralph Benjamin Singer, "Confederate Atlanta" [Ph.D. diss., University of Georgia, 1973] 255). After the intense bombardment of 9 August, Samuel Carter writes, "John Bell Hood was outraged and indignant at the stepped-up bombing and sent several messages, under flags of truce, to General Sherman (*The Siege of Atlanta,* 287). In an article for a Civil War buffs' magazine, Peggy Robbins once more got it all wrong. "The exchange of increasingly hostile messages between Generals Sherman and Hood—many of these several pages in length—began in early August, 1864....between Hood's headquarters in the city and Sherman's headquarters outside Atlanta, paper missiles were rushed back and forth under a flag of truce while the guns roared on....Hood started sending outraged, indignant letters about the increased bombing...." (Peggy Robbins, "Hood vs. Sherman: A Duel of Words," *Civil War Times Illustrated* 17/4 [July 1978]: 25). In his volume for the Time-Life series, Ronald Bailey states that after the heavy shelling of 9 August, "Hood sent a message to Sherman protesting the bombardment" (Ronald H. Bailey, *Battles for Atlanta: Sherman Moves East* [Alexandria VA: Time-Life Books, 1985] 140). Professors McDonough and Jones err, too: "Since mid-August Sherman and Hood had been waging a heated duel of words through letters, some of which were several pages in length and increasingly hostile. After thousands of shells delivered by Sherman's newly-arrived siege guns from Chattanooga struck Atlanta in a single day, leaving few blocks undamaged and numerous casualties, Hood began sending bitter letters about the increased bombardment" (*War So Terrible: Sherman and Atlanta* [New York: W. W. Norton & Company, 1987] 315).

Finally, in another buffs' magazine as recently as 1995, Roy Morris states that after Wallace Reed's "red day in August," with the deaths of the Warners and of Sol Luckie, "Hood, furious at the nonmilitary aspects of the bombing, wrote to Sherman at once" (Roy

Evidently someone in Hood's headquarters staff thought the peppery correspondence would make good reading, for the letters were leaked to the Southern press. In its issues of 14, 15, and 17 September, the *Macon Telegraph* printed eight letters exchanged by Sherman and Hood concerning the civilian expulsion and prisoner exchange. Within several days, Sherman was aware of the publicity, and he was annoyed. "I have seen that, in violation of all official usage, he has published in the Macon newspapers such parts of the correspondence as suited his purpose," Sherman wrote Halleck on 20 September. "This could have had no other object than to create a feeling on the part of the people; but if he expects to resort to such artifices, I think I can meet him there, too." So Sherman authorized his own press distribution, seeing that the correspondence was printed in Northern papers as well. Their response would have pleased him. "As trenchant with his pen as with his sword," exclaimed the *Washington Chronicle*. Even more than what he had done militarily, the *New York Herald* cried, his literary ripostes to Hood marked Sherman as "one of the great men of the time." The *Cincinnati Gazette* hailed his evacuation order as "the blast of the war trumpet," sure to further unnerve the Rebels. One of Sherman's soldiers, Edward Allen, joined in this general acclaim when he wrote his parents on 25 September about the Sherman-Hood letters printed in the newspapers. Sherman's "removal of the women and children," Allen wrote, reflected "the sentiments of this whole army," and showed that Sherman was "not afraid to treat...them as they deserve."

Even while Sherman and Hood were exchanging correspondence, the people of Atlanta had begun their forced evacuation. For every household, the initial process was about the same: decide whether to go north or south, register with the Federal authorities for transport, select which possessions to take, pack for the trip, have the Yankees search their stuff for "contraband," and await the time for departure. Registration for southbound departure began on 10 September. Lieutenant Colonel Le Duc, who had moved from the Neal house into Richard Peters's at Mitchell and Forsyth, sat at a table on the porch as people lined up to get their travel permits. Citizens had to provide number of adults, children, servants, and a count of packages or parcels they would be taking with them. A record kept by Le Duc eventually listed 1,651 individuals registered between 10 and 20 of September. The tally enumerated 705 adults, 860 children,

---

Morris, "As the Shells Exploded over Atlanta in 1864, the Opposing Generals Opened a War of Words," *America's Civil War* 7/6 [January 1995]: 6).

The Hood-Sherman correspondence of *7–14 September 1864* has been published in the *Official Records* for over a century. Let us hope that sloppy historical writing regarding its dates and circumstances has come to an end. A promising sign is "Fighting Words," *America's Civil War* 23/4 (September 2010) 30–37, which excerpts and correctly dates five letters of Hood and Sherman during 7–14 September, essentially atoning for Roy Morris's mistake in the same magazine fifteen years before.

and 86 servants. They carried altogether 8,842 "packages of baggage." Also registered were thirty-four horses, cows or calves, and eight wagons, drays, carriages or buggies. Historians have long known of these numbers and have reprinted them, but with few making an important, and indeed tragic observation: over half of Sherman's southbound expellees were children. Eight hundred and sixty youngsters (seventeen years or younger) had been driven from their homes, forced into an ordeal of refugeeing, and facing the prospect of never returning to their homes.[37]

For this great exodus the US army offered initial assistance. In his letter to Hood of 7 September, Sherman had written that he would "provide transportation by cars so far as Rough and Ready, and also wagons." And in Special Field Orders 70 of 10 September, Sherman instructed his chief quartermaster, Colonel Langdon C. Easton, to "afford all the people of Atlanta who elect to go south all the facilities he can spare to remove them comfortably and safely, with their effects, to Rough and Ready, using cars and wagons and ambulances for that purpose."

---

[37] *Macon Telegraph,* 14, 15,17 September 1864; Sherman to Halleck, 20 September, *OR,* vol. 39, pt. 2, p. 414; "Sherman vs. Hood," *New York Times,* 22 September (as example of a Northern paper printing generals' letters); John F. Marszalek, *Sherman's Other War: The General and the Civil War Press* (Memphis: Memphis State University Press, 1981) 172 (on the *Chronicle, Herald,* and *Gazette*); Lisa Tendrich Frank, "Children of the March: Confederate Girls and Sherman's Home Front Campaign," in James Marten, ed., *Children and Youth during the Civil War Era* (New York: New York University Press, 2012) 114 (867 children), 116 (Allen to parents); Le Duc, *Recollections of a Civil War Quartermaster,* 129; Le Duc, "Official account of the people sent south."

I thank Anne Salter, then librarian and archivist at the Atlanta History Center, for directing me to this list of expellees, which was printed apparently only in the fourth edition (1892) of Sherman's *Memoirs*; it is the basis of Wilbur G. Kurtz, "Persons Removed from Atlanta," first printed in the *Atlanta Historical Bulletin* in February 1932. The list is also more recently printed as Robert S. Davis, Jr., "The General Sherman Census of Atlanta, September 1864," *Georgia Genealogical Magazine* 31/1–2 (1991): 132–41.

Le Duc's manuscript list of the southbound emigres has been located by Dr. Tom Dyer in the National Archives. Entitled "The Book of Exodus," the twenty-two-page handwritten enumeration is in RG 393, Records of the US Army Continental Commands, Military Division of the Mississippi, Letters Received, Misc., box 2 (Dyer, *Secret Yankees,* 360n65). It carries the subtitle printed in Sherman's *Memoirs*: "an account of people sent South, their number, and baggage under Special Field Order No. 67 issued by Maj. Gen. W.T. Sherman. Atlanta, Georgia, September 4, 1864."

Recently Prof. Wendy Venet has also found Le Duc's "Book of Exodus" manuscript in the National Archives microfilm, misfiled under "Confederate Papers Relating to Citizens or Business Firms" (microfilm M346, reel 114, Bryant-Bryu). The "Exodus" appears under name of J. M. Bryant (the first individual listed as registering on 10 September for transportation).

Despite these hints that both trains and wagons would carry Atlanta's Rebel exiles to Hood's lines, it became clear that only wagons would be used. To be sure, the railroad from Atlanta to Rough and Ready was in place and operating. James Crew, who had carried Sherman's initial letter to Hood, was apparently Mayor Calhoun's courier for his appeal against the expulsion, which Sherman rejected in his reply of 12 September, and which Crew evidently also carried back. That day a Federal quartermaster signed a pass, noting by "Committee" Crew's favored status as Atlanta citizen and hence entitled to a seat on the US Military Railroad. But Crew's access to the cars in this instance was exceptional. Federals may have used some train transport for Atlantans refugeeing south; Captain David Conyngham, a correspondent for the *New York Herald*, wrote, "those going within the rebel lines seemed to enjoy the thing. The cars taking them down were loaded with a miscellaneous cargo." Yet in the main, the Federals relied on quartermaster wagons for the trips to Rough and Ready. By terms of SFO 70, Northern officers were also permitted to use their regimental and staff teams to assist citizens in loading up their belongings.

The exodus of the southbounds began on the morning of Monday, 12 September, the start of the ten-day truce agreed upon by Sherman and Hood. Citizens had until the afternoon of Wednesday, 21 September, to get out of the city. (The last wagon train was scheduled to leave downtown at 4:00 P.M. that day; the truce would end at daybreak the following day.) Once deposited at Rough and Ready and accepted into Southern lines, the refugees would be loaded onto Confederate wagons and borne to Lovejoy's Station, 7 miles south of Jonesboro. (The Yankees had wrecked the railroad inbetween.) From Lovejoy, the exiles would be carried on the Macon & Western into Macon.

Rough and Ready at the time was a "breakfast station" on the M & W, 13 miles south by rail of the Car Shed. Named for General and President Zachary Taylor, it served as a railroad supply point (woodyard and water tank), and passenger service center (a few stores and of course a tavern, sometimes called the old Bagley house). Major William Clare, assistant inspector general for the Army of Tennessee, and Lieutenant Colonel Warner, inspector general on Sherman's staff, arranged the truce point. Warner had served as Sherman's courier for his letter to Hood of 10 September, and presumably subsequent ones as well, carrying them to Confederate lines under flag of truce. General Hood would thus have learned that Warner was to be Sherman's officer in charge of both the truce of 12–22 September and the ongoing prisoner exchange. Mindful of military protocol, Hood chose his own assistant inspector general, Major Clare, to be Warner's counterpart.

On the evening of 11 September, Clare received his orders, and at 7:30 the next morning was at Rough and Ready. He had a little time to meet Warner; the two rehearsed how the truce would work and how the people would be transferred to the Southern army's wagons. Then they waited for the first Northern wagons out of Atlanta. There was some delay in their arriving. By

Lieutenant Colonel Morse's order of 6 September, all refugees were to assemble at City Hall Park at 9:00 A.M. Assigning wagons and loading passengers with cargo would have been confusing and time-consuming; on top of that was the slow ride over 14 miles of road, so the first wagon train probably arrived in the early afternoon. After that, as Morse noted in a letter on 13 September, a long wagon train went out each day, carrying families to Hood's lines.[38]

For those heading south, the indignity of having Yankees searching through their private possessions for contraband proved to be an overbearing insult. Young Mary Rawson recorded in her diary for 11 September that even though her mother had no idea of where they would go, packing would have to begin. "Scarcely was the work begun," she wrote, "when we heard that all those who went South would have their trunks searched and all goods not ready made be removed." Northern soldiers soon arrived to conduct their contraband search. "While we were in the midst of our work Aunt Charlotte came over from Grandmas and told us they had already opened Auntys trunks twice and came to perform the same detestable office again," Mary wrote. Her Aunt Delia (Mrs. Sidney Root) stood firm: "Aunty refused decidedly to open her baggage any more." Fortunately, Colonel Amos Beckwith, whom Mr. Rawson had earlier befriended, intervened and gave the Federal pertinacious package-prowler "a sound cudgeling." Aunty's goods suffered no further meddling. Later it was a sad sight for Mary to see her aunt's possessions loaded onto Yankee wagons. Walking to the Rootses' house on the morning of 12 September, she recorded, "I found two huge Army wagons and two ambulances at the gate and men hurrying to and fro with trunks and other baggage. At last they all came out and took their places in the ambulances and after a sad adieu they slowly departed."

The evacuation of prominent citizens provided even more houses for Union officers' quarters. After the family of James Clarke left, their house at Washington and Jones streets was soon occupied by Colonel Beckwith. The

---

[38] Sherman to Hood, 7 September 1864, *OR,* vol. 39, pt. 2, p. 415; Special Field Order 70, 10 September, *OR,* vol. 39, pt. 2, p. 356; T. D. Killian, "James R. Crew," *Atlanta Historical Bulletin* 1/6 (January 1932): 12 (Crew's train pass, 12 September); Conyngham, *Sherman's March through the South,* 225; Kurtz, "'Leave Atlanta within Five Days,'" 1; Annie Kurtz, "Atlanta's Envoys," 9; Wilbur Kurtz interview with James Bell, 21 June 1935, notebook 10, 234 (on Rough and Ready), Wilbur G. Kurtz Collection, Atlanta History Center; Annie Laurie Fuller Kurtz, "'While Atlanta Burned,'" *Atlanta Constitution Sunday Magazine,* 12 March 1939 (with Wilbur G. Kurtz illustration of "the old Bagley house, or Tavern"); "Railroads," *Barnwell's Atlanta City Directory,* 109 (distance to Rough and Ready from the Car Shed); Brooks D. Simpson and Jean V. Berlin, eds., *Sherman's Civil War: Selected Correspondence of William T. Sherman, 1860–1865* (Chapel Hill: University of North Carolina Press, 1999) 707 (noting Sherman's use of Colonel Warner and a truce flag, which is not shown in *OR,* vol. 39, pt. 2, p. 416); report of Maj. William Clare, 22 September, *OR,* vol. 38, pt. 3, p. 993; "Sherman's Third Order of Exile," *Atlanta Intelligencer,* 18 September; Morse, *Letters,* 190.

Rootses' home suffered a similar fate. Mary Rawson had already recorded in her diary that "Aunt Delia" Root had been "asked" by a Yankee colonel to vacate her home as early as 6 September. After the Root family left on 12 September, the place was doubtless occupied by Northern officers.

The *Intelligencer* announced on 15 September that "the exodus of the inhabitants of Atlanta began on Monday morning," 12 September. From its quarters in Macon, the paper announced that "amongst the most prominent civilians who have arrived here are Mr. Jas. Clark and family and Mr. Sidney Root's family." The *Intelligencer* made a point of recording what the exiles from Atlanta had to say. "A great deal of suffering and distress exists in the city, the general condition of which is represented as being terrible. The citizens who come South are not permitted to bring any household stuff of any consequence, the quantity being very limited, whilst those who have chosen to go North carry what they wish. The negroes, with but few exceptions, have elected to remain with the Yankees." With these reports coming in, the paper could not refrain from issuing its editorial judgment.

> This expatriation policy of Sherman merits the condemnation of civilized nations.—It is the very summit of brutality, and could only have been invented by a fiend whose soul is stamped with the devil's own hideous image. In it, we see revived the most barbarous principle of war that has ever disgraced the most uncivilized nations of earth, together with his favorite principle, that destruction and annihilation is the object of war, the barbarism is perpetrated with the cold hearted purpose and action of an executioner.

The *Intelligencer* of 17 September carried a report from Lovejoy's Station three days before: "the banished citizens from Atlanta continue to arrive. Some five hundred families have already come through. Many of them report the most deplorable condition of the Atlanta populace." "Scarcely any of them saved anything but a few articles of clothing and furniture," the paper added; the rest of the people's possessions had been left behind, inanimate casualties of war. In addition to their loss of property, some apparently suffered the loss of their dignity. "The Federal soldiery," the *Intelligencer* related, "though not permitted to commit personal outrage, were insulting to a degree." One lady related that "a Cerulean" had accosted her on the street, in unmistakable New England twang.

> "Where you going—North?"
> "No sir—seen enough of the North—We are going South!"
> "Then you are going to H—l!"
> "Well," was the redoubtable dame's rejoinder, "If we do, old Sherman will have a chance to flank us out of it, for he is mighty certain to get there first!"

"Some of the families who came out were transported by wagons over a rough road, and are naturally much fatigued and travel stained from their toilsome pilgrimage," the newspaper added. "Altogether, the procession is a sad one, reflecting with pathetic eloquence upon the cowardice and brutality of the Federal commander at Atlanta, who aspires to the dignity of statesman as well as warrior, to say nothing of his contemptible and absurd pretentions to epistolary distinction"—a snide swipe at Sherman's correspondence with Hood, already being printed in the Southern press.[39]

During their pilgrimage, some citizens could not help but convey their resentment toward the Yankees. "Some of them are very Saucy and independent," recorded Sergeant William B. Miller of the 75th Indiana, "and it hurts their feelings to be hauled out in a wagon with a Yankee driver." As with all such traumatic events, there were many sides to the story. One was offered by Sherman's engineer, Captain Poe, who wrote to his wife Eleanor on 18 September about how he had ridden in one wagon train with Atlantans who seemed to be of the less privileged classes. Poe hoped to see at the checkpoint—two little shacks, separated by a few hundred yards—an old army friend, Robert F. Beckham, now Hood's chief of artillery. At his destination, Poe was disappointed not to find Colonel Beckham. But he encountered several Southern officers, who conversed with him so politely that it seemed they were trying "as hard as possible to forget that a state of war existed."

Another tale was offered by a lady of Atlanta who appealed to Sherman that she be allowed to stay, and who actually secured an interview with the general. To be sure, she was ultimately denied exemption from the expulsion, and she made her way to Eatonton. There, however, she told the story of her meeting with Sherman, and emphasized how kind-hearted he was, even as he ordered her out of town. One George MacDonell of Eatonton set down in a long letter to J. A. Turner an account of his conversation with the unnamed lady. MacDonell took pains to include detail, as Turner—Joseph Addison Turner of Eatonton, publisher of a weekly journal, *The Countryman*—had evidently requested it for publication. MacDonell prefaced, "I have written it hastily, and leave it for you to condense, as you may deem proper. Hoping its publication may prove of some interest to your readers, I proceed, as follows:"

> The lady with whom I conversed, was under the necessity of calling upon Sherman, after the publication of the edict of banishment, and she represents him as being very kind, and conciliatory in his deportment towards her, and others who visited him. He expressed much regret at the necessity which compelled him to order the citizens of Atlanta from

[39] Rawson, diary, 6, 11–12 September 1864, Atlanta History Center; "The Exodus" and "The Enemy in Atlanta" (including Beckwith's occupancy of the Clarke residence), *Atlanta Intelligencer*, 15 September; "From the Front, Lovejoy Station, September 14, 1864," *Atlanta Intelligencer*, 17 September.

their homes, but stated, in justification of his course, that he intended to make Atlanta a second Gibraltar; that when he completed his defensive works, it would be impregnable; and as no communication could be held with their friends, in the south, they (the citizens) would suffer for food; that it was impossible for him to subsist his army, and feed the citizens, too, by a single line of railroad; and that as he intended to hold Atlanta, at all hazards, he thought it was humanity to send them out of the city, where they could obtain necessary supplies. He took the little child of my friend in his arms, and patted her rosy cheeks, calling her "a poor little exile," and saying he was sorry to have to drive her away from her comfortable home, but that war was a cruel, and inexorable thing, and its necessities compelled him to do many things which he heartily regretted.

As if taking cue from their commanding general, other Federals emphasized their efforts to help the southbound pilgrims. Colonel Le Duc himself travelled with one family. Mrs. George W. Adair (whose husband, editor of the *Southern Confederacy,* had fled the city in General Hood's evacuation) was left with her children at their home on Peters Street when they had to pack up for the trip to Rough and Ready. On Le Duc's register, she was #45: "Mrs. G.W. Adair...2 adults, 4 children, 2 servants...53 packages, 2 horses, carriage, cow and calf." One of the children was four-month-old Forrest Adair, who late in life remembered his mother telling him how Le Duc had held him in his arms during part of the journey to Hood's lines.

A number of Northerners recorded their impressions of the civilians' exodus, often stressing their work in helping to haul them. A Wisconsan, Alonzo Miller, recorded in his diary on 20 September having seen "something like 75 wagons loaded with citizens and their goods leaving Atlanta for the country." Sergeant Rufus Mead of the 5th Connecticut noted that twenty wagons from each of the three brigades in his division were assigned "to carry stuff south to Rough & Ready.... The wagons carry the stuff only, while the citizens walk or the women & children ride in Ambulances." Quartermaster Lieutenant Edgar Shannon supervised the loading of fifteen families and their belongings onto a train of seventy wagons. Included among his charges were a number of young women. After the eight-hour trek to Rough and Ready, and a few hours' fraternizing with the Rebels, Shannon climbed under a wagon to fall asleep and dream, as he put it, of "the fair ones" he had helped move.

Captain David Conyngham accompanied a wagon train and commented on its "heterogeneous medley of poodle dogs, tabby cats, asthmatic pianos, household furtiture, cross old maids, squalling, wondering children, all of which, huddled together, made anything but a pleasant travelling party." George W. Herr, a soldier in the 59th Illinois, made a point in his postwar regimental history of emphasizing the Federals' kindness to the departing civilians. "It was a curious and touching sight," he wrote, "to see the gentleness, the almost womanly delicacy, with which Sherman's soldiers treated the stricken and sorrowing people. Their hearts were touched, and many a big hulking fellow, who feared neither God, man or devil, was melted to tears."

> In every possible way the soldiers made themselves useful to the people. Some aided the old, endeavoring to cheer them, meanwhile, by trying to impress upon their minds that it were better to go to their friends than to remain in Atlanta, where fire and famine and bloodshed was all that the future promised. Others brought coffee and "hard tack" to the little ones, built fires for the women, aided in packing bundles and moving furniture; and one bearded Hoosier, a corporal, was seen trudging along with a moving family carrying two sick children, one upon each arm. They were puny creatures, sick and cross. One moaned feebly; the other cried incessantly, while the bearded soldier, endeavoring to soothe and quiet them, cooed as tenderly as a mother.

Captain Conyngham was struck by the sympathetic reception given the exiles by the Confederates at Rough and Ready. "Some even carried their enthusiasm so far as to welcome them with warm kisses and embraces," he noted. Union officer Ward Nichols observed a line of wagons and ambulances arrive at the truce point. To Nichols "these people seemed to be almost entirely of the lower class"; the more prosperous, he assumed, had already left the city. He nevertheless made acquaintance with a charming young lady and soon found himself subjected to considerable abuse as she remarked, "it is very hard to be obliged to leave our home. We have not felt the war before, except in the cost of luxuries of life. We did not believe your army would ever penetrate so far south; but I suppose our removal is one of the necessities of the situation, and we would much rather give up our homes than live near the Yankees. We will get far enough away this time." The woman said she was heading for Augusta, "where your army can't come." Nichols cautioned her not to be so certain: "it is a long way from Nashville to Atlanta, and we are here."[40]

---

[40] Patrick and Willey, eds., *Fighting for Liberty and Right,* 253; Orlando M. Poe to Eleanor, 18 September 1864, in Taylor, *Orlando M. Poe,* 86; George G. N. MacDonell to J. A. Turner, Eatonton GA, 4 November 1864, in Richard B. Harwell, ed., *The Confederate Reader: As the South Saw the War* (New York: Longmans, Green and Co., 1957) 317–18; Louis T. Griffith, "Joseph Addison Turner," in Kenneth Coleman and Charles Stephen Gurr, eds., *Dictionary of Georgia Biography,* 2 vols. (Athens: University of Georgia Press, 1983) 1009–10; Lawrence Huff, "'A Bitter Draught We Have Had to Quaff': Sherman's March through the Eyes of Joseph Addison Turner," *Georgia Historical Quarterly* 72/2 (Summer 1988): 306–309; "Concert after Atlanta Fell," *Atlanta Journal Magazine,* 6 November 1927 (on Colonel Le Duc accompanying Mrs. Adair); Alonzo Miller, diary, 20 September, MSS 237f, Atlanta History Center; Mead, diary, entry of 13 September ("our Brigade sent 20 teams to carry off stuff for the refugees beyond our lines"), Rufus Mead, Jr., Papers, Library of Congress; Padgett, ed., "With Sherman through Georgia and the Carolinas," 313, 315 (Mead to "Folks at Home, 13

A number of those who registered to go southward changed their mind—or changed their course. The Northern officer in Atlanta counted 1,651 people as ready to depart for Confederate lines under Sherman's order. But apparently not all of them made it to Rough and Ready. Major Clare was keeping his own list, and by the end of the transfer operation he counted 500 fewer people than Le Duc, 1,168 individuals received into his lines: 98 men, 395 women, 605 children and 70 servants. Either a number of people did not get listed by the Southern officer in Rough and Ready, or they never made the trip out of Atlanta in the first place. Some of the difference between Le Duc's and Clare's counts could have been accidental; there might have been clerical errors in trying to count a thousand-plus troubled civilians struggling to get out of town.

Having carried some of Sherman's and Hood's correspondence setting up the truce and expulsion, as well as Mayor Calhoun's protest of it, James R. Crew registered to have himself, wife, three servants, and fifteen packages borne to Rough and Ready. Even Crew, former member of the Atlanta City Council, had to undergo the baggage check that all refugees experienced. Among Crew's papers at the Atlanta History Center is this small scrap from the provost marshal's office: "I hereby certify that the baggage and household property belonging to Mr. James Crew has been examined and that they contain no contraband articles."

Entry 395 on Le Duc's list was none other than the mayor himself, "J.M. Calhoun, 1 adult, and 4 servants, 30 packages." The mayor registered with Le Duc on 17 September, which may have been the day of his travel to Rough and Ready. Major Nichols of Sherman's staff, who took a train to Rough and Ready on 16 September bearing a message for Colonel Warner, recorded in his diary that another train was scheduled the next morning to "transport several hundred of the citizens going south." If so, Mayor Calhoun may have been among them. Despite having to share the hardships of his fellow expelled citizens, in true gentlemanly fashion Calhoun sent a note of commendation if not of gratitude to General Sherman.

Atlanta, Sept. 20.—On leaving Atlanta I should return my thanks to Gen. Sherman, Gen. Slocum, Gen. Ward, Col. Coburn, Maj. Beck, Capt. Mott, Capt. Stewart, Capt. Flagg, and all the other officers with whom I have had business transactions in carrying out the order of Gen. Sherman for the removal of the citizens, and in transacting my private business. For their kindness to, and their patience in answering, the many inquiries I

September); Dunkelman, *Marching with Sherman*, 33; Conyngham, *Sherman's March Through the South*, 225–26; George W. Herr, *Nine Campaigns in Nine States: A Sketch...in which is Comprised the History of the Fifty-Ninth Regiment Illinois Veteran Volunteer Infantry* (San Francisco: Bancroft Company, 1900) 299–300; George Ward Nichols, *The Story of the Great March. From the Diary of a Staff Officer* (New York: Harper & Brothers, 1865) 21, 23.

had to make on the duration of the delicate and arduous duties devolving on me as Mayor of the city. Jas. M. Calhoun.

Entry 170, having registered on 14 September, was "Mrs. M. Bell," with another two adults and fully seven children, along with thirty-eight packages and a cow. This was the wife of Marcus Aurelius Bell, owner of the Calico House. Although evidently not with his wife, Mark Bell was able to compose a poem on the heartbreak of having to leave the city, and it was published in the *Atlanta Intelligencer* of 17 September. Entitled "Take Back Atlanta, My Home. Written for his wife, and respectfully dedicated to the Army of Tennessee," Bell's unmemorable verses exhorted the Confederate army with the chorus, "Take, O take back Atlanta, now marred by the shells / Of the foe, who possess and destroy; / O, we then shall be free—midst the ringing of bells, / We will sound loud our proud nation's joy!"

Entry 195 was another Bell, "Mrs. C. Bell...1 adult and 2 children...28 packages." Wilbur Kurtz was lucky enough to interview one of the two children, James Bell, in June 1935—barely two weeks before Bell died. Though Bell, a lad of fifteen years in summer 1864, was in his seventies, Kurtz was impressed at the clarity of his recollection, so he painstakingly took down what the old man told him about the wagon ride to Rough and Ready, and entered it all into his meticulously kept notebooks.

On Friday, Sept. 16th, 1864, an army wagon stopped at the Bell domicile on Capitol Ave. (it was then called McDonough St.) and most of these 28 packages were loaded up, together with the mother and the two boys. James climbed aboard with his pet rooster. Their destination was...'Rough and Ready.'...It was dark when they got there. There were a lot of wagons there and a lot of bewildered people standing around in a dazed condition, wondering what it was all about. The highway and the adjacent yards in the tiny hamlet were cluttered with packages of cooking utensils—a few sticks of furniture, baskets of clothing— provisions and all the trumpery of a hasty removal.... They climbed aboard one of Gen Hood's army wagons and left the scene where both Confederate and Federal officers hastened the transfers under a flag of truce. At Lovejoy's, the Bells got aboard a train of cars and reached Macon in the early hours of Saturday the 17th. They camped in a lumber yard that day and Sunday, and the next day, Monday, James and William went to work in a Government bakery. A few days later, ...the rooster got away![41]

---

[41] Kurtz, "Persons Removed from Atlanta," 25, 30; Clare report, *OR*, vol. 38, pt. 3, p. 993; C. F. Morse baggage inspection voucher, 15 September 1864, folder 3, James R. Crew Papers, MSS 79f, Atlanta History Center; Nichols, *Story of the Great March*, 18; James M. Calhoun to W. T. Sherman, 20 September 1864, in *Buffalo* (NY) *Commercial Advertiser*, 28 September; "Take Back Atlanta, My Home, by Marcus A. Bell," *Atlanta Intelligencer*, 17

In the crowds of Atlantans making their sad way southward were many poor women who, with nowhere to go, had stayed in the city as long as they could. Private Al Pugh of the 119th Illinois disparagingly described some of the people still in Atlanta, in a letter of 16 September.

> They are a few inhabitants here, but they are nearly all women and children, and made up of the class usually called "poor white trash." That peculiar blank and vacant stare which characterizes stolid ignorance, is to be seen on almost every countenance. Old women in the coarsest homespun are laying around smoking with a relish, old pipes, they appear never to lose sight of, while here and there you occasionally meet one indulging with the utmost carelessness in the luxury of snuff. There are some families appearantly inteligent and cultivated, but they are the exception. I have a slight acquaintance with one of the latter. But she was such a Bitter Rebel that it was of poor consolation to be with her, however she sang very nice and played the Piano very well, her songs were all of the Rebel Kind. But she has gone South.... she did not want to go.

Thus did Sherman's expulsion order affect the poor and rich alike. Captain John Fox of the 2nd Massachusetts, whose regiment was quartered on the open ground surrounding city hall, wrote home on 15 September, "all these people, in fact, every man, woman and child in town, must leave the city within a few days. I don't question orders, and it may be a military necessity, but you have no idea of the terrible hardship of its practical working." Other Federals commented on the citizens' distress, but like Captain Fox, accepted the situation without qualm. "The citizens are all being sent away, according to Sherman's order," noted Sylvester Daniels in his diary on 16 September. "It must make a trying time for women and children to be taken from home and put outside of our lines with

---

September 1864; Wilbur G. Kurtz, notebook 12, 40–41 ("James Bell's account of his experiences as one of Atlanta's population who was evicted, and who made the trip south via Rough + Ready is the only personal narrative I've met with, which deals with this episode of the Atlanta saga."), Wilbur G. Kurtz Collection, Atlanta History Center.

Major Clare's list of Atlanta refugees accepted into Confederate lines is at least as important as Lt. Col. Le Duc's, but it is apparently lost. Clare's report in the *OR* mentions a nominal list with dates of arrival, but as an attachment to the report was not printed. De Anne Blanton, senior military archivist at the National Archives, has found Clare's report in RG 109, but only in typed copy, not original. She infers that Clare's report in the *Official Records* was printed from this typescript, which the War Department apparently secured from the original document's owner, who is not identified. On ex-Confederates' practice of lending documents in their possession for copying and printing in the *OR*, see Richard M. McMurry, "The *Official Records* of the Rebellion," in Clyde N. Wilson, ed., *American Historians, 1866–1912*, vol. 47 of *Dictionary of Literary Biography* (Detroit: Gale Research Company, 1986) 369. I sincerely thank Ms. Blanton for her search for Clare's list, the loss of which is a major blow to the historiography of Atlanta during the war.

very few things to do with," Daniels acknowledged, adding that it was "pretty rough." But he also knew that nothing else could be done: "cant help it."

Orders and military necessity were the grounds on which most of Sherman's officers and men approved of the citizens' expulsion. Typical was the comment of General Geary to his wife Mary, 8 September: Sherman's order was logically intended "to prevent them from becoming chargeable to our government and of eating up the rations and subsistence intended for the army." Ward Nichols, aide-de-camp to General Sherman, also stood strongly with his commander's decision. "Atlanta was a captured city. He was at a great distance from his base of supplies, with a precarious line of communication, which was frequently interrupted by the Rebel guerrilla raids," he reasoned. "It would have been an absurd incongruity daily to fill the mouths of the wives and children of men in arms against the government. The safety of his command was at stake; so he sent these people away."

A soldier in the ranks, Horatio Chapman agreed: "our army is hear and must be fed." Chaplain John J. Hight of the 58th Indiana recorded after a visit into the city on 19 September: "there are still a good many citizens here, notwithstanding General Sherman's order of banishment. Some harsh criticisms are made by many on account of Sherman's action in this matter. But, I think, under the circumstances, the order was a wise one. It is true, there is not much humanity about it, but there is not much humanity about war measures of any kind." New Yorker Sergeant Rice Bull thought the same: it was a "very difficult and unpleasant job in evacuating those civilians," but the general's orders had to be carried out. It was a matter of military necessity that the people had to go; they could not be fed—the military railroad to the North was being taxed enough bringing food just for the army at Atlanta. As it turned out, Bull and his company accompanied a wagon train of civilians to Rough and Ready. "They were mostly old men and women who were almost helpless to care for themselves." Still, "we did all we could to make them comfortable and show them how sorry we were that they had to leave their homes.... The Negro servants were very loyal to them and we were happy that they went with these old white people."

There were at least a few Federal officers, however, like Colonel Le Duc, who openly objected to Sherman's order and sympathized with the citizenry. "The order to remove fills them with dismay and grief," Le Duc wrote to his wife. "Suppose all men [were] required to leave Mt. Vernon within ten or twenty days and you can imagine the consternation it would produce. When will we go. What will we do for a home. How shall we live. Can we take our property with us." Captain Edwin E. Marvin of the 5th Connecticut, evidently one of those who also objected to the expulsion, recorded that Sherman's treatment of Atlanta's citizens would likely haunt him in future years. Because of his decision, Marvin thought Sherman would be "given a very bad character for almost any position in life," even "by some of his old friends and classmates."

Atlanta's "Union men" were of course shocked to learn that they, like the Rebels, would also be thrown out from their homes. Captain David Conyngham felt for them. While the city's Confederate sympathizers "were merely joining their friends" in their pilgrimage southward, "the men who had concealed themselves from conscription, who had been persecuted by rebel authority, whose friends had been shot down or hung up for their Union sentiments, who concealed our wounded men and fed them, and who screened our prisoners and aided their flight, who longed for us as their friends, did not well know what to do." Conyngham told of a conversation he had with a gentleman of Unionist loyalty, who justly "found our friendship as destructive as the rebels' enmity."

> "Could you tell me who are our friends?" said an old, respectable citizen to me.
> "If you tell me your politics, I will," said I.
> "At the breaking out of the war I owed large sums to northern merchants, and I paid them. I had neither hand nor voice in bringing on this war; I wanted to live under the old flag. During the war I gave every assistance in my power to relieve Union prisoners, and my only son was caught aiding one of them to escape, and shot. The rebels then stripped me of my property, and called me a d—d Yank. Only for my age, they'd hang me."
> "Well, I think you are a Union man," I replied.
> "I have given proofs enough, at least; and now what's my reward? You hunt me from my house and place in my old age. Do you think but I am suffering for my country? I have the alternative of going north and starve, or going into the rebel lines and being hung."[42]

General Sherman seemed to show no remorse for his evacuation order, especially after chief of staff Major General Henry W. Halleck commended him for it. "Not only are you justified by the laws and usages of war in removing these people," he wrote, "but I think it was your duty to your own army to do so." Thus supported by the brass in Washington, Sherman was prepared to face public criticism. To his wife Ellen he wrote on 17 September:

---

[42] Al G. Pugh to "Sister," 16 September 1864, Pugh Letters, Chicago Historical Society (copy courtesy of Dr. Albert Castel, Columbus OH); Fox to William, 15 September, Wiley Sword personal collection; Frank, "Children of the March," 115 (on Daniels and Chapman); Blair, ed., *A Politician Goes to War*, 200 (Geary to wife, 8 September); Nichols, *Story of the Great March*, 26; John J. Hight, *History of the Fifty-Eighth Regiment of Indiana Volunteer Infantry* (Princeton IN: Press of the Clarion, 1895) 369; Bauer, ed., *Soldiering*, 170; William G. Le Duc to Mary, 9 September, quoted in Dyer, *Secret Yankees*, 202; Marvin, *Fifth Regiment Connecticut Volunteers*, 336; Conyngham, *Sherman's March through the South*, 224–25.

I have had some sharp correspondence with Hood about expelling the poor families of a brave People [that phrase again], which correspondence in due time will become public, and I take the ground that Atlanta is a conquered place and I propose to use it purely for our own military purposes which are inconsistent with its habitation by the families of a Brave People—I am shipping them *all* and by next Wednesday [21 September] the Town will be a real Military town with no woman boring me every order I give. Hood no doubt thought he could make Capital out of the barbarity &c. but I rather think he will change his mind before he is done.

In the Northern press, Sherman's expulsion order received widespread support for the reasons outlined by the general himself, especially that of military necessity. Yet some, such as "Huguenot," writing in the *New York Times*, expressed regret that noncombatants would have to suffer.

From necessary causes the order operates harshly upon the aged, of whom there are many whose children are in the rebel ranks, and who are thus shorn of all power to support themselves when cut adrift from their present homes. This class beg earnestly to be exempted from the order, pledging to avoid calling upon the Government for support; but no distinction is made. From the imperative dictates of military necessity, all not of the army must leave its vicinity. Although reason tells us that Gen. Sherman is right in his assertions and conclusions, as expressed in his orders and letters on this subject, our sympathies—we cannot deny it— are strongly enlisted in behalf of the aged and helpless, many of whom cannot be held responsible for the crime of treason....

Even if "Huguenot" felt sympathy with the civilians kicked out of Atlanta, he sided with General Sherman on the necessity of expulsion. As news of the event spread in the Northern papers, Sherman remained sensitive to some reporting. When the Associated Press distributed a Confederate news report from Macon of 14 September that claimed that the first exiles from Atlanta had been robbed of all their belongings by Union soldiers, the general defended himself in a letter to George Tyler, AP agent in Louisville:

Your press dispatches of the 21st embrace one from Macon of the 14th, announcing the arrival of the first train of refugees from Atlanta, with this addition, "that they were robbed of everything before being sent into the rebel lines." Of course, that is false, and it is idle to correct it so far as the rebels are concerned, for they purposed it as a falsehood, to create a mischievous public opinion. The truth is, that during the truce 446 families were moved South, making 705 adults, 860 children, and 479 servants, with 1,651 pounds of furniture and household goods, on the average for each family, of which we have a perfect recollection by name and articles.

Sherman even appended a generous note written by Confederate Major Clare to Lieutenant Colonel Warner, thanking him for his courtesies during the truce, as they supervised the people passing through their lines. "I would not notice this," he added, "but I know the people of the North, liable to be misled by a falsehood calculated for special purposes, and by a desperate enemy, will be relieved by this assurance that not only care, but real kindness has been extended to families who lost their homes by the act of their male protectors." In this last statement, Sherman engaged in the same exculpatory calisthenics as elsewhere in his writing about war's harshness—the women and children of Atlanta were losing their homes because their "male protectors" had started a war and were fighting it still.[43]

---

[43] Halleck to Sherman, 28 September 1864, *OR*, vol. 39, pt. 2, p. 503; Sherman to "Dearest Ellen," 17 September, Simpson and Berlin, eds., *Sherman's Civil War*, 717; "Huguenot," "From Georgia," *New York Times*, 1 October; "Letter from General Sherman," 24 September, *New York Times*, 26 September.

Sherman's letter to Tyler, printed in the *Times* and elsewhere, presents a problem. Whereas Le Duc's registry of southbound exiles counts 1,651 individuals with a total of 8,842 packages, Sherman used the figure of 1,651 as *the number of "pounds of furniture and household goods, on the average for each family."* The discrepancy is too gross to be an accidental error of transcription. Either Tyler deliberately changed Sherman's numbers in the AP wire he sent out in order to make more strongly the point Sherman wanted to make (that the Atlanta refugees were not "robbed of everything before being sent into the rebel lines"), or *Sherman himself* deliberately changed Le Duc's numbers to make the same point. The discrepancy was not due to typesetting error in a single newspaper. Sherman's letter to Tyler of 24 September was printed in a New York newspaper on 26 September with the same assertion of "1651 pounds of furniture and household goods on the average for each family" (*Buffalo Commercial Advertiser*, 26 September 1864).

Publication of Sherman's letter to Tyler in the *Official Records* does not add clarification: it implies 1,651 as the *total number* of luggage pieces. Under date of 26 September (not 24), it asserts that the Atlanta exodus consisted of "705 adults, 867 children, and 79 servants, with 1,651 parcels of furniture and household goods" (*OR*, vol. 39, pt. 2, p. 481).

Students seem not to have caught on to the jumbled numbers. Indeed, if Sherman's purpose in writing Tyler were to emphasize the mass of baggage he allowed the emigres to take with them, Atlanta writers have accepted the Yankee general's bogus contention. "During the truce for the removal of the families from Atlanta, 446 families were removed south.... With each family there was carried 1,654 pounds of furniture, household goods, etc., on the average" (Reed, *History of Atlanta*, 204). "An average of 1654 pounds of furniture, household goods, etc., went along with each family" (Garrett, *Atlanta and Environs*, 1:642). "The Yankees were, at least, generous in their allowance of baggage—each family carried with them, 1,654 pounds of furniture and household goods" (Russell S. Bonds, *War Like the Thunderbolt: The Battle and Burning of Atlanta* [Yardley PA: Westholme

Thus Sherman stuck to his contention that in ejecting Atlanta's civilians from their houses he was actually being kind. Indeed, a story circulated that the general personally intervened to help a disabled woman who was unable to pack up her goods. The *Macon Telegraph* even reported it on 17 September. According to the *Telegraph*, General Sherman made a point of spending three hours that evening talking with the woman about his expulsion order, explaining its military necessity, arguing that he hoped to spare Atlanta's civilians the privations which he expected his army soon could face and so on.

Sherman also defended himself one night in late September when Episcopal Bishop Henry Lay, seeking a pass through the Union lines, secured an interview with the general. The bishop was the same diarist who had recorded the explosion of the first Northern shells on 20 July, and those near Hood's headquarters at Thrasher's on 9 August. After the fall of the city, Lay had written Federal authorities, asking permission to pass through the lines and visit friends in Huntsville, Alabama (then occupied by Union forces). The bishop's request reached all the way to General Sherman, who promised to grant the privileges if he should come to Atlanta. Accompanying Lieutenant Colonel Willard Warner (the Union officer who had overseen the exile transfer and prisoner exchange), Lay arrived in the city on the afternoon of 28 September. He was taken to the general's headquarters at the Neal house across from city hall. Sherman met the bishop in house slippers, greeted him, and engaged him in easy, wide-ranging conversation. Around 6:00 P.M., the general invited the bishop to stay for dinner, at which several staff officers and the wife of cavalry general Lovell Rousseau shared roast beef, vegetables, and pea soup served in tin plates. Lay and Sherman agreed that the late General McPherson had been a kindly man, although Sherman added that after the fall of Vicksburg McPherson had expelled several women for abruptly leaving an Episcopal church service when prayers were made for the president of the United States. Lay—who as a bishop of the Episcopal Church of the Confederate States would have led Southern parishioners in prayers for Jefferson Davis—commented that Episcopal prayer services customarily included prayers for the president, but at the moment there were two such presidents across the land. "To this he rejoined with some vague declaration about the clergy handling politics, which I thought not quite civil, and to which I made no reply."

After dinner, the pair stood on the piazza and enjoyed cigars as the conversation got even franker. Sherman complained that in their recent correspondence Hood had unfairly criticized him and that in giving their

---

Publishing, 2009] 318). Few seem to have checked the sources, or done the math: 446 families x 1,654 pounds per family = 737,684 pounds, or more than 368 tons of stuff. (Or followed the logic: Union quartermasters would have refused to carry such vast loads in their wagons to Rough and Ready.) After more than a century, Atlantans owe it to themselves to call General Sherman on his numerical error, or his outright lie.

correspondence to the Southern press, Hood was trying to "excite unreasonable prejudice against him." "To be sure," Lay quoted Sherman, "I have made war vindictively; war is war, and you can make nothing else of it; but Hood knows as well as anyone I am not brutal or inhuman." In fact, Sherman seemed to be quite sensitive to Hood's charges of barbarity, and spoke at length defending himself. The bishop recorded into his diary his recollection of what Sherman had said.

> As to the shelling of Atlanta, he denied that this was intended. He threw no shot at private dwellings. It was our fault in putting our lines close to the city. He was shelling the lines and the depot. After all, there was no damage in this part of the city (near the City Hall). I reminded him that I was in Atlanta all through the siege; the shells fell everywhere; the hottest fire I had been in was in private houses; shells struck St. Philip's Church near by and passed over the city.
>
> He insisted they could not help it. They had only the range and the smokestack of the railroad, and could not see the effect of the shot. I mentioned that we at General Hood's headquarters thought he had a special grudge against us. He said no; he knew the house was on Whitehall Street, but not in what part of it.

Bishop Lay's conversation with General Sherman was the closest thing to a verbal grilling that Sherman ever faced concerning the bombardment of Atlanta, and the general stuck to his original justifications. He also repeated his contention, made over the protests of Mayor Calhoun, that expelling Atlanta's civilians was an act of mercy. He could not feed them in the city and was allowing them to seek sustenance elsewhere, even assisting them in their hauling off of possessions. Finally, Sherman defended his decision not to engage in a full exchange of prisoners with Hood. He understood that at Andersonville Northern soldiers were not being adequately fed and clothed and for this reason, Lay wrote, "he could not be expected in the midst of a campaign to give us able-bodied men, who would go at once into the ranks, and receive half-starved men unfit for duty." At the end of their several hours' conversation, Sherman apologized that he could not put Lay up with him at the Neal house. He instead had a staff officer escort the clergyman to a nearby hotel. The next morning Sherman sent over the bishop's pass to Huntsville, and Lay set out on his journey, having recorded the most detailed account of conversation with General Sherman during the Federals' two-and-a-half-month occupation of Atlanta.

While both sides were counting the people of Atlanta banished into Confederate lines outside the city, an undetermined number of Atlantans opted to travel north. (A good estimate would run 1000–1500, as the *Intelligencer* at the time declared, "about one half of the population elected to go to Tennessee, and the rest were coming, or preparing to come, South.") Many would have been the "secret Yankees" in town, of Northern birth, now able to get through the lines without difficulty. An Atlantan of Confederate sympathies later noted that some citizens reputed to have gone north actually did not do so, but instead headed south to temporary lodgings. He affirmed, though, that "Markham, Schofield, the Dunnings, Banks, Edwardy, Boutelle, Lazaron, and a few others only went to the north." According to a member of the 5th Connecticut, "many of the Irish, and German, and colored people gladly availed themselves of the opportunity to get away north, but most of the native born preferred to go south." Patrick Calhoun, son of the mayor, remembered that his family still had about thirty black servants in the city; these all went north.

Unlike most of those transported to Rough and Ready by wagon, all Atlantans heading north were given access to the railroad. But it was not easy; to secure railway passes they had to be vouched for by the Markham-Dunning-Crusselle review committee. For Samuel Richards this posed a problem.

> I anticipated difficulty in procuring a pass to go North as it was said that only those who could get vouchers for their loyalty from some one of a committee of several *Union* citizens who had been appointed by the authorities—would be allowed passes to go. As I was only acquainted with one of these men and he was not inclined to favor me, I feared I should not be able to go North except *under guard* to be set at liberty upon taking the oath at Nashville or Louisville.

But Richards ran into some good luck as he was putting his household furnishings up for sale in preparation for his move. A Union officer came over to buy some furniture; in conversation Richards learned they had a mutual friend, "and hearing that we expected to find difficulty in getting a passport he offered to give me a note of recommendation." The officer turned out to be Major G. Ward Nichols, Sherman's aide-de-camp. With Nichols's note, plus testimony from another Atlantan that he had always spoken against secession, Richards got his pass from the citizens' review committee. Within a week, he was onboard the train for Nashville. He even got boxcar space for a large number of books he was bringing with him from his downtown store; he ended up selling them in Nashville.

Civilians travelling north seemed to have had an easier time taking their possessions with them than the wagon-borne exiles to General Hood's lines—at least they had access to big freight cars. William Solomon, who had shared his home with Colonel Cogswell and Lieutenant Colonel Morse, had a son-in-law in Nashville; he headed there along with his household furniture. Morse wished that they could stay, "so that we might continue to enjoy the nice beds and furniture." But the Solomons departed on 20 September, leaving Cogswell and Morse "in entire possession of their house...living in state and style," even without all of the place's furnishings. A similar case was that of the Ormonds, whose house on the southern reaches of Washington Street had been occupied by Colonel George Mindil. James Ormond, a lieutenant in the 2nd Georgia Reserves, served as post adjutant at Camp Sumter, the prison camp near Andersonville; he thus should have been in bad odor with the Federals. But Elizabeth, his wife, was courteous to the occupants of her home, and prepared the meals for Dr. Henry Van Aernam, surgeon of the 154th. When a Yankee made off with the household silver, Colonel Mindil had the thief arrested and the items returned. Upon learning of Sherman's expulsion order, Lieutenant Ormond secured furlough and managed to be allowed to enter the city. There he persuaded Lieutenant Colonel Le Duc to grant a pass for train travel to the north. He helped Elizabeth pack as many possessions as they could get aboard the freight car, saw his wife and three children onto the train, and promptly returned to his post at Andersonville. Mindil and his other officers stayed in the Ormonds' home.[44]

Some Atlantans had it easier than others. Unionist leader William Markham wanted to stay in the city, at least for awhile, but arranged with Lieutenant Colonel Le Duc for his daughter and son-in-law, Emma and Robert Lowry, to secure passage north. Le Duc was due for a month-long furlough, and offered to accompany the Lowrys as far as Nashville. As they were about to leave, even the colonel could not find seats. So he had a freight car furnished with a bed and privacy curtain for the couple, and straw on the floor for himself. The trio left the city in late September.

For many, the act of packing—deciding which possessions to take, worrying about what would happen to the rest—was as wrenching as saying goodbye to one's home. After Edward Rawson and his family on Tuesday, 13 September, determined upon Iowa as their destination, preparations began. "We had not time to spare," Mary wrote in her diary that day; "now began the work of packing in earnest, and from morning till night we were running up and down stairs assisting Mother in her work." The next day the bustle continued; then, on Thursday, a Federal officer informed them that cars would be available if they could board on the morrow. This news set everyone to work even faster, especially in packing food for the journey. For instance, chickens had to be killed and prepared, "and other goodies cooked, so many worked assiduously to get this done." While her father arranged for army wagons and ambulances to come and pick up their belongings, Mary watched angrily as some women came to her

[44] "From Atlanta," *Macon Telegraph*, 17 September; [Lay], "Sherman in Georgia," 167–69; "From the Front, Lovejoy Station, September 14, 1864," *Atlanta Intelligencer*, 17 September; "Letter from Atlanta," 15 December 1864, *Augusta Chronicle & Sentinel*, 21 December; Marvin, *Fifth Regiment Connecticut Volunteers*, 337; "Reminiscences of Patrick H. Calhoun," *Atlanta Historical Bulletin* 1/6 (January 1932): 44; Patrick H. Calhoun, "What Sherman *Really* Said," *Atlanta Journal Sunday Magazine*, 22 May 1932 ("about thirty of our negroes whom we had left in the city, went north"); Venet, ed., *Sam Richards's Civil War Diary*, 237–38 (21 and 27 September); Dyer, *Secret Yankees*, 196–97; Morse, *Letters*, 189–90, 193; Dunkelman, Marching with Sherman, 24, 31, 34; William Marvel, *Andersonville: The Last Depot* (Chapel Hill: University of North Carolina, 1994) 220 (on Ormond's return to duty).

home, asking if the Rawsons had anything they wanted to sell. "On answering in the negative they said 'well we dont care you have got to leave and when you are gone we will come and take what we want.'" At least the family home itself would be protected. General Geary, who was staying at a house on Pryor Street, had from the start of the occupation been eyeing the Terraces for his quarters. On the morning of the family's departure, 16 September, Geary had his headquarters tent pitched in the yard, and even had his furniture brought up. "Taking a sad farewell from servants and friends," Mary recorded, "we seated ourselves in the ambulance which slowly moved out of the yard." Later that day, they were aboard a boxcar packed with their things and another family as well, sixteen refugees in all—seventeen, counting a little dog. General Geary moved into the Terraces the next day. His aide, Lieutenant William C. Armor, recorded in his diary that the Rawson's house was a "delightful place."

At the train station, men from the 111th Pennsylvania supervised the loading of people and possessions onto the cars. Although the passengers were permitted a "reasonable" quantity of luggage and other items, invariably some civilians tested the bounds of reasonableness by hauling their pianos, hand irons, even grindstones to the station for loading aboard. Demand for this much train space meant that many people had to wait their turn to board. They camped in the depot buildings and outside them, pitching their quilts and blankets into makeshift pup tents. For those whose wait for a train ran into days, conditions could be hard. One poor and pregnant woman went into labor while waiting in the trainyard. Captain William L. Patterson of the 111th brought her into the ticket office, arranged a couch, and called the regimental surgeon. Unfortunately, both mother and child died in delivery. Soldiers also tried to help those who ran out of food by doling out rations. One Iowan pitied their huddled plight, terming it more wretched than even he and his comrades had had to suffer during the campaign. "I could only say, God pity them!" he concluded, "and return to my quarters, pondering on the cruelties of war."

There were other stories of clemency and kindness. John W. Bates, a musician in a brigade brass band of the XVI Corps, was in camp outside of the city on 16 September when "a little girl calling herself Sarah Fowler came into camp." Dressed in a homemade cotton dress and a dirty sunbonnet, she carried a small basket with her rag doll in it. Aged ten, she said her father, a Confederate soldier, had died in Maryland and her mother had died of consumption just two months before. Since then she had been living alone. She had heard that people were being sent north; she wanted to go, although she had no relatives there. Bates and his colleagues were touched. They fed her dinner and put some hardtack and meat rations in her basket. Bates then took her to brigade headquarters and sent her on her way to General Howard, who was requested to arrange for her passage north.

In their orders for the city's civilian evacuation, the Federals had granted a slim window of exemption for certain individuals: "citizens from the north...connected with the army and who have...authority from Major General Sherman or Major General Thomas to remain in the city." This provision allowed some Northern loyalists to seek permission to stay in Atlanta, and thus stay in their homes. William Farnsworth and his wife Emily, both from Massachusetts and among the city's most pronounced Unionists, found three Federal surgeons who agreed to advocate for them as well as for a dozen other families who had aided wounded and sick Union soldiers hospitalized in the city. Among them were, of course, William Markham and James Dunning, but also Cyrena Stone and Bridget Doyle, who had waved US flags at Northern soldiers marching into Atlanta. Luther Faught, who claimed he had not sent his plant's munitions machinery out of the city, was also named. The surgeons' appeal, dated 10 September, was sent through channels to Brigadier General William D. Whipple, General Thomas's chief of staff. When it reached him, Sherman agreed to let the named parties stay in town, so long as they knew that "even their homes might be leveled in the fortifications" that he envisioned for the city. "Secret Yankees" who were given dispensation to stay in the city sometimes left anyway. For instance, Cyrena Stone departed Atlanta sometime during the fall, reuniting with her husband in Nashville; the couple then made their way to New York and eventually to Vermont.

The commanding general's leniency apparently opened the door for more petitions from those wishing to remain in Atlanta. Dr. Noel D'Alvigny had not left the city in the panicked exodus of citizens on 1 September, and got to stay as surgeon under contract with Dr. George Cooper, medical director of the Army of the Cumberland. D'Alvigny tended to the sick and injured during the Federal occupation at the Medical College hospital. Father Thomas O'Reilly continued his ministry at Immaculate Conception. Robert McCroskey, downtown storeowner and well-known Unionist, won his appeal on the grounds that he had slipped military information out of the city to Union forces. Some were just lucky. John Mecaslin was a businessman and city council member; on 15 September his wife Mary wrote her parents, "We are quite well, thank God, but somewhat troubled as to what to do.... We do not know where to go.... I fear we could not live here even if we were permitted to stay." They were in fact permitted to stay, for reasons not evident, except for possible Unionist sentiment. The Berrys also managed to secure permission to stay in the city. Carrie's father Maxwell had not served in the Confederate forces, having won exemption on account of his clerkship with the Southern Express Company. Maxwell Berry was fortunate to have as his brother-in-law William Markham, the most prominent Unionist in Atlanta. Doubtless Markham helped Berry get his special dispensation; during the occupation he would work as a quartermaster's clerk. The family was obviously relieved. "Papa got into buisiness to day," Carrie wrote on 13 September, "and the rest of us went to wirk in good earnest thinking that we will get to stay. I hope that we will get to stay. Mama dislikes to move so much."[45]

Despite Southerners' denunciation of Sherman for his expulsion order, there were stories of a lighter tone, doubtless told by the many Federal soldiers who approved of the measure. George S. Bradley, chaplain of the 22nd Wisconsin, related the tale of a citizen who allegedly got all the way to General Sherman, whom he asked to be exempted and allowed to stay in the city in order to tend to his property.

> *Citizen*—General, I am a Northern man from the State of Connecticut; I have been living in Atlanta for nearly seven years; have accumulated property here, and as I see that you have ordered all citizens to leave within twelve days, I came to see if you would make an exception in my case. I fear, if I leave, my property will be destroyed.
>
> *General Sherman*—What kind of property do you own, sir? Perhaps I will make an exception in your case, sir.
>
> *Citizen*—I own a block of stores, three buildings, a plantation two miles out of town, and a foundry.
>
> *General Sherman*—Foundry, eh! What have you been doing with your foundry?

---

[45] Dyer, *Secret Yankees*, 81 (on McCroskey), 202–204 (Markham), 214–15 (Berry); Rawson, diary, 13–16 September, Atlanta History Center; William C. Armor diary, entry of 17 September, Emory University. John Richards Boyle, *Soldiers True: The Story of the One Hundred and Eleventh Regiment Pennsylvania Veteran Volunteers* (New York: Easton & Mains, 1903) 249; Kennett, *Marching through Georgia*, 210–11 (Patterson and the Iowan); John W. Bates, diary, 16 September, US Army Military History Institute, Carlisle Barracks PA (copy courtesy of Dr. Albert Castel); Cogswell's General Order 3, 5 September, in "Sherman's Third Order of Exile," *Atlanta Intelligencer*, 18 September; Thomas G. Dyer, "Vermont Yankees in King Cotton's Court: Cyrena and Amherst Stone in Confederate Atlanta," in John C. Inscoe and Robert C. Kenzer, eds., *Enemies of the Country: New Perspectives on Unionists in the Civil War South* (Athens: University of Georgia Press, 2001) 141; "Contract with a Private Physician," 6 September 1864, P. P. Noel D'Alvigny Papers, MSS 84f, Atlanta History Center; Garrett, *Atlanta and Environs*, 1:652 (on Father O'Reilly staying); John M. Harrison, "John Henry Mecaslin," *Atlanta Historical Bulletin* 3/13 (April 1938): 127, 129; Carrie Berry, diary, 12–13 September, Atlanta History Center.

The Berrys were among the more favored of Atlantan's remaining residents. Federal authorities assigned a guard to the Berry residence at Walton and Fairlie streets (Berry, diary, 30 October, Atlanta History Center).

Stories of Atlantans being allowed to stay in the city became the stuff of legend. Years after the war, Mrs. J. W. Wade told how because of her hospital work and aid to Union wounded, she had been permitted to remain in her home, even with a soldier posted as sentry outside (Wilbur G. Kurtz, notebook 3, 200 [re an Atlanta newspaper article, "Mrs. Wade, 102, Who Saw Atlanta Rise From Ruins, Dies at Grandson's Home," ca. September 1927], Wilbur G. Kurtz Collection, Atlanta History Center).

Citizen—Have been making castings.

General Sherman—What kind of castings? Shot and shell, and all that kind of thing?

Citizen—Yes, I have made some shot and shell.

General Sherman—You have been making shot and shell to destroy your country, have you? And you still claim favor on account of your being a Northern man! Yes, sir, I will make an exception in your case; you shall go South to-morrow morning at sunrise. Adjutant, see that this order is carried out. Orderly show this man to the door.

Citizen—But, General, can't I go North?

General Sherman—No sir. Too many of your class there already, sir.

In addition to an unknown number of newly freed African Americans, around fifty families were allowed to stay in the city during the occupation, according to a Confederate officer returning to Atlanta after the Yankees left (no document from Colonel Cogswell or other Federal officer has yet appeared to name them). With so many residences empty, Federal troops occupying Atlanta had virtually the entire city at their disposal. Sherman's Special Field Orders 67 of 4 September prescribed how the ordnance, commissary, medical and railroad departments could impound structures or open lots for operations. Union commissary and quartermaster officers had no trouble finding warehouses and other places of storage. (Colonel Coburn commented, however, that some of them had been damaged by the Union army's shelling of the city. "Many of the buildings," he wrote in his initial survey of the city, "were found to be much injured by our artillery, but such as will be needed for public use can be taken at once with slight repairs.") Special Orders 67 forbade any officer or soldier from occupying any house or shed unless it had been designated as within the camp zone of the several regiments occupying the city. "But"—and it was a big *but*— "the chief quartermaster may allow the troops to use boards, shingles, or materials of buildings, barns, sheds, warehouses, and shanties, not needed by the proper departments of government, to be used in the reconstruction of such shanties and bivouacs as the troops and officers serving with them may require."

With this casual clause ("the troops to use boards, shingles or materials of buildings") the dismantling of a good many of Atlanta's buildings began. The soldiers' need for wood, and residents' alarm over how they would get it, caused the provost marshal's headquarters to issue additional orders on 18 September. A soldier of the 2nd Massachusetts, whose regiment was quartered in City Hall Park, recorded the directive that no lumber was to be "brought into camp from any buildings torn down without leave from proper authority." But such leave was widely granted, and soldiers ransacked downtown buildings for wood to build their quarters. The camp of the 2nd Massachusetts in City Hall Park featured shacks the walls of which were entirely of wooden planking. Some were even equipped with windows. All the Yankees' construction materials had been taken from buildings in the city, including the bricks for their fireplaces.

Andrew J. Boies, a member of the 33rd Massachusetts, recorded that from 12 to 21 September he and his comrades were "busy laying out streets, fixing up our quarters." "We have torn down quite a number of houses and converted them to our use," Boies wrote on 25 September. He was quite proud of his hut: wood framed with two windows, 8 feet x 10 feet, large enough to hold two bunks, six shelves, and a table. Nearby, the 111th Pennsylvania also had a trim, well-laid out encampment in the city park between the Car Shed and Trout House, their wooden huts constructed from the boards and planks ripped off downtown buildings.

Altogether, the troops' building activity meant, as Ohioan James T. Holmes put it, that "Atlanta by slow degrees is passing away." Holmes wrote his parents on 19 September that

all around the city fine houses are leaving, by piece-meal, on the backs of soldiers, in wagons, carts, old buggies and every conceivable vehicle. A house is vacated by a family, some soldier steps inside with a chunk or a rail and bursts off a board; it's goodbye house, for you'll soon see a hundred soldiers carrying away windows, shutters, flooring, weather boarding, studding, etc., etc., ad infinitum. All these, to fix up quarters in adjoining camps. So you can see we are comfortable.

The demolition of buildings prompted some Federals to view the destruction as proper wages of war. "The soldiers have (as a general thing) built themselves comfortable quarters out of lumber from the neighboring houses," wrote David Nichol of Knap's Pennsylvania battery. "Many a house has been torn down for our accommodations and nothing left to mark the place except the chimney or the foundation stones." Then Nichol added his judgment: "this is a sad calamity upon the citizens. But such treatment they must expect. They brought this war on & therefore must abide by the consequences." Atlantans sadly observed the Yankees' levelling buildings to erect quarters. "Ella and I took a walk to see how the soldiers had torn down the fine houses," wrote ten-year-old Carrie Berry in her diary entry of 2 October. "It is a shame to see the fine houses torn down."[46]

---

[46] Bradley, *The Star Corps,* 159–60; "Atlanta as Left by the Enemy. Report of Gen. Howard," *Macon Telegraph,* 10 December 1864 (on estimate of fifty families allowed to stay in the city); Special Field Order 67, *OR,* vol. 38, pt. 5, p. 837; report of Col. John Coburn, 12 September, *OR,* vol. 38, pt. 2, p. 393; Alonzo H. Quint, *The Record of the Second Massachusetts Infantry* (Boston: James P. Walker Co., 1867) 245; Boies, *Thirty-Third Massachusetts,* 90, 93; Strayer and Baumgartner, eds., *Echoes of Battle,* 333 (Maj. James. T. Holmes's letter); Brady, comp., *Hurrah for the Artillery!,* 374; Carrie Berry, diary, 2 October, Atlanta History Center.

Destruction of buildings was not limited to downtown; Union troops encamped near the Rebel works and beyond also stripped structures for the wood they needed. In so doing, Federal soldiers continued the suburban property destruction that had been begun by Confederate troops occupying the fortifications outside the city. "The houses on the outskirts of the city are being torn down to furnish lumber for the soldiers' huts," Captain Alfred Hough of the 19th US Infantry wrote home on 21 September, the last day of Sherman's expulsion of civilians into Confederate lines. Hough saw a train of wagons carrying out a lot of displaced people and their possessions, heading toward Rough and Ready, "and on each side of them were a detachment of soldiers demolishing their houses and casting off the lumber." Yankees' destruction thus affected a large area of Atlanta, both downtown and suburbs. When Corporal Charles Smith of the 32nd Ohio got a chance to go touring, he observed that "a large portion of the buildings in the outskirts had been torn down by our soldiers and converted into soldiers houses." Another regiment, the 5th Connecticut, had taken position in the old enemy works east of the city and established their camps with wood expropriated from surrounding structures. "The boys have good houses nearly built now," wrote commissary sergeant Mead in his diary on 24 September. They were neatly in line, with streets laid out as if by a city planner.

Everywhere the Yankees camped, buildings came down. Southwest of the city, General Howard's Army of the Tennessee concentrated at East Point and there, too, soldiers built quarters with all materials at hand. "As soon as the Infantry had 'stacked arms' and 'broken ranks,'" recorded Private J. P. Snell,

> ...every soldier deployed out, on his own hook, to pick up boards, slabs, shakes, rails, poles, etc. to contrive a house, bed and board for "No. 1". They were very successful, as the rebs left a good supply of boards, etc., scattered around, and the deficiencies were supplied by tearing down vacant houses, barns and cotton gins. Our own Hd. Qrs. were "fixed up" by the Pioneer Corps, in excellent style this P.M.—the ground cleared and policed—a railing built all around it, tents pitched and floored, etc.

Where houses were more resplendent, the soldiers made off with even better goods. From the "Homestead," suburban residence of John J. Thrasher, family legend later recounted how Yankees "tore out and carried away the marble mantels, melted the outside ornamental ironwork and used the library as a blacksmith's shop."

North of Atlanta, the same kind of property destruction occurred. Pvt. Laforest Dunham of the 129th Illinois had marched on 16 September from near Vinings, where his regiment had guarded the railroad bridge, to a new position outside the city. "We have got first trate quarters fixt up again," he wrote his parents with evident pride; "to make our shanties, we tore down houses some nice ones to. That is the way the army does." A few days later he wrote his sister,

I wish you could see how we have got our shanties fixt up. Thare is four in a shantie. The eaves ar about four feat high and our roof is our purp tents. We carried the boards about a mile—tore down houses to get them. We have two bunks in one end one above the other and we made a table out of ruff board and each one made a stool and we have places (or hooks rather) to hang our guns up and other things fixt according. So you see that we ar right at home and board at the same place.

In the general wrecking of civilians' homes, even Northern sympathizers were victimized. Amy Dyer, widow of the William Dyer who had been killed by a shell on 20 August, had her house and storehouse taken down by Northern soldiers, who also made off with her livestock and a buggy. After the war, she appealed to the Southern Claims Commission, which collected testimony of Unionist Southerners, and paid claims for property damage suffered during the war. The commissioners did not doubt the Dyers' Unionism, only their $1,430 estimate of damage. They gave her a few hundred dollars.

In the widespread dismantling of houses, blacks were also targeted. Henry and Polly Beedles lived in a house near the fairgrounds (she was free; he was "owned" by the Georgia Railroad until the Yankees arrived). They had worked hard, bought land, and built a house and stable. One day, not long after Federal troops occupied the city, 150 soldiers arrived with wagons. The men started tearing down the fencing around the property and soon set to work knocking down the plank walls of both residence and outbuilding. Henry and Polly begged them to stop. "Old man," answered a Union officer, "we must have your house and fence. My boys and myself have no tents and we must have your house to build some tents." "They came with wagons, saws and hammers," Polly recalled, "ordered us to get out of our house, and began to tear the house down." Dejectedly, the Beedles watched as their homestead, board by board, rolled off in the Northerners' wagons. After the war, Henry submitted a claim for compensation to the government: "they took down all my house, my dwelling, stable, well house, fence and posts. They did not leave a stick of anything on the place."

Commissary officer Henry Dean, whose Michigan unit occupied the former Rebel lines southeast of town between the McDonough road and the railway to Augusta, recorded in his diary on 10 October that his comrades were building wooden quarters for themselves, complete with cozy hearths. "There is a perfect chimney mania rageing in the Regt," Dean wrote. "Every man is a Mason & every tent surrounded by Brick and mud. The boys are getting up very nice fire places & chimneys." After observing that "many houses are being torn down, and the materials transported to camp to shelter the troops," Chaplain John J. Hight of the 58th Indiana explained, "there can be no objection to this. It seems a pity to destroy the houses, but the men are better than the buildings." The chaplain thus justified the demolition: "our people have long been exposed, and must now have protection and rest." Carrie Berry's parents had a different perspective, as she expressed in her diary: "Mama and Papa took a walk this evening and they say that they never saw a place torn up like Atlanta is." Perhaps they were talking still of shell-damage, but just as likely they were describing the demolition of city buildings by Union soldiers seeking wood planking. "Half of the houses," Carrie wrote, "are torn down." The destruction was not at an end, for whenever new Federal units arrived in town those troops too would dismantle buildings for their shanties. Companies D and E of the 1st Michigan Engineers and Mechanics arrived in Atlanta on 29 October—"today noon we fetched up at the City of Atlanta and was surprised to find Such a fine looking city," recorded engineer Isaac Roseberry of Company D in his diary. Two days later Roseberry wrote of "Great Times in camp this morning as we got ourselves into Some little Trouble on account of Tearing Down a fine House."

Not only did noncombatants' homes provide the timber for Union soldiers' dwellings, they provided the furnishings, too, when soldiers expropriated not just buildings but also their contents. "I remember of one instance," a Federal wrote later, "where a soldier had a costly mirror which almost covered one side of his hut." By 12 September, Major Daniel H. Fox of the 101st Ohio, in camp 2 miles northeast of downtown, had his quarters fixed up. "Colonel McDonald and myself have a large new wall tent and have a good pine floor in it and have made a very comfortable bed and succeeded in getting a couple of good chairs and have a pine table." Ohio captain Ira Read was also settled in, as he wrote back home:

> Our camp is in a very pleasant place and I have my tent nicely "fixed up." I have a door and two windows in one end with board sides and end with tent cloth over. My "furniture" is a stand with three drawers in it a rocking chair, an armed chair, and a spring seat lounge. The latter article makes a "gay" bed. I have white dishes to eat off and china cup and saucer. I procured some of my things with coffee, some with Secesh money and some I "went for." If they will let us stay here this winter I think I can live quite comfortably.[47]

---

[47] Athearn, ed., *Soldier in the West,* 216; Cryder and Miller, comps., *A View from the Ranks,* 443; Mead, diary, 24 September, Rufus Mead, Jr., Papers, Library of Congress; Snell, diary, 8 September, Illinois Historical Society; Fancher, "Historic Home" (on "Cousin John" Thrasher's "Homestead" in southwest Atlanta); DeRosier, ed., *Through the South with a Union Soldier,* 150 ("to make our shanties we tore down houses" is also quoted in Robert Gibbons, "Life at the Crossroads of the Confederacy: Atlanta, 1861–1865," *Atlanta Historical Journal* 23/2 [Summer 1979]: 51); Dyer, *Secret Yankees,* 198, 254 (on the Beedles' and Dyers' homesteads dismantled by Union troops); Arthur Reed Taylor, "From the Ashes: Atlanta During Reconstruction, 1865–1876" (Ph.D. diss., Emory University, 1973) 21–22 ("they came with wagons, saws and hammers"); John Hammond Moore, "In Sherman's Wake: Atlanta and the Southern Claims Commission, 1871–1880," *Atlanta Historical Bulletin* 29/2 (Summer

Meanwhile, in the city and around it, Sherman's soldiers settled into a routine camp life that, after the rigors of a hard four months' campaign, became rather enjoyable. The first train from the north entered Atlanta on the afternoon of 3 September, and thereafter, for most of the period of occupation, the army was well supplied with rations and clothing. On 6 September, a correspondent for the *Louisville Daily Journal* reported, "sutlers, artisans and news-dealers are fast coming in, and receiving permits to occupy houses"; these vendors sold amenities that Sherman's troops had not seen for months and now could purchase. Of course, there were always grumblers. Captain Alfred Hough of the 19th US Infantry wrote home to his "Dearest Mary" on 18 September that not enough transportation was being given to the army sutlers to bring in all their goods, and those sold were at "immense cost." As a result, he added, "we don't live very well…we get very little beyond army food, but plenty of that." Hough might have missed out on sutlers' delicacies, but other soldiers appreciated any new fare. In his diary entry a week later, Rufus Mead of the 5th Connecticut made a point of noting, "soft bread for the first time." Indeed, the "army food" being delivered to the troops included items which previously had been in short supply: vegetables. During the campaign, officers and men alike had received hardtack, pork or bacon, sometimes beef, coffee, and sugar. The fare had not been sufficient to prevent scurvy and the resulting night blindness. Private Dunham commented on this in a letter to his parents in late September: a comrade was doing well, but he was "blind after the sun goes down. Thare is a good many that way. Thare is four or five in our Regt. the same way." Commissary officers were now tending to the problem, as Corporal Charles Smith observed on 23 September: "Sherman orders eight tons of antiscorbutics to be sent to this army each day," allotted proportionally to each of his three armies (e.g., "two and a half tons to the Tennessee Army near East Point"). Fresh

---

1985): 14 (on Henry Beadles' claim for $1,120 and the claims commission's award of only $272); Henry Stewart Dean, diary, 11 October, University of Michigan (copy courtesy of Dr. Albert Castel); Hight, *History of the Fifty-Eighth Indiana,* 370; Kennett, *Marching through Georgia,* 213 ("a soldier had a costly mirror"); Carrie Berry, diary, 23 October, Atlanta History Center; Mark Hoffman, *"My Brave Mechanics": The First Michigan Engineers and Their Civil War* (Detroit: Wayne State University Press, 2007) 217 (on arrival of Cos. D and E in late October); Isaac Roseberry, diary, 29, 31 October, MSS 391, Emory University; Strayer and Baumgartner, eds., *Echoes of Battle,* 322 (letter of Major Fox, 12 September); Harwell, ed., "Campaign from Chattanooga to Atlanta," 277.

A few downtown houses dismantled by the Union soldiery have been identified. A correspondent of the *Augusta Chronicle & Sentinel,* walking through the then-burned shell of the city in mid-December 1864, reported that during the Northern occupation ("the interregnum"), S. J. Pinkerton's and T. R. Ripley's residences had been "carried off. The residence of Rev. Dr. Quintard and J. I. Brown of the *Register,* were considerably defaced—the weatherboarding and ceiling being removed" ("Letter from Atlanta," *Augusta Chronicle & Sentinel,* 21 December).

vegetables from the countryside, sweet potatoes and other delectables, were also vital, but often only available when locals were approved by authorities as licensed sutlers. "Officers and soldiers can purchase such things from persons authorized to sell them at government prices," noted Smith.

Among the civilians coming into Atlanta from the countryside were a large number of former slaves who had left their owners and now sought safety in the Union lines. Dr. James Patten, surgeon of the 58th Indiana, recorded in his diary on 6 October that "some contrabands" had entered Northern lines that day, claiming that they had traveled 60 miles to reach their new haven. Colonel James Selfridge, commanding a brigade of the XX Corps guarding the city's periphery, reported that during the occupation, "sixty-six negroes came into our lines"; some were sent to the quartermaster department to be employed as teamsters and workers, "while others were retained as officers' servants." Either way, African Americans adrift in the war zone gravitated to the Union lines. Doubtless all felt that their new condition was better than their old one, and usually it was. General Sherman allowed freedpersons entrance into Federal lines, but they were put to work: men as teamsters and pioneers, women as cooks and hospital laundresses. Officers also retained blacks as servants. Regardless, their freedom was strictly regulated. Just as slaves had done in Southern cities, officers' servants had to carry passes issued by the provost marshal identifying the individual by age, height and facial characteristics. Yet in the end, if blacks in Northern-held Atlanta found their lot demeaning, they could at least relish their new emancipation. William Ward was one former slave who, after initial worry as to how the Yankees would treat him, gladly accepted work as a teamster for Union ammunition wagons. He stayed with Sherman's army until the end of the war.[48]

As the Yankees settled into their occupation, "life became rather pleasant again," recalled Captain Henry Comey of the 2nd Massachusetts. After sleeping in a real bed under an actual roof and drinking his first glass of milk in months, another soldier wrote, "Golley, it is most like a ferlow." Indeed, many of Sherman's soldiers were getting more than a furlough; as their three-year

---

[48] Kennett, *Marching through Georgia,* 205 (first train, 3 September; Mead, "soft bread"), 213 (*Louisville Journal* on sutlers); Athearn, ed., *Soldier in the West,* 216; Byron Stinson, "Scurvy in the Civil War," *Civil War Times Illustrated* 5/5 (August 1966): 24 ("Sherman's men suffered from some scurvy during the battles for Atlanta in the summer of 1864"); Stinson, "Night Blindness," *Civil War Times Illustrated* 4/9 (January 1966): 33; DeRosier, *Through the South with a Union Soldier,* 150, 154; Cryder and Miller, comps., *A View from the Ranks,* 441; Athearn, ed., "An Indiana Doctor," 414; report of Col. James L. Selfridge, 26 December 1864, *OR,* vol. 39, pt. 1, p. 654; Clarence L. Mohr, "The Atlanta Campaign and the African American Experience in Civil War Georgia," Lesley J. Gordon and John C. Inscoe, eds., *Inside the Confederate Nation: Essays in Honor of Emory M. Thomas* (Baton Rouge: Louisiana State University Press, 2005) 288–89; Dunkelman, *Marching with Sherman,* 35 (on Ward).

enlistments expired, soldiers could choose to go home or reenlist. The US War Department offered considerable inducement for the men to re-up: a month's pay, a bounty of $400, a thirty-day furlough with free transport home, and a special chevron of red and blue braid for the soldier's left sleeve, distinguishing the wearer as a "Veteran Volunteer." But a month's pay for Billy Yanks was only $13.00; the bounty was to be paid periodically through the soldier's term of service; and a month at home substituted poorly for staying home permanently. Thus during the occupation at least several thousand—the number is hard to confirm—of Sherman's troops boarded the trains to go home. Some regiments such as the 32nd Indiana dissolved when most of their members opted to leave. Ohio Captain Ira Read wrote home on 18 September that "the cars come in heavily laden with rations and go out loaded with soldiers whose time has expired." Their rationale was voiced by a member of the 6th Kentucky, who asserted, "let the young men sitting at home come out and carry their share of the load."

Soldiers leaving the service signaled the relaxed atmosphere of the Federals' occupation. Adding to it was the troops' opportunity to refit when new clothing and other uniform replacements began to arrive. As the men turned in their old uniforms and worn-out shoes, they also received new haversacks, canteens and other items. A Michigander wrote in his diary, 11 September, "the men were looking splendidly with their new clothing I think I never saw them look any better." Lieutenant Colonel Philip C. Hayes of the 103rd Ohio recorded in his journal that the "complete new suit of army blue" transformed every soldier. "This so changed the appearance of some of the men," he wrote, "that their nearest friends scarcely recognized them."

Everyone was dressing up, even General Sherman. Sometime between his arrival in Atlanta and probably 28 September, George Barnard took a series of pictures at a Confederate fort west of the city that Union engineers had remodeled by lowering the earthen parapets and replacing the interior revetments with new wooden planks. Barnard's subjects were the Northern cannoneers manning the fort as well as Sherman, Captain Poe, and a number of other officers. In one scene Barnard focused on Sherman alone, mounted on his horse Duke, the general looking sternly ahead, every bit the confident, victorious commander. It is obvious that Sherman dressed up for the occasion; ordinarily indifferent to apparel, here he is smartly attired in full tunic with epaulettes, even a sash at his waist. Sherman was so proud of Barnard's photographs that he sent some home to his wife Ellen, including the one showing himself on Duke. On 1 October he wrote her, "I sent you a few days ago some photographs, one of which Duke was very fine. He stood like a gentleman for his portrait, and I like it better than any I ever had taken."[49]

[49] Comey, *Legacy of Valor*, 196; Kennett, *Marching through Georgia*, 205 ("Golley...ferlow"); McPherson, *Battle Cry of Freedom*, 719–20 (on Veteran Volunteers); Bell

To be sure, all was not leisure for Sherman's troops, as his officers ordered the drills, inspections, and parades. "We had dress parades every day and the usual brigade and division reviews and inspections," remembered Lieutenant Charles Dana Miller of the 76th Ohio. Miller was inspector for his brigade, so he was kept busy. "Every musket had to be handled, the appearance of the men criticized, their knapsacks, clothing and accoutrements examined," he wrote, "and everything pertaining to all the departments of the Brigade required a rigid examination." All the fuss caused considerable complaint among the men. "Our promised rest is pretty well taken up between Co & Reg drill 4 hours each day," Wisconsan Edward Allen wrote on 16 September; more time went to "cleaning camp, guns & accouterments, Inspections, parades, &c., &c." Indeed, parade marches became commonplace. On 21 September, troops of the XX Corps marched in a grand review for General Sherman, held in open fields outside town, after which, wrote Captain Edwin E. Marvin of the 5th Connecticut, "we moved into the city and gave General Sherman and General Thomas a marching salute at their headquarters"—a route that would have taken the infantry down Peachtree (past the Leyden house) to city hall (and the Neal home). All of this activity became tiring after awhile for the rank and file. "For my part thare is little to mutch marching about," grumbled Private Laforest Dunham in a letter to his sister. "We ar a going to have grand review of the hole corps some time next weak by General Tommas," he wrote; "I tell you what it will be a grand sight for a person to stand and look on, but I don't care mutch about it."

After such marches, many Yanks found time to write home and mend their uniforms. Some would-be bards even engaged in poetizing as a way of whiling time. A member of Company D, 13th New Jersey, composed ten stanzas of rhyme as a narrative of the Federals' victorious campaign: "Atlanta, the stronghold of treason, rebellion, / Has fallen at last in the hands of the brave; / And now, let the voice of the North's twenty million / Proclaim that its army the nation can save." The justly anonymous rhymer—unidentified in his regimental history—then recounted from Ringgold the Federals' four months' struggle against Johnston through North Georgia, until they came upon Hood at Atlanta.

So, in the defenses he rallied his forces,

Irvin Wiley, *The Life of Billy Yank: The Common Soldier of the Union* (Indianapolis: Bobbs-Merrill, 1951) 343 (red and blue chevrons); Joseph R. Reinhart, trans. and ed., *August Willich's Gallant Dutchmen: Civil War Letters from the 32nd Indiana Infantry* (Kent OH: Kent State University Press, 2006) 167, 204n52 ("let the young men…come out"); Harwell, ed., "Campaign from Chattanooga to Atlanta," 277; Dean, diary, 11 September, University of Michigan; Philip C. Hayes, *Journal-History of the Hundred & Third Ohio Volunteer Infantry* (Toledo: Commercial Steam Printing House, 1872) 123; "Sherman Strikes a Pose," *Civil War Times Illustrated* 8/9 (January 1970) 15–17; Poe to wife, 28 September, O. M. Poe Papers, Library of Congress ("I…enclose a couple of pictures of Genl. Sherman & staff"); Simpson and Berlin, eds., *Sherman's Civil War*, 728 (Sherman to wife, 1 October).

The Georgia militia and veterans combined,
But soon, to his sorrow, he received leaden doom
From right, then left, and then from behind.

Now the rebels gave way to depression,
And they burned up munitions of war there in store,
And soon the gate city was in the possession
Of Joe Hooker's veterans, the Twentieth Corps.

Others also felt the urge to set their thoughts and feelings to rhyme. Henry Neer of the 25th Michigan was one; for his wife, he penned some three dozen quatrains on both his pride as participant in Sherman's campaign and his animosity for the Rebels:

Here I am in the state of Georgia and town of Decatur
Where they cant raise even an Irish potatoe
But where they raised treason by voting secession
Which brought out the yanks and they took possession.

Now homeless and dejected they wander around
With the armies of Davis and sleep on the ground
Like the soldiers and dupes of that old traitor
Mourning for their homes in the town of Decatur.

But their homes in Decatur we use for the purpose
Of hospitals for sick with doctors and nurses
Their churches we use for commissaries too
By Uncle Sams boys in coats of blue.[50]

Throughout the occupation "there were suppers, and parties and even dances," remembered Captain Marvin. Members of the 3rd Wisconsin organized a "variety troupe" that presented amusing plays in the Atheneum, the theater downtown on Decatur Street. The men could attend these, as Cogswell's provost guards allowed foot traffic downtown until 10:00 P.M. Members of Knap's

---

[50] Stewart Bennett and Barbara Tillery, eds., *The Struggle for the Life of the Republic: A Civil War Narrative by Brevet Major Charles Dana Miller, 76th Ohio Volunteer Infantry* (Kent OH: Kent State University Press, 2004) 207; Steven E. Woodworth, *Nothing But Victory: The Army of Tennessee, 1861–1865* (New York: Alfred A. Knopf, 2005) 584 (Allen to father, 16 September); Marvin, *Fifth Regiment Connecticut Volunteers*, 338; *Historical Sketch Co. "D," 13th Regiment N.J. Vols...Compiled and Printed...by the Authority of "D" Society* (New York: D.H. Gildersleeve & Co, 1875) 33–35; Henry Neer, diary (undated verses), University of Michigan.

Battery organized a glee club, which gave free chorales for the entertainment of all. Some musical troupes charged audiences and made a little money. The "National Minstrels" of one New Jersey regiment put on "quite a creditable show," according to one report, allowing the minstrels to charge 50, even 75 cents, per attendee. The 33rd Massachusetts regimental band played frequently at night before the William Solomon house, according to Lieutenant Colonel Morse; staff officers came to visit and hear the music from the balcony. "Isn't a soldier's life a queer one?" he wrote on 25 September. "One month ago, we were lying on the ground in a shelter tent.... now we are in an elegant house, ...we smoke good cigars on the piazza and have a band play for us."

Colonel Bill Le Duc arranged concerts at the Atheneum, even though it "had suffered from a shell or two through the roof during the bombardment." Le Duc had the theater repaired, and organized a series of performances by the 33rd Massachusetts band, even printing the handbills on the small press used for issuing army orders. Performing with the band was a local songstress, Rebecca Welch. Welch had lost her husband in the army and had four children to support. Evidently she managed to win permission to stay in the city through Masonic connections with Federal officers; her late husband had been the Masonic grand master of the state. Le Duc came upon the idea of a "Vocal and Instrumental Concert" with ticket proceeds going to Welch's family. The first event was held on 24 September. Welch sang and played the piano to such tunes as "Then You'll Remember Me," and the army band rendering such airs as the "Anvil Chorus." For New Yorker Russell Tuttle of the 107th, "the familiar notes of old operas [he] had listened to from other stages," the bright lights, the crowded galleries, the applause and encores, all reminded him of the opera season back in Rochester. He noticed a few civilians in the audience, but mostly officers and soldiers—including generals Sherman and Barry, who "applauded most heartily." The next day Le Duc presented Welch with her share of the gate, $273. In successive concerts, the 33rd Massachusetts band performed, though the $1 ticket prices (set to help Mrs. Welch) "were rather high for enlisted men, getting only $13 a month," recalled one soldier. The price must not have mattered to the officers, or the events themselves must have been very popular. On the evening of 10 October, commissary officer Henry Dean rode into town with his regimental commander Colonel Heber Le Favor to attend the 33rd Massachusetts concert "but found such a crowd that we came home." As a variant of the musical recitals, a member of the 33rd expanded the regiment's repertoire to include comic plays performed by soldiers, Welch, and her daughter. "The Cobbler's Frolic" was the bill for the evening of 29 October, with a woman of color, "Miss Hattie," performing as "Dolly—Maid of all work." The theatrical season lasted four weeks, right up to the night before Sherman's armies marched out of Atlanta. Lieutenant Tuttle attended the performance of 8 November: "I never saw the Atheneum more full or the audience more noisy." In all, the band took in some $8,000, giving a quarter of it to Welch, who used the money to move her family north before the Federals destroyed the city.[51]

The commingling of soldiers and civilians involved some "sparking," as the men eyed the women about town and found some attractive. Sergeant Mead, with his tent pitched in one household yard, espied among the residents inside one young widow who was "quite pretty and charming—not over 22 or 23 years old." He might have taken up thoughts of romance, but then he learned that she not only had three children, but that the oldest was thirteen years old. "It took away the romance considerably," he recorded. On 15 September, Private John Brobst of the 25th Wisconsin wrote home about the "large warehouses full of tobacco, plenty of dry goods, plenty of everything but money" that the Federals had captured in the city. "But the greatest prizes that we had the good fortune to capture," he made a point to add, "was a fine lot of secesh war widows and girls" in town and seeking companionship. Some were seeking more than that, he explained: "those fairs of the south will tell a very pitiful and heart-rending story and the boys must marry them to get them out of their misery." Some soldiers evidently resolved to tie the knot, as Brobst estimated that there had been fifty weddings in the city between soldiers and local women (a surprisingly high figure, representing quick work indeed by both sides).

All romance aside, one Federal observed that some local women would for a few dollars "part with their good name, if ever they claimed to have one." Dr. Patten of the 58th Indiana noted:

A good many women came in as usual to trade for something to eat. Some of them bring in beans, some chinkapins and muscadines, while some I have reason to believe resort to more questionable means of obtaining the desired food. But who shall blame them, when their children are starving. Shame on the man who will take this advantage. But I have no doubt it is done every day, and that too by men whose position should be the guarantee of their good conduct.

In perfect innocence, the need for food drove some mothers to send their daughters into the Yankees' camps to beg. Pennsylvania artilleryman David Nichol commented on the "little girls…in our camp asking crackers & meat from

---

[51] Marvin, *Fifth Regiment Connecticut Volunteers*, 337; Samuel Toombs, *Reminiscences of the War, Comprising a Detailed Account of the Experiences of the Thirteenth Regiment New Jersey Volunteers* (Orange NJ: Journal Office, 1878) 172; John G. Zinn, *The Mutinous Regiment: The Thirty-Third New Jersey in the Civil War* (Jefferson NC: McFarland & Co., 2005) 156; Dunkelman, *Marching with Sherman*, 26 (Benson and Graves); Morse, *Letters*, 190, 193; "Concert After Atlanta Fell" (including Le Duc's letter to Forrest Adair, 31 January 1910 and text of the concert program; also in Garrett, *Atlanta and Environs*, 1:645–47); George Tappan, ed., *The Civil War Journal of Lt. Russell M. Tuttle, New York Volunteer Infantry* (Jefferson NC: McFarland & Company, 2006) 155, 168; Underwood, *Thirty-Third Mass. Infantry*, 236–38; Dean, diary, 10 October, University of Michigan.

us, I suppose sent by their Mothers." "They have a very hard life now since the Rebs left this place," Nichol observed; now "they have to rely on the liberality of us soldiers."

Sherman's men found the attitudes of females in Atlanta baffling. As one Federal put it, "as a general thing the ladies of Georgia were most bitter in their hatred of the Yankees." The writer, Sergeant Henry C. Morhous of the 123rd New York, could, however, cite an exception from personal experience. Morhous was at Rough and Ready when the southbound exiles were coming through. One young lady started talking with him, and before long "expressed her willingness to give her heart to the keeping of some good and handsome young Yankee officer or soldier, if he would marry her and send her North." Morhous and his buddies "admitted possessing these necessary qualifications," but there was one hitch: "the three years lease of our service to Uncle Samuel." The prospect of matrimony fell through for both parties.

At the same time, a number of Federals expressed no attraction at all for the womenfolk about town. Andrew Boies of the 33rd Massachusetts, for instance, was not complimentary of the Southern females he had met. "The women remind me of our 'Down East' squaws, the difference being that the squaws are more tasty and neat in their persons. They can beat the world for smoking and chewing. It is quite common, while on guard, to ask a woman for a chew, and forthwith it comes, just as freely and willingly as though it was a comrade from whom I had asked it." John Brobst concurred that the "ragamuffin gals" made for "a hard looking nation.... They want more hoops, because it is a Yankee invention, and the nicest fashion they have down here is that of snuff-dipping. The way that it is done, they take a small stick, such a one as they can get into their mouth, and wind a rag around the end of the stick, and wet the rag, then dip it in the snuff and chew it, spit and slobber around, just like an old tobacco chewer." Private James Clements of the 154th New York also found the local women disagreeable. "They're most all built like a ten-foot slab," he wrote home. He noticed many "a little round on the belly," and also of a peculiarly dark complexion, which he attributed to their practice of chewing tobacco and dipping snuff.

When Northern soldiers could ponder the indigenous females, clearly the campaign was over and Atlanta was safely occupied. The feeling of peacefulness in the city was helped by the disciplined duty of Colonel Cogswell's provost guards. "There is most excellent order in the city," observed one Federal; "the inhabitants are well pleased with our conduct and say openly they are better protected personally than they were by the rebel army." The surgeon for a Pennsylvania regiment wrote his wife on 19 September, "the men have behaved themselves the best I saw them either home or abroad. Every man has seemed to be on his best behavior since we entered Atlanta. The women have been dressed up waiting for our men to commence *Raping* but they have waited in vain. There has not been a single outrage committed in this city, a circumstance that the people say they cannot say for the Rebel Army."[52]

Amidst the general civility in the city, there was even opportunity for renewed religiosity. On Sundays, church services were conducted at several places of worship downtown, including the Second Presbyterian and Methodist churches as well as at Immaculate Conception Cathedral. On the Federals' first Sabbath as occupiers, 4 September, some attended church at Saint Philip's Episcopal. Lieutenant Russell Tuttle of the 107th New York was impressed when the rector, the Reverend Andrew F. Freeman, reading from the *Book of Common Prayer* that part that addresses civil authorities, actually intoned, "We beseech thee to behold and bless thy servant the President of the United States." All went well the next Sunday, too. At the Presbyterian church on 11 September, the chaplain of the 2nd Massachusetts sermonized under the title "What Wilt Thou Have Me Do"; Lieutenant Tuttle was again in the congregation, impressed by the playing of the church organ. "On the 11th," recorded a soldier in Cogswell's 2nd Massachusetts regiment, "the bells rang for church, and all was as quiet as Sunday at home." Yankee use of downtown worship places was not confined to the Sabbath. There were services each weeknight, organized by the thirty chaplains of the XX Corps, who formed an association during their stay in Atlanta to look after the spiritual needs of the men. Russell Tuttle attended one such prayer meeting on Tuesday evening, 27 September, at the Baptist Church.

But churches were used by the Federals for other purposes than worship. Just as the occupiers had taken over warehouses and depot buildings, even the Masonic Hall, for their army stores, so too did Union soldiers occupy many other buildings. Churches were not off limits. After the Reverend Freeman of Saint Philip's left town (traveling northward), the army took over the church and rectory—such that the US government following the war paid the parish $800 for use of the property. According to local legend, Trinity Methodist also served as a

---

[52] Kennett, *Marching through Georgia,* 206–207, 214 (including diary of William A. Pepper, 6 October, on "sparking" between a soldier and a widow [evidently *sparking* was a Yankee term for romance, as it appears in Washington Irving's "The Legend of Sleepy Hollow": when Brom Bones's horse could be seen tied to the hitch-rail in front of Baltus Van Tassel's home, it was "a sure sign that his master was courting—or, as it is termed, 'sparking'—within"]; Padgett, ed., "With Sherman through Georgia and the Carolinas," 311, 314; Margaret Brobst Roth, ed., *Well Mary: Civil War Letters of a Wisconsin Volunteer* (Madison: University of Wisconsin Press, 1960) 84–85; Athearn, ed., "An Indiana Doctor," 413; Brady, comp., *Hurrah for the Artillery,* 374; Henry C. Morhous, *Reminiscences of the 123d Regiment, N.Y.S.V., Giving a Complete History of Its Three Years Service in the War* (Greenwich NY: People's Journal Book and Job Office, 1879) 131; Boies, *Thirty-Third Massachusetts,* 98; Dunkelman, *Marching with Sherman,* 32.

warehouse. The basement of Central Presbyterian was even turned over to commissary department butchers; horses were stabled in its classrooms.[53]

With leisure time to walk about the city, Northern soldiers trekked out to Atlanta's City Cemetery, a mile east of the Car Shed. Like its Victorian counterparts in other American cities, the cemetery grounds offered spacious landscaping for visitors' strolling recreation and meditation upon the funerary monuments. Lieutenant Tuttle was quite impressed, as he recorded on 10 October: "It was 'a beautiful spot,' ...so nicely laid out, and so carefully kept. Many fine monuments are there. Some neat and beautiful, some stylish and for show. Shrubs and flowers everywhere, grass plots and terraces, and lots enclosed by neat fences and hedges, on all sides touching and beautiful reminder of enduring love of bereaved ones for their lost." Then came "a large field just east of the cemetery proper," a new section for the Confederate soldiers who had died in Atlanta of wounds or disease.

> But what touched me most was a sight of the countless headboards marking soldiers' graves.... Side by side they making long rows that stretch across the field, and so many of those rows! No carefully tended grass plots and flowers there, no trees and no avenues, no room left even to walk among the graves, but lain closely together side by side. There lie Colonels, Captains, and privates from every state in the South from Virginia to Texas, from Kentucky to Florida. Yes, and there are some Northern graves there also in one part of the field, with these words on the headboard, "From Prison Hospital." Poor fellows these, who had not even the poor consolation of dying under the folds of the 'Old Flag.' Ah! But the old flag now waves over their last resting place.... I have a deep interest in these captive dead, for a good friend of mine is sleeping among them. We had thought him killed at Dallas (25th May), but here we found his name, company and regiment, the date of his death, June 7 and those three words that mean so much sorrow—"From Prison Hospital."

Tuttle was pleased to see the cemetery being patrolled by a US soldier, "to guard the place from desecration." But some desecration had already occurred. When Chaplain John Hight of the 58th Indiana toured the cemetery on 19 September, he noticed part of the fencing torn away and some gravestones destroyed. Worse, he saw a burial vault opened and coffins looted by thieves—a

---

[53] Tappan, ed., *Civil War Journal of Lt. Tuttle*, 152, 154; Quint, *Second Massachusetts Infantry*, 245; Bartlett, *"Dutchess County Regiment,"* 122; Audria B. Gray, "History of the ʿal Parish of St. Philip's in the City and Diocese of Atlanta," *Atlanta Historical* ʾecember 1930): 6; "Georgians to Get Their War Claims," *Atlanta Constitution*, ʾVilbur G. Kurtz, notebook 12, 266, Wilbur G. Kurtz Collection, Atlanta

"sickening, loathsome sight" so revolting to Hight that he swore he would be buried deep in the ground, safe from post mortem plunderers.[54]

In early October, the opportunity for leisurely walks about town was cut short when Sherman decided to take most of his forces into North Georgia. Hood's army had been resting and refitting 20 miles southwest of Atlanta at Palmetto, but on 29 September the Rebels began crossing the Chattahoochee, heading north. Sherman had already determined they would be marching that way, probably to strike his supply line, the Western & Atlantic. His first aim was to protect the railroad from damage. On 25 September, he sent a division of the IV Corps to Chattanooga, and the next day sent another from the XV Corps to Rome. He then dispatched General Thomas on 29 September to Nashville to begin organizing an army there; Thomas took with him another division (Morgan's of the XIV Corps). By these dispositions, Sherman's army group of seven corps began to be whittled down. Already, on 22 September the XVI Corps (which had only two divisions) was broken up; its units were reassigned to the XV and XVII corps.

On 3 October, Sherman wired Thomas that he would leave the XX Corps in Atlanta and march with the rest of the army (IV, XIV, XV, XVII, and XXIII corps) northward to protect the railroad to Chattanooga and perhaps strike a blow at Hood. As predicted, the Rebels hit the W & A on 4 October, bending rails and burning ties for about 10 miles between Big Shanty and Acworth. On the day that Sherman and his troops set out from Smyrna, 5 October, Confederates unsuccessfully attacked the Union garrison at Allatoona. Hood then marched on, cutting the railroad north of Resaca to around Tunnel Hill, on 12 and 13 October, tearing up 20 to 25 miles of track. Sherman pursued rather leisurely, as he figured Hood would move out of North Georgia and into North Alabama—which he did. By 15 October, Hood was at Gaylesville, Alabama, and Sherman was at Dalton. Five days later, Hood was at Gadsden and Sherman at Gaylesville. For the rest of the month Federal forces hovered there, keeping watch on the Rebel army. After Sherman had confirmed Hood's intention of marching into Tennessee, in late October he ordered the IV and XXIII corps to join Thomas so as to confront Hood at Nashville. Meanwhile Sherman, with his three remaining corps (XIV, XV, and XVII) remained in North Georgia. As he put it in a dispatch to Slocum, "I think I will leave you at Atlanta and will swing around in the country for forage and adventure. Look out for yourself and hold Atlanta. You have plenty of grub, and I will turn up somewhere."

All during this time, the men of the XX Corps occupied Atlanta. There was little chance of a Rebel assault on the city, but the Federals took precautions anyway. Sherman and Slocum wanted a new line of fortifications built with a far

---

[54] Diana Williams Combs, "'All that Live Must Hear,'" *Atlanta Historical Bulletin* 20/2 (Summer 1976): 61–63 (on Oakland Cemetery); Tappan, ed., *Civil War Journal of Lt. Tuttle,* 163; Hight, *History of the Fifty-Eighth Indiana,* 370.

shorter circumference than the enemy lines, so as to be more efficiently manned. As early as 4 September, Sherman had ordered his chief engineer, Captain Orlando Poe, to "reconnoiter the city and suburbs, and indicate the sites needed for the permanent defense of the place." In the construction of the new Union works, civilians' buildings and lands would be as expendable in the work as they had been when Johnston's and Hood's engineers were building their fortifications. In his orders to Poe, Sherman had instructed his engineer to mark "any houses, sheds or shanties that stand in his way, that they may be set apart for destruction." Poe travelled the circumference of the enemy works and judged them to be about 12 miles in length. He then mapped out an interior line on high ground along the city's southern and western edges, with a tangent extending into the very heart of town. The proposed line ran less than 3 miles and cut through the northern part of the city; this necessitated, as Poe acknowledged, "the destruction of a great many buildings." Poe commenced his line-building on 1 October, when he laid out six batteries. Supervising the labor were Poe's engineers, both a regiment of Missourians and the 1st Michigan Engineers, who had arrived in town a week earlier. At times, several thousand soldiers of the XX Corps worked away, assisted by gangs of freedmen (an order had gone out on 3 October: "seize every negro that may be found in this city without proper authority...and put them to work on the fortifications"). On the evening of the 5 October Poe reported to Sherman that he already had positions for thirty cannon; "the platforms are laid and the embrasures revetted for that number, and I can finish quite a number more to-morrow." Poe sited twenty-two artillery forts on the line; installation 1 with its adjoining rifle pits ran right up to the front porch of the William Solomon residence on Mitchell Street, across from city hall (in which Lieutenant Colonel Morse was staying). The yard was gouged, but the house itself was untouched.

Other homes were not so lucky. General Geary predicted on 1 October that construction of the new Federal fortifications "will destroy many of the finest edifices in the city." "Every day," wrote Pennsylvanian James L. Dunn to his wife, "splendid mansions disappear and an unsightly earthwork with two or three of Uncle Sam's persuaders takes their place." The parsonage attached to St. Philip's Episcopal Church on Washington Street (then vacated by Father Freeman) was taken down in order to make room for an earthwork. "We are tearing down some of the finest buildings in the city to make room for forts," wrote William Wallace of the 3rd Wisconsin to his wife Sarah on 16 October. "We have built two large ones in the court house square and now we are taking down the female Seminary to make room for another, and so we go." The three-story, brick Atlanta Female Institute on Ellis Street was probably the most notable structure in the city to fall victim to the Federal demolition. "One of the finest & most prominent buildings in the city," Sergeant Mead termed it. From its tall cupola, photographer George Barnard had viewed the city and taken his magnificent "stereoscopic" photograph. Sergeant Mead recorded in his diary on

9 October, "it seems a pity to destroy such buildings but...down comes the Seminary." Captain Poe had wrestled with the need to tear down the tall institute, recording in his diary his "desire to save the building but fear it will be impossible." On 13 October, Poe even issued orders that the Michigan engineers cease its demolition, but then reversed himself a week later. On 23 October, pulling on ropes and tackles, the engineers brought down the structure in two sections, creating "an awful crash," according to engineer Martin Westcott in his diary. "That seminary," wrote Rufus Mead in a letter home, "is a mass of rubbish." He estimated the property loss at $20,000. "Such is the work of ruthless war."

Once the Federals' new line was built, even more houses went down as soldiers cleared a field of fire before their fortifications. "A line or irregular circle had been determined upon for our interior line of defense," recalled Captain Hough in his autobiography; "outside of this circle were many houses, some of them fine dwellings." Material from buildings marked for destruction would be used in construction of the soldiers' encampments near the new works. Hough recorded how the landscape could be changed with just two days' work.

> About 8 o'clock in the morning the troops were notified that they could take any lumber or other material from these houses that they might need to make huts of, as they were to be torn down. Before sunset every vestige of these houses, except the mortar that had fallen from the bricks, was gone. An equally effective establishment of property was then made, for before another 24 hours had passed, long rows of comfortable huts were to be seen, all made of the material from these houses.

Even though General Slocum had written on 6 October that the new line was finished, digging and clearing for the Northern fortifications took place throughout much of October. In Geary's division of the XX Corps, a thousand men worked almost every day for two weeks until the middle of October, when work slackened. Much had been achieved, according to Lieutenant Colonel Morse of the 2nd Massachusetts: "The old rebel works bear no comparison to ours; with our corps, we could easily stand a siege by Hood's whole army." Yet the lines were incomplete when construction ended altogether about 1 November. By that time Hood had marched his army well away from Atlanta, into North Georgia and North Alabama. Sherman's order suspended further fortification "until greater necessity should arise." Apparently, the Federal works in Atlanta would not be tested in combat.[55]

---

[55] Richard M. McMurry, *John Bell Hood and the War for Southern Independence* (Lexington: University Press of Kentucky, 1982) 157–63; Frank J. Welcher, *The Union Army, 1861–1865: Organization and Operations,* 2 vols. (Bloomington: Indiana University Press, 1993) 2:300, 343,583–84; Sherman to Thomas, 3 October, *OR,* vol. 39, pt. 3, p. 55; Charles Elihu Slocum, *The Life and Services of Major-General Henry Warner Slocum* (Toledo OH:

The Rebels' wrecking of the Western & Atlantic railroad—over 30 miles of track between Big Shanty and Tunnel Hill during 4–13 October—issued in a period of pinched subsistence among all the Yankees in Atlanta. Until the road was repaired, men and animals of the XX Corps garrison were without supplies coming into town. Union engineers therefore worked quickly to restore the rail line. The 10-mile break north of Big Shanty was repaired by 16 October, but the 20-plus mile span of wreckage north of Resaca took longer. Colonel William W. Wright, General Thomas's chief engineer, put 1,500 men to work out of Chattanooga; from Atlanta chief quartermaster L. C. Easton also traveled to help supervise the work. The repairs took a week and a half. Wright had enough men on hand, but there were complicating factors. Absence of roads in some stretches hindered transport of equipment; "men have to carry materials and tools," one officer noted; "makes work slow." Occasional raids by guerrillas were also disruptive; on 23 October, Colonel Wright complained of fifty or sixty of his men being captured, along with many of his work-oxen and even a trainload of rails. Finally, there was the problem of rails. The iron was being brought from Nashville, but not fast enough. To supplement, some rails were brought from Atlanta. On 21 October, for instance, Major Thomas Elliott's 60th New York marched south from the city and from those stretches of railroad not yet wrecked, yanked up the rails "till all railroad iron was removed from East Point to Atlanta." This iron was moved northward to help with the repairs. At last by the end of the month, the workers completed Atlanta's northern supply line. Colonel Amos Beckwith, chief commissary officer, advised General Sherman on

---

Slocum Publishing Company, 1913) 209 ("new line finished"), 212 ("I think I will leave you in Atlanta"); Poe's report, 8 October 1865, *OR*, vol. 38, pt. 1, p. 138; O. M. Poe, "Map Illustrating the Siege of Atlanta," Calvin Cowles, comp., *Atlas to Accompany the Official Records of the Union and Confederate Armies*, 3 vols. (Washington, DC: Government Printing Office, 1891–1895) vol. 2, plate 88 [on layout of the Federal fortifications in the city] (hereafter cited as *OR Atlas*); Hoffman, *"My Brave Mechanics,"* 217, 220–21; Mohr, "The Atlanta Campaign and the African American Experience," 287; Taylor, *Orlando M. Poe,* 187; Poe, diary, 1 October1864, box 1, folder 2, O. M. Poe Papers, Library of Congress; Rose, *Atlanta,* 112 (Barnard photograph of Solomon house), Blair, ed., *A Politician Goes to War,* 207 (Geary to wife, 1 October); Kennett, *Marching through Georgia,* 213 (James Dunn to wife, "splendid mansions disappear"); James R. Crew to wife, 1 December 1864, ("St. Philip's parsonage was taken down and a large fort in its place"), Crew Papers, Atlanta History Center; Holzhueter, ed., "William Wallace's Letters," 111; Mead to folks, 23 October, in Padgett, ed., "With Sherman through Georgia and the Carolinas," 320 (Mead to "Folks at Home," 8 October); and James A. Padgett, ed., "With Sherman through Georgia and the Carolinas: Letters of a Federal Soldier: Part II," *Georgia Historical Quarterly* 33/1 (March 1949); Athearn, ed., *Soldier in the West,* 216n3; report of Col. James S. Robinson, 28 December 1864, *OR,* vol. 39, pt. 1, p. 659; Morse, *Letters,* 194–95.

30 October, "the cars passed over the entire road both ways yesterday for the first time."[56]

Until the rail line in north Georgia was restored, General Slocum had to reduce food allotments issued to the men and animals in Atlanta. Worse, there was not just the XX Corps to feed, but convalescents and unarmed soldiers left behind by the several corps with General Sherman in North Georgia. These mouths belonged to fully 12,700 officers and men; plus there were some 5,000 horses and mules, "a force in men and animals almost equal in numbers" to the XX Corps itself, complained one of Slocum's officers. Indeed, the large number of animals in and around Atlanta—combined with the fact that the area about the city had been stripped of crops—caused General Slocum to wire Sherman on 9 October, seeking permission to send out a foraging party to bring back corn for the horses and mules. "We need forage," he wrote: "I have not a pound for my private horse, and all our animals have been out several days." The plight of the army's animals was indeed dire. "Starvation stairing us in the face," wrote a Union teamster, Michael Forry, on 10 October. He complained that he had only hardtack and coffee for subsistence, but the livestock had nothing at all: "mules & horses dying by the gross," he noted. "It seems so pitiful to see a fine large mule worth $200," lamented commissary sergeant Rufus Mead, "lie down and die just because he is too weak from starvation to stand up."

Sherman approved Slocum's request. Sherman, always logistically minded, knew the situation. "There is some forage on South River southeast of Atlanta," he instructed, advising Slocum that a division of troops and a hundred wagons should be sent out, both to collect the grain and to fend off guerrillas and Rebel cavalry, which were starting to be seen outside of Atlanta. Thus on 11 October,

---

[56] McMurry, *John Bell Hood*, 159 (on 10 miles of track wrecked between Big Shanty [Kennesaw Station] and Allatoona), 161 ("from Resaca northward to Tunnel Hill"); Col. William W. Wright to General Thomas, 18 October 1864, *OR*, vol. 39, pt. 3, p. 353 ("altogether twenty-four miles of railroad was destroyed"); Sherman to Grant, 16 October, *OR*, vol. 39, pt. 3, p. 305; Thomas to Grant, 18 October, *OR*, vol. 39, pt. 3, p. 351; Easton to M. C. Meigs, 23 October, *OR*, vol. 39, pt. 3, p. 409; J. C. van Duzer to Maj. T. T. Eckert, 19 October, *OR*, vol. 39, pt. 3, p. 366 ("makes work slow"); Wright to Thomas, 23 October, *OR*, vol. 39, pt. 3, p. 409 ("we are much annoyed by guerrillas. I have lost 50 or 60 men, one train of iron, and nearly all our oxen"); report of Maj. Thomas Elliott, n.d., *OR*, vol. 39, pt. 1, p. 674; Col. Amos Beckwith to Sherman, 30 October, *OR*, vol. 39, pt. 3, p. 510 ("the cars passed on the entire road both ways yesterday").

A relic of the Confederates' wrecking of the Western & Atlantic was discovered in the first year of the Civil War Centennial, when someone found a bent railroad rail at the bottom of the Oostanaula River near Resaca. Identified as of 1850s vintage and doubtless from the W & A, the iron was bent to a *j*. Observers concluded that it was a product of railroad-wrecking during the Civil War; my hunch is that the bent rail was the handiwork of Hood's soldiers in October 1864 (Mike Edwards, "Rail, Dated in 1850s, Gets Big Role at Big Shanty," *Atlanta Journal*, 4 January 1962).

General Geary led out some 2,900 men and a battery with not just a hundred, but over 400 wagons 20 miles southeast of the city near Flat Rock on the South River. Three days later, after combing the area, they returned with more than 6,000 bushels of corn. In addition, Geary proudly reported that the very wagon teams had lived off the land: "upwards of 3,500 horses and mules were amply fed for three days, and returned to Atlanta in a much better condition than when they left."

General Sherman directed Slocum on 14 October to "repeat the expeditions for forage and accumulate all you can." Again, the Federal columns headed east and southeast of Atlanta, countryside which had previously least been "eaten up" by the contending armies in their summer campaign. When the next foraging raid went out, 16 October, the men of the Atlanta garrison were continuing to feel the pinch. Michigander Allen Campbell wrote his brother that he and his comrades were "getting pretty hard up for rations." Federals in Atlanta looked to the repair of the railroad for relief. "If the road is not opened soon we will see some hard times," Campbell predicted; "our horses and mules are dying of starvation every day." Cattle in the commissary yards were also becoming emaciated; a Missouri engineer at the time commented on "the beeves becoming very thin and poor." When they were too weak to stand, he noted, they were simply slaughtered and dressed.

Thus both for rations and fodder, four Union expeditions went out during October. Each brought back in, according to Brigadier General Alpheus Williams, "over 650 wagon-loads of corn and fodder, besides considerable supplies of cattle, sheep, poultry, sweet potatoes, honey, sirup and the like." Major William C. Stevens of the 9th Michigan Cavalry rode on several of these foraging missions and rather enjoyed them. "We are saving the inhabitants a great deal of trouble in gathering their corn for them, digging their sweet potatoes, killing their hogs, fat cattle &c," Stevens wrote to his brother on 20 October, "in fact there will be nothing left within twenty five miles of Atlanta should the Rebels continue to cut our communication." Laforest Dunham of the 129th Illinois also enjoyed his foraging expedition. "We had a big scout last weak," he wrote home on 23 October. "We was gon three days. We had a tip top time. I tell you what we made the chickens, sheap, and hogs git." For Private Dunham, it was the little things that made a soldier's life pleasant. "I got a cantean full of molasses. It goes off first trate on hard tack and then we take hard tack and pound them up fine and mix them up with water and bake it and it goes down first trate with a little molasses on it."

Sergeant Rufus Mead of the 5th Connecticut, whose role in the commissary focused on his comrades' diet, enjoyed the plunder brought in by foragers from his regiment. "I never ate so many sweet potatoes in one week," he wrote approvingly to the folks back home on 29 October. A buddy, Tom, was on the second raid of 16–19 October and brought back a calf, a goose, and two chickens.

"It makes me feel like a countryman again to be woke up in the morning by goose gabble and rooster crowing," Mead recorded; "I enjoy it hugely."

Clearly the farmers and landowners in the raided areas were helpless to protect their property against the Yankees' depredations. Thomas Maguire owned the plantation Promised Land at Rockbridge some 14 miles east of Atlanta. On 23 October, as the Federals' third foraging expedition came his way, Maguire recorded in his diary his hope that the Yankees would stay away, but he feared that "we will have to drink the bitter cup as others have done." The next day, he had his slave hands drive off most of his hogs, cattle, and sheep to a more remote area just in case the foragers came. "We are now as well fixed as we will get to stand the Yankees," he cautiously wrote. Fortunately for Maguire, on 24 October the Federals headed back to Atlanta with their plunder but without a visit to the Promised Land.

On 26 October, Lieutenant Colonel Charles Morse of the 2nd Massachusetts recorded that a mess wagon had delivered to him at William Solomon's house "two barrels of flour, two or three sacks of sweet potatoes, a dozen chickens and ducks, a jar of honey, a keg of sorghum, and several other small articles; so you see that we are not likely to starve for some time to come." The army's livestock also fared better after the forays. One member of the 3rd Wisconsin recalled that his foraging expedition brought in 800 loads of corn, at least enough to give "the poor catle life enough to stand up and be killed." General John Geary pronounced his satisfaction with all the spoils: "I have procured from the enemy (here, following General Sherman's lead, Geary equated Southern civilians with Confederate soldiers) over 2,400 wagon loads of corn, and ravaged the country for 25 and 30 miles around the place. And besides the corn, the spoils captured in cattle, hogs, sheep and horses has been large," he wrote on 1 November. "We take every thing from the people without remorse". Expressing his own lack of remorse was Connecticut sergeant Mead. "It may seem barbarous to you to rob henroosts," he wrote in a letter of 22 October, "but Hood cut off our R R communication and forced us to forage for corn & of course we dont refuse to accept any thing better that offers. All is fair in war you know."

The commanding general himself encouraged this attitude. As General Slocum was sending out his foragers against farmers and villagers, Sherman placed the blame on the Rebels. "If Georgia can afford to break our railroads" [note *our*], he wrote, "she can afford to feed us. Please preach this doctrine to the men who go forth, and are likely to spread it." Still, not every Northerner approved of taking food from the people in the countryside. "I cannot say that this kind of business suits my notion," wrote Dr. John Bennitt, surgeon for the 19th Michigan. "But killing and stealing are legalized in war," and one had better get used to it, he reasoned, if a soldier intended to stay in the army. Geary came to the same conclusion about the foraging, which he did not find pleasant: "I suppose it is excusable, as necessity is said to be entirely unacquainted with *law.*" Wisconsin corporal Harvey Reid, after taking part in one of the foraging expeditions, judged them to be "really a curse to the army, for all the discipline seems to be laid aside. The men take everything that is fit to eat leaving families nothing to make another meal of—they kill chickens, pigs, sheep and calves, take the last particle of corn meal, flour, and so forth that they can find."

Thus, the Federals in Atlanta kept themselves provisioned until train traffic resumed on 29 October. Throughout the occupation, sutlers and open-air vendors were allowed in the city so the men could acquire vegetables and fresh fruit, always a delight for soldiers looking for antiscorbutics and variety. A bakery also set up operation, but prices were high, particularly when the sutlers tried to gouge for scarce items. John R. Boyle, an officer of the 111th Pennsylvania, remembered the costs of a certain major's eggnog party: "one bottle of brandy, twenty-five dollars; one gallon of whisky, one hundred dollars; five dozen eggs, twenty-five dollars; one jug, twenty dollars; one eggbeater, five dollars—or one hundred and fifty dollars for a treat of eggnog."

The situation worsened when army paymasters failed to arrive to issue the soldiers their monthly cash. (They did not show up till late October, when they distributed up to eight months' pay to the men.) Until then soldiers had to barter; the streets were filled with soldiers walking about, trading with the local women offering food for sale. John Hight commented that people from the countryside brought in "butter, buttermilk, green beans, chickens, tomatoes, muscadine grapes, etc." to exchange for goods in lieu of money. Private John Brobst of the 25th Wisconsin remarked in mid-September on the abundance of fruit and produce that country folk were bringing into the city, seeking "to trade them for stuff that we have and do not want," such as coffee, salt, and sugar. Yet aside from comestibles, other merchandise was more elusive to buy or trade in the city. George Cram, of the 105th Illinois, was delighted to discover a bookstore still open downtown, but found it only possessing "a few periodicals of ancient date, some musty old books and a very limited amount of stationery that could be obtained at fabulous prices." Cram ended up buying a bottle of ink for 25 cents. Still, at least for their basic needs, the Union occupants of Atlanta found themselves decently situated. Barber shops sprouted for officers and men who had not had a good shave in months. "Bake shops, commisaries & barber shops are very numerous," recorded Pennsylvania artilleryman David Nichol in a letter from Atlanta on 26 October. Express and post offices were also open; so long as the trains ran, the soldiers could reach the folks back home.

The war seemed far away in occupied Atlanta, except when an artillery shell exploded every now and then, the undetonated relics of the Federals' own bombardment. Their occasional explosion led, according to Samuel Toombs of the 13th New Jersey, "to many narrow escapes from serious injury." Still, Toombs wrote, "we led a happy life in Atlanta." For officers (as always), life was even better. Lieutenant Colonel Morse, living in the grand Solomon house south of city hall, wrote on 26 October, "we keep a cow in our back garden, and have cream in our coffee and new butter every day; we also keep ducks and pigeons."

Lieutenant Tuttle of the 107th New York, a lover of music, found that throughout the occupied city beautiful sounds could be heard. On the evening of 7 October, he strolled the streets under bright, starlit skies. "Brass bands in every part of the city, their music came blended, and confused from all parts," he wrote in his journal. Glee clubs of soldiers were singing, some amateurishly, others with fine voices. Near the Leyden house on Peachtree, "a splendid quartette" sang "Annie Laurie." Solo performers were also to be seen: here a blue-uniformed flutist, there a violinist. From one house came the graceful playing of a piano; Tuttle recognized "The Maiden's Prayer." He also heard hymns being sung from prayer services held in a downtown church; Tuttle was moved by the "the goodly company of worshipers" singing the doxology. Not everyone shared Tuttle's view; Private Al Pugh of the 119th Illinois could do without all the music. Writing home on 16 September, he complained of being stuck "in this Godforsaken land," having to endure "a never ceasing Pounding of Drums and Blowing of Bugles. Oh Dear I am so tired of hearing them. They are no less than twenty Brass Bands near here and some of them playing all the time. I am very fond of music but too much of a good thing spoils it all."[57]

---

[57] Report of Brig. Gen. Alpheus S. Williams, 9 January 1865, *OR*, vol. 39, pt. 1, pp. 649–50; Slocum to Sherman, 9 October, *OR*, vol. 39, pt. 3, p. 163; W. R. Johnson, ed., "'Enough to Make a Preacher Sware': A Union Mule Driver's Diary of Sherman's March," *Atlanta History* 33/3 (Fall 1989): 32; Padgett, ed., "With Sherman through Georgia and the Carolinas," 321; Sherman to Slocum, 10 October, *OR*, vol. 39, pt. 3, p. 178; report of Brig. Gen. John W. Geary, 15 October, *OR*, vol. 39, pt. 1, pp. 663–64; L. M. Dayton to Slocum, 14 October, *OR*, vol. 39, pt. 3, p. 270; Kennett, *Marching through Georgia*, 235 (Allen Campbell); William N. Neal, *An Illustrated History of the Missouri Engineer and the 25th Infantry Regiments* (Chicago: Donohue and Henneberry, 1889) 145; report of Col. Daniel Dustin, 26 December 1864, *OR*, vol. 39, pt. 1, pp. 679–80 (on dates of the four foraging expeditions, 11–14, 16–19, 21–24, and 26–29 October); Albert Castel, ed., "Scouting, Foraging and Skirmishing: The Federal Occupation of Atlanta as Seen in the Letters of Major William C. Stevens, Ninth Michigan Cavalry," *Atlanta Historical Journal* 23/2 (Summer 1979): 81; DeRosier, ed., *Through the South with a Union Soldier*, 157 (Dunham to parents, 23 October); Padgett, ed., "With Sherman through Georgia and the Carolinas: Part II," 49, 51; Thomas Maguire, farm diary, 23–25 October 1864, Thomas Maguire Papers, MSS 145, Atlanta History Center; Morse, *Letters*, 191, 195; Bryant, *Third Wisconsin*, 273; Blair, ed., *A Politician Goes to War*, 212 (Geary to wife, 1 November); Sherman to Slocum, 23 October, *OR*, vol. 39, pt. 3, p. 406; Bennitt to "My Dear Lottie," 21 October, in Robert Beasecker, ed., *"I Hope to Do My Country Service": The Civil War Letters of John Bennitt, M.D., Surgeon, 19th Michigan Infantry* (Detroit: Wayne State University Press, 2005) 324; Byrne, ed., *Uncommon Soldiers*, 197; Hinkley, *Third Wisconsin Infantry*, 146 (on 29 October as date of reopening of the W & A); Boyle, *Soldiers True*, 250; Hight, *History of the Fifty-Eighth Indiana*, 373; Roth, ed., *Well Mary*, 85–86; Bohrnstedt, ed., *Soldiering with Sherman*, 147; Brady, comp., *Hurrah for the Artillery*, 374; Toombs, *Thirteenth New Jersey*, 168, 172; Tappan, ed., *Civil War Journal of Lt. Tuttle*, 161; Pugh to sister, 16 September, Chicago Historical Society.

Amidst their comfortable camps and plentiful provisions, the Yankees enjoyed their time in Atlanta. But all about were signs that the Federals occupied only a half-city—plenty of buildings without many people, a fact depicted in the drawings of Captain David R. Brown of the 20th Connecticut. Like those Federals who wrote columns for newspapers, Brown was a Union officer who sold his drawings to *Harper's* as a sideline. During the Federal occupation, he had time to walk about Atlanta and compose his pictures. "Whitehall Street, Atlanta Georgia.—Sketched by D.R. Brown" appeared in the *Harper's* of 8 October. With only a few people in the streets or sidewalks, the main subject in Brown's drawing is on the buildings in the background and the Union troops in the fore. The picture, rendered into a woodcut by artisans in New York, makes the obvious point that the Gate City of the South was firmly under Federal control. A column of infantry bearing United States colors and a line of US wagons cross the foreground; atop a tall building flies a "white star" flag, the banner of the Union's XX Corps. Atlanta was clearly, as one Federal put it, a "Yankee town"; there were few Atlantans left in it. "Blue jackets rule the day," as David Nichol, artilleryman in Knap's Pennsylvania battery, wrote to this mother on 26 October. "The streets are crowded with them from day to night."

In the "Yankee town," some of the civilians who had secured permission to stay now thought about leaving. The Confederates' breaking of the railroad to Chattanooga for a period in October, however, upset any civilian plans for departure. "Markham, Rawlins, Moore, Schofield & others are still there anxious to go but cannot," wrote James Ormond on 31 October, himself an Atlantan who had already made his way out of the city. The sense of desperation among the civilians was palpable. "A few citizens still remain," wrote Sergeant Cram; they "walk the streets with a mournful absent look or stand like statues gazing at the 'Boys in blue' as they pass." Without work or business, the noncombatants in the city settled into a routine of deprivation. "There are some families yet remaining," wrote Lysander Wheeler of the 105th Illinois to his parents on 2 November; he added that Atlanta "is the most poverty stricken place I have yet been in." With "most every building...marked either with Bomb Shells or bullets," Wheeler concluded that the former Gate City was now the "Gate to Purgatory...."

"The houses are closed; blinds drawn tightly down and everything has a sad deserted appearance," Sergeant Cram observed. "The handsome streets are dug up in crazy places for fortifications; fine shade trees are hacked to pieces; magnificent stores are smoldering ruins; desolation prevails. Atlanta, the beautiful, the 'Gate City' is dead." The ghost-town feeling of the place affected Ward Nichols, an officer on Sherman's staff. "The houses are vacant; there is no trade or traffic of any kind; the streets are empty. Beautiful roses bloom in the gardens of fine houses, but a terrible stillness and solitude cover all." Yet Nichols found the fate of Atlanta to be a just retribution: "In the peaceful homes at the

North there can be no conception how these people have suffered for their crimes."[58]

As much as Atlanta had suffered in this war, the city would suffer still more.

---

[58] John W. Storrs, *The "Twentieth Connecticut": A Regimental History* (Ansonia CT: Press of the "Naugatuck Valley Sentinel," 1886) appendix, ix (Co. F: "2d Lieut. David R. Brown, pro. Capt. Cash'rd for misbehav. in face of en."); "Whitehall Street, Atlanta Georgia.—Sketched by D.R. Brown" (lithograph), *Harper's Weekly*, 8 October 1864; Bruce Catton, "Foreword," in Stephen W. Sears, ed., *The American Heritage Century Collection of Civil War Art* (New York: American Heritage Publishing Co., 1974) 7 (on New York woodcut engraving of field artists' drawings); Brady, comp., *Hurrah for the Artillery!*, 374; Ormond to McNaught, 31 October 1864, McNaught Papers, Atlanta History Center; Jennifer Cain Bohrnstedt, ed., *Soldiering with Sherman: Civil War Letters of George F. Cram* (DeKalb IL: Northern Illinois University Press, 2000) 148; Lysander Wheeler to "Parents, Bro and Sister," 2 November 1864, Illinois Historical Society (copy courtesy of Dr. Albert Castel); George Ward Nichols, *The Story of the Great March. From the Diary of a Staff Officer* (New York: Harper & Brothers, 1865) 38.

6

THE BURNING, 11–15 NOVEMBER

The wartime wrecking of Atlanta and its environs had thus far proceeded through seven stages, with both armies contributing to the property damage. Beginning a year prior to the Yankees' approach, Confederates themselves had dismantled buildings at the suburban edges, to make way for the engineers' fortifications, clear fields of fire, and obtain wood for building. Then, in summer 1864, came the perforations and fires downtown caused by Sherman's bombardment of July and August. Federals' encroaching lines also left their scars in no-man's land; sometimes (as with the Troup Hurt house) an unlucky structure became part of the battlefield. The Yankees cleared away all wooden buildings behind their lines, resulting in more "exurban" destruction. Confederates' burning of the rolling mill, their detonation of the army ordnance train east of Atlanta, and razing of buildings filled with abandoned supplies in the Southern army's evacuation of 1-2 September (as noticed by General Geary and Sergeant Bull) added to the city damage. Then ensued the occupation, when Sherman expelled most remaining inhabitants. In his two-and-a-half-month's stay, he allowed his troops to commandeer houses and other buildings, sometimes dismantling them for their wood or bricks. As seventh cause of demolition, other structures were destroyed in the construction of Captain Poe's interior lines of fortifications (e.g., the Atlanta Female Institute). Atlanta was indeed just as Sherman had said he wanted: "a used-up community."

Some Federal soldiers grasped the process by which Atlanta had been used up; it had taken months, and it had been done by both armies. John J. Hight, chaplain of the 58th Indiana, entered into his diary on 15 November a very telling recital of several causes of city wrecking.

> I have spoken before of the fact that the rebels burned many houses, in the outskirts of the city, when they occupied it. When they evacuated, they destroyed some buildings containing supplies and ammunition. Many houses were badly torn by shot and shell, during the siege. Some buildings were burned at the same time, by us, to give free range to our guns, or uncover the rebel sharpshooters. After the capture of the city many frame houses, especially in the suburbs, were torn down to make

huts for the soldiers. They were in need of houses, and in no other way could these have been easily and quickly constructed.[1]

Atlanta was thus definitely "used up." No power could soon restore it to anywhere near the position of economic prestige and strategic prominence it had enjoyed before summer 1864. Yet this did not matter to Sherman. Before he marched his men out of Atlanta, the Union commander ordered one final wave of demolition and arson.

General Sherman did not have to issue orders on destruction of the railroads around the city, because three of them had already been destroyed. Only the Western & Atlantic to Chattanooga was still functioning and that to serve the supply needs of the Union forces in Atlanta. The other three railways, though, had already been wrecked and Southerners were not able to repair the damage. To make the thing sure, as Sherman would have said, in late August when he moved his forces in his "movement round Atlanta by the south," he halted his columns for a day and a half, 28–29 August, and set the men working further to destroy the railroad between Atlanta and West Point (the railroad town near the state boundary, where the Montgomery & West Point line continued into Alabama). "Let the destruction be so thorough that not a rail or tie can be used again," he instructed General Thomas. Then, typifying his compulsion when it came to the wrecking of Rebel rails, Sherman detailed how the work should be done:

My own experience demonstrates the proper method to be: To march a regiment to the road, stack arms, loosen two rails opposite the right and two opposite the left of the regiment, then to heave the whole track, rails and ties, over, breaking it all to pieces, then pile the ties in the nature of crib work and lay the rails over them, then by means of fence rails make a bonfire, and when the rails are red-hot in the middle let men give the rail a twist, which cannot be straightened out without machinery. Also fill up some of the cuts with heavy logs and trunks of trees and branches and cover up and fill with dirt.

Following these instructions, Union soldiers thus further cut the Atlanta & West Point. When it was over, one Federal thought they had torn up about 20 miles of track.

Similarly the Georgia Railroad, running eastward from Atlanta to Augusta, had been put out of operation a month earlier. On 18 July, McPherson's Army of

---

[1] Sherman to Halleck ("used up community"), 7 August 1864, US War Department, *The War of the Rebellion: A Compilation of the Official Records of the Union and Confederate Armies*, 128 vols. (Washington, DC: Government Printing Office, 1880–1901) vol. 38, pt. 5, p. 409 (hereafter *OR* and all references will be to series 1 unless otherwise indicated); John J. Hight, *History of the Fifty-Eighth Regiment of Indiana Volunteer Infantry* (Princeton IN: Press of the Clarion, 1895) 409.

the Tennessee, marching southeast from Peachtree Creek, struck the Georgia line between Decatur and Stone Mountain. Kenner Garrard's cavalry tore up a mile of track, and Union infantry marching west toward Atlanta tore up another 1 1/2 miles. All carefully followed Sherman's thorough process.

However scrupulously performed, this damage to the Georgia Railroad by McPherson's army was not enough to satisfy Sherman. Two days after his artillery opened fire on the city, he sent Garrard's cavalrymen riding east toward Covington and Social Circle. Along the way, they burned three railroad trestle bridges (across the Yellow and Alcovy rivers and Cornish Creek) and wrecked 6 miles of track on 22 July. This damage was not repaired by the Confederates during the campaign. Major William Stevens, a Union cavalryman, writing near Decatur on 9 September, commented that "the Augusta R.R. has not been repaired since it was destroyed by our army...." Even after Atlanta's capture, Sherman wanted still more wreckage of the Southern rail system, and on 1 November ordered Slocum to send out a force to tear up the railroad east of Lithonia. That very day, Colonel Ario Pardee reported, his 147th Pennsylvania marched out and tore up 2 1/2 miles of track; Pardee made a point of adding that the work had been done according to the commanding general's well-known specifications. A Confederate engineer's report, prepared after the Yankees left in November, toted up the demolition performed by enemy troops along the 82 miles running from Atlanta through Stone Mountain, Conyers and Covington to the Oconee River: almost half had been ruined in some manner. Fully 38 miles of track was either "torn up," "twisted" or "burnt." The Federals apparently also took up long sections of iron rails and hauled them off, presumably to use in repairing the Western & Atlantic whenever Rebel cavalry raiders tore it up (as Sherman constantly expected them to do). "Outline," reporter for the *Columbus Times,* wrote in late August that "the Yankees before falling back from our right, were engaged...in effectually destroying the Georgia railroad from Decatur as far down as Covington. They also hauled away about seven miles of the iron, which they conveyed to their rear." William A. Neal, member of the 1st Missouri Engineer Regiment, commented on the "large quantities" of Rebel iron hauled away by train to Chattanooga.

Last to receive the Yankees' treatment was the Macon & Western. In striking the railway on 31 August, Union troops had done relatively little damage to the track; their mere presence on the line below Morrow had been enough to force Hood's evacuation of the city. But in the first week of September, as they leisurely moved north from Jonesboro to Atlanta, Union soldiers applied themselves to ruining the Macon road. At least for a while, the Federals kept the railroad functional north of Rough and Ready into the city, if only to transport such émigrés as Atlanta Councilman Crew on 12 September. After the conclusion of the truce on 22 September, when the last of Atlanta's southbound citizens had been expelled, the Yankees had no pity on the Macon road. When all was said and done, Union captain David Conyngham estimated that they had wrecked 15 miles of the Macon & Western, which would have been three-fourths of its 23-mile length from Jonesboro to Atlanta. The CS engineers' report on the damage to the Augusta railway also calculated the loss to the Macon line after the Yankees had left.

—Between Atlanta and East Point: "3 1/4 miles completely destroyed rails twisted & ties burnt"; "3 miles iron carried off Ties not disturbed"
—Between East Point and Rough & Ready: "2 1/4 miles of rail carried off Ties in good order & not disturbed"; "1 3/4 miles of Road in good order"
—Between Rough & Ready and Morrow: "6 3/4 miles ties burnt & rails bent"
—Between Morrow and Jonesboro: "1 3/4 miles rail destroyed—ties burnt & iron bent"; at another place, "1 mile ties burnt & iron bent."

The Yankees knew they had done a job on Atlanta's vaunted railroad system. With much certainty, Federal cavalryman Major Stevens wrote his father on 10 November, "Atlanta can never be much use to the Rebels and it will be a long time before they can use it [at] all as a base of operations, in fact when we have gone there will be a good many miles of Rail Road to repair before the next Locomotive passes through its streets."[2]

All the railroad-wrecking was just another signal to Sherman's officers and men that they would not stay in Atlanta indefinitely; the commanding general had told them in his orders of 4 September that they would occupy the city for about a month before setting out on "a fine winter's campaign." In the end, they enjoyed an extra month of occupation as Sherman spent much of October chasing Hood out of Georgia, sending troops to contest the Rebels' advance into Tennessee, and preparing for his next operation.

---

[2] David Evans, *Sherman's Horsemen: Union Cavalry Operations in the Atlanta Campaign* (Bloomington: Indiana University Press, 1996) 80–83 (Garrard), 166 (Rousseau); Sherman to Thomas, 28 August 1864, *OR*, vol. 38, pt. 5, pp. 688–89; Special Field Order 37, 18 July, *OR*, vol. 38, pt. 5, p. 179; Albert Castel, ed., "Scouting, Foraging and Skirmishing: The Federal Occupation of Atlanta as Seen in the Letters of Major William C. Stevens, Ninth Michigan Cavalry," *Atlanta Historical Journal* 23/2 (Summer 1979): 76, 88; Sherman to Slocum, 1 November, *OR*, vol. 39, pt. 3, p. 578; report of Col. Ario Pardee, 1 November, *OR*, vol. 39, pt. 3, p. 579; unnamed and undated document on damage to Georgia and Macon & Western Railroads, box 7, folder 12, Lemuel P. Grant Papers, MSS 100, Atlanta History Center; "Outline," "Special Correspondence of the Times" (Atlanta, 30 August), *Columbus Times*, 1 September; "Items from Atlanta" (letter of 30 August), *Columbus Sun*, 3 September ("The Georgia Railroad is utterly demolished, as far down as Stone Mountain, and the iron hauled off"); William N. Neal, *An Illustrated History of the Missouri Engineer and the 25th Infantry Regiments* (Chicago: Donohue and Henneberry, 1889) 144–45; David P. Conyngham, *Sherman's March Through the South* (New York: Sheldon & Co., 1865) 223.

Meanwhile, Sherman was communicating with the powers in Washington regarding his ideas for what his "fine winter's campaign" would be. General Slocum's corps had barely marched into the city on 2 September before Sherman started thinking of what he would do next. Pursuing Hood for an open-field fight was not an option; he had already allowed the Rebel army, beaten at Jonesboro, to slip away (some Northerners thought this was a mistake). At the same time, with Grant and the North's other big army static in the trenches at Petersburg, the authorities in Washington expected some movement by Sherman to bring the rebellion closer to collapse. Sherman began thinking of another destructive march through the tottering Confederacy, as he had done earlier in the year through Misissippi. In a wire to Halleck on 4 September, he tossed out the idea of some move against Columbus, Georgia, one of the few remaining Rebel industrial sites, a hundred miles southwest of Atlanta. But he was also thinking of a march in the other direction, perhaps to Augusta or to Savannah. "I can sweep the whole State of Georgia," he wrote Grant on 10 September. Indeed, any Federal march across Georgia would be a "sweep," as there was no Confederate army left to contest his advance; Hood and the Army of Tennessee were too weak for an open-field fight. Sherman's plans thus did not focus on the conquest of Southern military forces so much as the destruction of the rebels' railroads, factories, and shops, as well as the consumption or spoiling of Southern noncombatants' foodstuffs and perhaps the destruction of their property. "I would not hesitate to cross the State of Georgia with sixty thousand men," he added on 20 September, "hauling some stores, and depending on the country for the balance. Where a million people find subsistence my army won't starve." By such a campaign, Sherman looked to the end of the war, with himself and Grant as the glorious conquerors. "If you can whip Lee and I can march to the Atlantic," he wrote on 20 September, "I think Uncle Abe will give us a twenty days' leave of absence to see the young folks."

On the first of October—when Hood's army was marching toward Tennessee, and Thomas at Nashville was preparing to meet it—Sherman continued to make his case: "Why would it not do for me to leave Tennessee to the force which Thomas has and the reserves soon to come to Nashville, and for me to destroy Atlanta, and then march across Georgia to Savannah and Charleston, breaking roads and doing irreparable damage?" Sherman stated his objective clearly: "I propose we break up the railroad from Chattanooga, and strike out with wagons for Milledgeville, Millen, and Savannah." He intended to turn his men loose upon the Southerners' countryside and "cripple their military resources." And he was very confident of their ability to do so: "I can make the march, and make Georgia howl."

General Grant was not quick to give his approval, believing that the destruction of Hood's army should be Sherman's main objective. Indeed, President Lincoln himself may have had reservations about the idea of a march to the sea. And if Sherman wanted to head to salt water, General Halleck thought for awhile it should be toward Mobile, not Savannah. Yet Sherman continued pushing his idea, and eventually won Grant over by 11 October. "On reflection, I think better of your proposition," Grant wrote, as he gave permission for Sherman to make his march. To Sherman, though, it was more than a march. Indeed, he saw his forthcoming campaign through Georgia as a military feat with enormous economic and psychological consequences. As he explained to Thomas, "I propose to demonstrate the vulnerability of the South and make its inhabitants feel that war and individual ruin are synonymous terms." In the days to come, he called it "the grand move into Georgia," "my big raid," and "the grand march." "I propose to act in such a manner against the material resources of the South as utterly to negative [sic] Davis's boasted threat and promises of protection," he wrote Grant on 6 November. "If we can march a well-appointed army right through his territory, it is a demonstration to the world, foreign and domestic, that we have a power which Davis cannot resist."

As a key element of his campaign through Georgia, Sherman intended to destroy railroads, wreck facilities useful to the Rebel war effort, and plunder the people's farms and plantations. He was confident that his men could live off the land and became rather jaunty at the prospect. "Convey to Jeff. Davis," he wrote Secretary Stanton on 20 October, "my personal and official thanks for abolishing cotton and substituting corn and sweet potatoes in the South. These facilitate our military plans much, for food and forage are abundant." Indeed, Sherman had already rehearsed his march eight months before, and knew that it could be done. In February–March 1864 he had led 25,000 men across the width of Mississippi, from Vicksburg to Meridian, tearing up railroads, burning militarily useful shops, and robbing private farms. All along the march, Corporal Charles Smith of the 32nd Ohio recorded in his diary, Sherman's troops "ransacked the dwellings, then made for the ranks loaded down with Hams, shoulders, bacon, and chickens." Sherman intended to do as much and more in Georgia, and he did not care if the people protested—in fact, he looked forward to them doing so. Before setting out for Savannah he wired a reporter in Louisville, "you will hear worse stories than when I went to Meridian." Besides property loss, Sherman intended to inflict psychological hurt on the people themselves. In mid-October, he wrote General Halleck that Southern civilians "don't know what war means, but when the rich planters of the Oconee and Savannah see their fences and corn and hogs and sheep vanish before their eyes, they will have something more than a mean opinion of the 'Yanks.'" To Brigadier General James H. Wilson, he bragged that he proposed "to leave a trail that will be recognized fifty years hence."

And there was Atlanta. As early as 1 October, Sherman had written Grant that as part of his "grand move into Georgia," he pledged to "destroy Atlanta." He used the same phrase in a wire to Thomas on 19 October. On 1 November, he ordered General Slocum to "make preliminary preparations for the absolute destruction in Atlanta of the railroad track, depots, car and store houses, shops, and indeed everything that might be used to our disadvantage by an enemy." Finally, to General Grant on 6 November, he pledged that before he led his army into the interior, he would see that "Atlanta itself is utterly destroyed."[3]

After Grant approved the campaign, Sherman set an overly ambitious timetable for it. Initially, he thought he could set out about 1 November. But too much had to be done in preparation. To Thomas on 19 October, the commanding general outlined the work ahead. "I will send back into Tennessee the Fourth Corps," he wrote, in order to deal with Hood. Then he would strip down his army for hard marching, sending to the rear "all dismounted cavalry, all sick and wounded, and all incumbrance whatever, except what I haul in wagons." It would also take time to get his forces then with him in North Georgia back to Atlanta. With the Western & Atlantic broken by the Rebels between Resaca and Tunnel Hill, and with the XX Corps in Atlanta having to forage in order to feed itself, it made sense for Sherman to keep the rest of his army in North Georgia and close to his supply base at Chattanooga. On his eventual march back to Atlanta, Sherman intended to "break up the railroad and bridges" of the Western & Atlantic.

Even while the W & A was under repair, Sherman ordered his chief commissary officer in Atlanta, Colonel Amos Beckwith, to start sending to the rear all supplies not needed for the "big raid." "On the 1st of November I want nothing but what is necessary to war," he wrote on 19 October; "send all trash to the rear at once and have on hand thirty days' food and but little forage." Sherman repeated this order a few days later: "don't accumulate more than thirty days' supply anywhere, except at Chattanooga. Rather diminish than increase our supplies, and send back all surplus and worthless stores." By 28 October, Sherman knew that in addition to the IV Corps he would also send back to Thomas the XXIII Corps, then in northeast Alabama. This would leave the

---

[3] Field Order 64, 4 September 1864, *OR,* vol. 38, pt. 5, p. 801; Sherman to Halleck, 4 September, *OR,* vol. 38, pt. 5, p. 794; Sherman to Grant, 10, 20 September, 1, 9 October, 6 November, *OR,* vol. 39, pt. 2, pp. 356, 412–13; pt. 3, 162, pp. 660–61 (Grant, "on reflection, I think better of your proposition"); B. H. Liddell Hart, *Sherman: Soldier, Realist, American* (New York: Dodd, Mead & Co., 1929) 314–28 (including Grant, "I think better of your proposition"); Noah Andre Trudeau, *Southern Storm: Sherman's March to the Sea* (New York: HarperCollins, 2008) 40–41 (Lincoln's reservations about Sherman's plan); Lee Kennett, *Sherman: A Soldier's Life* (New York: HarperCollins, 2001) 259; Sherman to Thomas, 17, 20 October, *OR,* vol. 39, pt. 3, pp. 333 ("the grand move into Georgia"), 378; to Col. Amos Beckwith, 19 October ("my big raid"), *OR,* vol. 39, pt. 3, p. 358; Sherman to Slocum, 20 October ("the grand march"), 1 November, *OR,* vol. 39, pt. 3, pp. 370, 578; Sherman to Stanton, 20 October, *OR,* vol. 39, pt. 3, p. 369; Margie Riddle Bearss, *Sherman's Forgotten Campaign: The Meridian Expedition* (Baltimore: Gateway Press, 1987) 173 ("ransacked the dwellings"); Sherman to George W. Tyler, 8 November; to Halleck, 19 October; and to Wilson, 19 October, *OR,* vol. 39, pt. 3, pp. 700, 358.

XIV, XV, XVII, and XX corps for the Georgia campaign, 50,000 to 60,000 men for Beckwith to feed.

Despite Sherman's order to "rush things," Beckwith's work took time. When the railroad to Chattanooga reopened on 29 October, it could not run at full capacity. "Trains have to move slow," Beckwith explained to his commander on the 30th. The sidings and switches, destroyed by the Rebels, and the trackside water tanks burned by them, had not yet been finished; "nor is the road ballasted." With all the supplies still needing to be brought forward, and all the "trash" being sent back, the colonel could not predict when he would be ready. Within a week, however, Beckwith reported that he had collected the rations and fodder needed for the upcoming march.

Colonel Langdon C. Easton, chief quartermaster, received the same kinds of orders. Once the railroad was repaired, Sherman wrote on 19 October, he wanted Easton "to bring back to Chattanooga the sick, wounded, and surplus trash," as well as "all unserviceable stock, wagons, and stores." Sending back the XXIII Corps, however, required so many train cars that both Easton and Beckwith wired General Sherman on 31 October, "the removal of stores to the rear will have to stop in great measure." More, the two supply officers still needed to bring forward more food and supplies. As late as 4 November, Colonel Easton wired Sherman from Atlanta, "I am much disappointed in the working of the road. I have urged everybody and everything, but have been able to get in here only seventy-seven cars in the last twenty-four hours, all of which have been promptly unloaded, reloaded, and started back. I am sorry to disappoint you, but am doing my very best. They have accumulated more plunder in the last two months than I supposed could have been got here in six. We have an abundant supply of grain which I wish you would send animals here to eat up." This did not matter; General Sherman was impatient. Telegraphing from Kingston on 9 November, he told Easton if he did not have cars enough to send back unneeded ordnance, he was to destroy it: "I will delay for nothing." The Federal commander held the same view for sick soldiers awaiting transfer to hospitals northward. "The doctors have had plenty of notice," he snapped, "and if we were to wait a month it would be the same thing. The sick must march or fall into the hands of the enemy."

All the movement of men and material stirred talk among the soldiers in Atlanta. As Captain Henry Comey of the 2nd Massachusetts wrote, "all sick and disabled men, including all who were not in condition for continued marching, were sent to the rear. Everything in the way of property and impedimenta of every description was also sent to the rear, and the army was brought down to the lightest marching order." Among the civilians still in the city, the activity presented a dark omen of the Yankees' departure: who knew what they would do before leaving? Already times were hard for the remaining residents. The curtailment of commerce meant no one could make any money, only eke out an existence. Joshua Hill, a prominent Unionist from Madison, visited his friends in the city in late October and found many "in a pitiable condition with small available means and no market." Thus those who had endured this long now were forced to consider leaving town. William Markham took his family to New York City, as did Lewis Scofield. James Dunning took his family to New Jersey. Another prominent citizen, Alfred Austell, went south in early November. These were the affluent, but the poor had to clear out, too. Some blacks had been able to stay in the city as laborers or servants for the Federals. It was doubtless these stuggling civilians whom Union soldier Cy Titus observed as they clustering about the Car Shed, waiting for a northbound train to God-knew-where. "It was a very pitiable sight," he said, "to behold little children almost naked and many women barefooted. I was at the cars where they are loading today and I could not help but feel sorry from the very bottom of my heart to see what destitution this cruel war has brought upon these people."

At some point, Sherman issued orders to Colonel Cogswell that his garrison should begin plans to wreck what remained of the city. Professor Thomas G. Dyer of the University of Georgia has discovered in a Massachusetts archive a previously unknown small cache of papers relating to the widespread destruction, which Cogswell quietly kept and never published. The papers reveal that in late October Cogswell ordered officers in his three provost regiments downtown to start planning the demolition of designated buildings in areas of the city assigned to them. This "Plan of Destruction" was to include methods (e.g., gunpowder explosion, planted artillery shells or fire), manpower (specific companies assigned to individual buildings), tools and equipment required, as well as number of days estimated to complete the work. The 33rd Massachusetts got Whitehall and Peachtree; the 2nd Massachusetts was assigned the Car Shed and structures to its east (Georgia Railroad buildings, the old Peters flour mill, and so on), and the 111th Pennsylvania would target things to the northwest, including the Western & Atlantic roundhouse and gas works. In addition, a provisional brigade (four regiments from the three divisions of the XX Corps, working for Colonels Beckwith and Easton) would tear up the railroad track in the city.[4]

---

[4] Sherman to Col. Amos Beckwith, 19, 24, 28 October 1864, *OR,* vol. 39, pt. 3, pp. 358, 414, 477; Sherman to Thomas, 19 October, *OR,* vol. 39, pt. 3, p. 365; Beckwith to Sherman, 30 October and 5 November, *OR,* vol. 39, pt. 3, pp. 510, 641; Sherman to Easton, 19, 23 October, 9 November, *OR,* vol. 39, pt. 3, pp. 359, 404, 711; L. C. Easton and A. Beckwith to Sherman, 31 October, *OR,* vol. 39, pt. 3, p. 530; Easton to Sherman, 4 November, *OR,* vol. 39, pt. 3, p. 626; Trudeau, *Southern Storm,* 43, 50–53; Lyman Richard Comey, ed., *A Legacy of Valor: The Memoirs and Letters of Captain Henry Newton Comey, 2nd Massachusetts Infantry* (Knoxville: University of Tennessee Press, 2004) 202; Thomas G. Dyer, *Secret Yankees: The Union Circle in Confederate Atlanta* (Baltimore: Johns Hopkins University Press, 1999) 204–210 (including plans for building destruction submitted by the three provost guards regiments); Lee Kennett, *Marching through Georgia: The Story of Soldiers and Civilians during*

The officers involved found it hard to keep their work secret. On 1 November, as he prepared to send to Washington a batch of George Barnard's photographs, Captain Poe wrote General Richard Delafield, chief engineer in Washington, "long ere this reaches the Department the city of Atlanta will have ceased to exist, and the ground upon which it stood will have passed out of our hands." Lieutenant Colonel Morse, the provost general, wrote home on 3 November with a similar prediction.

> I am now going to let you into some of our mighty secrets, which, probably, when you receive this, will be no secret at all.
>
> We are going to abandon Atlanta, first utterly destroying every railroad building, store, and everything else that can be of any use to the rebels. The railroad from here as far north as Resaca will be entirely destroyed. Then, cutting loose from everything and everybody, Sherman is going to launch his army into Georgia.
>
> We shall probably march in two or three columns to Savannah, destroying all railroads and government property at Macon and Augusta, and taking up all rails on our line of march. Isn't the idea of this campaign perfectly fascinating? We shall have only to "bust" through Joe Brown's militia and the cavalry, to take any of these inland cities. Of course, the taking of Savannah is only the preface to taking Charleston.

Sherman's Campaign (New York: HarperCollins, 1995) 238 (Cy Titus, "It was a very pitiable sight").

Dyer's discovery of the demolition documents in the William Cogswell Collection (MSS 212, Phillips Library, Peabody Essex Museum, Salem MA) is arguably the most important archival find in the scholarship of Atlanta's wartime ruin. "Until recently, these documents have lain undiscovered and unread in an archive in Cogswell's home state of Massachusetts," he writes modestly (*Secret Yankees*, 208). The key documents are six in number, including two maps that have never been published: (a) Lt. Col. Thomas M. Walker, commander of the 111th Pennsylvania, to Cogswell, 2 November; (b) Lt. Col. Charles F. Morse, commander of the 2nd Massachusetts, to Cogswell, 3 November; (c–d) an undated, unsigned "Plan of Destruction" with accompanying map, identifying structures to be destroyed by the 33rd Massachusetts; and (e–f) Lt. Col. Eugene Powell, commander of the 66th Ohio and Provisional Brigade, to Cogswell, 4 November, with accompanying map showing lengths of downtown railroad track to be destroyed by the four regiments of the brigade.

I wish to express my sincerest gratitude to Irene Axelrod, head research librarian at the Phillips Library, for photocopies of these essential documents.

On the Provisional Brigade, sources are Lt. Col. Eugene Powell to Cogswell, 4 November 1864, Cogswell Papers, Phillips Library, Peabody Essex Museum, Salem MA; report of Brig. Gen. John W. Geary, 6 January 1865, *OR*, vol. 39, pt. 1, p. 668 (66th Ohio assigned to Beckwith); and "Orders," 14 November, Cogswell Papers, Phillips Library ("the Regts detailed for duty in the Qr. Mr. and Commy Departments").

"The proposed movement is the most perfectly concealed I have ever known one to be," Morse beamed (with satisfaction at being in on the plan); "scarcely an officer on the staff or anywhere else knows our destination or intention."

Thus the commanding general's plan for wrecking Atlanta was known to at least a few, although Sherman himself was slow to lay it out on paper. To Poe on 1 November, Sherman gave instructions on preparations for the march. As for "all the trash" accumulated in the city that could not be carried back by train, he advised, "I will use fire freely, both on our own and the enemy's property." To General Halleck in Washington on 3 November, Sherman predicted that "when I leave Atlanta it will contain little that will be of use or comfort to the enemy." General Geary, commanding a division in the XX Corps, knew enough to write home on 5 November, "Atlanta will be destroyed and all the Rail Roads leading into it." To Grant on 6 November, Sherman affirmed that before he left on his march across Georgia he would see that the Western & Atlantic was destroyed all the way from Resaca to Atlanta, a track length of 84 miles.

Just as General Sherman slowly informed his superiors of what he wanted to do with his army, so too did he try to withhold information from the men in the ranks on his plans for the upcoming campaign. But rumors flew among his officers and men. Amidst these a sergeant in an Illinois regiment, George Cram, wrote his mother on 30 October that "today we have received orders to prepare for a fifty-days campaign.... Not a soul knows where we are going or what we are to do, but conjectures are multiplied by mystery. Undoubtedly we shall go somewhere, but it matters little." A diarist in the 33rd Massachusetts set down on 2 November: "Marching orders have come. We will soon go. Our destination is unknown; we may go to Savannah; some say Mobile, others say back to Alabama, but I guess we shall all know when we get there." After a serenade by the 33rd Massachusetts band, Lieutenant Tuttle of the 107th New York set down in his journal on the night of 2 November what he had heard: "the impression is almost universal. I find that we are going 'To Seek Salt Water.' Is it Mobile, or is it Savannah?" He could not answer. In the midst of such uncertainty, soldiers let their imaginations fly. Robert H. Strong, a private in the 105th Illinois, later wrote, "we became convinced that we were going somewhere, no one knew where. Some guessed one place, some another. The most general guess was Baton Rouge, Louisiana, where there was reported to be a large Rebel Army. Others thought we were going to Andersonville to release the prisoners held there." "For once the army was completely nonplussed," recalled Stephen J. Fleharty of the 102nd Illinois. Captain Charles Wills of the 103rd Illinois heard the talk, and recorded in his diary, 6 November, "We are preparing for a huge campaign, and are glad of it; 50 days' rations is the word. Don't know when we start. Montgomery or Augusta are probably the points. We are going to shake up the bones of the rebellion. I would not miss this campaign for anything." On 6

November, Sergeant Cram only knew that the army was ordered to be ready to march at a moment's notice, yet "everything was still as mysterious regarding our intended movement as ever and no one had any idea which direction we were to take."

Part of the soldiers' anticipation, if not excitement, was their belief that Atlanta would be burned before they left. After Colonel Cogswell's provost guards, Captain Poe's engineers were probably the next to know. Isaac Roseberry of the 1st Michigan Engineers and Mechanics entered in his diary on 2 November, "it becomes a Military Necessity for to Destroy Some Valuabel Property which might again get into the hands of the [Rebels] after our leaving it in our Rear." "I think it is beyond a doubt that we will go south this winter," wrote William Wallace to his wife Sarah on 7 November; he added, "and burn up the Gate City, for it dont do us any good now." That same day Alonzo Miller of the 12th Wisconsin wrote his sister, "The story is in Camp that we are going to Mobile, but it is hard telling where we will go. Old Sherman is doing something—he is cleaning everything between Atlanta and Chattanooga. He has burnt Rome and is sending all the artillery north and everything. Marked US on it north and is cleaning Atlanta and is going to burn the place and the railroad up to Chattanooga. Something is going to be done."

Amidst all the rumors, somebody must have talked to the press. A correspondent for the *Boston Journal* filed his report from Nashville, 6 November: "Rumors prevail that Atlanta was to be evacuated yesterday by our troops, who would first totally destroy it by fire." The newspaperman showed no remorse at the prospect. Sherman had already rendered Atlanta "of no strategic importance." Its destruction was nevertheless necessary to prevent the Rebels from trying to rebuild it into the war center it once was. And General Sherman was the kind of commander who could make these decisions easily. "He wears gauntlets, not kid gloves. He knows that war is cruelty and implies not conservatism but annihilation."

Press leaks on Sherman's plans for the destruction of Atlanta were one thing; they would not have disturbed the general. He vehemently objected, however, when on 8 November the *Indianapolis Journal* printed a news dispatch that not only gave a surprisingly accurate outline of the Federal armies' dispositions, but also their future plans—all stated in the past tense as if they had happened, even though they had not. "Officers...report that General Sherman returned to Atlanta early last week, with five corps of his army, having left two corps in Tennessee, under General Thomas, to watch Hood. They say that Sherman first destroyed the railroad from Chattanooga to Atlanta, and is now sending the iron to the former city. He then burned Atlanta and marched with his entire army in the direction of Charleston."

When the *New York Times* reprinted the brief column on 10 November, it added even more details of Sherman's plans.

His objective point was boldly asserted to be Savannah, for which place, it was given out, he would leave on the 8th, having first destroyed Atlanta. It was thought he would touch at Macon, and would reach Savannah in a march of 25 days. The route is 200 miles, with no rivers and few creeks of importance to pass, and leading through the most flourishing part of Georgia. Milledgeville, the capital of the State of Georgia, could be reached in six days from the date of starting. He will have rations for thirty days, but is expected to find supplies and forage on his route. His force for this great march will be between forty and seventy thousand men, and he will have a large amount of ordnance, a construction corps and pontoon bridges.

With good reason, General Grant in Virginia called the *Times* article "the most contraband news I have seen published during the war." Secretary of War Stanton blamed Sherman for the breach of intelligence; staff officers (the apparent sources of the leaks) should not be talking with the press. Sherman himself attempted to deal with the situation by planting counter-stories in the papers. "If indiscreet newspaper men publish information too near the truth, counteract the effect by publishing other paragraphs calculated to mislead the enemy," Sherman lectured the assistant secretary of war, Charles A. Dana. He gave an example of what he wanted to see in print: "Sherman's army has been much re-enforced, especially in the cavalry, and he will soon move by several columns in circuit, so as to catch Hood's army." He provided another possible press line: "Sherman's destination is not Charleston, but Selma, where he will meet an army from the Gulf."[5]

---

[5] Poe to Brig. Gen. Richard Delafield, 1 November 1864, in Keith F. Davis, *George N. Barnard: Photographer of Sherman's Campaign* (Kansas City MO: Hallmark Cards, Inc., 1990) 84; Charles F. Morse, *Letters Written During the Civil War* (Charles F. Morse, 1898) 196; Sherman to Poe, 1 November; to Halleck, 3 November; and to Grant, 6 November, *OR*, vol. 39, pt. 3, pp. 577, 614; Blair, ed., *A Politician Goes to War*, 213 (Geary to wife, 5 November); Jennifer Cain Bohrnstedt, ed., *Soldiering with Sherman: Civil War Letters of George F. Cram* (DeKalb IL: Northern Illinois University Press, 2000) 146–48; Andrew J. Boies, *Record of the Thirty-Third Massachusetts Volunteer Infantry from August 1862 to August 1865* (Fitchburg MA: Sentinel Printing Co., 1880) 98; George Tappan, ed., *The Civil War Journal of Lt. Russell M. Tuttle, New York Volunteer Infantry* (Jefferson NC: McFarland & Company, 2006) 167; Ashley Halsey, ed., *A Yankee Private's Civil War* (Chicago: Henry Regnery Company, 1961) 97; S. F. Fleharty, *Our Regiment: A History of the 102d Illinois Infantry Volunteers* (Chicago: Brewster & Hanscom, 1865) 107; Mary E. Kellogg, ed., *Army Life of an Illinois Soldier* (Carbondale IL: Southern Illinois University Press, 1996) 318; Roseberry, diary, 2 November, Emory University; John O. Holzhueter, ed., "William Wallace's Civil War Letters: The Atlanta Campaign," *Wisconsin Magazine of History* 57/2 (Winter 1973–1974): 111; Alonzo Miller to sister, 7 November, Miller, diary and letters, MSS 237F, Atlanta History Center; *Boston Journal*, quoted under "The Rumored Destruction of Atlanta—Campaign against Mobile by Sherman," *New York Tribune*, 12 November; "From General

While Northern press correspondents predicted Atlanta's doom, the scope of destruction was being meticulously planned out, as Colonel Cogswell had directed. On 2 November, Lieutenant Colonel Thomas M. Walker of the 111th Pennsylvania listed his assignments and recommendations for handling them. First was the Macon & Western "Stone Freight Depot" (Pryor Street and the railroad, across from the Car Shed). It was so solidly built—locally called the Rock Depot, distinguishing it from the brick-built Car Shed—that it would have to be mined with explosive charges under the stone floor. The roof could then be burned (assigned to Captain James M. Wells and Company B). Second, the bridge across the railway between Forsyth and Whitehall would be set afire at both ends and its center. Four blocks to the west (where Spring Street intersected the railroad) was the formidable Western & Atlantic roundhouse. It required "pulling down the iron pillars" supporting the inside and mining the wall at several points; the roof and turntable were burnable. The nearby machine shops would have to be mined. The W & A freight depot could also be fired. Finally, farther north, the gas works and adjoining buildings would be burned (two companies under Captain Furguson). Winship's foundry, and Pitt and Cook's planing mill/carpentry shop and related sheds would also be destroyed. Four companies under Captain William J. Alexander were assigned to the W & A roundhouse and machine shops, Winship's foundry and planing mills. Just one company, E under Captain William L. Patterson, was put in charge of the W & A engine house and freight depot, nearby cotton warehouses, and the bridge over the tracks west of Whitehall. Walker estimated that one full day would be needed to "get these details in readiness," once the requisite powder, fuse, axes, picks, spades, and crowbars had been procured.

On 3 November, Lieutenant Colonel Morse of the 2nd Massachusetts submitted to Colonel Cogswell his proposal for the demolition of the structures in the central and eastern parts of the city assigned to his regiment. Like Walker, he saw the need for combinations of burning down and blowing up. On the Car Shed, he "propose[d] to mine the large brick passenger depot at the four corners and to complete its destruction by fire"; adjacent wooden sheds and stables

Sherman's Army," *Indianapolis Journal,* 8 November; "Extraordinary News. Sherman's New and Grand Campaign. Great Military March through Georgia. Stupendous Flank Movement upon Savannah and Charleston. The Railroad to Chattanooga Removed and Atlanta Burned. Atlanta as a Point of Advance upon the Atlantic," *New York Times,* 10 November; J. Cutler Andrews, *The North Reports the Civil War* (Pittsburgh: University of Pittsburgh Press, 1955) 577; Sherman to Dana, 10 November, *OR,* vol. 39, pt. 3, p. 727.

On the day after its leak of 8 November, the *Indianapolis Journal* added more of its peculiarly future-perfect reporting, as it reported in its edition of 9 November: "Nothing has been heard from Sherman since he cast off all moorings and swung out toward the salt water. We may soon look for a report of his movements through rebel sources, as we shall probably hear nothing from him direct till he strikes ocean communication" ("Late News," *Indianapolis Journal,* 9 November).

would also be torched (the work was assigned to Captain Parker, with Companies C and D). The Georgia Railroad roundhouse two blocks over would be mined in three places; "all other adjacent R.R. buildings can be sufficiently destroyed by fire," Morse wrote (he delegated this task to Captain R. B. Brown and three companies). Railroad workshops were to be burned, "the large chimney in yard to be mined" (Companies F and I, under Captain J. I. Grafton). The regiment would also demolish the Atlanta & West Point freight house north of the rail line between Butler and Pratt streets. Industrial sites along the railway heading out of the city would be taken care of, such as the Atlanta Machine Works (Captain G. A. Thayer and Company K), and the Peters steam flour mill/Spiller & Burr pistol factory (building to be burned and chimney blown up by Captain Francis W. Crowninshield's Company H). Every one of the ten companies in the regiment received an assignment; to Captain Henry N. Comey and E Company went the Georgia Railroad warehouse and loading platforms, "to be destroyed by fire." For those structures to be exploded, Morse carefully described and illustrated how a bag of powder, set in a wooden box, would be placed down an excavated chamber beneath the base of the building wall; a wooden tube would carry the fuse to the surface whence it would be run out a distance from the building to be safely lit. "All the space about the box and tube to be filled with earth and stone and rammed hard," Morse noted, to increase the force of the explosion. Besides shovels, picks, and axes needed for this work, Morse estimated that he would need 1000 feet of fuse line and 500 pounds of powder.

The "Plan of Destruction" designated for the 33rd Massachusetts listed seven buildings or areas to be burned or blown up. Unsigned, it would have been submitted by Lieutenant Colonel Elisha Doane, commander of the 33rd Massachusetts while Colonel Cogswell served as post commander. Accompanying it was a carefully drawn map of the downtown section assigned to the regiment, running from Mitchell Street and the railroad four blocks southwest of the Car Shed to the "Dome Building" three blocks northeast of the passenger depot. The seven sets of targets follow, with bracketed annotations referring to the map.

Plan of Destruction

No. 1. The stable on Mitchell Street with brick walls, burn the inside out. Corral burn. Half round [Macon & Western] Engine house mine under the four Corners & blow up. Turn table belonging to the Same—burn.

No. 2. Two brick blacksmith shops on Hunter Street burn the inside out. large wooden building (store house) on the Corner of Mitchell & Forsyth St. burn, one blacksmith and carriage maker Shop between Forsyth St. & Whitehall street burn. [The map shows three more structures marked for demolition as "2," two blocks south of Mitchell, between Forsyth and Whitehall streets.]

No. 3. Burn each side of Whitehall Street from Mitchell St. to the railroad crossing. [The east side of Whitehall for these two blocks is shaded in as "Brick Block."]

No. 4. Burn Peach Tree St. each side except the N.E. corner as per plan. [Marked here are "Bank" (the Georgia Railroad Bank Agency), the Atlanta Hotel, and evidently all other buildings on the block bounded by the railroad, Peachtree, Decatur and Pryor streets. Also marked are both sides of Peachtree up to Luckie St.]

No. 5. Burn Rebel Barracks [marked as "Prison" near Peachtree and Harris Streets].

No. 6. Burn Trout House, Washington Hotel & Barracks in vicinity [The barracks was the old City Hotel at Decatur and Loyd.].

No. 7 Burn College (marked "Dome Building" on plan).

Each of these seven tasks was assigned to various of the ten companies in the 33rd Massachusetts. The burning of Whitehall was deemed the biggest job: three companies were given the assignment.

Some noteworthy elements appear in the demolition plans developed by Cogswell's three provost regiments. Private homes were not marked for arson, in keeping with Sherman's attitude that military facilities and public buildings were enough for proper targets, not civilian houses. Railroad structures were to be thoroughly wiped out (including the Georgia Railroad Bank Agency at the railroad and Peachtree). Of course, the track itself running through the city would be wrecked. Just as Colonel Cogswell directed his three provost regiments to prepare plans for wrecking buildings, so did he instruct a provisional brigade of four additional regiments of the XX Corps serving as augments to the provost guards to plan the wrecking of all railroad track remaining in the city. Lieutenant Colonel Eugene Powell, commanding the brigade, submitted on 4 November a drawing of the downtown railway complex, with notes on how each of his regiments would be assigned to various sections of track; all would be torn up in General Sherman's famously specific style. Powell affirmed, "I intend to twist all of the rail that is possible in addition to bending," and that he would scour the city for crowbars needed in the work. Powell estimated some 8 miles of track were thus to be wrecked, plus another 2 miles of side lines. From the headpoint of the Macon & Western at Whitehall out to the earthworks, 200 men from the 141st New York were assigned; for the Western & Atlantic out from Whitehall, 400 men (Powell's 66th Ohio); for the central lines of track from Whitehall to the Georgia Railroad roundhouse at McDonough Street, 250 soldiers of the 107th New York; and from the roundhouse eastward out of town, another 250 (19th Michigan).

In the carefully planned destruction, major manufacturing sites were also to be blown up or burned, even if the machinery inside them were long gone. For instance, in the old three-story flour mill once owned by Richard Peters, Lieutenant Colonel Morse specifically stated that the "chimney of flouring mill will be mined." Some major public buildings were to be torched, including three hotels (Atlanta Hotel, Trout House, and Washington Hotel). All of Silvey and Glazner's block, across from the Trout House north of Marietta, was marked for demolition, including the Atheneum Theater, where Mrs. Welch and the 33rd Massachusetts band had performed for the entertainment of Northern troops. Even the domed medical college building at Jenkins and Butler in the northeast part of town was slated for the torch, despite the fact that Dr. D'Alvigny was treating sick Union soldiers there. The planned destruction of hotels, a theater and even a hospital—all structures serving civilian purposes, not military—can only be explained by passing comments from two Federals, both writing on 15 November, the night of the Northerners' most widespread burning. Major Henry Hitchcock recorded in his diary that Sherman intended for demolition "only such buildings as are used or useful for war purposes, whether for producing, *storing*, or transporting materials, etc., of war" (emphasis added). Corporal Harvey Reid wrote, "it was argued that the rebels could use the large buildings for hospitals, warehouses and so forth." It was thus understood that everything *brick* would go. This rationale explains also why Lieutenant Colonel Doane's plan of destruction for the 33rd Massachusetts marked the "Brick block" on Whitehall as target for razing. As he had written on 6 November to General Grant, he wanted to see Atlanta "utterly destroyed."[6]

Thus Colonel Cogswell proceeded in his preparations for the destruction of Atlanta. Men of the 2nd Massachusetts prepared walls and chimneys for their powder charges. According to a regimental chronicler, Lieutenant Colonel Morse even "tried a perfectly successful experiment with a small house," testing his explosives. But then work halted. On 7 November, Sherman reassigned responsibility for the city's destruction to Captain Poe of the engineers. To Poe he ordered, "I want you to take special charge of the destruction in Atlanta of all depots, car-houses, shops, factories, foundries, &c., being careful to knock down all furnace chimneys, and break down their arches; fire will do most of the work.

---

[6] Walker to Cogswell, 2 November and Morse to Cogswell, 3 November, Cogswell Collection, Peabody Essex Museum, Salem MA; Morse to home, 3 November 1864 ("Colonel Cogswell, with five regiments, has been ordered to prepare this place for destruction; he has given me the charge of about half of it. I have just submitted my proposition how to do it"), Morse, *Letters*, 196; "Plan of Destruction" and accompanying map, and Lt. Col. Eugene Powell to Cogswell, 4 November with accompanying map, Cogswell Collection, Peabody Essex Museum, Salem MA; M. A. DeWolfe Howe, ed., *Marching with Sherman: Passages from the Letters and Campaign Diaries of Henry Hitchcock* (New Haven: Yale University Press, 1927) 57; Byrne, ed., *Uncommon Soldiers*, 203; Sherman to Grant, 6 November, *OR*, vol. 39, pt. 3, p. 661.

Call on General Slocum for details and be all ready by the 10th." Sherman did not explain to Cogswell why he and his provost regiments were being taken off the task of destruction, but one of Sherman's staff officers, Major Henry Hitchcock, saw the letter that influenced the general. "Saw at Kingston joint letter of E. [Colonel Langdon Easton, chief quartermaster] and B. [Colonel Amos Beckwith, chief of commissary and subsistence] to General, recommending that the destruction here be specially in Poe's charge—'to prevent irregularities, he having reliable men under him.'" Easton and Beckwith's letter apparently warned of the "irregularities" that could befall the city when non-engineers were to carry out its destruction, referring to the damage to unauthorized structures that Cogswell's men might inflict; on the other hand, Poe, the engineer, had his two regiments of Michigan and Missouri engineers, men trained in such tasks as structural demolition. The plans submitted by Cogswell's three regiments had stressed fire and explosives, while engineers would know how to wreck buildings with battering rams and other devices. Besides, apparently General Sherman worried that with four infantry corps gathering for the upcoming campaign and marching into and through the city in the last days of the occupation, the men might take up the torch and engage in unauthorized arson if they saw soldiers burning buildings. Cogswell's provost guards would have to be ready to enforce order if the men started burning Atlanta. (Indeed, a Massachusetts soldier in the provost contingent recorded in his diary on 11 November that they had orders to "shoot on the spot all incendiaries.") Sherman took Easton and Beckwith's advice, and on 7 November ordered that Poe, not Cogswell, would see that "Atlanta is utterly destroyed."

Noncombatants still in the city could tell something was up. Young Carrie Berry, in her diary for 30 October, observed that because of how "the soldiers are moving about," her friends the Lowrys "are all ready to move and it looks like every body is going to leave here." A disturbing omen was the withdrawal that day of the Northern soldier who had been standing guard at the Berry's house. "Our sergeant left us this morning," Carrie wrote. "We all were sorry to part with him. He has been a very good friend to us." Several days later Carrie recorded, "It is the repote that the federals are going to have to leave Atlanta and we are afraid that we will have to leave too." An obvious omen of the Federals' plans was to be seen downtown at the passenger depot: northbound trains were being loaded with all kinds of impedimenta, the stuff not needed by an army during a long march. Colonel Easton, the chief quartermaster, told Sherman on 4 November that he was using the railroad as energetically as he could, but the lack of cars was delaying the loading operations. Sergeant Alexander Downing, 11th Iowa, recorded in his diary on 7 November that "the general quartermaster is loading every train going north with the surplus commissariat and all extra army baggage." All the commotion stood as a sure sign that "our army is preparing to evacuate Atlanta." Residents who had remained this long now learned that they would have to part with prized belongings. Captain Poe,

Sherman's engineer, wrote his wife on 2 November that he was sending home a nice box of books; he had bought them from "a man who was going north from Atlanta, and could not carry them."[7]

What everyone in the city—whites, blacks, soldiers, and civilians—apparently knew was confirmed by General Sherman in his special field orders of 8 November, which announced to his army that it would soon embark upon a "long and difficult march." "All surplus servants, noncombatants, and refugees should now go to the rear," he ordered (meaning to the north), "and none should be encouraged to encumber us on the march." Anxious affluent Atlantans were taken advantage of by devious Northern quartermaster officers and railroad conductors who, according to David Conyngham of the *New York Herald,* "saw that the thing could be made to pay, and they did make it pay." Though the Federals had promised everyone free rail transport northward, the coveted car space was apparently up for bribes. Passenger space, according to Conyngham, went for as much as $100. In lieu of cash, furniture or other prized stuff was accepted. Conyngham named a "Captain S—" as one of the chief extortionists who apparently "acted in collusion with railroad conductors and officials" to pack civilians' furniture northward. (Conyngham noted that "these fellows were afterwards court-martialed, I do not know with what result.") In addition to panicked citizens struggling to board the trains, people from outside the city also came in and added to the crush. Observed Iowa sergeant Downing on 9 November: "Citizens all around Atlanta, hearing that the Yankees are going to leave the place, are coming in larger numbers to go North. Women leave their homes and all they have, and with their children walk a distance of thirty miles, for the sake of getting to the North." Downing concluded that because of the Federals' foraging, these country folk "are destitute—haven't anything to eat"; given the coming winter and the threat of starvation, a free ride to the North seemed to offer more hope than staying home.

Freedpeople were particularly anxious to get north before the Union army, their protector, marched off. Carrie Berry noted on 7 November, "every boddie seems to be in confusion. The black wimmen are running around trying to get up north for fear that the Rebels will come in and take them." Major General Slocum took note of this rising excitement: "The few white people remaining after their

---

[7] Alonzo H. Quint, *The Record of the Second Massachusetts Infantry* (Boston: James P. Walker Co., 1867) 246; Sherman to Poe, 7 November 1864, *OR,* vol. 39, pt. 3, p. 680; Howe, ed., *Marching with Sherman,* 56 (diary entry, 15 November 1864); Dyer, *Secret Yankees,* 210 ("fire and explosives used in Cogswell's plan would have provided much wider destruction"); Joseph T. Glatthaar, *The March to the Sea and Beyond: Sherman's Troops in the Savannah and Carolinas Campaigns* (New York: New York University Press, 1985) 139 ("shoot on the spot all incendiaries"); Carrie Berry, diary, 30 October and 4 November, Atlanta History Center; Easton to Sherman, 4 November, *OR,* vol. 39, pt. 3, p. 626; Olynthus B. Clarke, ed., *Downing's Civil War Diary* (Des Moines: Historical Department of Iowa, 1916) 227; Poe to "Nell," 2 November, box 2, folder 1, O. M. Poe Papers, Library of Congress.

families were sent away, are alarmed, and many are leaving the city, giving up houses, lands, furniture, negroes, and all. The black want to go North, and the Car House is surrounded by them. Hundreds of cars are literally packed with them." Brigadier General Williams, division commander, recorded in his journal for 8 November:

> There is a great scramble at the depot to get away. Thousands of Negroes are striving to get transportation. We sent away a family of blacks which came in about forty miles soon after we got here. Part of them have been with us. There are two women and one boy that I should like to get to Detroit. They are the best and steadiest Negroes I have ever seen. One of the women washed and sewed for our mess and cooked part of the time. She cooks, sews, and washes splendidly, and withal is a steady home body and a most excellent character. She calls herself "Pibby," not *Phoeby.* If anybody wants a superb house-servant let them get her or her sister also with her. I gave them a letter of commendation to Lew Forsyth at Louisville.

This frantic exodus of the city's remaining civilians clogged and crammed the last trains heading north from Atlanta. "The Depot is lined with citizens or Refugees on their way to 'Gods country,'" observed Sergeant William Miller, 75th Indiana, in his diary on 10 November; "they are mostly women and children.... of the poorer class of people." Wrote Russell Tuttle of the 107th New York in his journal, Friday, 11 November:

> It is plain to be seen now that we are going to evacuate this place. The citizens have taken the scare and have been moving out in great numbers for the past day or two. The rail road depot presents an extraordinary scene. The cars loaded first with government property, then chinked in with families, men, women, and children, placed in among the old wagons, boxes and barrels, wherever there was a place large enough for a person to sit or stand or lie.
>
> A few box cars were filled with families and their goods. Very few goods could they take with them either, a trunk or two, a little bed clothing and the bundles they could take in their hands. It is sad to think of the amount of furniture that has been abandoned and destroyed in this city. I saw a fine piano lying by the track, whose owner had offered five hundred dollars to any one who would transport it North. It has been cut up for firewood. Indeed a fire had been built against one corner of it.

General Sherman originally had hoped to start his "grand move into Georgia" around 1 November, but the launch-date was pushed to 10 November for several reasons. First, the Rebels' railroad breaks from Big Shanty to Tunnel

Hill knocked out the W & A from 4 to 29 October, hindering the accumulation of supplies in Atlanta; at one point Sherman had told Slocum he wanted 1 ½ million rations of bread, coffee, sugar, and salt, plus ½ million rations of salted meat. Second, Sherman felt obliged to hover awhile longer in North Georgia. The Rebels were headed into Tennessee, but Sherman wanted to make sure they were well departed before he returned to Atlanta with the XIV, XV, and XVII corps. As he wrote General Halleck on 3 November, "I…am waiting to be more certain that Thomas will be prepared for any contingency that may arise." Additionally, some of Sherman's troops still had not been paid for the past several months; the paymasters were at work and the men were sending their money back home before setting out on the new campaign.[8]

Then, too, there was a United States presidential election coming up, and for the first time in history US soldiers would be allowed to vote in the field. President Lincoln was locked in a worrisome bid for re-election against the Democratic nominee, none other than Major General George B. McClellan of Ohio, who had led the Army of the Potomac during 1861–1862. McClellan had been nominated on a party platform that declared the North's three-year war for restoration of the Union to be a failure and called for an end to the war "at the earliest practicable moment," presumably through armistice. War-weariness in the North had risen during summer 1864, to the point that in late August Lincoln feared that he would lose the election.

Yet if there were any part of the electorate Lincoln could reliably count on, it was the soldier vote. Northern troops, having fought hard to conquer the rebellion thus far, were not about to give up the fight when victory seemed more attainable than ever. To be sure, in Virginia many in McClellan's former command, the Army of the Potomac, still felt warmly for their old leader, but in Sherman's army most expressed overwhelming support of Lincoln. Because of the peace plank in the Democrats' platform, wrote one, "'Mac' has lost thousands of votes." Major Thaddeus Capron of the 59th Illinois recorded that the army "now understands the party and principles" of the Democrats, and consequently "will be overwhelmingly for 'Old Abe.'" Another of Sherman's soldiers,

---

[8] Special Field Orders 119, 8 November, *OR*, vol. 39, pt. 3, p. 701; Conyngham, *Sherman's March through the South*, 234–35; Clarke, ed., *Downing's Civil War Diary*, 227; Carrie Berry, diary, 7 November, Atlanta History Center; Charles E. Slocum, *The Life and Services of Major-General Henry Warner Slocum* (Toledo OH: Slocum Publishing Co., 1913) 217; Milo M. Quaife, ed., *From the Cannon's Mouth: The Civil War Letters of General Alpheus S. Williams* (Detroit: Wayne State University Press, 1959) 351; Patrick and Willey, eds., *Fighting for Liberty and Right*, 271–72; Tappan, ed., *Civil War Journal of Lt. Tuttle*, 169; Sherman to Slocum, 20 October, *OR*, vol. 39, pt. 3, p. 370 ("I want to be near Atlanta, and ready by November 1"); Sherman to Halleck, 3 November, *OR*, vol. 39, pt. 3, p. 614; Sherman to Howard, 5 November, *OR*, vol. 39, pt. 3, p. 644 ("collect all your men to get paid and do everything necessary to make a clear start about the 10th"); Sherman to "Commanding officers," 6 November, *OR*, vol. 39, pt. 3, p. 661 ("the sending back of the soldiers' money").

Chauncey B. Welton, reflected the feeling in the ranks that a vote for McClellan would be a vote for secession. To his parents Welton advised, "if you wish to crush every hope of the rebel army...vote for A. Lincoln." Dr. Edwin Hutchinson, a surgeon in Slocum's corps, wrote his father three weeks before the election, "I would hide my head with shame sooner than vote for any man nominated under the Chicago banner." About the same time, on 19 October, General Geary predicted to his wife, "nine-tenths of the soldiers in this army will vote for Lincoln."

With the soldier vote so predictable, Northern authorities worked to record it. In the weeks before 8 November, state commissioners circulated among the troops, collecting their absentee ballots. Captain John C. Van Duzer, Sherman's telegrapher, sent word to Washington on 11 October that Ohio soldiers in hospitals plus other qualified voters already totaled 1,800 early votes, with "only 200 for Mack." Soldiers from other states waited for election day to make their preferences known. Alonzo Miller of the 12th Wisconsin wrote home that in his regiment "the boys are looking...to elect Old Abe," adding his prediction, "and he will be elected too."

On Tuesday, 8 November, soldiers of some units both voted and received pay. David Nichol of Knap's Pennsylvania battery pocketed $235.40 and like most of Sherman's troops cast his ballot for Lincoln. His unit went overwhelmingly for the president: "polled 113 votes, 95 for Lincoln & 18 for Mac (just 18 too many)." In the 3rd Wisconsin, each man filed through a tent and on an "old rickety table," as William Wallace described it, picked up one of two paper tickets—one for Abe, the other for Mac—and dropped it into a cigar box. "The election was conducted with as good regularity as if we were at the old school house," Wallace observed. No one attempted to sell his ballot, and rules against underaged voting were commendably enforced. When all were counted, it was 30 to 2 for Lincoln in Wallace's Company E, and 325 to 23 in the regiment as a whole. Lincoln's margin was just as great in other regiments. In the 75th Indiana, the number of those abstaining (14) was twice the number of McClellan voters; Lincoln got 310. In the 20th Illinois, the president received ninety-seven votes and General McClellan got only one—with its caster, Allen Geer, resolving in his diary to keep quiet about it.

In the end, the Union soldier vote spoke loudly for a continued prosecution of the war. Of the total Northern popular vote, Lincoln won just 55%, but among all Northern soldiers he got 78 percent. Sherman's men were even more supportive: fully 86 percent of them went with Lincoln, 14 percent McClellan. All during this political activity, General Sherman kept himself aloof, but he recognized that the men had to vote. "By the 10th," he had written to Grant on 6 November, "I...will have the troops all paid, the presidential election over and out of the way"; he would then be ready to start his campaign.

In the meantime, the XVII Corps and most of the XV left Cave Spring in North Georgia on 1 November heading toward Atlanta; they reached the area around Smyrna and Marietta about 5 November. The XIV Corps stayed with Sherman near Kingston; Corse's division of the XV was at Rome. On 9 November, the commanding general announced a reorganization of his forces. Special Field Orders 120 of that date referred only to "this army," but military stationery began circulating with a new name, "Army of Georgia." Sherman was deliberately playing with the custom of the two sides in naming their armies from bases of operation, e.g., "Army of the Potomac," "Army of Northern Virginia"; henceforth he would command an army named for the *enemy territory* he proposed to march through and devastate. The newly retitled army was divided into a left wing under General Slocum (XIV and XX corps), and a right, under General Howard (XV and XVII corps).

But the start date of 10 November got pushed further to 15th or 16th November. Heavy rains during 8 and 9 November kept Sherman at Kingston. On 11 November, he wired Halleck that the XIV Corps would start its return to Atlanta on the morrow, but that it would take three days. Adding in time it would take for Captain Poe's engineers to complete their destruction of the city, Sherman calculated he would be ready "to start on the 16th on the projected grand raid."

Meanwhile Poe and his engineers awaited orders to begin their destruction of the designated targets downtown. "I am all ready to do the work assigned me," wired Poe to Sherman on 9 November, "and will act the instant I get your order to do so." Soon everything was set in motion when the troops got word to pack their provisions for the march. Illinois sergeant George Cram wrote his mother on 9 November that his unit had gotten its orders. "We are to carry 2 days hard bread and pork, 10 days coffee and salt and 5 days sugar in our haversacks, regular forage parties are to scour the country continually on either side of our line of march. And in all probability every enterable house we find will be burned. Atlanta will no doubt be abandoned and mostly destroyed. Where we shall go I know not, perhaps to Savannah, or Mobile, though our destination may depend on circumstances...." All this loading and refitting took a few days. Thus it was on 11 November that Sherman directed his chief engineer, Captain Poe, "you may commence the work of destruction at once, but don't use fire until toward the last moment." Poe affirmed his understanding: Sherman did not want uncontrolled burning in Atlanta, "which would endanger other buildings than those set apart for destruction."[9]

---

[9] David E. Long, *The Jewel of Liberty: Abraham Lincoln's Re-Election and the End of Slavery* (Mechanicsburg PA: Stackpole Books, 1994) 61–62, 189, 224–25, 283 ("at the earliest practicable moment"); Blair, ed., *A Politician Goes to War*, 210 (Geary to wife, 19 October); Steven E. Woodworth, *Nothing But Victory: The Army of Tennessee, 1861–1865* (New York: Alfred A. Knopf, 2005) 587; J. C. Van Duzer to Eckert, 11 October, *OR*, vol. 39, pt. 3, p. 213; Alonzo Miller to sister, 7 November, Miller, diary and letters, Atlanta History Center; James P. Brady, comp., *Hurrah for the Artillery!: Knap's Independent Battery "E," Pennsylvania*

The engineers and troops began tearing up of the railroad track in the city on 12 November. General Sherman, at Kingston, planned the start of his march back to Atlanta with the XIV Corps when the last trains from Atlanta had passed northward toward Chattanooga, allowing the soldiers of the corps to begin destroying the railroad. Three southbound trains bringing the last rations and forage for the great march were on their way from Chattanooga on the evening of 11 November. The cars were unloaded quickly and sent back north sometime on the morning of 12 November. Early that day Sherman wrote Howard, then at Smyrna, "as soon as all the trains have passed north you may begin work on the railroad." Major Hitchcock, with Sherman at Cartersville by noon, observed the three trains heading north. Atlanta, the Gate City that had risen to prominence and wealth on the rails of the locomotive industry, had seen its last chugging train for a while. Lieutenant Tuttle of the 107th New York noted on 12 November that "the last trains have come and gone sure enough. There has not been a train today, and not a railroad man to be seen."

After the last train northward had passed Kingston, the Federal destruction of the Western & Atlantic began; in addition, the extension rail line westward from Kingston to Rome was torn up. Moreover, in their march to Atlanta, the men of the XIV Corps were under orders to destroy bridges, railroad shops, foundries, and warehouses wherever found. Sherman ordered Brigadier John Corse's division to destroy such structures in Rome "in the most effective manner by fire or otherwise." In this heady, vengeful atmosphere, soldiers interpreted the orders liberally, extending the scope of their destruction to houses, barns, and other private buildings. Much of Rome thus went up in flames. "The country is light with the burning of Rome," wrote one Federal on 10 November; "it seemed melancholy to see the property being destroyed. It is against orders—but the soldiers want to see it burn." On the other hand,

---

Light Artillery (Gettysburg: Thomas Publications, 1992) 375; Holzhueter, ed., "William Wallace's Letters," 111, 113 (Wallace to Sarah, 7 November); Patrick and Willey, eds., *Fighting for Liberty and Right*, 271; Stephen W. Sears, *George B. McClellan: The Young Napoleon* (New York: Ticknor & Fields, 1988) 385–86; Sherman to Grant, 6 November, *OR*, vol. 39, pt. 3, p. 660; itinerary of Union forces, 1 November–31 December 1864, *OR*, vol. 44, pp. 44, 25, 28, 32; Special Field Order 120, 9 November, *OR*, vol. 39, pt. 3, p. 713; "Orders, Atlanta Geo November 14th 1864," on stationery printed "ARMY OF GEORGIA, Head-Quarters, Left Wing," Cogswell Collection, Peabody Essex Museum, Salem MA (see also *OR*, vol. 39, pt. 3, pp. 701, 743, 745, and 762 for references in correspondence, 10–13 November, to the "Army of Georgia"); Sherman to Easton, 9 November, *OR*, vol. 39, pt. 3, p. 711; Sherman to Halleck, 11 November, *OR*, vol. 39, pt. 3, p. 740; L. M. Dayton to Beckwith, 7 November, *OR*, vol. 39, pt. 3, p. 680 (from Kingston "to Atlanta will be about three days"); Paul Taylor, *Orlando M. Poe: Civil War General and Great Lakes Engineer* (Kent OH: Kent University Press, 2009) 190 ("I am all ready to do the work assigned me"); Bohrnstedt, ed., *Soldiering with Sherman*, 150; Sherman to Poe, 11 November, *OR*, vol. 39, pt. 3, p. 741; Poe's report, 8 October 1865, *OR*, vol. 44, p. 60.

sometimes Sherman's officers actually issued orders for the burning of entire towns where residents were suspected of harboring guerillas. On 30 October, Brigadier General John E. Smith (commanding the 3rd Division, XV Corps) ordered a regiment of Ohio cavalry to ride to Canton, "permit the citizens to remove what they desire, and burn the town, after which you will proceed to Cassville and make the same disposition as at Canton." Civilians remembered for a long time when Federal soldiers swept through. "I saw a Yankee officer riding toward my house," recalled a Cassville woman in 1931. "He came up and said, 'Madame, I have orders to burn your house. You have twenty minutes to get your furniture out.'"

License to conduct wholesale burning made an impression on Sherman's soldiers. Sherman's soldiers had always known that manufacturing facilities were targets for destruction. After the Roswell textile mills had been burned in July, Ohioan Edwin Woodsworth had written his mother, "this country is noted for its manufactories establishments but if they don't quit fiting they will get them all burnt that is general shermans orders to burn pubic buildings and any things that would help the rebs." But now, torching homes was something new. "The Government is now Entering upon a new policy," wrote Ohioan Joseph Hoffhines. "We are ordered to burn Cities and Barns and Houses where Ever we go and lay waste the Entire Country." The same happened in Kingston, Cartersville, Acworth, and Big Shanty (today's Kennesaw). As one soldier noted, on 13 November at Cartersville, "this morning all that is burnable is burned.... Most of the families have gone either north or south but a few, for some cause, have failed to get away and now they are weeping over their burning homes. The sight is grand but almost heartrending." Dr. E. P. Burton, surgeon for the 7th Illinois, was among Corse's troops marching southward. His diary entries make clear the arson which was being committed along the Federals' route.

> Saturday eve, Nov. 12.... Started at 4 in the morning, by moonlight. Came 3 or 4 miles & passed the ruins of Cassville. Seemed to have been a nice town of 3 or 4000 inhabitants. Every building but the churches have been burned.... About daybreak passed a house in flames. Passed Cartersville at 10 A.M. Near the place was a nice house in flames....
> Ackworth Sabbath Morning Nov. 13. Here amid the smoking ruins of Ackworth. The hallowed Sabbath is disturbed not only by the usual camp noise, but by the sacking of this town—town had mostly been burned before we arrived—& now the soldiers are tearing up the R.R.— burning the ties with rails crossed.... At 1 1/2 came to Big Shanty— found it also burned.... One mile further on.... R.R. track burned up and rails bent around the trees.... .
> [From atop Kennesaw Mountain,] I had an extensive view on all sides.... all the way to Allatoona and along the line of the R.R. was a continuous cloud of smoke, evidently some houses burning as well as the

R.R.... Southeast at the foot of the mountain lay Marietta all in flames. All over the country, south and southeast were unnumerable columns of smoke showing where buildings were burning....

Monday Nov. 14.... Left camp near Marietta this morning at 7. All Marietta was a smouldering heap except the churches & most of the private residences. Nearly every house on the road today had been burned....

Illinois major James Connolly was in Acworth on 13 November when that town went up in flame and smoke.

We reached our point on the R.R.... destroyed an allotted portion of the Road—our soldiers burned the village of Acworth *without orders*.... Acworth has been a thriving R.R. village, but to-night it is a heap of ruins. I was the only one of the General's staff [Brigadier General Absalom Baird, division commander in the XIV Corps] in the town when the fires began, and I tried to prevent the burning, but while I watched one house to keep it from being fired, another some where else would take fire; so I concluded to give it up. I succeeded in saving a few houses, occupied by "war widows," and their families, but all the rest of the town went up in smoke.

The soldiers were right in thinking that while Sherman had issued strict orders for only military structures to be torched, the commanding general would not mind if firebrands were flung more freely, as happened in Marietta. Union soldiers marched southward through that town and Indiana sergeant William Miller was among them: "All the Buildings but a few was burned and it was almost suffocateing with heat and smoke. Our men would have to break ranks and run out to get their breath while marching." Men breaking ranks were indeed the perpetrators of much of Marietta's destruction. "Half of Marietta was burned up," recorded Major Ward Nichols, Sherman's aide-de-camp, in his journal for 13 November. "Stragglers will get into these places, and dwelling-houses are leveled to the ground." Wisconsan Michael Fitch, among the Union troops marching from Big Shanty to the Chattahoochee and entering Marietta, saw that "all the principal buildings around the public square in this town were burning as we passed." Fitch pointedly noted that "General Sherman was standing looking on."

Major Henry Hitchcock, on Sherman's staff, was with the general on 13 November when Marietta burned. In the square, soldiers with a fire engine were trying to put out a fire in the courthouse, unsuccessfully. Big stores and other buildings sprung ablaze, even while some fires were being extinguished by conscientious soldiers. In fact, guards were posted around downtown, but as the troops marched southward, the guards joined in the columns toward Atlanta. That was when "fire was set *without orders*," Hitchcock recorded in his journal.

While the courthouse burned, Hitchcock conversed with the commanding general.

"'Twill burn down, Sir."
"Yes, can't be stopped."
"Was it your intention?"
"Can't save it—I've seen more of this sort of thing than you."
"Certainly, Sir."

Sherman and Hitchcock rode past a column of soldiers. Sherman pointed to them. "There are the men who do this," he told the major. "Set as many guards as you please, they will slip in and set fire. That Court House was put out—no use—dare say whole town will burn, at least the business part. I never ordered burning of any dwelling—didn't order this, but can't be helped. I say *Jeff. Davis burnt them.*"

Sherman's evident vindictiveness was shared by his soldiers. Sergeant Miller of the 75th Indiana entered into his diary on 12 November that his regiment had marched past Cartersville that day and burned both it and Kingston.

All the building was burned along our line of march and the Rail Road distroyed and it looks as though we are going to devastate or burn out the confederacy. That has always been my policy. That we must make them feel our power and give the Rebel Soldiers to understand that we will not protect their famlies while they remain in the Army. It looks hard to see women and children driven out without shelter but it seams to be the only remedy that will cure the disease. When they learn that unless they submit their families will suffer for their folly the war will end. If we go across the country and destroy the property as we have to day there will be sufferin all over the south and I think forbearance has long ago ceased to be a virtue. The thousands of men who lay in Soldiers graves cry for vengeance. The widows and orphans Scatterd all over our land and the hardships endured by those of us who are left in the field cry for vengeance and now we will either wind up the war suddenly or make them suffer the consequences.

While Sherman's columns marched toward Atlanta along the line of the Western & Atlantic Railroad, Northern soldiers tore it up. The W & A, which had kept Sherman's forces supplied up to this point, was now going to receive the same treatment the Yankees had already applied to the rail lines leading from the Gate City to Augusta, Montgomery, and Macon. To Grant on 6 November, Sherman had written, "I will see that the road is broken completely between the Etowah and the Chattahoochee, including their bridges." And it was. All three army corps marching toward the city participated in the destruction. Each division got a stretch of the roughly 30 miles of rail line from the Etowah to the Chattahoochee.

XIV Corps (coming in from Cartersville)
—2nd Division: Etowah bridge to bridge over Allatoona Creek [ca. 4 miles]
—3rd Division: bridge at Allatoona Creek to "a point one mile beyond Acworth" [ca. 4 miles]
—1st Division: from that point to Big Shanty [now Kennesaw; ca. 4 miles]
XVII Corps (in vicinity of Kennesaw)
—4th Division: from Big Shanty to Noonday Creek [ca. 3 miles]
—1st Division: from Noonday Creek "to a point one-half mile south of Marietta" [ca. 5 miles]
—3rd Division: from a half-mile south of Marietta to Ruff's Station [ca. 2 miles]
XV Corps (near Smyrna)
—from Ruff's Station to the Chattahoochee River [ca. 8 miles].[10]

---

[10] Sherman to Easton, 11 November 1864, *OR,* vol. 39, pt. 3, p. 741; Sherman to Howard, 12 November, *OR,* vol. 39, pt. 3, p. 750; Howe, ed., *Marching with Sherman,* 50; Tappan, ed., *Civil War Journal of Lt. Tuttle,* 169; Sherman's report, 1 January 1865, *OR,* vol. 39, pt. 1, p. 584; Kennett, *Marching through Georgia,* 232–33 ("The country is light"; "This government is now Entering"; "this morning all that is burnable"); Woodworth to mother, 14 July 1864, MSS 645, Atlanta History Center; Clay Mountcastle, *Punitive War: Confederate Guerrillas and Union Reprisals* (Lawrence: University Press of Kansas, 2009) 94 (on the orders to burn Canton and Cassville); Capt. S. M. Budlong to Col. T. T. Heath, 30 October 1864, *OR,* vol. 39, pt. 3, p. 153 (orders to burn Canton and Cassville); Kellogg, ed., *Army Life of an Illinois Soldier,* 310 (on guerillas' murder of nine US soldiers near Cassville and burning of town); Lily Milholland, "Grandma's War Memories," *Atlanta Journal Sunday Magazine,* 5 April 1931; *Diary of E.P. Burton Surgeon 7th Reg. Ill. 3rd. Brig. 2nd Div. 16 A.C.* (typescript) (Des Moines IA: Historical Records Survey, 1939) 39–41; "Major [James A.] Connolly's Diary," *Transactions of the Illinois State Historical Society for the Year 1928* (Springfield: Phillips Bros. Print, 1928) 398; Patrick and Willey, eds., *Fighting for Liberty and Right,* 273–74; Michael H. Fitch, *Echoes of the Civil War as I Hear Them* (New York: R.F. Fenno & Co., 1905) 232; Howe, ed., *Marching with Sherman,* 52–53 ("I say *Jeff. Davis* burnt them" [emphasis original]); Sherman to Grant, 6 November, *OR,* vol. 39, pt. 3, p. 661; A. C. McClurg, Special Field Orders (to XIV Corps), 12 November, *OR,* vol. 38, pt. 3, p. 754; Samuel L. Taggart, Special Field Orders (to XV and XVII Corps), 9 November, *OR,* vol. 38, pt. 3, p. 715; C. Cadle, Jr., Special Order 277 (instructions to three divisions of XVII Corps), 9 November; *OR,* vol. 38, pt. 3, p. 716.

Sherman's placing of blame for the burning of Marietta on Jeff Davis fits with his general view of war and culpability. "In his view, war is entirely and singularly the curse of those who begin it," writes Michael Walzer, "and soldiers resisting aggression (or rebellion) can never be blamed for anything they do that brings victory closer" (*Just and Unjust Wars: A Moral Argument with Historical Illustrations* [New York: Basic Books, 2000] 32).

All this work took place 12–15 November, as recorded by Poe in his diary.

Nov. 12. Commenced destruction of Rail Road between Atlanta and Etowah Bridge. The 14th Corps being between Etowah & Big Shanty. The Army of the Tenn. between Big Shanty & Chattahoochee Bridge. The 20th Corps between Chattahoochee Bridge & Atlanta, and the Michn. Engrs. in Atlanta.
  Nov. 13. Destroying Rail Road in Atlanta & Northward.
  Nov. 14. Work of destruction of Rail Road in Atlanta & Northward—going on preparatory to marching.
  Nov. 15. Work of destruction of Rail Road & depots in Atlanta going on.

The men applied themselves diligently to their work. Captain Charles Wills of the 103rd Illinois in the XV Corps recorded in his diary for 12 November:

The Rubicon is passed, the die is cast, and all that sort of thing. We to-day severed our own cracker line. At 11 A.M. ours and the 17th Corps were let loose on the railroad, the men worked with a will and before dark the 12 miles of track between here and Marietta were destroyed. The ties were piled and burned and the rails, after being heated red hot in the middle were looped around trees or telegraph poles. Old destruction himself could not have done the work better. The way the Rebels destroyed our road on their raid was not even a fair parody on our style.

Surgeon James Patten of the 58th Indiana recorded in his diary entry of the 13th what it all looked like: "Last night we could see fires all along the r.r. where our men were destroying the track." And they were destroying bridges, too. Dr. Patten recorded how 400 men worked on one trestle for four hours; forty soldiers hacked away at the wooden beams, while the rest pulled with ropes.

To help the men with their work, Captain Poe and a railroad man named E. C. Smeed even devised a little tool for prying up the rails, "a small but very strong iron 'cant hook.'" The device was very effective. "It was found that forty men with hooks and levers could tear up and destroy four-fifths of a mile per hour," recorded Missouri engineer William Neal. Major Hitchcock of Sherman's staff witnessed the work riding into Atlanta from Marietta. "Saw Poe's men at work yesterday with his new contrivance for quickly tearing up R.R'd tracks: simply a large iron hook, hung on a chain whose other end has a ring to insert a crow-bar or other lever. The hook is caught on the inside of the rails, but supported against the outside, at the ring and end of lever. With these, the heaviest rails are easily and quickly turned over."[11]

A special target was the W & A bridge across the Chattahoochee, which Poe's engineers had rebuilt by 5 August as a wooden trestle over the stone piers left standing from the retreating Rebels' bridge fire in July. On 13 November, Colonel George P. Buell's 58th Indiana tore down the wooden structure. Stephen F. Fleharty of the 102nd Illinois was on hand to watch the work. The men of the regiment tied a strong cable to the bridge, bringing both ends to the riverbank. Then the soldiers began a heave-ho pulling of the cable that, in Fleharty's words, created "a swaying motion that increased to a pendulum-like swing, until at length it began to give way; then huge beams swung loose in the air, iron rails struck fire as they fell upon the stone piers, and several spans came crashing down into the turbulent river."

Of course, tearing down the trestle bridge over the Chattahoochee was just part of the overall destruction of Atlanta's railroad complex. After the last train left on the morning of 12 November, the Poe's engineers and their work crews began wrecking the three rail lines from their junction downtown out to the old Rebel works. (Captain Poe thought that the total track within the perimeter of the Confederate lines was about 10 miles, but Captain Grant's map suggests it was closer to 6.) Corporal Reid recorded on 12 November that the engineers "have commenced tearing up the railroad track in the city. They take up both rails and ties, pile the ties up, lay the rails across them, and fill around with kindling wood all ready for the torch." The first line to be targeted was the Georgia Railroad running eastward toward Augusta. One member of the 1st Michigan, Isaac Roseberry, recorded this work in his diary: "Nov 12. After getting our Diners we was Ordered to go on the Augusta Rail Road and Destroy it Effectualy which we done in Good Shape by Burning the Ties and twisting the Rails. Such a Destruction of Property I never before Saw." Companies H and I of the 1st Michigan completed their demolition of the Augusta road on 13 November.

The engineers were at work on the other lines as well. Isaac Roseberry noted in his diary that 13 November was a Sabbath, "but not with us for we are Still tearing up the Different R. R. Tracks leading from this city." Three companies of the 1st Michigan targeted the Western & Atlantic, aided by fatigue

---

[11] Poe Diary, 1864, box 1, folder 2, O.M. Poe Papers, Library of Congress; Kellogg, ed., *Army Life of an Illinois Soldier*, 318–19; Robert G. Athearn, ed., "An Indiana Doctor Marches With Sherman: The Diary of James Comfort Patten," *Indiana Magazine of History* 49/4 (December 1953): 417; "Hook used by General Sherman's army for twisting and destroying railroad iron. From print lent by Gen. O.M. Poe," illustration accompanying Oliver O. Howard, "Sherman's Advance from Atlanta," Robert Underwood Johnson and Clarence Clough Buel, eds., *Battles and Leaders of the Civil War,* 4 vols. (New York: Century Co., 1888) 4:664; Poe's report, 8 October 1865, *OR,* vol. 44, p. 60; Mark Hoffman, *"My Brave Mechanics": The First Michigan Engineers and Their Civil War* (Detroit: Wayne State University Press, 2007) 241; Howe, ed., *Marching with Sherman,* 58.

crews from the XX Corps (a brigade from each division). The soldiers' orders were clear: "Let the destruction be as complete as possible by burning the ties and bending and twisting the rails." The men set to their task. The 58th Indiana, attached to the XX Corps as "pontoniers," was one of the regiments helping the engineers with their work. Even John Hight, the regimental chaplain, knew the process: the piling and burning of ties, the heating of rails at their center, and the use of handspike, hook and ring to twist the bars. "A rail, simply bent, can be used again, without being taken to the shop for repair," Hight wrote in General Sherman's own style, "but a twisted bar cannot." "This is hard, hot work," the chaplain added, but "the boys all like the fun." Evidently there were not enough of Captain Poe's cant hooks to go around. On 13 November, Colonel Ezra A. Carman's brigade pried up a lot of track, but Carman had to report that his men could only burn ties and bend rails but not twist them; they had no tools for such work. Notably, as they torched the wooden ties, the engineers took precautions to prevent the spread of the flames, such as taking down wooden structures near the piles of burning wood. Corporal Reid observed their efforts, noting "much of the railroad track was fired today—all that would not endanger buildings by its burning."[12]

When they were done with it, the Yankees had essentially made the Western & Atlantic Railroad disappear. According to one authority, 84 miles of track between Atlanta and Resaca had been destroyed in Sherman's favorite rail-twisting style; another 20 miles of iron farther north had simply been taken up

---

[12] Report of Col. George P. Buell, 58th Indiana Infantry, 7 January 1865, *OR*, vol. 44, p. 160 ("November 13, 1864, my command destroyed the railroad bridge over the Chattahoochee River near Atlanta, Ga."); Lt. Col. Henry W. Perkins to "Col. Franklin C. Smith, Chattahoochee Bridge," 13 November, *OR*, vol. 39, pt. 3, p. 763 ("you will not destroy either the road or railroad bridges at the river; that is to be done by Colonel Buell"); Hight, *History of the Fifty-Eighth Indiana*, 411; Fleharty, *Our Regiment*, 108; Hoffman, "My Brave Mechanics," 217 (arrival of eight companies at Atlanta, 28 September); 240–41; Poe report, 8 October 1865, *OR*, vol. 44, p. 60; Frank L. Byrne, ed., *Uncommon Soldiers: Harvey Reid and the 22nd Wisconsin March with Sherman* (Knoxville: University of Tennessee Press, 2001) 200; Roseberry, diary, 12–13 November, Emory University; Tappan, ed., *Civil War Journal of Lt. Tuttle*, 170; report of Brig. Gen. Alpheus S. Williams, 9 January 1865, *OR*, vol. 39, pt. 1, p. 650 ("November 13, a brigade from each division was sent to destroy the railroad between Atlanta and the Chattahoochee River, which was reported the next morning as effectually done"); H. C. Rodgers to A. S. Williams, 13 November, *OR*, vol. 39, pt. 3, p. 762 (orders for destruction); Carman to Lt. George Robinson, 13 November, *OR*, vol. 39, pt. 3, p. 763.

Captain Poe states that his engineers completed rebuilding the Chattahoochee railroad bridge on 5 August. Before that, especially during the week of Sherman's troop crossings (10–16 July), Poe had overseen the construction of various pontoon and wooden trestle bridges to get Sherman's troops over the river and allow wagon traffic to keep them supplied (Poe's report, 1 October 1865, *OR*, vol. 38, pt. 1 pp. 130–34).

and hauled to Chattanooga. The act of cutting their own "cracker line" for food and supplies from the North made an impression among Union soldiers in Atlanta. For Daniel Oakey of the 2nd Massachusetts, "there was something intensely exciting in the perfect isolation" that troops in the city began to feel, once they realized that there would be no further supplies from the north. Sergeant William Miller of the 75th Indiana put it more figuratively: "we have crawled into the hole and pulled the hole in after us."

Adding to the excitement—to use Oakey's wording—was the apprehension of more destruction still to come. In addition to railroad track, Sherman wanted a thorough demolition of what remained of Atlanta's once-vaunted Confederate manufacturing, logistical, and transportation complex. To do the work, Poe divided his regiment of Michigan engineers into detachments and gave each an assignment, stressing (as he made clear in his report) that they were "to be careful not to use fire, which would endanger other buildings than those set apart for destruction." For example, on 12 November Captain Williamson's detachment was assigned to destroy the Western & Atlantic roundhouse, "being careful not to use fire in doing it." The engineers' demolition tasks along the railroad east of the Car Shed were quite specific: "You will please take the detachment under your charge, to the Georgia Round House, and destroy the chimneys, arches &c of that building, being careful not to use fire in doing so, as the high wind, now blowing would endanger other buildings which it is not intended to destroy." Lieutenant J. W. Spoor's men were to knock down a tall factory chimney north of the Georgia roundhouse; Lieutenant Benjamin A. Cotton's detachment would take care of "all the Steam Chimneys [and] Furnace Arches" near the roundhouse to the old Peters mill/Spiller & Burr factory. Lieutenant Walter F. Hubert would start at the pistol factory and "destroy all the Steam Chimneys, Furnace Arches, and Steam Machinery from there to the Old Rolling Mill, being careful not to use fire in doing the work."

The engineers obeyed orders, and Poe proudly confirmed in his post-campaign report that "neither fire nor powder was used for destroying buildings until after they had been put in ruins by battering down the walls, throwing down smokestacks, breaking up furnace arches, knocking steam machinery to pieces, and punching all boilers full of holes." Onlooking Federal soldiers documented the destruction around town, including the area of the Georgia Railroad roundhouse. "On the Augusta Railroad a little east of the main business street," recorded Corporal Harvey Reid of the 22nd Wisconsin, "is a large wooden mill or warehouse that was partly torn down a week ago. They are now finishing it." Reid then saw the engineers turn their attention to the stone roundhouse, using a swinging battering ram. "A bar of railroad iron is hung near the center with chains to a high 'horse' and swung back and forth against the solid stone wall until one of the rocks is knocked out, then another taken and so on until a portion of the wall between two windows is undermined when it falls and they commence at another window." Captain Comey of the 2nd

Massachusetts also saw how the battering rams worked, a process he termed "systematic and effective." "Cranes were rigged, from which were suspended chains and heavy iron rails. The cranes were set up near the walls of the buildings to be destroyed, and a detail of men took the rail by the long end and operated it after the manner of an ancient battering ram. A very few blows were sufficient to start moving the most solid stone in the wall, and in a very short time what had been a fine building would be reduced to a pile of ruins." Comey described how the industrial chimneys slated for demolition, such as the tall stacks of the old Peters flour mill/Spiller & Burr pistol factory, were broken down. They were "destroyed very much as a tree is cut down," he recorded in his diary. "A rope was attached as near the top as possible; the battering ram would cut a gash near the ground, and then a large force of men would sway on the rope until the stack would fall; a broken mass of brick work." After seeing the Georgia railroad torn up, the stone roundhouse battered down and surrounding smokestacks toppled, Lieutenant Tuttle on the afternoon of 12 November noted the obvious: "looks like this place will be no use to anybody after we all have left it."

Wisconsan Harvey Reid recorded Sunday, 13 November, as "the most unquiet Sabbath I have seen in a long time." After breakfast, he walked to where the engineers were completing the smashing of the Georgia roundhouse. He saw General Slocum talking with an officer in charge of the demolition; Slocum was apparently making sure that the work was being done according to General Sherman's orders against uncontrolled burning. Also on 13 November, the engineers turned to the Western & Atlantic roundhouse and complex of surrounding shops—"the largest and most complete I ever saw," Reid observed. Tuttle saw how "they were tearing down the 'State Shop,' once a splendid building."

On 14 November the last key structures of Atlanta's once-great railway hub crashed to the ground. Tuttle recorded that day as well: "the Lugrang Depot destroyed," meaning the facilities of the Atlanta & West Point line (which ran through LaGrange), one of the three rail lines leading from the city. Their nexus, of course, was the Car Shed at the center of downtown, which Tuttle noted was "laid low" on 14 November. According to a letter written shortly afterward by Captain John C. Van Duzer, Union engineers used "a large sawhorse about ten feet high" with "a 21-foot bar of railroad iron poised with the chain at its center" as battering ram, suspended from the top of the wooden frame. Half a dozen men pulled the big bar, which hammered into the brick walls of the depot. Indeed, two such wreckers may have been applied to the huge building, as Harvey Reid wrote that on the morning of 14 November he "went down town pretty early...and was surprised to see the large passenger depot gradually crumbling before the blows of two railroad-iron battering rams." Reid thought that the Car Shed crashed down more readily than the Georgia Railroad's stone roundhouse. "One of the narrow brick pillars would soon give way and in about three hours that elegant structure was a mass of ruins." Massachusetts Captain Comey was also onhand as a witness. "There was one very large railroad station, the sides of which were composed of a series of brick arches" (the distinctive features, with its curved roof, of the downtown depot). "In the destruction of this building, every alternate pier was battered down, and, as the last of these was broken through, the thrust of the great roof carried the entire building to the ground with a resounding crash." Others said the same. In his diary entry of 14 November, Captain John M. Carr of the 100th Indiana mentioned the morning destruction of "that magnificent structure," the Car Shed, "and the crash was terrible indeed." With all this destructive drama, and so many onlookers, no wonder a Northern infantryman wrote, "the pioneers were having all the fun."[13]

Indeed, the desire for "fun" may have been Northern soldiers' motive in setting unauthorized fires in Atlanta. For days, Federals such as William Wallace had been talking about burning the Gate City ("it dont do us any good now," as he had put it on 7 November). Now others predicted that the engineers' controlled demolition would get out of control. Moreover, amid so many signs of Atlanta's impending destruction, soldiers could count on officers looking the other way if they broke the rules. "I don't believe that Sherman contemplates destroying anything but the public buildings," Harvey Reid wrote in his diary, "but it is very evident that acts of vandalism by the men will be winked at." Reid knew that among the men in the ranks "there are plenty of them who will not be slow to avail themselves of such tacit license."

The unauthorized arson that apparently many in Federals expected began late on 11 November. "Toward Evening a tremendious Fire Broke Out in the City," recorded Isaac Roseberry, the Michigan engineer, in his diary that night. "Atlanta commenced burning on the night of Friday, the 11th of November," according to Captain Conyngham, who filed a report for his paper, the *New York Herald.*

---

[13] Hoffman, *"My Brave Mechanics,"* 241–42; Daniel Oakey, "Marching through Georgia and the Carolinas," Johnson and Buel, eds., *Battles and Leaders of the Civil War* 4:672; Patrick and Willey, eds., *Fighting for Liberty and Right,* 274 ("we have …pulled the hole in after us"); Poe report, 8 October 1865, *OR*, vol. 44, p. 60; Poe to Williamson, Spoor and Cotton, 11–12 November 1864, Poe Letterbook, box 12, O. M. Poe Papers, Library of Congress; Poe to Wooding and Hubert, Davis, *George N. Barnard,* 85; Byrne, ed., *Uncommon Solders,* 200–202; Comey, ed., *Legacy of Valor,* 206, 208; Tappan, ed., *Civil War Journal of Lt. Tuttle,* 170; Charles J. Brockman, ed., "The John Van Duser Diary of Sherman's March from Atlanta to Hilton Head," *Georgia Historical Quarterly* 53/2 (June 1969): 220–21; Trudeau, *Southern Storm,* 67 ("half a dozen men knocked away"); John M. Carr, diary, 14 November, Kennesaw Mountain National Battlefield Park (thanks to Willie R. Johnson, historian at KMNBP, for making this source available); Taylor, *Orlando M. Poe,* 191 ("the pioneers were having all the fun").

The fire broke out in a block of cheap tenement houses on Decatur street, near the edge of the town, where eight buildings were destroyed. Within an hour large fires were burning in five other localities, and the eager watchers in the camp began to think that the last days of the Gate City had come. The fire-engines had been loaded on cars for transportation to Chattanooga, and it was some time before they could be brought to work against the flames, which threatened the destruction of the entire southern portion of the city. The patrol-guard was doubled, and orders issued to them to shoot down any person seen firing buildings.... Twenty-two buildings, principally dwelling-houses, were burned by incendiaries that night, and a dense cloud of smoke hung over the town when the sun rose. Soldiers had labored faithfully during the night to save what they would have gladly destroyed, if the destruction had been sanctioned by order. Next morning General Slocum offered a reward of five hundred dollars for the detection of any soldier engaged in the incendiarism, but no traces of the perpetrators were discovered. The fires of Friday night were subsequently declared to be the work of some soldiers exasperated at the murder of a comrade.

Conyngham later wrote that the house fires "were the works of some of the soldiers, who expected to get booty." "In evening fires in town," recorded Major Lewis D. Warner of the 154th New York in his diary of the 11th. "Hot times," wrote New York sergeant Joshua Pettit, who added that soldiers set thirty buildings on fire that night. Other Northerners tried to shrug off the vandalism. "The fires were supposed to be set by citizens," an historian of the 2nd Massachusetts observed. Mead of the 5th Connecticut recorded in his diary that the fires of 11–12 November were even "supposed to have been done by rebel incendiaries." The few civilians still in the city knew better. Young Carrie Berry recorded in her diary: "Sat. Nov. 12. We were fritened almost to death last night. Some mean soldiers set several houses on fire in different parts of the town. I could not go to sleep for fear that they would set our house on fire. We all dred the next few days to come for they said that they would set the last house on fire if they had to leave this place." On 12 November, there was more unauthorized burning. "Large fire in the City again to Day," recorded Isaac Roseberry, who as a Michigan engineer knew well Captain Poe's orders not to use fire till the very last. The next day brought more of the same, according to Carrie Berry: "Sun. Nov. 13. The federal soldiers have ben coming to day and burning houses and I have ben looking at them come in nearly all day."[14]

[14] Holzhueter, ed., "William Wallace's Letters," 111; Byrne, ed., *Uncommon Soldiers*, 202; Roseberry, diary, 11–12 November, Emory University; Conyngham, *Sherman's March through the South*, 236; Dunkelman, *Marching with Sherman*, 38; Quint, *Second Massachusetts Infantry*, 247; Mead, diary, 12 November, Rufus Mead, Jr. Papers, Library of Congress; Carrie Berry, diary, entries of 12–13 November, Atlanta History Center.

The Federals coming in were those of the XIV, XV, and XVII corps, returning from Northwest Georgia with Sherman. Marching into the city on the road from Marietta, they were able to see widespread destruction of targeted works in northwest Atlanta. "A great deal going on in the way of destroying property," noted Lieutenant Tuttle on 13 November, adding, "Saw Windships Foundry burned." In that area was the gas works, and it was also set ablaze. "Some soldiers had thrown in a brand to 'see how it would burn,'" according to Wisconsin corporal Reid. Reid saw that "an officer came dashing up on horseback, seemingly much excited," and in accordance with Slocum's orders, "offered $500.00 to any one who would tell him who set it on fire." There were no takers. Eventually the excited officer gave up and, according to Reid, "coolly remarked—'How fine it burns!'" Soon General Slocum himself arrived, and watched the demolishing of the gas works. "See that the retort is broken and thoroughly destroyed," the general said before riding off. As the historian of Atlanta's gas company commented, "the retort was not all that was broken"; the gas works were thoroughly ruined.

Captain Charles Wills, of the 103rd Illinois, was one of the soldiers marching into the city on 13 November; he recorded in his diary that "coming through Atlanta the smoke almost blinded us." After taking a walk about the city with another officer that same day, Captain Edwin E. Marvin of the 5th Connecticut noted that "for three days the fires have been raging like a furnace, and every depot, round house and machine shop has been reduced to ruins, and of course the fires have spread considerably among the residences, there being no effort to save or destroy them." From outside the city, Confederate horsemen could see what was going on. General Hood had sent his cavalry chief, General Wheeler, with troopers back toward Atlanta to observe enemy activity. "For the last two days," Wheeler reported on 13 November, "the enemy have been burning something in Atlanta and some of the scouts think they are preparing to evacuate." Later that same day, Wheeler sent a message to General Howell Cobb at Macon: "Smoke & fires in Atlanta observed all yesterday & this morning."[15]

On 14 November, Poe's engineers, having knocked down round houses, depots, and chimneys, prepared to burn the rubble. Old wagons and abandoned camp equipment were piled up on the ruins of the Car Shed as tinder for the coming fire. Some structures too solid to have been battered down were mined

[15] Tappan, ed., *Civil War Journal of Lt. Tuttle,* 170; Byrne, ed., *Uncommon Soldiers,* 201; "Georgia Scenes," *Cincinnati Commercial,* 31 December 1864 (reprint of Conynham's column in the New York *Herald*); Conyngham, *Sherman's March through the South,* 237; James H. Tate, *Keeper of the Flame: The Story of the Atlanta Gas Light Company, 1856–1985* (Atlanta: Atlanta Gas Light Company, 1985) 15; Kellogg, comp., *Army Life of an Illinois Soldier,* 319; Castel, ed., "Scouting, Foraging and Skirmishing," 89; Wheeler to Hood and Cobb, 13 November 1864, Joseph Wheeler Letterbooks, 1863–1865, Alabama Department of Archives and History.

and set for explosion. One was the Macon and Western freight depot, called the Rock Depot to distinguish it from the Car Shed. Engineers packed kegs of gunpowder in and under the building and waited for orders to detonate. Corporal Harvey Reid of the 22nd Wisconsin noted in his diary that day seeing the powder being placed and that workmen were busy tamping it down.

The fire that Sherman had ordered Poe not to use till the last moment, according to two sources, began to be applied to all the wreckage on 14 November. "To Day we are at work tearing up Track and Committing all Kinds of Destruction fire to," Isaac Roseberry entered into his diary that day; "We have burnt up 2 large Depots and a Round House which was large Enough to hold 50 or more Engines we allso Blowed up a Stone Depot with 700 lbs of Powder. Weather Pleasant." From his plantation at Rockbridge, well over a dozen miles east of downtown, Thomas Maguire could see what was happening, as he recorded in his journal entry for 14 November: "considerable smoak at Atlanta this morning."

The engineers' most extensive and conclusive burning occurred on 15 November. "In the morning, some of the depots and machine shops were blown up, and in the afternoon all were given to flames," observed Chaplain John Hight of the 58th Indiana in his diary. Union engineers had planted shells in some structures, he noted, "which favored us with frequent explosions." Lieutenant Benjamin Cotton and a detachment of the 1st Michigan blew up the Rock Depot on the afternoon of 15 November. Union telegraph officer John Van Duzer recorded in his diary that day that "the stone warehouse" (Macon & Western freight depot) and "brick depot" (the Car Shed) had been demolished.

The destruction was not all in downtown; the Fair Grounds Hospital complex—two score wooden buildings, once holding 800 beds—was well of out of town to the southeast, but it too was burned on the morning of 15 November by engineers from Captain McCrath's Company B of the 1st Michigan. Chaplain Hight recorded the process in an entry to his diary. "This morning, a large cluster of frame hospitals in the eastern part of the city were simultaneously given to the flames.... First, there was a hammering and banging within, as the kindling was being prepared; and soon flames began to rise from the numerous small buildings. The lumber used in the construction of the houses was pine, hence the flames spread rapidly." Corporal Reid observed that the hospital buildings were "long wooden houses, admirably adapted to that purpose, so of course they must go."

The map accompanying the "Plan of Destruction" for the 33rd Massachusetts clearly indicates that the several blocks of Whitehall-Peachtree south and north of the railroad were targeted for destruction; they were burned on 15 November. (Hight recorded in his diary that "the compact business blocks in the center of the city were spared until the afternoon.") In addition, Captain Skidmore and thirty men from the 1st Michigan torched the deserted Rebel barracks off Peachtree. The Trout House and Washington Hall had been marked for burning; these also went up in flames, as well as most buildings surrounding the Car Shed square. "The Atlanta Hotel, Washington Hall, and all the square around the railroad depot, were soon in one sheet of flame," recorded Conyngham. Captain Van Duzer wrote a friend on the evening of 15 November, "this afternoon 'Bri' office and buildings all around it were set on fire. And now while I am writing you the Trout House our office and the whole business portion of Whitehall Street is in a perfect blaze." In the block of Whitehall near the tracks was the building that had housed Thomas Ripley's china and glass store, as well as Crawford, Frazer & Company's market for "auction and Negro sales." The destruction of this eyesore was particularly gratifying to the Northerners. Colonel Adin Underwood of the 33rd Massachusetts, writing well after the war, remembered the destruction of the city's foundries and machine shops, and of the downtown hotels, but especially the "negro markets...never to be set up again."

While these fires raged, Sherman's "Army of Georgia" prepared to set out on its long anticipated march to the Atlantic. Elements of the XIV, XV, and XVII corps were still marching through Atlanta on 15 November to their places of encampment to the east and southeast of the city. (Michigan engineer Ike Roseberry entered in his diary that "the 14th Army Corps came in to Day," adding that "large fires are Raging all over the City.") These men had witnessed—and taken part in—the burning of Rome, Kingston, Cartersville, Cassville, Acworth, Big Shanty, and Marietta, numerous buildings both public and private, and thus had little reason to believe that the torch would be withheld from Atlanta. They could already see that fires had been set, and the smoke from the engineers' blazes downtown doubtless encouraged many men to take up the torch on their own. Dr. E. P. Burton (7th Illinois) marched into the city with his regiment that morning. "Many houses had been burned," he recorded in his diary, "and all day long the fires kept increasing in number." Captain James R. Ladd of the 113th Ohio was one of those entering the city, witnessing the arson. "We arrived in the suburbs of Atlanta at 2 P.M.," he noted in his diary; "no sooner did we arrive than the boys commenced burning every house in [the northwestern] part of the town. The wind was blowing hard at the time and soon that part of the city was gone." Once in their bivouacs, the men were able to look back at the fires. After marching through the city, the 150th New York took a rest southeast of Atlanta on a hill. "I beheld a column of black smoke ascending to the sky," Charles Benton of the 150th recalled. "Then another column of smoke arose, and another, and another until it seemed that they all merged together and the whole city was in flames."[16]

[16] Conyngham, *Sherman's March through the South*, 238 ("worn-out wagons and camp equipage were piled up in the depot"; "the men plunged into the houses"; "the Atlanta Hotel, Washington Hall, and all the square around the railroad depot, were soon in one sheet of flame"); Michael Rose, *Atlanta: A Portrait of the Civil War* (Charleston SC: Arcadia

Major James Connolly, a Union staff officer, described how chaos ensued on the afternoon of 15 November. Commissary officers had that morning been issuing rations, clothing, and shoes to the troops before the big march. "Up to about 3 P.M. this issuing was carried on with something like a show of regularity," Connolly noted, "but about that time fires began to break out in various portions of the city, and it soon became evident that these fires were but the beginning of a general conflagration which would sweep over the entire city and blot it out of existence." Quartermasters and commissaries gave up distributing their supplies, and told the soldiers to just take what they wanted; it was all going to be burned up anyway. Among the stores, soldiers found liquor, and the resulting intoxication led to more fire-setting. "All sorts of discordant noises rent the air, drunken soldiers on foot and horseback raced up and down the streets while the buildings on either side were solid sheets of flame," Connolly wrote. In the spirit of chaotic merriment, some sang "Rally around the

---

Publishing, 1999) 25, 107 (on the M & W "Rock Depot"); Byrne, ed., *Uncommon Soldiers*, 202; Roseberry, diary, 14, 15 November, Emory University; Thomas Maguire, diary, 14 November, MS 145, Atlanta History Center; Hight, *History of the Fifty-Eighth Indiana*, 409–10; Hoffman, *"My Brave Mechanics,"* 242 (on the destruction of the Rock Depot, and the burning of the Rebel barracks and Fairgrounds hospital complex); Brockman, ed., "John Van Duser Diary," 220–21; untitled map, and "Orders, Atlanta Geo November 14th 1864. Army of Georgia, Head-Quarters Left Wing," Cogswell Collection, Peabody Essex Museum, Salem MA; Dyer, *Secret Yankees*, 210 ("Plan of Destruction"); "Thirty Years Ago. The Old Trout House Fell Under the Torch of General Sherman," *Atlanta Constitution*, 8 April 1894; Underwood, *Thirty-Third Mass. Infantry*, 240–41 (especially "negro markets never to be set up again"); *Diary of E.P. Burton*, 41; James Royal Ladd, diary, 15 November, "From Atlanta to the Sea," *American Heritage* 30/1 (December 1979): 6 (printed as "Sherman's March through Georgia Recounted in Soldier's Historic Diary," *Atlanta Journal-Constitution*, 14 January 1979); Charles E. Benton, *As Seen from the Ranks: A Boy in the Civil War* (New York: G. P. Putnam's Sons, 1902) 211.

During the Federal occupation, George Barnard photographed the storefront of the Crawford slave market, featuring an African-American soldier seated in front, reading while on leisurely duty. On the other hand, Union forces occupying Atlanta in fall 1864 likely had no United States Colored Troops among them. The photographer's image therefore seems to be "staged." For Sherman's aversion to African-American regiments serving among his combat troops and his refusal to feed or house "contrabands" (newly freed slaves), see Anne J. Bailey, "The USCT in the Confederate Heartland, 1864," in John David Smith, ed., *Black Soldiers in Blue: African American Troops in the Civil War Era* (Chapel Hill: University of North Carolina Press, 2002) 227–32. On the other hand, at least three regiments of US Colored Troops—the 110th, 113th and 116th regiments—probably served as support troops behind the front during the Atlanta Campaign. The evidence comes from the graves of 258 United States Colored Troops buried in Marietta National Cemetery, the burial ground established after the war for Union soldiers who died in North Georgia during the war (Bill Hendrick, "Historian aims to identify unknown Union soldiers," *Atlanta Journal-Constitution*, 13 April 2011).

Flag" in front of buildings afire. Along with the burning and drinking, came the looting. "The men plunged into the houses, broke windows and doors with their muskets," commented Captain Conyngham, "dragging out armfuls of clothes, tobacco and whiskey, which was more welcome than all the rest. The men dressed themselves in new clothes, and then flung the rest into the fire."

Officers gave up trying to restrain their men, and Colonel Cogswell's provost guards soon found it impossible to keep order. Cogswell confessed that it was hard to prevent indiscriminate arson "at a time when many stragglers were passing through the town and when the excitement of so great a conflagration was almost overpowering." Captain Poe acknowledged that "many buildings in the business part of the city were destroyed by lawless persons who, by sneaking around in blind alleys, succeeded in firing many houses which it was not intended to touch." Apparently, he could not admit that they were soldiers from three Federal corps, all marching through the city.

Under these powerful influences, even the most disciplined soldier could succumb. Harvey Reid of the 22nd Wisconsin recorded that "many soldiers set fire to the houses they had been occupying as they left them"; clearly the places would be of no future use to Sherman's troops, and might as well be burned. Sergeant Allen Campbell of the 1st Michigan Engineers knew well the orders against unauthorized burning, but even he took up a firebrand to a private dwelling. "As I was about to fire one place, a little girl about ten years old came to me and said, Mr Soldier you would not burn our house would you. If you do where are we going to live." The little girl's innocent question shamed the sergeant. "She looked into my face with such a pleading look that I could not have the heart to fire the place So I dropped the torch and walked away."

Soldiers may have had different motives for wanting to burn. For Campbell, it was the knowledge that a few months before, Rebel cavalry had burned much of downtown Chambersburg, Pennsylvania (ordered by General Jubal Early in retaliation for Federals' devastation in the Shenandoah Valley). Campbell recorded that some people still in Atlanta "left their houses without Saying a word for they heard the cry of *Chambersburg* and they knew it would be useless to contend with the soldiers." Thus under the cry of "Chambersburg," some Federals apparently took up the torch. When it was over, Campbell concluded, Chambersburg had been "dearly paid for."

Vengeance may have been on some men's minds, but on such a rowdy, riotous day the men simply gave way to abandon and recklessness, especially when they got hold of whiskey. The soldiers' understanding that private residences were off limits made it more mischievous, and therefore more fun, to burn them. The sight of the homeowners themselves scurrying before the torch added drama to the scene and the act. Chaplain Hight watched "a company of poor people, huddled together in an open lot, ...collecting their scant property from their houses, either now burning, or soon expected to burn." As he recorded in his diary, "a little house, near our camp, was burned. Another fine frame residence, nearby, was soon in flames." In his diary entry for 15 November, Ohio Captain Ladd confessed even to enjoying the sight of civilian residents scrambling amidst the flames: "to witness them getting away from the fire was decidedly rich."

Obviously, many in Sherman's army enjoyed the burning of Atlanta. The regimental band of the 33rd Massachusetts even played while the city burned. That night the musicians were conducting their last performance in the Atheneum downtown. "As the band was playing in the theatre," wrote Colonel Underwood of the 33rd, "the flaming red light from the approaching fire, which flooded the building, the roar of the flames and the noises of the intermittent explosions, added scenic effect which were not down in the bills, and will never be forgotten." The band had to leave the Atheneum when its whole block was put to the torch. The musicians then moved to the front of the Neal house and serenaded General Sherman; Major Henry Hitchcock wrote that he would always remember "the Miserere in 'Trovatore'" in connection with "this night's scenes and sounds." At one point, the band played "John Brown's Body." Major Ward Nichols recorded the scene in his diary: "to-night I heard the really fine band of the Thirty-third Massachusetts playing 'John Brown's soul goes marching on,' by the light of the burning buildings. I have never heard that noble anthem when it was so grand, so solemn, so inspiring." To Underwood, the hellish blend of flames, billows of treacherous smoke, and symphonous wafts of music "seemed like a demoniacal triumph over the fate of the city that had so long defied Sherman's armies."

A number of Northern officers and men documented that infernal night. One of them was Colonel Oscar L. Jackson, whose 63rd Ohio had marched through the city on 14 November and camped southeast of it that next evening. "It is dark and as we look back we see that Atlanta is in flames," he recorded in his diary. "It will be utterly destroyed. The glare of the light against the sky is beautiful and grand. A terrible but just punishment is meted out to the Gate City." F. Y. Hedley, adjutant of the 32nd Illinois, observed that from the engineers' fires applied to the railroad facilities, "the flames spread rapidly, and when morning came, it is doubtful whether there were a score of buildings remaining in the city, except in the very outskirts." Major Nichols described the night sky as "one expanse of lurid flame." Captain Oakey of the 2nd Massachusetts recalled that "there could be no 'taps' amid the brilliant glare and excitement."

The fierce flames consuming the city roared so high and lit the night so brightly that Axel Reed, a Minnesota soldier encamped 1 1/2 miles outside, recorded in his diary (likely with exaggeration), "we could see to read newspapers at midnight at our camp from the light of burning buildings." Sergeant Jerome Carpenter's regiment, the 87th Indiana (XIV Corps) had also marched through the city and beyond it, so he too could watch the flames. "I verily believe there have been few, more terribly grand and terrific sights than that which the city of Atlanta presented on the night of the 15th of Nov'r as witnessed by our troops. A whole city, as it were, on fire and the smoke and flame ascending and mingling with the clouds. Were I to live a thousand years I never should forget the scene." Captain Ladd, encamped with the 113th Ohio east of the city, described downtown Atlanta burning as "one of the most beautiful and terrific scenes I ever had the pleasure of witnessing." W. C. Johnson of the 89th Ohio also viewed the huge fires from outside the city. It was an "awfully grand sight...an ocean of fire as we look down upon the great volumes of fire and smoke, the ruinous flames leaping from building to building." Soon, Johnson wrote, there would only be left the "smoldering ruins of this once beautiful city."[17]

General Sherman also witnessed the burning of Atlanta. Having arrived back in Atlanta by noon of 14 November and resuming his residence downtown at the Neal house, he was a close observer of the destruction. Major Henry Hitchcock was with Sherman that night at the general's headquarters. From it they viewed the flames, which Hitchcock termed "the grandest and most awful scene." That night the major made his diary entry:

From our rear and E. windows, 1/3 of horizon shows immense and raging fires, lighting up whole heavens—probably, says Sherman, visible at Griffin, fifty miles off. First bursts of smoke, dense, black volumes, then tongues of flame, then huge waves of fire roll up into the sky: presently the skeletons of great warehouses stand out in relief against and amidst sheets of roaring, blazing, furious flames,—then the angry waves roll less high, and are of deeper color, then sink and cease, and only the fierce glow from the bare and blackened walls, etc. Now and then are heavy explosions [probably from undenotated Northern shells], and as one fire sinks another rises, further along the horizon, till for say 1/3 of the circle,

---

[17] Paul M. Angle, *Three Years in the Army of the Cumberland: The Letters and Diary of Major James A. Connolly* (Bloomington: Indiana University Press, 1959) 301; Cogswell's report, 26 December 1864, *OR,* vol. 39, pt. 1, p. 652; Poe's report, 8 October 1865, *OR,* vol. 44, p. 60; Glatthaar, *The March to the Sea and Beyond,* 139 (Allen Campbell and Axel Reed); Howe, ed., *Marching with Sherman,* 59; Nichols, *Story of the Great March,* 41; David P. Jackson, ed., *The Colonel's Diary: Journals Kept before and during the Civil War by the Late Colonel Oscar L. Jackson of New Castle, Pennsylvania, Sometime Commander of the 63rd Regiment O.V.I.* (n.p.: Sharon PA, 1922) 162; Fenwick Y. Hedley, *Marching through Georgia* (Chicago: Donohue, Henneberry & Co., 1890) 257; Oakey, "Marching through Georgia and the Carolinas," 4:672; Jack K. Overmyer, *A Stupendous Effort: The 87th Indiana in the War of the Rebellion* (Bloomington: Indiana University Press, 1997) 155 (quoting Carpenter in the Rochester [Indiana] *Chronicle,* 12 January 1865); W. C. Johnson, "The March to the Sea," Sydney C. Kerksis, comp., *The Atlanta Papers* (Dayton OH: Press of Morningside Bookshop, 1980) 809.

N.E. and E. of us, and some on the N.W., it is a line of fire and smoke, lurid, angry dreadful to look upon.

As they watched the burning, Hitchcock recorded his belief that "Gen. S. will hereafter be charged with indiscriminate burning, which is not true." The major affirmed that the commanding general ordered the destruction of "only such buildings as are used or useful for war purposes, whether for producing, storing, or transporting materials, etc. of war: but all others are to be spared, and *no dwelling touched.*" Hitchcock was mistaken regarding "no dwelling touched" in the city, as numerous house-burnings occurred. But downtown at least, Colonel Cogswell's provost guards kept order. Captain Comey of the 2nd Massachusetts remembered after the war how the men of his regiment stood their posts while all the burning was taking place around them; they were enforcing their orders "to guard all other structures, houses and churches from those who would torch such private property." Major Hitchcock left Sherman's headquarters for a walk to the wrecked and smoldering train depot. Coming back he was impressed that guards at two downtown churches directed him out into the street; they would not let him pass on the sidewalk in front of the church buildings. "This is right," the major concluded. Finally, around 11:30 P.M. the fires were "pretty much burnt out," according to Major Hitchcock.

The last ember had not cooled before Sherman's officers and men began recording their opinions and comments on what had been done: the devastation of a major American city. Many found justification for the act, starting with the commanding general himself. On the evening of 15 November, apparently over dinner, and with smoke and flame on the horizon around them, Major Hitchcock heard Sherman comment that Atlanta deserved to be burned because it had harbored the Rebels' extensive military manufactories. "At table he remarked— 'this city has done and contributed probably more to carry on and sustain the war than any other save perhaps Richmond. We have been fighting *Atlanta* all the time, in the past: have been capturing guns, wagons, etc., etc., marked *"Atlanta"* and made here, all the time: and now since they have been doing so much to destroy us and our Government we have to destroy them, at least enough to prevent any more of that.'"

Others felt the same. "The fate of the city was a terrible one," wrote Captain George Collins in his postwar recollections of the 149th New York, "yet its destruction was deemed a military necessity and was richly deserved, for next to Richmond it had supplied more arms and munitions to carry on the war than any city." By extension of this idea, Atlanta had to suffer as retribution for its role in starting the war. "Heaven and earth both agree in decreeing a terrible punishment to those perfidious wretches who concocted this wasting and desolating war," recorded Captain George W. Pepper of Ohio in his memoir, published a year after the war had ended. On the very night of the burning, Sergeant William B. Miller of the 75th Indiana entered in his diary, "the entire city was distroyed but a few accupied houses." To Miller, this punishment was meted out for general iniquity. "It reminds me of the distruction of the city of Babalon as spoken of in the Bible whis was distroyed because of the wickedness of her people and that is the case with Atlanta."

Some soldiers thought that since the city—for so long their objective—now belonged to them, they could have their way with it. In his diary for 15 November, Major Connolly imagined what General Sherman would then have been thinking: "well, the soldiers fought for it, and the soldiers won it, now let the soldiers enjoy it." That the soldiers' "enjoyment" entailed the burning throughout a whole city would not have mattered. Indeed, Connolly conjectured, General Sherman "is somewhere near by, now, looking on at all this, and saying not one word to prevent it." (The major was correct.) Other officers shared this attitude as well, and stood by while the men set their fires. A member of the 104th Illinois saw some of his comrades "set fire in many places" as higher-ups actually observed. "Several general officers were there, but they stood back and said nothing." Thus Atlanta deserved to be burned, the officers did not mind, and the men obliged—so went the reasoning. As John Hight put it, "a notion has possessed the army that Atlanta is to be burned."[18]

On the other hand, some Northerners tried to minimize the extent of the unauthorized arson, or to find some impersonal cause for it. In the writings of Sherman's soldiers, one sees several approaches to the issue of culpability. The easiest tack was to deny that any inappropriate structures had been damaged at all. Major Hitchcock led the way here in the affirmation that he made in his diary on the night of 15 November that "no dwelling has been touched, nor the Court House, nor any church." Others followed, such as Captain Hartwell Osborn, 55th Ohio: "great care was taken to burn only buildings of public importance, and very few if any dwellings were destroyed."

Conversely, some soldiers acknowledging that private residences and other off-limits buildings had been burned justified the destruction as part of a pattern, somehow sanctioned. Northern soldiers, after having burned Rome, Cassville, Marietta, and other places, and having to catch their breath amid the arson-smoke as they marched into Atlanta, would have assumed that Atlanta was doomed to the same fate, a logical extension of the soldiers' fiery march through those other communities.

---

[18] Howe, ed., *Marching with Sherman*, 55 (Hitchcock, diary, 15 November, "arrived yesterday by noon"), 57–59; Comey, ed., *Legacy of Valor*, 208; George K. Collins, *Memoirs of the 149th Regt. N.Y. Vol. Inft.* (Syracuse: George K. Collins, 1891) 288; George W. Pepper, *Personal Recollections of Sherman's Campaigns in Georgia and the Carolinas* (Zanesville OH: Hugh Dunne, 1866) 239; Patrick and Willey, eds., *Fighting for Liberty and Right*, 278; Angle, ed., *Three Years in the Army of the Cumberland*, 301–302; William Wirt Calkins, *The History of the 104th Regiment of Illinois Volunteer Infantry* (Chicago: Donnohue & Henneberry, 1895) 252; Hight, *History of the Fifty-Eighth Indiana*, 409.

Similarly, with the engineers knocking everything down, prying up the rails, and planting charges to demolish all that is left standing, some soldiers adopted the idea that, as Captain David Conyngham phrased it, "everything in the way of destruction was now considered legalized."

A fourth approach accepts that some unauthorized arson had occurred, but it was by accident—the wind did it. J. E. P. Doyle, correspondent for the *New York Herald,* mentioned the high wind that spread the flames from house to house, until he thought half the city was ablaze. Sergeant Samuel Toombs of New Jersey agreed: "the high wind which prevailed forced flames across wide streets and spread in all directions, until the greater part of the city was a mass of seething fire." Others said the same. "It was not intended to injure private residences," affirmed Captain Collins of New York, "yet many were destroyed by fires ignited by flying sparks."

As always, one could blame the liquor which Major Connolly claimed helped start new fires. Chaplain Hight concluded that "drunken men have destroyed whole blocks."

Or finally, in the broadest generalization, a Yankee could say that this was war, and hard things happened to people. "This is war, as Napoleon took it into Russia," reasoned Captain H. H. Tarr of the 20th Connecticut, "and, I suppose, history will vindicate us." As W. C. Johnson of the 89th Ohio gazed upon "the great volumes of fire and smoke, the ruinous flames leaping from building to building," he recorded in his diary, "surely the terrors of war are being fearfully felt." Wisconsin officer Michael H. Fitch agreed: "war is made up of cruelty and destruction. It destroys in a night what it took years of peaceful industry to construct." In this vein, an Illinois soldier, Harvey Trimble, viewed Sherman's destruction of Atlanta as a moral and historical lesson for the world about the nature of war.

> After what General Sherman did, and what he said about it, there was much keener appreciation generally throughout the civilized world, that war was organized cruelty. What he did was not materially different from what had always been done before, and what he said had always been known before. But the manner in which he wrought all kinds of destruction to the enemy, and to the people who gave encouragement and aid to the rebellion, and the reasons he assigned for it, and the terse manner in which he expressed himself about it, caused thoughtful men and women everywhere to realize the extreme cruelty of war more fully than they had ever done before. In this, he did the world a great service.

When war is essentially sanctioned by society as "organized cruelty," those participating in it are exonerated. Such was the feeling of Indiana sergeant W. B. Miller when he wrote, "I feel Sorry for some of the people but a Soldier is not supposed to have any conscience and must lay aside all scruples he may have."

Of course, Northern soldiers did have consciences, and for some the devastation of Atlanta created feelings of guilt. After being told by an officer just in from downtown that the business area was aflame, Lieutenant Russell Tuttle recorded in his diary that "such wholesale destruction will load us with merited disgrace and infamy." "Let the railroad be destroyed, say we all, and the warehouses and arsenals," Tuttle concluded, "but touch no private property, especially that devoted to trade and the common avocations of life, and most of all private dwellings." Corporal Harvey Reid of the 22nd Wisconsin wrote in his diary, under date of 15 November, one of the most thoughtful commentaries on what had gone on that day.

> I know not what others may think, but I believe this destruction of private property in Atlanta was entirely unnecessary and therefore a disgraceful piece of business. It was argued that the rebels could use the large buildings for hospitals, warehouses, and so forth but every one knows that temporary buildings can still be built, just as suitable for such purposes, even if the destruction of the Railroads and depots had not rendered the city almost valueless as a military post. The cruelties practiced on this campaign toward citizens have been enough to blast a more sacred cause than ours. We hardly deserve success. It is not that indiscriminate destruction of private property is *ordered*—quite the contrary. A guard is placed at every house we pass with orders to admit no soldiers, but he only remains while his division is passing—then come the trains accompanied by a thousand "bummers,"—stragglers under nobody's charge—and they ransack the house, taking every knife and fork, spoon, or any thing else they take a fancy to, break open trunks and bureaus, taking women or children's clothing, or tearing them to pieces, trampling upon them and so forth besides taking everything eatable that can be found. I have never heard however of personal violence being offered to any citizen, but they are insulted in every other way possible. There is certainly a lack of discipline in our army, and then, thanks to the malignity of some of our Northern philanthropists, many of the soldiers seem to think that a *rebel* is without the pale of humanity, and the greater the indignity offered them the more meritorious the action.

Even Captain Poe of the engineers, who in his report observed that "for military purposes the city of Atlanta has ceased to exist," was compelled to acknowledge in his personal diary on 15 November, "much destruction of private property by unauthorized persons." To Poe, this behavior was a "great scandal" for the army.[19]

---

[19] Howe, ed., *Marching with Sherman,* 59; Hartwell Osborn et al., *Trials and Triumphs: The Record of the Fifty-Fifth Ohio Volunteer Infantry* (Chicago: A. C. McClurg, 1904) 174; Conyngham, *Sherman's March through the South,* 237; Andrews, *The North Reports the Civil*

General Sherman himself seemed to show no regret at all when, on the morning of 16 November, he rode out of the city with his staff and the three regiments of Cogswell's provost guard, the last troops to leave. The Union "Army of Georgia" with its 60,000 veterans was heading eastward toward the sea. While they marched, the 33rd Massachusetts band again played "John Brown's Body." "Who that ever heard it, will ever cease to remember the glorious harmonies?" recalled one Northern soldier. The men sang along with the band. Sherman recalled that "the men caught up the strain, and never before or since have I heard the chorus of 'Glory, glory hallelujah!' done with more spirit, or in better harmony of time and place." The celebratory music seemed to herald both Sherman's triumph over Atlanta as well as the start of the new campaign. The men were in a festive mood. "They stepped high and long," remembered Hosea Rood of the 12th Wisconsin; "they sang and made merry," anticipating a "glorious march." The troops had had their way with the city for which they had fought so long and hard. "Behind us lay Atlanta," Sherman wrote in his memoirs, "smouldering and in ruins, the black smoke rising high in the air, and hanging like a pall over the ruined city."[20]

A few Federals gauged the extent of the damage before they marched out with Sherman to the sea. On 16 November, Major Henry Hitchcock wrote that he "saw no dwelling destroyed, and outside of central business part of town comparatively little damage. Should say 1/4 of area of town destroyed but this is the largest and best built business part." On the other hand, some Northerners gave sweeping overstatements of the destruction, such as Major Ward Nichols of Sherman's staff. Watching the burning, he wrote that "buildings covering two hundred acres are in ruins or in flames." A similarly broad estimation of the damage was made by Sergeant Rice C. Bull of the 123rd New York in writing

---

War, 577 ("Jep" Doyle of the *Herald*); Samuel Toombs, *Reminiscences of the War, Comprising a Detailed Account of the Experiences of the Thirteenth Regiment New Jersey Volunteers* (Orange NJ: Journal Office, 1878) 176; Collins, *Memoirs of the 149th N.Y.,* 288; Angle, ed., *Three Years in the Army of the Cumberland,* 301; Hight, *History of the Fifty-Eighth Indiana,* 409; John W. Storrs, *The "Twentieth Connecticut": A Regimental History* (Ansonia CT: Press of the "Naugatuck Valley Sentinel," 1886) 149; Johnson, "The March to the Sea," 809; Fitch, *Echoes of the Civil War,* 233; Harvey M. Trimble, ed., *History of the Ninety-Third Regiment Illinois Volunteer Infantry* (Chicago: Blakely Printing Co., 1989) 139; Patrick and Willey, eds., *Fighting for Liberty and Right,* 278; Tappan, ed., *Civil War Journal of Lt. Tuttle,* 171; Byrne, ed., *Uncommon Soldiers,* 203; Poe's report, 26 December 1864, *OR,* vol. 44, 56; Poe, diary, 15 November, Poe Papers, Library of Congress.

[20] "Orders," 14 November 1864, Cogswell Collection, Peabody Essex Museum, Salem MA (the three provost guard regiments "will remain in Atlanta until all troops have passed through the City"); Hedley, *Marching through Georgia,* 257; Burke Davis, *Sherman's March* (New York: Random House, 1980) 8 ("They stepped high and long"); William T. Sherman, *Memoirs of General William T. Sherman,* 2 vols. (New York: D. Appleton and Company, 1875) 2:178–79.

about the engineers' fires downtown: "their destruction meant the whole city; for when the blaze started there was no one to prevent its spread to all the business and residential districts." Probably the highest estimate of the destruction from Sherman's burning came from the adjutant of the 32nd Illinois, Fenwick Hedley, who asserted that "it is doubtful whether there were a score of buildings remaining in the city, except in the very outskirts."

The truth, if it can be had, lay somewhere between Hitchcock's and Hedley's estimates. With an engineer's sure grasp of detail, Captain Poe judged the structural loss as 37 percent of the city. General Sherman himself glossed over these particularities. More than a month later, in Savannah, Sherman included in his campaign report the brief statement that before his army left for the sea, "Captain O.M. Poe had thoroughly destroyed Atlanta, save its mere dwelling-houses and churches." More telling was Sherman's special field order of 8 January 1865 congratulating his troops for their success in the just-concluded Georgia campaign. As for the city damage, the general was brief and to-the-point: "we quietly and deliberately destroyed Atlanta." This is as close to a full and unapologetic confession as we have in print from Sherman on what he did to the city.[21]

One Northern soldier had termed the devastation of Atlanta "so widespread that I don't think any people will want to try and live there now." He was wrong, because some Atlantans never left—as in the case of the Berry family. Young Carrie had kept her diary during the last days of the Union occupation.

---

[21] Howe, ed., *Marching with Sherman*, 60; Nichols, *Story of the Great March*, 38; Bauer, ed., *Soldiering*, 174; Hedley, *Marching through Georgia*, 257; David Nevin, *Sherman's March: Atlanta to the Sea* (Alexandria VA: Time-Life Books, 1986) 46 ("Captain Poe estimated that 37 percent of Atlanta was destroyed"); report of W. T. Sherman, 1 January 1865, *OR*, vol. 44, p. 8; Special Field Order 6, 8 January 1865, copy at the time of this writing in possession of Kenneth Hosley and the Grey Parrot Gallery in Atlanta.

I have been unable to find the original source for Captain Poe's rather precise estimate of building damage (37 percent). Nevin's reference to Poe is not annotated in his Time-Life volume. In his biography of Sherman, Lloyd Lewis states that "approximately 37 per cent of the city's area was in ashes" by 7 A.M. of 16 November, though without mentioning Poe (Lewis, *Sherman: Fighting Prophet* [New York: Harcourt, Brace and Company, 1932] 435).

I wish to thank Mr. Hosley and Dr. Gordon Jones of the Atlanta History Center for showing me Sherman's Special Field Order 6, not only for its crisp admission ("we quietly and deliberately destroyed Atlanta"), but also because this document is not published in the *Official Records*—at least in vol. 47, pt. 2, which carries several other Special Field Orders issued in Savannah at the time (e.g., no. 1 [2 January], no. 7 [9 January] and no. 8 [10 January], pp. 9, 29, 33).

Mon. Nov. 14. They came burning Atlanta to day. We all dread it because they say that they will burn the last house before they stop. We will dread it.

Tues. Nov. 15. This has ben a dreadful day. Things have ben burning all around us. We dread to night because we do not know what moment that they will set our house on fire. We have a gard a little while after dinner and we feel a little more protected.

Wed. Nov. 16. Oh what a night we had. They came burning the store house and about night it looked like the whole town was on fire. We all set up all night. If we had not sat up our house would have ben burnt up for the fire was very near and the soldiers were going around setting houses on fire where they were not watched. They behaved very badly. They all left the town about one o'clock this evening and we were glad when they left for no body knows what we have suffered since they came in.

She observed that on 17 November some Confederate cavalrymen rode into town; Wheeler's troopers had been keeping a distant eye on the columns of smoke emanating from Atlanta. But after the first cautious, probing Southern horsemen, there came visitors of another kind: looters. "The town is full of country people seeing what they can find," Carrie recorded. Fortunately, more responsible citizens also began to arrive into the city. By 19 November, there were enough people—some eighty men, Carrie thought—to hold a meeting at city hall to begin talking about what they should do. First task was to stop the rummaging by the looters; Carrie wrote on 20 November that "the country people" were still plundering. But eventually the leading citizens restored order, and Atlantans began to evaluate what was left of their city.

The wreckage was widespread throughout the city and its suburbs, but worst of all was the destruction of downtown: the wrecking and torching conducted by Poe's engineers and the soldier-set arson in the final days of the Federal occupation. The demolition of the central railroad facilities would alone have astonished returning Atlantans, as well as the disappearance of once-stately hotels and prominent factories. Some recorded their shocked impressions of the damage, offering probably our best information on what exactly the Yankees had done to us. In all, seven eyewitness reports have come to light.

I. The first of these was written by Atlantan Zachariah Rice just four days after Sherman rode out of the city. Rice had been a prominent businessman in antebellum Atlanta (see "Watkins & Rice, slave dealers" in *Williams' Atlanta Directory* of 1859). He had served in the Confederate cavalry, resigned, returned home, and served as lieutenant colonel in the Fulton County militia in 1864. He probably left in the panicked flight of civilians as Hood's army abandoned the city, and was one of the first Atlantans to return after the Yankees left. On 20

November, he wrote a column describing the devastation (evidently for the *Memphis Appeal*, which had resumed publication in Montgomery). "You have heard before this that the federals have burned and evacuated Atlanta," he explained, "but for information to the refugees and the exiles who have been driven from their homes, allow me to trouble you with a few lines, as all will be anxious to know whether their homes have been spared by the vandal hands." Rice made broad observations on extensive arson along several of the city's main thoroughfares (keyed to the accompanying sketched map).

1. "There is not a house standing on Whitehall street from Roark's corner to Wesley chapel on Peachtree street [meaning... axis]...."
2. "All the houses on Marietta street are burned except a short space from Dr. Powell's to Robinson's house, opposite the State depot."
3. "Except Norcross's mills, L. Dean's and B.O. Jones's, no houses are burned on Peachtree Street beyond Wesley chapel."
4. "There is not a house standing.... down Decatur street a short distance below Colonel Cowart's building."
5. "The jail is burned, and all all the buildings between that and the fair ground."
"The churches are all unhurt, except the new Episcopal [6] and Pain's churches."

Rice stated also that the city jail on Fair Street was torched, as were all the buildings on Fair to the fairgrounds, four blocks to the east. In the rest of his column Rice also estimated that "most all of the residences in the city have been burned that were unoccupied." The Yankees had apparently heard about which homes belonged to Confederate officers living in the city, and these were deliberately torched. "Colonel L.P. Grant's and Dr. Grant's houses are burned, also Colonel Gartrell's house." "Colonel" [sic: Captain] Grant, the CS engineer, was the architect of Atlanta's fortifications; Doctor Grant was a contract surgeon for the Confederate army, and ran a military hospital early in the war; Lucius Gartrell was a Confederate brigadier general.

Rice also made mention of some saved areas. His statement that burning ceased at Wesley Chapel meant that destruction along Peachtree stopped after the first three blocks or so north of the passenger depot, the city's center. Homes on the south side, according to Rice, fared better. Rice made a point of noting that Luther Glenn's and Edward Rawson's residences, both on Faith's Alley eight blocks south of the Car Shed, were untouched. Similarly, "only three or four houses are burned on McDonough Street, one of which is Mrs. Rucker's" (Mrs. Louisa Rucker lived at McDonough and Faith's Alley). In the same vicinity "the house adjoining and just above William Watkins is burned" (Fair Street, two blocks south of city hall).

Rice confirmed destruction of the Federals' obvious targets downtown. "All the railroad depots are burned—including the passenger depot. All the hotels, foundries, railroad shops, government works and mills are burned." Rice noted that "the female college was pulled down to put up a fort on the spot"—the work of Captain Poe and his engineers in October. Yet some notable public buildings survived the rampage. Engine house 1 (east side of Bridge Street between Alabama and Hunter) and 2 (on the north end of Washington) were unhurt, although the Federals had earlier sent north the water-wagons and fire-fighting equipment. Rice observed that the Masonic Hall (Decatur Street, between Ivy and Pryor) had been saved. He wrote that city hall had been spared "by appeals and petitions of Mrs. Holcombe, who lives only a few steps from it," but such a claim is discredited by the fact that the 2nd Massachusetts, one of the three provost guards regiments posted downtown, had its shanties in the park area all around city hall. Dr. D'Alvigny was credited with saving the Medical College. All churches of note were also unharmed, Rice reported, save for "Pain's" (Payne's) Methodist chapel out at the northwest edge of the town—and "the new Episcopal," Confederate Chaplain Quintard's place of worship on Walton Street. It had been burned by Federals who evidently had picked up on its founder's identity. (Atlantan John Henderson remembered that they called it "the Rebel Church.")[22]

II. James R. Crew, Mayor Calhoun's emissary to General Sherman, had left the city in the mass exodus of civilians (on Lieutenant Colonel Le Duc's list of those going south, he was 317). He returned to Atlanta within two weeks of the Yankees' departure and penned a long letter to his wife on 1 December describing wreckage in the city. "At least two thirds has been distroyed," Crew judged, and specified it in some detail, confirming as well some of Zachariah Rice's observations.

Crew affirmed that all the railroad shops and depots were destroyed, as well as the bridge over the tracks and the Georgia Railroad bank building His observation that almost all of the structures had been burned on Marietta Street from Judge Clayton's (at Spring Street) out to the Ponder house by the old Confederate lines encompasses a full 1 1/2 miles. Crew also confirmed that of the downtown churches, Dr. Quintard's "Rebel" chapel had disappeared, but the

[22] Ronald H. Bailey, *Battles for Atlanta: Sherman Moves East* (Alexandria VA: Time-Life Books, 1985) 170 (unnamed Union private); Carrie Berry, diary, 14–20 November, Atlanta History Center; letter of Z. A. Rice, Atlanta, 20 November 1864, quoted in "Atlanta When It was Left in Ashes," *Atlanta Constitution*, 24 July 1898; Stephen Davis and William A. Richards, "An Atlantan Goes to War: The Civil War Letters of Maj. Zachariah A. Rice, C.S.A.," *Atlanta History* 36/1 (Spring 1992): 21, 36; Wilbur G. Kurtz, "St. Luke's Baptized by War," *Atlanta Journal Magazine*, 3 July 1932, 16; Hitz, "St. Luke's Church," 4; John Henderson to William L. Calhoun, 6 August 1895, Calhoun Family Papers, 1834–1960, MSS 50, Atlanta History Center.

others were all right. At the Presbyterian church across Washington from city hall, Crew saw "not a thing missing. They left us a fine lot of hymn books." "About half the houses" destroyed on McDonough Street meant that Federal troops marching out of the city on 15 November by that principal thoroughfare had broken ranks and committed arson on private dwellings, orders or no orders.

On the other hand, Crew recorded that a number of residences were noticeably untouched, such as Mark Bell's Calico House. Judge Lyon's/John Neal's house was also unhurt, of course—it had been General Sherman's headquarters. Among the unharmed houses and outbuildings were his own on Alabama Street. Suspecting that the Union soldiers spared the homes of those known to be sympathetic to their cause, Crew asked his wife, "wonder what will be said about it?" when their fellow citizens returned. Crew that day thought that some sixty families were in the city, some of whom had never left.[23]

III. William Pinckney Howard, an officer in the state militia, had come to Atlanta in late November to inventory state property and report to Governor Brown on its loss or damage. On 7 December, he wrote his report, which within days was widely printed in Confederate newspapers. His judgments were far ranging, beginning with his guess that fifty families had remained in the city during the occupation, and that another fifty had returned. Unfortunately, others had come to Atlanta as well—not to rebuild, but to plunder. Howard had not been in the city a week when he complained to the governor, "parties are constantly committing depredations on public and private property with a lawlessness unheard of." General Howard told the governor that when he arrived, he found

> about two hundred and fifty wagons in the city...loading with pilfered plunder, pianoes, mirrors, furniture of all kinds, iron, hides without number, and an incalculable amount of other things, very valuable at the present time. This exportation of stolen property had been going on ever since the place has been abandoned by the enemy. Bushwhackers, robbers and deserters, and citizens from the surrounding country for a distance of fifty miles have been engaged in this dirty work.

The pillagers were not just after furniture, but anything that could be sold for profit. This included iron and tools to be found among the debris left by the Yankee engineers. Howard believed, "could I have arrived ten days earlier, with a guard of one hundred men, I could have saved the State and city a million of dollars." Howard proceeded in his report to tell Governor Brown what was yet salvageable in the state-owned Western & Atlantic railroad complex.

---

[23] Crew to wife, 1 December 1864, James R. Crew Papers, MSS 79F, Atlanta History Center; T. D. Killian, "James R. Crew," *Atlanta Historical Bulletin* 1/6 (January 1932): 12–13.

The property of the State was destroyed by fire, yet a vast deal of valuable material remains in the ruins. Three-fourths of the bricks are good, and will be suitable for rebuilding if placed under shelter before freezing weather. There is a quantity of brass in the journals of burned cars and in the ruins of the various machinery of the extensive railroad shops; also, a valuable amount of copper from the guttering of the State depot, the flue pipes of destroyed engines, stop cocks of machinery, &c., &c. The car wheels that were uninjured by fire were rendered useless by breaking the flanges. In short every species of machinery that was not destroyed by fire, was most ingeniously broken and made worthless in its original form—the large steam boilers, the switches, the frogs, &c. Nothing has escaped.

Howard paid attention to the city's four fire houses, although they were not technically "state property": "The fire engines, except Tallulah No. 3, were sent North. Tallulah has been overhauled, and a new fire company organized. Nos. 1 and 2 fire engine houses were saved." Of the downtown water cisterns, he advised that "all the city pumps were destroyed, except one on Marietta street." He added the obvious: "The car shed, the depots, machine shops, foundries, rolling mills, merchant mills, arsenals, laboratory, armory, &c., were all burned."

Having assessed the loss in government property, General Howard proceeded to add to his report information on the Yankees' destruction of private citizens' business property and homes. On the basis of four days' perambulation of the city, he had drawn "a penciled map of the city, showing the position of every house left unburned." He explained:

In the angle, between Hunter street, commencing at the City Hall, running east, and McDonough street, running south, all houses were destroyed. The jail and calaboose were burned. All business houses, except those on Alabama street, commencing with the Gate City Hotel, running east to Loyd street, were burned. All the hotels, except the Gate City, were burned. By referring to my map, you will find about four hundred houses standing. The scale of the map is four hundred feet to one inch. Taking the car shed for the centre, describe a circle the diameter of which is twelve inches, and you will perceive that the circle contains about three hundred squares. Then, at a low estimate, allow three houses to every four hundred feet, and we will have the thirty-six hundred houses in the circle. Subtract the number of houses indicated on the map, as standing, and you will see by this estimate the enemy have destroyed thirty-two hundred houses. Refer to the exterior of the circle, and you will discover that it is more than a half a mile to the city limits, in every direction, which was thickly populated, say nothing of the houses beyond, and you will see that the enemy have destroyed from four to five thousand houses. Two-thirds of the shade trees in the park and city, and of the timber in the suburbs have been destroyed. The suburbs present to the eye one vast naked, ruined, deserted camp. The Masonic Hall is not burned, though the corner stone Is badly scarred by some thief, who would have robbed it of its treasure, but for the timely interference of some mystic brother.

The City Hall is damaged but not burned. The Second Baptist, Second Presbyterian, Trinity and Catholic Churches and all the residences adjacent between Mitchell and Peter streets running south or east, and Loyd and Washington streets running south of west, are safe, all attributable to Father O'Riley, who refused to give up his parsonage to Yankee officers, who were looking out fine houses for quarters, and there being a large number of Catholics in the Yankee army, who volunteered to protect their Church and Parsonage, and would not allow any houses adjacent to be fired that would endanger them. As proof of their attachment to their Church and love for Father O'Riley, a soldier who attempted to fire Col. Calhoun's house, the burning of which would have endangered the whole block was shot and killed, and his grave is now marked. So, to Father O'Riley the country is indebted for the protection of the City Hall, Churches, &c.

Dr. Quintard's, Protestant Methodist, the Christian and African Churches are destroyed. All other churches are saved. The Medical College was saved by Dr. D'Alvigny who was left in charge of our wounded. The Female College was torn down for the purpose of obtaining the brick with which to construct winter quarters.

Howard's observations are important. In his penciled map he had drawn a circle less than a half-mile within the city limits, and in that area he estimated there had been 3,600 houses, all but 400 of them destroyed. Then he extrapolated the possible number of private dwellings beyond his circle to the city limits and beyond and generalized on the damage done to them. In such a way he concluded, "you will see that the enemy have destroyed from four to five thousand houses." This estimate of the burn damage to Atlanta was clearly much greater than Hitchcock's 25% and Poe's 37%. Howard's calculations cannot be confirmed, but they represent the result of several days' walking about in the city, and therefore deserve serious consideration as one of the most thorough eyewitness accounts of the destruction within the city.

The key lay in the general's penciled map, sent to Governor Brown with his report. The *Macon Telegraph* was the first newspaper to get hold of the report, which it printed on 10 December and again on 12 December. No Confederate newspaper publishing the Howard report—and there were plenty—had the capacity to publish the map, given the constraints of the nineteenth-century newspaper industry, and the limited woodcutting/engraving capacity of

Southern newspapers as a whole. It is therefore doubtful that few, save Governor Brown, actually saw Howard's map. And to this day it has not been found. This invaluable document, which would have been able to pinpoint the extent of the Yankees' burning, is presumably lost. Without Howard's map, historians are unable to compare the extent of Atlanta's burning with that of other cities that suffered widespread, deliberate arson by soldiers in the Civil War. The literature is replete with accounts of towns being burned (e.g., Lawrence, Kansas, and Darien, Georgia). But among American cities, Atlanta was in league with at least two other contenders in terms of large numbers of structures fired: Chambersburg, Pennsylvania, and Columbia, South Carolina. Extensive areas of Chambersburg (as Sergeant Campbell of the Michigan engineers knew) had been torched by Confederate cavalry under Brigadier General McClausland on 30 July 1864. According to a Chambersburg newspaper, *The Old Flag,* 549 buildings were razed: 278 residences and businesses, 98 barns and stables, plus 173 other outbuildings. The Confederates' burning was in deliberate reprisal for Union depredations in the Shenandoah Valley. The fires in Columbia had more complex origins. As Sherman's forces approached the South Carolina capital in mid-February 1865, Confederate officers ordered all cotton in the city to be burned. Winds whipped these fires out of control as Federals entered on 17 February. Some Yankees got hold of whiskey and spread the blazes. Afterward William Gilmore Simms, South Carolina's famed man of letters, recorded a building-by-building list of those burned, on whose basis historian Marion B. Lucas has concluded that 265 residences and 193 businesses and public structures were burned—458 all told, about one-third of Columbia.[24]

---

[24] "Atlanta as Left by the Enemy. Report of Gen. Howard;" *Macon Telegraph,* 10 Dec. 1864; Chambersburg *The Old Flag,* 25 August 1864, in Ted Alexander, Virginia Stake, Jim Neitzel and William P. Conrad, *Southern Revenge!* (Shippensburg PA: White Mane Publishing Company, 1989) 142; Marion Brunson Lucas, *Sherman and the Burning of Columbia* (College Station: Texas A & M University Press, 1976) 12–13, 127–28.

Discovery of the Howard map would be a richer find than even Professor Dyer's discovery of the "Plan of Destruction" in the Cogswell Papers. My search for it has only extended to the governor's papers at the Georgia Archives and University of Georgia. One example of General Howard's correspondence with the governor is Howard to Joseph E. Brown, 30 November 1864, Governor's Office/General Executive Records/Governor's Incoming Correspondence, box 35, Georgia Department of Archives and History.

Alexander et al. and Lucas have produced maps of the burned areas in their respective studies. See "Portion of Chambersburg Burned during the Confederate Raid Led by John McCausland, July 30, 1864" in *Southern Revenge,* 130–31, and "Columbia: Buildings Burned February 17–18, 1865," f.p. 96 in *Sherman and the Burning of Columbia.* William Gillmore Simms' *Sack and Destruction of the City of Columbia, S.C. to Which Is Added a List of the Property Destroyed* (Columbia: Press of the Daily Phoenix, 1865), was reprinted in 1937, edited by A. S. Salley, and again in 1971 (Freeport NY: Books for Libraries Press). See also maps by David E. Roth accompanying Ted Alexander, "The Burning of Chambersburg,"

Howard's report gave rise to two legends of the Yankees' burning that persist today. The first concerns the Medical College, which had been marked as the "dome building" designated for burning in the "Plan of Destruction" laid out for the 33rd Massachusetts. Yet, as Howard confirmed, the structure was left standing, and the surgeon in charge there, Dr. Noel D'Alvigny, was given the credit. No contemporary source provides the details, but over the years a story has evolved about how the good doctor resorted to trickery in order to save the building. Before any Yankees came, he had instructed his assistants to pretend they were sick and wounded men, lying about and not able to be evacuated. When the torch squad arrived, the doctor told the officer in charge that there were still ailing patients inside, Union soldiers. To convince the dubious officer, D'Alvigny threw open the doors, whereupon his aides commenced audible groans. The officer gave the doctor till dawn to clear out his patients, but on the morning of 16 November the last Federals were already marching out of Atlanta. The medical college had been saved.

The militia general's story of Dr. D'Alvgny is more plausible than his statement that Fr. Thomas O'Reilly of the Catholic Immaculate Conception Cathedral saved the downtown churches, city hall, and a block of residences. There are several reasons to doubt the story. Chief among them is its vagueness. Just how did O'Reily save the churches? On the night of the great fire, did he patrol the several blocks of streetfront near Washington and Mitchell, chasing off torch-brandishing Federals? Reading Howard's text more closely, what was the connection between O'Reilly's alleged defense of his parsonage (located behind the Catholic church) and the Protestant churches nearby? If Catholic Northern troops "volunteered to protect their Church and parsonage," why is there no mention of this in the abundant memoirs left by Sherman's soldiers?

Other facts need to be considered as well. Federal officers had issued strict orders against unauthorized burning (e.g., General Slocum's $500 reward); much more than residences, churches would of course have been off limits. Moreover, Colonel Cogswell's provost guards, charged with enforcing the orders, were concentrated downtown; the 2nd Massachusetts was quartered in City Hall Park, just across the street from the "saved" churches. This fact alone should discredit Howard's claim that "to Father O'Riley the country is indebted for the protection of the City Hall" (not to mention Zach. Rice's counter-contention that a "Mrs. Holcombe" had "saved" city hall). Indeed, Howard's statement that a Union soldier had been shot while trying to torch Mayor Calhoun's house on Washington Street attests to the heavy guards in the area. The presence of armed

---

Blue & Gray 11/6 (August 1994): 47 (slightly revised in Ted Alexander, *History and Tour Guide of the Burning of Chambersburg* [Columbus OH: Blue & Gray Enterprises, 2004] 44) and accompanying Tom Elmore, "The Burning of Columbia, February 17, 1864," *Blue & Gray* 21/2 (Winter 2004): 18. Against this defining cartography, the study of Atlanta's burning will remain comparatively handicapped.

sentries with orders to shoot arsonists would clearly have deterred any would-be church-burner far more than a pleading clergyman. Further, there is Major Hitchcock's authoritative diary entry of 15 November, stating that in his downtown walk that night he had been shooed away by a sentry and not allowed even to approach the churches. Finally, Sherman was staying in the Neal house in the block across from city hall (the very block of homes which Howard said O'Reilly had "saved"); the area of the commanding general's headquarters would have been even more strongly guarded.

All of these considerations seem not to matter. In Atlanta, Howard's story has sprouted a sturdy legend, and to this day Father Thomas O'Reilly is locally credited with having saved the city's downtown churches, city hall, and surrounding dwellings.[25]

IV. In an abrupt change of tone from Howard's report came the description of city damage composed by the editors of the *Atlanta Intelligencer*. The paper's staff had returned to the city in the first days of December, so that they could publish their first extra, a front-only broadside, on 10 December. In it was a column entitled "The City," with a summary of what had escaped the Yankees' fires. The editors' intent was to emphasize what was standing, not destroyed, in order to encourage former citizens to consider coming back home. Their text, below, has thus far not been published in the literature of wartime Atlanta.

> Whitehall street from Roark's corner up to Peachtree street is one entire mass of ruins.
> Alabama street from Bridge to Pryor is destroyed. The property standing embraces the block of buildings from the Planter's Hotel to the Confederate smoke house.
> On Pryor street the buildings from Hunter street are all standing.
> Lloyd street.—With the exception of the block on which the Washington Hall was situated, the buildings are all standing.
> Hunter street—From Whitehall to the Court House and beyond, all the houses are standing.

---

[25] Dyer, *Secret Yankees,* 210; F. Phinizy Calhoun, "The Founding and the Early History of the Atlanta Medical College," *Georgia Historical Quarterly* 9/1 (March 1925): 45–46; Robert R. Otis, "High Lights in the Life of Father Thomas O'Reilly," *Atlanta Historical Bulletin* 8/30 (October 1945): 18–20. As example of the Father O'Reilly legend, see Camille Kunkle, "Atlanta's Churches in 1896," *Atlanta History* 33/1 (Spring 1989): 39 ("Father O'Reilly approached General Sherman with a request to spare his church and all other Atlanta churches. His request was partially granted, and guards were placed around five of the city's churches as Atlanta was destroyed."). In Oakland Cemetery, a stone memorializes Father O'Reilly for his help in "defending and preserving the city during the Civil War." The memorial was placed by the Hibernian Benevolent Society.

Mitchell street—All the residences on this street, with few exceptions, are standing.

Marietta street—From Dr. Powell's residence nearly all the residences are standing.

Peachtree street—From Wesley Chapel nearly all the houses are standing.

Washington street—From Col. Calhoun's residence to Knox's lot all the houses are in a good state of preservation.

Decatur street—From Hunnicutt & Taylor's Drug Store up to Masonic Hall the buildings have been destroyed. The balance of the street from the Masonic building, with some exceptions, the residences are standing. The residences on this street in the rear of the Trout House are all destroyed.

McDonough street—with the exception of Judge Clark's house and two others, all the buildings are standing.

Walton street—Nearly all the dwellings on this street are standing.

All the churches with the exception of the Episcopal Church, on Walton street, are preserved.

The depots of the four connecting roads, together with the car shed, are destroyed.

The report of the *Intelligencer* repeats several observations made by Rice and Crew. Whitehall, from the corner of Mitchell to the railroad, had been leveled. On Peachtree, no damage had been done north of Wesley Chapel. At the same time, the editors added some new information on the Yankees' burning. A block and a half of Alabama Street running east from the bridge had been torched, but the next block, from Pryor (Planter's Hotel) to the Confederate smokehouse (at Alabama and Loyd) still stood. The first block and a half of Decatur Street (from Hunnicutt's drug store at Peachtree to the Masonic Hall) was gone. Included was the Trout House and buildings in the block behind it.

On the other hand, with its repetition of all the structures "standing" and "preserved," the report of the *Intelligencer* accentuated the positive for would-be returning Atlantans. In a couple of cases, the column seems to contradict the reports of others. For instance, the claim that on McDonough Street only three houses had been burned does not conform to James Crew's statement that "about one half the houses on this street distroyed." And the editors' statement that on Marietta Street, "from Dr. Powell's residence [southwest corner of Marietta and Wadley] nearly all the residences are standing" is true only if one were considering the several blocks of Marietta running south from Wadley to Peachtree. If looking north, according to James Crew, nearly every house had been burned. Nevertheless, the editors' community spirit was quite evident as they urged Atlantans to come back and help rebuild the city. "To our absent citizens we would say return as soon as possible, and with one mind commence to extricate ourselves from the ruin detailed upon us by the God-forsaken, miserable and deluded Yankee crew."[26]

V. Another primary source on the destruction of Atlanta is the undated letter by "a correspondent of the [Knoxville/Griffin] Register," reprinted in the *Augusta Chronicle & Sentinel* of 14 December. The *Register*'s reporter offered little new information, but confirmed what others had observed, such as the vandalism described by General Howard.

> From the best information I can get there have been from fifty to three hundred wagons per day in Atlanta, since the Federals left, hauling off iron, furniture, wagons, window blinds, door locks, books, lumber, &c., amounting to about fifteen hundred wagon loads. They come from fifty to one hundred miles in every direction. They broke open all the houses that were left, including the churches in which the exiles' furniture was stored, and plundered indiscriminately.

On the city's churches there was both old and new information. "Wesley Chapel and Trinity, the First and Second Baptist, First and Second Presbyterian, and Catholic Churches are standing. The First Episcopal Church [St. Philip's] is standing, but badly damaged. The Yankees used it, I have been told, for a ten pin alley.... The African church [a block from the Medical College] is standing but all cut to pieces with axes." The reporter also made the dramatic statement that the Federals had drawn some line of demarcation through the western part of the city as a kind of boundary for their burning. "Sherman ran a line from Walton Springs south, one house below Judge Clayton's on Marietta street, by the mineral spring, to Mr. Thomas Scrutchen's, then east by the old White Hall, crossing on the Macon road to the Protestant Church, thence east to Col. L.J. Glenn's, and nearly every house outside of the line is destroyed. About two-thirds of the houses inside the line are also destroyed."[27]

VI. A week after the *Augusta Chronicle & Sentinel* printed the column from the *Register*, it published a longer letter by its own correspondent, "Civis," who sent a letter from Atlanta under date of 15 December. It represents a strong reiteration of the damage-reports already printed and adds new particulars, evidently based on the writer's own walking-about of the ruined city. The reporter judged that "about three fourths of the buildings have been torn down or burned, and about nine-tenths of the property value destroyed." He specified areas of damage, as keyed to the accompanying map.

---

[26] "The City," *Atlanta Daily Intelligencer Extra,* 10 December 1864.
[27] "From Atlanta," *Augusta Chronicle & Sentinel,* 14 December 1864.

1. "On Peach tree street from Mrs. Lipham's to the fortifications there is not a house standing…"

2. "…and from Winship's Block to the corner of Decatur street all the stores have been destroyed."

3. "In the Forsyth settlement in rear of the Trout house a clean sweep was made of the buildings."

4. "On Marietta street, from Hamilton Goode's to Mrs. Ponder's residence there are but few houses left."

5. "On the left hand side from Dr. Powell's former residence to the corner of Decatur and Peach tree streets is another space made vacant by the devouring flame."

6. "The Atlanta Hotel with all the buildings on that block were destroyed…"

7. "…as well as the Concert Hall,…"

8. "…and the Atheneum and all the buildings adjacent to them."

9. "From the railroad crossing to Roark's corner on Whitehall, not a building escaped the ravages of the fire."

10. "From Major Bacon's residence on Whitehall street out to the fortifications, there are but three houses standing, two of Braumuller's, and one opposite his residence. Hammock's house is seen in the distance as an oasis in the Great Desert."

11. "From Alabama street to Mitchell, between Whitehall and Forsyth streets, there are but two buildings standing, both on Hunter street, opposite each other, just above where Gardner's carriage shop stood."

12. "From the corner of Alabama and Whitehall streets to Pryor street the fine buildings all fell victims to the ignifluous flame. From the Gate City Hotel to Lowery's store, the buildings are all standing unhurt."

13. "The Trout House was burned, but the Masonic Hall and the four wooden buildings below it were saved."

14. "Hubbard & Chisolm's corner, and the houses occupied by Kehoe and Buchanan, were destroyed."

15. "On the Washington Hall square only three buildings are standing—Judge Owen's residence, and the two on Decatur just below Cowart's house; the one on the corner being almost cut down."

16. "On the left hand side of Decatur street, going down, from the Armory to Gartrell's house, there are only two or three buildings standing—Dr. Beach's, Kennedy's, and one opposite Nace's mill."

17. "The Armory—Peck's old shop—and all the buildings on the square, except Walker's fronting on the Georgia Railroad, were consumed."

18. "Along the line of the Georgia Road from the rolling mill up to T.L. Thomas' residence, not a building is standing. [A] Dunning's old foundry [the Atlanta Machine Works], the [B] Atlanta and LaGrange depot, the [C]

pistol factory, the [D] Georgia Railroad workshop, depot and round house, were destroyed."

19. "The jail and all the buildings from thence to the fair ground were swept away by the devouring breath of flame."

20. "On the right hand side of the Macon & Western Railroad, from Dr. Ford's as far as the eye can reach, not a house is standing."

21. "From Evans' Chapel to the fortifications,..."

22. "...and from Scrutchin's house to the fortifications the sites of buildings can alone be discerned."

23. "The [a] Passenger depot, the [b] Macon & Western depot, and the [c] State shop and depot, are masses of ruins."

"Civis" documented the Federals' destruction of the Car Shed, the railroad depots, roundhouses, and workshops. He also confirmed that in addition to railroad facilities, the city's "business part," around Whitehall Street, was largely burned. Major thoroughfares used by Union troops, such as Marietta and Decatur streets, suffered extensive arson. Gaps in the devastated areas, such as the half-mile or so on Peachtree to just north of the Corporation Line, suggest that Federal provost guards prevented house-burning in those areas. Where they were likely not present, however, as in the city suburbs, widespread arson was committed by Northern soldiers. "Civis'" statement that most houses on Marietta Street from Goode's (at Spring) to Ponder's implies that the white brick and stucco house which had been the target of Federal artillerists probably succumbed to Union arsonists. Decades later, Wilbur Kurtz told an audience of Atlanta Historical Society members that the Ponder place was "demolished during the general conflagration throughout the city." The same suburban torching is evident in the "Civis" observations about four major thoroughfares in the southwest quadrant of the city. On Whitehall, Peters, Nelson, and Stockton Streets, the reporter specified points from which, extending all the way out to the Confederate fortifications, almost every structure had been torched.

Among the city's places of worship, "Civis" confirmed the downtown churches as unhurt, although the Episcopal parsonage of the Reverend Freeman "was removed to make room for a line of works." Farther out, Payne's chapel had been burned (as noted by Rice, Crew, and Howard); so had Evans Chapel west of the Macon railroad, as well as the Christian Church (Decatur Street between Collins and Loyd). "Civis" also noticed buildings damaged in the "interregnum," meaning the Federals' occupation of the city. The houses of S. J. Pinkerton and T. R. Ripley had been "carried off" by soldiers for their timber. The home of one Dr. Brantley had also been "completely demolished, all the debris, fencing and orchard being removed." The residences of Confederate chaplain Dr. Quintard and one J. I. Brown had merely been "defaced"; Yankees had removed their weatherboarding and ceilings. Similarly, the home of Colonel Luther J. Glenn, at Cooper and Rawson Streets, had been "sadly mutilated."

Finally, around city hall, the newspaper correspondent noticed the park "filled with little wooden huts"—the quarters of the 2nd Massachusetts—and "much of the shrubbery removed."[28]

VII. In their broadside issue of 10 December, editors of the *Intelligencer* claimed that they only gave "a description of those portions of city we have visited, and will in a future number notice more." That fuller report was published in the paper on 20 December, which rounded out the observations and reporting of earlier eyewitnesses. Approaching Atlanta from its periphery, the editors stated that the first thing a traveler into the city would notice is that from Kennesaw Mountain south, and from Stone Mountain westward, forests had disappeared: "For miles around, scarcely a tree is standing, and near and within a few miles of the city *fire and the axe* have destroyed the habitations of the rich and of the poor, and laid waste the country round." Even more unpleasant was the ubiquitous bad smell surrounding the place: "But a few days ago, the putrid carcasses of dead horses and mules met the eye, while the stench that exhaled from them filled the air, producing a loathing on the part of all who ventured into the city, unutterably disgusting; nor were they relieved from this oppressive sensation when they entered it, for within its corporate limits lay the last remains of man and beast emitting the same disgusting odor." The editors then gave an estimation that two-thirds of Atlanta had been wrecked and ruined.

> Here you will see the awful effects of one vast extended conflagration—a city destroyed by FIRE—two-thirds at least of it devoured by flames— naught remaining of that portion of it doomed to destruction by a remorseless and cruel foe, but what could not be destroyed—the stone, and the brick, and the mortar—ashes alone remaining of what had been combustible in its nature. We sicken as we present this picture of Atlanta to our distant readers. Even now as we look upon the smoked and blackened ruins, familiar at last to our view, by which we are surrounded, we are amazed and appalled at the savage ferocity of our Yankee foes, and at the *fiery* vengeance they have inflicted upon the city.... Doomed to utter destruction, one third of Atlanta lives.

To identify specific areas of damage the editors conducted a walk along the city's main streets. They started "where the four principal streets converge, to wit: the streets of Whitehall, Peachtree, Marietta and Decatur" (Atlantans today call the intersection "Five Points"). The newspapermen made a number of observations (marked on sketched map). (1) Hunnicutt's drug store at Decatur and Peachtree was "a heap of ruins." (2) Opposite, the structure used as a

[28] "Letter from Atlanta," *Augusta Chronicle & Sentinel,* 21 December 1864; "Kurtz Describes Historic Homes of Atlanta," *Atlanta Journal,* 28 April 1935 (on fate of Ponder house), 8B; *Williams' Atlanta Directory,* 22 (location of the Christian Church).

Confederate barracks was destroyed ("Burn Rebel Barracks" had been one of the tasks originally assigned to the 33rd Massachusetts). In the several blocks of Peachtree to the north, including Cherokee block, some twenty tall ("three stories high, with cellars") commercial structures had been burned; the editors noted that "a great deal of the business of Atlanta was done in these buildings." (3) Wesley Chapel was "horribly desecrated. It is left more in the condition of a hog pen than the House of God." From this point on, little damage was seen on Peachtree until the suburbs, where "occasionally we find a house torn down to build huts."

On Marietta Street, "all the business houses...are destroyed," meaning those for a block or so west of Peachtree. Then for a few blocks beyond Marietta's commercial strip none of the residences was torched, but all bore signs of the enemy shells. (4) The home of Hamilton Goode at Marietta and Spring was still standing, but "after passing Mr. Goode's house, the torch has been applied to every building on this street, its entire length," with the exception of only three houses. The editors noticed that (5) Marshall's sword factory (farther out Marietta near Thurmond), the button factory and a grist mill had been special targets of the Federals' destruction. (6) The editors assessed that "Whitehall street is an entire ruin," except for a two-block length from Roark's corner at Mitchell Street to V. A. Gaskill's near Garnett, which had been saved, the writers heard, because someone had told the Yankees that an old man named Baker lay "in the agonies of death" and would have been burned alive. The area destroyed was at the heart of the city's commercial sector. "Those acquainted with the city will know what amount of destruction this implies," the editors lamented; "full one-half of the business houses are included in this count." The burning extended well out Whitehall, as "the tasteful and ornamental residences near the Macon & Western railroad have ceased to be," including the home of John S. Thrasher, superintendent of the Confederate Press Association.

For their next trek, the perambulating editors started at the ruins of the Car Shed and headed east along Decatur Street. The Trout House and buildings behind it had been burned; nearby so had the Atlanta Hotel and Washington Hall. (7) "The business houses on Decatur street have all been consumed except the one under the Masonic Hall," which itself had not been harmed; the editors assumed it had been saved by "the square and compass, the symbols of the mystic brotherhood." (8) "For the space of three hundred yards on this street, beginning with the spot where stood the Christian Church [Decatur, between Ivy and Collins] and ending where the Government Armory was located [north of the railroad, between Pratt and Moore], the private dwellings have been left." (9) "After these, for the remainder of the street, some three miles in the direction of Decatur," the writers estimated, "all the dwellings on either side have been burned, with two or three trifling exceptions."

The same thing was to be seen on the south side. On Pryor and McDonough, long stretches of buildings remained undisturbed closer in town, but at a point toward the suburbs extensive arson had been committed: (10) "on McDonough street.... from Mr. Ball's [corner Rawson] out, all destroyed"; (11) "on Prior street.... from Rawson's out all destroyed except the one Mr. Coleman built." (12) Moreover, the editors repeated the observation, made by the *Knoxville Register* correspondent quoted in the *Augusta Chronicle and Sentinel*, that one could draw a line from (a) Walton Spring, southwest past (b) Judge Clayton's, on to (c) the Mineral Spring, past (d) Thomas Scrutchin's (Stockton and Mangum), to (e) the Methodist church at Forsyth and Garnett, down to (f) Colonel Luther Glenn's at Cooper and Rawson streets, a distance of at least 1 mile, beyond which extending to the periphery, "nearly every house is destroyed."

Elsewhere in the city, the editors witnessed uneven evidence of torching. Only one house was burned on Butler Street (Toon's) and on Calhoun, one block over, every house stood except one. On Ivy Street, paralleling Peachtree to its east, they saw only isolated houses burned, but among them was a whole block destroyed between Houston and Wheat. On Houston itself, which ran eastward from Peachtree, a number of houses were destroyed. But of the three homes identified by the editors as spared, one belonged to Bob Yancey, the quasi-free African-American barber and trader, suggesting that the Yankees might have known the homeowner's identity and saved his property.

The editors confirmed that the city's main churches survived: First and Second Baptist, Wesley Chapel and Trinity Methodist, First and Central Presbyterian, the Catholic cathedral, and St. Philip's Episcopal. On the other hand, the central rail facilities had been completely demolished. The Car Shed had been knocked down by a battering ram. "The Railroads are destroyed in the completest manner by burning the cross ties, and bending and twisting the iron. As you stand on the crossing on Whitehall and look up the Western & Atlantic Road, the piles of cross-ties are so numerous and spread out to such an extent, as to remind one of the ocean when its waves are raised by a brisk wind. It is an ocean of ruins." Even the city's firefighting capacity had been stripped out. "All the pumps are ruined"; the Yankees shipped fire engines 1 and 4 off to the north before they cut the railroads; they burned engine 2 and the accompanying equipment of its Hook and Ladder Company; and left engine 3 "in a badly damaged state."

Assessing all of this structural ruin, the *Intelligencer* estimated that "nearly one out of three" private residences escaped the conflagration, although it ascribed this result not so much to good fortune as to "the failure of the fire-fiends to perform the task assigned them." The paper's editors judged soberly and starkly that "of the whole real estate of the city fully five-sixths in value have been laid in ashes." Beyond the shocking statistics, however, was the gloomy feeling of returned Atlantans that their once-thriving city was now something of a ghost.

The stillness of the grave for weeks reigned over this once bustling, noisy city. No whistle from railroad engines, no crowing of cocks, no grunting of hogs, no braying of mules, no lowing of cows, no whirring of machinery, no sound of the hammer or saw—nothing but the howling of dogs was in our midst. Profound silence reigned in our streets, no pedestrians on Whitehall, no children in the streets, no drays, no wagons, no glorious sound of the Gospel in the churches, the theatre was hushed in the silence of death. Ruin, universal ruin was the exclamation of all.

Altogether, the editors bemoaned the loss of Atlanta's "thousands of burning tenements, its splendid mansions, its vast warehouses, its magnificent and costly mechanical workshops, down to the humble cottage residence." They made a point of reminding their readers that the blame for this destruction lay squarely on the fiendish Yankees and their unprincipled leader, "than whom no vandal Captain of ancient times left a blacker, or more cruel record for the historians to indite."[29]

Taken in sum, the *Intelligencer* article of 20 December and the six other contemporary accounts tell us as much about the extent of destruction in Atlanta as we are likely ever to know until the Howard map appears. These accounts allow for several conclusions.

First, we can confirm that from the corner of Whitehall and Mitchell to Peachtree/ Pryor/ Houston, the Whitehall-Peachtree axis was destroyed for a length of half a mile, a fact supported by three of the accounts. Second, the Federals' destruction was thorough but had its limits as several reports listed areas as undamaged. Similarly, the Yankees seemed to have granted reprieve to other major downtown streets, as reported in the Crew and the *Intelligencer* evaluations.

But after that, moving toward the city limits/corporate line and the suburbs, observers noted more extensive arson. Both James Crew and "Civis" wrote that only a few houses still stood on Marietta between Spring Street and the Ponder estate—about 1 1/2 miles. "Civis" implied that Peachtree from Wesley Chapel to the corporate line, over a half-mile, had been spared, but "from Mrs. Lipham's to the fortifications there is not a house standing." The same was to be seen on McDonough: "from Mr. Ball's out, all destroyed" (*Intelligencer*).

---

[29] "Atlanta—Her Past, Her Present, and Her Future," *Atlanta Intelligencer*, 20 December 1864; Thomas G. Dyer, "Half Slave, Half Free: Unionist Robert Webster in Confederate Atlanta," in Lesley J. Gordon and John C. Inscoe, eds., *Inside the Confederate Nation: Essays in Honor of Emory M. Thomas* (Baton Rouge: Louisiana State University Press, 2005) 301 (on Yancey); Ken Denney, "Map indicating the principal landmarks, features and structures within the city of Atlanta during the year 1864," copy courtesy of the author (on Hamilton Goode house and Marshall sword factory); Franklin M. Garrett, *Atlanta and Environs: A Chronicle of Its People and Events*, 2 vols. (New York: Lewis Historical Publishing Co., 1954) 1:656–57 (on Gaskill's and Ball's houses).

And also on Whitehall: "from Major Bacon's residence on Whitehall street out to the fortifications, there are but three houses standing" ("Civis"). This arson, not authorized by Colonel Cogswell or Captain Poe, and flouting Sherman's much-publicized orders against the burning of private homes, was probably perpetrated by the soldiers as they were marching into the city (Marietta Street) about 15 November, and marching out of it. The road to Decatur, for instance, was repeatedly prescribed as the march route for Federal columns leaving the city; according to the *Intelligencer,* almost all of the houses on both sides of that thoroughfare were burned for 3 miles. Another part of the explanation may lie with Cogswell's provost guards, who were charged with preventing and punishing house-burning. They were posted on city streets only for a distance; where the watchful guarding ended, the wanton burning started. This would explain "Civis'" observation that on Peachtree north of Winship's block (area of Houston Street), a half-dozen blocks were untouched. But then, at "Mrs. Lipham's" (just north of the corporate line), burning began, extending all the way to the Confederate fortifications (about half a mile).

Furthermore, we know that scattered buildings were fired by deliberate arsonists as early as 11 November; that night, according to Union Captain Conyngham, blazes consumed over twenty houses. Carrie Berry's diary of 12 November reports that "mean soldiers set several houses on fire in different parts of the town" the night before. This kind of arson accounts for several observers' mention of widely scattered residences burned throughout Atlanta: as example, Thomas G. Healey's, two blocks west of the Macon & Western (Crew), and E. Buice's on Crew Street and Joseph Barnes' on Calhoun Street (*Intelligencer*).

Federals also apparently singled out some structures for their Rebel associations. More than one observer noted that Confederate General Gartrell's house was burned on Decatur Street. While the downtown churches were not touched, St. Luke's Episcopal on Walton was burned, as noted by Rice and Crew; the latter was known to the Federals as the "Rebel church," having been established in spring 1864 by Confederate Chaplain Quintard.

Several commentators also made a point of mentioning Yankees soldiers' plundering of the City Cemetery. Zachariah Rice, in his letter of 20 November, commented on this ghoulish misconduct, such as the burning of cemetery fences and plundering of burial vaults. State militia general Howard closed his report on the same inglorious note: "Horses were turned loose in the Cemetery to graze upon the grass and shrubbery. The ornaments of graves, such as marble lambs, miniature statuary, souvenirs of departed little ones, are broken and scattered abroad. The crowning act of all their wickedness and villainy was committed by our ungodly foe in removing the dead from the vaults in the cemetery and robbing the coffins of the silver name plates, and tippings, and depositing their own dead in the vaults." The *Register* correspondent added even harsher details:

The Cemetery fence is all destroyed. The Yankees have buried their dead all over the city, and have taken the fence from around the Cemetery to build some separate lots for themselves. They have put their dead in private vaults, and have stolen tomb stones from Mr. Oatman's marble yard to put at their heads. They have taken the moss and shrubbery from other graves to cover the graves of their dead. And have robbed our dead in the vaults of the silver coffin plates to make finger rings.

The *Intelligencer* of 20 December added its own observations on this "general bad behavior." The Northern soldiers' ransacking of the vaults of the dead and taking down of the cemetery fencing struck the editors as conduct "more characteristic of Goths and Vandals than of Christian men of the 19th century." Almost as bad as the Yankees' desecration of citizens' gravesites was their establishment of burial plots for their own troops. The *Intelligencer* disdainfully stated that the Federals had created two graveyards for dead comrades evidently reinterred from the battlefield of Peachtree Creek. They had even fashioned a monument to "Our Dead Heroes" with marble taken from Oatman and Judson's funeral yard, and planted turf of bluegrass dug up from citizens' yards. A third burial plot had been created in a back lot belonging to Colonel Whitaker; the remains of some forty Northern soldiers had been interred in it. The paper also noted another Yankee grave on the southeast corner of where the Atlanta Hotel once stood. The editors implied a feeling of resentment that the Yankees had left behind these graves as offensive reminder of their conquest and occupation.

Yet the *Intelligencer* remained optimistic. "That which built Atlanta and made it a flourishing city, will again restore it," the editors predicted. "Her citizens must 'put their own shoulders to the wheel,' and pull hard themselves to draw her out of the slough into which Yankee ferocity and Yankee vengeance have cast her." Businessmen would return and reestablish their shops, stores and offices, they promised. The railroads to Augusta, Macon, Montgomery and Chattanooga would be rebuilt, and Atlanta would regain her stature as transportation center. "Efforts like these," concluded the *Intelligencer,* "will soon restore her to her former greatness."[30]

---

[30] "Atlanta When It was Left in Ashes." Rice's letter is an important eyewitness account of the damage left by Sherman's armies. Robert R. Otis claims that it was published in the *Atlanta Intelligencer,* 20 November 1864, but it does not appear there or in the *Macon Telegraph* at the time (Otis, "Father Thomas O'Reilly," 23). Its reprint in the Atlanta papers thirty years after the war (mentioning "From the Memphis Appeal") is apparently our only source until the newspaper issue (*Appeal, Constitution,* or *Journal*) carrying it comes to light. No historian, even Garrett, has thus far cited it.

Crew's letter of 1 December is quoted in Annie Laurie Fuller Kurtz, "Atlanta as Sherman Left It—Burning of the City," *Atlanta Journal Magazine,* 19 January 1936, with modern references to named sites. Wilbur G. Kurtz transcribed Crew's letter and also

The citizens did indeed return, and they rebuilt, although the task was herculean. "After the war was over," wrote Cornelia Venable, "we returned home to find our house in ruins and the city a heap of ashes and debris." Another returnee was Thomas W. McArthur, a Virginian who had come to Atlanta in 1855, opening a store on Whitehall. He had stayed in Atlanta throughout the semi-siege; in the expulsion he went to Nashville. When he returned he found all his property in the city leveled, but he set to work in rebuilding. "Working early and late," contemporaries observed, "he soon made enough to replace his burnt houses, destroyed by Sherman's army." Another

---

annotated sites mentioned; the document is in the Wilbur G. Kurtz Collection, box 35, folder 13, Atlanta History Center.

Howard's report was printed by numerous Confederate newspapers, beginning with the *Macon Telegraph,* 10, 12 December 1864; *Columbus Times,* 13 December; *Augusta Chronicle & Sentinel,* 16 December; *Augusta Constitutionalist,* 17 December; *Atlanta Intelligencer,* 20 December; and of course other papers outside the region. Edmund Ruffin, the diehard Southern nationalist in Virginia, included a clipping of the report in his diary entry of 27 December 1864 (probably from a Richmond paper), presumably as a testament to Yankee malignancy (John Bennett Walters, *Merchant of Terror: General Sherman and Total War* [Indianapolis: Bobbs-Merrill Company, 1973] 236n86). Garrett includes the full text of Howard's report with notes for sites in *Atlanta and Environs,* 1:653–55. Russell Bonds reprints it as appendix in *War Like the Thunderbolt: The Battle and Burning of Atlanta* (Yardley PA: Westholme Publishing, 2009) 408–10.

"Civis'" "Letter from Atlanta" is reprinted as "Ten Years Ago. Atlanta Then and Now," *Atlanta Constitution,* 15 December 1874; also as "Atlanta as Sherman Left It Atlanta Then and Now," *Atlanta Historical Bulletin* 3 (May 1930): 15–20 (with notes on locations by Meta Barker, Kate Shivers Logue, and Sarah Huff).

A version of the *Atlanta Intelligencer* article of 20 December, severely edited by Susan Simonton Padgett, appears as "Atlanta as Sherman Left It," *Atlanta Journal Magazine,* 7 August 1932, and is reprinted in Garrett, *Atlanta and Environs,* 1:655–59, with annotations on site locations and some individuals named. The *Journal Magazine* states that the article is drawn from the "Atlanta Daily Intelligencer of December 22, 1864," but there is no issue of 22 December in *Atlanta Intelligencer* microfilm at Emory and the Atlanta History Center; the editors should have given the date as 20 December.

Elizabeth Perkerson, in a letter dated 2 December 1864 to her brother Angus, is sometimes quoted as an early witness to the burning in Atlanta (as in Katherine M. Jones, *When Sherman Came* [Indianapolis: Bobbs-Merrill Company, 1964] 3), but in her letter "Lizzie" confessed, "I haven't been there yet" (Medora Field Perkerson, ed., "A Civil War Letter on the Capture of Atlanta," *Georgia Historical Quarterly* 28/4 [December 1944]: 260).

Col. Isaac Avery claimed that he rode into Atlanta with General Howell Cobb, commander of Confederate forces in Macon, in what he called "the first visit to the destroyed and deserted city," although he gives no date for it. He may have recorded what he saw, though it was not till decades later that his impressions of Atlanta's "sad spectacle of ruin and desolation" appeared in print. Upon close reading, he merely paraphrased W. P. Howard's report, as in numbers of houses burned ("in and about Atlanta the destruction of houses was four thousand five hundred") (Avery, "Atlanta," 29).

citizen told a Northern visitor that he had returned a month after the war ended: "when I came back in May, the city was nothing but brick and ruins. It didn't seem it could ever be cleared. But in six weeks new blocks began to spring up, till now you see more stores actually in operation than we ever had before." The return of the railroads was of course an occasion of civic pride. The first to be repaired into the city was the Atlanta & West Point, a month before Lee's surrender at Appomattox. On Sunday, 5 March 1865, the *Intelligencer* beamed, "we take great pleasure in announcing to the public, that on Friday last, about one o'clock in the afternoon, the shrill whistle of the steam engine announced the *first* arrival of a train of cars within the corporate limits of Atlanta since its abandonment by the enemy." The locomotives' return signalled Atlantans' determination to try to put the war's ravages behind them. John H. Kennaway, an Englishman touring the South in fall 1865, remarked on all the rebuilding he saw. "Wooden-frame work-houses were springing up on all sides," he wrote, and "buildings of a more substantial nature" were even beginning to be seen. Another tourist-correspondent, John Richard Dennett, walking about the city on Christmas Day 1865, commented, "unfinished houses are to be seen on every hand; scaffolding, mortar-beds, and lime-barrels, piles of lumber and bricks and mounds of sand, choke every street, and the whole place on working days resounds with the noise of carpenters and masons."[31]

Atlantans gradually removed signs of war's wreckage. The *Intelligencer*, which had resumed publication as a weekly, in July 1865 noticed the improvements underway in merely cleaning up the city streets, including Alabama, which "for months has been almost a nuisance." "We hope that this good work will be continued," the editors added, "until all our streets are free from rubbish and obstructions." Rebuilding of fire-ravaged downtown was particularly important. Focusing on the Cherokee Block on Peachtree north of the railroad, the *Intelligencer* in early January 1866 commended the business firms— Huff & Cox, Taylor & Hall, Cox & Hill—that had established themselves in the block "since it has risen from its ashes." Nor was the city transfiguration confined to downtown. Russell Conwell, a Union veteran and newspaperman visiting Atlanta in 1869, commented on farmers plowing through the earthworks around it. In town, "many building spots made vacant by the war still remain

---

[31] Rose, *Atlanta*, 114 (Venable, "we returned home"); [Louis L. Parham, ed.], *Pioneer Citizens' History of Atlanta, 1833–1902* (Atlanta: Byrd Printing Company, 1902) 263 (on Thomas McArthur); Gordon Carroll, ed., *The Desolate South 1865–1866: A Picture of the Battlefields and of the Devastated Confederacy by John T. Trowbridge* (Boston: Little, Brown and Company, 1956) 238 ("when I came back in May"); Franklin M. Garrett, "The Phoenix Begins to Rise: The *Atlanta Daily Intelligencer* Announces the Return of the Railroads," *Atlanta History* 37/4 (Winter 1994): 5–8; John H. Kennaway, *On Sherman's Track; or, The South After the War* (London: Shelley, Jackson, and Halliday, 1867) 115–16; John Richard Dennett, *The South as It Is: 1865–1866*, ed. Henry M. Christman (New York: Viking Press, 1965) 268.

unoccupied," Conwell noted, "and a few shell-torn houses remain unrepaired. But the greater portion of the city is looking fresh and cheerful."

As the evidence of war-damage disappeared, commentators sought to put it in some kind of context. Sidney Andrews, a Northern traveller through the Carolinas in fall 1865, observed that Columbia seemed to have more "massive and impressive" ruins than Atlanta, from its fire of mid-February 1865. In his "Condensed History of Atlanta," published in 1867, V. T. Barnwell agreed that Atlanta's "destruction of public and private property has not been witnessed in any city during the war, except, perhaps, Columbia, South Carolina." Others seemed to contend that Atlanta deserved the dubious distinction of most-extensively-burned Southern city of the war. In his history of Georgia (1881), Confederate veteran-turned-newspaperman Isaac W. Avery, working from General Howard's estimates (400 houses standing out of 5,000), did some math and concluded, "eleven-twelfths of the place, shops, depots, mills, dwellings, stores, were burned." A decade later, further echoing estimations from the Howard report, Avery wrote, "in the city limits it is estimated that there were three thousand eight hundred houses, and, of these, four hundred were left standing. In and about Atlanta the destruction of houses was four thousand five hundred." Avery's dramatic numerator/denominator resonated. Fellow journalist Wallace P. Reed used it in an article for the *Constitution* in 1893: "The fire destroyed eleven-twelfths of the city"—a dramatic conclusion which would have far overshadowed the extent of arson-damage suffered both by Columbia and Chambersburg.[32]

More recently, historians and professional writers have tried to help determine the exact extent of the damage wreaked in the days of Sherman's burning, but have discovered no new sources of information. Hence Professor T. Conn Bryan (1953) accepts Avery's estimate of 11/12 of the city destroyed. John B. Walters, in his exposition on Sherman's practice of waging "total war," also cites Colonel Avery's postwar estimates as his source in stating, "there were an estimated 3,800 houses within the city limits of Atlanta. When the explosions ceased and the flames died down there remained approximately 400 standing. It is estimated that eleven-twelfths of the city was burned, including shops, depots, mills, dwellings and stores." Professor Frederick Nash Boney also accepts

---

[32] "The City," *Atlanta Weekly Intelligencer,* 26 July 1865; "Cherokee Block, Peach-Tree Street," *Weekly Intelligencer,* 3 January 1865; Joseph C. Carter, *Magnolia Journey: A Union Veteran Revisits the Former Confederate States* (University: University of Alabama Press, 1974) 157; Sidney Andrews, *The South Since the War: As Shown by Fourteen Weeks of Travel and Observation in Georgia and the Carolinas* (Boston: Ticknor & Fields, 1866) 339; Barnwell, *Atlanta City Directory,* 31; I. W. Avery, *The History of the State of Georgia from 1850 to 1881* (New York: Brown & Derby, 1881) 307; Avery, "Atlanta," 29; Wallace P. Reed, "Two Epochs in the History of Atlanta in the Sixties," *Atlanta Constitution,* 18 June 1893.

Howard and Avery's arithmetic: "in the ensuing holocaust only four hundred dwellings survived."

Other writers tend to side with Northerners' observations. In his popular history of the war (1974), Shelby Foote seems to draw on Captain Poe's estimated 37 percent of the city destroyed when he settles on "more than a third of the town" as lying in ashes on the morning of 16 November. Burke Davis, in his *Sherman's March* (1980), accepts Major Ward Nichols's conclusion: "by dawn [of 16 November] some two hundred acres of Atlanta lay in ashes." Professor Joseph Glatthaar (1985) repeats General Howard's judgment that the Northerners' fires in Atlanta "eventually consumed an estimated 4,000 to 5,000 homes and buildings," adding that this was a higher number of structures fired than "in any other large city," including Columbia.

Earl Schenck Miers (1951) also draws on Howard's estimate, but pointedly suggests that such attempts at counting were beside the point: "four thousand or five thousand houses destroyed in a single night—would the one figure seem less disheartening than the other?" Miers has a point. Perhaps for this reason some scholars have refrained from house-counting, instead offering broad generalizations on the Federals' burning. "Thus Sherman marched out of Atlanta, torching the city," note Professors McDonough and Jones. Hattaway and Jones go further: referring both to Sherman's depopulation and burning, they dramatically conclude, "thus Atlanta not only fell, it disappeared." Marc Wortman in *The Bonfire* (2009) sides with those who contend that Atlanta suffered more than any city during the Civil War. The conflict "struck Atlanta with a greater ferocity than...any American city," he writes; Sherman's hard hand of war ended up "squeezing and crushing it with greater fury than any ever unleashed on an American city before." Ultimately the best conclusion on the entire question of the extent of Atlanta's burning is offered by Sherman's biographer John Marszalek: "there will perhaps always be controversy as to the exact extent of damage to Atlanta, but the historical facts are clear that the entire city was not destroyed and that Sherman was not solely responsible for the part that was."[33]

---

[33] T. Conn Bryan, *Confederate Georgia* (Athens: University of Georgia Press, 1953) 165; Walters, *Merchant of Terror*, 151; F. N. Boney, "War and Defeat," Kenneth Coleman, ed., *A History of Georgia* (Athens: University of Georgia Press, 1977) 201; Foote, *The Civil War*, 3:641; Davis, *Sherman's March*, 7; Glatthaar, *The March to the Sea and Beyond*, 139; Earl Schenck Miers, The General Who Marched to Hell: William T. Sherman and His March to Fame and Infamy (New York: Alfred A. Knopf, 1951) 218; James Lee McDonough and James Pickett Jones, *War So Terrible: Sherman and Atlanta* (New York: W. W. Norton & Company, 1987) 318; Herman Hattaway and Archer Jones, *How the North Won: A Military History of the Civil War* (Urbana: University of Illinois Press, 1983) 625; Marc Wortman, *The Bonfire: The Siege and Burning of Atlanta* (New York: Public Affairs, 2009) 2, 6; John F. Marszalek, *Sherman: A Soldier's Passion for Order* (New York: Free Press, 1993) 299.

A century and a half after the war, it is time to take a long view. Such a perspective would remind us that Atlanta—the physical city itself—suffered damage and destruction in nine distinct ways.

1. Confederate engineers' stripping of suburban houses for wood in fortifications, and burning of others in the field of fire, summer 1863–1864.

2. The Federal bombardment, 20 July–25 August.

3. The destruction, by both sides, of houses in no-man's land (e.g., the Troup Hurt).

4. Federals' demolition of "exurban" houses behind their fortified lines to the Chattahoochee for shelter and firewood, as reported by the *Augusta Chronicle & Sentinel*, 31 August 1864.

5. Confederate's burning of the rolling mill, demolition of the reserve ordnance train east of Atlanta (the explosion of which leveled surrounding structures) and burning of buildings with supplies being abandoned in their evacuation, 1–2 September.

6. Federal dismantling of structures for wood and so on in building their huts during the occupation.

7. Federal destruction of buildings in the way of their inner line of defenses built in October (e.g., the Female Seminary).

8. Union engineers' "authorized" destruction of railroad roundhouses, factory chimneys, rail freight depots, etc.: first by smashing, then by burning.

9. Northern soldiers' unauthorized arson, 11–15 November.

All of this, as we have seen, has led commentators to estimate the extent to which Atlanta had been wrecked. Yankees, obviously, set a lower figure, as in Major Hitchcock's 25 percent or Captain Poe's 37 percent. Southern calculations include the *Intelligencer*'s estimate of 2/3 of buildings in the city and "Civis'" judgment that 2/3 of the buildings had been torn down or burned, extending all the way to General Howard's guess of 4,000 to 5,000 and Colonel Avery's 92 percent (11/12). To Atlantans, such mathematics can seem academic and almost pointless. Such fractions—1/4 of the city destroyed, or 11/12ths? —are really only gradations of hell.

In assessing the fiery damage to Atlanta, some scholars slip up, as Mary DeCredico does in stating—without explanation— that before the Federals evacuated "fifteen fires were set to complete the destruction begun by the Confederates just two months previously" (*Patriotism for Profit: Georgia's Urban Entrepreneurs and the Confederate War Effort* [Chapel Hill: University of North Carolina Press, 1990] 113). From her sources cited, it appears that she misread one: "On the 15th, fires were set to complete the destruction" (Julian, "Atlanta's Last Days in the Confederacy," 10).

The salient point is that Atlanta suffered immensely during the war, and therein lies the cornerstone of our city's history and the nub of our civic identity. As a result, for a long time many Atlantans had their own stories of Sherman's burning. One such was that of Patrick Lynch, the builder and rock contractor. He had refugeed during the shelling at his farm outside town, but had returned to the city at the end of the bombardment. He was apparently allowed to stay in Atlanta during the occupation, and was even present on the last night of the Federals' stay, as he was years later credited for putting out fires in his neighborhood. According to one account, Northern soldiers had started to burn the house of Joseph Meade at Ivy and Gilmer Streets, when Lynch intervened with his servants and told a Yankee to extinguish the fire. "A Federal soldier...told him he would shoot him if he put the fire out," ran the story. "The negro replied, 'No you won't shoot me while my old master is around.' This so amused the Yankee that the house was saved."

Lynch's story was published in 1902, thirty years after his death. At that time other Atlantans were still alive to tell their tales. In 1909, Lucy Pittman Ivy—whose father Daniel had come to the city in 1855, bought a house on Collins Street, and managed to stay in Atlanta during the bombardment and occupation—remembered that the Yankees deliberately fired stores and houses, to the point of strewing straw and other flammables to feed their blazes. On the night of the burning, however, "my father went around after them," Mrs. Ivy said, "and put out as much of the burning things as he could, and in that way saved a great many buildings." Another chronicler was a Mrs. Peel, who in 1922 told the local press of the destroyed Winship house. Mrs. Isaac Winship had helped organize women's relief efforts for Confederate hospitals, and the newspaperman dutifully took down Mrs. Peel's account. "Mrs. Winship lived in a beautiful home, a large old-fashioned white house. It stood on a hill where Broughton's tabernacle now stands and then known as Walton Springs.... When Sherman captured Atlanta, Mrs. Winship's house was burned to the ground; her beautiful mansion demolished; and the flower bushes in her yard pulled up and thrown away. There was not a brick nor a plant left standing. She herself went as a refugee to Macon and there lived in a tent." A decade and a half later, Atlantans were still telling stories about Yankees wanting to burn their houses. Maria Trabert was quoted in the *Atlanta Constitution* in 1937 about their home on Marietta Street. The newspaper related the exchange when Yankees came calling.

"We are ordered to burn this house and you will please vacate at once."

She replied: "You are soldiers and you will obey orders, but I will not leave."

They left and did not return. The house was saved.[34]

Such yarns, passed down, give Atlantans a heritage of knowledge about war and its hardships. To the extent that historical understanding is shared today (or even remembered), the Yankees' wrecking and burning of our city can give Atlantans a feeling of distinctiveness. A half-century ago, the renowned Southern historian C. Vann Woodward recounted how Arnold Toynbee phrased it. Toynbee had been a lad in England at the heyday of the British empire, and like most of his countrymen he felt on top of the world. "There is, of course, a thing called history," Toynbee wrote, "but history is something unpleasant that happens to other people. We are comfortably outside all that. I am sure, if I had been a small boy in New York in 1897 I should have felt the same." But then came Toynsbee's, and Woodward's point: "Of course, if I had been a small boy in 1897 in the Southern part of the United States, I should not have felt the same; I should then have known from my parents that history had happened to my people in my part of the world."[35]

We Atlantans can say the same. History, relentless and unforeseen, has happened to us.

---

[34] [Parham, ed.], *Pioneer Citizens' History of Atlanta,* 318; Lollie Belle Wylie," Interesting Sketches of Pioneer Women" (Mrs. Lucy P. Ivy), *Atlanta Journal,* 20 June 1909; "Mrs. Peel Recalls Events of the Civil War," *Atlanta Constitution,* 24 September 1922; Ball, "Monument of Service."

[35] C. Vann Woodward, "The Irony of Southern History," *Journal of Southern History* 19/1 (February 1953): 5.

AFTERWORD
ATLANTANS AND THE MEMORY OF SHERMAN

John Potter, Methodist chaplain of the 101st Illinois during the war, happened to visit Atlanta three decades after his regiment had occupied the city. "I casually observed to an old resident that I had been one of the men who had assisted in pulling their town to pieces and burning it up," he wrote.

> "Oh," said he, "that was the best thing that ever happened to us. Of course I didn't see it that way then, and was all-fired mad about it at the time. Why, we've built a good deal better town, and if Sherman had not destroyed it as he did it's likely the old dingy buildings would have been standing yet. Now we've got everything new, and many thousand more people than we had then, and I doubt if there is another city that can show such prosperity in the land.[1]

Reverend Potter's anecdote perfectly reflects Atlantans' ambivalent attitudes toward William T. Sherman and his soldiers: they destroyed our city, yet turned it into something better. These mixed feelings were evident when Sherman himself visited Atlanta a decade and a half after he had left in fall 1864. On the day of his arrival, 30 January 1879, the *Atlanta Constitution* ran a long column on Sherman's "First Visit" to Atlanta—his occupation of September–November 1864. Recounting the expulsion of the citizenry and extensive burning, the paper's tone was restrained, even a bit light. "The general is doubtless a fine man in his way," it concluded, "but whenever he feels his bump of destructiveness feeling tender again, we trust he will find it convenient to dodge Atlanta. One visit of that sort is about all a town can stand." At the same time, the *Constitution* beamed that the returning general would find "a proud city, prosperous beyond compare, throbbing with vigor and strength, and rapturous with the thrill of growth and expansion." On 31 January, the *Constitution* even opened a column on its front page with the welcoming headline, "Wm. T., Come, Sir!"[2]

During his stay, everyone was cordial and friendly to Sherman. Crowds gathered to see him during his three-day visit, and he was entertained by the mayor, governor, and other dignitaries. Far from bitter remembrances of their wartime sufferings, Atlantans could almost joke about them. As Sherman's train

---

[1] John Potter, *Reminiscences of the Civil War in the United States* (Oskaloosa IA: Globe Presses, 1897) 105.

[2] "The First Visit," "Two Receptions," *Atlanta Constitution*, 30 January 1879; "Wm. T., Come, Sir!," *Atlanta Constitution*, 31 January.

approached the downtown station, someone called out, "Ring the fire-bells! The town will be gone in 40 minutes!" The general returned the pleasantries, commenting repeatedly during his stay on the fine renascence of Atlanta. The message was plain: Atlantans had experienced Sherman's wartime brutality, but with the return of peace could rise above it and treat their former enemy with hospitality, even kindness. Demonstration of this mood was the request of *Constitution* editor E. P. Howell, written just after Sherman had left Atlanta, that the general compose a boosterish hailing of Atlanta's advantages as an urban center. Sherman complied in a letter widely reprinted in papers across the country. If Atlantans forgot the pretensions of the South's past and embraced talented newcomers from the North, their city could become one of America's greatest, "an end which I desire quite as much as you do."[3]

Atlantans' mood was different a few years later, when Sherman visited the city again, this time to take in the International Cotton Exposition, November 1881. To be sure, he was treated politely as he toured the Exposition's exhibits, which showcased the South's economic progress since the war. Yet on 18 November, the *Constitution* chose to reprint a wartime account of the Yankees' extensive destruction of the city. It also reprinted a passage from Jefferson Davis's memoir, *The Rise and Fall of the Confederate Government*, which was particularly critical of Sherman's order expelling civilians from Atlanta. As the ex-Confederate president wrote, and as the newspaper lengthily quoted, "since Alva's atrocious cruelties to the noncombatant population of the low countries in the sixteenth century, the history of war records no instance of such barbarous cruelty as that which this order designed to perpetrate." Davis also blamed Sherman for the devastation of Atlanta, Rome, Marietta, and other towns in north Georgia, and this too was quoted in the newspaper column. In the ex-president's words, Northern soldiers were "carrying out General Sherman's order to 'enforce a devastation more or less relentless' along the line of his march where he only encountered helpless women and children. The arson of the dwelling houses of noncombatants and the robbery of their property, extending even to the trinkets worn by women, made the devastation as relentless as savage instincts could suggest."

To all observers, the *Constitution* was deliberately insulting the city's famous guest. Sherman took the hint, and left Atlanta the next day. To make sure there was no mistaking of their sentiments, the editors of the *Constitution* on 19 November sought to tamp down rumors that during the exposition there might be a "Sherman's Day," celebrating the general's visit. The paper made adamantly clear that there had been no such talk of that in the city, and that Sherman was

---

[3] John F. Marszalek, "Celebrity in Dixie: Sherman Tours the South, 1879," *Georgia Historical Quarterly* 66/3 (Fall 1982): 373–74; Wesley Moody, *Demon of the Lost Cause: Sherman and Civil War History* (Columbia: University of Missouri Press, 2011) 66; Lewis, *Sherman*, 635.

visiting as a private citizen, as he had every right to do. Recognizing that a "Sherman's Day" would insult Georgia's Confederate veterans, the *Constitution* affirmed that Atlantans would do no such thing: "Georgians need never fear that Atlanta will do anything to disgrace the name of the state, lower the dignity of its people, or sacrifice the least particle of the respect due its history or traditions. In war or peace, in politics and in business, in sentiment or sense, she has always borne herself worthily as the capital city of the empire state."[4]

We Atlantans have thus waffled in our moods toward Sherman. A few years after the *Constitution* insulted the general out of town, *Constitution* editor Henry Grady famously toasted him in his celebrated "New South" speech delivered in New York, 22 December 1886. With Sherman in the audience, Grady declared, "I want to say to General Sherman, who is considered an able man in our parts, though some people think he is a kind of careless man about fire, that from the ashes he left us in 1864 we have raised a brave and beautiful city."

Within a year of Grady's speech, and in keeping with his magnanimous sentiment, the Atlanta City Council voted to change the official city seal. Its central image had been from 1854 the somewhat graceless etching of a locomotive. In 1887, though, the council adopted a more majestic visual: a broad-winged phoenix, the legendary eagle-like creature mythically rising out of flames. The word "Resurgens" replaced "City Council" at the top of the circle, and two dates were added: "1847," the year of the city's incorporation and "1865," the end of the war and a time of rebuilding for Atlanta.

A few years later the *Constitution* again turned its editorial attention to Sherman, as the old soldier neared death in February 1891. The editors affirmed that Sherman "has been more bitterly hated than any other northern general. The ruined houses and the general devastation he left behind him naturally made his victims unwilling to forgive or forget." After all, the editors noted, "he burned Atlanta and Columbia, and other towns, and stripped the people of all they had." Yet the paper acknowledged that once the war was over, "he showed a softer side, and men and women, even among his former foes, found him a very lovable man." The editors noted that General Sherman had shown this softer side in his two previous visits to Atlanta: "the rebuilding and subsequent prosperity of Atlanta gratified him very much, and he was a firm believer in the future greatness of this region." In this conciliatory vein, the *Constitution* honored the dying general by calling him "one of the greatest soldiers of the age." "We do not

---

[4] Marszalek, "Celebrity in Dixie," 382; "The Destruction of Atlanta. Sherman's Inhuman and Ferocious Conduct—Two Accounts From Widely Different Sources That Substantially Agree," *Atlanta Constitution*, 18 November 1881; "General Sherman's Visit to Atlanta," *Atlanta Constitution*, 19 November 1881. Atlanta became the capital city of Georgia in 1868 by provision of the new state constitution, proposed and ratified that same year (James C. Bonner, *Milledgeville: Georgia's Antebellum Capital* [1978; repr., Athens: University of Georgia Press, 1985] 220–24).

believe," the editors claimed, "that the civil war developed on the union side a more unique and picturesque figure than this great soldier."

But that was not the whole story. A week later, as the paper reported Sherman's funeral, it also placed on its front page an article about how the Yankee general allegedly ransacked a South Carolina plantation, had the seventy-five year-old owner, James Ingraham, clapped in irons and thrown in jail, ordered all the farm buildings burned save the big house, and confiscated all food and livestock on the place, leaving the desperate Mrs. Ingraham a pile of cowpeas for her subsistence. When she protested that she could not live on mere peas, the paper quoted Sherman's alleged angry outburst: "'D-n you, they are good enough for an G-d d-d rebel like you are!' and off he rode." Perplexed, the *Constitution* posed a question in another column entitled "A Man of Moods": "How shall we judge a man who was one day all fire, and the next day all ice; forgiving one moment, and relentless the next?" The editors were frankly unable to answer their question.[5]

It has been that way ever since: Atlantans waffling in their attitudes toward Sherman, sometimes vilifying, sometimes admiring; first cursing his destruction of the city, then thanking him for it. As an example, a *Constitution* column in 1932 on three antebellum homes still standing in Atlanta headlined that they had "Withstood Sherman's Attacks," as if the Yankees had burned everything else in the city. At the same time, the columnist acknowledged that "this very vigor of destructiveness became, in the end, an unconscious philanthropy," as it spurred the rebuilding that led to Atlanta's postwar boom. Two curious anecdotes from the 1930s make the point that Atlantans could remember the Yankees' depradations, yet somehow separate Sherman from association with them. John Ryan, a dry goods merchant, lived on Whitehall Street in January 1931, when his stately home was about to be demolished. The *Atlanta Constitution* carried a column on the house and its wartime history, as related by Mr. Ryan. "A captain of the Union army, making the home his headquarters, removed some of the Ryan household [furnishings] and had them shipped to his own home in a

[5] Harold E. Davis, *Henry Grady's New South: Atlanta, a Brave and Beautiful City* (Tuscalooosa: University of Alabama Press, 1990); Franklin M. Garrett, *Yesterday's Atlanta* (Miami: E. A. Seemann Publishing, 1974) 8 (on the city seal of 1887); "General William T. Sherman," *Atlanta Constitution*, 13 February 189; "Sherman's Funeral," *Atlanta Constitution*, 20 February; "A Man of Moods," *Atlanta Constitution*, 18 February.

Grady's quip about Sherman's carelessness with fire heralded a long Atlanta tradition of Sherman-with-matches humor. In 1957, Georgia governor Marvin Griffin engaged in it with a letter to an Augusta resident who asked his views on Sherman's life and loves. "As for his 'loves,'" the governor answered, "in common with other pyromaniacs, he had a great fondness for fire, apparently. Certainly," Griffin affirmed, "he left the impression that he loved to play with matches, especially when he got to Atlanta" (Robert W. Dubay, "No Love Lost—A Governor Reflects on William T. Sherman," *Atlanta Historical Journal* 25/2 [Summer 1981]: 96).

distant state," the article explained. "General Sherman, on learning of the captain's act, issued orders that the belongings not only should be returned, but that no other possessions should be disturbed or taken from the house." Ryan's story contains enough vagueness to arouse suspicion: the Union captain who stole the furniture goes unnamed; his home state is unspecified; and records show Ryan did not even own the house during the war (he bought it in 1865). No matter; Ryan's was a good story about General Sherman and his kindness, which Atlantans were still talking about two generations after the war.

Another tale comes from longtime Atlantan James Bell, who in the mid-30s was relating his memories of the war to Wilbur G. Kurtz. Bell had been fifteen years old during the Atlanta Campaign; he and his family lived on Marietta Street. Kurtz interviewed the old man repeatedly, remarking on his sharp memory of wartime incidents. During the Federal shelling, James's mother had been wounded; seeking shelter, the Bells moved to the south side of the city. Later, Mrs. Bell and her two sons were among the Atlantans forced to leave, and were expelled into Confederate lines. Eighty-six-year-old Bell therefore had plenty of reasons to be angry at Sherman. Yet when Kurtz interviewed him in May 1935, the old man actually exonerated the Yankee general for the burning of Atlanta. "Bell stated that Sherman never ordered anything of the city burned, but public buildings—such as the Car Shed—freight + round house, and such business structures that would be serviceable to Confederates," Kurtz wrote. Bell thus accepted the statements of General Sherman, Major Hitchcock, Captain Poe and other Northerners who exculpated Sherman for the burning of the city. So how did the old Atlantan explain it? "The indiscriminate and wanton destruction wrought by the irresponsible Federal soldiery was motivated by revenge for the hanging of Andrews + his men," Kurtz faithfully recorded. "Bell said that this Andrews affair was well known among the western boys in Sherman's army, and this inspired most of the 'spot' fires over the city." Less than a month later, Kurtz interviewed Bell again, and recorded the same thing: "Bell...reiterated that the Ohio soldiery in Sherman's army were bent on revenge when they got here and wreaked vengeance on the town by doing a lot of burning—of residences. (Sherman authorized destruction of public buildings only.)" Thus James Bell, who grew up in Atlanta during the war, not only excused Sherman for his soldiers' fires, but through some pretty tortuous reasoning indirectly put the fault on the Confederate authorities who had hanged the Andrews train raiders two years before. Kurtz recorded that "Bell said the hanging of Andrews + the seven men was the worst thing that ever happened to Atlanta!" This was strong stuff indeed. Among defenders of his reputation decades after the war, General Sherman would have found few as stalwart as Atlantan James Bell in 1935.

Within a decade, the mood had swung back. Among the members of the Atlanta Historical Society, venerable guardians of our city's past, someone must have remembered the assertions of state militia general Howard back in 1864 that Sherman's soldiers had tried to burn the downtown churches, and that

Father O'Reilly of Immaculate Conception saved his and three other houses of worship. At its membership meeting in October 1943, the society passed a resolution calling for a memorial to O'Reilly's heroism. Funding was secured, and two years later, in October 1945, O'Reilly was recognized as a local hero when a marble monument to his memory was placed on city hall lawn, the very site where Sherman had spent the night of the big burning. The good father was hailed as "The Priest Who Stood Up to Sherman," and as the "stubborn Catholic priest who feared neither fire nor William Tecumseh Sherman." The implication of all this was that Sherman had wanted or even had ordered Atlanta's downtown churches to be burned. Nowhere in the society resolution, or the news accounts of the marble monument, is there any explanation of how one solitary man of the cloth "stood up to Sherman." For good measure, no one seems to have thought about what would have happened if word of Sherman's alleged intent had gotten back to Ellen, his devout Catholic wife. If Sherman had ordered Immaculate Conception Cathedral to be burned, Cump (as they say down here in the South) would have had a whole lot of "splainin" to do when he got home. Nevertheless, the monument to O'Reilly stands today outside Atlanta City Hall. The tale of the Catholic priest who stood up to a Yankee general seething to burn downtown churches is literally etched in stone.[6]

Atlantans' tradition of mood-swing continues; we can absolve Sherman of blame for the burning of private homes, yet accuse him of unholy church arson. Inherent in this ambivalence (recalling John Potter's story) is Atlantans' habit of cursing Sherman for the burning of Atlanta while thanking him for setting our city on a course to greatness. A generation after the placing of the memorial to Father O'Reilly, Norman Shavin captured the latter mood in his column, "Thanks, 'Cump," in *Atlanta Magazine*, May 1976. As the issue paid tribute to individuals who had helped shape the city, Shavin did not forget General Sherman. He reminded his fellow citizens of the obligation to "acknowledge that man whom Atlantans once hated most: William Tecumseh Sherman." We owe him a debt, Shavin wrote, for "if he hadn't torn hell out of the place, it might have remained a sultry, small-smug southern town. But when Sherman ignited it, he unwittingly torched another fire—a blaze of determination among Atlantans (and many an opportunistic Yankee) to rebuild." Shavin concluded that since the war, Atlanta's growth was among the "civic achievements unparalleled in the nation's history," and for it, Shavin thanked Cump.

---

[6] Mary Ralls Dockstader, "Fine Old Atlanta Homes of Present Day which Withstood Sherman's Attacks," *Atlanta Constitution*, 24 April 1932; Frank C. Gilreath, "Famous Ryan Home, Early Atlanta Mansion, Soon to Disappear from Whitehall Street," *Atlanta Constitution*, 1 February 1931; Wilbur G. Kurtz interviews with James Bell, 31 May and 21 June 1935, notebook 10, 222, 238, Wilbur G. Kurtz Collection, Atlanta History Center; "Monument to Priest Who Stood Up to Sherman," and "Monument for Priest Who Saved Five Churches," *Atlanta Journal*, 19 and 14 October 1945.

The same kind of attitude has permeated since. In July 1988, when the Democratic National Convention was held in Atlanta, I went downtown and bought a campaign button. It was not for Governor Dukakis, but one that read, "General Sherman for President: The Father of Urban Renewal." In this little lapel ornament, the Yankees still clearly enjoyed their peculiar twin legacy: they burned Atlanta to the ground, but somehow made it better. When Atlantans buy buttons celebrating the burning of our city, history has turned to commercial marketing, and everyone is in on the joke. Driving through Buckhead in spring 1990, I pulled over to record a billboard for the Atlanta Ballet: "Atlanta hasn't sizzled like this since Sherman left town." The Atlanta History Center, of course, is clearly aware of what people think of when it comes to the city's past. A promotional magnet from the AHC reminds folks, "There's more to Atlanta's past than Tara and some guy named Sherman."[7]

There are thus many history-conscious Atlantans who still "remember" the Union general; there are also many who don't, and who might need a memory jog. An example comes from the *Atlanta Journal-Constitution* article of 14 November 1954, "Atlanta Put to Torch 90 Years Ago Today," reminding citizens of the razing of our city. From time to time we have called attention to the event, as when the Atlanta History Center sponsored an evening lecture by James M. McPherson of Princeton, 14 November 1989, on the 125th "anniversary" of the burning of our city. The history center's McElreath Auditorium was so packed that to accommodate the crowd we had to arrange an overflow room with Professor McPherson on closed-circuit television. It was clear to me that Atlantans wanted to learn, or relearn, what the Yankees had done to us.

Even as we do, we continue to differ in opinion about it. A *Journal-Constitution/* Georgia State University poll of 750 Georgians, conducted in January 1995, asked the question, "Did you grow up thinking William Sherman was one of American history's heroes or one of its villains?" The results split almost evenly: 29 percent said "hero"; 28 percent said "villain." More important, 43 percent had no opinion. In other words, Atlantans' attitude of ambivalence toward Sherman, evident a few decades after the war, has persisted to this day. For example, accompanying an article on John F. Marszalek's just-released biography of Sherman, the *Constitution* in December 1992 ran a side column quoting a few of the general's writings. One of them captured Sherman's vindictiveness against the Southern people for having started the war: "I have not one word of apology to offer, but on the contrary reassert that for the forcible

---

[7] Norman Shavin, "Thanks, 'Cump," *Atlanta Magazine* 16/1 (May 1976): 11. Shavin added, "We wish Sherman could come back and revisit Atlanta. We're sure the Hyatt Regency, the Peachtree Center Plaza, the Omni, the Hilton, the Marriott or one of the other fine downtown hotels would provide a room free."

I touch on these themes in my essay, "Coming to Terms with General Sherman—At Last," *Georgia Historical Quarterly* 77/2 (Summer 1993): 318–35.

hauling down of the U.S. flag by the people of Georgia in 1861 and submitting their own, they deserved all the punishment they received and more, too." Yet the man who wanted to punish the South continues to get off the hook, as Cameron McWhirter observed in "Sherman Still Burns Atlanta" (*Journal-Constitution*, 9 May 2004). "Many Southerners have been reared to believe he ordered his troops to burn the entire city," McWhirter noted, even as he explained the general's orders for only "military targets" in the city to be razed. Indeed, the columnist concluded, "by the standards of war at the time, 'that devil Sherman' really wasn't that bad a guy."[8]

In the same vein, former University of Georgia professor Lee Kennett wrote an article for the *Atlanta Journal-Constitution* in September 2001 under the title, "Burned by History: Man Who South Loves to Hate May Not Have Been So Bad." "Sherman should not be considered 'the Attila of the West,'" Kennett argued. The Yankee commander "fought the war in Georgia pretty much by the book," he stated, acknowledging only that in not giving Atlantans a twenty-four-hour warning of impending bombardment did he violate the "rules of war." Kennett's article dealt more with Sherman's legacy for the march to the sea and his reputation as "Sherman the Destroyer" through Georgia, but his point was that the Northern general did not deserve the black mark in history that he had (at least in some circles) incurred. The seven responses in the next Sunday edition expressed a decidedly opposite view. "May you soon join your hero, Sherman, for eternity," snapped one reader. "Burn with him, you hypocrites." "Lee Kennett's effort to sell Sherman as a nice guy is about as effective as selling a skunk as a perfume factory. After 157 years, Sherman still smells!" wrote John Black. "He was a terrorist, plain and simple." Beau Williamson, resident of Marietta, affirmed, "The man is no hero. If on Earth in 2001, Sherman would be on trial in The Hague and would make a great war criminal." His trial, Williamson added, would be "a field day for the press."

The idea of a war crimes trial for William T. Sherman was behind the public debate twenty years ago hosted by the Atlanta History Center entitled, "Sherman: Brilliant Commander or War Criminal?" (The judges and audience could not agree on which side won.) The very idea of war criminality at all suggests the harshness of some Southerners' continued memory of the general. Indeed, the shelling, forced evacuation and burning of Atlanta are three charges

---

[8] Lauren Irby, "Atlanta Put to Torch 90 Years Ago Today," *Atlanta Journal-Constitution*, 14 November 1954; "Let Us Destroy Atlanta: A Symposium on the 125th Anniversary of the Burning of Atlanta and Its Rise after the Civil War," Atlanta Historical Society, November 1989; "Good guy/bad guy?," *Atlanta Constitution*, 2 February 1995; "In Sherman's Own Words" and Pama Mitchell, "Sherman's March to the Sea lingers in Southern psyche," *Atlanta Constitution*, 22 December 1992; Cameron McWhirter, "Sherman Still Burns Atlanta," *Atlanta Journal-Constitution*, 9 May 2004.

leveled against Sherman by Walter Brian Cisco in his *War Crimes against Southern Civilians* (2007).[9]

But if Sherman was not a "war criminal," was he crazy? The allegation of Sherman's insanity started during the war in fall 1861 when a Cincinnati newspaper trumpeted "General William T. Sherman Insane," after he claimed that he needed 200,000 men in Kentucky. In January 1863, Thomas Knox, correspondent for the *New York Herald*, reported seeing Sherman "so exceedingly erratic that the discussion of...his sanity was revived with much earnestness." Sherman emerged unscathed from these episodes, but he maintained a reputation, in the words of one Northern general, as "a splendid piece of machinery with all of the screws a little loose." Decades after the war, the institutionalization of Sherman's son Thomas kept the "insanity" story alive. Historians have weighed in with their own assessments. In the early 1930s, Professor Merton Coulter of the University of Georgia sagely judged Sherman as one whose "mercury was never quite fixed." A half-century later, in a symposium on Sherman held at Kennesaw College, north of Atlanta, psychologist Janet Franzoni addressed the subject of "Was Sherman Crazy?" She answered that he was not; but the bipolar disorder he suffered from allowed him to say that he loved the South, but then burned it to the ground. To this day, Sherman's mental state still plays in the local press. Example is "Sherman's Demons," which appeared in *Atlanta Magazine*, November 2006, written by professor of psychiatry at Emory University School of Medicine, Nassir Ghaemi. Recounting the publicized allegations of Sherman's insanity in fall 1861 and other evidences of "major depressive episodes," Ghaemi concluded that the Yankee general who wrecked our city suffered from a manic-depressive illness which may have led him to practice the deliberately punishing warfare which he waged on noncombatants.[10]

---

[9] Lee Kennett, "Burned by History," *Atlanta Journal-Constitution*, 2 September 2001; "Sherman Takes Heat," *Atlanta Journal-Constitution*, 9 September; Cisco, *War Crimes against Southern Civilians*, chaps. 15, 16, and 19. An interesting perspective on the question of Sherman as "war criminal" is offered by Thomas G. Robisch, an attorney in the Judge Advocate General's Corps, US Army Reserve. Robisch examines Sherman's bombardment of Atlanta and expulsion of civilians not by nineteenth-century understandings, but modern legal standards applicable to US forces. In this light, Robisch finds the Union shelling without notice to be "questionable." Regarding the noncombatants' expulsion, Sherman "was in compliance, albeit minimally, with current international law" ("General William T. Sherman: Would the Georgia Campaign of the First Commander of the Modern Era Comply with Current Law of War Standards?" *Emory International Law Review* 98/2 [Fall 1995]: 477, 480.

[10] Marszalek, *Sherman's Other War*, 64–65; Norman Rourke, "The Newsmen," *Civil War Times* 40/6 (December 2001): 63; David Hardin, *After the War: The Lives and Images of Major Civil War Figures After the Shooting Stopped* (Chicago: Ivan R. Dee, 2010) 43 (on Tom Sherman's insanity); Kennett, *Sherman: A Soldier's Life*, 101; E. Merton Coulter, "Sherman

As a result of all this talk, up North when you say you're from Atlanta, it's almost expected that you're not a fan of the Union general. When I visited Sherman's boyhood home in Lancaster, Ohio, a decade ago in the company of my good friend Dave Roth, we were greeted at the door. Dave told our hostess that I was from Atlanta. She blanched: "Should I call the police?" A year later I participated in a "mock trial" of General Sherman, staged by the historical society in Lancaster, Ohio, as a fictional event set in 1872. The "war crimes" charges against him included "the pillage and plundering of towns": I was invited up to serve as prosecutor. We lost, of course; the three judges were Lancastrians playing United States generals, and the gallery was also stacked against us. It didn't matter; I and my Southern witnesses argued our case strongly and passionately. In my closing statement, I addressed the judges: "Go ahead and justify him! Nobility, decency and civility have already been vanquished, ground into the red clay of Georgia by the heels of 100,000 Yankee soldiers under the direct command of William Tecumseh Sherman!"[11]

It was with these incongruous notions—detesting Sherman for conquering and ruining our city, yet somehow forgiving him for it—that some years back I accepted an invitation to address a Civil War conference in St. Louis. The general is buried there, I told my hosts, and I asked them to make sure they would drive me to Calvary Cemetery so I could pay my respects. All during the seminar people asked me what I would say and do at the general's gravesite. I thought about it all weekend, up to the drive on Sunday morning to the airport by way of the cemetery. Finally, I had it written down, and with my throng of friends standing behind me, I read my statement before Sherman's tall, granite monument, its large, crossed flags grandly sculpted. I felt as if I were addressing the general himself: "I hate you, you son of a bitch, for what you did to my people, and my city, and that you won. But I admire you as a soldier. Peace to your ashes. An Atlantan." I folded my note, and placed it at the foot of the stone monument. I had done my duty. And so had he.

---

and the South," *Georgia Historical Quarterly* 15/1 (March 1931): 29; Janet Franzoni, "Was Sherman Crazy?" Kennesaw College Civil War Symposium, 5 May 1988; Dr. Nassir Ghaemi, "Sherman's Demons: An Emory Psychiatry Professor and Civil War Aficionado Believes the General Who Torched Atlanta was Bipolar," *Atlanta* 46/7 (November 2006): 76–82.

Along related lines, as writers over the years have noted Sherman's psychoses, I like the observation of two recent historiographers that it was not the general who was mad; it was the kind of work in which he was engaged: "Sherman knew that war itself was insanity. He put the war on the couch" (Edward Caudill and Paul Ashdown, *Sherman's March in Myth and Memory* [Lanham MD: Rowman & Littlefield, 2008], 82).

[11] "The Military Court of Inquiry of William T. Sherman," program brochure, 30 September 2000, Lancaster OH.

WORKS CITED

Abbott, Henry L. *Siege Artillery in the Campaigns against Richmond.* New York: D. Van Nostrand, 1866.

Adamson, Robert. "Isham G. Harris as Warrior and Fugitive." *Atlanta Constitution,* 1 August 1897, 2.

Al G. Pugh Letters. Chicago Historical Society. Includes Pugh to "Dear Sister," 16 September 1864. Copy courtesy Dr. Albert Castel, Columbus OH.

Albaugh, William A. and Edward N. Simmons. *Confederate Arms.* Wilmington NC: Broadfoot Publishing Company, 1993.

———. *Confederate Edged Weapons.* New York: Harper, 1960.

———, Hugh Benet, Jr., and Edward N. Simmons. *Confederate Handguns.* Philadelphia: Riling and Lentz, 1963.

Aldrich, C. Knight, editor. *Quest for a Star: The Civil War Letters and Diaries of Colonel Francis T. Sherman of the 88th Illinois.* Knoxville: University of Tennessee Press, 1999.

Alexander, Ted. "The Burning of Chambersburg." *Blue & Gray* 11/6 (August 1994): 11–18, 46–61.

———, Virginia Stake, Jim Neitzel, and William P. Conrad. *Southern Revenge!* Shipppensburg PA: White Mane Publishing Company, 1989.

"Andrew West Sought Marker for Lamp Post." *Atlanta Constitution,* 1 September 1942, 12H.

Andrews, J. Cutler. *The North Reports the Civil War.* Pittsburgh: University of Pittsburgh Press, 1955.

———. *The South Reports the Civil War.* Princeton: Princeton University Press, 1970.

Andrews, Sidney. *The South Since the War: As Shown by Fourteen Weeks of Travel and Observations in Georgia and the Carolinas.* Boston: Ticknor & Fields, 1866.

Angle, Paul M., editor. *Three Years in the Army of the Cumberland: The Letters and Diary of Major James A. Connolly.* Bloomington: Indiana University Press, 1959.

Armor, William C. diary, 20 August-23 September 1864. Emory University.

Ash, Steven V. *When the Yankees Came: Conflict and Chaos in the Occupied South, 1861–1865.* Chapel Hill: University of North Carolina Press, 1995.

Athearn, Robert. G., editor. "An Indiana Doctor Marches with Sherman: The Diary of James Comfort Patten." *Indiana Magazine of History* 49/4 (December 1953): 405–22.

———, editor. *Soldier in the West: The Civil War Letters of Alfred Lacy Hough.* Philadelphia: University of Pennsylvania Press, 1957.

"Atlanta as Left by the Enemy. Report of General Howard." *Macon Telegraph,* 10 December 1864, 2.

"Atlanta as Sherman Left It." *Atlanta Journal Magazine,* 7 August 1932, 7, 17.

"Atlanta as Sherman Left It—Atlanta Then and Now." *Atlanta Historical Bulletin* 3 (May 1930): 15–20.

Atlanta City Council Minutes, 1861–1865. Atlanta History Center.

"Atlanta—Her Past, Her Present, and Her Future." *Atlanta Intelligencer,* 20 December 1864, 2.

"Atlanta Made Armor for the Famous Merrimac." *Atlanta Journal,* 21 September 1930, 4.

Atlanta Pioneer Women's Society Collection. MSS 391, Atlanta History Center. Includes Austell, Mrs. Alfred, typescript recollections, box 1, folder 30.

"Atlanta Police. From the Days of Marthasville, in '44, to Atlanta, in '88." *Atlanta Constitution*, 12 August 1898. 2.

"Atlanta When It Was Left in Ashes." *Atlanta Constitution*, 24 July 1898, 7. Includes Zachariah Rice's letter of 20 November 1864, apparently first printed in the *Memphis Appeal*, describing damage to the city.

Austerman, Wayne. "Case Shot and Canister: Field Artillery in the Civil War." *Civil War Times Illustrated* 26/5 (September 1987): 16–29, 43–48.

Austin, J. P. *The Blue & Gray*. Atlanta: Franklin Publishing Co., 1899.

Avery, Isaac W. "Atlanta. Its History and Advantages." In *City of Atlanta. A Descriptive, Historical and Industrial Review of the Gateway City of the South*. Louisville KY: Inter-State Publishing Company, 1892–1893.

————. *The History of the State of Georgia from 1850 to 1881*. New York: Brown & Derby, 1881.

Bailey, Anne J. "The USCT in the Confederate Heartland, 1864." In *Black Soldiers in Blue: African American Troops in the Civil War Era*, edited by John David Smith, 227–48. Chapel Hill: University of North Carolina Press, 2002.

Bailey, Ronald H. *Battles for Atlanta: Sherman Moves East*. Alexandria VA: Time-Life Books, 1985.

Baker, B. Kimball. "The Memphis Appeal." *Civil War Times Illustrated* 18/4 (July 1979): 32–39.

Baker, Thomas H. "Refugee Newspaper: The *Memphis Daily Appeal*, 1862–1865." *Journal of Southern History* 29/3 (August 1963): 326–44.

————. *The Memphis Commercial Appeal: The History of a Southern Newspaper*. Baton Rouge: Louisiana State University Press, 1971.

Baldwin, Lucy. Autobiography. Typescript #849. Southern Historical Collection, University of North Carolin Carolina at Chapel Hill.

Ball, Lamar Q. "Monument of Service Left City in Long Life of Anton Louis Kontz." *Atlanta Constitution*, 24 January 1937, 5K.

Barker, Meta. "Schools and Teachers of Ante-Bellum Atlanta." *Atlanta Historical Bulletin* 4/16 (January 1939): 31–33.

Barnwell, Valentine T. *Barnwell's Atlanta City Directory and Stranger's Guide...for the Year 1867*. Atlanta: Intelligencer & Job Office, 1867. Includes "Condensed History of Atlanta," and "Railroads" (mileage from Atlanta to other points on the four lines).

Bartlett, Edward O. *The "Dutchess County Regiment" (150th Regiment of New York State Volunteer Infantry)*. Danbury CT: Danbury Medical Printing Company, 1907.

Bates, John W. Typescript diary. U.S. Army Military History Institute, Carlisle Barracks, Pennsylvania. Copy courtesy Dr. Albert Castel.

"Battles of Atlanta. Short Sketch of the Battles Around, Siege, Evacuation and Destruction of Atlanta, Ga., 1864...Prepared under the Direction of the Committee of the Atlanta Camp, United Confederate Veterans." Atlanta: n.p., 1895.

Bauer, K. Jack, editor. *Soldiering: The Civil War Diary of Rice C. Bull, 123rd New York Volunteer Infantry*. San Rafael CA: Presidio Press, 1978.

Bearss, Edwin C. *The Siege of Jackson, July 10–17, 1863*. Baltimore: Gateway Press, 1981.

Bearss, Margie Riddle. *Sherman's Forgotten Campaign: The Meridian Expedition*. Baltimore: Gateway Press, 1987.

Beasecker, Robert, editor. *"I Hope to Do My Country Service": The Civil War Letters of John Bennitt, M.D., Surgeon, 19th Michigan Infantry.* Detroit: Wayne State University Press, 2005.

Beers, Fannie A. *Memories: A Record of Personal Experience and Adventure During Four Years of War.* Philadelphia: J. B. Lippincott Company, 1889.

Bell, Earl, and Kenneth Crabbe. *The Augusta Chronicle: Indomitable Voice of Dixie 1785–1960.* Athens: University of Georgia Press, 1960.

Bell, Piromis H. "The Calico House." *Atlanta Historical Bulletin* 1/3 (May 1930): 28–38.

———. "Drama Behind the Oil Footlights." *Atlanta Journal Magazine,* 31 July 1932, 9.

Bell, Pyromis H. "Bombardment of Atlanta Described by Letter Written Amid Falling Shells." *Atlanta Constitution,* 8 October 1919, 6.

Benedict Joseph Semmes Papers, 1848–1865. MSS 2333, University of North Carolina, Chapel Hill.

Bennett, Stewart, and Barbara Tillery, editors. *The Struggle for the Life of the Republic: A Civil War Narrative by Brevet Major Charles Dana Miller, 76th Ohio Volunteer Infantry.* Kent OH: Kent State University Press, 2004.

Benton, Charles E. *As Seen from the Ranks: A Boy in the Civil War.* New York: G. P. Putnam's Sons, 1902.

Berry, Carrie. Typescript diary, 1 August 1864–26 January 1866. MSS 29f. Atlanta History Center.

Black III, Robert C. *The Railroads of the Confederacy.* Chapel Hill: University of North Carolina Press, 1952.

Blair, William Alan, editor. *A Politician Goes to War: The Civil War Letters of John White Geary.* University Park: Pennsylvania State University Press, 1995.

Blight. David W. *Race and Reunion: The Civil War in American Memory.* Cambridge: Harvard University Press, 2001.

Bogle, James G. "Civil War Railroads—Georgia and Tennessee." *Atlanta Historical Bulletin* 12/3 (September 1967): 23–37.

———. "The Great Locomotive Chase or the Andrews Raid." *Blue & Gray* 4/6 (July 1987): 8–24, 46–62.

Bohrnstedt, Jennifer Cain, editor. *Soldiering with Sherman: Civil War Letters of George F. Cram.* DeKalb: Northern Illinois University Press, 2000.

Boies, Andrew J. *Record of the Thirty-Third Massachusetts Volunteer Infantry from August 1862 to August 1865.* Fitchburg MA: Sentinel Printing Company, 1880.

Boland, Frank K. "Atlanta's First Physician." Atlanta Historical Bulletin 7 (June 1993): 14–19.

Bonds, Russell S. "Sherman's First March through Georgia." *Civil War Times* 46/6 (August 2007): 30–37.

———. *Stealing the General: The Great Locomotive Chase and the First Medal of Honor.* Yardley PA: Westholme Publishing, 2007.

———. *War Like the Thunderbolt: The Battle and Burning of Atlanta:* Yardley PA: Westholme Publishing, 2009.

Boney, F. N. "'Retribution Will Be Surely Given': *Harper's Weekly* Looks at Confederate Georgia." *Georgia Historical Quarterly* 72/2 (Summer 1988): 327–31.

———. "War and Defeat." In *A History of Georgia,* edited by Kenneth Coleman, 187–204. Athens: University of Georgia Press, 1991 [1977].

Boom, Aaron M., editor. "Testimony of Margaret Ketcham Ward on Civil War Times in Georgia." *Georgia Historical Quarterly* 39/3 (September 1955): 268–93.

Bowlby, Elizabeth Catherine. "The Role of Atlanta During the Civil War." Master's thesis, Emory University, 1938.

Bowlby, Elizabeth. "The Role of Atlanta during the War Between the States." *Atlanta Historical Bulletin* 5/22 (July 1940); 177–96.

Boyle, John Richards. *Soldiers True: The Story of the One Hundred and Eleventh Regiment Pennsylvania Veteran Volunteers.* New York: Easton & Mains, 1903.

Bradley, G. S. *The Star Corps; or Notes of an Army Chaplain, during Sherman's Famous "March to the Sea."* Milwaukee: Jermain and Brightman, 1865.

Brady, James P., compiler. *Hurrah for the Artillery! Knap's Independent Battery "E," Pennsylvania Light Artillery.* Gettysburg: Thomas Publications, 1992.

Brantley, Rabun Lee. *Georgia Journalism of the Civil War Period.* Nashville: George Peabody College for Teachers, 1929.

Breeden, James O. "Medical Shortages and Confederate Medicine: A Retrospective Evaluation." *Southern Medical Journal* 86/9 (September 1993): 1040–48.

Brockman, Charles J., editor. "The John Van Duser Diary of Sherman's March from Atlanta to Hilton Head." *Georgia Historical Quarterly* 53/2 (June 1969): 220–40.

Brown, Russell K. *To the Manner Born: The Life of General William H. T. Walker.* Athens: University of Georgia Press, 1994.

Bruffey, E. C. "Atlantan Tells of Siege of City—Pat Calhoun Gives Vivid Description of Time When Whitehall Street Was Mass of Ruins." *Atlanta Constitution,* 10 October 1919, 8.

———. "The Siege of Atlanta—and Afterwards. *Atlanta Constitution Magazine,* 5 October 1919, 5–6.

Bryan, T. Conn. *Confederate Georgia.* Athens: University of Georgia Press, 1953.

Bryant, Edwin F. *History of the Third Regiment Wisconsin Veteran Volunteer Infantry.* Madison: Veteran Association of the Regiment, 1891.

Burton, E. Milby. *The Siege of Charleston 1861–1865.* Columbia: University of South Carolina Press, 1970.

Burton, E. P. *Diary of E.P. Burton Surgeon 7th Reg. Ill. 3rd. Brigadier 2nd Div. 16 A.C.* Typescript. Des Moines IA: Historical Records Survey, 1939.

Bush-Brown, Harold. "Architecture in Atlanta." *Atlanta Historical Bulletin* 5/23 (October 1940): 278–83.

Bussel, Alan. "The Atlanta *Daily Intelligencer* Covers Sherman's March." *Journalism Quarterly* 51/3 (Autumn 1974): 405–10.

Byrne, Frank J. "Rebellion and Retail: A Tale of Two Merchants in Confederate Atlanta." *Georgia Historical Quarterly* 79/1 (Spring 1995): 30–56.

Byrne, Frank L., editor. *Uncommon Soldiers: Harvey Reid and the 22nd Wisconsin March with Sherman.* Knoxville: University of Tennessee Press, 2001.

Calhoun Family Papers, 1834–1960. Atlanta History Center, MSS 50. Includes "Affidavit of James M. Calhoun, Mayor of Atlanta as to Facts in Regard to Surrender of Atlanta September 2, 1864." 31 July 1865; and John Henderson to William L. Calhoun, 6 August 1895.

Calhoun, Patrick H. "What Sherman *Really* Said." *Atlanta Journal Sunday Magazine,* 22 May 1932, 9.

Calhoun, F. Phinizy. "The Founding and the Early History of the Atlanta Medical College." *Georgia Historical Quarterly* 9/1 (March 1925): 34–54.

Calkins, William Wirt. *The History of the 104th Regiment of Illinois Volunteer Infantry.* Chicago: Donnohue & Henneberry, 1895.

Campbell, Steve B. "History of Atlanta Volunteer Fire Companies 1846–1882." Microfilm, n.d., Atlanta History Center.

Candler, Allen D., editor. *The Confederate Records of the State of Georgia.* 6 volumes. Atlanta: Charles P. Byrd, 1909–12.

Cannan, John. *The Atlanta Campaign, May–November 1864.* Conshohocken PA: Combined Books, 1991.

Carr, John M. Diary, Kennesaw Mountain National Battlefield Park.

Carroll, Gordon, editor. *The Desolate South 1865–1866: A Picture of the Battlefields and of the Devastated Confederacy by John T. Trowbridge.* Boston: Little, Brown and Company, 1956.

Carter, Joseph C. *Magnolia Journey: A Union Veteran Revisits the Former Confederate States.* University: University of Alabama Press, 1974.

Carter III, Samuel. *The Siege of Atlanta, 1864.* New York: St. Martin's Press, 1973.

Cash, William N., and Lucy Somerville Nugent, editors. *My Dear Nellie: The Civil War Letters of William L. Nugent to Eleanor Smith Nugent.* Jackson: University Press of Mississippi, 1977.

Castel, Albert. *Decision in the West: The Atlanta Campaign of 1864.* Lawrence: University Press of Kansas, 1992.

———. "Order No. 11 and the Civil War on the Border." *Missouri Historical Review* 57/4 (July 1963): 357–68.

———, editor. "Scouting, Foraging and Skirmishing: The Federal Occupation of Atlanta as Seen in the Letters of Major William C. Stevens, Ninth Michigan Cavalry." *Atlanta Historical Journal* 23/2 (Summer 1979): 73–89.

———. *Winning and Losing in the Civil War: Essays and Stories.* Columbia: University of South Carolina Press, 1996.

Cate, Wirt Armistead, editor. *Two Soldiers: The Campaign Diaries of Thomas J. Key, C.S.A. December 7, 1863– May 17, 1865 and Robert J. Campbell, U.S.A. January 1, 1864–July 21, 1864.* Chapel Hill: University of North Carolina Press, 1938.

Catton, Bruce. Foreword. In *The American Heritage Century Collection of Civil War Art*, edited by Stephen W. Sears, pp. 6–11. New York: American Heritage Publishing Company, 1974.

Caudill, Edward, and Paul Ashdown. *Sherman's March in Myth and Memory.* Lanham MD: Rowman & Littlefield, 2008.

Christie, Anne M. "Civil War Humor: Bill Arp." *Civil War History* 2/3 (September 1956): 103–19.

Cisco, Walter Brian. *War Crimes against Southern Civilians.* Gretna LA: Pelican Publishing Co., 2007.

"The City." *Atlanta Intelligencer Extra,* 10 December 1864.

City of Atlanta tax digest, 1858–1860. Atlanta History Center.

Clark, Charles T. *Opdycke Tigers 125th O.V.I.: A History of the Regiment and of the Campaigns and Battles of the Army of the Cumberland.* Columbus OH: Spahr & Glenn, 1895.

Clarke, Olynthus B., editor. *Downing's Civil War Diary.* Des Moines: Historical Department of Iowa, 1916.

Clauss, Errol MacGregor. "The Atlanta Campaign, 18 July–2 September 1864." Ph.D. dissertation, Emory University, 1965.

Coffey, David. *John Bell Hood and the Struggle for Atlanta.* Abilene TX: McWhiney Foundation Press, 1998.

Cogswell, William Collection, MSS 212, Phillips Library, Peabody Essex Museum, Salem MA. Includes unlabeled map detailing the "Plan of Destruction" for 33rd Massachusetts, and map showing downtown railroad track to be destroyed by Powell's Provisional Brigade.

Cohen, Stan, and James G. Bogle. *The General & the Texas: A Pictorial History of the Andrews Raid, April 12, 1862.* Missoula MT: Pictorial Histories Publishing Co., 1999.

Collins, George K. *Memoirs of the 149th Regt. N.Y. Vol. Inft.* Syracuse CA: George K. Collins, 1891.

Combs, Diana Williams. "'All that Live Must Hear.'" *Atlanta Historical Bulletin* 20/2 (Summer 1976): 61–96.

Comey, Lyman Richard, editor. *A Legacy of Valor: The Memoirs and Letters of Captain Henry Newton Comey, 2nd Massachusetts Infantry.* Knoxville: University of Tennessee Press, 2004.

"Concert after Atlanta Fell." *Atlanta Journal Magazine,* 6 November 1927, 19.

Connelly, Thomas Lawrence. *Autumn of Glory: The Army of Tennessee, 1862–1865.* Baton Rouge: Louisiana State University Press, 1967.

Connolly, James A. "Major Connolly's Diary." *Transactions of the Illinois State Historical Society for the Year 1928.* Springfield IL: Phillips Bros. Print, 1928.

Conyngham, David P. *Sherman's March through the South.* New York: Sheldon & Co., 1865.

Cook, Ruth Beaumont. *North Across the River: A Civil War Trail of Tears.* Birmingham AL: Crane Hill Publishers, 1999.

Cooke, Chauncy H. "Letters of a Badger Boy in Blue: The Atlanta Campaign. *Wisconsin Magazine of History* 5/1 (1921–1922): 63–98.

Cooper, Walter G. *Official History of Fulton County.* [Atlanta]: History Commission, 1934.

Cope, Alexis. *The Fifteenth Ohio Volunteers and Its Campaigns, 1861–1865.* Columbus OH: Edward T. Miller Co., 1916.

Coulter, E. Merton. *The Confederate States of America, 1861–1865.* Baton Rouge: Louisiana State University Press, 1950.

———. "Sherman and the South." *Georgia Historical Quarterly* 15/1 (March 1931): 28–45.

Cowles, Calvin D., compiler. *Atlas to Accompany the Official Records of the Union and Confederate Armies.* 3 volumes. Washington DC: Government Printing Office, 1891–1895.

Cox, Jacob Dolson. *Military Reminiscences of the Civil War.* 2 volumes. New York: C. Scribner's Sons, 1900.

Cralle, Richard K., editor. *The Works of John C. Calhoun.* 6 volumes. New York: D. Appleton and Company, 1856.

Crawford, Frank, editor. "Your Charlie." *Civil War Times Illustrated* 31/6 (January–February 1993): 20, 62–69. The letters of Major Charles Loop.

Crew, James R. Papers. MSS 79f, Atlanta History Center. Includes Crew to wife, 1 December 1864, describing fire-damage to city.

Crist, Lynda Lasswell, Mary Seaton Dix, and Kenneth H. Williams, editors. *The Papers of Jefferson Davis* 12 volumes. to date. Baton Rouge: Louisiana State University Press, 1971–.

Cryder, George R., and Stanley R. Miller, compilers. *A View from the Ranks: The Civil War Diaries of Corporal Charles E. Smith*. Delaware OH: Delaware County Historical Society, 1999.

Cuttino, George Peddy, editor. *Saddle Bag and Spinning Wheel, Being the Civil War Letters of George W. Peddy, M.D., Surgeon, 56th Georgia Volunteer Regiment, C.S.A. and his Wife Kate Featherston Peddy*. Macon GA: Mercer University Press, 1981.

Daiss, Timothy, editor. *In the Saddle: Exploits of the 5th Georgia Cavalry During the Civil War*. Atglen PA: Schiffer Military History, 2004.

D'Alvigny, P. P. Noel. Papers. MSS 84f. Atlanta History Center.

Daniel, Larry J. *Cannoneers in Gray: The Field Artillery of the Army of Tennessee, 1861–1865*. Tuscaloosa: University of Alabama Press, 1984.

Daniel, Larry J., and Riley W. Gunter. *Confederate Cannon Foundries*. Union City TN: Pioneer Press, 1977.

Davis, Burke. *Sherman's March*. New York: Random House, 1980.

Davis, Harold E. *Henry Grady's New South: Atlanta, a Brave and Beautiful City*. Tuscaloosa: University of Alabama Press, 1990.

Davis, Keith F. *George N. Barnard: Photographs of Sherman's Campaign*. Kansas City MO: Hallmark Cards, 1990.

Davis, Mary. "Shell-Scarred Lamp Post Relic of Atlanta War Days." *Atlanta Constitution*, 5 August 1928. 7A.

Davis, Robert S., Jr. "The General Sherman Census of Atlanta, September 1864" *Georgia Genealogical Magazine* 31/1–2 (1991): 132–41.

Davis, Robert Scott, Jr., editor. *Requiem for a Lost City: A Memoir of Civil War Atlanta and the Old South*. Macon GA: Mercer University Press, 1999.

Davis, Robert Scott. *Civil War Atlanta*. Charleston SC: History Press, 2011.

Davis, William C., editor. *The South Besieged: Volume Five of the Image of War 1861–1865*. 6 volumes. Garden City NY: Doubleday & Company, 1983.

Dean, Henry Stewart. Diary. University of Michigan. Copy courtesy of Dr. Albert Castel, Columbus OH.

DeCredico, Mary A. *Patriotism for Profit: Georgia's Urban Entrepreneurs and the Confederate War Effort*. Chapel Hill: University of North Carolina Press, 1990.

Denkler, Kirk, editor. *Voices of the Civil War: Atlanta*. Alexandria VA: Time-Life Books, 1996.

Dennett, John Richard. *The South as It Is: 1865–1866*. New York: Viking Press, 1965.

DeRosier, Arthur H., Jr., editor. *Through the South with a Union Soldier*. Johnson City: East Tennessee State University Research Advisory Council, 1969.

"The Destruction of Atlanta. Sherman's Inhuman and Ferocious Conduct—Two Accounts from Widely Different Sources that Substantially Agree." *Atlanta Constitution*, 18 November 1881, 1.

Dew, Charles B. *Ironmaker to the Confederacy: Joseph R. Anderson and the Tredegar Iron Works*. New Haven: Yale University Press, 1966.

Dockstader, Mary Ralls. "Fine Old Atlanta Homes of Present Day which Withstood Sherman." *Atlanta Constitution*, 24 April 1932, 5.

"Dodging Federal Shells." *Atlanta Journal Sunday Magazine*, 12 October 1930, 8, 14.

Downey, Fairfax. "Field and Siege Pieces." *Civil War History* 2/2 (June 1956): 65–74.

———. *Sound of the Guns: The Story of American Artillery from the Ancient and Honorable Company to the Atom Cannon and Guided Missile*. New York: David McKay Company, 1955.

————. *Storming the Gateway: Chattanooga, 1863*. New York: David McKay Company, 1960.

"Dr. E.L. Connally, Beloved Physician and Leader of Atlanta Progress, Passes." *Atlanta Journal*, 17 March 1930, 1.

Dubay, Robert W. "No Love Lost—A Governor Reflects on William T. Sherman" *Atlanta Historical Journal* 25/2 (Summer 1981): 95–96.

DuBose, Beverly M., III. "The Manufacture of Confederate Ordnance in Georgia." *Atlanta Historical Bulletin* 12/4 (December 1967): 8–21.

DuBose, Beverly Collection. MSS 1020, Atlanta History Center.

Dumond, Dwight Lowell. *The Secession Movement 1860–1861*. New York: Macmillan Company, 1931.

Dunkelman, Mark H. *Marching with Sherman: Through Georgia and the Carolinas with the 154th New York*. Baton Rouge: Louisiana State University Press, 2012.

Dunlop, Colin. Typescript of letters, MSS 96f, Atlanta History Center.

Dyer, Thomas G. "Atlanta's Other Civil War Novel: Fictional Unionists in a Confederate City." *Georgia Historical Quarterly* 79/1 (Spring 1995): 147–68.

————. "Half Slave, Half Free: Unionist Robert Webster in Confederate Atlanta." In *Inside the Confederate Nation: Essays in Honor of Emory M. Thomas*, edited by Lesley J. Gordon and John C. Inscoe, 295–315. Baton Rouge: Louisiana State University Press, 2005.

————. *Secret Yankees: The Union Circle in Confederate Atlanta*. Baltimore: Johns Hopkins University Press, 1999.

————. "Vermont Yankees in King Cotton's Court: Cyrena and Amherst Stone in Confederate Atlanta." In *Enemies of the Country: New Perspectives on Unionists in the Civil War South*, edited by John C. Inscoe and Robert C. Kenzer, pp. 121–47. Athens: University of Georgia Press, 2001.

Edwards, Mike. "Rail, Dated in 1850s, Gets Big Role at Big Shanty." *Atlanta Journal*, 4 January 1962, 2.

Elliott, Sam Davis, editor. *Doctor Quintard, Chaplain C.S.A. and Second Bishop of Tennessee: The Memoir and Civil War Diary of Charles Todd Quintard*. Baton Rouge: Louisiana State University Press, 2003.

Ellis, B. G. *The Moving Appeal: Mr. McClanahan, Mrs. Dill, and the Civil War's Great Newspaper Run*. Macon: Mercer University Press, 2003.

Ellis, Barbara, and Stephen J. Dick. "'Who Was "Shadow"?' The Computer Knows: Applying Grammar-Program Statistics in Content Analysis to Solve Mysteries about Authorship." *Journalism & Mass Communication Quarterly* 73/4 (Winter 1996): 947–62.

Elmore, Tom. "The Burning of Columbia, February 17, 1864." *Blue & Gray* 21/2 (Winter 2004): 6–27.

"Eternal Flame to the Confederacy Dedication Ceremony, Atlanta, Georgia, December 14, 1939." Wilbur G. Kurtz Collection, MSS 130, box 15, folder 1, Atlanta History Center.

"'Eternal Light' Flickers as Bus Hits Lamppost." *Atlanta Journal-Constitution*, 29 January 1956, 1.

Evans, Clement A., editor. *Confederate Military History*. 12 volumes. Atlanta: Confederate Publishing Co., 1899.

Evans, David. "The Atlanta Campaign." *Civil War Times Illustrated* 28/4 (Summer 1989): 13–61.

————. *Sherman's Horsemen: Union Cavalry Operations in the Atlanta Campaign*. Bloomington: Indiana University Press, 1996.

Fancher, Laureita. "Historic Home May Be Razed." *Atlanta Journal Sunday Magazine*, 21 December 1930, 2.

Feldman, Ruth Elaine. "A Checklist of Atlanta Newspapers, 1846–1948." Master's thesis, Emory University, 1948.

Fellman, Michael. *Citizen Sherman: A Life of William Tecumseh Sherman.* New York: Random House, 1995.

———. *Inside War: The Guerrilla Conflict in Missouri during the American Civil War.* New York: Oxford University Press, 1989.

"Fighting Words." *America's Civil War* 23/4 (September 2010): 30–37.

"The First Shell Fired into Atlanta." *Kennesaw Gazette*, 15 October 1888. Reprinted from Atlanta *Constitution* (n.d.).

"The First Visit." *Atlanta Constitution*, 30 January 1879, 1.

Fitch, Michael. *Echoes of the Civil War as I Hear Them.* New York: R. F. Fenno & Co., 1905.

Fleharty, S. F. *Our Regiment: A History of the 102nd Illinois Infantry Volunteers.* Chicago: Brewster & Hanscom, 1865.

Foote, Shelby. *The Civil War: A Narrative.* 3 volumes. New York: Random House, 1958–1974.

"Forts to Defend Atlanta." *Atlanta Journal*, 25 May 1941, 6.

Fox, John A. to "My Dear William," 15 September 1864. Copy of typescript in author's possession. Courtesy of Wiley Sword, Suwanee, Georgia.

Frank, Lisa Tendrich. "Children of the March: Confederate Girls and Sherman's Homefront Campaign." In *Children and Youth during the Civil War Era*, edited by James Marten, pp. 110–24. New York: New York University Press, 2012.

Freemon, Frank R. "Administration of the Medical Department of the Confederate States Army, 1861 to 1865." *Southern Medical Journal* 80/5 (May 1987): 630–37.

———. "The Medical Support System for the Confederate Army of Tennessee During the Georgia Campaign, May–September 1864." *Tennessee Historical Quarterly* 52/1 (Spring 1993): 44–55.

French, Samuel G. *Two Wars: An Autobiography of General Samuel G. French, an Officer in the Armies of the United States and the Confederate States, a Graduate from the U.S. Military Academy, West Point, 1843.* Nashville: Confederate Veteran, 1901.

"From an Old Diary which Was Kept by Mr. Lewis Lawshe During the War." Newspaper clipping [ca. 1898], Edda Cole Scrapbook (MSS 267), Atlanta History Center, 113.

"From Atlanta." *Augusta Chronicle & Sentinel*, 14 December 1864. A *Knoxville Register* correspondent's description of damage to the city.

Funeral Services at the Burial of the Right Rev. Lenidas Polk, D.D. Columbia SC: Evans & Cogswell, 1864.

Garrett, Franklin M. *Atlanta and Environs: A Chronicle of Its People and Events* 2 volumes. New York: Lewis Historical Publishing Co. 1954.

———. "Civilian Life in Atlanta." *Civil War Times Illustrated* 3/4 (July 1864): 30–33.

———. "The Phoenix Begins to Rise: The *Atlanta Daily Intelligencer* Announces the Return of the Railroads." *Atlanta History* 37/4 (Winter 1994): 5–8.

———. *Yesterday's Atlanta.* Miami: E.A. Seemann Publishing, 1974.

[———, and Wilbur G. Kurtz]. "Key to Map." *Atlanta Historical Bulletin* 2/8 (September 1934): 5–29.

Garrison, Webb. *Atlanta and the War.* Nashville TN: Rutledge Hill Press, 1992.

Gay, Mary A. H. *Life in Dixie During the War.* Atlanta: Charles P. Byrd, 1897.

Geary, John W. Papers. Typescript copies of Geary's wartime letters are at both the Atlanta
    History Center (MSS 55) and Georgia Historical Society, Savannah (MSS 2030).
"General William T. Sherman." *Atlanta Constitution,* 13 February 1891, 4.
Ghaemi, Nassir. "Sherman's Demons: An Emory Psychiatry Professor and Civil War
    Aficionado Believes the General Who Torched Atlanta was Bipolar." *Atlanta* 46/7
    (November 2006): 76–82.
Gibbons, Robert. "Life at the Crossroads of the Confederacy: Atlanta 1861–1865." *Atlanta
    Historical Journal* 23/2 (Summer 1979): 11–72.
Gilreath, Frank C., Jr. "Famous Ryan Home, Early Atlanta Mansion, Soon to Disappear
    from Whitehall Street." *Atlanta Journal,* 1 February 1931, 8D.
Glatthaar, Joseph T. "Sherman's Army and Total War: Attitudes on Destruction in the
    Savannah and Carolinas Campaigns." *Atlanta Historical Journal* 29/1 (Spring 1985): 41–
    52.
———. *The March to the Sea and Beyond: Sherman's Troops in the Savannah and Carolinas
    Campaigns.* New York: New York University Press, 1985.
Goldy, James M. "The Swamp Angel." *Civil War Times Illustrated* 28/2 (April 1989): 22–27.
"Good guy/bad guy?" *Atlanta Constitution,* 2 February 1995, G3.
Goodrich, Thomas. *Black Flag: Guerrilla Warfare on the Western Border, 1861–1865.*
    Bloomington: Indiana University Press, 1995.
Gordon, Leslie J., and John C. Inscoe, editors. *Inside the Confederate Nation: Essays in Honor of
    Emory M. Thomas.* Baton Rouge: Louisiana State University Press, 2005.
"Gov. Harris at the Close of the War." *Confederate Veteran* 5/8 (August 1897): 402–405.
"Grant Home, Built in '50s, Historical Site." *Atlanta Constitution,* 1 September 1942. 4E.
Grant, Lemuel P. Papers, MSS 100. Atlanta History Center. Includes Grant Letterbook
    1862–1865.
Grant, L. P. "Sketch of the City of Atlanta and Line of Defenses" (map). In *Atlas to
    Accompany the Offical Records of the Union and Confederate Armies,* compiled by Calvin D.
    Cowles, vol. 1, plate 51, 2. 3 volumes. Washington, DC: Government Printing Office,
    1891–1895.
Gray, Audria B. "History of the Cathedral Parish of St. Philip's in the City and Diocese of
    Atlanta." *Atlanta Historical Bulletin* 1/4 (December 1930): 5–11.
Griffith, Louis T. "Joseph Addison Turner." In *Dictionary of Georgia Biography,* edited by
    Kenneth Coleman and Charles Stephen Gurr, 2:1009–11. 2 volumes. Athens: University
    of Georgia Press, 1983.
Griffith, Louis Turner, and John Erwin Talmadge. *Georgia Journalism, 1763–1950.* Athens:
    University of Georgia Press, 1951.
Grimsley, Mark. *The Hard Hand of War: Union Military Policy toward Southern Civilians, 1861–
    1865.* New York: Cambridge University Press, 1995.
———. "'Rebels' and 'Redskins': U.S. Military Conduct toward White Southerners and
    Native Americans in Comparative Perspective." In *Civilians in the Path of War,* edited by
    Mark Grimsley and Clifford J. Rogers, 137–61. Lincoln: University of Nebraska Press,
    2002.
Halley, R. A. "A Rebel Newspaper's War Story: Being a Narrative of the War History of the
    Memphis Appeal." In Tennessee Historical Commission, *Tennessee Old and New,* 2:247–72.
    2 volumes. Nashville: Tennessee Historical Commission, 1947.
Halsey, Ashley, editor. *A Yankee Private's Civil War.* Chicago: Henry Regnery Company,
    1961.

Hardin, David. *After the War: The Lives and Images of Major Civil War Figures after the Shooting Stopped.* Chicago: Ivan R. Dee, 2010.

Harris, Joel Chandler. *Tales of the Home Folks in Peace and War.* Boston: Houghton, Mifflin, 1898.

Harwell, Richard and Philip N. Racine, editors. *The Fiery Trail: A Union Officer's Account of Sherman's Last Campaigns.* Knoxville: University of Tennessee Press, 1986.

Harwell, Richard B., editor. "The Campaign from Chattanooga to Atlanta as Seen by a Federal Soldier." *Georgia Historical Quarterly* 25/3 (September 1941): 262–78.

Harwell, Richard Barksdale. "Atlanta Publications of the Civil War." *Atlanta Historical Bulletin* 6/25 (July 1941): 165–200.

———. "Civilian Life in 1862." *Atlanta Historical Bulletin* 7/29 (October 1944): 212–19.

———, editor. *The Confederate Reader: As the South Saw the War.* New York: Longmans, Green & Company, 1957.

———, editor. *Kate: The Journal of a Confederate Nurse.* Baton Rouge: Louisiana State University Press, 1964.

"Isham G. Harris as Warrior and Fugitive." *Atlanta Constitution,* 1 August 1897, 2.

Harrison, John M. "John Henry Mecaslin." *Atlanta Historical Bulletin* 3/13 (April 1938): 120–39.

Hartsfield, William B. "Document in Handwriting of Atlanta's War-Time Mayor Describes Formal Surrender of the City to Federal Army." *Atlanta Sunday Constitution Magazine,* 31 May 1931, 12.

Hattaway, Herman, and Archer Jones. *How the North Won: A Military History of the Civil War.* Urbana: University of Illinois Press, 1983.

Hayes, Philip C. *Journal-History of the Hundred & Third Ohio Volunteer Infantry.* Toledo: Commercial Steam Printing House, 1872.

[Haygood, Greene B.]. "Sketch of Atlanta." In *Williams' Atlanta Directory, City Guide and Business Mirror,* 9–15. Atlanta: M. Lynch, 1859.

Hazen, W. B. *A Narrative of Military Service.* Boston: Ticknor Company, 1885.

Hazlett, James C. "The 3-Inch Ordnance Rifle." *Civil War Times Illustrated* 7/8 (December 1968): 30–36.

———. "The Parrott Rifles." *Civil War Times Illustrated* 5/7 (November 1966): 27–33.

Hedley, Fenwick Y. *Marching through Georgia.* Chicago: Donohue, Henneberry & Company, 1890.

Hendrick, Bill. "Digging into Downtown's History." *Atlanta Constitution,* 24 December 1994, E1.

———. "Historian aims to identify unknown Union soldiers." *Atlanta Journal-Constitution,* 13 April 2011, B5.

———. "Treasure beneath Rich's Revealed in Bits, Pieces." *Atlanta Constitution,* 30 August 1994, C1.

Henry Champlin Lay Papers, 1841–1885. MSS 418, University of North Carolina at Chapel Hill. Includes diary, May 1863–December 1865.

Henry, Robert Selph. *"First with the Most" Forrest.* Indianapolis: Bobbs-Merrill Company, 1944.

"Here Are Some Last Farewell Views of the Old Leyden House." *Atlanta Journal,* 23 February 1913, 8.

Herr, George W. *Nine Campaigns in Nine States: A Sketch...in which Is Comprised the History of the Fifty- Ninth Regiment Illinois Veteran Volunteer Infantry.* San Francisco: Bancroft Company, 1900.

Hight, John J. *History of the Fifty-eighth Regiment of Indiana Volunteer Infantry.* Princeton IN: Press of the Clarion, 1895.

Hilde, Libra R. *Worth a Dozen Men: Women and Nursing in the Civil War South.* Charlottesville: University of Virginia Press, 2012.

Hillyer, Elinor. "New City Hall Where Sherman Made Headquarters." *Atlanta Journal Magazine,* 4 September 1927, 11.

Hinkley, Julian Wisner. *Narrative of Service with the Third Wisconsin Infantry.* Madison: Wisconsin History Commission, 1912.

Hinman, Wilbur F. *The Story of the Sherman Brigade.* Alliance OH: Wilbur F. Hinman, 1897.

Historical Sketch Co. "D," 13th Regiment N.J. Vols.... Compiled and Printed...by the Authority of "D" Society. New York: D. H. Gildersleeve & Company, 1875.

"History of the Atlanta Gas Light Company." Undated typescript, box 29, folder 9, Wilbur G. Kurtz Collection, MSS 130, Atlanta History Center.

"History of Trinity Methodist Church, 1853–1867." *Atlanta Historical Bulletin* 3/15 (October 1938): 286–88.

Hitt, Michael D. *Charged with Treason: Ordeal of 400 Mill Workers during Military Operations in Roswell, Georgia, 1864–1865.* Monroe NY: Library Research Associates, 1992.

Hitz, Alex M. "The Origin and Distinction Between the Two Protestant Episcopal Churches Known as St. Luke's Church, Atlanta." *Georgia Historical Quarterly* 34/1 (March 1950): 1–7.

Hoehling, A. A. *Last Train from Atlanta.* New York: Thomas Yoseloff, 1958.

Hoffman, Mark. *"My Brave Mechanics": The First Michigan Engineers and Their Civil War.* Detroit: Wayne State University Press, 2007.

Holzhueter, John O., editor. "William Wallace's Civil War Letters: The Atlanta Campaign." *Wisconsin Magazine of History* 57/2 (Winter 1973–74): 91–116.

Hood, J. B. *Advance and Retreat: Personal Experiences in the United States and Confederate States Armies.* New Orleans: Hood Orphan Memorial Fund, 1880.

Hornaday, John R. *Atlanta: Yesterday, Today and Tomorrow.* Atlanta: American Cities Book Company, 1922.

Howard, Oliver O. "Sherman's Advance from Atlanta." In *Battles and Leaders of the Civil War,* edited by Robert Underwood Johnson and Clarence Clough Buel, 4:663–66. 4 volumes. New York: Century Co., 1888.

Howe, M. A. DeWolfe, editor. *Home Letters of General Sherman.* New York: Charles Scribner's Sons. 1909.

———. *Marching with Sherman: Passages from the Letters and Campaign Diaries of Henry Hitchcock.* New Haven: Yale University Press, 1927.

Hubner, Charles W. "Some Recollections of Atlanta During 1864." *Atlanta Historical Bulletin* 1/2 (January 1928): 5–7.

Huff, Lawrence. "'A Bitter Draught We Have Had to Quaff': Sherman's March through the Eyes of Joseph Addison Turner." *Georgia Historical Quarterly* 72/2 (Summer 1989): 306–26.

Huff, Sarah. *My Eighty Years in Atlanta.* Atlanta: n.p., 1937.

Hughes, Nathaniel Cheairs, Jr. *The Civil War Memoir of Philip Daingerfield Stephenson, D.D.* Conway AR: University of Central Arkansas Press, 1995.

Hunter, Benjamin. Typescript diary. MSS 179f, Atlanta History Center.

Hurt Family Papers. Alabama Department of Archives and History.

"In Sherman's Own Words." *Atlanta Constitution*, 22 December 1992, A3.

"Indigenous Remedies of the South." *Confederate States Medical & Surgical Journal* 1/7 (July 1864): 106–108.

Instruction for Heavy Artillery: Prepared by a Board of Officers, for the Use of the Army of the United States. Washington, DC: Government Printing Office, 1862.

"Interesting Sketches of Pioneer Women: Mrs. Frank P. Rice." *Atlanta Journal*, 6 June 1909, S2.

"Interesting Sketches of Pioneer Women." Typescript. Atlanta Women's Pioneer Society Collection. MSS 391, box 1, folder 35. Atlanta History Center.

Irby, Lauren. "Atlanta Put to Torch 90 Years Ago Today." *Atlanta Journal-Constitution*, 14 November 1954, 13B.

Irvine, William Stafford, editor. "Diary and Letters of Dr. William N. White, a Citizen of Atlanta Written 1847, 90 Years Ago." *Atlanta Historical Bulletin* 2/10 (July 1937): 35–51.

Jackson, David P., editor. *The Colonel's Diary: Journals Kept before and during the Civil War by the Late Colonel Oscar L. Jackson of New Castle, Pennsylvania, Sometime Commander of the 63rd Regiment O.V.I.* Sharon PA: n.p., 1922.

Johnson, W. C. "The March to the Sea." In *The Atlanta Papers*, compiled by Sydney C. Kerksis, 801–30. Dayton OH: Press of Morningside Bookshop, 1980.

Johnson, W. R., editor. "'Enough to Make a Preacher Sware': A Union Mule Driver's Diary of Sherman's March." *Atlanta History* 33/3 (Fall 1989): 21–36.

Jones, Jenkin Lloyd. *An Artilleryman's Diary*. Madison: Wisconsin History Commission, 1914.

Jones, Katherine M. *When Sherman Came*. Indianapolis: Bobbs-Merrill Company, 1964.

Jones, Virgil Carrington. *Gray Ghosts and Rebel Raiders*. New York: Henry Holt & Company, 1956.

Jordan, Mildred. "Georgia's Confederate Hospitals." Master's thesis, Emory University, 1962.

Joslyn, Mauriel Phillips. *Immortal Captives: The Story of the Six Hundred Confederate Officers and the United States Prisoner of War Policy*. Shippensburg PA: White Mane Publishing Company, 1996.

Julian, Allen Phelps. "Atlanta's Last Days in the Confederacy." *Atlanta Historical Bulletin* 11/2 (June 1966): 9–18.

Julian, Allen P. "Atlanta's Defenses." *Civil War Times Illustrated* 3/4 (July 1964): 23–24.

[———]. "Tour of the Peachtree Creek Battle Field Area." Typescript, box 26, folder 6. Wilbur G. Kurtz Collection. MSS 130, Atlanta History Center.

"Just up the Street from Us Lived Scarlett and Aunt Pittypat." *Atlanta Journal*, 15 December 1939, 50.

Kellogg, Mary E., editor. *Army Life of an Illnois Soldier*. Carbondale: Southern Illinois University Press, 1996.

Kennaway, John H. *On Sherman's Track; or, the South After the War*. London: Shelley, Jackson, and Halliday, 1867.

Kennett, Lee. "Burned by History." *Atlanta Journal-Constitution*, 2 September 2001, D1, D3.

———. *Marching Through Georgia: The Story of Soldiers and Civilians During Sherman's Campaign*. New York: HarperCollins, 1995.

———. *Sherman: A Soldier's Life*. New York: HarperCollins, 2001.

Kerksis, Sydney C., compiler. *The Atlanta Papers.* Dayton OH: Press of Morningside Bookshop, 1980.

Key, William. *The Battle of Atlanta and the Georgia Campaign.* New York: Twayne Publishers, 1958.

Killian, T. D. "James R. Crew." *Atlanta Historical Bulletin* 1/6 (January 1932): 5–15.

King, Alvy L. *Louis T. Wigfall, Southern Fire-Eater.* Baton Rouge: Louisiana State University Press, 1970.

Kirwan, A. D., editor. *Johnny Green of the Orphan Brigade: The Journal of a Confederate Soldier.* Lexington: University of Kentucky Press, 1956.

Knight, Lucian Lamar. *History of Fulton County Georgia.* Atlanta: A.H. Cawston, 1930.

Kremenak, Ben, editor. "Escape from Atlanta: The Huntington Memoir." *Civil War History* 11/2 (June 1965): 160–77.

Kunkle, Camille. "Atlanta's Churches in 1896." *Atlanta History* 33/1 (Spring 1989): 35–47.

Kurtz, Annie Laurie Fuller. "Atlanta as Sherman Left It—Burning of the City." *Atlanta Journal Magazine,* 19 January 1936, 10–11.

———. "Atlanta's Envoys to Sherman." *Atlanta Journal Magazine,* 7 January 1934, 9, 18.

———. "Atlanta's First Jail Break." *Atlanta Journal Magazine,* 11 February 1934, 10, 18.

———. "Departed Glory of State Square." *Atlanta Journal Magazine,* 1 December 1935, 2, 16.

———. "'While Atlanta Burned.'" *Atlanta Constitution Sunday Magazine,* 12 March. 1939. 3.

Kurtz, Anne Laurie Fuller. "Surrender of Atlanta—Evacuation of Its Citizens." *Atlanta Journal Magazine,* 12 January 1936, 10–11.

"Kurtz Article Is Given Praise by Old Atlantan." *Atlanta Constitution,* 24 June 1930, 4.

"Kurtz Describes Historic Homes of Atlanta." *Atlanta Journal,* 28 April 1935, 8B.

Kurtz, Wilbur G. "At the Dexter Niles House." *Atlanta Constitution Sunday Magazine,* 28 September 1930, 5–6, 20.

———. "At the Troup Hurt House." *Atlanta Constitution Sunday Magazine,* 25 January 1931. 4–5, 20.

———."The Augustus F. Hurt House." *Atlanta Constitution Sunday Magazine,* 22 June 1930, 5–6.

———. "Dugout Home in Atlanta." *Atlanta Journal Magazine,* 10 July 1932, 3, 27.

———. "A Federal Spy in Atlanta." *Atlanta Constitution Magazine,* 8 June 1930, 5, 14.

———. "Fort Hood and the Ponders House." *Atlanta Constitution,* 1 June 1930, 5, 14.

[———]. "How St. Luke's Was Built." *Atlanta Journal Magazine,* 6 October 1935, 13.

———. "'Leave Atlanta Within Five Days.'" *Atlanta Journal Magazine,* 12 October 1941, 1.

———. "Map of Atlanta as of 1938 Showing the Field and Fortified Lines of the Confederate Forces, Together with Those of the Federal Armies—Also the Fields of the Three Major Engagements, During the Summer of 1864." Atlanta Chamber of Commerce, 1938. Kurtz Collection, FF 148, T2, folder 2, Atlanta History Center. My thanks to Melanie Steffan of the Atlanta History Center for locating this invaluable map.

———. "Embattled Atlanta" (map). *Atlanta Constitution,* 20 July 1930, 12–13.

———. "Environs of the present State Capitol and City Hall, Atlanta, Ga." (map). *Atlanta Historical Bulletin* 8/30 (October 1945): 32.

———. "McPherson's Last Ride." *Atlanta Constitution Magazine,* 29 June 1930, 8–9, 14.

———. "Persons Removed from Atlanta by General W.T. Sherman, September 4, 1864." *Atlanta Historical Bulletin* 1/6 (January 1932): 21–32.

———."St. Luke's Baptized by War." *Atlanta Journal Magazine,* 3 July 1932, 5, 16, 21.

———. "Shells for Dinner." *Atlanta Journal Magazine,* 7 September 1941, 9.

———. "Some Unpublished Glimpses of General John B. Hood." Wilbur G. Kurtz Collection, box 33, folder 6, Atlanta History Center.

———. "Walter Q. Gresham at Atlanta." *Atlanta Constitution Magazine,* 24 August 1930, 8–9, 21.

Lack, Paul D. "Law and Disorder in Confederate Atlanta." *Georgia Historical Quarterly* 66/2 (Summer 1982): 171–95.

Ladd, James Royal. "From Atlanta to the Sea." *American Heritage* 30/1 (December 1979): 4–11.

Lash, Jeffrey N. *Destroyer of the Iron Horse: General Joseph E. Johnston and Confederate Rail Transport, 1861–1865.* Kent OH: Kent State University Press, 1991.

Latimer, Carolyn, and Nancy Lee, editors. *Civil War Letters Written by Elder Ira Lawson Gunter, M.D.* McDonough GA: self-published, 1993.

———. "Sherman in Georgia by the Right Reverend Henry C. Lay." *Atlantic Monthly* 149/2 (February 1932): 166–72.

Leckie, Robert. *The Wars of America.* New York: HarperCollins, 1992.

Le Duc, William G. "Official Account of the People Sent South, Their Numbers and Luggage, under Special Field Order No. 67, Issued by Major-General W.T. Sherman, Atlanta, Georgia, September 4, 1864." In *Memoirs of General W.T. Sherman,* 546–53. 2 volumes. 4th edition. New York: Charles L. Webster & Co., 1891.

———. *Recollections of a Civil War Quartermaster: The Autobiography of William G. Le Duc.* St. Paul MN: North Central Publishing Co., 1963.

Lepa, Jack H. *Breaking the Confederacy: The Georgia and Tennessee Campaigns of 1864.* Jefferson NC: McFarland & Co., 2005.

"Let Us Destroy Atlanta: A Symposium on the 125th Anniversary of the Burning of Atlanta and Its Rise after the Civil War." Symposium pamphlet, Atlanta Historical Society, November 1989.

"Letter from Atlanta." *Augusta Chronicle & Sentinel,* 21 December 1864.

Lewis, Lloyd. *Sherman: Fighting Prophet.* New York: Harcourt, Brace & Company, 1932.

Liddell Hart, B. H. *Sherman: Soldier, Realist, American.* New York: Dodd, Mead & Company, 1929.

Lin Family Papers. MSS 849. Atlanta History Center.

Lindqvist, Sven. *A History of Bombing.* Translated by Linda Haverty Rugg. New York: New Press, 2001.

Livingood, James W. "The Chattanooga Rebel." *East Tennessee Historical Society Publications* 39 (1967): 42–55.

Long, David E. *The Jewel of Liberty: Abraham Lincoln's Re-Election and the End of Slavery.* Mechanicsburg PA: Stackpole Books, 1994.

Longacre, Edward G., editor. "From Atlanta to the Sea: The Civil War Letters of Corporal Eli S. Richer, 1862–1865." Typescript. In author's possession. Courtesy of Dr. Albert Castel, Columbus OH.

Longacre, Glenn V. and John E. Haas, editors. *To Battle for God and the Right: The Civil War Letterbooks of Emerson Opdycke.* Urbana: University of Illinois Press, 2003.

Lord, Francis A. "'Greek Fire' Enflamed Beauregard at Charleston." *Civil War Times Illustrated* 2/8 (December 1960): 9.

Losson, Chrisopher. *Tennessee's Forgotten Warriors: Frank Cheatham and His Confederate Division.* Knoxville: University of Tennessee Press, 1989.

Lucas, Marion Brunson. *Sherman and the Burning of Columbia.* College Station: Texas A & M University Press, 1976.

Luraghi, Raimondo. *The Rise and Fall of the Plantation South.* New York: Franklin Watts, 1978.

Mallet, J. W. "Work of the Ordnance Bureau." *Southern Historical Society Papers* 37 (1909): 1–20.

Malone, Henry T. "Atlanta Journalism During the Confederacy." *Georgia Historical Quarterly* 37/3 (September 1953): 210–19.

———. "The Weekly Atlanta Intelligencer as a Secessionist Journal." *Georgia Historical Quarterly* 37/4 (December 1953): 278–86.

"A Man of Moods." *Atlanta Constitution,* 18 February 1891, 4.

Manufactures of the United States in 1860; Compiled from the Original Returns of the Eighth Census. Washington DC: Government Printing Office, 1865.

Marszalek, John F. "Celebrity in Dixie: Sherman Tours the South, 1879." *Georgia Historical Quarterly* 66/3 (Fall 1982): 368–83.

———. *Sherman: A Soldier's Passion for Order.* New York: Free Press, 1993.

———. *Sherman's Other War: The General and the Civil War Press.* Memphis TN: Memphis State University Press, 1981.

Marten, James, ed. *Children and Youth During the Civil War Era.* New York: New York University Press, 2012.

Marten, James. *Sing Not War: The Lives of Union & Confederate Veterans in Gilded Age America.* Chapel Hill: University of North Carolina Press, 2011.

Martin, Thomas H. *Atlanta and Its Builders: A Comprehensive History of the Gate City of the South.* 2 volumes. Atlanta: Century Memorial Publishing Company, 1902.

Marvel, William. *Andersonville: The Last Depot.* Chapel Hill: University of North Carolina, 1994.

Marvin, Edwin E. *The Fifth Regiment Connecticut Volunteers: A History Compiled from Diaries and Official Reports.* Hartford: Wiley, Waterman and Eaton, 1889.

Mason, James Walter. "Atlanta's Matronymic." In Walter G. Cooper, *Official History of Fulton County,* 68–71. [Atlanta]: History Commission, 1934.

Massey, Mary Elizabeth. *Refugee Life in the Confederacy.* Baton Rouge: Louisiana State University Press, 1964.

McBride, John R. *History of the Thirty-Third Indiana Veteran Volunteer Infantry.* Indianapolis: Wm. B. Burford, 1900.

McDonough, James Lee, and James Pickett Jones. *War So Terrible: Sherman and Atlanta.* New York: W. W. Norton & Company, 1987.

McGregor, Laura. "Trinity Methodist Spared by Sherman." *Atlanta Journal,* 17 August 1957, 4.

McKee, Robert. "New Sherman Letter Shows General's Iron Will." *Atlanta Journal,* 24 January 1956. 14.

McKenzie, Ellie Lou. "Five Men Who Fought in the War." *Atlanta Journal,* 2 November 1930, 15.

McKinney, Francis F. *Education in Violence: The Life of George H. Thomas and the History of the Army of the Cumberland.* Detroit: Wayne State University Press, 1961.

McMurry, Richard M. "The Confederate Newspaper Press and the Civil War: An Overview and a Report on Research in Progress." *Atlanta History* 42/1, 2 (Spring–Summer 1988): 59–75.

———. *John Bell Hood and the War for Southern Independence.* Lexington: University Press of Kentucky, 1982.

———. "The Mackall Journal and Its Antecedents." Unpublished typescript of Lieutenant Thomas B. Mackall's diary. In author's possession.

———. *The Road Past Kennesaw: The Atlanta Campaign of 1864.* Washington, DC: US Department of the Interior, 1972.

McPherson, James M. *Battle Cry of Freedom: The Civil War Era.* New York: Oxford University Press, 1988.

McWhirter, Cameron. "Sherman Still Burns Atlanta." *Atlanta Journal-Constitution,* 9 May 2004, E1, E2.

Melton, Maurice. *The Confederate Ironclads.* New York: Thomas Yoseloff, 1968.

———. "Major Military Industries of the Confederate Government." Ph.D. dissertation, Emory University, 1978.

Merrill, James M. "Personnne Goes to Georgia: Five Civil War Letters." *Georgia Historical Quarterly* 43/2 (June 1959): 202–11.

Merrill, Samuel. *The Seventieth Indiana Volunteer Infantry.* Indianapolis: Bowen-Merrill Company, 1887.

Miers, Earl Schenck. *The General Who Marched to Hell: William T. Sherman and His March to Fame and Infamy.* New York: Alfred A. Knopf, 1951.

———. *The Web of Victory: Grant at Vicksburg.* New York: Alfred A. Knopf, 1955.

Milholland, Lily. "Grandma's War Memories." *Atlanta Journal Sunday Magazine,* 5 April 1931, 3, 27.

Miller, Alonzo. Typescript of diary and letters. MSS 237f. Atlanta History Center.

Miller, Paul W., editor. *Atlanta Capital of the South.* New York: Oliver Durrell, 1947.

Miller, William J. *Great Maps of the Civil War.* Nashville TN: Rutledge Hill Press, 2004.

Mink, Charles R. "General Orders No. 11: The Forced Evacuation of Civilians During the Civil War." *Military Affairs* 34/4 (December 1970): 132–36.

"Miss Abby." Diary. MS 1000. University of Georgia.

Mitchell, Pama. "Sherman's March to the Sea Lingers in Southern Psyche." *Atlanta Constitution,* 22 December 1992, A3.

Mitchell, Stephens. "Atlanta the Industrial Heart of the Confederacy." *Atlanta Historical Bulletin* 1/3 (May 1930): 20–27.

[———]. "Colonel L.P. Grant and the Defenses of Atlanta." *Atlanta Historical Bulletin* 1/6 (February 1932): 32–35.

Mohr, Clarence L. "The Atlanta Campaign and the African American Experience in Civil War Georgia." In *Inside the Confederate Nation: Essays in Honor of Emory M. Thomas,* edited by Lesley J. Gordon and John C. Inscoe, 272-94. Baton Rouge: Louisiana State University Press, 2005.

Molineaux, Emily E. *Lifetime Recollections: An Interesting Narrative of Life in the Southern States before and during the Civil War, with Incidents of the Bombardment of Atlanta by the Union forces, the Author Being Then a resident of that City.* San Francisco: C. W. Gordon, 1902.

"Monument for Priest Who Saved Five Churches." *Atlanta Journal,* 14 October 1945, 9–B.

"Monument to Priest Who Stood Up to Sherman." *Atlanta Journal,* 19 October 1945, 29.

Moody, Wesley. *Demon of the Lost Cause: Sherman and Civil War History.* Columbia: University of Missouri Press, 2011.

Moore, Frank, editor. *The Rebellion Record: A Diary of American Events.* 11 volumes. New York: G. P. Putnam, 1861–1863; D. Van Nostrand, 1864–1868.

Moore, John Hammond. "In Sherman's Wake: Atlanta and the Southern Claims Commission, 1871–1880." *Atlanta Historical Journal* 29/2 (Summer 1985): 5–18.

Moore, Kent. "Atlanta's Pride and Problem." *Atlanta Historical Bulletin* 20/2 (Summer 1976): 19–41.

Morgan, Chad. *Planters' Progress: Modernizing Confederate Georgia.* Gainesville: University Press of Florida, 2005.

Morhous, Henry C. *Reminiscences of the 123rd Regiment, N.Y.S.V., Giving a Complete HIstory of Its Three Years Service in the War.* Greenwich NY: People's Journal Book and Job Office, 1879.

Morris, Roy. "As the Shells Exploded over Atlanta in 1864, the Opposing Generals Opened a War of Words." *America's Civil War* 7/6 (January 1995): 6.

———. "The Chattanooga Daily Rebel." *Civil War Times Illustrated* 23/7 (November 1984): 16–18, 20–24.

Morse, Charles F. *Letters Written During the Civil War 1861–1865.* Charles F. Morse, 1898.

Moses H. Wright Papers. MSS 386f. Atlanta History Center.

Mountcastle, Clay. *Punitive War: Confederate Guerrillas and Union Reprisals.* Lawrence: University Press of Kansas, 2009.

Munson, Gilbert D. "Battle of Atlanta." In *The Atlanta Papers,* edited by Sydney C. Kerksis, 409–29. Dayton OH: Press of Morningside Bookshop, 1981.

Murphy, John M., and Howard Michael Madaus. *Confederate Rifles & Muskets: Infantry Small Arms Manufactured in the Southern Confederacy 1861–1865.* Newport Beach CA: Graphic Publisher, 1996.

Myers, Robert Manson, editor. *The Children of Pride: A True Story of Georgia and the Civil War.* New Haven: Yale University Press, 1972.

Naisawald, L. Van Loan. *Grape and Canister: The Story of the Field Artillery of the Army of the Potomac, 1861–1865.* New York: Oxford University Press, 1960.

———. "Field Artillery in the War." *Civil War Times* 3/3 (June 1961): 4–7, 24.

Neal, Andrew Jackson. Letters. MS 218. Emory University.

Neal, William N. *An Illustrated History of the Missouri Engineer and the 25th Infantry Regiments.* Chicago: Donohue and Henneberry, 1889.

Neely, Mark E., Jr. "Was the Civil War a Total War?" *Civil War History* 37/1 (March 1991): 5–28.

Neer, Henry. Diary. University of Michigan. Copy courtesy of Dr. Albert Castel, Columbus OH.

Nellie Peters Black Papers. MSS 32F. Atlanta History Center.

Nevin, David. *Sherman's March: Atlanta to the Sea.* Alexandria VA: Time-Life Books, 1986.

Newlin, William Henry, compiler. *A History of the Seventy-Third Regiment of Illinois Infantry Volunteers.* Springfield IL: Regimental Reunion Association, 1890.

Nichols, George Ward. *The Story of the Great March. From the Diary of a Staff Officer.* New York: Harper & Brothers, 1865.

Niepman, Ann Davis. "General Orders No. 11 and Border Warfare During the Civil War." *Missouri Historical Review* 66/2 (January 1972): 185–210.

Niesen, William C. "'The Consequences of Grandeur': A Union Soldier Writes of the Atlanta Campaign." *Atlanta History* 33/3 (Fall 1989): 5–19.

Nisbet, James Cooper. *Four Years on the Firing Line.* Edited by Bell Irvin Wiley. Jackson TN: McCowat-Mercer Press, 1963.

Noll, Arthur Howard, editor. *Doctor Quintard Chaplain C.S.A. and Second Bishop of Tennessee Being His Story of the War (1861–1865)*. Sewanee TN: University Press, 1905.

Norman, Matthew W. *Colonel Burton's Spiller & Burr Revolver: An Untimely Venture in Confederate Small-Arms Manufacturing*. Macon GA: Mercer University Press, 1996.

———. "Spiller & Burr: One Confederate Manufacturing Firm's Struggle for Survival During the War Between the States. *Man at Arms* 17/1 (January-February 1995): 30–38.

O. M. Poe Collection. United States Military Academy, West Point, New York.

Oakey, Daniel. "Marching through Georgia and the Carolinas." In *Battles and Leaders of the Civil War*, edited by Robert Underwood Johnson and Clarence Clough Buel, 4:671-79. 4 volumes. New York: Century Company, 1888.

Oakland Cemetery Collection, MSS 618, Atlanta History Center.

"Obsequies of Father O'Reilly." *Atlanta Constitution*, 11 September 1872, 3.

"Old Lamp Post, Relic of Battle of Atlanta, Attracts Attention." *Atlanta Constitution*, 8 October 1919, 10.

"Old Newspapers; Relics of the War." *Atlanta Constitution*, 20 July 1898, 5.

Olmstead, Edwin, Wayne E. Stark, and Spencer C. Tucker. *The Big Guns: Civil War Siege, Seacoast, and Naval Cannon*. Alexandria Bay NY: Museum Restoration Service, 1977.

O'Neill, Charles. *Wild Train: The Story of the Andrews Raiders*. New York: Random House, 1956.

Osborn, Harwell et al. *Trials and Triumphs: The Record of the Fifty-Fifth Ohio Volunteer Infantry*. Chicago: A. C. McClurg, 1904.

Otis, Robert R. "High Lights in the Life of Father Thomas O'Reilly." *Atlanta Historical Bulletin* 8/30 (October 1945): 13–31.

Overmeyer, Jack K. *A Stupendous Effort: The 87th Indiana in the War of the Rebellion*. Bloomington: Indiana University Press, 1997.

Padgett, James A., editor. "With Sherman Through Georgia and the Carolinas: Letters of a Federal Soldier." *Georgia Historical Quarterly* 32/4 (December 1948): 284–322. "Part II" in 33/1 (March 1949): 49–81.

[Parham, Louis L., editor]. *Pioneer Citizens' History of Atlanta 1833–1902*. Atlanta: Byrd Printing Company, 1902.

Parker, David P. *Alias Bill Arp: Charles Henry Smith and the South's "Goodly Heritage."* Athens: University of Georgia Press, 1991.

Parks, Joseph H. *Joseph E. Brown of Georgia*. Baton Rouge: Louisiana State University Press, 1977.

Patrick, Jeffrey L., and Robert J. Willey, editors. *Fighting for Liberty and Right: The Civil War Diary of William Bluffton Miller, First Sergeant, Company K, Seventy-Fifth Indiana Volunteer Infantry*. Knoxville: University of Tennessee Press, 2005.

Paul, Franc M. "The Chattanooga Rebel." In *Tennessee Old and New*, 2:273–79. 2 volumes. Nashville: Tennessee Historical Commission, 1947.

Peacock, Jane Bonner, editor. "A Wartime Story: The Davidson Letters, 1862–1865." *Atlanta Historical Bulletin* 19/1 (Spring 1975): 8–121.

Pepper, George W. *Personal Recollections of Sherman's Campaigns in Georgia and the Carolinas*. Zanesville OH: Hugh Dunne, 1866.

Perdue, Theda, and Michael D. Green. *The Cherokee Nation and the Trail of Tears*. New York: Penguin Books, 2008.

Perkerson, Meda Field, editor. "A Civil War Letter on the Capture of Atlanta." *Georgia Historical Quarterly* 28/4 (December 1944): 251–69.

Peterson, Harold L. *Round Shot and Rammers.* Harrisburg PA: Stackpole Books, 1969.

Phelps, W. Chris. *The Bombardment of Charleston, 1863–1865.* Gretna LA: Pelican Publishing Company, 2002.

"Photograph of 'Little Sallie' Found in Atlanta in September, 1864." *Atlanta Constitution,* 20 July 1898, 2.

Pinckney, Roger. "Iron Angel of Death." *Civil War Times Illustrated* 38/5 (October 1999): 26–32, 66.

Poe, O. M. Map Illustrating the Siege of Atlanta." In *Atlas to Accompany the* Offical Records of the Union and Confederate Armies, compiled by Calvin D. Cowles, vol. 2, plate 88, 2. 3 volumes. Washington, DC: Government Printing Office, 1891–1895.

Potter, John. *Reminiscences of the Civil War in the United States.* Oskaloosa IA: Globe Presses, 1897.

"Protestants Honor Priest." *Atlanta Historical Bulletin* 8/30 (October 1945): 56.

Quaife, Milo M., editor. *From the Cannon's Mouth: The Civil War Letters of General Alpheus S. Williams.* Detroit: Wayne State University Press, 1959.

Quint, Alonzo H. *The Record of the Second Massachusetts Infantry.* Boston: James P. Walker Company, 1867.

Quintard, Charles Todd. *Nellie Peters' Handkerchief and What It Saw: A Story of the War.* Edited by Arthur Howard Noll. Sewanee TN: University Press, 1907.

Rains, George W. *History of the Confederate Powder Works.* Augusta GA: Chronicle & Constitutionalist Printing, 1882.

Rawson-Collier-Harris Family Collection. MSS 36, Atlanta History Center. Includes Mary Rawson's typescript diary, 31 August–22 September 1864.

"Records of Ordnance Establishments at Dalton, Savannah, Augusta, and Atlanta, Ga., and Nashville, Tenn." National Archives Record Group 109, microfilm at University of Georgia and Atlanta History Center.

Reed, Wallace P. *History of Atlanta, Georgia, with Illustrations and Biographical Sketches of Some of Its Prominent Men and Pioneers.* Syracuse NY: D. Mason & Co., 1889.

———. "Two Epochs in the History of Atlanta in the Sixties." *Atlanta Constitution,* 18 June 1893, 36.

Reinhart, Joseph R., translator and editor. *August Willich's Gallant Dutchmen: Civil War Letters from the 32nd Indiana Infantry.* Kent OH: Kent State University Press, 2006.

"Reminiscences of Patrick H. Calhoun." *Atlanta Historical Bulletin* 1/6 (January 1932): 41–47.

Rice, Ralsa C. *Yankee Tigers: Through the Civil War with the 125th Ohio.* Edited by Richard A. Baumgartner and Larry M. Strayer. Huntington WV: Blue Acorn Press, 1992.

Rice, Thomas. "Fredericksburg Under Fire: All the Imps of Hell Let Loose." *Civil War Times Illustrated* 22/4 (June 1983): 8–15.

Richards, William A. "'We Live Under a Constitution': Confederate Martial Law in Atlanta." *Atlanta History* 33/2 (Summer 1989): 26–35.

Ripley, Warren. *Artillery and Ammunition of the Civil War.* New York: Promontory Press, 1970.

Risley, Ford. "The Confederate Press Association: Cooperative News Reporting of the War." *Civil War History* 47/3 (September 2001): 222–39.

Robbins, Peggy. "Hood vs. Sherman: A Duel of Words." *Civil War Times Illustrated* 17/4 (July 1978): 22–29.

Robinson, William M. *Justice in Grey: A History of the Judicial System of the Confederate States of America.* Cambridge: Harvard University Press, 1941.

Robson, Kate Hester. "Autobiography." Typescript. MSS 291F. Atlanta History Center.

Romances of Atlanta Real Estate, Reprinted from the Atlanta Journal. Atlanta: Sharp-Boylston Company, 1927.

Rose, Michael. *Atlanta: A Portrait of the Civil War.* Charleston: Arcadia Publishing, 1999.

Roseberry, Isaac. Diary. MSS 391. Emory University.

Roth, Margaret Brobst, editor. *Well Mary: Civil War Letters of a Wisconsin Volunteer.* Madison: University of Wisconsin Press, 1960.

Rourke, Norman. "The Newsmen." *Civil War Times Illustrated* 40/6 (December 2001): 56–70.

Rufus Mead, Jr., Papers, 1861–1865. Library of Congress.

Russell, James Michael. *Atlanta, 1847–1890: City Building in the Old South and the New.* Baton Rouge: Louisiana State University Press, 1988.

Russell, Lewis C. "Georgia Towns Moved in War." *Atlanta Journal Magazine,* 28 February 1932. 6.

Samuel Hollingsworth Stout Papers. MSS 274. Emory University. Atlanta, Georgia.

Samuel P. Richards Papers, MSS 176. Atlanta History Center. Includes Richards' wartime diary, now published as Wendy Hamand Venet, ed., *Sam Richards's Civil War Diary: A Chronicle of the Atlanta Home Front* (Athens: University of Georgia Press, 2009).

Scaife, William R. *The Campaign for Atlanta.* Saline MI: McNaughton & Gunn, 1993.

Schroeder-Lein, Glenna R. *Confederate Hospitals on the Move: Samuel H. Stout and the Army of Tennessee.* Columbia: University of South Carolina Press, 1994.

Scott, Carole E. "Total War Comes to New Manchester." *Blue & Gray* 12/2 (December 1994): 22–26.

Scott, James G., and Edward A. Wyatt IV. *Petersburg's Story: A History.* Petersburg: Titmust Optical Company, 1960.

Sears, Stephen W. *George B. McClellan: The Young Napoleon.* New York: Ticknor & Fields, 1988.

Secrist, Philip. "Life in Atlanta." *Civil War Times Illustrated* 9/4 (July 1970): 30–38.

Selby, John. *Stonewall Jackson as Military Commander.* London: B. T. Batsfords, 1968.

Shannon, Margaret. "Court Asked to Save Historic Home Here." *Atlanta Journal,* 10 December 1947, 1, 20.

———. "New Plaque Slated for 'Eternal Flame.'" *Atlanta Journal,* 25 April 1949, 14.

Shavin, Norman. "Thanks 'Cump." *Atlanta Magazine* 16/1 (May 1976): 11.

Sherman, William T. *Memoirs of General William T. Sherman.* 2 volumes. New York: D. Appleton and Company, 1875.

"Sherman Takes Heat." *Atlanta Journal-Constitution.* 9 September 2001, D7.

"Sherman's Character Assessed." *Atlanta Constitution,* 20 February 1891, 1.

"Sherman's Funeral." *Atlanta Constitution,* 20 February 1891, 1.

"Sherman's Shells Burst on Street Where Vets Unite." *Atlanta Journal,* 5 October 1919, 3.

"Sherman Strikes a Pose." *Civil War Times Illustrated* 8/9 (January 1970): 15–17.

Shingleton, Royce. *Richard Peters: Champion of the New South.* Macon GA: Mercer University Press, 1985.

Simms, William Gillmore. *Sack and Destruction of the City of Columbia, S.C. to Which Is Added a List of the Property Destroyed.* Columbia: Press of the Daily Phoenix, 1865.

Simpson, Brooks D., and Jean V. Berlin, editors. *Sherman's Civil War: Selected Correspondence of William T. Sherman, 1860–1865.* Chapel Hill: University of North Carolina Press, 1999.

Singer, Ralph Benjamin. "Confederate Atlanta." Ph.D. dissertation, University of Georgia, 1973.

Sinks, Alva E. Letter to "Dear Father," 20 September 1864. MSS 732. Georgia Historical Society, Savannah.

Slocum, Charles Elihu. *The Life and Services of Major-General Henry Warner Slocum.* Toledo OH: Slocum Publishing Co., 1913.

Smith, Charles H. *Bill Arp's Peace Papers.* New York: G. W. Carleton & Co. 1873.

———. *Bill Arp, So Called. A Side Show of the Southern Side of the War.* New York: Metropolitan Record Office, 1866.

Smith, George Gilman. "Recollections of an Atlanta Boy 1847–1855." *Atlanta Journal,* 2 October 1909, 7.

Smith, Gustavus W. "The Georgia Militia about Atlanta." In *Battles and Leaders of the Civil War,* edited by Robert Underwood Johnson and Clarence Clough Buel, 4:331–35. 4 volumes. New York: Century Company, 1888.

Smith, John Robert. "The Day Atlanta Was Occupied." *Atlanta Historical Bulletin* 21/3 (Fall 1977): 61–70.

Smith, Mollie. "Dodging Shells in Atlanta." *Atlanta Journal Magazine,* 24 March 1929, 13.

Smith, Ralph. "In Crackerland." *Atlanta Journal,* 17 December 1936, 9.

Snell, James P. Typescript diary, Illinois Historical Society. Copy courtesy of Dr. Albert Castel, Columbus, Ohio.

Speed, Thomas. Manuscript letterbook. Filson Club, Louisville, Kentucky. Copy courtesy of Dr. Albert Castel.

Speer, Lonnie R. *Portals to Hell: Military Prisons of the Civil War.* Mechancsburg PA: Stackpole Books, 1997.

Spiller and Burr Pistol Factory Records, 1861–1863. MSS 334F. Atlanta History Center.

Stackpole, Edward J. *Drama on the Rappahannock: The Fredericksburg Campaign.* Harrisburg PA: Stackpole Company, 1957.

Stanley, Henry D. Diary. MSS 645. Atlanta History Center.

Steele, Christy, and Anne Todd, editors. *A Confederate Girl: The Diary of Carrie Berry 1864.* Mankato MN: Blue Earth Books, 2000.

Still, William N., Jr. *Confederate Shipbuilding.* Columbia: University of South Carolina Press, 1987.

———. "Facilities for the Construction of War Vessels in the Confederacy." *Journal of Southern History* 31/3 (August 1965): 285–304.

Stinson, Byron. "Night Blindness." *Civil War Times Illustrated* 4/9 (January 1966): 30.

———. "Scurvy in the Civil War." *Civil War Times Illustrated* 5/5 (August 1966): 20–25.

Storrs, John W. *The "Twentieth Connecticut": A Regimental History.* Ansonia CT: Press of the Naugatuck Valley Sentinel, 1886.

Strayer, Larry M., and Richard A. Baumgartner, editors. *Echoes of Battle: The Atlanta Campaign.* Huntington WV: Blue Acorn Press, 1991.

Strong, William E. "The Death of General James B. McPherson." In *Military Essays and Recollections,* 1:311–44. Chicago: A. C. McClurg & Company, 1891.

Sumner, David E. "Everybody's Cousin: John J. Thrasher Was One of Atlanta's Founders and Most Colorful Figures." *Georgia Historical Quarterly* 84/2 (Summer 2000): 295–307.

Swain, Craig. "Yankee Super Gun." *Civil War Times* 49/4 (August 2011): 49–51.

Sylvester, Lorna Lutes. "'Gone for a Soldier': The Civil War letters of Charles Harding Cox." *Indiana Magazine of History* 48/3 (September 1972): 181–239. Cox's manuscript letters are in the Charles Harding Cox Papers, MSS 330 (box 1, folder 2), Emory University.

Tappan, George, editor. *The Civil War Journal of Lieutenant Russell M Tuttle, New York Volunteer Infantry.* Jefferson NC: McFarland & Company, 2006.

Tate, James H. *Keeper of the Flame: The Story of the Atlanta Gas Light Company, 1856–1985.* Atlanta: Atlanta Gas Light Company, 1985.

Taylor, Arthur Reed. "From the Ashes: Atlanta During the Reconstruction, 1865–1876." Ph.D. dissertation, Emory University, 1973.

Taylor, F. Jay, editor. *Reluctant Rebel: The Secret Diary of Robert Patrick, 1861–1865.* Baton Rouge: Louisiana State University Press, 1959.

Taylor, Paul. *Orlando M. Poe: Civil War General and Great Lakes Engineer.* Kent OH: Kent State University Press, 2009.

"Ten Years Ago. Atlanta Then and Now." *Atlanta Constitution,* 15 December 1874, 4. Reprint of "Civis," "Letter from Atlanta," *Augusta Chronicle & Sentinel,* 21 December 1864.

"Thirty Years Ago. The Old Trout House Fell Under the Torch of General Sherman." *Atlanta Constitution,* 8 April 1894, 4.

"This House Used by General Sherman." *Atlanta Constitution,* 20 July 1898, 23.

Thomas, Dean S. *Cannons: An Introduction to Civil War Artillery.* Gettysburg: Thomas Publications, 1985.

Thomas, Emory M. *The Confederacy as Revolutionary Experience.* Englewood Cliffs NJ: Prentice-Hall, 1971.

———. *The Confederate Nation, 1861–1865.* New York: Harper & Row, 1979.

Thomas, Isabelle Ormond. "Pioneer Woman Tells Interesting Story of Early Days in Atlanta." *Atlanta Journal,* 24 November 1912, S17.

Thomas Maguire Papers. MSS 145, Atlanta History Center.

Thompson, C. Mildred. *Reconstruction in Georgia: Economic, Social, Political, 1865–1872.* New York: Columbia University Press, 1913.

Thornton, Ella Mae. "Mr. S.P. Richards." *Atlanta Historical Bulletin* 3/12 (December 1937): 73–79.

Toombs, Samuel. *Reminiscences of the War, Comprising a Detailed Account of the Experiences of the Thirteenth Regiment of New Jersey Volunteers.* Orange NJ: Journal Office, 1878.

Tower, R. Lockwood, editor. *A Carolinian Goes to War: The Civil War Narrative of Arthur Middleton Manigault, Brigadier General, C.S.A.* Columbia: University of South Carolina Press, 1983.

Trask, W. L. War Journal. Microfilm at Emory University, Atlanta, Georgia. Typescript at Kennesaw Mountain National Battlefield Park.

Trimble, Harvey M., editor. *History of the Ninety-Third Regiment Illinois Volunteer Infantry.* Chicago: Blakely Printing Co, 1989.

Trudeau, Noah Andre. *Southern Storm: Sherman's March to the Sea.* New York: HarperCollins, 2008.

———. *The Last Citadel: Petersburg, Virginia, June 1864–April 1865.* Boston: Little, Brown and Company, 1991.

Turner, Maxine. *Navy Gray: A Story of the Confederate Navy on the Chattahoochee and Apalichicola Rivers.* Tuscaloosa: University of Atlanta Press, 1988.

Tuthill, Richard S. "An Artilleryman's Recollections of the Battle of Atlanta." In *The Atlanta Papers,* compiled by Sydney C. Kerksis, 431–49. Dayton OH: Press of Morningside Bookshop, 1980.

"Two Receptions." *Atlanta Constitution,* 30 January 1879, 1.

Underwood, Adin B. *The Three Years' Service of the Thirty-Third Mass. Infantry Regiment, 1862–1865.* Boston: A. Williams & Company, 1881.

Unidentified Union soldier's letter. "Before Atlanta Georgia Monday Night August 15th 1864." Beverly DuBose Collection, MSS 1020. Atlanta History Center.

Unidentified Union soldier's letter. "Camp near Atlanta," 16 August 1864, MSS 2355. Georgia Historical Society, Savannah. Typescript copy courtesy of Dr. Todd Groce.

US Navy Department. *Official Records of the Union and Confederate Navies in the War of the Rebellion.* 31 volumes. Washington, DC: Government Printing Office, 1894–1922.

US War Department. *The War of the Rebellion: A Compilation of the Official Records of the Union and Confederate Armies.* 128 volumes. Washington, DC: Government Printing Office, 1880–1901.

"Unveiling of Marker in Memory of Father Thomas O'Reilly." *Atlanta Historical Bulletin* 8/30 (October 1945): 8–9.

Vandiver, Frank E. "A Sketch of Efforts to Equip the Confederate Armory at Macon." *Georgia Historical Quarterly* 28/1 (March 1944): 34–40.

———. *Ploughshares into Swords: Josiah Gorgas and Confederate Ordnance.* Austin: University of Texas Press, 1952.

Venet, Wendy Hamand, editor. *Sam Richards's Civil War Diary: A Chronicle of the Atlanta Home Front.* Athens: University of Georgia Press, 2009.

"Veterans Here During Battle of Atlanta Back for Reunion." *Atlanta Constitution,* 8 October 1919, 10.

Walker, Mary Hubner. *Charles W. Hubner: Poet Laureate of the South.* Atlanta: Cherokee Publishing Company, 1976.

Walker, Peter F. *Vicksburg: A People at War, 1861–1865.* Chapel Hill: University of North Carolina Press, 1960.

Walker, Scott. *Hell's Broke Loose in Georgia: Survival in a Civil War Regiment.* Athens: University of Georgia Press, 2005.

Wall, Joseph Frazier. *Henry Watterson, Reconstructed Rebel.* New York: Oxford University Press, 1956.

Walters, John Bennett. *Merchant of Terror: General Sherman and Total War.* Indianapolis: Bobbs-Merrill Company, 1973.

Walzer, Michael. *Just and Unjust Wars: A Moral Argument with Historical Illustrations.* New York: Basic Books, 2000.

Weddle, Kevin. "'Old Stars': Ormsby MacKnight Mitchel at the Gates of the Confederacy." *Blue & Gray* 4/6 (July 1987): 25–29.

Weiman, David F. "Urban Growth on the Periphery of the Antebellum Cotton Belt: Atlanta, 1847–1860." *Journal of Economic History* 48/2 (June 1988): 259–72.

Welcher, Frank J. *The Union Army 1861–1865: Organization and Operations.* 2 volumes. Bloomington: Indiana University Press, 1993.

Wells, Tom Henderson. *The Confederate Navy: A Study in Organization.* University: University of Alabama Press, 1971.

Welsh, Jack D. *Two Confederate Hospitals and Their Patients: Atlanta to Opelika.* Macon GA: Mercer University Press, 2005.

"West End Thinks Japs Are Here When Civil War Shell Explodes." *Atlanta Journal,* 22 April 1942, 5.

Wheeler, Joseph. Letterbooks, 1863–1865. Alabama Department of Archives and History.

Wheeler, Lysander. Letter, 2 November 1864. Typescript, Illinois Historical Society. Copy courtesy of Dr. Albert Castel, Columbus OH.

[Wigfall, Louise]. *A Southern Girl in '61: The War-Time Memories of a Confederate Senator's Daughter.* New York: Doubleday, Page & Company, 1905.

Wilbur G. Kurtz Collection. MSS 130, Atlanta History Center.

Wiley, Bell I. "A Story of 3 Southern Officers." *Civil War Times Illustrated* 3/1 (April 1964): 6–9, 28–34.

Wiley, Bell Irvin. *The Life of Billy Yank: The Common Soldier of the Union.* Indianapolis: Bobbs-Merrill, 1951.

Wilkens, John A. to "Dear Sister," 5 September 1864. Wilkens Collection, Indiana Historical Society. Copy courtesy of Dr. Albert Castel, Columbus OH.

William M. McNaught Papers. MSS 156. Atlanta History Center.

Williams' Atlanta Directory, City Guide and Business Mirror. Atlanta: M. Lynch, 1859.

Williams, Noble C. *Echoes from the Battlefield: or, Southern Life During the War.* Atlanta: Franklin Printing Company, 1902.

Wills, Brian Steel. *A Battle from the Start: The Life of Nathan Bedford Forrest.* New York: HarperCollins, 1992.

Wilson, Charles Reagan. *Baptized in Blood: The Religion of the Lost Cause, 1865–1920.* Athens: University of Georgia Press, 1980.

Wilson, Quintus. "Confederate Press Association: A Pioneer News Agency." *Journalism Quarterly* 26/4 (June 1949): 160–66.

Winship-Flournoy Family Papers. MSS 209. Atlanta History Center.

Winters, John D. *The Civil War in Louisiana.* Baton Rouge: Louisiana State University Press, 1963.

Wise, Stephen R. *Gate of Hell: Campaign for Charleston Harbor, 1863.* Columbia: University of South Carolina Press, 1994.

———. *Lifeline of the Confederacy: Blockade Running During the Civil War.* Columbia: University of South Carolina Press, 1988.

Wittenberg, Eric J. "The Shelling of Carlisle." *Blue & Gray* 24/2 (Summer 2007): 41–46.

"Wm. T., Come, Sir!" *Atlanta Constitution,* 31 January 1879, 1.

Woodward, C. Van. "The Irony of Southern History." *Journal of Southern History* 19/1 (February 1953): 3–19.

Woodworth, Edwin C. Letter to mother, 14 July 1864. MS 645, box 2, folder 19. Atlanta History Center.

Woodworth, Steven E. *Nothing But Victory: The Army of Tennessee, 1861–1865.* New York: Alfred A. Knopf, 2005.

Wortman, Marc. *The Bonfire: The Siege and Burning of Atlanta.* New York: Public Affairs, 2009.

Wright, Moses H. Compiled Service Record. RG 109, National Archives. Microfilm copy, Georgia Department of Archives and History.

Wylie, Lollie Belle. "Interesting Sketches of Pioneer Women." *Atlanta Journal,* 13 June 1909, S3.

———. "Interesting Sketches of Pioneer Women." *Atlanta Journal,* 20 June 1909, **[PAGES?]**.

———."Interesting Sketches of Pioneer Women." *Atlanta Journal,* 1 August 1909, S4.

———. "Interesting Sketches of Pioneering Women." *Atlanta Journal,* 8 May 1910, S9.

Zaworski, Robert E. *Confederate Sections at Oakland Cemetery Atlanta Georgia: History and Restoration.* 2 volumes. Self-published, 1996.

————. *Headstones of Heroes: The Restoration and History of Confederate Graves in Atlanta's Oakland Cemetery.* Paducah KY: Turner Publishing, 1998.

Zinn, John G. *The Mutinous Regiment: The Thirty-Third New Jersey in the Civil War.* Jefferson NC: McFarland & Company, 2005.

A FURTHER WORD ABOUT SOURCES

Any history of Atlanta must begin with the monumental work of Franklin Miller Garrett (1906–2000). Renowned as Atlanta's official historian, he compiled the basic history of the city in his two-volume *Atlanta and Environs,* published in 1954, with subsequent reprint by the University of Georgia Press. Garrett's encyclopedic style, often quoting *verbatim* long documents, may not make for light reading, but *Atlanta and Environs* is the *sine qua non* for serious study of Atlanta's past.

Aged publications add details. *Williams' Atlanta Directory, City Guide, and Business Mirror of 1859* places residences and store locations just before the war; a copy is at the Atlanta History Center. (We still don't know its compiler; even Garrett only refers to "Mr. Williams, of Cincinnati.") One example of the entries is "LUCKEY SOLOMON. Barber Shop and Bathing Saloon, ss. Decatur b Whitehall and Pryor, Atlanta Hotel Bldg." Sol Luckie is the only known African-American victim of Sherman's shelling.

Edward A. Vincent's map of the city, the first (1853), shows street names of the time, which of course have been changed. Reproductions are to be found at the Atlanta History Center, although the best published version can be found in Russell, *Atlanta 1847–1890,* 30. An adaption of 1878 is printed in Garrett's *Atlanta and Environs,* 1:354. Robert Scott Davis has a helpful close-up of Vincent's downtown sector in his *Civil War Atlanta,* 15.

The Confederate arsenal was the city's largest wartime employer. Microfilm records of its work reside at the Atlanta History Center and the University of Georgia. Compiled service record of Moses H. Wright, the arsenal commander, is on microfilm at the Georgia Department of Archives and History in Atlanta; some of Wright's papers also reside at the Atlanta History Center. Stephens Mitchell's short article "Atlanta, the Industrial Heart of the Confederacy" (*Atlanta Historical Bulletin* [May 1930]) contains bits of information on other manufactories not found elsewhere.

The Atlanta History Center has numerous manuscript holdings, including the widely quoted diary of wartime Atlantan Samuel P. Richards (MS 176). Professor Wendy Venet of Georgia State has now edited and published its main part (October 1860–August 1865) as *Sam Richards's Civil War Diary: A Chronicle of the Atlanta Home Front* (2009). With Richards in print, the diary of Carrie Berry (MS 29f), young chronicler throughout August 1864, is probably now the History Center's most important manuscript source on the bombardment.

Essential for an understanding of the city's fortifications are the Lemuel P. Grant Papers (MS 100, Atlanta History Center). Grant's map of the entrenchments around the city as of 12 April 1864 is one of the most important images in Confederate Atlanta's history; it is reproduced in the *Official Records Atlas* as plate 54, 2. Stephens Mitchell quotes some of Grant's correspondence in "Colonel L.P. Grant and the Defenses of Atlanta," *Atlanta Historical Bulletin* (February 1932). Colonel Allen P. Julian (then director of the Atlanta Historical Society) describes Grant's work in "Atlanta's Defenses," *Civil War Times Illustrated*, July 1964. Some manuscript material in the Center archives have been published. One source I have found useful is Jane Bonner Peacock, "A Wartime Story: The Davidson Letters, 1862–1865" *Atlanta Historical Bulletin* (Spring 1975): 8–121, drawing on Julia's letters to her husband (Davidson Family Correspondence, MSS 78). In her letter of 4 August to John, for instance, Julia writes of the shelling deaths of "Mr. Warner & his little daughter Lizzie," who had been neighbors.

Among secondary works on the Atlanta Campaign, the place to start for military operations is always Albert Castel's *Decision in the West: The Atlanta Campaign of 1864* (1992). Richard M. McMurry's *Atlanta 1864: Last Chance for the Confederacy* (2000) is commendable for the author's trademark concision. Russell S. Bonds's *War Like the Thunderbolt: The Battle and Burning of Atlanta* (2009) offers an Atlantan's informed perspective on the campaign, occupation, and burning. Marc Wortman's *The Bonfire: The Siege and Burning of Atlanta* (2009) is less successful. A. A. Hoehling's *Last Train from Atlanta* (1958) presents a documentary history of life in the war-torn city from July to November 1864. Lee Kennett's *Marching through Georgia* (1995), drawing on the author's impressive manuscript research, has material not to be found in other books.

In the past generation of scholarship on the Atlanta Campaign, the signal research in manuscript sources has been admirably conducted by Drs. Castel and Kennett. I have provided little here, but will cite the Joseph Wheeler Letterbooks, 1863–1865, at the Alabama Department of Archives and History. General Wheeler's report from outside of Atlanta on 13 November ("[F]or the last two days the enemy have been burning something in Atlanta and some of the scouts think they are preparing to evacuate....") is important not only for documenting the first fires in Atlanta on 11 November, but also for establishing that Confederate authorities knew of the impending burning of Atlanta. To my knowledge, Wheeler's reports have not been previously cited.

I cover individual Confederate newspapers in the following section, but here I emphasize the bombardment-reporting of Isaac B. Pilgrim, foreman of the *Atlanta Intelligencer*, who stayed in the city when his paper fled to Macon, witnessed the shelling, and filed columns about it. Pilgrim's balanced, detailed reports are arguably the best reporting we have on the Federal cannonade. An example is his remarkable column, "The Houses Shelled in Atlanta," printed in the *Intelligencer* on 6 August. Wallace Reed includes a lengthy, close paraphrasing of it in his *History of Atlanta* (1889), but otherwise Pilgrim's account has gone unrecognized in the literature. On Confederate newspapers as a whole, the basic source remains J. Cutler Andrews, *The South Reports the Civil War* (1970).

Soldiers of both sides wrote in their letters and diaries of the bombardment. Among those published, I have found two of particular value: K. Jack Bauer, ed., *Soldiering: The Civil War Diary of Rice C. Bull, 123rd New York Volunteer Infantry* (1977) and Wirt Armistead Cate, ed., *Two Soldiers: The Campaign Diaries of Thomas J. Key, C.S.A. December 7, 1863–May 17, 1865 and Robert J. Campbell, U.S.A. January 1, 1864–July 21, 1864* (1938). Because I consider the killing of Joseph F. Warner and his daughter Elizabeth on 3 August to be the central incident of Sherman's shelling, Emily F. Molineaux's *Lifetime Recollections...* (1902) is an important source, especially when linked to John E. Haye's story about the tragedy, printed in the *New York Herald*, 9 November 1864.

The chief source on the expulsion of civilians from Atlanta into Confederate lines in September 1864 is the list kept by Lieutenant Colonel William G. Le Duc, "Official account of the people sent south, their numbers and luggage...," first printed as an appendix in the fourth edition of Sherman's *Memoirs* (1892). Wilbur G. Kurtz oversaw its reprinting as "Persons Removed from Atlanta by General W.T. Sherman, Sept. 4, 1864" in the *Atlanta Historical Bulletin* (February 1932). In his research for *Secret Yankees: The Union Circle in Confederate Atlanta*, Thomas G. Dyer found this "Book of Exodus" in the National Archives' record group 393. More recently, Professor Venet has chanced upon it also in National Archives microfilm, misfiled as M 346, roll 114. The Confederate officer in charge at Rough and Ready, Major William Clare, kept his own list of persons received into the lines, but it was not printed with his report of 22 September in the *Official Records* (vol. 38, pt. 3, 993–94). Because of numerical differences with Le Duc's list (1,651 in Le Duc versus 1,168 in Clare) and omissions in Le Duc's of persons we know to have left (e.g., Sidney and Delia Root), the Clare list is an important document that is yet to surface (but is presumably lost. I express my sincere gratitude to DeAnne Blanton, senior archivisit at the National Archives, for her diligent efforts to find Major Clare's listing.).

On the occupation, I find Professor Dyer's *Secret Yankees* to be essential. It was Dr. Dyer who found in the Cogswell Papers (Salem, Massachusetts) the invaluable documents indicating the Federals' plans of destruction. No wartime history of Atlanta should henceforth fail to cite this great achievement, although a couple since its publication in 1999 have done so. Here I wish to thank Irene Axelrod, head research librarian of the Phillips Library, Peabody Essex Museum in Salem, for copies of these key manuscripts.

A number of observant Yanks recorded their impressions during the Federals' occupation and destruction of Atlanta. Their publication, as letters, diaries, and regimental histories, offers a rich body of material. Very important are volumes from the units that served as provost guards during the occupation. For the 2nd Massachusetts: Lyman Richard Comey, ed., *A Legacy of Valor: The Memoirs and Letters of Captain Henry Newton Comey, 2nd Massachusetts Infantry* (2004); and Alonzo H. Quint, *The Record of the Second Massachusetts Infantry* (1867). For the 33rd Massachusetts: Andrew J. Boies, *Record of the Thirty-Third*

Massachusetts Volunteer Infantry, from Aug. 1862 to Aug. 1865 (1880); and Adin B. Underwood, *The Three Years' Service of the Thirty-Third Mass. Infantry Regiment 1862–1865* (1881). For the 111th Pennsylvania: John Richards Boyle, *Soldiers True: The Story of the One Hundred and Eleventh Regiment Pennsylvania Veteran Volunteers, and of Its Campaigns in the War for the Union, 1861–1865* (1903). Charles Fessenden Morse, lieutenant colonel of the 2nd Massachusetts, served as provost marshal of the city during the occupation; his *Letters Written during the Civil War, 1861–1865* (1898) provides information I have not found in other sources.

Beyond these, the more useful titles come from units of the XX Corps, which spent the most time in Atlanta. I note in particular John J. Hight, *History of the Fifty-Eighth Regiment of Indiana Volunteer Infantry* (1895); Edwin E. Marvin, *The Fifth Regiment Connecticut Volunteers* (1889); Frank L. Byrne, ed., *Uncommon Soldiers: Harvey Reid and the 22nd Wisconsin March with Sherman* (2001); and George Tappan, ed., *The Civil War Journal of Lieutenant Russell M. Tuttle, New York Volunteer Infantry* (2006).

When I was reading Dr. Castel's draft of *Decision in the West* in summer 1990, Albert told me that he had researched beyond Sherman's capture of the city, into its occupation by Union troops. He had once thought of including in his book the Federal occupation, and had accumulated research material on it; but by then he had sufficient text already for a sturdy volume. Subsequently, in the rarest display of scholarly generosity I have ever encountered, Dr. Castel sent me his photocopies of Union soldiers' manuscript letters and diaries concerning the occupation, most from Northern libraries and archives that I could never hope to visit, essentially allowing me to use his research work for this present work. In my notes for chapter 5 and the Union occupation, I have credited Albert for these gifts (for instance, the letters of Private Al G. Pugh, Company H, 119th Illinois Infantry, at the Chicago Historical Society). But here I must add further words of thanks to a great scholar of the Civil War's western theater, and to a fine friend.

Of the seven contemporary descriptions of Atlanta's wreckage after the Federals left, Georgia Militia General William P. Howard's is the most valuable, and the most often cited, having appeared (without map) in the *Macon Telegraph*, 10 December 1864, and subsequently in numerous other Southern newspapers. Garrett reprints it entirely in *Atlanta and Environs* (1:653–55) as does Russ Bonds in an appendix of *War Like the Thunderbolt* (408–10). Zachariah A. Rice's letter from Atlanta (20 November 1864), apparently first published in the *Memphis* (Montgomery) *Appeal*, was reprinted in "Atlanta When It Was Left in Ashes," *Atlanta Constitution*, 24 July 1898. It is mentioned by Robert Otis in the *Atlanta Historical Bulletin* (October 1945, 23–24) as from "the Atlanta *Intelligencer* of November 20, 1864," but I do not see it there. James R. Crew's letter of 1 December 1864 is in the Crew Papers (Atlanta History Center) and is published with notes in Annie Laurie Fuller Kurtz, "Atlanta as Sherman Left It," *Atlanta Journal Magazine*, 19 January 1936. The *Atlanta Intelligencer* article "The City" (10 December 1864) has to my knowledge not been reprinted. Nor have "From

Atlanta" in the *Augusta Chronicle & Sentinel* (14 December 1864) and Civis' "Letter from Atlanta," in the *Chronicle & Sentinel* (21 December). The *Atlanta Intelligencer* column "Atlanta—Her Past, Her Present, and Her Future" (20 December 1864) is reprinted in Garrett, *Atlanta & Environs*, I, 655–59, with notes as to sites.

Part of the fun of research and learning—*gaudium eruditionis*, I call it—is finding, even at this late date, manuscript sources not yet cited in other works. An example is Captain John Carr's diary ("Atlanta like Sodom and Gomorrah is doomed") at the Kennesaw Mountain National Battlefield Park (thanks to Willie R. Johnson, park historian). Dr. Todd Groce, president of the Georgia Historical Society in Savannah, generously informed me of a letter in the society holdings (MS 732) by Alva Sinks of the 71st Ohio to his father on 20 September 1864: "the Major part of the Houses on the north side of the city are completely Riddled with shot & shell." Isaac Roseberry of Company D, 1st Michigan Engineers and Mechanics, kept a diary; microfilm copy (MSS 391) is in Emory University's Manuscript, Archives, and Rare Book Library; I learned of it from the Kurtz notebook 10 at the Atlanta History Center, in which was pasted Frank Daniel's article, "Union Soldier's Personal Diary Gives Insight to Atlanta's Past" (*Atlanta Journal*, 18 March 1962). Fortunately, Marc Hoffman's recent history of the 1st Michigan Engineers cites Roseberry's diary. Let us hope that such manuscript nuggets continue to appear, adding to the richness—if that is the word—of the story of Atlanta's demolishment.

I close by recognizing the invaluable work of Wilbur G. Kurtz (1882–1967), the hero for those of us studying Atlanta's Civil War history. His many articles and illustrations, many of which were published in the *Atlanta Constitution* and *Journal*, document information which Kurtz indefatigably pursued and which he struggled to get precisely correct. Kurtz's writings, especially in the 1930s, are especially important because Kurtz often based them on information he obtained by interviewing old-time Atlanta residents. For instance, "Dugout Home in Atlanta" (*Atlanta Journal Magazine*, 10 July 1932) about the Willis bombproof in southwest Atlanta, was based on Kurtz's interview with Joseph Willis's daughter, just months before she died in September 1932.

Kurtz's maps are also treasures. Most useful to me are "Embattled Atlanta" (*Atlanta Constitution*, 20 July 1930) and "Map of Atlanta as of 1938" (prepared for the Atlanta Chamber of Commerce and as yet unpublished, I think). Perambulating the city in the 1920s and '30s, when Civil War entrenchments were still to be found, Kurtz discovered the three earthwork redoubts which held the Federals' 4.5-inch siege cannon north of the city, and quietly inked them into these two maps.

More untapped treasure lies in Kurtz's as-yet-unindexed manuscript notebooks, all reverently stored by the Atlanta History Center. One example is the letter to Kurtz of Augustus F. Hurt (18 September 1913) explaining that his house, behind Federal lines northeast of Atlanta, had been taken down for its wood "to make fire for cooking and other purposes. I know this to be a fact, as I saw hinges and locks and pieces of marble mantels scattered at many places where the soldiers built fires" (notebook 3, p. 241; notebook 6, p. 105–106). The Augustus Hurt house had been Sherman's headquarters on 22 July during the battle of Atlanta, and is depicted in the Cyclorama. Its site is presently that of the President Jimmy Carter Center. To my knowledge, the fate of the A. Hurt house is not in the literature; without Kurtz, we would today be ignorant of it. Heaven knows what else we would have lost had it not been for Wilbur Kurtz and his work.

BIBLIOGRAPHIC REVIEW:
CONFEDERATE NEWSPAPERS AND
THE BOMBARDMENT OF ATLANTA

More important, I think, than a bibliographic list of works cited will be a review of the Confederate newspaper articles that I used to put together the story of Sherman's shelling of Atlanta. Without these contemporaneous and sometimes eyewitness descriptions, no history of the Yankee bombardment would be possible. Indeed, one might judge that the Federal artillery barrage of Atlanta, 20 July–25 August, has not found fuller historical chroniclers to date precisely because Confederate newspapers have been overlooked. Nevertheless, I am very aware that my newspaper research, more extensive on the bombardment than any yet in the literature, is far from complete. More newspapers remain to be consulted by scholars, and their work in years to come will only add more drama and detail to the story of the Yankee bombardment of Atlanta. Dr. Richard McMurry, who probably has done more research in Confederate newspapers than any other scholar, himself acknowledges that his work is incessant and ongoing. As he wryly remarked in a symposium at the Atlanta History Center in February 1998 on "The Press and the American Civil War," "with any luck I may complete the project sometime in the twenty-third or twenty-fourth century."[1]

For these reasons I here list the newspaper articles which I have cited, with a word or two on their most important content. As to names, when the papers refugeed around the South, I adhere to their city of origin, as in *Knoxville Register* and *Memphis Appeal*.

Press Association of the Confederate States. This organization, established in March 1863 in Atlanta by the veteran journalist John S. Thrasher, brought together correspondents, newspapers across the South, and telegraph companies in an effective system of distributing daily news columns—the AP and UPI of the Confederacy. "Probably its greatest accomplishment was the mutual system whereby member editors sent news from their localities to newspapers in other cities," writes the chronicler of the Confederate press, J. Cutler Andrews. Despite considerable obstacles, "it kept on reporting news throughout the war and proved a valuable asset to Confederate journalism."[2]

---

[1] Richard M. McMurry, "The Confederate Newspaper Press and the Civil War: An Overview and a Report on Research in Progress," *Atlanta History* 42/1, 2 (Spring–Summer 1998): 73

[2] J. Cutler Andrews, *The South Reports the Civil War* (Princeton: Princeton University Press, 1970) 58. See also Quintus Wilson, "Confederate Press Association: A Pioneer News Agency," *Journalism Quarterly* 26/4 (June 1949): 160–66; and Ford Risley, "The Confederate

The C.P.A. "Telegraphic" columns appeared in many of the papers I have read; here is a review of the columns that refer to the bombardment of Atlanta, with dates of the column as posted from Atlanta and the newspapers that carried it, typically entitled, "Telegraphic," "By Telegraph" or "Telegraphic Reports of the Confederate Press Association."

25 July: *Macon Telegraph*, 26 July. "Many shells from the enemy's batteries have entered the city. A few houses have been struck, but no material damage done."

"From the Georgia Front. Yankees Shelling the City. No Notice Given to Noncombatants," 26 July: *Mobile Register & Advertiser*, 27 July. "No notice of the intention to shell the city was given to enable women and children to be removed to a place of safety. The enemy's barbarous violation of the usages of civilized warfare only enabled him to murder a few noncombatants."

30 July: *Augusta Chronicle & Sentinel*, 2 August. "A most furious shelling of Atlanta has been going on during the last two days. A lady on the train was killed by a shell at Atlanta this morning."

2 August: *Macon Telegraph*, 3 August. "The enemy shelled the city half an hour last evening."

"Latest from the Front. Shelling of Atlanta. A Young Lady Killed," 4 August: *Augusta Chronicle & Sentinel*, 5 August. "The city was vigorously shelled…during the night, and one young lady was killed by a piece of shell."

5 August: *Atlanta Intelligencer*, 6 August. "There was comparative quiet in the city throughout the night, and but few shells thrown, resulting, as usual, in no damage."

6 August: *Macon Telegraph*, 8 August. "Comparative quiet reigned in the city last night."

8 August: *Macon Telegraph*, 9 August. "No shells were thrown into the city yesterday."

"Latest from Atlanta. Heaviest Shelling of the City Yet. One citizen killed and a child wounded," 10 August: *Atlanta Intelligencer*, 11 August. "The heavy cannonading yesterday ceased at 5 P.M.… In the city one citizen was killed and a child was wounded. The fire upon the city was the heaviest yet experienced, many buildings being struck."

12 August: *Macon Telegraph*, 13 August. "The batteries upon Marietta Street and east of the State road opened upon the city at one o'clock this morning and continued up to the present time striking a number of houses on McDonough street. No casualties reported."

13 August: *Augusta Chronicle & Sentinel*, 14 August. "No shells were thrown into the city during last night or to-day."

Press Association: Cooperative News Reporting of the War," *Civil War History* 47/3 (September 2001): 222–39.

"Enemy Furiously Shell Atlanta. A Warehouse Fired. Noble Conduct of the Firemen. The Flames Extinguished. No one Hurt," 14 August: *Augusta Chronicle & Sentinel*, 16 August. "The enemy opened fire upon the city with six batteries at eight last night.... The firing was very heavy and continued till 4 A.M. About midnight a shell entered the frame storehouse of Biggers & Co., on Marietta street, between that and Peachtree church, setting fire to some loose cotton. The flames spread rapidly and the buildings were soon in flames. The fire bell was rung, and the engine No. 3 reported promptly. The enemy immediately concentrated his fire on the point, but the firemen nobly stood their ground, and despite the rain of shells, succeeded in saving the large warehouse of Kyle & Co. The other buildings on the square were consumed. Not a citizen was injured, the women and children having sought safety in the bomb proofs."

15 August: *Augusta Chronicle & Sentinel*, 16 August. "But few shells were thrown into the city.—Some of them had Scriptural quotations in Hebrew pasted on them."

17 August: *Atlanta Intelligencer*, 18 August. "A slow fire was kept up all night, which resulted in the killing of one person."

"Shelling of the City. Several Citizens Killed and Wounded," 19 August: *Augusta Chronicle & Sentinel*, 23 August. "This morning the enemy's batteries in front of the city opened heavily.... A forty two pounder Sawyer shell exploded in the house of Mr. Peters in Atlanta, killing Captain Garrison of the 14th Texas Cavalry, and two children, and wounding several ladies." [In this telegraphic news column as published in the Savannah *Republican*, 23 August, "Captain Garrison of the 14th Texas Cavalry" is printed as "Captain Davidson, formerly of the 14th Texas Cavalry."]

22 August: *Augusta Chronicle & Sentinel*, 23 August. "No shelling yesterday. The enemy deny the charge of shelling the city, and claim that their shots were aimed at the defences."

23 August: *Atlanta Intelligencer*, 24 August. "The enemy shelled the city at intervals all night.... A lady was killed near the Express Office last evening by a shell, and a soldier lost his leg."

24 August: *Atlanta Intelligencer*, 25 August. "The enemy shelled the center of the city steadily last night. McDaniel's warehouse on Hunter street between Pryor and Whitehall was destroyed by fire this morning at 6 o'clock. Five hundred bales of cotton were consumed. The City Fire Battalion was promptly on hand and checked the spread of the conflagration under a heavy fire from the enemy's batteries. A small frame building near the State Railroad Shop was also burned last night. Both buildings were fired by shells. No casualties resulted from the shelling."

25 August: *Atlanta Intelligencer*, 26 August. "For some cause the Federal batteries are silent this morning. Last night a shell struck the First Presbyterian Church, on Marietta street, and exploded in the basement, where a number of

citizens had sought shelter. A fragment of the shell cut off an arm of a citizen lying on a bed in the basement. There were no other casualties."

26 August: *Macon Telegraph*, 27 August. "With the exception of three shells fired from the right last night, before the enemy withdrew from that point, the enemy have not shelled the city for twenty four hours."

Atlanta Intelligencer (microfilm files at Emory University and at the Atlanta History Center). *Intelligencer* microfilms at Emory and Atlanta History Center show 10 July as the last issue in Atlanta before the paper left for Macon, but Ralph Singer's dissertation cites an issue of the *Intelligencer* for the 11 July as well.[3] The microfilms show daily issues resuming on 3 August, but the *Augusta Chronicle and Sentinel* of 27 July states that the first issue of the relocated *Intelligencer* was issued on "Saturday last," *i.e.*, 23 July. The *Columbus Enquirer* of 30 July quotes an *Intelligencer* column of the 24 July. During the Federals' semi-siege and bombardment, the paper's foreman, Isaac B. Pilgrim, remained in Atlanta, and sent to Macon frequent reports on the shelling of the city. A brief review of the paper's wartime experience is Alan Bussel, "The Atlanta *Daily Intelligencer* Covers Sherman's March," *Journalism Quarterly* 51/3 (Autumn 1974): 405–10.

"The Position in Georgia," 24 July (as quoted in *Columbus Enquirer* of 30 July). "The smallest amount of damage to life has been effected by their explosions."

"The Position in Georgia," 26 July (as dated in *New York Times*, 16 August; also reprinted in *Macon Telegraph*, 26 July; and in *Augusta Constitutionalist*, 29 July). One of the first lengthy reports of the bombardment: "Several persons have been killed and wounded by these explosions.... A great many houses on Peachtree street have been completely torn to pieces by the destructive shots that rained on it."

"From the Front," *Atlanta Intelligencer* (n.d.): quoted in *Augusta Chronicle & Sentinel*, 28 July. "Several persons have been killed and wounded by the explosions."

Isaac B. Pilgrim, "The Houses Shelled in Atlanta" (Atlanta, 4 August): *Atlanta Intelligencer*, 6 August. The most comprehensive account of shell-damage to Atlanta buildings after two weeks of bombardment; obviously based on Pilgrim's walks through the city. He also recounted what he had heard of casualties. Pilgrim's column is lengthily paraphrased in Reed, *History of Atlanta*, 177–79. Later local writers, drawing on Reed's text, also rephrased Pilgrim's observations in "Houses Shelled"; see Bruffey, "The Siege of Atlanta—and Afterwards," *Atlanta Constitution Magazine*, 5 October 1919.

---

[3] Ralph Benjamin Singer, "Confederate Atlanta" (Ph.D. diss., University of Georgia, 1973) 247.

"P.," "For the Intelligencer" (Atlanta, 4 August): *Atlanta Intelligencer*, 6 August; also in *Columbus Times*, 8 August. Despite frequent comments on the city's depopulation, "P." (presumably Isaac Pilgrim) observed, "in perambulating the town,…about two-thirds of the residences of the city are occupied by families, and several of them the oldest inhabitants of the place."

"C-," "Editor of the Intelligencer" (Atlanta, 12 August): *Atlanta Intelligencer*, 14 August. Describes a "bomb proof" in the yard of a dwelling on Peachtree Street.

[Isaac B. Pilgrim], "Atlanta": *Atlanta Intelligencer*, 13 August. Reprinted in *Savannah Republican*, 15 August. "It is impossible to enumerate all the buildings that have been struck either by shells or fragments…. You can find evidences of the enemy's barbarity in almost every house or lot in the city, except in the Southern and Southeastern portion." Given this considerable physical damage, "the wonder is that so few of the citizens have been hurt."

"Atlanta": *Atlanta Intelligencer*, 14 August. Residences of William Solomon and Judge Lyon (John Neal) reported as struck by shells; "the former being severely injured."

"Fire in Atlanta—Shelling of the City" (Atlanta, 14 August): *Atlanta Intelligencer*, 16 August; reprinted in *Columbus Times*, 17 August. Identifies buildings damaged or destroyed by the fire of 13–14 August. "Since the 22nd of July last, there has been scarcely any provisions for sale here."

"MIRGLIP," "Special Correspondence" (Atlanta, 17 August): *Atlanta Intelligencer*, 19 August. The industrious Isaac Pilgrim relates a shell explosion he actually witnessed while writing a column for his paper, and names several victims, including one Francis Hale, employee of the Western & Atlantic, killed when a shell struck the railroad woodshop.

"MIRGLIP," "Special Correspondence": *Atlanta Intelligencer*, 18 August. A ball was held at the Medical College, 12 August. Pilgrim also examined damage to the *Intelligencer* building caused by an unexploded shell; the fire battalion was keeping the projectile as a relic.

PILGRIM, "Special Correspondence" (Atlanta, 18 August): *Atlanta Intelligencer*, 20 August. "There has been several persons wounded in the city to-day by fragments of shells, but I have been unable to learn their names."

"From Atlanta" (22 August): *Atlanta Intelligencer*, 23 August. A shell explosion killed a Captain Garrison and two children. (See C.P.A. "Telegraphic" column in *Augusta Chronicle & Sentinel*, 23 August.)

PILGRIM, "Special Correspondence" (undated, but 23 August): *Atlanta Intelligencer*, 25 August. "The city is terribly torn to pieces by the shells, especially Marietta street. Some houses on this street have been literally torn to pieces." Pilgrim claims to have heard "a prominent physician" in the city say that there had been 107 amputations among civilians as a result of the bombardment.

"The Position": *Atlanta Intelligencer*, 24 August. "The city is very desolate. There are few people remaining who could get away…. The shelling process has been increased in intensity during the past four or five days...that portion of Atlanta lying along Marietta street, has been furiously bombarded, making the avenues of travel perfectly untenable and the destruction of property almost unprecedented, yet it only effects the ruin of property, nothing else is gained by all his furious work."

PILGRIM, "For the Intelligencer. Special Correspondence. Atlanta, Aug. 24, 1864": *Atlanta Intelligencer*, 26 August. On fires in city set by Union artillery night of 23 August, and work of city firemen.

"B.," "Atlanta Correspondence" (24 August): *Atlanta Intelligencer*, 27 August. Describes structures burned in fires of 23–24 August, including the Holland warehouse on Alabama Street, which housed cotton; recommends removing cotton and tobacco from city to reduce fire hazard. "B." was probably William D. Barr, who also wrote as "B." for the *Memphis Appeal*.

"Our Atlanta Friends": *Atlanta Intelligencer*, 2 September. Of some 300 firemen, only 70 or 80 remained in the city in late August to fight the fires started by Northern shells.

"An Atlanta Refugee," "Atlanta Calumniated"; editorial, "Atlanta Calumniated": *Atlanta Intelligencer*, 16 October. On the disputed estimate of 497 civilians killed and 691 wounded by the Union bombardment.

Atlanta Southern Confederacy (microfilm files at University of Georgia). *Confederacy* microfilm files in Athens stop at 9 July, but the *Augusta Chronicle & Sentinel*, 12 July, quotes from the issue of 10 July. The *Augusta Chronicle & Sentinel* of 21 July quotes the *Atlanta Confederacy*, suggesting it had resumed publication in Macon by that date. Its format was likely a shortened "extra," according to Andrews.[4] Griffith and Talmadge cite an issue of the *Southern Confederate Extra* issued from Macon on 1 September, the day Confederate troops evacuated Atlanta.[5]

"Georgia" (quoting "Macon *Confederate* of Saturday" [30 July]): in *Richmond Sentinel*, 1 August. "Atlanta is completely stripped of everything in the way of army material, and the greater portion of its private and personal movable property. If the enemy capture it, they will not get much in that respect."

"Correspondence Atlanta Confederacy. From the Front" (10 August): *Columbus Enquirer*, 14 August. Claims Sherman himself ordered his arterillists not to fire upon the Rebel fortifications, but upon the city itself.

Augusta Chronicle & Sentinel (microfilm files at University of Georgia and Emory University). Earl Bell and Kenneth Crabbe, *The Augusta Chronicle: Indomitable Voice of Dixie, 1785–1960* (Athens: University of Georgia Press, 1960)

---

[4] Andrews, *The South Reports the Civil War*, 455.
[5] Louis Turner Griffith and John Erwin Talmadge, *Georgia Journalism, 1763–1950* (Athens: University of Georgia Press, 1951) 81.

is a history of the paper, albeit with only slight reference to the Atlanta Campaign.

"From Atlanta": *Augusta Chronicle & Sentinel*, 26 July. "A gentleman who left Atlanta on Saturday [23 July] says that…several buildings had already been destroyed, among them the large one occupied by Mr. Honnecut as a drug store."

"Rover," "Letter from the Georgia Front. Special Correspondence" (Atlanta, 3 August): *Augusta Chronicle & Sentinel*, 7 August. "Four casualties only have occurred. An old lady was killed in her bed, on the north end of Marietta street; one teamster was killed and another wounded, near the Macon depot; and a negro boy killed." "Rover" also points out that Sherman's bombardment "was commenced without any notification to noncombatants to leave."

"Rover," "Letters from the Georgia Front" (Atlanta, 4, 5 August): *Augusta Chronicle & Sentinel*, 9 August. The death of the Warners, 3 August; only one shell thrown into the city, night of 4 August.

"Rover," "Letter from the Georgia Front" (Atlanta, 8 August): *Augusta Chronicle & Sentinel*, 12 August. Judges that supplies of beef, bacon and cornmeal entering Atlanta were adequate to feed Hood's army, though vegetables were scanty.

"Rover," "From the Georgia Front" (Atlanta, 12 August): *Augusta Chronicle & Sentinel*, 16 August. "Within the past two days, on two occasions we have been visited with a shower of shells, each time of several hours in duration.… One lady and a child were severely bruised by heavy splinters knocked about, and one soldier killed. The escape from personal damage was wonderful."

"Rover," From the Georgia Front" (Atlanta, 13 August): *Augusta Chronicle & Sentinel*, 19 August. The downtown fire on the night of 12 August.

"Rover," "From the Georgia Front" (Atlanta, 15 August): *Augusta Chronicle & Sentinel*, 20 August. Since the bombardment of night of 13 August, "the city has received but little attention from the enemy; the occasional shells since thrown scarce attract momentary attention. Why we have been thus favored no one pretends to conjecture, but all rejoice at the apparent neglect."

"Rover," "Letter from the Georgia Front" (Atlanta, 17 August): *Augusta Chronicle & Sentinel*, 21 August. "We are beginning to witness the opening of a little trade in the City," with some vendors profiting from high prices.

"From Atlanta" (19 August): *Augusta Chronicle & Sentinel*, 23 August. In a rare instance, a shell victim is named, Captain Garrison of the 14th Texas Cavalry, killed 19 August. (See also the *Intelligencer*, 23 August.)

"Rover," "From the Georgia Front" (Atlanta, 19 August): *Augusta Chronicle & Sentinel*, 25 August. "Since my last [17 August] two men and a child have been killed, and a few wounded—none of the latter, however, seriously."

"Rover," "Special Correspondence" (Atlanta, 23 August): *Augusta Chronicle & Sentinel*, 28 August. Casualties for the previous twenty-four hours were two women killed and one soldier and a boy severely wounded.

"Rover," "Letters from the Georgia Front" (24 August): *Augusta Chronicle & Sentinel*, 28 August. On the fires of 23–24 August.

"The Georgia Front": *Augusta Chronicle & Sentinel*, 24 August. Editorial castigates Sherman for claiming that this artillery was aimed only at Confederate fortifications.

"Rover," "From the Georgia Front" (Atlanta, 25 August): *Augusta Chronicle & Sentinel*, 30 August. "Not a single shell has been fired since sunrise this morning."

"Rover," "Letter from the Georgia Front" (Atlanta, 27 August): *Augusta Chronicle & Sentinel*, 31 August. "Throughout the twenty-four hours ending yesterday morning...the exemption of the city from the usual visitation of the enemy's shells, created no little wonderment."

"From the Front": *Augusta Chronicle & Sentinel*, 31 August. "Several unexploded Yankee shells have exploded in Atlanta from careless handling recently—killing and wounding many citizens." States that "all the houses vacated between the Yankee fortifications and the Chattahoochie have been demolished."

"From the Front": *Augusta Chronicle & Sentinel*, 1 September, Hood's army is reported to be "abundantly supplied with provisions of all kinds."

Augusta Constitutionalist (microfilm files at Emory University and University of Georgia).

"The Front": *Augusta Constitutionalist*, 26 July. "The Yankees are shelling the city, but as to the amount of damage resulting from the fire we are without information."

"Grape," "The Siege of Atlanta" (Atlanta, 26 July): *Augusta Constitutionalist*, 29 July. A shell incident of 26 July: several members of a family wounded, one child killed. ("Grape" is identified as Henry Watterson in Andrews, *The South Reports the Civil War*, 551.)

"Grape," "From Atlanta" (3 August): *Augusta Constitutionalist*, 10 August. Observes that the "unfortunate citizens of the town, most of them of the poorer classes, who have been compelled to remain" face both shells and meager food supply.

"Car," "From Atlanta" (16 August): *Augusta Constitutionalist*, 20 August. Estimates 5,000 shells were fired into the city during the night bombardment of 15–16 August.

"Lavengro," "From Atlanta" (23 August): *Augusta Constitutionalist*, 28 August. "Can you imagine anything more brutal than the bombardment of a city, crowded with poor people, who are unable to get away, and are forced by their poverty to remain and suffer?"

"Grape," "From Atlanta. The Situation Unchanged" (undated, ca. 24 August): *Augusta Constitutionalist*, 28 August. Henry Watterson complains poetically of "shells all night, shells all day, shells for breakfast, dinner and tea."

"Grape," "From Atlanta. Trying to Burn Atlanta" (26 August): *Augusta Constitutionalist,* 28 August. Bitter denunciation of Sherman, "the intolerable wretch."

Chattanooga Rebel (microfilm, Tennessee State Library and Archives). The *Rebel* left its home city in August 1863, moving to Marietta. By the third week in June it had relocated in Griffin, south of Atlanta.[6] Microfilm copy at the Tennessee State Library and Archives in Nashville shows issue only of 22 August during the period of bombardment, 20 July–25 August, but its columns of other dates were occasionally reprinted in the Confederate press. The *Rebel* was apparently circulated in Atlanta during the semi-siege; Union General Thomas stated in his report of 13 September 1864, "for details I have the honor to refer you to...an article in the Chattanooga Rebel, published at Griffin, Ga., August 25."[7]

"Effects of the Bombardment": paraphrased in *Columbus Sun,* 10 August. Another account of the Warners' deaths. "The same shell struck his little daughter, aged seven years, tearing out her bowels. The shell did not explode."

"Special Correspondence of the Rebel" (Atlanta, 2 August): quoted in *Columbus Times,* 4 August. General John C. Carter's brigade donated a day's rations for the poor civilians in Atlanta.

Columbus Enquirer (microfilm copy at University of Georgia).

"J.T.G.," "From Our Correspondent with General Hood's Army": *Columbus Enquirer,* 30 July. Reports one woman and two children killed by shells.

"J.T.G.," "From Our Correspondent with General Hood's Army" (Atlanta, 30 July): *Columbus Enquirer,* 7 August. Reports significant Union shellfire on area of downtown railroad depot, 27–28 July.

"General Hood Increases His Army," quoted in *Atlanta Intelligencer,* 10 August. "For two days [Sherman] has not thrown a shell into the place."

"J.T.G.," "From Our Correspondent with General Hood's Army" (Atlanta, 16 August): *Columbus Enquirer,* 20 August. On Union bombardment of ca. 12–15 August.

Columbus Sun (microfilm copy, University of Georgia).

"Confederate" (Atlanta, 23 July): *Columbus Sun,* 28 July. "The city is almost entirely abandoned, and it presents a sad and gloomy appearance."

---

[6] James W. Livingood, "The Chattanooga Rebel," *East Tennessee Historical Society Publications* 39 (1967): 51; Roy Morris, "The Chattanooga Daily Rebel," *Civil War Times Illustrated* 23/7 (November 1984): 22, 24.

[7] *OR,* vol. 38, pt. 1, p. 163.

"J.A.B." (Fayetteville, Georgia, 28 July): *Columbus Sun,* 4 August. "The Yankees...know that there are hundreds of women and children in such a city as Atlanta, that can't get away."

"Confederate" (Atlanta, 5 August): *Columbus Sun,* 9 August. Besides the two Warners killed on the night of 3 August, "a young lady whose name I have been unable to learn" was also slain.

"Distress in Atlanta": *Columbus Sun,* 14 August. "Nocturnal thieves" stealing from citizens' private gardens.

"Mentor," "Letter from Atlanta" (17 August): *Columbus Sun,* 21 August. "Every citizen has a bomb proof in his yard."

"S.D.L.," "Correspondence of the Daily Sun" (Atlanta, 20 August): *Columbus Sun,* 25 August. "A soldier in town was killed by a shell and a Mrs. Baldwin had both feet badly injured" on 19 August. Mentions Confederate soldiers stripping suburban houses for wood to build trench-line shelters.

Columbus Times (microfilm at University of Georgia).

"Occasional," "Correspondence of the Times" (Atlanta, 13 August): *Columbus Times,* 17 August. "The Yankees continue their uncivilized and brutal mode of warfare of shelling the women and children of the city. So far, thanks to a kind providence, but few casualties have occurred."

"Outline," "Special Correspondence of the Times" (Atlanta, 24 August): *Columbus Times,* 27 August. "The Express and Post Offices, and the stores and dwellings situated between Whitehall street and the City Hall, are being battered pretty severely just now."

"Outline," "Special Correspondence of the Times" (Atlanta, 26 August): *Columbus Times,* 29 August; also quoted in *Augusta Constitutionalist,* 3 September; and in Richmond *Sentinel,* 2 September. Explosion of a shell in the basement of the First Presbyterian Church downtown, the night of 24 August; the lard oil factory/Holland warehouse fire of 24 August.

"Outline," "Special Correspondence of the Times" (Atlanta, 30 August): *Columbus Times,* 1 September. After the bombardment had ended, unexploded Union shells continued to cause casualties.

"Outline," "Special Correspondence of the Times" (Atlanta, 31 August): *Columbus Times,* 2 September. "The city is gradually resuming its usual bustling aspect, and fresh beef is once more offered for sale in the market house."

Jackson *Mississippian.*

"The Position of Affairs Before Atlanta": quoted in *Richmond Examiner,* 1 September; reprinted in *New York Tribune,* 5 September. "The garden to almost every house which does not boast a cellar is now supplied with its artificial 'bomb-proof.'"

Knoxville Register (microfilm at Atlanta History Center, 1860–8 April 1864). The *Register* relocated to Atlanta in September 1863; the *Intelligencer* on 15 September announced that it would resume publication on the next day: "Tennessee refugees and soldiers are invited to call at 'Tennessee Headquarters,' at the Register office," on Whitehall Street. "Bill Arp" (Charles H. Smith), the "runagee" from Rome, assumed the assistant editorship of the *Register,* according to the *Intelligencer* of 25 June 1864. After its departure from Atlanta in July it relocated to Augusta. The *Augusta Constitutionalist* of 30 August announced: "THE ATLANTA REGISTER.—This excellent journal, formerly published in Atlanta, but compelled to leave that unfortunate city, in consequence of the proximity of the Yankees, is now published in our city. The first number was issued yesterday afternoon."

"Sherman's Murders" (undated): quoted in *Richmond Sentinel,* 22 August, citing the *Atlanta Register:* also in *Mobile Register & Advertiser,* 13 August. "On the 3rd a lady, a gentleman and his little daughter were killed in Atlanta by fragments of Yankee shells, and about 11 o'clock at night Mr. Warner, the Superintendent of the Gas Works, and his little daughter, lying in the same bed, were killed by a round shot. The child was severed in two, dying instantly, the father had both thighs cut off close to the body and lived about two hours."

Macon Telegraph (microfilm file at Emory University).

"From the Front": *Macon Telegraph,* 22 July; also in *Augusta Chronicle & Sentinel,* 23 July. On first shells falling on Atlanta.

"Refugees": *Macon Telegraph,* 22 July. Some Atlantans were coming into Macon, fleeing the bombardment.

"Orion" (Atlanta 21 July, 7 P.M.): *Macon Telegraph,* 23 July. On 21 July, the second day of the bombardment, several shells burst near Female College, doing no damage.

"For the Daily Telegraph" (Atlanta, 25 July): *Macon Telegraph,* 27 July. "A lady was wounded and a child killed by a shell on Saturday," 23 July. Also, a correspondent's personal encounter with a shell, and "miraculous" escape.

"W.P.H.," "From the Front" (Atlanta, 26 July, 6 P.M.): *Macon Telegraph,* 27 July. "Mrs. Weaver was wounded, the same shell killing her child in her arms."

"St. Clair" [Alexander St. Clair Abrams], "Special Correspondence of the Telegraph" (Atlanta, 26 July): *Macon Telegraph,* 28 July. Casualties so far: two women and a child dead, another child severely wounded. Asserts that because Atlanta was only semi-invested, Sherman was not obliged to warn residents of the impending bombardment.

"Shelling Atlanta": *Macon Telegraph,* 2 August; reprinted in *Columbus Enquirer,* 3 August. "The enemy is now throwing from five hundred to a thousand shells daily, in all parts of the town, and every noncombatant should be removed from it."

"From Atlanta.—A New Movement": *Macon Telegraph*, 30 August. Mentions death and injury caused by Union shells exploding after the end of the bombardment.

Memphis Appeal (microfilm files at University of Georgia, Emory University and Atlanta History Center). A good history of the *Memphis Daily Appeal* is Thomas Harrison Baker, *The Memphis Commercial Appeal: History of a Southern Newspaper* (Baton Rouge: Louisiana State University Press, 1971); see also Thomas H. Baker, "Refugee Newspaper: The Memphis *Daily Appeal*, 1862–1865, *Journal of Southern History* 29/3 (August 1963): 326–44. Barbara G. Ellis, *The Moving Appeal: Mr. McClanahan, Mrs. Dill, and the Civil War's Great Newspaper Run* [Macon: Mercer University Press, 2003] adds much more detail on the war years. On 22 July 1864, the paper's owner and chief editor, John R. McClanahan, packed up in Atlanta with most of his staff and his Hoe press and moved to Montgomery, there to resume publication on 20 September (Ellis, *The Moving Appeal*, 313, 324). The big press is pictured in B. Kimball Baker, "The Memphis Appeal," *Civil War Times Illustrated* 18/4 (July 1979): 32. During the bombardment, Assistant Editor John B. Dumble remained in Atlanta and in the Franklin Printing House on Alabama Street cranked out one-page, front-only "extras" of the *Appeal*, the only newspaper operating in the city. Its information was consequently much sought and reprinted by numerous Confederate newspapers. Microfilm copies at Emory and Georgia have no issue between 4 July and 3 November 1864. Microfilm copy at the Atlanta History Center has the "extra" of 15 August, which is also the only number cited from the original by Ellis in her study. Information provided by the *Appeal* during the semi-siege therefore must be obtained from columns reprinted in other papers, as shown below.

"Army News" (Atlanta, 2 August): quoted in *Atlanta Intelligencer*, 4 August. Regarding shell-death of "an old lady" on north Marietta Street.

"The Immediate Front" (Atlanta, 5 August): quoted in *Atlanta Intelligencer*, 6 August. "Since noon yesterday the city has received more than the usual attention of the enemy's batteries…. One young lady and a gentleman and his little daughter" killed.

"The Immediate Front" (Atlanta, 6 August): quoted in *Atlanta Intelligencer*, 9 August and in *Augusta Chronicle & Sentinel*, 11 August. "But few shells were thrown yesterday, and we learn none last night. One lady was struck yesterday, and her foot severely cut."

"The Immediate Front" (Atlanta, 8 August): quoted in *Columbus Times*, 12 August. "Saturday afternoon [6 August] the city was subjected to one of the fiercest fires from the enemy's batteries it has yet sustained…. We have a report of three casualties having occurred, but on investigation conclude it is without foundation, and that no personal damage was sustained whatever."

Undated editorial, *Memphis Appeal:* quoted in *Atlanta Intelligencer,* 9 August. Criticizes Sherman for bombardment of civilians.

"The Immediate Front" (Atlanta, 9 August): quoted in *Atlanta Intelligencer,* 11 August; and (undated) in *Macon Telegraph,* 11 August. "Quite a number of shells were thrown into the city yesterday, the firing commencing at 10 o'clock A.M. No person was injured by the spiteful demonstration."

"Death of Mr. Warner and Daughter" (no date): quoted in *Augusta Constitutionalist,* 10 August. The much-talked-about event occurred on the night of 3 August.

"The Immediate Front" (Atlanta, 10 August): quoted in *Columbus Times,* 13 August; also in *Atlanta Intelligencer,* 13 August, although incorrectly dated 9 August. "The amount of Federal spite vented against the city yesterday far exceeded any demonstrations our enemies have yet made.... But two casualties have been reported. A gentleman in the outskirts of the city had both legs taken off by a shell, while sitting on his doorstep, and died before a surgeon could be procured. The other was a child, who was severely bruised by a lump of earth set in motion by a shot." "Many buildings were struck, and strange to say, most of these were private residences." Argues that the barrage was unwarrantable— "unwarrantable because no notice has ever been given."

"The Immediate Front" (Atlanta, 14 August): quoted in *Atlanta Intelligencer,* 16 August; *Augusta Constitutionalist,* 18 August; and in *Columbus Enquirer,* 17 August. On the fire of Saturday night, 13–14 August.

"The Immediate Front": *Memphis Appeal,* 15 August. Only one man wounded in heavy shelling of Saturday night, 13–14 August. "The escape of our citizens is remarkable, when it is considered they were subject to an incessant fire from five batteries for a period of ten hours."

"The Immediate Front" (Atlanta, 16 August): quoted in *Atlanta Intelligencer,* 18 August; *Columbus Enquirer,* 19 August; and *Macon Telegraph,* 19 August. "Very few shells were thrown yesterday but during the night their visitations were more numerous."

"The Immediate Front" (Atlanta, 18 August): quoted in *Columbus Enquirer,* 21 August; and in *Mobile Register & Advertiser,* 23 August. Another civilian's death, an unnamed railroad employee. (Isaac Pilgrim was able to name him: Francis Hale of the Western & Atlantic.)

"From the Front" (citing undated *Memphis Appeal*): *Augusta Chronicle & Sentinel,* 23 August. Notes that Federal artillery fire for the past two days has been very slight, leading to speculation that Union gunners may be low on ammunition.

"The Immediate Front" (Atlanta, 19 August): quoted in *Atlanta Intelligencer,* 24 August. A Union shell exploded in a house: one child killed, one soldier mortally wounded, two women injured.

Untitled column of *Appeal*, 22 August, quoted in *Columbus Sun*, 25 August. "Throughout Saturday night [20 August], Sunday and Sunday night, only an occasional shell was directed at the city."

"The Immediate Front" (Atlanta, 23 August): quoted in *Atlanta Intelligencer*, 26 August. The *Appeal* is able to identify a shell-victim as a Mrs. Cook, killed on Marietta Street.

Untitled column of *Appeal*, 25 August, quoted in *Richmond Sentinel*, 31 August. "A heavy fire was kept up on the city yesterday [24 August] until evening, when it slackened, and during the night only occasional shells were thrown. A few casualties occurred during the day, but none of a fatal character have been reported to us."

"The Immediate Front" (Atlanta, 27 August): quoted in *Mobile Register & Advertiser*, 1 September. On Northern artillery positions, which Atlantans observed after the Federals' departure for Jonesboro.

Mobile Register & Advertiser (microfilm at University of Georgia). "Shadow," the paper's correspondent in Atlanta, has been identified as Henry Watterson. J. Cutler Andrews surmised as much in *The South Reports the Civil War*, 543–47; Barbara Ellis affirms it, based on content analysis (*The Moving Appeal*, 576–84).

"Wounded by the Enemy Shells in Atlanta": *Mobile Register & Advertiser*, 3 August. "The casualties from the shells have been two white women, one white child, and one white man killed. One white woman wounded, one negro man killed and another wounded. The child was killed in the mother's arms, and she was also wounded by the same missile."

"Sherman's Murders": *Mobile Register & Advertiser*, 13 August. Relates the deaths of J. F. Warner and his daughter, 3 August.

"Atlanta, Aug. 14": *Mobile Register & Advertiser*, 16 August. Report of fire started by Union shells, night of 13 August.

"Shadow," "Letter from Atlanta" (24 August): *Mobile Register & Advertiser*, 28 August. Watterson actually saw "a poor woman killed this morning on Alabama street." Relates story of a woman castigating a Yankee artillery officer for claiming that their guns never aimed for the city.

"Shadow," "Letter from Atlanta" (26 August): *Mobile Register & Advertiser*, 30 August. "Last night Marietta Street was knocked into a cocked hat"— confirming the night of 25 August as the Federals' last shelling of the city.

"Shadow," "Letter from Atlanta" (Atlanta, Sunday evening, 28 August): *Mobile Register & Advertiser*, 1 September. Watterson rejoices at the cessation of the Union bombardment. He reports that "not a gun has been fired for two days."

"Shadow," "Our Army Correspondence. Letter from General Hood's Army" (Atlanta, 30 August): *Mobile Register & Advertiser*, 3 September. "The casualties during the bombardment are reported to be 691 wounded and 497 killed. At least 47 houses were destroyed by fire, involving a loss of five millions of dollars worth of property."

Mobile News.
"Atlanta Correspondent of the Mobile News," "Getting Out of Atlanta" (no date): quoted in *New York Times*, 7 August. Colorful account of panicked civilians' flight from city. Quoted also in Foote, *The Civil War*, 3:491–92; and in Castel, *Decision in the West*, 341.

Richmond Enquirer (microfilm at University of Georgia).
"Cedric," "From Atlanta" (18 August): *Richmond Enquirer*, 30 August. Two people wounded by a shell, 13 August.
"Cedric," "From Atlanta" (23 August): *Richmond Enquirer*, 1 September. "The incessant picket firing, the constant shrieking of shells—which occasionally kills a woman, child or negro in the city; the rumbling of an ambulance—now and then bearing a wounded soldier to the hospital—are all that break the almost Sabbath-like stillness."

Richmond Sentinel (microfilm at Atlanta History Center, 5 July 1864–27 February 1865; gift of A. A. Hoehling).
"Murder of the Innocents": *Richmond Sentinel*, 31 August. "We learn that the sexton in Atlanta reports thirty children killed by the enemy's shells in that city."

Savannah Republican (microfilm at Georgia Historical Society, Savannah).
"F.G. de F." [Felix G. de Fontaine], "From the Army of Tennessee" (Atlanta, night of 22 July): *Savannah Republican*, 27 July; also quoted in *Macon Telegraph*, 28 July; and *Mobile Register and Advertiser*, 4 August. On the morning of the 22nd, "shells were dropping in the streets, and sad groups of women and children, with a temporary supply of provisions, were wending their way to the woods."
"F.G. de F." (Atlanta, 23 July, 10 A.M.) [postscript to above column]: *Savannah Republican*, 27 July. "Several houses have been badly damaged—many narrow escapes made, but I hear as yet of no loss of life."
"F.G. de F.," "From the Army of Tennessee" (Atlanta, 23 July evening): *Savannah Republican*, 4 August. With a shell exploding every five minutes, "since about noon to-day the citizens have enjoyed the privilege, for the first time on a systematic scale, of studying the science of ferruginous conchology."
"F.G. de F.," "From the Georgia Front" (Atlanta, 25 July): *Savannah Republican*, 27 July. "At mid-day the Yankees opened again with shells upon the city, and are shelling now with some vigor. No notice was given of the enemy's intention to shell the city and enable us to remove the women and children to safer places, but his barbarous violation of the usages of civilized warfare has only caused him to murder a few noncombatants."

INDEX

Augusta Constitutionalist, 137, 213, 216, 230, 232-33
Augusta gunpowder works, 37
Austell, Alfred, 166, 262; leaves city, 364
Austell, Mrs. Alfred, recalls bombproof shelter, 210
Austin, C.S. Capt. J.P., 110
Avery, Isaac W., 423n30; estimates destruction in city as 11/12, 425
"B." *(see William B. Barr):* correspondent for *Atlanta Intelligencer,* 216; and for *Memphis Appeal,* 220; on fires in city, 221; on shells striking Car Shed, 235
Bacon, CS Maj. William, 30
Bailey, Ronald H., 167
Baker, US Lt. George W., 272-73
Baker Street, 223
"Bald Hill"/Leggett's Hill, 114-15; occupied by Federals, 118; in battle of Atlanta, 123
Baltimore, Maryland, 37
Ball, James, M., emissary between Sherman and Hood, 296-97, 301
Bank Hospital, 23
Bank of Fulton, first Atlanta bank, 6
Banks, Isaac T., 10
Banks, US Maj. Gen. Nathaniel, expels New Orleans civilians, 298
Barber Greenwood & Company, 36
Barnard, George, 284-85; photographs Sherman, 337; 365; photographs city from Female Institute cupola, 346; photographs Crawford slave mart, 394n16
Barnes, William B., metal works owner, 10; and Confederate Iron and Brass Foundry, 36; home of, 164
Barnesville, Georgia, 77
Barnett, US Capt. Charles M., 119
Barnum, US Col. Henry A., occupies Windsor Smith house, 253, 285
Barnwell, V.T., compares Atlanta's burning to Columbia's, 425
Barr, William D., newspaper correspondent, 216, 220-21

Barracks on Peachtree Street, as prison, 54, 54n34; designated for destruction, 371; burned, 392, 418
Barry, US Brig. Gen. William F., chief of Sherman's artillery, 115-16; 340
Barth, Carl, drum-maker, 43
Bartlett, US soldier Edward, 264
Bartow County, Georgia, 35
Bates, US musician John W., 327
Bates County, Missouri, 298
Battery F, 2nd US Artillery, 179
Battery H, 1st Illinois Light Artillery (DeGress'), fires first shells into city,106; 123; moves to west of city, 149
Battery H, 1st Michigan Light Artillery, 122
Battery I, 1st New York Light Artillery (Winegar's), 136-37; fires every five minutes, 149; in shelling of 9 August, 171, 181
Battery I, 2d Illinois Light Artillery (Barnett's), 119
Battery K, Confederate artillery fort/Fox Theatre hill, 223
Battery M, 1st Illinois Light Artillery (Spencer's), 146
Battery M, 1st New York Light Artillery (Woodbury's), 120, 130, 136
"Battle Cry of Freedom" played by Federal bands, 272
"Battle of Atlanta," U.C.V. pamphlet of in 1895, 108
Beach, John, Atlanta merchant, 14
Beach & Root building, on Whitehall, 14; damaged by fire, 92; hit by shell, 207-208
Beatty, Henry, 212
Beatty, CS Col. Taylor, 82
Beauregard, CS Gen. Pierre G.T., commander at Charleston, 99, 104, 247-48
Beck, Cora Warren, on entrance of Federal troops, 268
Beckham, CS Col. Robert F., 313
Beckwith, US Col. Amos, chief commissary officer, 311; moves

Canton, Georgia, burned by Federals, 533

Capitol Avenue, 443

Capron, US Maj. Thaddeus, 376

"Car," correspondent for *Augusta Constitutionalist*, 213

Car Shed/Passenger Depot, completed in 1854, 7-8; described, 9; 11, 17, 20, 23-24, 30, 34, 51, 69, 74, 89, 110, 124, 133, 141; as Federals' target, 143-45; little damage to, 164; 251, 263, 331, 344, 364; designated for destruction, 369; pulled down and burned by Federals, 388, 391-92, 406, 416

Carlisle, Pennsylvania, shelling of, 101

Carman, US Col. Ezra, 270, 386

Carr, US Capt. John M., on demolition of Car Shed, 389

Carter, CS Brig. Gen. John C., 90; brigade gives up rations for city's poor, 292

Carter, US Capt. Lewis, 54n34; 61-62

Carter III, Samuel, 167

Carter Center and Presidential Library, as Sherman's headquarters site, 121

Cartersville, Georgia, 36; burning in, 382

Cass County, Missouri, 298

Cassville, Georgia, 67; burned by Federals, 380, 393, 399

Casualties during bombardment: none reported 20 July 107; mother and child allegedly killed, 133; reports of, 134, 137-41, 151; daughter of John M. Weaver allegedly killed by shell, 138; two African-American children allegedly wounded, 139; *Intelligencer* on casualties, 184, 198; Pilgrim reports on, 164-65; Geary judges to be numerous, 172-73; rumors concerning 214-16; lack of medical records concerning, 193; 213; difficulties in determining, 243-44; Richards estimates twenty deaths, 243; Pilgrim and Semmes allege 107 amputations, 243, 245; *Richmond Sentinel* alleges 30 children killed, 244; "Shadow" states 497 killed and

691 wounded, 244-45; rumor of 100 killed, 246; *Intelligencer* estimates 10 killed and 40 wounded, 245; caused by later shell-detonations, 246-47; rumor of 200 women and children killed, 276

Castel, Albert, 167, 298

Cave Spring, Georgia, 378

Cedar Bluff, Alabama, 55

"Cedric," correspondent for *Richmond Enquirer*, 184

Census, Atlanta, local of 1854, 8

Census, US, of 1850, 5, 8; of 1860, 8

Central Avenue (originally Loyd Street), 4

Central Presbyterian Church (see also Second Presbyterian): opens 1860, 11; 70; struck by shell, 205; 211, 344; spared burning, 407

"Cerulean abdomens," US troops as, 72, 75, 436

Chaffee, US Sgt. Newton, 276

Chambersburg, Pennsylvania, Confederates' burning of, 395, 410

Chambersburg Old Flag, 579

Chapman, US soldier Horatio, 319

Charleston, South Carolina, 7, 27n6, 50, 52, 85. 98; shelling of, 99-100, 104, 180; longest-range bombardment of war, 99, 248; longest duration of bombardment, 100, 248; 167, 228; buildings damaged by shells, 247

Charleston Courier, 51

Chattahoochee River, 1-2; fortifications at, 56-58, 61-62, 68, 72, 75, 80-81, 83, 87-88, Sherman crosses, 80-81; XX Corps stationed at, 195, 225; 260, 271; Hood's army crosses northward, 345; Federals tear down bridge, 385

Chattanooga, Tennessee, 1, 4, 7, 22, 27, 41, 47-49, 51, 54, 57, 61-63; 64; shelled, 100; 168-69, 195, 348, 362-63

Chattanooga Gazette, 278

Chattanooga Rebel, 28n7; 152, 203, 258

206, 237; 406; residence "defaced," 416

Race track, in southwest Atlanta, 40; site of C.S. ordnance laboratory, 40, 43, 56

Railroad destruction by Federals: *see individual rail lines*

Rawson, Edward E. *(see also "Terraces"),* 16, 262-63, 282, 293-94; leaves for Iowa, 295; 302, 326, 405

Rawson, Mary, 282, 285; on expulsion order, 292-94; 311-12, 327

Rawson Street, 17, 177

Read, US Capt. Ira, 150, 276, 279, 337

Receiving and distributing hospital (Gate City Hotel), 24, 69, 193

Reed, US soldier Axel, 396

Reed, Harvey, tannery owner, 10

Reed, Wallace, writes for *Constitution* and author of city-history, 108; on Sol Luckie's death, 188-90, 207

Reese, US Surg. A.W., 129

Reid, US Cpl. Harvey, 286, 351; on selection of certain buildings for burning, 372; 385-88; on demolition of Car Shed, 388; predicts officers will ignore unauthorized arson, 389; 395; on burning, 401

Reynolds, CS Brig. Gen. A. W., 74

Resaca, Georgia, 64, 366

Rhodes, Mrs. A.D., 164

Rhodes, T.V., 162

Rhodes Street, 152

Rice, US Brig. Gen. Elliott, 149

Rice, Frank, 17, 44, 108

Rice, US Lt. Ralsa, 197

Rice, Zachariah, writes of devastation in city, 404-406

Richards, Jabez, 67, 125

Richards, Sallie, 82, 246

Richards, Samuel, receives exemption from military service as publisher of *The Soldier's Friend,* 67, 82; 197-98; 71, 73, 89, 190, 303; home of at Washington and Peters Sts., 89, 133; on Confederates' march through city 21-22 July, 125; bookstore owner 125-26; grocery owner, 133;373; robbed

by Confederate soldiers, 125-26; describes shelling near home, 133, 219; on shell-casualties, 152; on food supply in city, 200; 204-205, 208, 212; bookstore hit by shell, 207, 219; on end of bombardment, 225; guesses twenty shell-deaths, 243, 246, 351; describes Confederate evacuation, 250; bookstore looted, 267;353, 373-74; deals with Sherman's expulsion order, 295, 325

Richardson Street, 208

Richer, US Cpl. Eli S., 275

Richmond, Virginia, 10, 27n6, 36-37, 45, 47, 50, 57-59, 62-63, 77, 89, 102, 143, 194

Richmond Armory, 37

Richmond Arsenal, 42

Richmond Enquirer, 184

Richmond Sentinel, alleges thirty children killed in bombardment, 244

Ripley, Thomas, china and glass store, 393; house dismantled, 416

Rise and Fall of the Confederate Government, Davis' memoir, 431

Roark, William W., grocery store of, 29

Roark's Corner (Whitehall and Mitchell), 29, 405, 412, 418

Roberts, Albert, editor of *Atlanta Southern Confederacy,* 67, 80; stays in Atlanta, 83; 253, 258

Robson, Sion, 162

"Rock Depot," freight depot of Macon & Western 396, 392

Rockbridge, Georgia, 351, 392

Rocky Face Ridge, Georgia, 64

Rodgers Tannery, on Whitehall Street, 176

Rome, Georgia, 54-55, 67, 127, 165; burning in, 379-80, 393, 399

Rood, US soldier Hosea, 402

Root, Delia (Mrs. Sidney), 311

Root, Sidney, 14, 204, 312

Roseberry, US Pvt. Isaac, 1st Michigan Engineers, 334, 367, 385, 392; on arson of 11 November, 389; unauthorized fires, 12 November,

Stevenson, Alabama, 49

Stevenson, CS Maj. Gen. Carter L., 184

Stewart, CS Lt. Gen. Alexander Peter, corps commander in Army Tennessee, 85; 196

Stewart, James A., flour manufacturer, 10; owner of Greenwood Mills, 44

Stewart, US Capt. John, 432

Stone, Amherst, leaves Atlanta, 117

Stone, Cyrena, Union sympathizer in Atlanta, 50, 66, 71; house comes under bombardment, 116-18; stays with friends, 185; welcomes Federal troops, 272; leaves city for North, 328

Stone Mountain, Georgia, 20, 358, 417

Stone Mountain depot, on Georgia Railroad, 88

Stoneman, US Maj. Gen. George, 148, 300n34

Stout, Dr. Samuel H., Army of Tennessee's hospital director, 26, 29, 193

Streight, US Col. Abel, 54; cavalry raid of, 55-56

Strong, Judge C.H., 208

Strong, US Pvt. Robert H., 366

Stuart, CS Maj. Gen. James E. B. ("Jeb"), orders shelling of Carlisle, Pa., 101

Sullivan, US Lt. John, 115

Sumner, US Maj. Gen. Edwin V., 98

"Sumner Oscillating Breechloading Rifled Gun," 34

Sutermeister, U.S. Capt. Arnold, commanding 11th Indiana Battery (XX Corps siege artillery), 120, 130; aims for Car Shed, 144; oversees 4.5-inch cannon, 169-70; 181, 219

Sutlers, in city during occupation, 352

"Swamp Angel," Union cannon at Charleston: *see 8-inch Parrott rifle*

Sweeny, US Brig. Gen. Thomas, division commander in battle of Atlanta, 123

Sweetland, US Pvt. Emory, 265

Sweetwater textile factory, workers expelled by Sherman, 81n19

Swett, CS Capt. Charles, 251, 256, 258

Swiftsure, locomotive struck by shell, 235

Tallulah Fire Company (No. 3), *see fire companies*

Tarr, US Capt. H.H., 400

Taylor, James A., drugstore owner, 29

Taylor, President Zachary, 310

Telegraph office in Atlanta, opens, 4; in Dougherty Building, 14; at Gate City Hotel, 89

10-pounder Parrott rifled cannon, range and ammunition of, 115

Tennessee, CSS, 31

Tennessee House, hotel in 1859, 9

Tennessee troops: **9th Infantry Regiment**, 110

Terminus, early name for Atlanta, 1-2

"Terraces," residence of Edward Rawson, 17, 282; occupied by Geary, 327; not burned, 405

Texas, locomotive, 30

Texas troops: **6th Infantry Regiment**, 185; **14th Cavalry**, 215

13-inch seacoast mortar ("Dictator"), 102

30-pounder Parrott rifled cannon, 168-69

32-pounder smoothbore cannon, 73, 196, 256

Thomas, US Maj. Gen. George H., commander of Army of the Cumberland, 88; as "Rock of Chickamauga," 88; 91, 95, 97; advances 22 July, 118; artillery shells Atlanta, 130; orders heavier cannon for bombardment, 168; 169; proposes to shell Hood's HQ on Whitehall Street, 169; directs 4.5-inch cannon positioned on his front, 169, 179-80; 218, 234, 237, 243, 282; moves into Leyden house, 284; sent to Nashville to confront Hood, 345, 360

Thomas, T.L.., 415

Thomaston, Georgia, 76

Thomasville, Georgia, 18

Thompson, James, early Atlanta hotel owner, 8

Thompson's Hotel, 223

Thrasher, John J., "Cousin John," early resident, 2, 5, 352